CONVENT CHRONICLES

Convent Chronicles

Women Writing About Women and Reform in the Late Middle Ages

Anne Winston-Allen

The Pennsylvania State University Press
University Park, Pennsylvania

LIBRARY OF CONGRESS CATALOGING-IN-PUBLICATION DATA

Winston-Allen, Anne, 1942–
    Convent chronicles : women writing about women and reform
    in the late Middle Ages / Anne Winston-Allen.
        p.   cm.
    Includes bibliographical references and index.
    ISBN 0-271-02460-7 (alk. paper)
    1. Christian literature, German—Women authors—History and criticism.
    2. Christian literature, Dutch—Women authors—History and criticism.
    3. German literature—Early modern, 1500–1700—History and criticism.
    4. Dutch literature—1500–1800—History and criticism.
    5. Nuns as authors.
    6. Women and literature.
    7. Reformation—Germany—History.
    8. Reformation—Netherlands—History.
    I. Title.
    PT255.W56 2004
    830.9'38230'082—dc22
                          2004012982

The Pennsylvania State University Press is a member of the
Association of American University Presses.

It is the policy of The Pennsylvania State University Press to
use acid-free paper. Publications on uncoated stock satisfy
the minimum requirements of American National Standard
for Information Sciences—Permanence of Paper for Printed
Library Materials, ANSI Z39.48-1992.

FOR MY SISTER *Jane*

CONTENTS

ILLUSTRATIONS

Map Convents from which primary sources by women are cited.

1 Petrarca-Master, woodcut from [Francesco Petrarca,] *Von der Artzney beyder Glück, des guten und widerwertigen* (About the Medicine of Both Kinds of Fate: The Good and the Vexatious). Book 1, chapter 13. Edited by Georg Spalatin and Peter Stahel. Augsburg: Steyner, 1532.

2 Tapestry (detail): two Dominican nuns weaving. Late fifteenth century. Bamberg, Diözesanmuseum (photo: Diözesanmuseum).

3 Benedictine nun and school child. Illustration from a song book (detail). Cloister Archive, Ebstorf, MS V 3, fol. 200v. Fifteenth century (photo: Lüneburger Klosterarchive).

4 *Hoofkijn van devotien* (Garden of Devotion), Antwerp, Gerhard Leeu, 1487. Reproduced by permission of the Koninklijke Bibliotheek, The Hague (No. 150 B 48).

5 *Somme le Roi*. Bodleian Library, Oxford, MS 283, fol. 99v. Fifteenth century. Reproduced by permission of the Bodleian Library, Oxford (photo: Bodelian Library).

6 Illustration (c. 1490) from a choir book of Cloister Heilig Kreuz, Regensburg, showing beside the donor and her niece (novice in white veil) four reforming sisters from St. Katharina in Nuremberg (photo: Bischöfliche Zentralbibliothek Regensburg).

7 The handwriting of Sister Regula, "Buch von den heiligen Mägden und Frauen" (Book of Holy Maidens and Women, c. 1460), MS L69, fol. 1r (Kloster Lichtenthal) Badische Landesbibliothek Karlsruhe (photo: Badische Landesbibliothek Karlsruhe).

8 Illustration of Elsbeth Stagel (d. c. 1360), composing the *Lives of the Sisters of Töss*. Manuscript copied c. 1454 in the scriptorium of St. Katharina in Nuremberg, Stadtbibliothek Nürnberg, MS Cent. V 10a, fol. 3r (photo: Stadtbibliothek Nürnberg).

9 Clare of Assisi with Pope Gregory IX. One of 33 illustrations by Sibilla von Bondorf for a Life of St. Clare (c. 1490). Badische Landesbibliothek Karlsruhe, MS Thennenbach 4, fol. 138r (photo: Badische Landesbibliothek Karlsruhe).

10 Illustration by Sibilla von Bondorf of Clare of Assisi writing with pen and scraper. Badische Landesbibliothek Karlsruhe, MS Thennenbach 4, fol. 157r (photo: Badische Landesbibliothek Karlsruhe).

This book took shape in the summer of 1999. I had received a DAAD (German Academic Exchange Service) grant to work at the Staatsbibliothek in Berlin as guest of the project researching unpublished vernacular sermons in German archives. Originally, what I had wanted to study were the concepts of reform expressed by popular preachers in the period just prior to the Reformation. Because virtually all the sermons in German that survive from the Middle Ages were written down or copied by women who heard them in convent parish churches, a good place to look was in the sermon collections that nuns made for their cloister libraries. Perhaps the best collection is that of the former great library of the Strasbourg cloister of St. Nicolaus in undis, remnants of which are now in Berlin and contain some 850 sermons. Wanting to learn more about the women who made this remarkable collection, I had been looking at cloister annals and other historical writings. But I had not thought of making these the focus of a study until Hans-Jochen Schiewer, co-director of the sermon project, remarked that women's convent chronicles struck him as a particularly interesting topic. It was this comment that stayed with me and changed the direction of my research.

Already I had run across a few chronicles while searching for women's writings about their activities in the fifteenth-century Observant reform, a movement to which the sisters at St. Nicolaus as well as most of the other sermon transcribers belonged. This movement, originating in Italy in the previous century, was an initiative to revive piety and reform religious orders that spread in the 1400s throughout the German-speaking territories and other parts of Europe. Observant groups gained adherents in most religious orders but they also affected the laity through an increased focus on the care of souls, the founding of lay religious confraternities, and the influence of popular reform preachers. Trying to find accounts of it written by women, I had scoured the footnotes of the large collection of German dissertations on individual cloisters in the Theological Seminar library at the University of Freiburg. Here I had come across references to several nuns' chronicles, which until only recently were of little interest to anyone. But I was convinced that there were more of them.

Besides writing historical accounts and collecting sermons, women in the movement had compiled, translated, and copied large numbers of devotional works. Other researchers had already noted an astonishing amount of scribal activity in Observant women's houses in the fifteenth century. Some three hundred volumes were copied by sisters at St. Katharina in Nuremberg alone. And yet, despite this voluminous production, I discovered that there was no comprehensive study in German or English of convent chronicles nor was there a survey of fifteenth-century women's writings. Where were the studies examining the transition from the sister-books of the fourteenth century to women's religious pamphleteering in the sixteenth century? Where were texts by women of the fifteenth century at all?

If such texts had been neglected by German researchers, they were totally absent from English-language surveys of women's writing. The *Encyclopedia of Women in the Middle Ages* (2001) lists German visionary writers from the twelfth and thirteenth centuries—Hildegard of Bingen, Elisabeth of Schönau, Herrad of Landsberg, and the Helfta mystics—but no women later than that. Conspicuously absent are the known authors of fourteenth-century sister-books: Anna von Munzingen, Christina Ebner, Katharina von Gueberschwihr, Elisabeth of Kirchberg, Elsbeth Stagel, and mystical writers Margareta Ebner and Adelheid Langmann. Although the *Encyclopedia* lists fifteenth-century writers Christine de Pizan and Margery Kempe, it lists none from the Dutch- and German-speaking areas, even though women's contributions there are considerable. Clearly, this is a problem that needs to be addressed.

Many of the chronicles had been transcribed from old manuscripts by scholars, local historians, and antiquarian collectors in the eighteenth and nineteenth centuries and simply printed verbatim in collections of historical documents, local or regional periodicals, and ethnological or church history journals. But they had not been studied as a group. Rather, women's historical writings from the Middle Ages have been almost completely ignored in articles and monographs on the chronicle as a literary genre. A few have been examined in works on individual convents or regions, such as Gudrun Gleba's book (2000) on women's houses in Westphalia and Heike Uffmann's articles (1997, 2000) on chronicles in the area of Lüneburg. But I wanted to look at a larger group. Accordingly, this present study is the first to survey nun's convent chronicles and historical writings collectively across orders and regions in the fifteenth and early sixteenth centuries.

What connects these texts scattered over a wide area and representing many orders is their relationship to the Observant movement. The Observance itself is a relatively well-kept secret compared to the much better known *devotio moderna* movement, or Brothers and Sisters of the Common Life, which emerged in the Netherlands in the late fourteenth century. Looking at the collection of articles in the widely used volume *Christian Spirituality: High Middle Ages and Reformation* (1989), for example, one finds an entire chapter devoted to the *devotio moderna* but none to the Observant movement, even though it was a widespread development affecting nearly all religious orders in the fifteenth century. In English there are two or three monographs dealing either with the Observance in individual orders or with reform actions by Observants initiated by the Council of Basel (1431–49). Yet German sources yield seventeen books (if one counts order-centered studies) and dozens of articles. Published proceedings of three symposia in Berlin, which include papers on Observant initiatives in fourteen different religious orders, underscore the need for wider recognition of the development as a whole, traversing order and national boundaries. About women's role in the movement at large there is no monograph in either language.

Present-day women's historians have tended to regard female Observants as the tools of men who wished to incarcerate and suppress them. At the same time they object that the nuns who refused to be reformed have been used in the master narrative as foils for the "good women" who accepted the Observance. I take up this issue because it seems to me that female Observants have been treated less seriously than were the movement's male supporters. Rather than categorizing the women as either pawns or protofeminists, I wanted to look at the complex social, political, and cultural reasons why women both supported and opposed the reform. Exploring these motives casts light on possibilities of female agency, the social power structures surrounding convents, and late medieval spirituality both in and outside the cloister. Ultimately, studying the past is looking at texts left behind by those who lived it. But the past reads differently according to whether one is examining texts by dominant or by subordinate groups and whether the texts are external or internal records. While previous studies of the reform have used only reports written by men, I wanted to examine women's accounts. Not surprisingly, these offer an alternative view of female agency, one that challenges the traditional narrative about women.

Almost all of what researchers know about medieval women's houses has come from external sources: official judicial and church records, *vitae* or reports of religious women by male writers. I wanted to know in what ways the accounts left by women confirm or contest the master narrative. This study is, thus, the first to draw on internal sources about convents, sources that reveal women's own representations of themselves and their lives in fifteenth-century German religious communities.

Jennifer Summit's *Lost Property: The Woman Writer and English Literary History, 1380–1589* (2000) demonstrates well how the "woman writer" was constructed by male authors, editors, translators, and printers and defined by her very "exteriority" to literary tradition as being absent or lost. In the same way, I argue that the fifteenth-century "convent woman" has been constructed by external authorities and sources as absent in the sense of silent, marginal, and walled-off from society. Nuns' writings, however, show that these women were intimately involved in close-knit family, social, and convent networks with connections throughout medieval society. Neither were they silent. Substantial numbers of still almost completely unknown works by women produced in the Dutch- and German-speaking regions exist and need to be taken into account. Theories that argue from convent women's silence must be reexamined in the light of actual texts. New judgments about the literary and social history of medieval women writers will follow as more of these works come to light. As the chronicles and historical texts dealt with here demonstrate, the visionary mode, so often regarded as medieval women's primary manner of self-expression, was not the only kind of writing in which women engaged. Such chronicles and other writings are texts that theorists need to carry their work further.

Recent colloquia on women's studies urge new ways of analyzing women's agency. They seek to identify its female forms, how agency functioned, the circumstances in which women were able to exercise power. Of particular interest are new paradigms that examine female power relations through women's connections with men. In this context the Observant movement offers a particularly well documented case study of an alliance of this kind as seen from the point of view of women who acquired positions of power through their involvement in it. The texts they left behind illustrate the relation between authority and text production by women. Like mystical and visionary works that conferred power or sister-books that represented social strategies, historical writings and chronicles are also political. Reform chronicles comprise a literary sub-genre that was both generated by the reform and at the same time constitutive of it, seeking to validate, construct, and perpetuate the Observance. A New Historicist approach looks at how these works function in a cultural-historical framework. Seeking to expand the textual base of women's literary artifacts, New Philologists deal with works further out on the margins of the literary realm. They view all texts as part of a discourse that has to be reconstructed in order to fully understand literary production. By using a discursive model in this study, I hope to underscore the particular importance in the fifteenth century of the increasing shift to vernacular language, a shift that allowed women to join in and to affect the nature of the religious discussion.

At the same time that women chronicled the Observance, they resisted the dominant discourse by portraying themselves differently from their male biographers. They protested earlier attempts to exclude women from religious orders and even left blank spaces in their manuscripts for visions that male censors refused to let them record. Participating in a literary Renaissance of their own, women in networks of Observant convents explored literary production and exchange as a form of agency. The authorization to write histories, copy and translate devotional literature into the vernacular, to transcribe, edit, and disseminate sermons all opened opportunities for more active engagement in the public discourse on spirituality. While women's importance as the largest audience for, and as the chief transmitters of, sermons in the vernacular has gone largely unnoticed, the cultural significance and force of their collective choices and participation as a reading community cannot long be ignored.

Women's preferences and alternative point of view as a majority subculture will become clearer as more of their texts are recovered and read. The images that women present of themselves in fifteenth- and early sixteenth-century chronicles correspond remarkably closely to those identified in two studies that have appeared since this manuscript was completed: Charlotte

Woodford's *Nuns as Historians in Early Modern Germany* (2002) and Rebecca Garber's *Feminine Figurae: Representations of Gender in Religious Texts by Medieval German Women Writers 1100–1375* (2003). Woodford's study of convent chronicles from the Reformation and Counter-Reformation period in Bavaria is historiographic, examining the history of the chronicle as a literary genre. Similarly, Garber's work examines three related sub-genres of women's writings from the twelfth to the fourteenth century: vision cycles, personal revelations, and sister-books. Although different in approach, these two new studies and mine reach similar conclusions about the complex functions served by women's writings, the constitutive role of women's communities in their production and reception, and above all, the different image that women put forward of themselves in their own works. With this study I hope to provide the link between these other two examinations of earlier and later writers. Together they constitute a much needed, first connected survey of women writers in the German-speaking region from the twelfth to the seventeenth century.

Ann Matter once characterized the ideal in scholarly research as "a generous exchange." That this spirit is alive and well has been amply demonstrated at critical points in the progress of this project. For generous help along the way, I would like to express my thanks chronologically to Sarah DeMaris for sharing her extensive knowledge of women and the Observance and for giving me the manuscript of her forthcoming edition of Johannes Meyer's *Ämterbuch*; to Richard Kieckhefer, Barbara Newman, and Merry Wiesner for generous recommendations in support of grant proposals; to Hans-Jochen Schiewer and Volker Mertens for invaluable advice and placing at my disposal the resources and library of the Berlin research project on sermon transcriptions; to Monika Costard, assistant on the project, for sharing with me her expertise, tea, M&Ms, and her articles on convent women and sermons; to Sabina von Heusinger for a guided tour of medieval Constance and a prepublication copy of her dissertation on Johannes Mulberg and the Dominican Observance; to Ulrich Ecker for his assistance in researching references at the Freiburg Stadtarchiv and a copy of his dissertation on the reform of Kirchheim; to Wybren Scheepsma for papers, articles, and his book on convent women in the Windesheim Congregation; to Thomas Mertens for an advance copy of his article on women as ghostwriters of sermons; to Werner Williams-Krapp for an unpublished conference paper on reformed cloisters in Nuremberg; to Abbess Irmgard von Funcke for an unpublished transcription of the chronicle of Ebstorf; to Sigrid Schmitt for her generous hospitality in Mainz and for two chapters of her soon to be published Habilitationsschrift on religious women in Strasbourg; to Anne Bollmann for her forthcoming article on Alijt Bake; to Sara Poor for two prepublication chapters of her monograph on Mechthild of Magdeburg; to Martina Backes for advance copies of articles on Magdalena Beutler and other medieval women, for helpful suggestions about archival materials, and especially for the courage to undertake with an amazingly unreliable automobile an excursion to the Archives départementales, Haut-Rhin, in Colmar; to Larissa Taylor for careful reading and insightful suggestions that greatly improved the present manuscript; and to Penn State Press Editor-in-Chief, Peter Potter, for listening, critiquing, advising, and supporting this project all along the way.

Special thanks go to the American Association of Teachers of German and the DAAD for summer research support, to the Southern Illinois University and Professional Women's Association for a grant to purchase microfilms, and to SIU for a year-long sabbatical to write this book. My hosts for many years in Freiburg, Ingrid and Werner Hoefel, not only took me to see the cloisters Schönensteinbach and Sylo, Sélestat, but insisted on hiking the eight kilometers around and up the hill to Herrad of Landsberg's famous abbey, St.-Odile, towing me the last part of the way. To them I want to express my long-term gratitude. Last, but chronologically first and always there with his support, not only towing but patching, jump-starting, and steadying the load on the long haul, I thank my perfect partner, Jim.

**Convents from Which Primary Sources by Women are Cited
(14th through Early 16th Century)**

1. Adelhausen (sb)
2. Alspach (lit)
3. Altomünster (c)
4. Bickenkloster (c, lit, r)
5. Brixen (lett)
6. Bronopia (lett)
7. Deventer and Diepenveen (sb, sb)
8. Ebstorf (c, c)
9. Engelport (lett)
10. Engelthal (sb)
11. Facons (lit)
12. Galilea in Ghent (lit)
13. Gertrudenberg (c)
14. Heiningen (c)
15. Herzebrock (c, c)
16. Inzigkofen (c)
17. Jericho in Brussels (lit)
18. Jerusalem in Utrecht (lit)
19. Katharinental (sb)
20. Kirchberg (Württemberg) (sb, r)
21. Kirchheim unter Teck (St. John Bapt.) (r)
22. Kirchheim am Ries (lit)
23. Lamme-van-Dieze House in Deventer (sb)
24. Lichtenthal (lit)
25. Maihingen (c)
26. Marienberg at Helmstedt (lett)
27. Marienthal (Niesing) (c)
28. Oetenbach (sb)
29. Penitents, St. Maria Magdalena, Strasb. (lit)
30. Pforzheim (r)
31. Pfullingen (c)
32. Preetz (m)

33. Rolandswerth (lit)
34. Söflingen (lett)
35. Sonnenburg (lett)
36. St. Agnes, Emmerich (sb)
37. St. Agnes, Mainz (lit)
38. St. Agnes, Trier (j)
39. St. Katharina, Colmar (lett)
40. St. Katharina, Nuremberg (r, lett)
41. St. Katharina, St. Gall (c, sb)
42. St. Klara, Freiburg (lit)
43. St. Klara, Nuremberg (lett)
44. St. Maria Magdalena an den Steinen (lit)
45. St. Nicholas in Undis (r)
46. Steinheim (j)
47. Töss (sb)
48. Überwasser (c)

49. Unterlinden (sb)
50. Wienhausen (c)
51. Weissfrauen Cloister, Erfurt (lit)
52. Zoffingen (r)

Primary Sources by Men about Women

53. Inselkloster, Bern (c)
54. Ribnitz (c)
55. Schönensteinbach (c, sb)

Legend:
c = chronicle
j = journal
lett = letter(s)
lit = devotional work, poem, sermon reconstruction, vita
m = manual, handbook
r = reform account
sb = sister-book

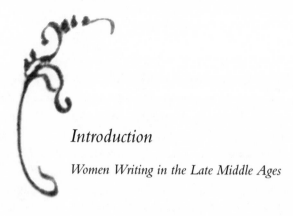

Introduction

Women Writing in the Late Middle Ages

In the year 1503, on the Feast of the Epiphany, an anonymous woman completed a *Book of Sisters,* an account of the lives of sixty-six nuns of the cloister of St. Agnes at Emmerich on the Rhine. Her narrative opens with these words:

> Here begins the prologue of the book of the sisters of St. Agnes in Embrick [Emmerich], under the rule of St. Augustine, the life and converse of the honorable sisters serving God at the cloister of St. Agnes, which was founded in the year of our Lord 1419. . . . Thus have I undertaken to write a little—to the honor of God and the Virgin—in praise of those who lived and for the edification of those who will come after [us]—a consolation to all devout souls. And because I am simple and uneducated, I desire that those who read or hear this should not disdain it, but examine the lives and virtues of those who are described in this book.[1]

Despite the author's request for remembrance, her book reached few readers and was all but forgotten for the next five hundred years. The one surviving copy was discovered and edited by Anne Bollmann and Nikolaus Staubach in 1998. This kind of literary-historical obscurity is more the rule than the exception for works by monastic women of the late Middle Ages. It has led to the mistaken assumption that they left no substantial written records about themselves. But, in fact, they did.

A survey of the remains of women's convent libraries turns up many similarly obscure vernacular convent chronicles, historical accounts, and other kinds of writings. This book surveys works composed by women in monastic orders during the fourteenth, fifteenth, and early sixteenth centuries in Germany, Switzerland, Italy, Belgium, and the Netherlands.

Produced in fifty-two different women's communities, they include, besides the Emmerich text, two other books of sisters, twelve women's cloister chronicles, five foundation narratives, six accounts by nuns of the reform of convents, plus numerous other annals and historical writings. While four of the women's accounts are in Latin, the others are all in dialects of German and East Netherlandish. Also included are three women's chronicles from a later period that cite verbatim from fifteenth- and early sixteenth-century annals. These works, along with letters, poems, and mystical and devotional texts comprise only a small part of medieval women's writings, which are still extant but unstudied in cloister, regional, and national archives.[2]

The female monastics who produced these works represented a significant presence in medieval society. Like many northern convents, the St. Agnes cloister in Emmerich had originally been founded as a house of Sisters of the Common Life but by the middle of the fifteenth century had become a monastic community. Women's houses of Devout Sisters were the first to be founded by the *devotio moderna* or Common Life movement, which began in the Netherlands toward the end of the fourteenth century, and constituted the majority of Common Life establishments. Even though only thirteen of the women's communities were officially admitted to the Windesheim Congregation (the movement's monastic branch), houses of Sisters of the Common Life outnumbered those of the Brothers by a ratio approaching three to one.[3] John Van Engen's more conservative estimate counts some forty male and ninety female houses spread throughout Holland and Germany at the end of the fifteenth century.[4] Despite their numerical majority, however, the women of the movement were largely ignored by the scholarly community until 1985, when Gerhard Rehm published a groundbreaking study of the Sisters of the Common Life in Germany. By Rehm's estimate German sister-houses numbered about seventy as compared to twenty-five for the Brothers.[5] Still, it took another twelve years before the first extensive study of the cloister life and writings of the women of the Windesheim Congregation appeared.[6]

In the more traditional monastic orders, the ratio of women's to men's houses is less imposing than in the Common Life movement but remains substantial. The number of female religious in Germany alone, c. 1250, has been estimated at between 25,000 and 30,000.[7] From its founding c. 1220, the women's branch of the Dominican order grew so rapidly that, by the early fourteenth century, there were seventy nunneries to forty-six friaries.[8] Particularly in southern German cities such as Strasbourg, which alone was home to no fewer than seven houses of Dominican nuns, religious women constituted an important presence.[9] In northern Germany, the high ratio of nunneries to priories was primarily in the Cistercian order. Here one finds in the sixteenth century forty-three women's as compared to fifteen men's houses.[10] Although nuns were outnumbered by male monastics in Europe as a whole, the number of women religious approached or even exceeded that of men in many places.[11]

Despite the significant numbers of these religious establishments, relatively little is known about the day-to-day lives of the many women who inhabited them from the point of view of the sisters themselves. Jeffrey Hamburger's recent books on medieval nuns as artists have provided essential information on the spiritual and artistic inner workings of German-speaking communities. Yet, as Hamburger points out, this geographic region and historical period have long been neglected by North American medievalists as compared with studies of French, Italian, and English nuns. Much research remains to be done.[12] Women were, for example, active participants alongside men in the reform movements that swept the German-speaking areas in the fifteenth century. They left behind accounts that offer a different perspective on the struggle for renewal and reform on the eve of the Reformation. Consequently, to fully understand the dynamics of change that resulted in the radical religious upheavals of the Protestant Reformation in the sixteenth century, those records require further study.

In their comprehensive history of women in Europe, Bonnie Anderson and Judith Zinsser argue against the idea that the "invisible majority" had "no history" or achieved little that is "worthy of inclusion in the historical record."[13] Other women's historians have asked provocatively whether a "master narrative," which does not include half of the population, is legitimate.[14] Clearly, the past looks different, Joan Ferrante asserts, "just with women sharing the stage."[15] Fortunately, it is a very large stage and there is plenty of room on it. The task now is to rewrite the action with faces, names, and firsthand accounts from the women whose own histories and works, like the Emmerich *Book of Sisters,* have long been gathering dust in the archives.

Aside from a few mystical works composed by female visionaries, almost all primary texts used by modern scholars to study medieval women were recorded by men.[16] In addition to the vitae of charismatic, radically ascetic, and even sometimes deranged women composed by their male confessors, the most common documents studied have been court protocols, visitations records, registers and charters.[17] Perhaps it should not surprise that the largest single source of information on the everyday life of medieval women has been criminal court proceedings.[18] A sampling of these kinds of protocols, along with scholarly and popular accounts, can be found in Eileen Power's classic *Medieval English Nunneries* (1922), still the most widely used authority on medieval convent life. For all its excellence and splendid wealth of information, however, Power's landmark study is almost entirely lacking in sources actually written by women. Worse yet, many of the popular songs, ribald and moral tales it includes depict nuns satirically as naive, silly, vain, spiteful, or sexually unchaste.[19] Critiquing these kinds of salacious sources, Shulamith Shahar cites a typical twelfth-century nunnery description attributed to Renart, in which a nun leaves her own infant unattended in order to serve as midwife to other nuns who are about to give birth.[20]

Reacting against such depictions, Caroline Walker Bynum asserts that "the stories men liked to tell about women reflected not so much what women did as what men admired or abhorred. . . . It is crucial not to take as women's own self-image the sentimentalizing or the castigating of the female in which medieval men indulged." To overturn stereotypes like these Bynum recommends studying "works in which women wrote about their own visions and mystical experiences and about life among the sisters in their households, beguinages, and convents."[21]

Unfortunately, these kinds of texts are hard to find. Although many prominent women mystics' writings can be documented, especially from the thirteenth century on, in most cases their revelations were edited or recorded not by the women themselves but with the assistance of well-meaning and sympathetic male collaborators. The philological difficulties this creates have led scholars to question whether a "female voice" can be distinguished at all.[22] A step in the right direction is Albrecht Classen's search for alternative sources. Classen suggests four areas or genres where female voices from the Middle Ages can be identified. Listed are (1) religious songs, (2) love poetry in books of popular song, (3) letters for public or private consumption, and (4) religious pamphlets of the Reformation era.[23] By broadening the range of texts to encompass writings that are less conventionally "literary," one can identify many more works by women. These include histories, eyewitness reform reports, and cloister annals, as well as more nontraditional sources such as prioresses' manuals, books of advice, and New Years' addresses to their communities, books of sisters, personal devotional books, meditational exercises and interpretations of biblical texts, and even student compositions. This study comprises these primary sources, along with more conventional types of writings.

One eye-opening effort to present some of these alternative tests to an English-speaking audience is Daniel Bornstein's translation of Bartolomea Riccoboni's chronicle and necrology of the convent of Corpus Domini in Venice (1395–1436).[24] Bornstein concludes that "far from being closed in upon themselves and interested exclusively in their own spiritual lives, the sisters of Corpus Domini were deeply engaged in the world beyond their walls." Indeed, the picture of women that emerges in Sister Bartolomea's chronicle diverges significantly from conventional wisdom about what nuns in the late Middle Ages thought and were like. Bornstein asserts that Sister Bartolomea's chronicle is noteworthy because it records and illuminates "a particularly dramatic moment in the long history of the Catholic Church," namely, the schism created by the election of three rival popes and the great church councils subsequently called to deal with it.[25] There are, however, other reasons for studying this and other women's accounts.

The texts collected in this study recall a similarly dramatic moment in the history of the medieval church: the intense struggle for reform waged by fifteenth-century activists in the Observant movement. But they also record another important juncture. From the point of view of women's history, the fifteenth century constitutes a critical period in religious women's efforts to find new avenues of engagement and self-expression. To these women, activism in the Observant movement, to which most of them belonged, offered alternatives to the old avenue of influence that had been closed off to women by censorship of mystical and visionary writings. At the same time that the Observance imposed a stricter rule, it placed some women in positions of authority and created conditions that encouraged literary production, new networks of exchange between women's cloisters, and a more active role in the late medieval discourse on religious piety and practice.

In the religious transformations that preceded the Reformation, both male and female monastics were deeply involved. The fifteenth century, dominated by the great church councils, calls for religious change, and efforts at top-down reform, was a time of intense religious ferment that spawned countless middle- and lower-level reform initiatives.[26] The Observant reform advocated, on the one hand, a return to the strict piety practiced by the founders of the orders and, on the other, a new spirituality similar to that of the *devotio moderna* or Common Life movement (which was spreading at the same time from the Netherlands across northern Europe).[27] Although the Observant revival was brought to prominence by the great reform councils, its origins date back to the previous century. Having begun in the 1330s among Franciscans in Italy, the reformed piety was promoted among Augustinians in the 1380s, Dominicans in the 1390s, and reached the upper Rhine valley by the turn of the century. From there the movement spread in the 1400s throughout the German-speaking territories. By the early sixteenth century, it had achieved a majority hold in the fatefully important province of Saxony, where Martin Luther, himself an Observant, was a leader in the reformed faction of Augustinians.[28] Local initiatives such as these and a growing participation by secular authorities in reforms paved the way for more radical and rapid changes to follow, affecting the whole populace.

Among Dominicans, an approximately equal number of men's and women's religious communities had joined the Observance by the 1480s. In spite of women's participation and eye-witness reports, studies traditionally have cited only accounts written by male activists, usually those by Dominicans Johannes Nider and Johannes Meyer, and Augustinian Johannes Busch. Even Constance Proksch's 1994 monograph on chronicles of the reform movement, which draws on thirty-five convent histories, uses only chronicles written by men.[29] The chronicles and accounts written by female reform activists have not been studied in a systematic way. Yet, in these accounts, one reads of prioresses soliciting help from other prioresses to introduce the Observance in their own communities, of groups of sisters accompanying male activists on missions to reform other cloisters, and of struggles inside convents between Observants and opponents of the reform. By examining these and other texts, this study thus explores the distinctive nature of women's religious and literary activities at a key moment in both the history of Western Christianity and the ongoing construction of a history for women. The accounts of the Observant reform from women's perspective are texts that must be integrated into the history of the Observant movement. Moreover, they call for a reconsideration of late medieval women's role, agency, and attitudes about themselves.

For the medieval female population, even more than for men, religion was of critical cultural importance. Feminist historian Gerda Lerner has called it "the primary arena on which women fought for hundreds of years for feminist consciousness."[30] Yet the fifteenth-century Observant reform presents something of a dilemma in the feminist context. On the one hand, the imposition of strict claustration on female monastics and the requirement that all goods be held in common are seen as attempts to subjugate women and to appropriate their wealth.[31] Understandably, then, feminist scholars applaud their plucky medieval sisters who fought the efforts of reformers to encloister them and place their private possessions in the convent's hands. In some convents women resisted physically, as did nuns at Nuremberg, who for a time held off male reformers by brandishing a large crucifix at them.[32] In many other places, nuns left reformed cloisters for other communities rather than join the Observance against their will. On the other hand, at the same time that many women opposed the reform there were others who supported it and were as committed to its goals as male activists. Voting with their feet, many joined the rapidly expanding new Observant communities. Others took part in the effort to spread the movement, working side by side with men and sometimes independently. What are scholars to do, for example, with women like Katharina von Mühlheim who set off with parties of reformers to introduce the Observance at three other cloisters, or with prioresses like Sophie von Münster, Margareta Zorn, and Margareta Regenstein, who each engaged in the reform of four cloisters? Clearly, it is difficult to decide who the heroines are here: the women who fought for the movement or those who fought against it. Most women religious opposed the strict seclusion, austerity, and renunciation of private property demanded by the reformers. But, while women who supported the reform constitute only a small group, they left numerous records. Pictured in their own writings, these women saw themselves as active agents with positive political and spiritual agendas. It is now clear that more studies are needed of women on both sides of the reform controversy, as well as examinations of their agency and relationships to their male mentors.

Feminists do not object to women launching reform efforts of their own but rather to programs imposed on them from outside, especially when what male reformers imposed was "control."[33] Yet to say that women were subject to the machinations of religious and secular overlords is not to say that female religious were uninterested in reform. What has been missing is women's own perspective on their situation, their struggles, aims, and hopes. In her 1997 study, historian Joan Ferrante cautioned that many medieval women may rightly be characterized as "victims," but for scholars to concentrate too much on misogyny and the negative is to play into the hands of the patriarchal view that "women were able to do little, therefore they did nothing valuable." Instead, Ferrante advocates studying what she calls "examples of positive practice," that is, women who "were active and effective" despite prejudices and the constraints placed upon them.[34] One does not have to look far to find such accounts. The sources this study examines are filled with portraits of active and effective women. These are not queens and saints but less high-profile, more ordinary women, though still of the patrician classes, whom female chroniclers celebrate for their practical resourcefulness, leadership and personal virtue.

Because so little is known about cloister life from the point of view of the women who lived it, Chapter 1 reviews recent scholarship, combining it with women's own depictions of life inside the walls of a medieval convent. Does the assertion that convent life was repressed and monotonous, a "horrible tedium," agree with nuns' own descriptions?[35] Can the conflicts that arose over reform justly be called "trivial nuns' squabbling," as another scholar asserts?[36] A look at women's own narratives about their lives inside the convent reveals a surprisingly broad range of theatrical, literary, and artistic pursuits. Far from a sense of repression, these nun's self-portraits convey a very positive opinion of themselves and their spiritual work. As educational and living establishments for the upper classes, medieval convents played an essential role in the "economy of social prestige." Admission to an exclusive convent was often a coveted position and a way of achieving higher social status. In narratives by medieval women, who had few options, often none desirable, the convent is frequently depicted as a safe haven offering them an alternative and a choice.

Besides preserving the extensive and influential family connections of the convents' inhabitants in medieval society, women's religious houses served important roles as money-lending institutions, adjudicators of legal disputes, and recorders of wills, deeds, and transactions. Beyond this, women's religious houses constituted a significant presence through the religious services their parish churches provided, their performance of the liturgical offices, the keeping of lists of the dead, and the offering of prayers for the souls of the deceased. The extent of these multiple, interlocking social, financial, and spiritual links between religious houses and the lay community are reflected in the intense engagement of the lay populace in conflicts over convent reforms that erupted in the fifteenth century.

Chapter 2 examines how the environment for women religious changed from the thirteenth to the sixteenth century, as reflected in fourteenth- and fifteenth-century narratives. In these works, the sisters depict the origins of their communities as beguine settlements. They celebrate how the "founding mothers" established religious houses in the thirteenth century and tell stories about women seeking an alternative religious lifestyle, setting up their own communities, supporting each other financially, and working together in strikingly nonhierarchical relationships with male advisors. Their foundation stories depict the women's struggle to achieve regular status, acceptance into religious orders, and the sanction of the church hierarchy. While some of the foundation histories were written in the fifteenth century, others date from the fourteenth century and earlier. All the stories, however, were written for female audiences and all feature female protagonists as active, self-directed agents.

By the fifteenth century, conditions had begun to change rapidly as divisions within the Catholic church reached crisis proportions. At the same time that church councils and new religious movements took up the banner of reform, city councils and territorial princes stepped in to demand greater control and oversight of religious institutions. Dominican women's houses—by then recognized fixtures of the religious establishment—became subjects of the newly influential laity's vision of a more pious society. Themselves members of the increasingly powerful and affluent urban non-noble class, Observant reformers questioned the privileges and immunities of the old religious elite and campaigned to open cloisters to a wider spectrum of the population. Thus, for some women of the burgher classes, reform gave access to positions of leadership in convents.

After tracing the development of the Observant movement, the following chapters will look at the women who supported and opposed it. Chapter 3 focuses on those who took part in spreading the Observance, both women who willingly undertook or even initiated it and those who were drafted to go out with reform parties. Not all of the nuns who participated as reformers wrote about it, but several of them left firsthand accounts. Like the convent foundation narratives, these reform artifacts place women in the foreground and portray them with agency and initiative, with strong, capable, and dedicated personalities. They particularly prize leadership abilities, the same qualities, ironically, that enabled women to successfully oppose the reform.

Chapter 4 looks at these opponents. Examining case studies of the reform's most famous failures, it reviews the strategies women used to fend off takeovers by reformers. In successful resistance campaigns, women were able to solicit effective support from their networks among the minor nobility. Rejecting any interference in the internal affairs of their houses, abbesses fought to stay in power and avert infringements of the convent's independence or social prestige. In elite houses, the critical issue was often loss of privileges for the nobility and the admission of women of lower rank. While some Conventual houses supported a more moderate kind of reform, they staunchly resisted the loss of private property and more austere practices, insisting that their traditional piety and way of life were in no way inferior.

Always at the core of this conflict was the difficult issue of enclosure. More complicated than merely an effort by the church hierarchy to further subjugate women, the move was bound up with public pressures of an economic, political, and social nature. Among the Observants, the ideal of withdrawal from the world was advocated as a spiritual necessity and proposed for men as well as women. Surprisingly, enclosure was used, in some instances, by women as a way to limit secular access and outside interference in their affairs. But the opponents of the reform were unmoved and resisted enclosure, often quite successfully, to defend their interests both as individuals and as communities.

Chapter 5 examines the explosion of scribal activity that occurred in Observant women's convents. Especially in the houses reached by the Bursfeld reform, primarily Benedictine and Cistercian communities, much effort was put into copying the new liturgical texts that had been mandated as part of the Bursfeld program to simplify and standardize the liturgy. But in all orders, books and often a program of education were some of the most important things reforming sisters brought with them. For Dominican women, reformer Johannes Meyer promoted a reading plan and a booklist. Under the Observance, communal and individual reading assumed significance as a means of introducing the newly reformed sisters to the spirituality of the movement.

The result was what Werner Williams-Krapp has called a "literary explosion" of text production.[37] Library collections expanded at a rapid rate as books were copied and exchanged among Observant houses through a network of interlibrary loans. Although almost all of the collections built up in this expansion of women's libraries have since been dispersed or destroyed, a few medieval catalogues of what was contained in them remain. These inventories are impressive. The largest library to have partially survived was that of the Dominican sisters of St. Katharina in Nuremberg, which comprised some 500 to 600 volumes. In its time, the library at St. Katharina constituted the largest collection of German-language manuscripts of the Middle Ages. In most houses, the greatest expansion occurred in the first fifty to seventy-five years following the reform. Even though only ten percent of cloisters belonged to the Observance, this small number of houses produced ninety percent of the manuscripts from the period.[38] At St. Katharina, approximately half of the volumes housed there were copied by the sisters themselves.

Authorized by the Observance to keep records, write histories, and copy works to supply the growing demand for devotional literature, the women began to make their own translations from Latin into the vernacular. They also composed original poems, interpretations of biblical texts, devotional works, tracts, books of practical advice, accounts of the reform, and convent chronicles. For their personal study and reflection they compiled collections of excerpts from religious works. In addition, they collected sermons by their own "house preachers" and by guest preachers. Some sermons were copied, others summarized or reconstructed from notes. The result is that virtually all of the surviving vernacular sermons were preserved and made into collections by women, producing a literature primarily for female audiences. Despite the long neglect of women's works, it is becoming clear that, in both Germany and the Low Countries, the fifteenth century constituted a period of extremely active religious literary and scribal engagement on the part of women.

Drawing some conclusions about the nature and aims of feminine writing and its distinctiveness, Chapter 6 considers the strategies used and roles played by religious women in late medieval piety. While in earlier centuries mysticism had given them a voice and a means of exercising power, by the fifteenth century this power had been heavily eroded through increased censorship. Deprived of visionary revelations as a route to influence, women began to focus on other literary modes. Accordingly, the portraits they draw of themselves in fifteenth-century chronicles differ from those of earlier mystical works and from what nineteenth- and twentieth-century literary historians asserted was innately and typically "female." The self-portraits of women in fifteenth-century chronicles are just as much literary fictions as those in earlier visionary writing, but they serve different aims. Instead of charismatics who fall into trances, the new heroines are portrayed as *in* the world rather than out of it. They are models of spiritual fervor but also of practical skills and attainable virtues. The chronicles depict convent inhabitants as aware of their history, contrast the old with the new, and celebrate the introduction and continuation of the Observance. Aimed at a new generation, they seek to inspire their audiences to persevere in the reform.

The larger range of texts that are available in the fifteenth century makes it possible to compare parallel works by men and women and circumvent some of the problems of mediation that have always plagued studies of "women's" writing. In form, convent writings do not conform to established models but tend to be idiosyncratic and eclectic. The language used by the female vernacular chroniclers is less educated and bears a closer resemblance to spoken than conventional written language. The tone is immediate and personal, unlike that of conventional chronicles. Women frequently use the first person, address the reader directly, and speak of the community as "we" and "our." Their texts concentrate much more than the men's on the religious life itself. Yet women's concentration on re-formed spirituality does not have only an internal focus. Perhaps the most surprising discoveries of my research are examples of convent sisters editing texts specifically for distribution to the laity. For these sermon transcribers and editors, the Observance provided an arena for active engagement in the religious conversation of the day.

The sources upon which this study relies illustrate many of the difficulties of working with women's texts. First of all, they are texts of many types, dispersed over a large region (see map, page xviii) and a 300-year timespan. Besides letters and various kinds of devotional works, they include fourteenth-century Dominican women's collections of mystical vitae that contain convent foundation narratives (Adelhausen, Engelthal, Katharinental, Oetenbach, Töss, and Unterlinden), fifteenth- and sixteenth-century vitae of sisters in houses of the New Devout (Deventer, Diepenveen, Emmerich), chronicles, housebooks, annals, and journals (Altomünster, Ebstorf [2], Heiningen, Herzebrock [2], Maihingen, Marienthal, Pfullingen, St. Gall, Überwasser, Zoffingen), reform accounts (Kirchberg, Kirchheim, Nuremberg, Pforzheim, Steinheim), and manuals or handbooks (Preetz, St. Gall). In addition, there are two chronicles in manuscripts that extend beyond this time period but cite excerpts verbatim from New Years' addresses by Prioress Ursula Haider in 1495 and 1496, and excerpts from the old Inzigkofen chronicle of 1525.[39] The Wienhausen chronicle, from a manuscript dated 1692, is included because it contains entries copied from the earlier Low German, fifteenth-century chronicle.[40]

The problems of establishing women's authorship are fewer than might be supposed. In the best cases, as in the Adelhausen sister-book, the writer identifies herself with the colophon, "I, Sister Anna von Munzingen, who composed this book."[41] Similarly, the "Book in the Choir" at cloister Preetz begins with the words, "In the year of our Lord 1487, on the vigil of St. Michael, this book, which was begun by me, Anna von Buchwald, in 1471, was completed and finished."[42] In other cases, a writer may be anonymous because she identifies herself only as "I, Sister Anna, Prioress," as in the Maihingen "Housebook," for example, where three prioresses have compatible dates and bear this first name.[43] Often the author does not name herself but interjects revealing personal comments, as does the chronicler of Pfullingen, who says, "As I write this, I have great hopes that the Lord will not abandon us," and "Pray to God for the writer, she composed this for you out of love."[44] In the chronicle of Ebstorf, the narrator uses the pronoun "we," and speaks of her colleagues as "the daughters."[45] In cases where sufficient internal clues in the text itself are lacking, the gender of the writer and sometimes even the name have been revealed by other convent documents. Because institutional documents were continually added on to, however, the issue becomes problematic when the earlier entries were recopied by later hands. Sometimes, as at Maihingen, the abbess collected the materials and prepared an outline, which scribes completed.

An example of the complicated, layered history of many of these texts is the case of the Töss sister-book, some, but clearly not all, of which was composed by Elsbeth Stagel (d. ca. 1360).[46] In the fifteenth century, a prologue, an epilogue, a vita of Henry Suso's mother and one of Elsbeth herself were appended to the work by Johannes Meyer (1422–1485) who copied and edited three of the nine sister-books (those of Töss, Katharinental, and Oetenbach). Meyer, one of the earliest and most radical of the Dominican Observants, realized that the women's texts of the previous century, with their emphasis on poverty, virtue, and spiritual devotion, could supply spiritually edifying vernacular readings for women in newly reformed cloisters. Yet Ruth Meyer, who compared other manuscripts of the St. Katharinental sister-book to Johannes Meyer's version of it (in the same manuscript with the Töss sister-book), finds that Meyer's changes to the body of the text were limited to modifying chapter headings, rewording unclear passages, and removing three sections that he did not consider sufficiently edifying. Meyer's prologue and epilogue are the only parts not found in other manuscripts of the Katharinental text.[47] Since they do not differ appreciably from the sister-books that Meyer did not edit, the three sister-books abridged by him are regarded as essentially the women's own work. Scholars agree that, unlike other women's texts of the fourteenth century, sister-books were conspicuously lacking in the influence of confessors either as initiators or as advisors to their composition.[48]

Another difficulty is that many of the sources in this study are accessible only as unpublished manuscripts or as transcriptions made in the eighteenth or nineteenth century and printed whole or in excerpted form in regional or difficult-to-access periodicals. Magdalena Kremer's chronicle of the reform of cloister Kirchheim is available, for example, in a collection of documents on the history of the counts of Württemberg, published in 1777. Except for the Dominican sister-books, preserved in multiple copies made by the Observants, almost all of the women's chronicles, manuals, journals, and reform accounts have survived from the Middle Ages in only one single manuscript copy, often still located in a convent library or regional archive. Like Magdalena Kremer's chronicle, printed because it recounts deeds of three of the counts of Württemberg, the parts of women's chronicles that have been published most often are those that contain accounts of wars and revolts. The only sections of the chronicle of Überwasser in print are episodes that relate the Anabaptist uprising in Münster in 1534–35.[49] Thus, in many women's works, the sections dealing with "important events" have been deemed worthy of publication, while the rest has not.

The question of genre is complicated by the fact that even internally these texts are not of one type. Typically, they are hodgepodge collections, combining letters, inventories, financial accounts, and general advice, interspersed piecemeal within a sort of chronicle format. As such, they do not conform to conventional notions of "literature" or belong to established genres. Indeed, many of these institutional annals are such idiosyncratic hybrids as to defy categorization. Rather, they constitute a subgenre of their own that has so far received no attention. Even institutional texts by named writers such as Anna von Buchwald and Magdalena Kremer are not included in the *Verfasserlexikon,* the standard reference work on German medieval writers. Because these and other women's institutional writings do not fall into traditional categories or qualify as literary texts in the conventional sense, they have long been excluded from the most broadly defined canon.

Their character as hybrid works makes dealing with them "whole" problematic, since they can be read in so many different ways. Anna von Buchwald's "Book in the Choir," although largely about liturgical reform, is also a chronicle and ledger book that can be read as an economic and social history of the cloister. Yet it is just as much an autobiography of Anna herself. Moreover, in dealing with texts that cover events extending from the thirteenth through the sixteenth centuries, a single study can focus only on a few of the many topics and in a limited time frame. Since the chronicles were written in the wake of the Observant movement, a primary theme in them is reform. As noted, the last chapter of this study examines the complex question of how they were composed, what political agendas the women had in mind, and the relationship between power and text production.

For the most part, these women's texts are not finished literary works or intended as such, but examples of utilitarian record keeping and narrative accounts that were written down "for the record," as a witness to current and future generations. Yet, despite all the factual, historical, and financial data contained in them, cloister chronicles are also representations that select out of the everyday certain events to which the writer wants to give particular significance. Although not considered "literature" in the traditional sense, chronicles are literary fictions just as much as they are "documents," a distinction that New Cultural historians have for the most part abandoned as moot, if not meaningless.[50] Indeed, the move of literary and cultural historians from an aesthetic to a more anthropological perspective has led to a more inclusive approach, one that views literary texts as parts of a larger cultural discourse encompassing all kinds of written artifacts. In this context, then, convent annals do not need to be upgraded to "literature" to be worthy of study.

Examining only parts of hybrid works, each one with its own complicated history, has its limitations. In drawing from a diverse set of writings from fifty-two different houses, this study cannot treat more than a few of them whole. Instead, I have attempted to put together a broader composite picture from the fragments and disparate sources that have survived—a mosaic like the works themselves. Dealing with the texts piecemeal and anecdotally does not assume, however, that they constitute a transparent window on the past. Clearly, each has, along with a complex textual genesis, its own recognized discursive agenda.

From the point of view of gender identity, however, the women's own words are also important. These surviving accounts from the Middle Ages have been neglected for so long that these female voices are heard here in many cases for the first time. It is exactly because they are so unfamiliar that they have been allowed to speak as much as possible, for themselves and anecdotally in their own words. No longer can it be said, as one scholar has observed: "Apart from a few exceptions—accounts about women in the Middle Ages were written only by men: at first almost exclusively by clerics, then more and more often lay persons, but again only men. Behind these [men's] accounts we perceive only the murmuring of numberless, nameless—or named but not consulted—unheard women."[51]

Before long, as more and more women's accounts are recovered, this statement will be ancient history. Women will acquire names, their murmuring will become distinct speech, and their contributions will be recognized. This study brings onto the stage and into the spotlight many women whose names, lives, and writings were previously little known. It demonstrates that women did not murmur but spoke distinctly in written records of many different kinds beyond the mystical works that are most often associated with them. In addition to examining the written records these religious women left behind, this study recognizes their contributions as users, selectors, and transmitters of texts. For in the late Middle Ages it was women who constituted the principle audience for sermons and devotional literature in the vernacular. Moreover, as makers of personal collections of extracts and sermon summaries, as well as compilers of anthologies, convent women's choices and collective reading preferences influenced the selection, promotion, and transmission of the works that have come down to us. By preserving these works in their libraries and repositories, by exchanging them among themselves and with the laity (even editing some), convent women were major participants in and helped to shape the vernacular discourse on religious piety and reform in the period leading up to the Reformation.

1

Late Medieval Nunneries

Accounts by Women

Although much has been said about the absence of women in the historical master narrative, little has been written about the histories that women themselves produced. Yet as far back as Hrosvit of Gandersheim's *Origins of the Convent of Gandersheim* (c. 973/83) and Sister Bertha's *Life of Adelheid, Abbess of Vilich* (1057) women have been writing chronicles, histories, and accounts of their own. The reason these and similar works have been neglected in the "grand récit" is illustrated by the comments of Carl Cornelius, mid–nineteenth-century editor of the "Chronicle of the Sisterhouse Marienthal" (c. 1541). In his introduction, Cornelius explains that the work "confines itself strictly to the fortunes of the cloister which in times of peace are insignificant and of no interest to a larger audience. Only where the uprising [of Anabaptists in Münster] intrudes into the quiet life of the women does it acquire historical import."[1] Today, however, historical import is being defined in new ways that recognize competing subcultures and encompass alternative points of view. Gender theorists argue, for example, that power can be understood in paradigms other than public authority, and feminists are looking for methods of analyzing women's agency through social processes and cultural transformations.[2] Most recently, attention has been drawn to feminine social networks, alliances, and to the cultural impact of these subgroups in medieval society.[3]

Although female religious were regarded in the nineteenth century and earlier as "insignificant" and as having no "historical import," newer secondary research and the narratives that medieval convent women themselves wrote have shown them to be much more intimately connected throughout medieval society than was previously recognized. Their letters to family members, for example, and the correspondence between prioresses recording exchanges of gifts and advice indicate some of the social networks in which convent women were engaged and the personal contacts they maintained. These and other artifacts demonstrate that female religious were by no means silent or cut off from society. Some of the texts to be looked at here highlight, for example, their social and economic presence as operators of boarding schools, employers of workers and artisans, producers of cloth and books, dispensers of food to the poor, and providers of places of retirement for widows and the elderly.

Fourteenth-century records for the city of Freiburg show that the city contained, besides five large women's cloisters, at least 300 women living in ten houses as unincorporated religious groups.[4] In 1450, men's and women's convents together owned one-sixth of all the properties within the central city and by 1500 they had increased their holdings to one-fifth.[5] Secular constituencies regularly borrowed from or invested capital with religious communities. In addition to their significant physical and financial presence, women's cloisters had familial ties to the townsfolk, as institutions where the sisters, daughters, aunts, and cousins of many of the most prosperous and prominent families lived. In convent parish churches, nuns and parishioners worshiped together, separated by a screen. This proximity to the holy women was valued because it was believed to heighten the power and significance of parishioners' prayers.[6] Moreover, to be buried near them and to have the nuns pray for one's soul would lessen time in purgatory. By maintaining lists of the dead for whom they prayed, nuns thus served as keepers of written records, which included also the wills, charters, deeds, and transactions of the secular community. Not least, for people living in the vicinity of the cloister, life was regulated by the ringing of the convent's bells.[7]

While the chronicles and literary texts that medieval convent women produced provide an alternative narrative to the dominant male-produced one, they do not contradict it on all points. Rather, as participants in the same institutional system, the female writers reflect and vary the ideological views that produced these institutions. Their perspective on institutional ideology differs significantly on one point, however, from that of the master narrative: in all of these texts women are at the center rather than at the margins or in the background. They are active and not passive agents. Beside the "women worthies" of the kind portrayed as models of feminine virtue by Plutarch, Bocaccio, or the authors of saints' lives, convent women's narratives include portraits of many more of the rank and file. By describing themselves differently, choosing other issues, images, and infor-

Fig. 1 Petrarca-Master, woodcut from [Francesco Petrarca,] *Von der Artzney beyder Glück, des guten und widerwertigen* (About the Medicine of Both Kinds of Fate: The Good and the Vexatious). Book 1, chapter 13. Edited by Georg Spalatin and Peter Stahel. Augsburg: Steyner, 1532.

mation from those presented by the dominant narrative, they call into question its ability to offer a whole or valid picture of medieval life. Certainly, the satirical stereotypes of nuns in the many ribald tales and songs that have come down to us, caricatures such as the popular sixteenth-century woodcut of nun as "cloister cat" (see Fig. 1), leave room for alternative representations.[8]

It is not that women's accounts are more "factual" than popular tales or depictions by male biographers. They are literary representations and self-fashionings just as imaginative as other medieval literary works, biographies, histories, and documents. But they differ in being unmediated by male collaborators, have different agendas, and address different issues. Though composed by women, they are not "voices" per se but literary self-depictions serving particular functions for the communities of female religious in which they were composed. Less the creations of individuals than of these communities, the chronicles, annals, and sister-books were often written and added on to by a succession of female contributors. As institutional texts, these collective portraits constructed a group identity by compiling a narrative about the community's past and providing role models for both present and future generations of sisters. They were intended to foster a sense of common mission and commitment to the community. Many works also function as reform literature, produced by women empowered by the Observance to write histories of their houses (see Chapter 3).

But before turning to the Observant movement and its implications for late-medieval women religious, this chapter will look at the situation of convent women from the point of view of recent secondary literature and also as represented in accounts by medieval women themselves on topics they chose to address. The questions of greatest concern to them, although relating to their own community, also reflect social issues and developments in the larger society of which convents were an integral part. Their anecdotes deal with a wide range of significant issues, including marriage, inheritances, social status, dowries and financial assets, the costs and problems of running a cloister, the economic impact of convent labor and its products on the secular community, poor relief, standards of living, hygiene, nutrition, longevity, literacy, education, patronage of the arts and artistic production, male-female friendships, working relationships with stewards, clerical overseers, and, of course, religious life.

The striking thing about these convent women's self-portraits in all types of texts—whether chronicles, vitae, manuals, letters, or student essays—is their depiction of themselves as self-determining, active agents taking the initiative in solving the problems that face them. Collectively, they express a strong sense of self-worth and, in first-person narratives, indicate many forceful personalities. While some portraits are hagiographic, idealized depictions, others are more realistic and sober biographies. Especially in these latter works, and in their everyday letters exchanging opinions and practical advice, convent women seem much more "normal" than in traditional external depictions of them, their lives more varied and often more difficult than in popular stereotypes. The stories women tell to women are clearly different from those that men tell to them or those that men tell about them to men. In the same way that audiences influence the nature of the narrative, these literary representations for female readers and hearers contain agendas that are specific to women's cultural situation. This situation will be considered below, as background to the reforms by combining secondary sources with accounts narrated by medieval women who viewed it from the inside.

Why Women Entered Cloisters: Nun's Stories

One of the foremost issues in the writings of inhabitants of convents was the question of why they were there. In some cases, entry into a convent is depicted as a trauma or crisis situation, in others a matter of course. Often women in the fourteenth and fifteenth centuries, before the Observant reforms, entered religious houses as young children, sometimes at the death of a parent. Typical is the comment on Elisabeth von Weiler who, as the author of the Weiler sister-book matter-of-factly relates, "was five years of age, when she came to the cloister."[9] Jutta Sperling remarks that patrician girls in sixteenth-century Venice were sent off to convents "as soon as they could walk, speak, and eat on their own." There they grew up and received a rudimentary education. If a marriage could not be arranged for them by their parents they simply remained in the convent where they had grown up among friends and female relatives.[10] Some scholars thus suggest that girls placed as children in a convent were not likely to be "fired by a sense of religious vocation," but in many accounts convent life seems rather to have fostered it.[11] Magdalena Kremer writes, for example, in her "Chronicle of Kirchheim" (c. 1490) of Subprioress Elisabeth Herwert, one of the reformers from Alsace, who had lived in a convent from childhood but transferred to join an Observant community.

> This sister had been from childhood at the cloister of St. Katharina in Augsburg, also of the Dominican order. And when she became an adult, God began to work in her conscience so that she conceived the desire to go to the cloister of Schönensteinbach, which was the first and oldest cloister of the Observance in the German provinces. And when she had received permission from her superiors and had traveled as far as Sélestat, she heard that there was fighting in the area [Alsace] and that she could not get to Schönensteinbach. So she asked for shelter in cloister Sylo at Sélestat [also

an Observant house]. This was granted, and she liked this cloister so much that she asked to remain there.[12]

Elisabeth later came with a party of seven sisters from Sylo to reform the cloister of Kirchheim (in Württemberg). The practice of taking in children was disapproved of, however, by the Observant reformers in the fifteenth century, who raised the cloister entrance age to fourteen and closed many convent schools for children.

In some cases, girls were placed in convents as orphans when one parent remarried, or simply because parents sought a secure, religious life for their daughter and spiritual insurance for themselves. The Emmerich *Book of Sisters* (1503) tells of Beel te Mushoel (d. 1481), whose father died. Her mother, wishing to remarry, placed her in the cloister on the advice of relatives. The account narrates in a very realistic way how the fourteen-year-old girl was homesick and had trouble adjusting to her new home among the Sisters of the Common Life.

> When she came to live here she was a nice, likeable girl of about fourteen years of age who in better days had been tenderly raised by her mother. And therefore it was exceedingly difficult for her when she had to leave her mother. But, because she saw that her mother desired it and it was her wish, she acquiesced, although it was trying and difficult for her. For she had been high spirited and merry and now had to behave in a restrained, subdued manner. Oh, this life seemed so unsettling to her that her heart failed her when she thought that she must spend her life here. But our Lord helped her, so that with time things got better. For when she learned to read the Holy Scriptures, she began to acquire the knowledge and love of God.
>
> She showed herself to be industrious and learned to do all the things that our sisters did. She came to the workhouse and there she was uncommonly useful and helpful and assisted those with whom she worked [spinning or weaving]. For she was reliable in her work and did not spare herself. It was her custom to do it vigorously, as though she were the strongest of all; such was her willing character. . . . When she was young, this good sister often had to master herself with great effort, for she was very merry and

lively by nature and loved talking with people. Thus her nature and this life were like light and darkness. And therefore she had a hard, difficult life and had to overcome her nature and break it. I believe that many a saint in heaven did not have as hard a time of it as this life was for her.

Beel successfully made the adjustment, according to the narrator, and then had to face another one when the sisterhouse became an enclosed Augustinian cloister in 1463. Beel struggled with the decision. Because of her reluctance, she sought the advice of a renowned holy woman, Mechthild van der Mollen, who "ignited" her heart with a vibrant spiritual vocation:

> [S]he was distressed and afflicted in her heart, for it seemed impossible to her to bear the restrictions of the rule. And she thought and considered that she would rather leave here, before she would do that. . . . [S]he wanted first to visit a holy woman who lived at Nijmegen and was called Mechthild van der Mollen, of whom she had heard many wonderful things, for example, that she received from God secret and hidden things and knew the future and made prophecies. She conceived a great desire to visit this Mechthild, received permission from her superiors, and traveled together with another sister to Nijmegen to see the woman and speak to her. . . . They talked affectionately and fervently with one another for a long time, such that through the working of the Holy Spirit and the earnest and ardent urging of the worthy woman Mechthild, Sister Beel's heart became completely ignited by the love of God and she resolved to join the holy order.[13]

This account goes on to tell of Sister Beel's spiritual transformation and later of a terrible accident in which she fell onto the point of a pole, which poked out her eyeball and blinded her in one eye. Yet Beel overcomes her grief at this accident, regains her natural cheerfulness, and becomes a model and inspiration to other members of the community.

Marriage Rejected?

In narratives composed by women from the fourteenth through the sixteenth centuries at both convents and sisterhouses of the Common Life, avoidance of an unwanted marriage is a frequent scenario.[14] The Emmerich *Book of Sisters* tells how Mechtelt van Diedem (d. 1476), the second woman to lead the young community, joined when she heard that she was to be shown to a man that her parents wanted her to marry. Mechtelt seems to have been traumatized by the prospect and was reluctant to be introduced. Her relatives' attempt to trick her into it precipitated a decision to seek the safe haven and the alternative of a religious life among the sisters. Although stressing the honorableness of the match, the story focuses on Mechtelt's mental state and her secret pondering of her decision. At last, the account reports, she took matters into her own hands.

> Mechtelt van Diedem was born in one of the best and most prominent families of this city of Emmerich. Her parents were good people who honored and served God and raised their daughter tenderly and honorably. And when she had reached her maturity, so that she was eighteen years of age, her parents decided, on the advice of friends and relatives, to fit the girl out richly and respectably in marriage to a well born established man of the world. So it happened that her friends were to travel to Wesel to a great wedding that was to be held there and they took this young woman, Mechtelt, with them. And they planned that the man to whom they wanted to give her in marriage should come there so that he could see her. For she was a very charming, attractive, pleasant person, whom one could very honorably and appropriately take to wife. After they had arrived at Wesel, this excellent young woman learned of what her friends wanted to do. Now when she heard this, she kept silent about it and went secretly aboard a ship and sailed back home so that her friends and relatives knew nothing of it. So she came in obedience to God and at the urging of the Holy Ghost to the sisters who had only recently started this community, and humbly asked that she might join them and serve God together with them.[15]

Narratives of this kind are so numerous in women's writings as to constitute a major theme in their works. A less realistic account, but more programmatic as a protest, is the case of Hedwig von Gundelsheim, narrated by Katharina von Gueberschwihr in the Unterlinden sister-book (c. 1320), which tells how Hedwig, who was not willing to wed, steadfastly refused to open her hand to swear the marriage vow.

> It was also the custom that a sword should be brought in upon which the groom and the bride were to place their thumbs so that the vows could be made valid. She, however, made her hand into a fist and clamped her thumb inside so tightly that no one, even using great force, could pull it out. When, however, some said, that her whole hand must be laid on the sword, she put up such resistance that no man by his strength could get her hand out of her pocket.

The story relates how the bridegroom sensibly felt pity for her, released her from the marriage contract and withdrew. But the distraught parents turned her over to an uncle who beat her and housed her in a pigsty. When the girl became dangerously ill, the uncle—afraid of being charged with homicide—called for advisers and his priest. The advisers declared, writes Katharina with passion: "The murderers are all those who treated the girl in such an inhumane fashion." The advisors decide that the girl, should she survive, must be allowed to enter a religious order, "since they had discovered how she could not be moved either by threats, flattery, or martyrdom, to enter the married state."[16]

While women's accounts do not differ from men's on the issue of chastity, the women's narratives pointedly and vigorously condemn all who would give women in marriage against their will. The girls in these stories defy parental authority by escaping to the safe haven of a religious community and devoting themselves to Christ. While the sober vitae composed at sisterhouses and convents of the New Devout use marriage-rejection stories to illustrate how an act of expediency develops into a true vocation for piety, the earlier Dominican sister-books tend to depict a radical commitment to chastity already fully developed from the beginning. They portray extreme situations in which heroic female spiritual athletes demonstrate charismatic power. More will be said about these kinds of narratives as a strategy for exercising agency in Chapter 6.

Other typical accounts describe sisters who were "married against their will" and then entered the convent after being widowed.[17] Bynum notes that young women were generally given in wedlock at fifteen or seventeen to men on average thirteen to fifteen years their senior,[18] an age discrepancy that—for the lesser partner, anyway—may have increased the unequalness and unhappiness of the relationship. Young widows might, thus, have chosen retirement in a convent over remarriage. Christine de Pizan (1365–c. 1430), widowed in her early twenties, chose the convent for her daughter but not for herself. She, however, advised women to remain in their widowhood, saying: "The lot of the married woman is sometimes no sweeter than that of one who has been taken captive by the Saracens."[19]

Women living in convents were not only free from the dangers of continuous childbearing but also less likely to contract contagious diseases, and lived well beyond the childbearing years. The average lifespan of abbesses in the Middle Ages—estimated at 56.4 years—exceeds by almost thirty years that of women outside the cloister who lived on average only 27.7 years.[20] On the vegetarian diet of many convents, some women survived to a very great age. The sister-book of Töss (c. 1340) mentions Adelhait von Lindow, who reached the age of one hundred, and Elsbet von Cellinkon who was ninety but senile.[21] Similarly, Anna von Munzingen's chronicle of Adelhausen (1318) tells touchingly of Sister Metzi von Walthershoven, who

> reached the age of one hundred years, and was so overcome with grace many years before her death that she cried out constantly by day and by night "Little Jesus, little Jesus, dear little Jesus, beloved little Jesus, happy little Jesus, sweet little Jesus." And she did this indefatigably and with such a loud voice that no one could get any rest. And her face was so rosy and her eyes so bright that one might say God showed her his wonders.[22]

One is tempted to ask how many husbands could have borne this with such equanimity.

To married women, especially those who had grown up and been educated at the convent, it offered a familiar place of retirement in widowhood, an asylum during periods of marital conflict, or a temporary retreat while husbands undertook long trips abroad.[23] To those who took the veil out of expediency and without a real vocation for the religious life, Shulamit Shahar asserts, the convent offered "relative freedom from male domination," education, and the opportunity—as abbesses or officers in the community—to exercise their talents of leadership and organization.[24] Here they could substitute religious pursuits for menial domestic duties. Indeed, great abbeys such as Gandersheim, Essen, and Quedlinburg offered intellectual training that was the best of its kind. There women could devote themselves to learning and the arts.[25]

Inheritances and Handicaps: The Daughters' Tales

Generally, the expense of placing a daughter in a convent was less than that of paying a dowry to secure an eligible bridegroom. In some cases, women were placed there by male relatives eager to both rid themselves of the responsibility of caring for them and come into control of the women's property.[26] The story of how Abbess Sophia von Münster successfully recovered her sisters' inheritances from the hands of their brothers is told with a certain indignant relish by Anna Roede in her second "Chronicle of Herzebrock" (c. 1553). As abbess, Sophia took out a loan for the financially strapped cloister from her wealthy father—1000 gulden at six percent interest—and had paid the interest on it for two or three years when her father died. At his death, her brothers demanded the return of the principal as part of their inheritance. But Sophia argued that she did not intend to pay it back, because her sister, Jutta, had received only fifty gulden as her patrimony and the other two sisters nothing at all. She reasoned that "they also belonged to the family and were legitimate children as well as she and the others; so she intended to keep the money for herself and her two sisters as their part."[27] Anna relates that the assertive Sophia won her case against the brothers.

Women's accounts do mention "backward" or retarded girls living in cloisters. The Oetenbach sister-book, for example, relates several anecdotes of the simple-minded Sister Agnes, a particular favorite of the cloister's benefactor, Count Rudolf von Rapperswil, who liked to converse with her. The author of the Oetenbach foundation account was especially fond of telling droll stories. In an anecdote featuring the ingenuous Sister Agnes and Count Rudolf, she writes:

> [H]e asked her how often the convent drank wine. And she answered, "Oh often, my Lord. Whenever the sisters take commu-

nion, we drink wine," meaning the wine in the communion chalice. And when he offered to send them bread, she said, "Lord, you keep it, I can't carry it." So he called for a boat and loaded it with wine, bread, and schmalz and sent this to the cloister often, especially on feast days.[28]

In another episode, the count offered her the choice of a robe, and the guileless Sister Agnes would have picked one of the cheapest ones. But his wife, the countess, the story relates, "pointed out to her secretly one that was good. And she took that." But other less humorous accounts tell of sisters unable to learn to recite the office such as Verena Senn at St. Katharina in St Gall who, the chronicle notes, was a hard worker but "simple minded so that she could not participate in reciting the hours like the others."[29]

Unlike men's narratives, women's seldom mention illegitimate girls such as Sophie, daughter of Duke Wilhelm of Braunschweig and Lüneburg, who repeatedly ran away from the cloister of Mariensee. Her story circulated in popular accounts decrying immorality in convents.[30] In a later century, Sister Arcangela Tarabotti (1604–1652), author of *Inferno monacale* (Hell of Nuns, written 1640–50), denounced the practice of forcing girls to enter convents. At the same time, she insisted on strict enforcement of the decrees of the Council of Trent, which mandated that no novice should be permitted to take vows unless ecclesiastical examiners made sure she was truly devout.[31]

The "Disadvantage" of Rank?

One of the important reasons young women entered cloisters was attributable to, Eileen Power asserts, "the disadvantage of rank," that is, the "narrowness of the sphere to which women of gentle birth were confined" due to the limited number of occupations considered appropriate to the nobility. For these families, the convent was "the refuge of the gently born," a finishing school and living establishment for the daughters of the upper classes.[32] As a nun, a woman of the nobility or urban patriciate could live among equals and enjoy a comfortable lifestyle that offered a respectable alternative, perhaps even superior to marriage. Many girls joined communities not only where sisters, cousins, or aunts were already in residence but also in which ancestors had resided for generations. In those elite families whose daughters routinely became abbesses, the cloister played an important dynastic role in administering patrimonial lands and benefices. In family dynastic strategies, the church had as important a role as marriage, and care was taken to retain hold of certain abbeys.[33] Even for the lower ranks of the elite, the monastery was no less a part of family strategy, a way of preserving fortunes and fortifying reputations. As Jutta Sperling has so insightfully pointed out, "patrician nuns were, so to speak, living metaphors of the nobility's mythical qualities." Symbolically, she identifies the "bodies of nuns" as "sites where the honor, purity, and distinction of the nobility as a class resided." Service to God on behalf of the family was a responsibility and a valued contribution to its well-being. Accordingly, Sperling estimates that in 1581, due partly to dowry inflation, over fifty percent of patrician women in Venice lived in convents.[34]

While monachization may have been involuntary, so was marriage or spinsterhood when no suitable groom could be found. Particularly in the case of noble women, sometimes none of the available choices was good. If no suitable partner could be arranged for by her family, a girl often simply remained where she had grown up, among friends and relatives in the community that had educated her. In some cases, such as that of a daughter of the Coronaro family cited by Sperling, a young woman insisted on entering a convent out of a sense of social superiority, that is, because she could not find a groom of status equal to hers. Indeed, it was quite possible for a family's wealth and standing in the "economy of prestige" to be too high for an appropriate husband to be found.[35] Although marrying "down" could lower a woman's standing, placing a daughter in an exclusive convent could actually upgrade the status of a less prominent family. At St. Katharina in St. Gall, Barbara Enzinger, the daughter of a stone mason, was admitted through the prerogative of a newly elected bishop to recommend one woman for admission. In gratitude, the girl's father presented the convent with a gold-plated monstrance.[36] While not all cloisters were exclusive in their admissions policies, especially after the reform, others such as Rijnsburg Abbey were extremely selective and, according to regulations issued in 1500, admitted "only nuns who were of noble descent on both paternal and maternal sides for at least four generations."[37]

With its exclusively aristocratic inhabitants, Rijnsburg Abbey maintained the customs of the secular court. Its abbesses, regularly chosen from the very highest nobility, were waited on by a chamberlain, a cupbearer, and pages. Hüfer notes that its account books record outlays for ceremonial dinners to receive new members that provided for instrumental music (drums, trumpets, fifes, cymbals, and violins).[38] Likewise, the abbesses of Überwasser in Münster invested their ministers with the lands owned by the convent as fiefs after the manner of secular rulers.[39] Lina Eckenstein points out that the women who headed the great Saxon abbeys had "the duties and privileges of a baron," distributing patronage in the form of leases on convent lands, holding legal jurisdiction over them, and employing judges to settle disputes.[40]

Canoness Houses

As living establishments for the daughters of the nobility, these canoness houses more closely resembled seminaries for young ladies or elegant boarding houses than religious monasteries. Unlike members of the regular orders, canonesses were not bound by formal vows and had no habit, common meals, common dormitory, or claustration. They were permitted to own property, to keep servants, and to eat their meals in the private apartments where they lived. Their chief duties entailed singing the Hours and attending religious services. The only vows taken were those that promised obedience to the abbess and chastity while in residence at the convent. With the abbess's permission women could travel, visit relatives, and might leave at any time to marry.[41] The abbey of Überwasser served, for example, as a religious foundation for the daughters of the Münsterland aristocracy. A fourteenth-century account described it as having a separate house and garden for the abbess, separate quarters for the prioress and for each of the other residents, all located abound a central ambulatory.[42]

The earliest great imperial abbeys were established by the newly christianized Saxon nobility in the ninth century. Here the old pagan cult of veneration of ancestors found expression in Christian prayers for the souls of the dead. Convents founded by the ruling families served as a means of assuring prayers and veneration of the dynasty's illustrious ancestors.[43] The oldest houses were often erected on the property of the foundress. A royal abbess was the best choice to lead the abbey, because she served as a link to the royal house and, as a family member, could keep the crown actively committed to the support of the monastery.[44]

The famous abbey at Gandersheim was founded toward the end of the ninth century by Oda and Liudolf, Duchess and Duke of Saxony (d. 860), for their daughter Hathumod (d. 874). Oda and Liudolf had four daughters, one of whom married, with the other three, Hathumod, Gerberga, and Christina, serving in succession as abbesses of Gandersheim. Hrosvit's chronicle of Gandersheim (c. 973/983) depicts Oda as the moving force behind the establishment of the abbey and its de facto head. After the death of Liudolf, Oda retired there and, Hrosvit asserts, survived to the age of 107. Considering Hrosvit's description, Oda's rule may well have seemed 107 years, for she is depicted as a stern disciplinarian and a bigger than life, awe-inspiring figure. Although canonesses had much greater freedom than women in the regular orders observing a monastic rule, life under Gerberga and her mother, Oda, was closely monitored. According to Hrosvit, Gandersheim was not a place for relaxation of discipline.

The august Oda, also staying within the cloister,
Inspected with vigilant concern
The deeds and devotion, the habits and even the manner of living,
Of the community of sisters very frequently
So that none of them would ignore the rule of the ancestors
And presume to order her life as according to her own judgment.
(ll. 409–414)[45]

Determining the exact status of canoness houses and their distinction from Benedictine convents is often difficult. From the tenth century onward, successive waves of reform initiatives attempted to place canoness houses under a monastic rule but met with little success.[46] In 1148, the Council of Reims decreed that "women called canonesses" must adopt either the Benedictine or the Augustinian rule.[47] At Münster, an attempt had been made even earlier to convert the Abbey of Überwasser to a Benedictine cloister. A habit and enclosure had been introduced there and the women lived under the Benedictine rule until the reformer, Bishop Egbert, died in 1132; they later reverted to their former way of life.[48] Jo Ann McNamara points out that many of the German houses took to calling themselves Benedictine, but their inhabitants continued to live as canonesses.[49]

It is often difficult to draw a line between "regular" and "extra-regular" groups of women's communities because of their diversity of status, organization, and function.[50] Likewise, the adaptability from informal to formal communities was much more typical for women than it was for men.[51] In many cases, however, it is simply not possible to tell with which order a community was affiliated or how closely.

Despite reform efforts of Hildesheim bishops Berthold I (1119–30) and Bernhard I (1130–53), Gandersheim remained a canoness house.[52] The Abbey of Vilich, however, converted itself early on to the Benedictine order at the instigation of its first abbess, Adelheid herself, as Sister Bertha's *Life of Adelheid* (1057) proudly relates. Bertha's portrait of Adelheid as a saintly reformer stresses the differences between the women's lives as canonesses and those of Benedictines. Bertha's idealized depiction, a kind of *plaidoyer* for the regular life of the Order, relates that the abbess began the transition to the Benedictine rule surreptitiously.

> Thus she held in contempt the daily hour of restoration, the meat and other food which was well selected and varied and was content only with monastic foods. This she did, however, without the knowledge of her table companions, except one good sister, who was a silent accomplice. In public she shone in linen garments but next to her skin she wore a rough woolen garment in the spirit of repentance and thus she subdued the soft nature of her noble body so that she might suffer the dictates of a hard law for the sake of God. When, after a year, she had summoned up the necessary strength and hoped that it would be sufficient to continue the work she had begun, Adelheid put into action the long-deliberated silent vow, not alone, but with the grace of God. Then she called upon the venerable abbess and the leaders of the Cologne convent of the Holy Mother of God [where her sister was abbess] and humbly put herself under their knowledgeable guidance so that through their teachings she would find the way into the order.[53]

As it turned out, not all of the residents of the house wanted to accept the Benedictine rule and some left the convent rather than do so.

Although abbess of an exclusive house of noble canonesses was a socially prominent position, the women whom Hrosvit and Bertha portray are distinguished rather for their religious zeal. Like the indomitable Oda, Adelheid, too, was a stern disciplinarian. Bertha recounts how Adelheid disliked sisters singing badly and berated those lying abed with illnesses.

> [I]t happened that one of the sisters could not keep the [tune] of the choir of loudly singing voices . . . and the good mother would correct her and box her ears, then for the rest of her life the sister had a beautiful voice and sang clearly. In this same manner she often reproached some sisters who suffered from long-term illnesses that they were wasting their time uselessly if they did not labor with their hands and shortly after she had reproached them, they were healed by the grace of the Lord.[54]

This anecdote gives a rather startling female perspective on what seems to have been considered proper discipline applied by a "good" woman to other women of the upper classes in the eleventh century, clearly a harsher age than our own.

Rank and Religiosity

Some houses admitted only women of the nobility, but the presence of those of the highest rank was considered an important asset even in houses of the mendicant orders. It was exceptional for a woman of the old free nobility to join either a Cistercian or a mendicant nunnery. She would more usually have entered a Benedictine house or a foundation of secular canonesses.[55] Yet there are cases of princesses, such as Anna of Stargard (d. 1498), niece of the Duke of Braunschweig and Lüneburg, who entered the Cistercian cloister of Wienhausen, which was not composed exclusively of noblewomen. One sees, in the account rendered in the cloister chronicle, the competition—not only within the house but between houses—over the issue of social rank. The chronicler relates how Princess Anna's uncle, the duke, ordered that she "should receive no preferential treatment because of her high standing, but be dealt with like the other sisters." The partisan chronicler asserts, however, that

> [s]he had spent three years in the cloister and, although still very young, she nevertheless outshone her companions in love, humil-

ity, and friendliness and exceeded them in obedience. This was a mighty thorn in the flesh of some resentful sisters and they worried that she would one day accede to the office of abbess. In order to forestall this, they falsely reported to her relatives (but under a pretense of kindness) that she was not behaving as was proper to her station. When her mother, Lady von Stargard, heard this, she asked the abbess to bring her daughter along with several other young sisters to stay at Celle for a few days. Now when the abbess was returning to the cloister with the daughter, the young woman was taken from the wagon by force and held captive despite her tearful protests. She was forced to put on secular clothing against her will, but nevertheless continued to wear her habit underneath. Finally, she was sent to a cloister called Ribnitz, which housed only noble women, under the pretense that Wienhausen was not strict enough.[56]

This tale of friction and competition for social prestige reflects the changes occurring at Wienhausen and at other cloisters during the fourteenth and fifteenth centuries. The Wienhausen incident took place during the term of reform prioress Susanna Potstock (1470–1501), the first prioress of the burgher class, and shows the tensions this shift brought about. Records at the Dominican cloister of Kirchberg in Württemberg, where formerly only daughters of noble families had been accepted, show that by the latter half of the fourteenth century, the majority of inhabitants were affluent non-nobles. In 1354 a commoner was for the first time named prioress there.[57]

In 1417 a Provincial Chapter of Benedictines decreed that when not enough noble candidates were available commoners could be accepted.[58] Throughout the fourteenth century, members of the wealthy urban merchant class accounted for an increasing number of convent admissions. In the Observant reforms of the fifteenth century, as will be seen in Chapters 3 and 4, removal of social barriers to cloister admissions became one of the goals of the movement, particularly in Benedictine houses reached by the Bursfeld reformers. Yet, although admissions generally became more open, they did not change the face of things altogether. For example, between 1424 and 1480 the Observant Dominican house of St. Maria Magdalena an den Steinen in Basel took in eighty-five new entrants. Of this group, thirty-five still belonged to the aristocracy. Indeed, of the thirteen Observant sisters who reformed the house in 1423, seven were themselves of noble birth.[59]

Lay Sisters and Fees

Women from less affluent families often entered cloisters as lay sisters. They paid a smaller dowry and, instead of reciting the monastic hours as the better educated choir nuns did, they were responsible for the washing, cleaning, and cooking at the convent.[60] Because they were not required to be able to read and write, their devotions consisted largely of repetitions of the Ave Maria, the Lord's Prayer, and similar devotions.[61] At the Clarissan house in Nuremberg, the lay sisters were instructed to pray twenty-four Our Fathers at matins; five at lauds; seven at prime, terce, sext and non; twelve at vespers; and seven at compline.[62] Not strictly enclosed, lay sisters could go in and out of the convent. On rare occasions, a lay sister might work her way up to choir-sister as did Sister Christina Reyselt, whose story is told in the chronicle of the cloister of Pfullingen. The account, written by one of the sisters (c. 1525), prizes Christina's resourcefulness, relating how she negotiated the right to become a choir nun. In tandem with the reform, the well-liked and capable Christina rose in the monastic ranks.

> This Christina had been a servant of the Sisters of Saint Clare in Nuremberg. When some of them were sent to Brixen to introduce the reform, the sisters wanted her to accompany them. But she did not want to go unless she could join the order of Saint Clare. She was accepted as a lay sister. So she traveled with them and was a great comfort on the way. When the reform had been instituted at Brixen they wished to keep her there, so they had Sister Christine educated and she became a choir nun.[63]

In this post-reform account, the women seem to applaud the enterprising woman's advancement. More will be said about Christina in the context of the aims of the Observance in Chapter 3.

For many young women, not only restrictive admissions policies but also expense prevented them from entering a cloister. Although the rule of Saint Benedict forbade the outlay of a dowry for a cloister entrant, some sources indicate the payment of a "voluntary" donation.[64] Others, such as the Cistercian cloister of Saarn on the Ruhr, had a fixed entrance fee in writing. In 1535 each young woman at the start of her Saarn novitiate paid 125 gold gulden, roughly six times the annual income of a stonemason (21 gulden).[65] Before ever becoming a novice, she would have paid nine gulden per year for her schooling. In addition, each entrant at Saarn was required to bring with her a substantial trousseau comprising two robes, one coat, three head cloths, a bed and bedding, a bed frame, a chest, table linens totaling 18 ells in length, towels also 18 ells in length, a silver beaker or bowl of at least 18 weight.[66]

According to Brigitte Degler-Spengler, in the fourteenth century there was no firm dowry at Gnadental in Basel but rather annual annuities paid to the cloister by the inhabitants. Entrants in the fifteenth century paid a sum of at least 100 gulden, with the daughters of the wealthiest families bringing 500 or 600 gulden. This was still a substantial amount, since according to city tax records before 1446–54, only ten to eleven percent of the population even paid taxes on 100 to 200 gulden.[67] Marie-Claire Däniker-Gysin estimates the worth of a dowry at the cloister of Töss as approximately the price of a farm.[68]

Records at the St. Katharina cloister at St. Gall, a Dominican house predominantly of wealthy urban-class women, show that the burgher daughters of St. Gall often brought assets in commodities rather than in money. Anna Krumm came with the deed to one and one-half vineyards producing 5,887 liters of wine annually, and Anna Sattler brought—besides 500 gulden and an annual endowment of 3 gulden for masses for her family—four bushels of grain, sixteen barrels of oats, and four chickens in perpetuity.[69] Usually these substantial dowries became the property of the cloister only upon the death of the sister or—as was the case at Söflingen— they could be willed to a relative residing in the cloister.[70] Often, however, the payments ceased when a sister died.[71]

Prioresses as Financial Managers

Despite the sizeable dowries paid to the them, most women's communities were far poorer than men's. Penelope Johnson estimates the mean worth of nunneries at only fifteen percent of that of priories, while the average number of inhabitants of a women's convent was much larger than that of a men's monastery. For example, in mid–thirteenth-century northern France women's convents averaged thirty-five nuns, the number in men's reaching only about twenty-three monks.[72] The nuns' inability to perform the sacraments may have diminished their attractiveness to donors wishing to establish foundations to have masses said after their deaths.[73] Women's cloisters, while owning extensive properties, were thus often in financial difficulties.

The chief sources of income for nunneries were donations for burials on the cloister grounds, endowments to finance prayers for souls, dowries, rents, and annuities for the upkeep of the sisters. Since rents were often paid in the form of grain, fruit, wine, cheese, eggs, or poultry, cash was often in short supply.[74] Repairs and enlargements to cloister buildings were dependent on donor gifts, which were encouraged by the granting of indulgences. When the Clarissan house at Nuremberg undertook a building program in 1474, thirty donors were permitted to tour the cloister in order to form an idea of the state of the buildings.[75] A special indulgence was conferred upon them, allowing each donor to choose a confessor to absolve him of all sins for ten years—even sins reserved to the pope. To avoid hard feelings, the city council selected the thirty recipients, and anyone who was not chosen, but had attended a service on certain holy days or made a donation to the convent church, could receive a lesser indulgence of forty days.[76]

Another source of cloister income was from the provision of housing for lay pensioners, who received a house or apartment and meals from the cloister kitchen for life in exchange for a sum of money or an annuity. Such an arrangement also provided for burial in the cloister cemetery and intercessory prayers. Some pensioners worked as gatekeepers, carpenters, gardeners, or provided other services to the convent. At cloister Klingental, an agreement made in 1452 with the widow, Elsi Sattler, states that

> in exchange for all her cash and property, the sisters would permit [the Widow Sattler] to live in the little weaver's house by the front gate and supply her with wood for heating and cooking, 274 liters of common wine, the same amount of superior vintage every fall, money for meat, fish, 300 eggs, a gallon of peas and lentils, a gallon of salt, two loaves of bread a day; and, after her death, burial within

the cloister and intercessory prayer services on the seventh and thirtieth anniversaries of her death.[77]

Emil Erdin cites the amount paid by a lay pensioner for lifetime care at the Magdalen cloister in Basel as between 100 and 150 gulden for each person. This was approximately equal to the dowry paid by a nun.[78]

Besides taking in pensioners, women's cloisters earned money by teaching children. While this worked for urban cloisters, it was not feasible for those lying outside centers of population. Inflation continually eroded the value of fixed rents paid to the cloister on its properties, so income from these sources steadily declined. By the second half of the fifteenth century, convent ledger books show increasing deficits and buildings in disrepair.[79]

For those cloisters already in poor financial health, the costs of instituting a reform sometimes dealt a fatal blow, especially since sisters who refused to accept the reform could transfer to other cloisters, taking their dowries and annuities with them. Although visitation protocols, such as those of Wendelin Fabri of St. Katharina (St. Gall), in 1511, state that in the case of a transfer annuities shall remain with the first cloister, there are numerous other records of sisters taking a pension or assets to another convent.[80] At St. Nicolaus in undis, Strasbourg, where prioress Agnes Vigin and a number of sisters proposed joining the Observance, the idea was rejected by eight residents, who elected to transfer to other houses, demanding to be recompensed not only for the funds and goods they had brought when they entered the cloister but also the monies paid for the festive meal served to the convent on the day of their entrance, plus the value of apartments left to them by the wills of deceased sisters, and even payment for services rendered in educating children. This huge sum was duly paid out, nearly impoverishing the remnant community.[81] In other cases, as at Medingen and Heilig Kreuz in Regensburg, property was divided equally between two houses.[82] But books the reformers brought with them had to be returned to the first cloister at their deaths.[83]

At Überwasser (Münster) in 1483, pensions were paid to sixteen canonesses who chose to leave the house rather than accept the reform (even though during the transition they could wear secular clothing, keep their servants, and were not required to sing the Hours). But their departure nearly bankrupted the convent. The cloister chronicle calculates the costs of the reform, for legal fees and pensions paid out, at 4500 gulden.[84] The reform abbess, Sophia Dobbers—who reports that she was required to pay pensions of 20 gulden a year to the women who had left—registers the financial toll and hard feelings on both sides over the financial arrangement. "In the year 1490 we were so poor that we could not give them [the sisters who had left] their money. This we regretfully reported to my Lord [the bishop] and showed our accounts. . . . But the women on the outside [who had left the house] threatened to have their friends rob and burn us."[85] Ordered to pay, Sophia says the cloister mortgaged everything, including its monstrances and a valuable painting of the Virgin, which the abbess later redeemed. Similarly, convents that sent out reforming sisters to introduce the Observance at other cloisters sometimes suffered substantial financial losses; St. Katharina, St. Gall, for example, was forced to pay out 400 gulden to Cloister Zoffingen for the dowries of the two reformers it had sent there.[86]

Because women could not perform the sacraments themselves, women's houses were obliged to pay for the daily masses and other services performed by their chaplains. The cloister rules of the Clarissan sisters of "auf dem Wörth" in Strasbourg state that the cost of each sung mass was usually one schilling.[87] The chronicle of the St. Katharina cloister at St. Gall records that in September of 1477 the sisters' new lector took up his duties, agreeing to read or sing mass daily, "according to the needs of the day." On Sundays and holidays he was to preach and administer the sacraments. For these services he received room and board plus a salary of twelve gulden (a little more than half the salary of a stonemason). The cloister chronicle records that this brother gave to the sisters, among other gifts, "four beautiful turned candle sticks" for their choir altar.[88]

Women's Comments on Provosts: Praise and Blame

Clearly, the men responsible for pastoral care or supervision of the convent's finances sometimes themselves contributed to the needs of the cloister out of their own pockets. At Ebstorf, wealthy provost Matthias von Knesebeck paid for the construction of a large and airy building where the sisters could work together. The Ebstorf sister who, c. 1490, chronicled the reform (1464/70) tells enthusiastically of the building of the new structure, which was extremely expensive: "One must assume that the costs for all of it exceeded 1200 florins. But he told us in chapter in the clearest terms that he had paid the costs himself out of monies that he had inherited and out of annuities and benefices that he had received from princes when he had served as chancellor and secretary. Thus he had spent none of our assets because it was to be a memorial to him."[89]

Because most provosts were clerics, they served as both financial and spiritual overseers of the cloister.[90] In Braunschweig and Lüneburg, provosts were usually ducal chaplains, secretaries, or chancellors, hand picked to represent the duke's interests as the cloister's representative in the provincial diet.[91] A provost was appointed, first, by a cloister's founding donor and, subsequently, by his successors, and usually selected by the prioress from a short list of names submitted to her. Gustav Voit asserts that all cloisters made efforts to shake off the burden of secular rule and frequently succeeded in supplanting and replacing the office of provost with stewards of their own.[92]

Not all relationships with the cloister's provost were as felicitous as the one at Ebstorf. Anna Roede laments bitterly in her *Chronicle of Herzebrock* over the dishonest stewards and businessmen who enriched themselves at the cloister's expense, saying, "[T]hey made themselves rich and us poor. God knows their names."[93] At Preetz, enterprising prioress Anna von Buchwald (1484–1508) recounts in her handbook for future prioresses and the convent) how difficult it was to get incompetent provosts to deliver wood from the cloister's own forests for use in the new fireplace in the refectory that Anna herself had built to replace the intolerable old smoky one.

> Finally I, Anna, had it torn down in 1484 and moved from the north side to the west corner of the same building where it was rebuilt and is now located so that it draws the smoke no matter how the wind blows. But when the fireplace was finished we had no wood to burn and did not know where we could get as much as was needed. I took the greatest trouble to urge the provosts [two in succession] to provide us with wood, but they ignored it and paid no attention to the lack of wood.

Finally, in desperation, Anna begged the Bishop of Lübeck to instruct the provost to bring wood, which the bishop did in a written communication to the habitually negligent Provost Dornebusch. Anna reveals her sense of relief and accomplishment when she writes, "And thus we were provided by God's grace with a fireplace and wood, which up that time had been unheard of." No shrinking violet, Anna adds, "This comfort, Beloved, you have obtained through my efforts, therefore remember me to God in your prayers!"[94] Indeed, guaranteeing prayers for their souls in the future was one of the reasons women wrote accounts of themselves.

The conflict over the fireplace at Preetz was not the only frustrating encounter Anna von Buchwald had with Provost Dornbusch. Anna and the oldest sisters of the convent had also asked him to repair the roof on one of the buildings, which had not been maintained for sixty years; it had such rotten wood that "the vaulting and walls were going to ruin." Provost Dornbusch's rude and sarcastic refusal embittered her so much that Anna reported it word-for-word in her book. Dornbusch said that he would only rebuild the kitchen "so that he might get something in the pot. [And] that would be difficult enough!" But he had no intention of making any other repairs.[95]

Living Conditions and Daily Life

With or without incompetent managers and inadequate supplies of wood, living conditions in medieval cloisters were harsh by modern standards. Women's accounts of it are recorded in texts such as a set of student essays from the fifteenth century written in Latin at Ebstorf and preserved in the cloister library. An essay by one young woman gives a glimpse of the hardships endured in the cold months of winter.

> In the winter time I suffer from lack of activity. I don't make good use of winter days because of the extreme cold from which I suffer. My hands are so numb that I can scarcely move them to write. Besides that my ink is frozen solid. I am resolving to make new gloves from a new shift that my parents bought me at market. A small piece of material is left over. And I will form them out of white sheep's wool. Then my hands will stay nice and warm when I cover them with the gloves.

Another essay describes elaborate preparations for a bath.

> Next week the convent will bathe. Wood has been brought in. The laborers cut it on the allodial land. We remunerated them well, sending them butter and cheese via the cook. The girls have come bringing a great stove for heating. The bath is ready. I will go quickly so that I arrive in time for vesper prayers. I will cover my head with a pillow so that my brain will not be overheated.[96]

At Preetz, one of the indefatigable Anna von Buchwald's first undertakings as a prioress who loved cleanliness and order was scrubbing and repairing the bathhouse. She writes about how she first hired two workers "who cleaned the entire bathhouse" and three more who cleaned up the overgrown area around it where overflow from the river had eroded and softened the ground around the bridge that formed the approach to the bathhouse. Then Anna had the workers bring in pebbles so that the courtyard approach, where "there was often standing water," would not be too muddy to walk across. Last, she put up a wall "so that [the sisters] could walk about in the yard when they wished and stroll about in the fresh air—more than they had before my time. For when there was no wall with gate, walkway and railing, no religious person could go outside the door of the bathhouse. For this pray to God for me when you use it." These changes were not merely cosmetic but necessary sanitary precautions since, as Anna shockingly relates, the channel was so shallow and overgrown that "in dry periods [the women] could have no water for cooking and it was unsanitary because all sorts of trash washed up there such as dead pigs, dogs, chickens and other filthy refuse which [they] often found in the ditch and complained to me about."[97] After digging a new channel and putting in flagstones outside, Anna added drains, fireplaces, tables, and benches to facilitate washing, drying, and ironing of clothes.

The benefits of the renovated bathhouse, no doubt, made life in Preetz more pleasant. At the wealthy Dominican cloister of Klingental in Basel, the sisters had greater comforts (two bathhouses) and more relaxed discipline. In summer they swam and romped in the Rhine while citizens watched in amusement from the bridge, a practice that brought protests from the city council.[98] While at Kingental most nuns had a room of their own, at Preetz Anna records that she struggled with a shortage of cells and dormitory beds for the younger sisters, twenty-two of whom had to sleep on the floor in the attic or wherever they could find a space. Anna managed to get fifteen small cells constructed for the eldest sisters and dark cubicles under the stairs for the seven youngest.[99]

Ulrich Faust comments that in Benedictine cloisters in Lower Saxony and Schleswig-Holstein nuns slept in common dormitories until the fifteenth century, when individual cells came into use.[100] The size of a nun's cell at the Magdalen cloister in Basel, where a new row of cells was added between 1510 and 1522, is given as "eleven shoes in length and nine shoes in width."[101] Even at Klingental not every nun had a cell as soon as she made her profession. Often she had to wait for one to be bequeathed to her by the death of a sister. In order to have the use of a cell for life, one had to pay the cloister twenty gulden. The amount for larger cells with a view of the Rhine was, of course, higher. Some sisters had the use of more than one cell, such as Prioress Clara zu Rhein who had nine of them. Indeed, records at Klingental indicate that the standard of living at such wealthy establishments was high. Besides furniture—beds, chests, chairs, benches, and tables—Klingental nuns were permitted to outfit their quarters with wall hangings and embroidered pillows, woven bed and sofa covers, coverlets of fur or serge, white linen tablecloths and hand towels, tin plates, bowls, and platters, silver and silver- or gold-plated drinking vessels, spoons, and salt cellars, tin or brass pitchers, jugs, and water or fish pots, as well as candle holders. psalters, breviaries, and other books.[102]

For women living enclosed, the garden was an important part of the cloister compound. Under the rules of the Bursfeld reform, all sisters were strictly required to work in the garden.[103] At Ebstorf, where the garden was replanted with trees in 1485, the author of the cloister chronicle (1487) rejoices over this improvement, saying, "It is for us no small pleasure to go walking there, for it is as though we could observe all the loveliness of earthly paradise."[104] At Preetz, each nun had her own garden plot where she could grow herbs or food for herself and her tablemates.[105] These plots were at the women's disposal and Prioress Anna von Buchwald's instructions state that "any sister may give her garden plot to another during her life and without explanation."[106]

Artifacts of day-to-day life in convents include letters written and received by nuns. In Observant houses of the regular orders, letters sent outside the cloister were to be read by the prioress, in part to prevent disputes within the cloister from being aired in public to the detriment of the convent's reputation.[107] Evidence that some correspondence reached the outside without the abbesses' knowledge is demonstrated by some very angry letters that Sister Maria von Wolkenstein sent to her brothers from the Clarissan cloister at Brixen in 1455, when Nicholas von Cusa was trying to reform it. Maria was the leader of a faction that was attempting to depose the abbess. Writing secretly to her brother Leo, she complained that "they [the abbess and her party] are closing every chink in the wall and even closing up holes that we never knew about. . . . Send only Ulrich here anymore and on Sunday or Monday. This I ask you faithfully. And . . . only send the letter by a messenger you are sure of."[108]

Another reason for a prioress to monitor letters was the correspondence between nuns and male "spiritual friends." In some places, convent women had what were understood to be special relationships, called "spiritual friendships," in which the partners exchanged missives of endearment. A large number of these letters, written at the unreformed Clarissan house of Söflingen, have survived. Editor of the Söflingen letters Max Miller asserts that these supposedly scandalous messages, written in the language of intimate affection, are artifacts of friendships between couples who regarded themselves as joined in a kind of "spiritual marriage" and even used each other's initials in signing their letters.[109] In 1482, for example, Sister Genoveva Vetter wrote to Father Johannes Spieß, signing herself with his initial G[enoveva] Sp[ieß].

> I wish you a blessed, joyful day, dearest. Your letter arrived and you gave me much joy and I ask you affectionately, if matters have been settled, let me know this evening by way of Heßlin, how things went and if he [Jodocus Wind] has been removed from office [in Ulm]. Know that I saw you yesterday most gladly with my whole heart, and I ask you to make me happy and send me good news today. Dearest, let me commend myself to you faithfully as I trust your faithfulness.[110]

Karl Suso Frank points out that these relationships were in no way secret.[111] The Söflingen women often had a portrait of their spiritual friend hanging in their cell. Jodocus Wind, who is mentioned in Genoveva Vetter's note, affectionately called his own spiritual mate, Magdalena von Suntheim, his "very lovely dear," his "dear miss," "dear little woman," or "true dear sweetie." Fearing for her reputation, Magdalena reminds him in another letter that she is "a very proper old thing."[112] These male-female friendships were neither carnal nor "mystical" in nature but more often political and, unfortunately, probably disruptive, since they arose from or created rivalries within the community.[113]

Even in a larger context, convent women were not as marginalized as is commonly thought. Ursula Peters points out that Dominican women of the fourteenth century dwelt in "flourishing convents" and enjoyed "a wealth of contacts with important religious and secular luminaries of their time."[114] Indeed, many female writers represent themselves as extremely content with life in a monastery. The fourteenth-century compiler of the *Lives of the Sisters at Töss* depicts Sister Margret Willin saying, "This is the most splendid life that ever was."[115] Similarly, a sister at Ebstorf c. 1490, citing St. Bernard exclaims, "If there is paradise on earth, it is either in books or in the cloister."[116] Where amity and true piety reigned, the sisters are liberal in their praise of one another. At St. Agnes's in Emmerich, the chronicler writes, one sister was often known to say of Sister Mechtelt von Kalker, "Being around Mechtelt is like being with an angel."[117]

A few letters that survive show that nuns kept up contacts with women in other cloisters and not only corresponded but also frequently exchanged letters and gifts. A letter from Prioress Kunigunda Haller of St. Katharina in Nuremberg to fellow Prioress Angela Varnbühler in St. Gall thanks the sisters for a gift of fine linen canvas. On another occasion, Prioress Haller writes, "[K]now that I and the sisters have received your precious package with great joy and thanks and I can write to you with satisfaction of the happiness and rejoicing with which the sisters received it. God be your reward for such kindness."[118]

Food

One of the topics that seems to distinguish women's writings from men's is the subject of food. Like women of the present day, medieval women often chose to write about food and record what they had (or did not have) to eat. As in other dormitory-like situations, satisfaction with cloister life did not always extend to the cuisine. At Ebstorf, a young sister wrote in a

Latin essay, "I am very hungry. Thus far I have fasted and eaten nothing at all [today]. Our entire midday meal was over salted. We pushed it away [and] I did not eat a bite. Yesterday I had [only] warm beer. Now I must eat bread dipped in sauce. . . . I prefer a soft-boiled to a hard egg. Hard-cooked and fried eggs lie heavy on my stomach."[119] Perhaps this was written during Lent when only one meal a day was eaten.[120]

The bill of fare was an important topic, since in most cloisters meat was forbidden throughout the year, except for patients in the infirmary, where it might be needed to restore an invalid's strength. The Bursfeld regulations in 1459, however, do allow nuns to have meat three times per week if they cannot do without it.[121] Using visitation records from 1512, Voit describes the diet at Engelthal as including, morning and evening, one-third liter wine and one-half liter of beer, soup, meat, cabbage, and carrots or turnips; in the evening, rice and barley in addition. On feast days, three types of vegetables and two types of fish were served.[122] In contrast, at St. Katharina, St. Gall, meat was not eaten and a warm meal was served only once a day, at noon. Here the evening meal consisted of a piece of bread or spice cake with dried fruit, and sometimes wine.[123] While St. Gall sisters ate only water and bread on Good Friday, at Klingental the sisters were served lamb.[124] In most cloisters special fare was served on days when anniversary masses were celebrated for the souls of deceased donors. The special dishes, such as a fish meal from Johann zum Thor for the nuns at St. Maria Magdalena an den Steinen in Basel, were gifts from the donors to the sisters, who would take part in the services with songs and prayers for donors' souls.[125]

Foundation narratives from Dominican houses, about the beginnings of their communities in the thirteenth century, tell stories of privations and hunger in the early days when they were poor beguine settlements. The author of the Oetenbach foundation narrative tells about the miserable food that the founding mothers had to eat.

> They had a holy sister named Mechthild von Schaffhausen who baked bread for them as well as she could, [but] it was so sour and doughy that they laid it in the sun to dry. On some loaves the crust fell away and on others the inside did, so that they had not enough. And often they were given beet chard to eat and this happened so often that it piled up in the bowls. [A]nd sometimes when someone wanted to help them they made them a cake without eggs and

that was dough cooked in fat. So they suffered such great privation that sister Beli von Ebnot said later that she was often very hungry and had a great desire for something to eat and to drink. They very seldom had wine and, if the sisters were ill, they boiled water with caraway and kept it in wooden containers and drank that for wine. Now the young ones and the sisters who could not fast after prime, they were given no more than a soup.

This author, whose love of earthy and amusing stories differentiates her lively style from Johannes Meyer's didactic additions, tells how one Sister Bertha had a bright idea for increasing the meat supply. By placing it under shingles, she grew maggots in it, which she cooked with the meat. The narrator reports that what was served "looked as though it had been sprinkled with maggots," so the sisters would not touch it "and ate nothing but dry bread."[126]

Other less comic narratives, such as Anna von Munzingen's Chronicle of Adelhausen (1318), likewise emphasize the hunger and privations of the cloister's early days. Anna tells of a miraculous incident when the women, having no more food at all, received a timely donation.

And once during Shrovetide, while they were singing vespers, the cellaress had not a single egg to give to the convent, and she sat down in misery and wept from her heart and asked Our Lord that he would advise her that she might have something to give the convent on Shrove Tuesday and in that hour a woman came and brought two hundred eggs, and she rejoiced and praised God heartily.

In another more miraculous, loaves-and-fishes kind of story, a youth whom the women had never seen before and whom they took to be an angel brought the convent a beautiful loaf of bread that, to their amazement, served all of them.[127]

While later accounts may be more realistic, they still tell of insufficient budgets. Writing in her account book for 1507, a glum Prioress Anna von Buchwald says, "For seven years I gave you each in Lent one pound of raisins, but this year they were too expensive, so you will not get them." We know from her accounts that the favorite delicacy at Preetz was almonds, which the sisters made into almond milk and marzipan. In her log for 1499 Anna writes, "At the end of the year I was 40 marks in debt for your sakes because of the almonds which I bought for you again . . . and you asked me for." Anna manages to pay the debt but writes, "God knows, I was greatly worried the whole year and I have not been able to give you the thirteen schillings this year. For if I had distributed them, as I have always done before and never failed to, I would have been in debt."[128] Elfriede Kelm comments that the fifty to ninety cloister inhabitants at Preetz had to manage on three cattle, thirty-two lambs, and two goats, while a vicar received each year for himself one-half of an ox (salted) and a fattened pig.[129]

Arts and Education

Despite economic privations, all was not grim at Preetz, however. As Anna reports, one of the reasons for the debts incurred by the cloister in 1499 was the building or repair of an organ.[130] This luxury is not uncommon in women's convents of the fifteenth century. The chronicle of St. Katharina at St. Gall records the purchase of an organ in 1484. Here a letter from Prioress Haller at Nuremberg warmly congratulates the St. Gall women on this acquisition: "I rejoice in my heart that you have an organ and over the sisters' joy and reverence for it. It is of great comfort to a choir in singing, especially when you have a proper organist."[131] With or without an organ, the singing of the Hours is often mentioned in women's writings as a very satisfying and fulfilling activity. Anna Roede portrays in her chronicle of Herzebrock of the enthusiasm of Abbess Sophia von Gozes (1500–1516).

> She never tired of the service. By day and by night she was always the first and the last one as she always managed to do. And when she thought the manner of singing was not up to standard, she brought in a sister from [the convent of] Vinnenberg, Hilleke Sternenberg. She instructed the convent and the children every day in singing and she [the abbess] took the lessons too and learned like a child, for she had a beautiful light voice. And in payment she gave the sister a new habit.[132]

Anna recounts that this same abbess embroidered for the sisters' choir two antependia of exceptional quality (a "Maria in sole" and a very large annunciation scene), as well as the best cover for the high altar.[133]

Women's expressed interest in describing these kinds of artistic and creative activities at their houses contrasts radically with the view expressed by Friedrich Techen that convent life was a "dreadful tedium."[134] Lina Eckenstein asserts, rather, that cloister life "ceases to appear monotonous" when one enters one of the old treasuries and reflects "on the aims and aspirations which were devoted to producing this wealth in design and ornamentation."[135] Calligraphers, painters of miniatures, embroiderers, and weavers all found creative expression in the making of myriad objects of sacred art. Besides needlework antependia and intricately embroidered vestments, convent women produced large numbers of tapestries on secular and religious themes both for their own use and on commission. That this was not unusual is shown by a fifteenth-century tapestry, now at the Diözesanmuseum in Bamberg, which depicts two Dominican nuns at a loom weaving (Fig. 2).[136]

Beyond producing works of their own, women's accounts record that prioresses were patronesses of the arts who frequently commissioned works for their houses. Chronicles describe some of these commissions, including the prioress's role in choosing the designs. At Ebstorf (c. 1490), a sister relates how

> the prioress had an exceptionally beautiful treasure made, namely, an ostrich egg, which had long lain in the cabinet of the sacristan. This she had covered with gold and silver. Also four apostles of silver and a silver incense container. All this she had made from small silver pieces of jewelry which the sisters had owned before the reform and had turned in [to the common chest]. The greater part—in silver and gold ornaments—she still keeps in a coffer.[137]

Besides expressing pride in the accomplishment, these kinds of chronicle entries served as proof of ownership of works of art. Among the most active patrons was the ever-enterprising Anna von Buchwald, who commissioned for her convent—besides an altar of unique design, numerous frescos and wall decorations—more than twenty-eight paintings.[138]

Besides the occupations of daily choral singing and recitation, convent

Fig. 2 Tapestry (detail): two Dominican nuns weaving. Late fifteenth century. Bamberg, Diözesanmuseum.

women describe the staging of imaginative and sometimes dramatic devotional productions (some of which will be described in Chapter 4). At the cloister of Villingen, the ever-creative Prioress Ursula Haider (d. 1498) continually organized pageants, undertook imaginary "pilgrimages," and invented devotional exercises inspired by the seasonal celebrations of the church year. The overall impression is one of lively amateur theatrical activity. The Bicken Cloister chronicle tells, for example, how at Advent Prioress Ursula Haider would designate a particular evening for a candle-light dinner of fish and wine, served "with her own hands," to which she invited the sisters and in which she herself would appear in the role of "the representative of eternal wisdom." When the meal was almost finished, Prioress Haider reportedly played her dramatic role with great success.

> [She] ordered all the lights to be put out and knelt before the whole convent with great humility and began to speak with such delightful words that the sweet women were moved to great piety and wept hot tears. . . . When she had finished her talk, which lasted at least half an hour, they lighted the candles again and rejoiced. Then the dear Mother came and bought a gift or two, as holy poverty would allow [a paper picture or a little straight pin], and distributed them to the whole convent, each one the same, [wishing each] a happy new year.[139]

Prioress Ursula was particularly imaginative in putting on spiritual pageants. Most well known are the imaginary "pilgrimages" to Rome and to the Holy Land, which she arranged with parchments representing the stations of the journey that the sisters undertook individually or in a procession. As the chronicle indicates, the sisters proceeded "with monstrance and lighted candles, with song and great devotion through the ambulatory—from one parchment letter [each representing a holy site] to the next as though they were present in the Holy Land."[140] Indeed, with her unceasing flow of ideas, Prioress Ursula seemed capable of organizing a theatrical production for almost any occasion.

Beyond choral singing, celebrating the feasts of the church year, creating artistic works, and devotionally contemplating the paintings and objects commissioned for their cloister churches, convent women write about opportunities to enrich their lives through education. They praise the benefits of being able to read Latin texts and understand the beauties of the liturgy. At Ebstorf (c. 1490), a sister writes candidly about the satisfactions of her education:

> Oh what sweetness it is in the divine service to hear and to read the sacred texts, the words of the holy Gospel from the mouth of the Lord, the words of the sacred teachers both of the Old and the New Testaments. . . . [And] conversely, how disagreeable it is to stand in choir, to read and to sing and not to understand.

The same sister, perhaps a novice, gives an account of the schooling-in-progress that she was receiving at Ebstorf:

> [Our teacher] explained to us declination, the "Donatus," and the "glossed Donatus" word for word completely. . . . And she proposes soon to explain to us the first part of Alexander [de Villa, *Dei Doctrinale*], if God preserves her health. [The teacher had recovered from a nearly fatal illness.] She makes every effort toward the goal that we may properly understand the declinations of words, cases, and tenses.

Telling of making her profession together with her classmates, the writer records the ages of novices at Ebstorf in the late fifteenth century and describes the girls' views of the significance of their vocation.

> [I]n the same year that our teacher came to the school, at advent of the sixth year of the priorate of our beloved abbess, we made our profession on the first Sunday of advent and were consecrated to the order. A noble and worthy state to which God in his excellence had preordained and chosen us before we were born. There were six of us and four laysisters. [T]wo of us were still very young, one eleven and the other ten, the other four were fifteen years of age.[141]

While the exact circumstances of the composition of this text are not known, it was apparently written to be read aloud to the convent community and expresses the young women's indoctrination into the literate cultural atmosphere at Ebstorf.

According to convent records, the average age of girls (some orphans) on being admitted to the elite Klingental cloister for schooling was between five and ten years of age. Here each child was placed in the care of an adult, sometimes a relative, who became the child's "cloister mother." An impression of nuns' activities as foster mothers and teachers may be gained from a fifteenth-century illustration made at Ebstorf showing a small child being instructed by a nun in music (Fig. 3). Each girl at Klingental lived in the cell of her cloister mother and owed obedience to her and to the older "cloister daughters." If she remained in the cloister, a grown "daughter" would often continue to live with her cloister mother and to care for her when she became old and enfeebled. At her death, the "mother" usually bequeathed to her "daughter" the use of part of her property and her cell.[142] In the fifteenth century, nearly all Observant houses raised the minimum age for profession of vows from twelve or even younger to fourteen or fifteen. The regulations from the cloister of Pfullingen, for example, state that "girls under the age of fifteen and women over the age of forty-six should not be accepted."[143] Bursfeld reformers, such as Johannes Busch, closed convent boarding schools for lay children, however, because they felt that the running of a school made contact with the world unavoidable and interfered in the house's character as a religious cloister.[144] The loss of this source of income no doubt added to the hardships of financially troubled convents that had previously depended on it.

Work

Many women's houses supplemented their meager incomes by copying manuscripts, weaving woolen and linen cloth, or doing washing and mending for men's houses.[145] At St. Agnes in Emmerich, formerly a house of sisters of the Common Life but after 1463 an enclosed Augustinian cloister, all the women worked at spinning and weaving woolen cloth and had a production quota to be met every day. The Emmerich book of sisters (1503) tells of Sister Griet van Gorchem who became blind at the age of seventy-three. Concerned, lest she become a burden to the house, she devoted herself industriously to spinning and weaving. The account states

Fig. 3 Benedictine nun and school child. Illustration from a song book (detail). Cloister Archive, Ebstorf, MS V 3, fol. 200v. Fifteenth century.

that in the fifteen years until her death at age eighty-eight, Griet spun each year enough yarn for fifty to sixty ells of cloth.[146]

Producing the necessary amount of thread or yarn for the day's weaving was not an easy task and the Emmerich *Book of Sisters* records that the older, faster spinners would sometimes help the young ones meet their quotas. The chronicler tells the story of how one day a tired younger sister came to an older sister, Beel te Mushoel, and said, "Dear sister, I don't know what to do. I think I would rather die than spin all the time." Beel advised her, "But my dear child, do not think that, but rather: with this spinning you shall gain heaven."[147] While work is depicted realistically as labor, the economic necessity of it is sublimated to the goal of enabling the pursuit of a religious life and ultimately salvation. The didactic function of the narrative is clearly to model the behavior of its female readers. Here women teach other women and spur them on to more earnest spiritual devotion. Unlike the earlier sister-books, these fifteenth-century collections of vitae focus on the unspectacular, depicting heroism in small deeds of the rank and file. At the sisterhouse of Marienthal (called Niesing) in Münster, weaving was the chief source of income. Yet the convent chronicle relates that when the sisters produced enough goods to affect the local market, the weavers' guild objected and demanded that the looms be destroyed, thus the women had to stop production. In the *Chronicle of Marienthal*, composed c. 1541, one of the sisters records the confrontation (1525), but not without irony.

> [T]here was one there who told the town council he would wager his neck that we had one hundred looms—he was named Claus Munt. And councilman Munsterman took him along and showed him the eleven looms and told him that he had said he would wager his neck that we had one hundred. To which he answered, "That's what was told to me!" Then we had to bring the looms outside the door where a great, nameless crowd stood with the wagons, [and] who could not wait until the looms were broken up.[148]

Despite their own financial hardships, part of convent women's work—in both poor and wealthy religious houses—was feeding the poor. In 1526 the town council of Basel issued orders on the care of the poor that required the individual cloisters on a specific day to give every poor person "a bowl of gruel and about a penny's worth of bread."[149] Maria Hüffer estimates that during the famine years of 1481–82, the wealthy canoness house of Rijnsburg fed an estimated 4,000 people every day.[150] From the beginnings, almsgiving was one of the chief means by which women of the nobility expressed not only their piety but also their authority. These rituals of charity guaranteed them a high-ranking place in heaven appropriate to their high status on earth.[151] Early vitae, such as Bertha's *Life of Adelheid, Abbess of Vilich,* celebrate in hagiographic fashion the abbess's compassionate giving. With the feminine writer's typical penchant for describing food, Bertha tells how Adelheid concerned herself with providing the proper kind of nutrition for each recipient of her alms.

> At one time, almost the whole world was afflicted by a bitter famine and great masses of the starving came from everywhere, to partake of her generosity, as from the breast of a mother. All through the streets and at every crossroad many lay half-dead and waited for the accustomed dispensing of her alms. Touched by their great need, Adelheid herself cared with devotion for everyone. To the healthy and robust she parceled out bread and bacon; the ill she served cabbage and vegetables carefully boiled with meat. The dying and those almost despairing of life she revived with broths mixed with water and flour and other nourishment, always watching with diligence that the body not be put in peril by overeating after a lack of proper food.

Bertha goes on to describe how the saintly Adelheid was known to take off her shoes and put them in the beggar's vessel.[152] Both poor and rich houses exercised patronage through spiritual giving and interceding for the souls of the "needy dead."[153]

Spiritual Life

Between reading and singing services for the dead and performing the monastic office, convent women spent at least four to five hours of their day in choral prayer.[154] Marie-Luise Ehrenschwendtner estimates that medieval nuns spent roughly eight hours a day in chapel performing their liturgical duties.[155] Accordingly, women write a great deal about choral prayer. Sometimes they characterize their performances as very hearty, as for example in the "Chronicle of Inzigkofen," a nineteenth-century abridgement of the older chronicle begun in 1525 by Apollonia Besserer (1492–1538) and Elisabeth Muntprat (d. 1555). "The women are said to have sung, as the old chronicle records, so eagerly and manfully that they could be heard clearly all the way to the bridge."[156] The *Housebook* of the newly established Brigittine cloister of Maihingen (founded 1473) tells how the initial meager group of eight, and sometimes only five, singers had difficulty putting together two choirs to perform the office. But the *Housebook* (begun in 1522) narrates how the women, in an equally manful way,

> sang their seven Hours industriously every day. . . . And when the sisters had sung matins they had to spin until it was time to sing prime. It was often very hard on them when several times there were not more than two in one choir, and the fifth sat in the middle and sang in both choirs. For often the worthy Mother had to be with another sister at the [convent] door, and the stewardess in the kitchen to prepare the food . . . so the five sisters had to sing, whether it went well or badly for them.

Somehow the food got prepared and the Hours sung creditably enough—at least, so it sounded to the townspeople, who reported, "Something is singing with you; its voice is as loud as if an angel were singing with you."[157]

At Preetz, however, Prioress Anna von Buchwald felt that the number of services the women were obligated to sing was exhausting her nuns. Always efficient and enterprising, Anna writes that she tried to reduce the burden on them by consolidating some of the services. On the day of her ordination as prioress, she threw herself on her knees before the bishop and the superiors of her order to lament the many "worries, strains, and hardships" endured by her sisters, who, "because of the quantity of singing, reading and other things, were taxed beyond their abilities and tormented." Anna requested permission to reduce the number of readings and to allow the sisters to use a written text (rather than having to learn all the offices by heart), as well as to read the first two masses at the same time. These requests were roundly rejected by the bishop and the abbot, who reprimanded her harshly before the entire convent. Then, unexpectedly, the next day, they approved the changes. Anna, intensely practical and always focused on the spirit rather than the letter of prescribed duties, asserts that she made the changes "not because I am averse to work or lazy, but so that my beloved sisters in Christ would not be too exhausted, weak, and dejected . . . [rather] so that they would serve God more ardently in other things and continue their service the more diligently."[158]

When not performing the monastic office, services for the dead, or other prescribed duties, nuns could devote themselves to private readings and devotions. In her *Lives of the Sisters of Unterlinden* (1310/20), Katharina von Gueberschwihr depicts the spiritual zeal of idealized charismatic predecessors in the convent, women striving to purify their consciences "in manly fashion" (a term frequently applied to women's feats of devotion or radical asceticism).

> Mornings and evenings they assiduously examined the secrets of their conscience. If they became aware of anything that even moderately affected their heart or darkened its purity, they disciplined themselves most strenuously and cleansed themselves through pure confessions. . . . Armed in manly fashion against all temptations of the flesh and the devil, they held aloft the shield of faith and carefully pulled out the thorn bushes of vain thoughts by the roots.[159]

In private exercises, requiring a kind of calisthenics, some women worked out like spiritual athletes, praying in different postures—with outstretched arms, kneeling, face to the ground, or prostrate—mentally weaving imaginary "gifts" for the Virgin and Child or a "mantle" to cloak a deceased sister in the other world.[160] Freeing souls from purgatory through prayer was one of religious women's primary vocations, one way of participating in "Christ's work in the world."[161] The sister-book of cloister Töss (c. 1340) narrates how, after a morning of prayer and sewing, Sister Beli von Liebenberg said she would dearly like to know "how many souls the sisters had released from purgatory by their prayers that forenoon."[162] Bynum cites 70,000 souls that the mystic Mechthild of Magdeburg was reputed to have saved from purgatory. Christ also appeared to Gertrude of

Helfta and told her exactly how many souls had been released "from exactly how much purgatory by exactly which devotions of the community."[163]

Through intercessory prayer and other works of piety, such as almsgiving, women offered their own spiritual merits on behalf of helpless souls since, as God had assured Mechthild of Hackeborn, "it was his habit to repay every gift of charity with an equal store of charity." Thus, McNamara explains, even women "who felt themselves to be far from assured of their own salvation still became convinced that they had spiritual wealth enough to save others," and part of a nun's contemplative mission was "repenting for the sins of others and suffering in their place."[164]

By suffering on earth, one could reduce one's own suffering after death but, more important, one could redeem others. As Bynum succinctly puts it, "[T]o suffer was to save and be saved."[165] In this way, prayer, fasting, and other austerities were regarded as "service," the substituting of one's own suffering for that of others. Even illness, if offered as a "gift," could become a source of merit and a way to exercise charity, that is, the winning of mercy for souls in purgatory.[166] Accordingly, in her *Lives of the Sisters of Unterlinden,* Prioress Katharina explains the mission of her nuns and their devotion to the Virgin by declaring that they "observed a stricter and harder discipline in life than usual," in order to gain more effectively "the Grace of the Lord and his mercy."[167]

As a place apart from the sinfulness of the world, the cloister in Prioress Katharina's view is a higher plane where holy women offer prayers for the needs of the whole community as a kind of "public work." Certainly, it was clear to the populace at large that the more holy the life of the intercessor, the more efficacious would be the prayers. Everyone knew of saints who had worked miracles with their supplications. Margaret of Hungary's prayers were reputed to have kept the Danube from overflowing and those of Clare of Assisi to have saved her town from an imperial army.[168] Yet, even in less dangerous times, the interests of the local community were intimately bound up with the spiritual life of its cloister. Ellen Ross underscores this relationship between monasteries, "whose raison d'être was prayer," and the society outside, which "provided both the need for prayer and financial support in return for prayer."[169] Thus, more important in medieval towns than the imposing physical presence of the convent, with its visible church and cemetery, was the vital spiritual presence it represented. Inside it, the women interceded in prayer for a populace—both the living and the dead—that needed security in this life and especially in the next. Indeed, for the soul's journey through purgatory, the populace required very powerful and efficacious intercession.

Accordingly, the writings of nuns like Katharina von Gueberschwihr express a very positive view of women, their mission, and the role they played in their religious life and work. For these women, religious practice and the dispensing of spiritual patronage to the needy were ways of exercising an authority that constituted a form of empowerment. To be sure, the stories of sisters who would not have chosen the religious life for themselves are rarely told. Only occasionally do the narratives include women such as Fye Vreysen, who, after visiting friends on the outside, lost her zest for living in the sisterhouse. She became depressed, physically ill, and died an early death.[170] The author of the Deventer book of sisters used Fye's story to illustrate the manifest dangers inherent in contact with the world. Certainly, women's options both inside and outside the cloister were limited. But for those who actively chose or developed a vocation for the religious life, entering a women's community could be a strategy for exercising agency that allowed for religious self-development and in which opportunities to teach, create, and hold positions of responsibility and leadership were many. Moreover, through spiritual patronage women could command respect and exert influence in the world beyond the cloister.

The stories that religious women composed about themselves constitute an alternative narrative that calls into question the popular caricature of the nun as "cloister cat." Their depictions of daily life, work, and spiritual activities within the cloister do not confirm the stereotypes in ribald tales about nuns. How, for example, does one liken Unterlinden's Prioress Katharina to her close contemporary, Madame Eglantyne, Chaucer's self-indulgent prioress in the *Canterbury Tales*? And how are Anna von Buchwald's accounts of hardworking nuns to be reconciled with modern descriptions of nunneries as "enclaves for female leisure."[171] Clearly, narratives differ in style and content according to the audiences for whom they are produced. They are culturally specific and shaped by users for specific ends that reflect spiritual and social anxieties, power relations, and strategies for dealing with them. From the medieval perspective, the spiritual condition of a cloister was of critical importance, since it was connected directly to the health and well being of the secular community. Accordingly, Chapter 2 will look at the publicly perceived state of health of women's cloisters in the fifteenth century, at changing expectations, societal pressures, and at idealist as well as opportunist reformers.

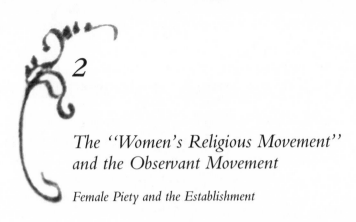

2

The "Women's Religious Movement" and the Observant Movement

Female Piety and the Establishment

Any discussion of women's religious activities in the late Middle Ages owes much to Herbert Grundmann's groundbreaking study, *Religious Movements in the Middle Ages*.[1] Since the book's publication in 1935, Grundmann's thesis of a "women's religious movement" has repeatedly come under fire for, among other things, conjuring up anachronistic associations with modern-day feminism. How can one speak of a "women's religious movement" in the late medieval period?[2] Did women at the time see themselves collectively as participants?

According to Grundmann's theory, the twelfth and thirteenth centuries gave rise to a growing pressure from women of all social strata for active participation in religious life.[3] Grundmann traces the origins of this pressure to the influence of wandering lay ministers who preached apostolic poverty and evangelism. Inspired by the ideal of the apostolic life, large numbers of lay people turned their backs on the world to embrace poverty and simplicity in the way that the earliest Christians did. The most popular of these charismatic preachers, Robert of Arbrissel (c. 1045–1116) and Norbert of Xanten (c. 1080–1134), established religious communities where their male and female followers could pursue a life of strict asceticism and discipline.[4] It was out of these foundations that Fontrevaud, with its double monasteries for men and women, and the new Premonstratensian order developed. By the mid-twelfth century, so many women had been attracted to the movement that there are reports of more than a thousand Premonstratensian sisters living in the diocese of Laon alone. Similarly, another chronicle from the year 1091 describes "innumerable women" taking up a religious form of life.[5]

Documenting a fourfold increase in new establishments for women in this period, scholars since Grundmann have suggested additional factors besides the apostolic life movement to explain the increase in women living as religious. These conditions include the much debated "surplus"of women and a decentralization of power in which the lesser nobility gained in influence and demonstrated its new prerogatives by founding convents.[6] Yet it is clear that even the large numbers of new foundations were unable to handle the press of patrician women wanting to live as religious. Jacques de Vitry (c. 1160–1240) asserted that these women were so numerous that "three times as many Cistercian cloisters would have been needed" to take them all in.[7] Overwhelmed by the applications for admission, both the new Premonstratensian and the older Cistercian orders declared a moratorium on admission of any more women's houses.[8] Concerned about the endangered situation of large numbers of "beguines," or religious laywomen, living in unincorporated groups throughout the diocese of Liège, Vitry obtained from newly elected Pope Honorius III (1216–27) his "verbal" consent for women to live in communal houses without belonging to an order or following a rule.[9] In the north the numbers of these unincorporated groups rose to some three percent of all women. In Cologne there were one hundred beguine houses and sixty in Strasbourg, where they constituted as much as ten percent of the female population.[10]

When the first Dominicans and Franciscans began to arrive in the south of Germany in the thirteenth century, they encountered similarly large numbers of women living together in groups without a rule and outside the institutional structures of the church. The mendicant friars promptly took over their spiritual care and advised them to adopt a rule and apply for admission to their orders. The response was overwhelming. Within its first twenty-five years, women's houses in the Dominican order grew from four in France, Spain, and Italy to thirty-two in the German provinces alone and to eighty there by 1303.[11] Providing pastoral care for so many religious women soon placed demands on the order that could not be met, and the Dominicans, like the Cistercians and the Premonstratensions, closed their doors to women. But this action did not eliminate the pressure to accept more women into the order, especially when popes continued to make exceptions. Finally, the Dominican order took the radical step of divesting itself even of those women's houses already admitted and decreed that the brothers must henceforth cease providing pastoral care to all female religious communities.[12] Only after some twenty years was a compromise worked out, allowing for sacramental duties to be delegated to secular priests serving as chaplains, and women were again admitted to the Dominican order.[13]

Women Writing about Beguines

Did women in their chronicles and foundation histories write about these events and do their narratives about beguines register a sense of belonging to a movement of religious women? Grundmann cites Hadewijch (fl. c. 1220–40), whose writings, he asserts, indicate "a consciousness of the interconnections of the new feminine piety." Hadewijch mentions beguines in Flanders, Brabant, Paris, Zealand, Holland, Frisia, England, and "beyond the Rhine."[14] That women knew the history of their collective struggle for acceptance into religious orders and were acquainted with writings by earlier women authors (as will be shown in Chapter 6) can be verified in a chronicle composed around 1490 by Magdalena Kremer at the cloister of Kirchheim unter Teck in Württemberg. Magdalena writes of the early days of women's efforts to gain admittance to the Dominican order and of their subsequent expulsion. Remarkably, however, she uses this account to tell of a successful collective counteraction by women in response to being denied recognition and pastoral care. Many women, she asserts, went on foot to Rome and joined together to protest their situation to the Pope. Attributing the resolution of the problem to women's collective effort, Magdalena describes their successful lobbying and the positive outcome:

> [F]rom many cloisters in German lands two or three sisters from each set out on foot, joined together, and traveled under great hardship to Rome where they protested their desperate situation and misery to our holy father the pope and besought him that he would again place them under the direction and protection of the Dominicans. The pope perceived their great earnestness and returned them to the care of the Dominicans. And where they previously had had one women's cloister, they now had seven to one.[15]

Magdalena rejoices in the sevenfold increase in Dominican women's houses, despite the hierarchy's attempts to keep them out. Her version of the events reflects not only the sisters' feeling of accomplishment at winning their suit but also a sense of solidarity in their growing strength of numbers. Certainly, Magdalena's picture of scores of German Adelheids and Hildegards marching on Rome in a kind of women's second Germanic invasion seems a startling one for a female author in the late Middle Ages.

Literary historian Peter Dinzelbacher has argued that formulations such as "we women" begin to appear for the first time in the fifteenth century.[16] He identifies Christine de Pizan (1365–c. 1430), author of the *Book of the City of Ladies,* as the first woman writer to express an awareness of women collectively in opposition to the masculine world. If Dinzelbacher's hypothesis is correct, it marks a significant watershed in women's thinking. As early as 1320, Dominican women had begun writing foundation accounts of the formation of their communities out of gatherings of beguines. Five of the nine Dominican sister-books composed between 1320 and 1350 at women's houses in Switzerland, Alsace, and Southern Germany were prefaced by foundation narratives that had already been added in the fourteenth century. Three of the nine were later edited by Johannes Meyer, who cut out visions that he objected to and supplied didactic prologues and epilogues.[17] Yet the ironic approach taken by the author of the Oetenbach sister-book clearly distinguishes her style from Meyer's. She, too, mentions the moratorium on Dominican pastoral care of women's communities but describes a different solution. In her narrative, the beguine founding mothers solve the problem by pitting the Dominicans friars against their rivals, the Franciscans. When the Dominicans hear that the women might join the order of the Poor Clares instead, they become alarmed and decide to take over their care again. In this way the women succeed in gaining the help of the men.[18]

In the Oetenbach sister-book, as in several foundation narratives, the author relates how two of the beguine women subsequently make the arduous trip to Rome to get confirmation of their community's acceptance. The chronicler tells how Hemma Walaseller and another sister took an elderly secular priest with them as their escort on their journey to Rome. Once there, the sisters again prove more effective than the men. With God's help they see their matter quickly arranged "ahead of many a great lord who had been there long before them."[19] The chronicler expresses evident satisfaction in the sisters' success, in spite of the disadvantages of being poor and female.

While fourteenth-century sister-books lack explicit "we women" wording, they celebrate female agency and initiative in the founding of beguine communities and in achieving the incorporation of these communities into the order. In these narratives, the beguine founding mothers observe the spirituality of the new men's mendicant communities and solicit their guidance and friendly advice. But the stories depict the women as the primary agents and initiators of the beguine "gatherings." Stressing the lay women's desire for a life devoted to religion, the foundation stories portray the extreme privations they endured in establishing and financing a house, helped by lay women of the neighborhood. Thus the Oetenbach foundation story relates with characteristic irony how a woman named Gertraut von Hilzingen, who lived in the city of Zurich,

> gained a burning desire to live such a holy spiritual life as [the Dominicans] and so she took with her two persons of good will and they moved to an abandoned house that was in that city and there they established a cloister. And when they entered the house, the rain was coming in everywhere so that it was almost filled with water. Thus they moved in, relying on God's mercy, and had at first nothing but water and bread. That was a poor state of affairs for such exalted brides of God.

Here, as in other foundation stories, solidarity is a prominent theme in descriptions of the way the beguine women supported one another. Thus the Oetenbach author relates, "Of the three sisters, one was named sister Mechthild von Woloshofen. She helped out in her father's inn, but she had such sympathy for the other two that she left it and ate water and bread with them."[20]

Often solidarity takes the form of women helping other women monetarily. The foundation account in the sister-book of cloister Katharinental (c. 1318/1343), near the Swiss town of Diessenhofen, tells of the community's origins in a beguine gathering at Winterthur.[21] In this narrative, the decisive initiative is taken by a widow named Williburg von Hünikon, a woman of considerable property. This enterprising and wealthy widow joins an already existing community of poor women and maintains them with her own funds while looking for a better situation for the group.

Where women and men work together in these narratives, it is in decidedly non-hierarchical relationships. Thus the foundation account states:

> [W]hen this blessed Sister Williburg came to them and became well acquainted with the holy and blessed life that [the beguines] led, she became very eager to better their condition and that she might help them to a secure and permanent place where they could serve our Lord undisturbed and in a proper manner. . . . And they heard of the good intention which the honorable priest Herr Hugh at Diessenhofen had to establish a cloister where forty women might serve the Lord. When Sister Williburg heard this, she hurried to him on foot and asked about his plans and told him of their needs and what she intended. This appealed to him and they agreed that they wanted to do all in their power to establish an honorable cloister of the Dominican order in that place. . . . Then sister Williburg brought her group from Winterthur and they lived in a house until the cloister was built.[22]

Acting in an equal partnership, Hugh becomes the chaplain and Williburg the prioress of the new community.

Unlike the accounts of Gandersheim, Quedlinburg, and Essen, great dynastic foundations for women established in earlier periods on the initiative of a noble patron, the fourteenth-century narratives stress the communities' humble and independent origins. Donors come into the picture only after a group of pious, spiritually dynamic women has banded together to start a community on their own.[23] Even though these stories were written a century or so after a community's first gathering, after the cloisters had become wealthy and secure, they depict the hardships and celebrate the initiative of the beguine "founding mothers" as a way of creating a communal identity and a fictive golden age of beguine spirituality.

Christina Ebner (1277–1356), who composed the foundation history and sister-book of Engelthal, the *Little Book of the Overwhelming Burden of Grace*, entered the cloister in 1289. Thus Christina may have known personally some of the former beguines who were present at the community's incorporation as a Dominican house in 1244.[24] Christina's narrative tells how a certain Adelheid Rotter left the entourage of Princess Elisabeth of Hungary to live as a penitent in Nuremberg. There she joined a group of beguines, who asked her to become their leader. The women did not have sufficient funds to establish a cloister, but each one brought all that she possessed. Emphasizing the beguines' earnest desire to live as a religious community, Christina depicts in the typical manner of the sister-books the women's charismatic spirituality. She tells how the beguines organized themselves and invented a rule of order, relying on Adelheid, who was literate and had been at court. Through their self-fashioned ritual, they acted out their religious devotion.

> They read the Hours as well as they were able. At compline they went to their mistress [Adelheid] and asked her what they should do on the following day, and that they did willingly. When they sat at table, their mistress sat at the head. After she had eaten a little, she read to them in German: and it occasionally happened that some of them fell into a swoon and lay unconscious like the dead, for they were totally absorbed in God, as though departed. . . . When people heard of their holy life, they gave them freely all that they needed, especially Kunigunde, the Queen of Bohemia, who was very generous to them.

In 1239, when Nuremberg was placed under interdict because of the excommunication of Emperor Friedrich II (Hohenstaufen), the group of beguines left Nuremberg and went to a manor outside of the city, where, the narrator continues, "they had to do heavy work and cut their grain themselves, wash, bake, and do all the chores. This they did with great devotion and patience."[25] After they had lived as a self-organized group for some time, turning for advice to a local pastor, the women petitioned the first Dominicans to arrive in their region to join their obedience. But, as in the other sister-book foundation stories, the focus here is on devout beguine women starting a community on their own.

While poverty is an important theme in the women's stories about their beguine foremothers, it is not a constant. It does not figure prominently, for instance, in the foundation story that Prioress Elisabeth Kempf (1415–1485) added to the Unterlinden sister-book (Colmar) when she translated it from Latin into German. The original, composed by Prioress Katharina von Gueberschwihr around 1320, had contained no account of the cloister's founding.[26] Elisabeth Kempf's addition draws from other convent documents and tells the story of two very enterprising, noble widows who established and managed a lay religious community. Hiring a priest to conduct services, they organized a manner of life patterned on what they call the "old cloisters." In planning the community, the first members consult their network of widow friends who offer their opinions and assistance.

> There lived in Colmar two widows, respected for their piety, upright life, and their noble families—Agnes von Wittelnheim and Agnes von Herkenheim. On the advice of Walther, a lector at the Dominican men's convent in Strasbourg. . . . God gave them the desire to found a convent. They made their intention known to other widows in the neighborhood in order to hear their opinions about it. These women responded joyfully with advice and eager assistance. The two widows rented out the houses that they owned in Colmar for a yearly sum and moved with their sons and daughters to the outskirts of town to a place called "under the Linden," where there was a house and some property around it. After a short time they left that place on the advice of two respected women who had joined their group, and moved, on the evening of the feast of St. John the Baptist 1222, to a place called Aufmühlen, which is next to the chapel of that saint. There were then eight of them. . . . Soon afterward they built on the same location some houses and a long, wide, and high stone dormitory. They enclosed themselves in this building and there led a pious life in the fear of God. After the manner of the old cloisters, they had maids and laborers work their fields and vineyards and paid a priest of spotless reputation at their own expense, who said the mass for them almost daily.

In Elisabeth's story, the two widows eventually make the arduous trip to the papal court to petition for incorporation into the Dominican order. In Rome, they do some research and visit the women's cloister of San Sisto, established by Saint Dominic, in order to study its physical construction and the nuns' habit and practices. Then, continues Elisabeth, "with great eagerness and persistence, they requested that Pope Innocent IV grant them the order and dress of the Dominicans and asked that they be placed under the care and direction of the order and enjoy its privileges."[27] The account includes the text of Pope Innocent's decree, issued in 1246.

In the Unterlinden case, as in the other narratives, it is primarily women who help beguine women. Its depictions agree with recent studies showing a high number of female patrons for beguine settlements. Forty-five percent were founded by women as the principle donors. Moreover, Walter Simons's study calls the beguine movement "the only movement in medieval monastic history that was created by women and for women."[28] The sister-book foundation narratives strongly emphasize female patronage and self-starting mutual support. The Katharinental account, for instance, not only mentions generous townspeople but also singles out by name specific women who helped the community financially.[29] Like other stories that women wrote for each other, the foundation account of the Clarissan cloister of Pfullingen, composed by an anonymous sister around 1525, tells how two noble women established a cloister themselves and then traveled to Rome to receive permission to incorporate the house into the order of the Poor Clares.

> On Saint Martin's day in the year of our Lord 1251 this cloister Pfullingen was begun by the noble, well-born lady Mechthildt and lady Irmel von Pfullingen, of the noble family of Rempen. And they went themselves in person to Rome and acquired permission, and with their property and with holy alms built this cloister. Let it be known that the first donation given was a little lamb or sheep that, by the grace of God, became an entire strain and herd. God be praised. Afterward, in the year 1252 on St. Otmar's day, the same women entered the holy order of Saint Clare.[30]

The narrative tells how years of military campaigns subsequently decimated the cloister's holdings. But the chronicler emphasizes the women's resourcefulness in protecting what little they could from the marauding soldiers. She recounts, for example, "Once the sisters took everything that they could carry and hid it in the refectory under the benches and [hiding the cache] stood before them close together in their cloaks."[31] Thanks to the women's clever collective stratagem, the soldiers found nothing to confiscate and left the cloister.

For most of the convents that grew out of thirteenth-century beguine settlements, the origins were small, poor, and obscure, making it difficult to identify to what order they first belonged. Particularly in "Cistercian" cloisters, it is often unclear exactly what the nature of the women's affiliation with the order was.[32] Likewise, many self-established convents that received pastoral care from the Dominicans were never officially accepted into that order. The stories about the founding mothers of these houses, which became part of the sister-books in the fourteenth and fifteenth centuries, are a far cry from the earlier women's narratives about great noble abbeys such as Gandersheim. Both Hrosvit's *Origins of the Convent of Gandersheim* (c. 973/983) and Bertha's *Life of Adelheid, Abbess of Vilich* (1057) relate splendid foundations.[33] In both of these accounts, the monasteries are organized by the wealthy and powerful parents of the first abbesses. Sister Bertha relates, for example, how at Vilich the noble father, Count Megengoz, and mother, Countess Gerberga, daughter of Duke Godfrey, took an active part in overseeing the building of a monastery for their daughter Adelheid. Bertha relates how Vilich Abbey, built some seventy years before, was closely supervised by the exacting Lady Gerberga, who "remained steadfastly at the place where the monastery was to be built, accelerating the pressing work on the structure with magisterial foresight." In this narrative, Adelheid's parents donate the building and its furnishings, recruit the women who are to inhabit it, and arrange the privileges and safeguards that will protect their daughter and their investment. Bertha relates:

> Then they collected together a community of virgins in that place who were to tend the Divine Service. From the convent of the Holy Virgins [where Adelheid was being schooled], they redeemed their daughter with a gift of land, and handed over to her the care of the future direction and government of Vilich. . . . When they had decorated the place worthily, they gave it into the hand of the Emperor Otto III, so that his protection would defend it in perpetuity. Graciously, he freed the place from all secular yoke and laws and bestowed upon it the liberties according to the laws and constitutions of the convents of Gandersheim, Quedlinburg and Essen, namely, that a judge or advocate could never demand ser-

vices thereupon nor could govern in the boundaries of the area of that convent unless it pleased the abbess and her congregation.[34]

Clearly, these much earlier foundation narratives—composed by women but with a male audience and the illustrious donor families in mind—were not the models for the accounts that fourteenth-century Dominican women composed. It is doubtful that they even knew about them. Rather, the foundation stories in the Dominican sister-books appear to have been modeled on Gérard de Frachet's (d. 1281) *Vitae Fratrum* (Lives of the Brethren of the Order of Preachers), which was compiled in response to a mandate from the Dominican Chapter General in 1256 to collect any "edifying occurrences" within the order so as to chronicle its origins and development. Frachet's *Lives* contains a number of monastic foundation histories of individual convents.[35]

Gertrud Jaron Lewis asserts that the sister-books are more than simply feminine versions of Frachet's work. Above all, they present a different view of women from the male-authored *Vitae patrum, Vitae fratrum,* and Vincent of Beauvais' *Speculum historiale,* all of which contain a few token saintly women but portray the vast majority of females as disreputable, silly, or, at worst, downright satanic. Lewis cites the "depressingly negative" and steady diet of misogynist tales offered to monastics, both male and female, in their daily reading as the backdrop against which the "unique and novel achievement of the authors of Sister-Books" stands out. If not an actual backlash, Lewis suggests, we have in sister-books at least images of virtuous women and—more important—a "consciously feminine perspective." Here women are not only the authors but also the subject and the audience for the texts. Women in the sister-books "talk directly about themselves, their own community, their values and attitudes."[36]

Wilhelm Oehl has called the sister-books "typically female, without a trace of objective history writing."[37] One wonders if a truly "objective" view would include such a categorization of what is female. But clearly these "histories," written by fourteenth-century women, must be seen in their late-medieval context. If patterned on Gérard de Frachet's work, they fit within a tradition of foundation narratives that is not female. Yet they differ in presenting a point of view that places women at the center rather than at the margins. These stories do not characterize women as subaltern, passive recipients of pastoral care or as persons who have been "sent" to nunneries but as women choosing and actively initiating an alternative life-style, one entirely devoted to religion. The portrait of enterprising, re-sourceful, and determined beguine founding mothers is, perhaps, not so unusual a view as has been supposed.

The literary genre to which these accounts belong and the political agenda they represent with be discussed in Chapter 6. The important point here is that these works were written with a particular aim in mind. Com-posed some one hundred years after the beguine communities had become wealthy and secure houses of regular Dominican nuns, the sister-books look backward to their beguine origins and the communities' most cele-brated visionaries for models, in order to combat what they perceive as a falling away from spirituality in their own time. The anecdotes of the fer-vent piety of women in the community's past are designed to inspire the contemporary generation to renew its spiritual devotion.[38] In the Töss sis-ter-book, for example, the narrator reports that she asked Sister Elisabeth Bechlin, a resident of the cloister for sixty-two years, to provide an anec-dote for her book. When Sister Elisabeth wanted to know what it was to be used for, the narrator replied that it was to provide a model, one that would inspire readers to strive for God's grace, because, as she laments, "the love of God is beginning to decline these days in many places in the hearts of men."[39] The sense of spiritual decline that worried the compiler of the Töss sister-book in the fourteenth century would become far more acute in the following century as the social and religious landscape under-went rapid and radical changes.

Religious Practice and Women's Convents

These worries were not unjustified, for by the late fourteenth century the church was, indeed, in a state of crisis, having two, and later three, rival popes. Religious orders were headed up by rival Masters General and at ground level mendicant friars were in competition with parish clergy. These divisions created confusion among the laity and undermined morale in the monastic ranks. Decimated by plague in the fourteenth century, the religious orders had not recovered. In southern Germany only 400 of what had been 1200 Franciscan friars remained.[40] In many institutions the state of religious practice was alarming, as can be seen in Bishop Matthias Rammung's reform regulations for the St. Guido chapter house at Speyer (1464–78). These directives state that no member "may bring a dog with him into the choir" or use "abusive language during a chapter meeting." During the singing of the psalms, "[o]ne side of the choir may not begin to sing or recite their verse until the other side has completed its psalm verse. . . . During the office the members of the chapter are required to sing or to read. They should not poke and tease each other [or] disturb others during the common singing and prayer."[41] In many women's houses the situation was not much better, since the male monastic orders were poorly equipped to supply them with qualified priests.[42] At Nuremberg the Clarissan sisters complained in a letter to the town council, circa 1410, that the Franciscan friars did not "keep an upright common life," or instruct them in "proper faith," but instead led them away from it.[43] Women at the Strasbourg convents of St. Mark, St. Katharina, and St. Nicolaus in undis objected that Dominican brothers had entered their cloisters without permission, wanting to dance.[44] In the fifteenth century, it had become a layman's sport in Zurich to scale the walls of the cloister of Oetenbach at Shrovetide and play pranks or dance with the sisters. Here, a New Year's Eve escapade in 1505/6, reported in the minutes of the town council, ended in a pillow fight.[45]

But it takes two to tango, and men were not the only dancers. At the Clarissan cloister of Söflingen it was rumored that the nuns wore shrovetide costumes. Officials in 1484 reported finding there "pointed shoes" and a "cleavage enhancing bodice."[46] The reforming Count Ulrich of Württemberg was horrified to learn that both his son and his brother had danced and carried on loudly with the sisters at the Dominican cloister of Kirchheim during a visit in 1476.[47] More serious, however, was a letter written to the bishop of Constance, c. 1450, by an unnamed clergyman who complained that at Klingental the women were not observing the rule of silence and stayed up so late at night that they slept through early mass—which only three or four of the forty nuns attended. The informant remonstrates that in choir the sisters chatted in loud voices and brought dogs and birds with them. When admonished to be quiet, they refused to sing. If the religious service were too long, the sisters would sneak out of the choir before the end instead of listening to the sermon and stroll chatting throughout the cloister. Furthermore, the writer complains, many did not take communion regularly. The anonymous whistle-blower identifies the prioress as the source of the problem, accusing her of currying favor with the younger sisters by letting them do anything they wished and herself keeping company with a man named Wilhelm.[48]

Other kinds of complaints cite gross inequities of wealth and poverty within women's cloisters. A tract from 1453/54 states that, while some convent women enjoyed jewelry, expensive clothing, valuable utensils, soft beds and good food, others sisters were poorly and thinly clothed and had to live on watery broths and pea soup. Some, it asserts, live "like lords" while others resemble shabby beggars.[49] Visitation records from the Cistercian cloister at Jena seem to corroborate this charge, showing that a few nuns there owned as many as fifty or one hundred veils, while the others had five or six.[50]

Despite the possession of substantial individual property, many women's houses in the fifteenth century were in serious financial trouble. Critics asserted that the nuns, rather than giving over all their assets to the cloister, were keeping some of them outside for their own private use.[51] More real and pervasive problems, however, were financial mismanagement, inflation, and the inexorable shift from an agricultural to a currency-based economy that had eroded many convents' financial base.[52] By 1450 the Augustinian cloister of Heiningen, for example, had run up 2,000 gulden in debts and was so poor that the women had no candles even to eat by in winter.[53] At Zoffingen, reforming sisters sent from St. Gall in 1497 were appalled to find the cloister out of food and nearly bankrupt. The newly arrived reformers record in the Zoffingen account book and chronicle, "When we arrived in the cloister, we found nothing that one could live on, only about six or seven measures of wine and about eight pounds of nuts. There was neither schmalz nor salt nor grain nor meal that we could survive on." Setting to work, the sisters succeeded in turning the situation around and by 1502 the convent's eight inhabitants (all but three of them over age sixty) had increased to twenty-six.[54] At the Benedictine cloister of Herzebrock Sister Anna Roede writes that feuds and military campaigns had so damaged her cloister that "the Divine Service could not be held night and day with such ardent devotion as had been their practice. This was due to the great uproar caused by the fighting."[55]

Even where the sisters could attend to spiritual matters, some cloisters were so lacking in good leadership and a common understanding of their

mission that destructive rivalries arose. At the Clarissan cloister in Nuremberg a particularly grievous rivalry came to light in which two factions
harassed each other on the feast days of their respective saints. Writing to
the city council, one group of sisters complained, "You should also know
that recently on Saint John the Evangelist's day a new book containing his
vita was brought out and read at table and that is against the wishes of the
majority of the convent . . . who are devoted to Saint John the Baptist [and]
will think up something new to do in retaliation. Thus the irritation never
ends and keeps escalating."[56] To escape conditions like these, sisters often
left troubled cloisters for better situations, as did Sister Guta Rüssin who
transferred in 1378 from the house of the Penitents of St. Maria Magdalena
an den Steinen at Basel to a Cistercian house. Sister Guta cites two reasons
for her move: the poverty of the convent and the constant traffic of secular
visitors, which she felt to be detrimental to the spiritual life of the house.[57]

Certainly not all reports of moral and spiritual laxity in women's houses
are reliable. Some were exaggerations, while others were simply false.
Often the reputation of the nuns was purposely defamed by fervent agitators trying to initiate a reform or justify one afterward. Even sincere reformers could sometimes be overzealous and politicians often opportunistic
or unscrupulous. A vigorous public debate at Strasbourg in 1454/56 led
popular Observant preacher and secular priest Johannes Kreutzer (d. 1468)
to denounce all unreformed cloisters as "brothels."[58] Sometimes financial
problems that were not of the nuns' making were, nevertheless, used as the
pretext for a reform. At the cloister of Medingen, for example, the sisters
were blamed when a dishonest male steward embezzled their funds and
fled. The nuns were then forced on pain of excommunication to pay the
unjustly incurred debts. And when, having undertaken to pay, they became
impoverished and their living conditions so intolerable that the nuns had
to go home to their parents, they were criticized for breech of the rule of
enclosure. Intervention to take control of the cloister's finances thus appeared to be justified.[59] In some cases the defamations were simply wrong,
as at Söflingen where, as has been mentioned, a critic claimed that there
were a large number of pregnancies at the cloister. Max Miller has since
demonstrated that this was a false understanding of terminology. For, in
context, the word that had been interpreted as meaning "pregnant" actually signified "puffed up, proud, or rebellious."[60]

Lest all women's religious houses be condemned out of hand as sorely in need of reform, some distinctions must be drawn. Polemics denouncing them for allowing ownership of private property, servants, separate living quarters and meals do not always distinguish between expectations for nuns living under a rule and canoness houses that, as has been shown, never prohibited any of the above. In many cases, and especially by the fifteenth century, the difference between nunneries of the regular orders and canoness houses of choir sisters was difficult to determine.[61] Some cloisters officially broke their connections to the regular orders, while in others the relationship was only loosely defined.[62] Perhaps the only thing that can be said with certainty is that the term "canoness" is not synonymous with "unreformed" and women's convents cannot all be lumped together.

The Church Regenerate

The church of the fifteenth century was not entirely in decline. In many parts it was healthy, and in others vigorously regenerating. Far from being an age on the wane, the period before the Reformation was one of intense religious ferment that gave rise to new forms of spirituality, driven by the increasing influence and demands of the urban burgher class and its religious needs.[63] The eagerness of the general populace for sermons in this period is only one measure of a vigorous upsurge in popular piety.[64]

As has been mentioned, one of the movements that arose toward the end of the fourteenth century and experienced its greatest expansion in the 1420s and 1430s was that of the New Devout or Brothers and Sisters of the Common Life. The movement offered the option of a third or "middle" way between lay status and the religious orders, a manner of living as "Devout" without being professed religious.[65] Seeking a more intense spiritual experience, the New Devout formed communities in private houses, where they began to emulate a life based on that of the apostles and the early church. The earliest of these communities was a house for women in Deventer that founder Geert Grote (d. 1384) organized by turning over to them his own residence. The Devout sisters required no vows or seclusion from the world but practiced a life of great simplicity centered on techniques of meditation. Like other parishioners they attended mass at the parish church. The sisters were expected to work to support the house, to live communally and, holding their goods in common, to devote themselves to reading devotional books and the liturgical Hours.[66] Over 130 such sister-houses were founded in the fifteenth century along the lower- and middle Rhine, as well as in other parts of Westphalia, lower Saxony, Hessen and the Baltic coast.[67] They constituted almost half of all cloister foundations in the fifteenth century.[68] Many of these sister-houses, like St. Agnes in Emmerich, later took on the Augustinian rule and lived enclosed. Some were reformed by Observants or themselves sent women to intro- duce their way of life at unreformed houses, as did the convent at Diepen- veen, a former sisterhouse that dispatched three sisters to reform Hilwartshausen on the Weser.[69] In this and other reforms carried out by Windesheim-trained Observant activists such as Johannes Busch, the devo- tionalist movement and the Observant reform initiative overlap.

Recent research has made increasingly clear that the New Devout movement did not arise in isolation but must be seen in relationship to other reform and Observant movements taking place in the religious orders at this same time.[70] Many orders developed a spirituality in the fourteenth and fifteenth centuries resembling that of the devotionalists or *devotio mod- erna* but that was spawned by the Observant reform movement. Both de- velopments were part of what Kaspar Elm calls the "new spiritual landscape" at the end of the Middle Ages.[71] Many of these independent initiatives, instigated locally by monastics themselves have, until recently, been ignored and little done to trace them beyond any strictly order-cen- tered compass or, as Katherine Walsch comments, to establish lines of de- velopment toward the reforming movements of the sixteenth century.[72]

The Observants: An Overview

While reform, "the leitmotif of German history in the fifteenth century," was a call that resounded from every quarter, the Observant movement itself did not originate in the fifteenth century or with the great reform councils.[73] Rather, it began earlier at a grassroots level and simultaneously within various orders.[74] A quick overview here of the Observant move- ments in the Franciscan, Augustinian, Dominican, and Benedictine orders will show the commonalities and general aims.

Among the Franciscans, an initiative to return to observance of the Rule of Saint Francis as it was first conceived is associated with the "Spirituals" of the early fourteenth century and the charismatic Angelus Clarinus (d. 1337).[75] These self-styled poor and devout brothers lived in hermitages and pursued a life of penitence and prayer. Toward the turn of the fifteenth century in France, Colette of Corbie (1381–1447), a former beguine who had become a Clarissan nun, launched her own reform of the order and was successful in founding twenty-two convents.[76] At the same time, radical eremitical initiatives among Franciscans in Spain urged not only a return to a life of poverty but also strict silence and seclusion. Following the Council of Constance, a more moderate form of observance was promoted by popular preachers Bernardino of Siena and John of Capistrano, but the issue of radical poverty ultimately split the Franciscan order into separate branches of Observants and Conventuals.[77]

In the Augustinian order, an Observant movement that was strongly influenced by the example of the Franciscan eremitical ideal developed in Italy about 1385. From the first Observant house at Lecceto, it spread in the fifteenth century throughout the Italian Augustinian provinces and developed strong followings in Spain and Saxony, where Martin Luther, early on, was himself a resident of three Observant houses. Besides penance, prayer, common life, and observance of the rule without exemptions, the Augustinian reformers devoted themselves with increased commitment to the sacramental life of the laity.[78]

Among Dominicans, the order from which the most documents in this study stem, the Observance was promoted by Master General Raymond of Capua (1380–99), biographer and confessor to Saint Catherine of Siena (d. 1380). But it was actually Catherine who is credited with having persuaded Raymond that a renewal of the order was possible and who pressed him to pursue it.[79] In 1388 at the general chapter meeting in Vienna, Raymond's plan was emphatically dramatized by the flamboyant Conrad of Prussia (d. 1426) who appeared at the meeting dressed as a penitent and with a rope about his neck. Before the assembled brothers, Conrad accused himself and the entire order of not living in accordance with the rule and the constitutions. Raymond placed Conrad in charge of organizing an Observant house at Colmar in Alsace. Within a year, the charismatic Conrad had recruited thirty like-minded brothers and proceeded to take over the house, much to the consternation of many former inhabitants and citizens of Colmar. Afterward, Master General Raymond decreed that each Dominican province should designate one convent as an Observant house for those who wished to keep the original rule of the order completely and strictly.[80] In

Italy, reformer Giovanni Dominici (1355–1419) was named vicar of San Domenico di Castello in Venice. There, in 1391, he founded the first Observant convent in Italy. Three years later, Corpus Domini was founded at the instigation of a group of Observant women who wished to establish an observant cloister with Giovanni Dominici as their confessor.[81] In the German territories, Conrad of Prussia organized the first Observant house for women (1397), locating it at Schönensteinbach (near Guebwiller in Alsace).

In the Benedictine order, reform movements sprang up in the fourteenth and fifteenth centuries at more than six different Observant centers in Italy, Austria, and Germany: Subiaco (1362), San Giustina in Padua (1408), Melk (1415–18), Kastl (1378–89), St. Matthias in Trier (1419–21), and Bursfeld-Clus on the Weser river (c. 1430).[82] The Council of Basel (1431–49) itself issued reform decrees mandating a new liturgy and new statutes for all Benedictine cloisters.[83] To the Bursfeld Union, one of the largest reform congregations (many of whose activists, like Johannes Busch, came out of the Windesheim Congregation of the New Devout), observance meant a strict adherence to the common life, shared meals, and the presence of everyone in choir. Bursfeld Observants reduced the length of their monastic office so that the monks would have time for individual meditation and spiritual exercises along with the manual labor that the reformers had reinstated. Because the liturgy had become so overladen in the course of the centuries with variations and special offices that took up an inordinate amount of time, it was cut back and returned to the simplest daily liturgy of the rule. Chanting was to be kept plain and performed mostly a capella. Moreover, the changes that the Bursfelders made in the breviary were aimed, they asserted, at allowing the office to be performed more slowly, more attentively, and with greater devotion.[84] Substantial negotiation and effort went into the construction of this new, simpler common liturgy, which was to replace with a uniform manner of worship all the divergent practices that had grown up around it.[85]

At the women's cloister of Ebstorf, which was refomed c. 1464/70, one of the sisters composed an account of the sweeping changes that were introduced there. She relates how the prioress of Hadmersleben came with two sisters to instruct the women of Ebstorf in the new liturgy and describes the considerable the labor this entailed for everyone.

> On the first Sunday after her arrival, we changed the choral singing and the entire music. And the women had an enormous amount

of work because they often copied out during the day what was going to be sung that night. Twelve sisters were appointed at the beginning, six in one choir and six in the other, to sing the office. All the others were exempted so as to watch until they had been instructed in the manner of it. All the books for the choral singing, as well as the readings, the graduals, and the antiphons had to be discarded. They were cut up and destroyed and new ones copied.[86]

Besides the simplification, standardization, and reanimation of the liturgy, which were carried out in Benedictine houses, Observant programs in other orders most often meant:

1. Revival of the rule of poverty and divestiture of private property,
2. Restoration of common meals and living quarters,
3. Institution of enclosure for women (or restricted time outside the convent for men),
4. Elimination of exemptions to the rule and special privileges for the nobility, and
5. Creation of more open admissions policies.

Despite these domestic program objectives, Dominican Master General Raymond of Capua insisted that the reform was not a matter of externals— not of "eating and drinking"—but of the inward mind, a restoration not of the letter but of the spirit of the rule.[87] What was sought was a renewal of fervor.

To Dominicans of the radical first generation of reformers, the Observance meant totally divesting the house of wealth. The men's convents at Chur and Guebwiller ridded themselves of accumulated property by turning their assets over to women's convents, which because of enclosure could not rely on begging. Several Franciscan houses accomplished divestiture by transferring their holdings to charitable institutions.[88] In women's cloisters, personal devotional paintings, statuettes, and private altars were relocated to the communal areas, where they could be venerated in common.[89] Bursfeld reformer Johannes Busch describes, for example, his party's arrival at Wienhausen, where

> in the choir behind the altar where [the women] stand and in their seats, most of the sisters each had images of Christ and the saints,

both sculpted and painted, for their own devotion. All of which we thence removed and placed toward the east in the space between their choir and church, so that all could see them equally, have devotion from them in common and not in private in the manner to which they were accustomed.[90]

Particularly among the houses of the Bursfeld Union, class privileges for the nobility were seen as inconsistent with the ideal of the common life and convents were to be opened to all ranks of society.[91] As might be expected, a democratization of admissions, which undermined the special position of cloisters as representations of the exclusivity and inaccessibility of the noble class, was staunchly opposed by the families of aristocratic nuns. But, in some cloisters, compromises were worked out so that a reform could be instituted and still only noble applicants admitted. This happened in 1483 at Überwasser, where the reform statutes state: "At the request of the ruling estates, the canoness house of Überwasser shall retain its old privileges, rights, and customs. In particular, only school children and young ladies who are of genuine and proper noble parentage on both sides will be admitted. For this purpose a genealogical examination . . . will be required."[92] Despite arrangements like this one, democratization was, nevertheless, a trend that would not be reversed as will be seen in the chapters to follow. Moreover, the opening of convents to more women of lower social standing was one of the most significant and far-reaching changes brought by the Observance.

Particularly in Dominican houses, and especially in its early, most radical phase, the Observance brought a major reorientation focused on reduced contact with the world in order that the community might pursue a contemplative life in common. The reform statutes of Dominican men's houses stressed the primacy of solitude, meditation, and life in a closed community instead of preaching, begging, and ministry in the world. At Basel, for example, the brothers were permitted to leave their house no more than once a week and were expected to live as a cloistered community devoted to prayer, study, and meditation.[93] This change to a more contemplative life in the early phase of the Observance later shifted to include an increased emphasis on pastoral activities and on spiritual revival among the laity, particularly through the founding of lay confraternities such as the new rosary brotherhood.[94] While some Observants early on stressed simplicity and regarded excessive learning with suspicion, others were strongly influenced by the Renaissance enthusiasm for academic study of Christian "sources": the Scriptures and the Church Fathers. Moreover, many of the second generation of Observants came from university circles. It was these so-called "cloister humanists" who stressed the importance of study for the spiritual renewal of convent life.[95] This development, as will be seen in Chapter 5, had a far-reaching effect on women.

Instituting the Observance and its program often necessitated the building of new common rooms, usually a new refectory and a dormitory or, at least, cells of uniform size;[96] in women's cloisters it meant building or completing an enclosing wall. At Überwasser, after a contentious reform, the convent was all but impoverished by the departure of most of the old residents. Nevertheless, reform abbess Sophia Dobbers installed a new refectory, a dormitory, and a new wall around the entire convent. The cost of her ambitious construction program ran to some 1300 gulden.[97] Changes like these were a financial strain on marginal women's cloisters and required donors as well as community support, which, in most cases, was there.

The Laity and the Reform

Despite the austerities of Observant life, the movement attracted adherents. Townspeople admired the Observants' religious zeal and the way they conducted services in their convent churches. To their credit, the Observant friars were regarded as more strongly committed to the care of souls than were local unreformed parish clergy.[98] In many places, a competition developed as soon as it became clear that the reformed monasteries were preferred by townspeople for burials, endowments, and religious services. Other cloisters were forced to make efforts to improve their way of life in order not to look bad by comparison with the Observants or to lose the support of the populace.[99] At Cologne, the city council went so far as to request that only professors and students from Observant convents be sent to university there.[100] But the reform often had financial consequences for cities. In Nuremberg, the extremely wealthy widow Kunigunde Schreiber informed the town council that she wished to enter the Observant cloister of Schönensteinbach in Alsace (taking her large fortune with her) because

Nuremberg had no Observant house of its own for women. Immediately, the council took steps to recruit sisters from Schönensteinbach to come and institute the Observance at the Dominican cloister of St. Katharina.[101]

More than merely an internal matter, reform of monastic houses was closely connected to the larger interests of secular constituencies. Often the arrival of a reform party was the occasion for a public ceremony in which the populace and lay officials expressed their support. The degree of lay interest and involvement is described by Prioress Adelheid von Aue in her account of the reform of Sylo in Sélestat. Adelheid, prioress of St. Katharina in Colmar, relates in a letter how the party of five sisters that she sent to Sylo in 1464 was met on the road by citizens and city magistrates, who acted as a welcoming committee and conducted the sisters into town: "And there rode out to [meet] them more than a mile from Sélestat the patrons and many men, and with a great show of respect escorted them into Sélestat and to the cloister. . . . The city magistrates and the town council were all present and promised to help and support them in all things."[102] The welcoming committee may also have been a bodyguard, since, as will be seen, this was also a hard-fought reform that was opposed by relatives of several of the Sylo sisters. As this and other accounts show, the lay authorities, both town councils and territorial rulers, were almost always deeply involved in the reform of convents.

Increasingly, and at all levels, the laity was coming to consider itself responsible for the church's performance and wished to exert greater control over it.[103] As part of this process, religious institutions were becoming more and more assimilated to municipal institutions and values.[104] Although contrary to church doctrine, the lay populace still believed that the effectiveness of prayers depended on the devoutness of those who offered them. Moreover, sins and vices could have dire consequences, bringing on God's wrath in wars, plagues, and bad harvests. Only true piety could avert punishments and bring God's blessings. In 1422, the city council of Basel wrote to Conrad of Prussia to request that female reformers be sent to Basel from Schönensteinbach. In its letter of request, the council explained why it wanted Observant sisters, citing the extraordinary power of these holy women's prayers. The council's letter asserts that "supplications offered by honorable religious people are more acceptable to God and more powerful than those of other sinners."[105]

Beyond security in the present life, the lay persons needed powerful and efficacious prayers to aid their helpless souls in purgatory. The continuance of earnest and regular performance of prayers, vigils, and religious offices was thus a matter of common concern. At the South Tyrolean convent of Brixen, religious services were placed under interdict in 1455, when the Clarissan sisters refused the reform mandate issued by newly appointed Bishop Nicholas von Cusa. In a letter, Sister Maria von Wolkenstein, leader of the resistance, reports with little sympathy how representatives of the city council came themselves to the convent and asked the sisters to accept the reform. Rather than acquiesce to rules she opposed, however, Maria transferred to another house.[106] With spiritual concerns like these on their minds, the lay public had a strong vested interest in securing the services of reformed religious for their community. And because of their material gifts to these houses, donors felt justified in expecting not only full value but also some control. Reform was thus anything but simply an internal matter of convents and orders; it was something everyone had a stake in.

One aspect of the Observant reforms that appealed strongly to the laity at large was the reassigning of "benefits" (of masses said for rich donors) to the entire civic community. At Nuremberg (1447) and Basel (1443), for example, the Observants decreed that anniversary masses for families of wealthy donors would be continued but would henceforth be said for all souls.[107] This move toward a more inclusive and egalitarian religious practice, like more open admissions to convents, was one of the changes supported by popular demand and arising from changes in lay attitudes and expectations. In general, townspeople, city magistrates, and local territorial rulers all saw greater access and control over cloisters as likely to benefit them.

On the other hand, patrician families, especially the lower nobility to which Maria von Wolkenstein belonged, and those who had made large endowments to benefit their cloistered daughters did not wish to see control of these annuities to pass into the common chest. They feared that stricter enclosure would restrict access to their daughters, as it did, for example, at St. Agnes in Strasbourg, where the visiting window was covered with a grille that could not be seen through.[108] These families staunchly opposed the reform, even where very moderate reform statutes, such as those issued in 1454 for the Benedictine abbey of Rijnsburg near Haarlem, specified only that the sisters could no longer receive overnight visitors for "more than three days."[109] Although nuns who refused to accept the reform were permitted to transfer to other cloisters, taking their dowries with them, even this option often placed them at an inconvenient distance from their families. The departure of too many sisters, with their assets, could weaken the financial health of a house, sometimes with disastrous consequences both for the house and the community, because its closing would deprive the leading families of a necessary institution for educating and housing their daughters.

In addition, families whose ancestors had endowed a cloister and been buried in its cemetery for generations understandably felt a proprietary interest. Those who could object sometimes rather spectacularly took the law into their own hands. At Klingental in Basel, for example, Albrecht von Klingenberg zu Hohentwil, a descendent of one of the patron families, protested the attempted reform of the cloister in 1480–82 as an affront to the women of the nobility housed there. Declaring a private war against both the reformers and the city of Basel, Klingenberg captured and thrashed Dominican friars, kidnapped townspeople, and threatened to burn the city.[110] Similarly, convent women of powerful families were not without recourse to weapons of their own. When Engelthal (near Nuremberg) was threatened with a reform in 1513, its prioress drafted a letter that was signed by seventeen influential nobles, warning that they would intervene. One letter in the exchange contained a death threat for the Observants.[111]

City Councils

In spite of disturbances and even armed protests by rural nobility who opposed the reform, cities and city councils generally saw advantages in it for them. One way for city magistrates to gain greater economic control over cloisters was to participate in the reform of these houses. Thus, it was at this critical juncture that the citizenry often stepped in to make its demands. At Villingen in 1480, for example, as a travel-weary party of reforming sisters from Valduna neared the city, having been on the road with their vicar for nine days, the burghers blocked the way into town and refused to let the reformers pass unless they promised to pay taxes and "fulfill all the obligations of citizens." The exhausted sisters had no choice but to agree, although, the Bicken cloister chronicle remonstrates, "it was a great hardship for a poor, unendowed, small cloister."[112]

On the other hand, as the Basel city council noted, observant cloisters remained desirable because they would attract the daughters of wealthy families seeking a convent with a good reputation, and these women would "bring with them very many [financial] assets."[113] Citizens wanted to have women's convents, especially Observant ones, within the city limits to provide schooling and pious institutions for the daughters of the increasingly affluent town patriciate. Yet they were loath to have too much property in the "dead" (i.e., non–tax-paying) hand of the church. Thus, whenever they could, they maneuvered to increase fiscal control. Even before the reforms, cities such as Zurich had passed laws prohibiting cloisters from purchasing additional houses, gardens, or other properties and decreed that whatever was bequeathed to a convent would have to be sold off within one year. Similarly, in 1362 Regensburg prohibited citizens from donating interest income to a cloister without notifying the town council. Other cities, such as Cologne (1385), decreed that all town properties must remain in the hands of citizens.[114]

The anonymous sister who wrote the chronicle of Marienthal (Niesing), an Augustinian house in Münster, illustrates the problem in her story of how her community was started as a house of Devout sisters by three women who had between them three schillings. Soon people began to give the sisters donations and a childless couple willed them a house. The small community of women joyfully moved into it. But then, the narrator recounts, "the burghers [of Münster] objected and did not want to allow this because [the man] was not a citizen. For this reason we had to purchase this place and give the city 1,000 gulden. Yet, with the help and support of good friends, we received back as many donations as if the city had given us a benefice to support a priest. And in this way we established this convent in the year 1459."[115] In these houses for women of lower social rank, founded in the fifteenth century and located in flourishing cities, powerful town councils often demanded oversight not only of the house's financial affairs but also of its internal organization and religious life. Accordingly, when the Marienthal women adopted the Augustinian rule in 1459, the house was placed under the protection of the city council. The magistrates then stipulated that two pious citizens would be appointed with visitation rights to evaluate whether or not the women were living according to the regulations. The town council also required a twice-yearly accounting of the house's finances.[116] At Nuremberg, the council was able to decree that only women born in the city could be admitted to its cloisters.[117]

Territorial Rulers and the Observance

Protection by a territorial lord, rather than by a city council, did not necessarily confer greater independence or immunity from the Observants. Clearly, townsfolk and urban magistrates were not the only ones interested in oversight and change. Following the failure of the Council of Basel (1431–49) to effect a thorough-going monastic reform, territorial lords themselves increasingly took over the prerogative to reform convents, seeing it as their natural responsibility and—not inconveniently—a way of consolidating power. The result was an increasing subordination of cloisters to the territorial state.[118]

Indeed, sovereignty and reform went hand in hand. Manfred Schulze points out that what moved many secular princes to support the Observants was neither "power hunger" nor personal "religious conviction" but rather both, that is, a political concern for divine protection of the realm. Even more than city magistrates, territorial princes felt that the church was their church and the piety of the people their responsibility.[119] To assure God's protection of the realm, the prudent prince needed both a devout populace and the prayers of pious monks and nuns, for only then would God bestow His blessings.[120] Like city councils, princes feared God's punishments, which could be meted out as war, pestilence, and bad harvests.

According to Johannes Uytenhove's treatise, *On Reform* (1471), a cloister reform was a work of merit equal to that accruing to the "founder" who had endowed the house.[121] Thus Duke Albrecht of Bavaria underwrote the costs of instituting a reform of the house of Poor Clares in Munich. He paid travel expenses for three Clarissan sisters to journey to the Observant house in Nuremberg and be trained in their way of life.[122] In Württemberg, Count Ulrich (d. 1480) urged the reform of the women's cloisters in his realm. He acquired a decree from Pope Pius II, solicited the help of the Dominican Master General, and selected the Observant houses from which reforming sisters were to be recruited. Along with his wife and his daughter-in-law, the count then wrote letters to prioresses in 1478 requesting them to send Observant sisters.[123] In Ulrich's letter to the Observant Dominican sisters at Sylo in Sélestat in 1478, he offers his justifications and makes an appeal for their help in undertaking the reform: "[F]or the sake of God's honor, the great blessings and good that may arise from it, and to avoid dishonor to God and sinful life in this cloister, we urge and request most earnestly and eagerly that you will favor our holy undertaking and send reforming sisters to us."[124] The prioress of Sylo agreed to send seven sisters and Ulrich supplied wagons to bring the women from Alsace to Württemberg. Magdalena Kremer's narrative of this reform effort describes a high-profile reception for the reform party, with secular and ecclesiastical dignitaries who met the sisters when they arrived at Kirchheim: "We were received honorably: There were the two lords of Württemberg, the elder Count Eberhard, who is called Eberhard of Urach, and the young Count Eberhard of Stuttgart [Ulrich's son and successor]. These two lords entered the convent along with us, other nobles, and learned masters and prelates, both ecclesiastical and secular persons."[125] In this reform, organized and orchestrated by the ruler of the realm, the change of leadership, as Magdalena describes it, went smoothly—at least in its initial stages. But soon the problems began. Once installed, the new Observant prioress and officers had to win over the rest of the cloister community, which, as Magdalena also relates, was a much more difficult task. Much of her narrative tells how a few years later five of the old sisters, aided by the new count, tried unsuccessfully to reverse the reform and take back control of their cloister.

Besides initiating the reform of convents in their territories, secular rulers also founded new religious houses. Between 1440 and 1517, twenty-three Observant convents were established in middle- and eastern Germany.[126] Like earlier foundations, these were not disinterested financial outlays but a move aimed at securing divine support for the sovereign. At the dedication of Schönensteinbach in Alsace, Catherine of Burgundy presented endowments to the sisters with the admonition, "Take these temporal goods, live piously, and pray to God for the House of Austria."[127]

The reform or founding of cloisters, while contributing to the consolidation of the state, might also be an expression of sincere personal piety. Returning from a pilgrimage to the Holy Land, the Duke of Cleves stopped over at Bologna, where he became acquainted with the Observant house in that city. Its thriving spiritual atmosphere is said to have impressed him so much that he recruited reformed monks from Rotterdam to found a similar house at Kalkar in 1456.[128] The Emmerich *Book of Sisters* reports how he urged the devout women of their sister-house, who were not bound by vows, to take on a rule. In her vita of Mother Mechtelt van Diedem, the chronicler, obviously a supporter of the reform, gives an account of what were clearly very controversial and much-debated changes at the time. Here, Mother Mechtelt tries to justify the wishes of the duke to the sisters:

> When [Mechtelt van Diedem] had been Mother [of this house] for two years, His Lordship the Duke and Prince of Cleves asked the sisters to take on the rule of Saint Augustine and live according to it, which the sisters were very unwilling and not prepared to do. And they repeatedly said to her in a troublesome and severe way that she should not allow it but should resist. And she would answer amicably, "Dear sisters, let us not oppose our superiors and go against the worthy ruler of our land who wishes and desires this that we and our house should not come into disrepute."[129]

Mechtelt decided not to go against the wishes of the duke. But not all the sisters accepted the change. Some, as will be seen in Chapter 4, continued to live in the house without taking the vows.[130] In his account of the reform of the cloister of Mariensee, Augustinian Observant Johannes Busch relates how the Duke of Brunswick himself accompanied Busch on his reform mission. The sisters at Mariensee defied the reform mandate and climbed up inside the roof of the church. Then the duke went into the choir and announced that the women would be taken away in the carriages, which he had parked at the door, and transported out of his lands if they did not accept the reform. Apparently, the women here had not organized their own militia of relatives, as sometimes happened. Now, faced with deportation, they decided to acquiesce.[131]

Not all secular princes were strong supporters of the Observance. Many, along with most of the lower nobility, were its most powerful and consistent opponents. And not all of the princes who supported the reform did so all of the time. Archduke Sigismund of Austria (1426–1496) first supported but then opposed the reform of Klingental in Basel.[132] Wooed by both sides, Sigismund, who owed the city of Basel a large sum of money, was offered 3,000 gulden by the reforming sisters to allow them to remain at Klingental but 8,000 by other sisters who opposed the reform. He accepted the higher offer.[133]

Clerical Politics

No less unpredictable and hard fought were conflicts within the church itself between proponents and adversaries of the Observant reform. Some bishops actually thwarted the efforts of the Observants because they resented intervention from outside or because they wished to carry out the reforms themselves, thereby strengthening their political position and bringing cloisters more closely under their own control. Thus within the religious orders, power struggles arose between Observants and Conventuals and led to strategic reform efforts for the control of certain areas. In the Dominican province of Teutonia (encompassing Austria, southern Germany, the Rhine valley, and the Low Countries), the Observants achieved a majority in the 1470s. But still the Conventuals controlled the cities of Freiburg, Hagenau, Speyer, Strasbourg, Weissenburg, and Zurich. When in Strasbourg the Dominican convent of St. Agnes was, nevertheless, made Observant in 1464 by authority of the city council, the opponents of the reform tried to derail the process by bringing the matter before the bishop of Strasbourg. The bishop's chancellor ordered the measure reversed and called reforming Father Heinrich Schretz to account, asserting that it was against the bishop's wishes for any "monk" to exercise such authority in his bishopric. This touched off a dispute between the bishop and the Strasbourg city council members, who announced that the bishop had "no authority over them." In the end, the reform was upheld by the order.[134] Yet even a master general such as Salvus Casseta (1481–83), who himself personally supported the Observants, nevertheless for the sake of peace and the unity in the order often had to forbid some efforts to reform the women's cloisters. This was the case, for example, in the Conventual-held area of Zurich (where Oetenbach and Töss were located).[135]

By most accounts, the great reform councils of Constance and Basel, which were organized to restore unity and renew the church "in head and members," had only limited success. Although the council at Constance (1414–18) successfully ended the papal schism, its achievements in instituting reform were less effectual.[136] Yet in 1435, the Council of Basel tasked the Windesheim Congregation with reforming the Augustinian cloisters. And in the following year, it launched an expanded Benedictine initiative.[137] The council itself encouraged secular rulers as well as city authorities to support the reform of cloisters. Significantly, it was the engagement of secular princes in cloister reform that paved the way for their more extensive activities in the next century. Thus, the increasing involvement of secular forces—both civic magistrates and territorial princes—in religious reform produced an essentially different environment, one that would become a political precondition for the Reformation.[138]

In all these conflicting interests, women were intimately involved, often finding themselves the focus of a power struggle among influential family networks to which most of them belonged. Against this background of power politics, popular sentiment, and Observant activism surrounding cloisters, issues of agency are hard to tease out. What was women's interest in reform when they supported it? And how did they implement their aims? In a few cases, women were themselves the primary initiators of reform and successfully solicited the help they needed to put it into place. But in most cases women worked together with male Observant activists. Certainly, not all female Observants wanted to be reformers. Many accepted the call to go out with reform parties as part of their vow of obedience. But all who went out took over the leading offices in the houses they reformed. Some may have been motivated by the desire to become prioresses themselves; others were committed to the ideals of the Observance. But whenever a reform took place, power was at stake. Abbesses and prioresses of the elite old guard stood to be deposed and replaced by others, often of lower rank, who rose to new positions of social status and influence. For many women of lower social status, the reform opened access to a religious vocation that was previously unavailable to them. Overall, the Observant initiatives to take control of religious houses succeeded because they were attempts to conform them to an ideal of piety that resonated with the interests of the laity and reflected the changing power structures of the fifteenth century.

Clearly, from 1300 to 1600 the religious landscape had changed radically. Between the time of the fourteenth-century Dominican sister-books, with their narratives about beguine founding mothers trekking to Rome to seek admittance for their communities, and the time of the fifteenth-century Observant movement, beguine settlements had been officially banned by church councils. The communities that grew from the earlier beguine "gatherings" had joined the establishment and become accepted fixtures of the regular orders. Despite this acceptance, however, expectations and constituencies were changing. The fifteenth century was a period of enormous ferment, an age of transition, in which a new political, social, and economic order was emerging, fueled by a commercial revolution and a century of rapid population growth. Disparate religious movements and an interval of almost unparalleled intellectual activity were beginning to affect long-held assumptions.[139] Whereas in the fourteenth century the laity had not yet begun to involve itself greatly in oversight of the church, a century of increasing of urban prosperity and influence brought a new self-confidence and a new relationship between the laity and its church. It was not that the new, more powerful urban populace opposed the church. On the contrary, despite the expressions of anticlericalism and dissatisfaction with religious institutions, what lay people wanted and envisioned was a more pious society of which the church was an integral part.[140]

As cities expanded, they encircled outlying convents along with the convent properties and, accordingly, sought to exercise jurisdiction over them. While this self-confident urban citizenry took a more active and proprietary interest in "its" convents and "its" church, the educated elite of Humanist circles began to engage more actively in discussions of religious problems. The privileges and immunities enjoyed in the religious communities by the old social elite were less readily taken for granted. It was not only women's but also men's religious communities that came under closer scrutiny. Many of the Observant reformers were themselves members of the new wealthy urban burgher families. Having the power to demand change, the laity exercised it. In this shifting environment, women too found a new role to play. Many took part along with men in the program of the Observants, as will be seen in the chapters to follow. In becoming participants in the Observant movement, women, like the population at large, began to take a more active part in the intense religious discussions being carried on during the fateful century of experimentation and change that preceded the Reformation.

3

Women of the Reform

With every good work the beginning is the most difficult part, especially in founding or reforming a cloister. For one must endure great worry and effort in building, as well as deprivations and poverty at the start.

—Magdalena Kremer, c. 1490

Not all of the sisters who participated in the reform wrote about it,[1] but a few, like Magdalena Kremer, left behind firsthand accounts. Written from the perspective of those who assumed power, these artifacts of the Observant movement are strongly partisan. They illustrate that "women's texts" are not just about women but overlap with other genres, in this case reform literature. Moreover, they constitute a unique example of how groups in power not only shape the kinds of texts that are produced but determine which ones will be preserved. As participants in the Observant movement and tasked with taking over the governance of reformed cloisters, women received authorization to write histories, keep records, and document the reform. Observant leaders, some guided by the growing Humanist interest in history writing or by a penchant for record keeping, encouraged women to compose house annals and copy devotional works and instructional texts in vernacular translations. For women, this authorization to write would be of enormous importance.

An overview of their role in the reform effort will help connect together the different kinds of narratives and records that have survived. These include letters by women who went on missions as reformers or as temporary teachers, other eyewitness accounts, house chronicles, handbooks, and vitae. Although these narratives tend to idealize the reformers and portray their actions in a positive light, they also describe women's opposition to the Observance and take particular pains to document the legality of the transitions of power in which their authors took part. Here both reform and anti-reform prioresses are depicted, engaged in conflicts with secular and ecclesiastical authorities, sometimes trying to implement a reform, at other times trying to avert one. In these battles, as will be seen in this chapter and the next, winners and losers were on both sides. This chapter will examine the Observant side, why and under what circumstances they took part in the reform effort. What were their responsibilities and how was the Observance implemented? What was their relationship to male superiors and activists in the movement and, above all, to the women they "reformed"? How much agency did they really have?

The account by Magdalena Kremer was perhaps the most detailed report of how a reform was carried out. Magdalena was a member of the party that came from Alsace to institute the Observance at the convent Kirchheim unter Teck (in Württemberg) in 1478.[2] She begins with a brief sketch of the beginnings of the movement among Dominicans, citing as her models the celebrated sisters of Schönensteinbach.

> When the blessed friars of our holy order saw that some sisters' cloisters were becoming secular houses and that they did not want to observe the rules of the order, these friars wanted to reform these cloisters and bring them back to their original, true character. But when one speaks of keeping the observance, that means keeping its early, real nature, like the sisters in Alsace at Schönensteinbach.[3]

Although scarcely a household word today, the cloister of Schönensteinbach was well known in the fifteenth century. The first Observant women's house in the German-speaking territories, Schönensteinbach had been founded by Conrad of Prussia, the same charismatic reformer who had appeared at the 1388 meeting of the Vienna chapter general dressed as a penitent and wearing a rope about his neck in order to publicize the order's sinfulness in not keeping the rule. As a consequence, or perhaps as an advance arrangement, Master General Raymond of Capua appointed Conrad to take over the men's convent at Colmar and to establish there a reformed community strictly devoted to observance of the original rule as in the order's early days. Conrad and thirty like-minded brothers succeeded in colonizing the Colmar house against the strong resistance of the original residents and objections from some townspeople.

Wishing to start an Observant house for women, Conrad located an abandoned Augustinian cloister about fourteen miles away in the forest at Schönensteinbach. To found and finance his new community, the enterprising Conrad approached Duke Leopold IV of Austria and his wife, Catherine of Burgundy, sovereigns of the Habsburg lands in Alsace. Both Leopold and Catherine liked the idea of founding an Observant cloister and endowed the project, giving Conrad a free hand to organize it and renovate the buildings. In his circuit preaching, Conrad had identified nuns at several Dominican convents who were interested in forming a new community based on the model of Conrad's Observant house for men. For this new foundation he chose thirteen women to represent symbolically Christ and his twelve apostles.[4] Most were nuns from cloisters in the area: Katharinental (near Constance), St. Katharina and Unterlinden (in Colmar), and Sylo (in Sélestat).[5] Included in the thirteen were three lay sisters whose previous convents are not known. The account of the founding of Schönensteinbach, related in Johannes Meyer's *Book of the Reform of the Dominican Order* (1468), is based on an earlier history (now lost) composed by Elisabeth Meringer (d. 1442), one of the thirteen founders and Schönensteinbach's second prioress.[6] Elisabeth herself had come from Katharinental, a cloister that in the fourteenth century had produced its own foundation history and a sister-book of the house's most famous inhabitants.

Soon after its founding, the Schönensteinbach community had developed a reputation for extraordinary piety and had begun to grow. By 1426 it had expanded to fifty-two members and had established two daughter-houses at Wijk-bij-Duurstede (1403) and Westroye (1407), both in the bishopric of Utrecht.[7] By 1483, the cloister had registered 182 entrants, many of whom had been sent out with reform parties to introduce the Observance at other cloisters.[8] From this center, the Observant movement spread during the first seventy years of the reform to twenty-two other Dominican women's convents. Parties from Schönensteinbach reformed Unterlinden (Colmar, 1419), St. Katharina (Nuremberg, 1428), St. Maria Magdalena (Freiburg, 1465), Engelport (Guebwiller, 1466), and St. Maria (Medlingen, 1468). From these cloisters, Schönensteinbach women went on with other groups to houses as far away as Brünn in Bohemia.[9]

Not only did Schönensteinbach itself experience extraordinary growth but also the houses it had reformed. St. Maria Magdalena in Pforzheim increased from twenty-six to fifty and Himmelskron at Hochheim (near

Worms) from thirty to seventy sisters.[10] St. Katharina at Nuremberg sent out four reforming parties to other cloisters, and St. Maria Magdalena an den Steinen at Basel dispatched contingents to five cloisters between 1423 and 1465.[11] Many of these reforms were bitterly contested, as was that at St. Agnes in Strasbourg (1465). Prioress Barbara von Benfelden, at the neighboring cloister of St. Nicolaus in undis, describes how St. Agnes first lost half of its inhabitants, but then more than tripled its original size. A supporter who sheltered the party of reform sisters during the hardest days of the struggle, when they were driven out of the cloister, Prioress von Benfelden reports with satisfaction:

> This blessed community became like the green palm standing by the flowing waters. Thus this convent put out green shoots and grew and increased in virtues and spirituality expanding in such a short time, that is, ten years, to fifty-seven persons, all taking the habit of the order of St. Dominic. [And] Before [it] was enclosed [the sisters] had numbered no more than sixteen—of whom only eight had remained.[12]

Reform in other orders proceeded in similar ways. Clarissans at Nuremburg, for example, dispatched missions to Brixen (1455), Bamberg (1460), Pfullingen (1461), Eger (1465), and the Angerkloster in Munich (1480).[13] Most spectacular was the Benedictine cloister of Marienberg at Boppard on the Rhine, which reported an increase from nine sisters when it became Observant in 1437 to one hundred during the tenure of its abbess, Isengard von Greiffenklau.[14]

Not all who entered Observant houses were new recruits. Many, in fact, were transfers and some, like Johanna von Mörsberg, changed monastic orders in joining.[15] On the other hand, many women left convents to avoid the reform. Yet overall, Observant cloisters showed greater fiscal and numerical growth than unreformed houses in the same period.[16] Some of the shift may be explained, of course, by the desire of male heads of households to send their daughters to strictly Observant nunneries. But in Württemberg, transfers to Observant houses outside the territory reached such alarming proportions that the ruling counts of Württemberg-Stuttgart declared a moratorium. At Kirchheim alone at least six nuns left for the Observant house of Sylo (at Guebwiller in Alsace).[17] Magdalena Kremer relates that when her party of Observant sisters arrived to reform Kirchheim in 1478, they found there some twenty-three sisters. Over the next ten years, the community grew to forty-eight. She attributes the increase to the response of the laity, saying that the reform "pleased all the townspeople; and this cloister had a good name so that many honorable young women joined us."[18]

Women's Role as Reformers

Perhaps partly because of the influence of Schönensteinbach, the Dominican Observance in its early days made more headway among women's cloisters than among men's.[19] Yet, even though reforms were often set in motion by city councils or initiated by secular rulers, nunneries seldom became successfully Observant without a strong reform prioress and cadre of sisters to implement the plan. Thus, although authorities might formulate a reform, women were necessary to make it work.[20] Still, despite the large number of women known to have participated—some as initiators—their role has generally been ignored or, as in the case of Magdalena Beutler, discounted. Critics mention, for example, the remarkable, single-handed reform of the convent of the Poor Clares at Freiburg, where Magdalena Beutler in 1429 induced the sisters to renounce private property. Nonetheless, Wilhelm Schleussner and Wilhelm Oehl disparage her actions as a "neurotically motivated imitation of similar activities by her mother," Margareta von Kenzingen.[21] (Margareta was one of a party from Unterlinden that six years earlier had reformed St. Maria Magdalena an den Steinen in Basel.) While Magdalena was certainly a flamboyant and even outrageous personality, it does not follow that she did not have a serious interest in making her cloister Observant, a plan in which she also succeeded. Pointing to Colette of Corbie's (1381–1447) reform of Clarissan convents in France and Flanders, Bynum states emphatically, "Women were not only followers, manipulated and circumscribed in their religious ideals by powerful clerics; they were leaders and reformers as well."[22]

It is clear that women have worked together with men in missionary and reform efforts throughout the history of the church. In the earliest days of the christianization of the Germanic tribes, the English monk Saint Boniface wrote to England asking Abbess Tetta of Wimbourne to send over as a help to his mission "the virgin Lioba, whose reputation for holiness and virtuous teaching had penetrated across wide lands."[23] Nor did the practice of sending parties of men and women on missions to other cloisters originate with the Observants.[24] In the previous century, the Oetenbach sisterbook (c. 1340) recounts, for example, that in 1294 four sisters from their house went in company with a brother to the new cloister of Brunnadern in Bern, where they by their "example, life, and teaching" instructed the sisters there "in all spirituality of the order and in godly virtues."[25] Still, fifteenth-century women reformers have been characterized as pawns and victims, described as "pitifully naive," and "unbelievably otherworldly" young women from simple, non-affluent backgrounds. A look at who these women were and the circumstances under which they engaged in the reforms will provide a more numanced view of a wide range of motivations.

Reluctant Reformers

Clearly, not everyone who was an Observant wanted to be a reformer. When one considers the hardships and sufferings recorded in some of the hard-fought struggles and failed attempts, it is not surprising that women would have been reluctant to leave their home communities. Their daunting task was to go out as reforming colonists into hostile environments where, if they were successful, they might have to remain permanently. In one particularly arduous and discouraging example, four Dominican sisters from Himmelskron and Liebenau in 1437 failed in their attempt to introduce the Observance at the house of the Penitents of St. Maria Magdalena in Strasbourg. The Strasbourg sisters had balked at adopting Dominican practices, claiming they were being made to "join another order." When the town council became divided over the issue, the Observant sisters were withdrawn and sent, instead, to reform the convent of St. Katharina in Colmar. There only two of the twelve inhabitants agreed to join the Observance, with the rest vehemently rejecting it. The ten who rejected reform vilified the reformers and objected so violently that the Master General threatened to incarcerate them. Eventually, the majority of the resisters departed for another cloister, leaving the traumatized Observants and the few sisters who stayed to rebuild a debilitated community.[27]

The reform of the convent of Gnadenzell in Offenhausen was so contentious that it took three tries. In the first attempt, when five Dominican sisters arrived from Pforzheim, they found that the residents had taken everything moveable out of the cloister so that it was almost uninhabitable. The residents then exercised such effective passive resistance that after a month the reformers became discouraged and left. In 1478 the original Gnadenzell women frustrated the efforts even of seasoned reformer Johannes Meyer, who tried to teach them the Observant way of singing. To warn of his approach and trip him up, they placed pans and plates on the dark stairs.[28] Finally, in 1480, a third reform party, this time from Sylo, succeeded—at least, nominally—but life for the reformers cannot have been pleasant. In the notorious failed reform of Klingental (1480–82), the resisters reportedly threatened to strangle the reforming sisters and set the cloister on fire.[29] The undoing of this reform came, at the last, not from violence but from the cloister's financial collapse. The defeated Observant sisters had to withdraw after a painful two-year ordeal. Such a difficult task required extraordinary fortitude and strength of character.[30] The most direct testimony to the exceptional character of some of the women who were sent on these missions is found in a letter from Prioress Kunigunda Haller at Nuremberg to Angela Varnbühler, prioress at St. Gall. Kunigunda laments that the Dominican Provincial wants to recruit for the reform effort Sister Veronika Bernhart, who, she asserts, is "capable in all things."[31]

Considering the difficulties and hostility groups of reforming sisters encountered at unwilling houses, it is no wonder that even committed Obervants paled at the thought of being sent out to undertake a reform. At Schönensteinbach, the prioress first declined when the Master General asked for volunteers to reform Unterlinden in Colmar in 1419, but later undertook it.[32] Sisters at St. Gall declined twice to send a party to Zoffingen at Constance but complied when the bishop threatened them with excommunication.[33] Reformers such as Johannes Busch were not loath to apply pressure to get the recruits they wanted. After Prioress Gertrud von Harlessem at Hildesheim refused to send sisters to Erfurt—objecting that it was too far away—Busch threatened her with the admonition that God would allow her to die within the year if she rejected this opportunity to work for His honor. She did, indeed, die within the year, but on her deathbed gave Busch the three sisters he asked for.[34]

Prioress Gertrud's hesitation was a grave failing, because Observants in

Benedictine cloisters of the Bursfeld reform were required to accept any reassignment if called upon to do so in the interest of the reform.[35] The call was, thus, usually accepted but often with expressions of dismay. The chronicle of the Bicken cloister reports that the Poor Clares of Valduna, chosen by Franciscan Provincial Heinrich Karrer to reform the Villingen house, "came forward with tears in their eyes."[36] Similarly, Magdalena Kremer, herself one of the Sylo sisters selected for the reform party to Kirchheim, tells how the group was chosen after Johannes Meyer came to their cloister with letters of authorization from the Dominican provincial and with requests from the Count of Württemberg. Magdalena relates:

> [A]nd this is how the selection was made: first the brothers gave the letters that they had brought from our worthy Father Provincial and from his Lordship and her Ladyship [the count and countess] to the Mother Prioress of Sylo and ordered her to read all the letters to the elders [the governing sisters] of the cloister. . . . Afterward the elder nuns were ordered to choose eight sisters for the reform party and to indicate to the brothers what offices they were selected to hold. . . . Thus they took six choir sisters and a lay sister. And these came forward and prostrated themselves, accepting the obedience. . . . And with full absolution of all their sins [they] indicated that they wished to accept dutifully without objections and to submit themselves to the ordeal to the honor of God.[37]

A Letter Home: Katharina von Mühlheim

In a letter she wrote to her former prioress at Schönensteinbach, Katharina von Mühlheim has left a rare, first-person account of how one woman felt about leaving her surrogate cloister family to go on three reforming missions. Katharina had first gone with a reforming party to Nuremberg in 1428, and was setting off in 1436 for a second cloister in Tulln, Austria, where she would become prioress. "[T]he Lord God has again called me on to another cloister in obedience to Him (as our Mother prioress will tell you in a letter) which has caused and still causes me some concern, but since I see that it could not be otherwise, I have surrendered myself entirely to God, however and wherever he wants me to go, I also want to go and even if it should cost me my life."[38] At this time, Katharina was looking back on ten years at Schönensteinbach and eight at Nuremberg. She would subsequently spend thirty years as prioress at Tulln before setting off a third time in 1466 for Brünn in Bohemia.[39] Her touching letter home reveals something of the special bond among the sisters at Schönensteinbach and of Katharina's own character and personality.

> Although I know that I am unfortunately truly unworthy and un-suited for such good, holy works, I am happy to see that God's honor and His praise are made perfect in all things. Therefore my dearest Mothers and Sisters, I remind you of all the faithfulness, love and zeal that you have always had especially for all of us from Schönensteinbach. Remember that you are our first mothers in the order and let me ask you to remember me to God. This I ask you humbly and desire from all of you in common, from each one individually, and [your prayers] also [for] all the sisters with whom I will have to live in the future. I would never have thought that I would have to spend my life alone with [only] one sister from Schönensteinbach. Know that it makes me very sad that I must live so far from Schönensteinbach and henceforward so far from all those sisters. Dear Mothers, give my regards to Father Heinrich your confessor, [asking] his faithful remembrance and prayers, which I do not doubt of, and let him know of this. No more at this time as God be with us eternally, amen. Written at Nuremberg with a heavy heart on Easter Wednesday, 1436.[40]

A prioress could refuse to answer the call to provide nuns for reform missions but rarely did so. This seems evident from the kind of moral pressure that Johannes Nider, the prior of the Nuremberg Dominican men's convent, applies in his letter written to the prioress of Schönenstein-bach in 1428, asking for ten "zealous and capable" sisters (the party that would include Sister Katharina von Mühlheim) to come to Nuremberg and reform the women's convent there. In his letter, Nider gives eight reasons why the Schönensteinbach sisters should comply. Looking at his persuasive arguments, one can see why they did. Nider appeals first to the women's sense of piety, their loyalty and honor. Then he moves on to duty and ends with a cry of distress from the men at Nuremberg. Summarized briefly, the arguments assert why the sisters should undertake the reform:

1. For the increase of God's honor.
2. For the sake of St. Dominic and the order.
3. For the betterment of the lay people who have requested it.
4. Because people are saying that the Hussite heresy has arisen "on account of priests, monks, and women in cloisters being unreformed," and the women "will undermine the health of the Christian faith" if they do not help by sending capable reformers.
5. Because it will not be a burden to the prioress financially, since the annuities of the sisters will remain at Schönensteinbach.
6. Because it is a worthy endeavor to renew an old cloister, since they will be responsible for all the good that comes of it.
7. Because they owe it to the Dominican brothers at Nuremberg for the prayers and services rendered to the sisters. Moreover, the brothers at Nuremberg will be shamed before the populace if they do not send sisters.
8. Because great anger will arise in the whole city of Nuremberg if the women should not hear their request. For, he asserts, "all the people here and round about now know that several attempts have been made to reform St. Katharina and if you do not send zealous and capable women, we will be a laughingstock."[41]

We know from Sister Katharina von Mühlheim's letter home after eight years at Nuremberg and from other sources that the women went, the reform was successful, and the men were not made a laughingstock.

Teachers and Office-holders

The role of the female reformers was not only to demonstrate the Observant way of life in practice but often also to teach Latin or introduce the new Benedictine liturgy. In 1462, Johannes Busch took three sisters from Bronopia (near Kampen)—Ida, Tecla, and a lay-sister, Adelheid—to reform Marienberg (at Helmstedt). During their three years at Marienberg, Ida, the eldest, took over as subprioress in charge of "spiritual matters," while the regular prioress, Helena, continued to oversee the material running of the cloister. Tecla instructed in singing, grammar, and school subjects. After her departure three years later, Tecla's pupils wrote in their newly acquired Latin to thank their teacher for all that she and the others had done, including the lay-sister Adelheid, whom they refer to as "our capitan" (capitanea). Tecla's letter in reply reflects pleasure in her pupils' accomplishments. "I rejoice with you that you have made so much progress that you could compose such a letter in Latin. Gladly, most gladly have I taught you, seeing your gratitude."[42] Prioress Helena wrote as well, thanking the visitors "for all the good done in spiritual and material things." Tecla's warm but modest response seems to reflect unusually amicable relations during the three-year stay.

> [F]rom the beginning, your zeal for God and love for the holy reform never waned and for us, his servants however unworthy, but you constantly strove to make progress, to acquire good virtues and knowledge of the Holy Scriptures. Thus, you yourselves have become stronger in the love of God and learning of true virtues, and have with God's help grown and advanced greatly in the necessary knowledge and understanding of the scriptures.

Concluding, Tecla writes, "You now have been educated as teachers of others in your own house and outside your house in cloisters that you will reform."[43] Marienberg sisters went on to reform Mariabrunn (near Helmstedt) and Stendal (in Altmark).

In order to institute the Observance, reform sisters were usually placed in charge of the chief offices. That they were not young and naive women, as critics have suggested, but usually experienced sisters who had held these positions in their home convents, can be seen in Magdalena Kremer's account, which provides enough information to ascertain their ages and qualifications. Magdalena reports how the reformers were installed in their offices. Barbara Bernheimer was invested with the office of prioress, a nun with thirty-eight years of experience whom Magdalena describes as "a wise, skillful, honorable, good sister in spiritual and material matters."[44] Adding up the years Barbara had spent at previous convents, one sees that she could not have been any younger than fifty. Similarly, Sub-Prioress Elisabeth Herwert, who had transferred to Schönensteinbach in 1423, was an intrepid sixty-seven. The third sister, Barbara von Speyer, who took over as bursar, was one of the reformers of Sylo itself fourteen years before and thus could not have been younger than twenty-six.[45] We do not know the ages of the other four Observants from Alsace, but the blanket assertion that reformers were young and inexperienced women does not hold for the known Kirchheim data.

In the few other cases where the ages of participants can be ascertained, there are sometimes reforming sisters of very advanced age, such as Katharina von Mühlheim. After ten years at Schönensteinbach, eight as a reformer at Nuremberg, then thirty years as reform prioress of Tulln (Austria), Katharina set off a third time for Brünn in Bohemia at the age of at least sixty-two.[46] Yet some reform prioresses were as young as Mechthild von Niendorf, who was only twenty when she became head of Ebstorf. From what we know of Mechthild in the Ebstorf chronicle, she was a woman with a very strong personality. Heike Uffmann suggests that Mechthild succeeded because she had an "integrative personality" and was "charming and friendly, but firm and definite."[47] Some reform prioresses, like Margaret Meyer, who headed the ill-fated effort at Klingental and died there, could only be called seasoned veterans. Sixteen years earlier Margaret had helped to reform Sylo and then had served as prioress at Engelport before being sent to Klingental. As a former prioress, Margaret would surely have known the ins and outs of managing convent finances. Thus suggestions that Klingental and other similar efforts failed because the women were inexperienced and incapable of handling money are also without support.[48]

In the annals of the Observance, there are many women who went on missions to two, three, and—in a few cases—even four or more cloisters. Of the original early sisters at Schönensteinbach, Margareta von Masmünster and Maria Magdalena Bettunger each went on to reform or found two more houses.[49] Mechthild and Truta von Bollwig went with reforming missions to Unterlinden (1419), St. Maria Magdalena at Basel (1423), and Himmelskron (1425 or 1429); Anna Minckhin, a prioress at Schönensteinbach, became reform prioress at Unterlinden and later at Liebenau.[50] Most remarkable of all were Margareta Regenstein of Unterlinden, who participated in four reform missions, and Margareta Zorn, who transferred to Schönensteinbach from the unreformed St. Margaret's in Strasbourg and then, in eighteen years, participated in three more successful reforms and one failed effort.[51]

Even those women who were reluctant to leave their home communities and encounter difficult and often hostile situations considered the ordeal part of their vow of obedience. Magdalena Kremer quotes Sister Elisabeth Herwert, one of the seven reformers drafted to come from Sylo to Kirchheim, as saying, "We were called here by obedience and for the praise of God, and we would rather be hacked to pieces like weeds than retreat against the will of our superiors."[52] But the ordeal was often a protracted one. Even long after a reform had been instituted, things did not always go smoothly, as opponents fought continual rear-guard actions. At Kirchheim, for example, after the old Count Ulrich died, several of the dispossessed women enlisted help from his son, Eberhard. The new sovereign reversed his father's policy and supported the resisters' plan to take back their cloister because it coincided with his own interests. Eberhard was already deeply in debt and happy to find an excuse to take control of the cloister's assets to ease his own financial problems.[53]

Magdalena's chronicle tells how Eberhard ordered the expulsion of the seven reformers, herself included. But, she asserts, the cloister resolved to resist and banded together with the Sylo sisters rather than give them up. So Eberhard blockaded the convent and tried to starve them out. Through three long seiges, with no food or firewood and their barns set ablaze, the nuns held out. In the third seige, Magdalena relates how the sisters consumed all their supplies and burned their furniture for heat. At last, the count's uncle, Eberhard the Elder, interceded on their behalf. Magdalena's narrative celebrates the women's solidarity and courage in standing up to the count. She portrays how the other sisters hid the reformers among themselves and declared that they were "all reformers." Fearing a breech of the walls, the women gathered together in the chapel.

> [Some of the sisters] thought they should stand in front, holding the crucifix before them. . . . And the reforming sisters thought [rather] that they should stand together so that the injustice would only come upon them and not upon the others. . . . But the other sisters said that they should not do that but should mix themselves together so that no one would know which were the reformers. . . . [And they said to the reformers,] "We will take your places in the choir, one in the prioress' chair, holding a crucifix before her, and she will say 'I am the prioress, what do you want?'" And two

or three wished to do the same in the place of the sub-prioress and in the places of the other reformers. Thus they called on the sisters to resist our opponents with a united front and truthfully. For they did not speak untruth when they said they were reformers too. . . . They were all reformers; for, indeed, the whole convent was united.[54]

This idealized report may or may not represent the sentiments of all the sisters, but it reveals those of one who was a reformer herself. Her conviction is expressed in the dramatic way she chooses to depict the events and the women's role in them.

Implementing a Reform

The way of introducing the reform was to allow a trial period, after which those sisters who did not want to accept it could transfer to an unreformed cloister. Trial periods varied from one year, as at Adelhausen in Freiburg (reformed 1465), to three months at the Bicken cloister in Villingen (1480), or only two months at Engelthal near Nuremberg (in 1513).[55] Johannes Meyer gives an account of how at St. Katharina in Nuremberg (in 1428) the master of the order, Bartholomeus Texerius, decreed "that all the sisters who had been in the convent previously should remain there and try [the Observance] humbly, as much as they were well disposed and desired it. And [he] set them a goodly time as their goal. And those who after that time did not want to remain should be found places in other houses of [the] order." Texerius charged the new reform prioress to "allow all the convent sisters to continue to live as they had been accustomed to: to eat meat, to forgo fasting, to sleep on soft mattresses, to wear their previous shifts and clothing, and the like, as long as the sisters were pious and did what was required gladly and with good grace, and of their own free will, but humbly and obediently."[56]

This account relates how the Nuremberg city council was still split over the issue of reform. Consequently, the party of reforming sisters from Schönensteinbach had to be housed temporarily in the home of one of the townspeople for a week while the council debated. But after a week, Master General Texerius was "filled with the Holy Spirit" and ordered that the

Observant sisters should be taken into the convent secretly at night. Meyer asserts that the superiors spoke "graciously" with both groups of sisters.[57] They agreed that the Observants should be installed into the offices, thus presenting the city council with a fait accompli. Another account, written by one of the St. Katharina sisters, probably one of the Observants, gives a different perspective. It mentions none of the external wrangling. Instead, it focuses on the sisters and their vote, saying, "[A]ll the sisters of this convent were present and gave their votes to said Father Johannes Nider to choose a prioress." After naming the new prioress and the officers, the chronicler writes:

> Afterward, the said master of the order gave the thirty-five sisters a period to think over whether they wanted to keep the Observance. Those who did not wish to could be accommodated in other cloisters. Thus the sisters agreed to the holy Observance, except for eight sisters who said that it was too difficult for them and that they did not wish to [do] it. . . . The eight sisters [whose names are listed] took with them books, clothing, jewels, annuities, rents, cash, chests, cabinets, and other household goods, more than belonged to them. But twenty-seven of the sisters remained and ten sisters from Schönensteinbach.

The writer goes on to tell how those who stayed gave over their private property to the convent: jewels, cash, chests, cabinets, extra clothing, including "coats of finely woven wool, of squirrel and other furs, cloaks and down comforters."[58] The items collected were sold and the proceeds invested. The sister's narrative differs from Meyer's in that it is primarily concerned with demonstrating the legitimacy of the takeover and with giving names and an exact accounting of the property that was collected. Unlike Meyer, she does not describe the sneaking in of the women at night or the men's exhortations to the sisters, but proceeds straight to the vote.

At Überwasser (Münster), in contrast, the trial period was one year. Until Easter, the nuns were permitted to wear long dresses, keep their servants, and were not required to take part in the singing of the Hours. Those over age sixty could have a room of their own as well as a servant. Yet after the trial year, fifteen sisters elected to leave and pensions had to be paid out to them as settlements.[59] Dominican officials expressed their concern that no one should be forced to join the Observance and Provincial Jakob von Stubach admonished reformers at Gmünd in 1478 that no one was to be driven out of the convent.[60] At the Clarissan cloister of Söflingen some of the sisters, who had left the house because of the reform, later returned and were allowed to live there under a modified form of the Observance with special dispensations, such as the privilege of visiting with their friends.[61]

In many cases, when sister-houses of the New Devout were "reformed" by the introduction of the Augustinian rule and enclosure, as was St. Agnes at Emmerich in 1463, not all the women accepted the change. The Emmerich sisters had already solemnly renounced ownership of property in 1439, but many felt that living under a monastic rule was incompatible with their freedom to pursue their own pious devotional exercises and live by the work of their hands.[62] Thus, even after the community accepted the rule, some of the sisters continued to live in the house without taking the vows or accepting enclosure. The Emmerich book of sisters tells, for example, of Sister Ide Ruijtkens, who said that keeping the rule of the order would overtax her abilities. "Sister Ide had not joined the order and this she explained by saying she had not taken orders because she was not strong of mind and was often overly worried and uneasy, that she could not do all the things properly and keep the order. And therefore she continued in her original simple ways and served God as best she could."[63]

In some accounts it is the resident abbess, converted by Observant preaching, who decides to join the reform. At least this is the explanation given by the chronicler at the Bridgettine cloister of Maihingen (1522–1552). She relates how Magdalena von Oettingen, abbess of the neighboring Cistercian cloister of Kirchheim am Ries (1446–1496), was converted by the preaching of Father Peter Karoli, Maihingen's confessor, and decided to become an Observant.

> Father Peter went often to Kirchheim, to the lady abbess and her convent, for she was a particular friend of the holy order and of all spiritually devout people. [He] told the lady abbess and the other women, who were all still unreformed, many good things about a blessed, reformed life and of the anxious situation that those who own property and are not reformed find themselves in.[64]

The Observant chronicler explains how as a result of Father Peter's preaching the abbess and some of the sisters decided to join the reform despite strong opposition from within the community.

> And he instructed them in many gracious teachings, so much so that their hearts became ardently inclined toward the reform. And he devoted special attention to the lady abbess with good teachings, for he saw that she was a person with a particular understanding and affinity for God. And with God's help, he led her to entirely accept the Observance, even though she faced strong resistance from several women in her cloister. There were some who were not willing to agree to it. . . . Several left the house, who did not want to be among the sheep of Christ the Lord. But those who remained henceforward led a devoutly spiritual life as an enclosed community, which still exists.[65]

Unfortunately, no further account of the implementation of this reform is given.

In some cases, women were motivated to join the reform by the desire to take part in the Jubilee indulgence proclaimed in 1450 by Pope Nicholas V (1447–55), in which only reformed cloisters could participate. Wishing to gain its benefits, Prioress Adelheid von Bortfeld and a faction of the canonesses at Heiningen solicited the help of the provost of Sülte, in Hildesheim, who after some hesitation, carried out a reform despite the opposition of the other women in the house.[66]

Women as Initiators of Reform

Beyond scenarios in which women took part in the reform effort out of obedience, as converts of Observant pastors, or sought to gain the Jubilee indulgence, many women initiated reforms on their own. In some cases, however, such as that of Alijt Bake (1415–1455), female reformers acted too independently and were reprimanded for their activities by church authorities. Inspired by the model of Colette of Corbie, Alijt Bake, prioress of the Windesheim house of Galilea in Ghent, worked to bring about a spiritual revival in her own cloister. But she ran into difficulties with the leadership of the Windesheim Congregation over her outspokenness and her mystical and "philosophical" writings. When Alijt failed to modify her activities sufficiently, she was removed as prioress and sent to another cloister.[67]

Other women were inspired by the example of Schönensteinbach or similar communities and requested help in introducing the Observance at their own houses. At the Clarissan convent of Gnadental in Basel, Abbess Clara Seckinger in 1447 petitioned for a reform of her cloister on the model of Alspach (in Alsace), the first Observant Clarissan house in the province.[68] More enterprising was Elisabeth Kröhl (d. 1480), abbess of the Cistercian convent of Heggbach. Under the pretense of taking a cure, Elisabeth visited several cloisters to find out the best practices before initiating a reform of her own house.[69]

Citing from the old chronicle begun in 1525 by the Augustinian sisters of Inzigkofen (near Sigmaringen), a seventeenth-century abridged version asserts that the sisters decided to institute "all the rules and good practices" of the Observant house at Pillenreuth (near Nuremberg). In 1430 they sent two lay sisters to request a copy of their reform statutes.[70] After studying the Pillenreuth reform statutes, the Inzigkofen sisters followed up with a list of forty-one written questions, asking for clarification and advice on how to implement the rules. In the close relationship that subsequently grew up between the two convents, the sisters at Inzigkofen refer to Pillenreuth in their chronicle as "our magistra, teacher, and instructor in the holy order of . . . Saint Augustine."[71]

Two accounts by Johannes Meyer in his *Book of the Reform* resemble others he is known to have solicited from prioresses. In these two accounts, Meyer reports how reforms were initiated by women who successfully agitated to join the Observance. One of the most high-profile efforts was led by prioress Agnes Vigin at St. Nicolaus in undis, Strasbourg. Meyer relates how Prioress Vigin and the sisters at St. Nicholas had earlier hosted a party of Observant sisters who stopped there on their way to reform Himmelskron at Hochheim (near Worms). Impressed by these reformers, Prioress Vigin and some of the sisters petitioned to join the Observance themselves, but their request was ignored because the Dominican men's convent at Strasbourg belonged to the Conventual, or unreformed, faction. So Agnes and her supporters then approached the town council and won its approval after threatening to transfer if their cloister did not join the

Observance. Finally, in 1431, the Dominican Provincial for Teutonia agreed to authorize Observant sisters from Unterlinden and Basel to undertake the reform with Father Peter Gengenbach. Meanwhile, inside the cloister, the situation was tense. Most of the younger sisters opposed the change and declared their intention to leave and take their property with them if the reform should be instituted. After much agitation in the convent, in the city council, and among friends and relatives of both sides, eight of the sisters elected to leave, at an almost debilitating cost to the cloister of 1,600 gulden.[72]

After St. Nicolaus had been reformed for about thirty years, Brid Melburgen, the new prioress of St. Agnes (in Strasbourg) began to organize support for a reform of her own cloister. Meyer reports that Prioress Melburgen and three supporters obtained the backing of a group of the cloister's trustees, friends, and some city councilors. They approached the Dominican Master General, who agreed to send Father Heinrich Schretz and four Observant sisters from Unterlinden in 1465. But the reform was opposed by other sisters in the convent and by their vicar, Johannes Wolfhart. When Wolfhart heard that a reform party was on its way, he ordered the gates to be locked. Prioress Melburgen and her three supporters, who tried to keep the gate open, were locked out. The matter was brought before the city council, Schretz's letters of authorization read out, and the council decided for the Observants.[73]

The details of these last two cases show particularly how involved women's family networks, townspeople, city councils, bishops, and Conventual congregations all were in decisions about the reform of women's cloisters. Sigrid Schmitt's study of Strasbourg illustrates the importance of the changing social composition in Observant convents and the strong pressure for the reform exerted by the burgher magistrate class to which Prioress Brid Melburgen and her three supporters belonged. This pressure was so strong that the minority party succeeded in forcing a reform of St. Agnes, even though the majority of the sisters opposed it. Subsequently, more women from the increasingly powerful city magistrate class were admitted to Strasbourg cloisters.[74]

Both the St. Nicolaus in undis and the St. Agnes accounts are in the Strasbourg manuscript of Meyer's *Book of the Reform,* which also contains additional chapters about St. Agnes that are not in the other manuscripts of Meyer's work. Annette Barthelmé suggests these were composed by one of the Strasbourg sisters.[75] This is confirmed by Meyer's "Open Letter to Dominican Sisters" (c. 1474), which lists his writings and says of the *Book of the Reform,* "to this book a considerable part was appended by the prioress of St. Nicolaus in Strasbourg [Barbara von Benfelden], as she herself was concerned with the work of the reform."[76] Meyer seems to be referring to the additional chapters about St. Agnes's merger with and reform of St. Margaret's in 1475, which are found only in the Strasbourg manuscript.[77] The accounts about Strasbourg cloisters St. Nicolaus and St. Agnes are also each far longer than his other reports. And in these narratives the prioress and principal figures are referred to by name, with the women playing a central role in spearheading the reform efforts. Thus it seems likely that Meyer was working from detailed sources supplied by Prioress von Benfelden.

Confirmation that Meyer used accounts from prioresses is found in Adelheid of Aue's letter to Meyer in 1464, in which she states, "You have asked for information about Sylo." Seraphin Dietler, who included the actual letter in his version of the *Chronicle of Cloister Schönensteinbach,* prefaces it by saying that Meyer had asked the prioress for the names of the sisters who participated in the reform and how it was carried out.[78] Prioress von Aue's account matches almost verbatim Meyer's version in his *Book of the Reform,* except for one important difference: Adelheid's narrative attributes more of the initiative to the women than does Meyer. Her account tells in the first person how she helped and advised the prioress and five sisters at Sylo who themselves wanted to join the Observance. Prioress Adelheid writes:

> And since you want to know about the cloister Sylo, be informed that some sisters of that house for a long time had a great desire and earnest longing to join the Observance, so much so that for ten years the prioress continually expressed her desire to transfer to our Observant cloister. But I always comforted her with letters and other gestures of friendship and asked her to endure and be patient, for her desire would soon be fulfilled and I would do my best for her. In the meantime, I wrote to the donors and spoke personally with them so that they agreed because there were five sisters in the cloister who wanted to be reformed.[79]

Adelheid goes on to tell how the six sisters and their spiritual mentors wrote to the master general who in 1464 appointed Father Heinrich Schretz to take five sisters from St. Katharina in Colmar to reform Sylo.

The profile of the reform party from Adelheid's cloister is similar in age and experience to the women whom Magdalena Kremer described in her account of the reform of Kirchheim. Among the party were Barbara Krebs, sub-prioress for twenty-six years, and Ursula Surgand. Both of them had been at St. Katharina since before it was reformed in 1438.[80] Barbara Krebs would go on to reform St. Gertrude in Cologne two years later and Margaret Meyer, also of the party, later headed missions to both Engelport (1466) and Klingental (1480).[81]

Here again city magistrates intervened in support of the Observants with offers of help and assistance. Prioress Adehleid states that, of the twenty inhabitants of Sylo, five favored and fifteen opposed the reform. One of the opponents left before the reformers arrived, and afterward four more did so without requesting permission, for which they were excommunicated. Yet the influence of the town council and the Dominican master general was sufficient to institute the reform, at least on a trial basis. Abbess Adelheid closes her letter to Meyer by asking for his prayers that the seeds planted at Sylo "will grow and bear fruit."[82]

As noted, Adelheid's version gives greater emphasis to the requests of the Sylo prioress during the ten years before the reform and to her own activities, which are in the foreground of her account. Meyer, however, attributes the initiative to the perspicacity of Master General Conrad Asti, who during a visitation "noticed that the prioress herself and some of the other good sisters desired wholeheartedly that their cloister should be reformed."[83] From this it is apparent that Prioress Adelheid, who gives less emphasis to Asti, perceived herself as more active in bringing about the reform than did her male mentors. Adelheid's narrative resembles earlier women's accounts in which beguines play the central roles as the founders of religious communities. Women, it seems, tended to perceive themselves as more active and instrumental than did their male co-participants.

Women on Their Own

The clearest description of women taking the initiative and instituting a reform by themselves is found in accounts left by sisters at St. Katharina in

St. Gall. The chronicle, begun by Prioress Angela Varnbühler (1441–1509) and the sister-book by Elisabeth Muntprat (d. 1531), provide a close look at both the reform and the extraordinary friendship between Varnbühler and Prioress Kunigunda Haller, her mentor in Nuremberg. It was Haller who provided the sisters at St. Gall with a written how-to course on the Observance. Thoma Vogler's 1938 history of the convent asserts that the initiation of reform at St. Gall shows no influence of the lector. "We do not even know his name, probably a Dominican of Constance. But this [men's] convent was itself not reformed and the women would have received little impetus from this quarter."[84]

Angela Varnbühler, who began the chronicle that covers the years 1450–1528, tells how she entered the cloister in 1453 at age thirteen. Together with the ardently religious Angela, a few like-minded sisters began to live in voluntary poverty. The prioress at the time, a friend of the Observance, was unable to gain majority support and was succeeded in 1455 by a strong opponent of the reform. But the situation was reversed four years later when Anna Krumm, one of the Observant group, was elected and instituted the common life for all. The sister-book, begun in 1483 by Elisabeth Muntprat, recounting the history of the cloister from 1228 to 1488, describes the first stage of the reform: "In the year 1459, we began a communal life which the worthy mother prioress and several sisters so greatly desired that they had begun it among themselves earlier, but in this year [1459] they initiated it for the [whole] convent. It was accomplished with great anguish and worry that would fill a book."[85] The chronicle gives a graphic account, reporting that "some sisters set themselves against it, so that one sister, screaming loudly, wounded our sub-prioress so that she almost died, but God showed his grace and she survived another twenty-two years." Eventually, all but three of the convent's fourteen sisters accepted voluntary poverty, and twenty new members joined the community under Prioress Anna Krumm's direction. Anna died in 1476 and was succeeded by the charismatic Angela Varnbühler, who proceeded to reform the entire life of the cloister. Under Varnbühler's leadership, the sisters decided that they wished to be an enclosed cloister and, in 1482, sent a delegation to the bishop of Constance for his approval, afterward also soliciting the approval of the St. Gall city council. Vogler comments that the first stage of the reform (voluntary poverty) was introduced with a great deal of opposition, but the latter stage (enclosure) with none.[86]

The decision to embrace voluntary poverty and asceticism may have been motivated by the model of Saint Catherine of Siena, whose biography can be found in at least six manuscripts in the cloister library. But the most important influence was Varnbühler's correspondence with Kunigunda Haller, prioress (1468–97) of the Observant Dominican cloister at Nuremberg. This correspondence, in which Haller acted as mentor, extended over many years. Although Varnbühler's half of the conversation has not survived, one can see from Haller's letters, which were copied into the St. Gall sister-book, how the friendship developed and how Haller guided the progress of the reform at St. Gall, a convent that had never been officially accepted into the order, even though the women repeatedly tried to gain admission. In one early letter, Prioress Haller writes her encouragement to Angela: "Not occasionally, but often and continually I rejoice over your great, earnest, scrupulous striving, that is appropriate to the order, to spirituality and the Holy Observance. May God grant me His grace that I may be equal to your desires [in guiding you.]"[87] With similar enthusiasm, she writes repeatedly, "your boundless love and zeal for the holy Observance are the great joy of my heart."[88]

Haller and the sisters at Nuremberg instructed the sisters at St. Gall, shared books and advice on the practices of the Observance, as Elsbeth relates in the sister-book.

In the year 1483, when we enclosed our cloister, the above mentioned worthy mother prioress [Haller] at Nuremberg began to help and instruct us in her most faithful and friendly letters and to advise us in all spirituality. And she and her dear daughters taught us with such faithfulness and love . . . lent us their books in a most friendly way, . . . [and] answered all our questions as we desired about how they observed the rule, as is written hereafter.[89]

Prioress Haller, who especially valued the rule of silence, writes in one example:

There is no part of the rule more suited to me than holy silence. It is as though rooted in my nature. When I assumed the office of prioress it was a great cross to my heart that I worried about my silence. . . . Our old, dear mother prioress told us often in chapter that the old monastics sometimes kept silence for the whole of Lent and Advent, not only in those places and times when talking is forbidden, but [also] other useless words.[90]

In her role as mentor, Haller calls silence "a key to all spirituality and a foundation stone of peace" as well as "the greatest basis of devotion and the resting place of the holy spirit."[91] Haller provided the St. Gall sisters with a detailed handbook (over 200 pages copied into the sister-book) on all aspects of the day-to-day implementation of an Observant regime and many letters of encouragement.

The women's reform at St. Katharina highlights the question of agency. How much maneuvering room did female religious have in shaping their own lives? It is clear, for example, that women sometimes chose enclosure as a way to limit outside interference in their internal affairs, as will be seen. Yet their options were limited. How did women operate in relation to ecclesiastical and secular authorities? In the accounts that women left about themselves one finds many portraits of self-confident, energetic, enterprising, innovative, and resourceful personalities. Often they tell stories about the frustrations endured from external powers that either thwarted the prioress's efforts to accomplish a goal or tried to tyrannize them. In some narratives the protagonists manage to accomplish their aims by exceptional entrepreneurship or resist the pressure applied to them through ingenuity or sheer courage. In dealing with ecclesiastical authorities they were bound by their vows of obedience, but in facing up to secular injustice and tyrannical exercise of power, the women portray themselves resisting boldly and resourcefully.

Prioress Anna von Buchwald

As members of the nobility and of the upper classes, nuns were not lacking in self confidence. Anna von Buchwald, prioress at Preetz (1484–1508) begins her "Book in the Choir" with a drawing of the coats of arms of both sides of her family and proudly announces herself as the author: "This book was written by Mother Prioress Anna von Buchwald, composed new by her. It is useful to all and eliminates most of the errors which can usually only be avoided with great effort. . . . If you read it, you will never go wrong."[92] This confident introduction prefaces Anna's advice to the sisters. Her careful record-keeping and practical spirituality show a concern with the well being of her community. Never afraid to innovate, Anna early in her term of office proposed changes in the performance of the liturgy that emphasized spirituality and understanding over rote memorization. As mentioned earlier, Anna suggested and received approval for her plan to shorten the numerous readings, masses, and special vigils, which taxed the strength the nuns in her cloister. But she also proposed to allow them to sing from books instead from rote memory. Anna writes that in the third year of her priorate she observed three novices endeavoring to sing the antiphons and graduals by heart as was the practice, and she noticed how those with lesser ability "labored greatly and with heavy anxiety" to learn the difficult texts.

> I observed their abilities and great efforts and permitted them—and not only them but all the other novices who will come to the school in the future—to sing these texts from books and no longer from memory . . . so that their health would not be too much affected by the extreme effort of learning by rote but [that they] could serve God with hearty singing and study the music more perfectly and more eagerly.[93]

Anna preferred a simpler liturgy and a smaller number of well sung pieces over many badly sung ones. After receiving the prelate's approval for her plan she writes unabashedly: "Yes, dearest sisters in Christ, I, the aforesaid Anna, ask with a full heart that you, now and in the future, all of you who, because of my efforts, will enjoy this alleviation—these changes and attenuations of your labor in this cloister—will remember in prayer my name which stands at the beginning and the end of this book."[94] Always practical, Anna even introduced warming pans for the early service so that all would take part.

Besides the liturgical reforms she introduced, perhaps the most telling example of Anna's remarkable capabilities and her resourceful agency, despite all the difficult restraints placed on her, was the renovation of the cloister. Anna had long had a running conflict with the provost who refused almost all requests to repair the facilities. When Anna repaired the sixty-year-old rotting roof at her own expense, the provost refused even to feed the workers, so that the sisters had to pay for their food out of the refectory funds.[95] Most of the cloister's buildings were sadly in need of repair. Lest one think that Anna was exaggerating the need for renovation, her description of the state of the bakery house gives an idea both of her reasons for concern and of the difficulties of life in fifteenth-century convents. Anna writes that the roof beams were so rotten that tiles frequently fell onto the floor.

> When it rained or snowed, our grain was flooded and sprouted. How our beer could agree with us after that, one can imagine! It rained into the flour bin and leaked into the vats when beer was being brewed and into the dough trough when sourdough was rising. We were constantly afraid that the bakery house would fall down and then we would not have been able to rebuild it for 1,000 gulden. Then we saw that the walls had separated from each other and were hollow so that they could no longer stand.[96]

By 1494, twenty-three years after Anna had begun her book, the last in a series of incompetent provosts had departed, leaving the cloister deeply in debt. Anna writes, "[B]ecause no one could be found who wanted to take on the office because of the debts," she was herself allowed to take over the financial management of the cloister for a period of four years.[97]

Anna set to work immediately. After making an inspection of the grounds with the eldest sisters, she and the other sisters undertook a fund-raising campaign among friends, relatives, townspeople, and associates with whom the convent did business. Under Anna's direct stewardship, the cloister was almost entirely rebuilt. She added a new bakery, mill, hospital, provost's house, stained glass windows, vaulting, as well as an organ for the church, all, she states, without incurring any new debts for the cloister. Convinced of the health benefits of fresh air, Anna replaced all of the old, stationary cloister windows with new ones that could be opened on fine days. Her considerable expertise in fund-raising included rewarding donors by including their coats of arms in the stained glass windows that they funded. By astute management and her capital funds campaign, organized with the equally astute help of her sister Dilla, Prioress Anna succeeded in paying off all the cloister's debts accumulated by the three previous provosts. Finally, in 1498 a new provost was appointed, this time a good manager with whom Anna worked harmoniously and in great mutual respect throughout her remaining years as prioress.[98]

Ursula Haider

In fiscal matters Anna von Buchwald was possibly the most effective prioress to leave an account of her activities, but she was certainly not the only enterprising one. Another was Ursula Haider (1413–1498), reform prioress at the Bicken cloister in Villingen, a house of Poor Clares. Hearing of the Jubilee indulgence announced in 1489 that would be granted for visiting the seven churches of Rome and which was augmented in 1491 to include the holy places in Palestine, Ursula placed descriptions of holy places (written on parchment) at certain locations in the cloister so that her nuns could make the pilgrimage "in spirit" without leaving the confines of their cloister.[99] Then Ursula decided to apply to Pope Innocent VIII for a bull officially granting the indulgence to her nuns for making the spiritual pilgrimage within their own cloister, since they lived enclosed. To support her application she solicited letters from the mayor and members of the Villingen city council as well as from many influential friends and acquaintances including Count Eberhard of Württemberg and sent them by messenger to Rome. But the messenger returned with the disheartening report that the application had not gotten past the office of one of the cardinals because it was not accompanied by the necessary gratuities. Ursula then started over again and solicited another set of letters of application, even though the Poor Clares could not offer the thousand ducats that would normally accompany such a request.

For the second attempt, the Bicken cloister chronicle states, Ursula recruited Father Conrad von Bondorf, who was an acquaintance and former classmate of Pope Innocent, to carry the request to Rome. This time the application reached the pope who granted the request of the poor sisters without requiring "one single kreutzer in payment." When the letter of indulgence was brought back to the Bicken cloister, the nuns carried it tearfully from station to station in a solemn procession with singing and candlelight.[100]

Ursula Haider was not only a determined woman but, like Anna von Buchwald, also very self-confident in her opinions. She left behind a book of her writings and revelations, some of which describe dream-visions of conversations with "a master and doctor of holy writ, a Dominican" (possibly Johannes Tauler). The Bicken cloister chronicle quotes extensive passages from Ursula's text. In one encounter she says assertively to her Dominican interlocutor, "[H]ear me and do not withdraw until I have explained my opinion to you." After she spoke, Ursula, never short on self-esteem, reports his reply, "God be praised that He created you, a creature in which His light of grace so shines," and tells her that her writings will become widely known.[101]

Dorothea Koler and the Sisters of Marienthal

Max Straganz refers to Dorothea Koler (d. 1463), leader of the party sent from Nuremberg in 1455 to reform the Clarissan cloister at Brixen, as "a woman of manly spirit."[102] The portrait of Abbess Koler, composed about seventy years later by a sister at the convent of Pfullingen (c. 1525), tells how she defied Duke Sigismund of Tirol by honoring a papal interdict that had been placed over him and, together with other Observants, refusing afterward to have religious services conducted in the convent church. The story of these events, narrated rather melodramatically in the Pfullingen chronicle, illustrates the involvement of the townspeople in the issues concerning the convent and its religious services.

> And from day to day the situation got worse, so that every day they were threatened with violence, sometimes that [the townspeople] would cut their clothes off at the belt and drive them out of town with sticks, sometimes other threats. And once they said that if they did not hold with the community [and stop honoring the interdict] they should know for sure that they would all be drowned, for "that's what they were good for"—that and a lot of other things. Then abbess [Koler], standing in the open door of the cloister clapped one hand in the other and replied, "I hope and trust God and all the Nurembergers that they will not let it go unpunished."[103]

The sisters went on refusing to ring the bells for services until at last the exasperated duke evicted the women from his lands (1461). But Abbess

Koler refused to go unless transportation was provided for the sick and elderly sisters. To this the duke, somewhat shamed, acquiesced.

A different kind of breach between the convent and citizenry is related in the chronicle of Marienthal (Niesing) in Münster, a house of Sisters of the Common Life that had taken on a rule and lived enclosed. The narrative tells how, during the Anabaptist uprising of 1534, the nuns were evicted from their cloister. The convent chronicle (c. 1540) relates how a mob of Anabaptist townsfolk came to the cloister, demanding that the women should join them and be baptized. But the sisters, as their chronicle states, were "harder than a stone, for a stone can be moved more than we." And so the mob drove them out of their cloister, although it was snowing heavily. Looking for each other on the outside a few days later in the aftermath of the snow and general chaos, the sisters discovered that three of their number were missing.

> [T]here was one sister who customarily took care of the sick, and she had remained in the infirmary with two elderly invalid sisters until Sunday. So three of our sisters, who had come out, went back and asked earnestly at the door that the three sisters should be brought out . . . but [the pillagers] refused and said they must go away or be shot. And so the sisters drew back very sad and the Anabaptists fired shots after them.[104]

Waiting at a distance, the women saw the infirmary sister coming out with the two invalids and, despite the danger to themselves, ran to help them. Their courage and concern for the sick—like Dorothea Koler's—mark them as women of more than "manly spirit." Rather than the spiritual warrior of the fourteenth-century sister-books, winning the Lord's grace and mercy through hard discipline and asceticism, the heroine in fifteenth- and sixteenth-century convent chronicles is portrayed standing up to the duke or risking her safety to care for the sick.

Barbara Bernheimer and Christina Reyselt

Magdalena Kremer's narrative tells how, under Prioress Barbara Bernheimer, the women of Kirchheim not only held out against the Count of

Württemberg through three seiges by his troops but also how the women launched a propaganda campaign to fight back. In order to mobilize public opinion, the nuns published a flier (which Magdalena includes) addressed to "all Christian princes, knights, noblemen, and all others" in which they detailed the injustices committed against them by Count Eberhard the Younger and the circumstances and course of the seige.

> [W]e cannot understand such fearful persecution and uncalled for violence from someone who is supposed to be our gracious sovereign or protector, he who not only does not protect us but himself undertakes to starve us. We urgently seek and cry out with flowing tears for help and comfort. [Signed] The Prioress and the entire Dominican Convent of St. John the Baptist at Kirchheim unter Teck.[105]

Whether it was this broadside that brought Eberhard's uncle with his troops to their rescue is not clear. But in this and other writings the sisters published the names of those who had helped them and those who had not. In this struggle against the count, Observant women mounted a very public resistance against a more powerful secular authority.

Sometimes the women's resistance to secular pressure was more individual, immediate, and direct. Christina Reyselt at Brixen in 1460, for example, took matters into her own hands when the papal interdict was issued against Duke Sigismund of Tirol. The Observants, as mentioned, upheld the interdict while the Conventuals did not. The Pfullingen chronicle recounts that, in order to prevent the cloister's bells from being rung for services by the duke's men, Christina climbed up to the bell towers, took the clappers out of the bells, and hid them so well that even later they could not be found.[106] This audacious strategem is typical of the capable and ambitious Christina, the former servant who had worked her way up to choir sister. In the chronicle narrative she shows her resourcefulness again during the long and arduous journey from Brixen to cloister Pfullingen (near Reutlingen in Württemberg), after the duke evicted the women in 1461. The chronicler portrays graphically how the astute Christina took charge in this crisis:

> In the night when the sisters were told that they were to be expelled, she took cord and sacking and had the wagons covered

with it. And [she collected] all the things that might be of use on the journey, particularly all the chickens and capons, which she beheaded with a cleaver and stuffed into sacks and pillowcases, also spice cakes and whatever was at hand. And [on the road] whenever they came to honorable people who were friendly to the sisters and did anything to help them, Christina always had something with which to show their gratitude, perhaps a spice cake or the like. And when they came to an inn, she usually had something that was good to cook.[107]

In these women's writings, Observant nuns are not represented as otherworldly and docile. Their self-portraits sketch them as self-directed and purposeful. The convent chronicles depict everyday life in a fifteenth-century religious house as less sterile, monotonous, and detached than is often assumed. The celebrated sisters of Schönensteinbach had to evacuate their cloister four times when maurading armies crossed through their territory.[108] Frequently, they received letters and reports back from members of their community who had gone to reform cloisters as far away as Bohemia. Women in different Observant convents knew about the history of the reform in their order and wrote in their chronicles not only about their accomplishments but also those at other houses.[109] Moreover, they knew the political situation at court, to which they sent representatives to plead their cause, when they were being harassed by a local territorial lord. They knew where the levers of ecclesiastical and secular power lay and how to access them through the right influential connections. They struggled with economic hardships and rejoiced at their successes in dealing with these authorities. As in any surrogate family, the most highly valued acts in these stories are those of selflessness or of resourcefulness that benefited the community. What is, perhaps, most surprising today are monastic women's extensive networks and the close relationships among members of different cloistered communities.

Where larger political conflicts were concerned, especially the struggle for church reform and renewal, nuns were intently engaged and cloister life was far from quiet and detached. Daniel Bornstein has shown how avidly and with what partisan interest the nuns at Corpus Domini followed papal politics, the struggles of rival papal candidates, and the efforts of the councils of Pisa and Constance to end the schism. Although convent women were not at the same levers of power, they were participants in the political conflicts, class struggles, and economic reorganizations of their time. At Brixen and Kirchheim Observant women agitated politically against secular overlords. While they lost in the confrontation at Brixen, they won at Kirchheim and Maihingen.[110] In these encounters with those in power, the women acted resourcefully and courageously, despite their subordinate position. Agency, solidarity, and compassionate concern for one another are prominently depicted in their accounts: Anna von Buchwald's efforts to ease the burdens on her novices, Ursula Haider's exertions to gain the jubilee indulgence for her community, Dorothea Koler's audacity in demanding transport for the sick and elderly, and the unnamed sister at Marienthal's choice to remain with the invalids and care for them while her cloister was being sacked. Yet this is but one half of the picture. What about the agency of their sisters on the other side of the reform issue? It is to these women that this study will now turn.

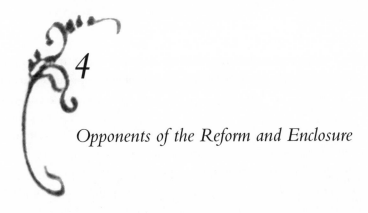

4

Opponents of the Reform and Enclosure

This was the way of life I found kept in this monastery [when I entered it] forty years ago; for as many years I myself have kept it and will continue to serve in this way and no other.

—Katharina von Hoya, Abbess of Wienhausen (d. 1474)

Although women who supported the reform left behind many accounts, those who opposed it did not.[1] Either they did not write them at all or the texts were not preserved in the archives of their Conventual or Observant houses. Occasionally, the chronicle of an Observant house contains entries by sisters who were not kindly disposed to the reform, but these, too, are rare. Thus, for reports of women's resistance, one must rely mainly on male reformers' records or other documents. Yet these relate a number of examples of women's strong—sometimes successful—opposition.

In his account of reform activities among Benedictine, Cistercian, and Augustinian houses for both men and women in the diocese of Hildesheim, Johannes Busch tells of his appointment as father confessor to the nuns of Derneburg (1440–42). He relates how he was caught off guard when one of the women ambushed him as he undertook to transfer the women's individual property into a common chest. Accompanying him to inspect the last of the private cellars in which the Derneburg nuns kept their beer and other personal stocks, the seemingly guileless sister who owned this store said to Busch, "[Y]ou go first now, Father, for my cellar is the same as those of the other sisters." Then, he recounts,

> without thinking, I did so. But when I went down into it, she suddenly clapped to the door or vault over my head and stood upon it. I was shut up alone in there, thinking what would have happened if the nuns had shut me up there secretly. . . . At length

after some delay they opened the trap-door of the cellar and let me come out. After that I was never willing to go first into any closed place in any nunnery. . . . The sister who did this was good enough and very simple, whence I was astonished that she should think of such a thing.[2]

Busch may have underestimated the "simplicity" of the sister who trapped him, though he should not have. For women did not take kindly to having their jewelry, and especially their beer, taken away, even if it was placed in common use.

The sisters at Derneburg were not the only ones to take violent measures to prevent the imposition of Observant practices. At St. Katharina in Augsburg, women wielded sticks and skewers to drive away workmen who were heightening the wall around their cloister.[3] At St. Katharina in Nuremberg, nuns fended off the first wave of male reformers by brandishing a large crucifix at them.[4] When outraged families of the nuns at Glaucha retaliated against the Observants by withholding donations that would go into the common purse, Busch countered by announcing to the townspeople in their churches that the nuns would all be transferred if the cloister became too poor to support them.[5] Sometimes armed friends and family members attacked reformers on the roads or issued death threats.[6] In nearly all cases involvement of the lay populace was intense and feelings ran very high.

The nuns were usually quite willing to accept improvements to their education and even the discipline of conformity to the rule but they adamantly opposed infringements of the cloister's prestige and independence, especially where bishops, secular lords, or city councils tried to tighten control over them. The participation of secular authorities in the reforms, as well as the handing over of cloister offices to "foreign" sisters who had no familial ties to the local nobility, tended to isolate a convent and strengthen the grip of centralized secular and ecclesiastical authorities on it.[7] For resisting these measures nuns were labeled "worldly" or "wild, roguish women" by the frustrated reformers.[8]

To make matters worse, teams of visitors often had different ideas about reform and the officials got into conflicts with one another.[9] The author of the account in the chronicle of Wienhausen, a sister hostile to the Observance, complained bitterly that even after reform had been instituted, different groups kept issuing conflicting sets of instructions.

> [N]evertheless her Highness the Duchess of Braunschweig and Lüneburg, Anna von Nassau [who had requested the reform] and Provost Heinrich Wetemann called for many visitations by fathers and Dominicans, who often entered the cloister without the bishop's authority and either introduced or forbade this thing or that thing under the pretext of improvement, as, for example, that the principal mass should not be performed as it previously had been by the clergy and the assembled sisters, but must be sung by the women alone. Also that there should be no more organ or instrumental music at matins and vespers. That the chapel of St. Fabian and Sebastian for particular reasons—which are unclear and conjured-up deceptions—should be closed.[10]

Most Conventuals did not feel that they were in need of reform and argued that they were not living in violation of established rules. In fact, many Conventual cloisters kept the rule in only a moderately less stringent way than Observants and in complete conformity to papal dispensations on the holding of property. Matthias Döring, a leader of the Franciscan Conventuals, argued that their manner of life was "entirely correct."[11]

Attempting to head off the Observants, the sisters at Oetenbach wrote to Peter Wellen, the provincial for Teutonia, to ask what they would have to do to preempt a reform. Wellen's answer was that if they would sing the choral Office, live together peaceably, and follow the rules of enclosure, they need not fear being reformed against their will.[12] Because both Töss and Oetenbach were under the care of the Conventual, or unreformed, Dominicans of Zürich, who objected to any incursions by the Observants, attempts to reform these houses failed. Some Conventuals, such as Franciscan Johannes Pauli, openly accused Observants of smugness and a "holier-than-thou" attitude.[13]

Women such as Abbess Katharina von Hoya (d. 1474) at Wienhausen saw no reason for change. Abbess Katharina asserted unabashedly that she had been "living this way for forty years" and did not intend to change.[14] Indeed, it can hardly be called stiff-necked disobedience for women to want to keep to established practices that were guaranteed in writing by their charters. Renée Weis-Müller identifies the unreformed nuns as "traditionalists" and the reformers as the "representatives of modernity." Weis-Müller argues that the clash between Observants and Conventuals over the nature of piety was a clash between the old and the new, the status quo and changing expectations.[15] Other scholars stress the importance of class pressures.[16] Traditionally, many women's houses had never been intended to be strictly subjected to a rule but were founded as patrician finishing schools and living establishments for the unmarried daughters of the nobility. Some convent women could even honestly claim ignorance of the rule, as did two sisters at Rechentshofen (near Pforzheim).[17] The inhabitants of the most elite religious foundations, in many cases, had entered them as part of a dynastic strategy or family tradition. Despite the unsuccessful attempts of earlier popes to convert secular into regular canonesses by placing them under a rule, Pope Alexander VI in 1493 confirmed the rights of certain houses to forgo vows and habits. They were permitted to own private property, to live in individual quarters on a fixed income, and even to take a yearly leave to visit parents and family.[18] Often it is difficult to establish the exact status of a particular house centuries after its founding. When at Rechentshofen, nominally a Cistercian house, hearings were held about a projected reform (c. 1422), the families of the women disparaged the idea of enclosure as too "ignoble" and "rustic" a life for their privileged daughters. "The nobility and our ancestors . . . founded this and similar cloisters so that their and their posterity's daughters would be cared for, but not under enclosure or in such strictness as that under which you and your monks live or 'those ignoble types and rustics in your enclosed monastery.'" Moreover, these young women could not keep the Observance because of their "delicate constitutions."[19] At Engelthal, when a similar reform attempt was initiated in 1512, Sub-prioress Martha von Kürmreuth and a few of her sisters actually visited several reformed Dominican cloisters and afterward wrote a letter to their vicar; they had seen "great strictness and unendurable hardship, . . ." which their own "parents, ancestors, and other friends had not intended them to be subjected to." Furthermore, the city of Nuremberg had promised them and their servants "conditions appropriate to the princely classes."[20] Even men, Abbot Johannes Trithemius (d. 1516) reports, claimed that they were "noble, sensitive and of delicate health" and therefore could not endure "fasting, austerity, vigils, flagellation and other such exercises."[21] Not surprisingly, then, the number of entrants coming from the rural nobility declined drastically in many houses after the reform.[22] Here the division between supporters and opponents of the reform was along class lines.

The Abbess and the Cardinal

One of the most prominent battles in which ecclesiastical authorities tried to assert control over a house of noble canonesses was the attempted reform of the abbey of Sonnenburg. The resulting conflict between the powerful abbess, Verena von Stuben, and the newly appointed cardinal, Nicholas von Cusa (1401–1464), was a match of the strongest wills from which neither emerged unscathed. A larger than life struggle, it has been the subject of several literary works.[23]

The wealthy abbey of Sonnenburg was located in the bishophric of Brixen to which Cardinal Cusa was appointed in 1452. Named papal legate two years before, Cusa was charged with instituting reform in all of the German-speaking territories. Yet this assignment turned out to be most difficult in his own bishophric because, as Morimichi Watanabe points out, Cusa was "a bourgeois Rhinelander" and the women of Sonnenburg were daughters of the Tyrolese nobility, who considered him an upstart.[24] Besides having a higher social rank than Bishop Cusa, Sonnenburg's abbess had the status of a minor territorial ruler and exercised control over the abbey's extensive lands.[25] One of Cusa's sucessors wrote, after a visitation to Sonnenburg in 1612, that the nuns there

> are noble and, in spite of many attempts, could not be enclosed even up to the present day, because they rely [for support] on the nobility of this province. This reliance is so great that, although they recognize the bishop in spiritual matters, in secular matters— even those closely related to spiritual ones—they call on the territorial princes and the nobility for their protection and rebel against the bishop.[26]

Cusa encountered exactly these difficulties. Having issued a decree in 1452 that all the convents of the province "must be reformed within one year" and that all women's cloisters were to be enclosed, Cusa expected compliance from Sonnenburg, nominally a Benedictine house. But the nuns there had never been cloistered and were in the habit of traveling about freely. Abbess Verena, in particular, was often away from the convent to attend weddings, to appear at social functions, and to administer the financial and legal affairs of her cloister's lands and villages. While her nuns might devote themselves to religious matters, the abbess saw her own office primarily as political and administrative rather than as religious. She realized clearly that enclosure would make it impossible for her to administer her holdings in the accustomed way. As an alternative she suggested to Cusa that he might reform the nuns but exempt her.

This proposal did not suit the cardinal. Indeed, the reform statutes that Cusa drew up after an official visitation of the cloister in 1453 stress emphatically his view that in a reformed cloister the abbess must be the spiritual leader of her community; she should set an example by being present for the performances of the liturgical offices.

> Each abbess must give the greatest attention to the preservation of her own soul and those of all the sisters and guide them with wholesome teaching and her good example. . . . She is required by the rules and holy ordinances to be present with the others as much as possible at the proper times: in choir, in chapter, the refectory, the dormitory, and especially at matins, high mass, vespers, compline, so that by her presence a greater discipline and integrity will be observed and the Divine Office performed with greater application.[27]

Abbess Verena's almost total ignorance of the rule and her focus on material and political matters made her unsuited to the role of spiritual leader that Cusa and the reform tried to impose on her. Well practiced and skillful in political maneuvering, the abbess managed to hold Cusa at bay for six years. She stalled, repeatedly asking for extensions, filing petitions at the papal court, negotiating over details of procedure and jurisdiction, without ever instituting any of the mandated changes.[28]

Early on Cusa demanded that Verena resign as abbess and appointed Afra von Velseck as administrator in her place. When Verena refused to resign, Cusa excommunicated her, placed Sonnenberg under interdict, and forbade that any rents be paid to the cloister or any supplies delivered. When the village of Enneberg refused to pay its rents, Verena appealed to her brother-in-law, Jobst von Hornstein, who gathered a troop of supporters and mercenaries to attack the village. When the troops approached, the villagers let loose an avalanche of stones and counterattacks, killing fifty of the mercenary soldiers and capturing their leader, Jobst von Hornstein. When a contingent of the cardinal's men stormed the convent, Verena escaped and then returned after Duke Sigismund of Austria's forces retook the cloister. Eventually, a peace agreement was worked out that called for Verena's resignation and transfer, but granted her a handsome annual pension to be paid by the cloister.

Verena left Sonnenberg but continued to negotiate with Cusa about the conditions for removing the ban he had placed on her, conditions that were humiliating and held her entirely responsible for the deaths at Enneberg.[29] Cusa's demands caused Verena to make repeated written protests to Rome, decrying the cardinal's treatment of her. Finally, after seven years of conflict, Verena was absolved from the ban. Future abbesses of Sonnenberg proved to be no more compliant in accepting Cusa's stipulations or those of ensuing bishops, however. The cloister was never successfully reformed.

The cardinal's dogged attempt to institute reform by force and without the cooperation or support of the secular authorities—with whom he was also in conflict—was doomed from the outset. For her part, Verena neither understood the goals of the reform nor trusted Cusa's motives in pursuing it. Knowing nothing about the Observance and having no contact with any reforming Observant nuns, she was convinced of Cusa's duplicity. His motives, she believed, had nothing to do with religious observance, and the reform was only a fabricated excuse to take away the cloister's property. Matters of spirituality do not figure prominently, if at all, in Verena's objections. Her concern is rather with issues of authority. In a memorandum explaining her reasons for resigning, Verena writes sarcastically, "First of all, it is His Grace's [Cusa's] opinion, that I as abbess should have no power other than to assign penances to the women, and I should be obedient to them and they to me and should in all things be like them and they like me. . . . And I, as abbess, shall not contradict."[30] One can hear in this memorandum Verena's contempt for Cusa's stipulations.

Although Cusa himself may have been sure of his intentions, modern scholars are not. One of his aims was to regain the episcopal possessions that had been ceded by his predecessors. To this end he carefully examined the titles and legal records on properties that had formerly belonged to the bishops of Brixen. These measures made it difficult for him to convince Verena that he was interested only in the spiritual condition of her cloister. Sadly, Cusa never understood Verena's motivations and her suspicions of him but referred to her simplistically as a "Jezebel."[31] Their resentful exchanges and the failed outcome of the reform did Cusa and the Observance little credit and left Verena embittered.

Rijnsburg Abbey

Another case involving an exclusive Benedictine abbey for daughters of the highest nobility was Rijnsburg, a house that only admitted women of noble parentage on both maternal and paternal sides for four generations. Located near Haarlem, Rijnsburg had long been the most exclusive convent of the area. Although ostensibly a Benedictine house, it was inhabited by women who were little acquainted with the rule. Life in Rijnsburg followed the ceremonies of the court; and the abbess was daily attended by her chaplain, three servants, and a chamberlain, all of whom strode in order before her when she went to mass.[32]

In 1451, as part of his reform mission to the northern provinces, Nicholas von Cusa visited Rinjsburg. He had issued a proclamation that all men's and women's convents in the diocese of Utrecht were to return to strict observation of the rules and statutes of their order. Only the year before, Abbess Margareta van Oostende (d. 1452) had successfully fended off a reform attempt by protesting that Rijnsburg was an exempt cloister and not subject to the bishop of Utrecht but under the direct protection and jurisdiction of the Pope. Abbess Margareta had appealed successfully to Philip of Burgundy (d. 1467), himself no opponent of reform but a ruler unwilling to allow an exempt cloister in the bishop's diocese to be reformed by people "from outside."[33] Philip could not, however, refuse the visit of papal legate Nicholas von Cusa, who had been commissioned and empowered by the pope himself to institute reform.

At Rijnsburg, Cusa mandated that the nuns follow the rule of St. Benedict, divest themselves of personal property, give up consumption of meat, share common meals and a common dormitory, wear the habit, and observe enclosure. His visit incited a series of protests by the nuns against these infringements of their rights. To prevent encroachments on his sovereignty, Philip of Burgundy then decided to appoint his own personal reformers for the diocese of Utrecht. Thus, in 1454, Rijnsburg was visited again, this time by appointees of the bishop of Utrecht. They issued new, milder reform statutes for the women that allowed the older sisters to go in and out of the cloister in pairs, with the approval of the abbess. Guests could also be received but not for longer than three days. Yet the women objected to these restrictions as well and launched a counteroffensive by composing their own new set of regulations, which their new abbess, Beatrix van Reimerswaal (1494–1529), succeeded in getting approved. The new regulations allowed more freedom, including walks as a group to a nearby cloister in the summer months. Male guests and persons on business could enter the cloister between the hours of 8 a.m. and 9 p.m. As a preemptive measure against any further Observant reformers, the Rijnsburg nuns solicited an official legal opinion as to whether reformers could impose a stricter rule than that which had customarily been followed in the cloister "as far back as human memory could recall." This important legal ruling affirmed that they could not.[34]

Nevertheless, in 1498 a new visitation by the reform abbots was ordered at the request of successor Philip the Handsome (d. 1506). This time, eight Observant sisters were brought in from the cloister of Hagenbusch. The situation of the reformers was untenable, however, because, despite their presence, Abbess Beatrix remained head of the cloister. The women soon segregated into two camps, singing the hours separately and eating separately, as the old Rijnsburgers carried on a silent but determined resistance to the reforms. Before two months were up, the Observant sisters had requested and received permission to leave. Philip was not pleased and another group of four reform sisters was sent from Klaarwater, an Observant house in the diocese of Utrecht. This time the two groups accommodated each other's liturgical practices and lifestyles. The Observants remained for eight months.[35]

The Rijnsburg sisters then tried a new strategy to reverse the reform. This time they hired expensive lawyers to take five requests to Rome. Their influential chartered procurers acquired for them the five separate papal proclamations affirming all of their exemptions and then presented the sisters with an enormous bill, which the wealthy women were, fortunately, able to pay.[36] In the meantime, Abbess Beatrix had cultivated an improved relationship with Philip the Handsome, then installed his banner and coat of arms at the entrance to the cloister as symbols of Phillip's protectorate over them. Although the Bursfeld congregation continued to try to reform Rijnsburg, the efforts had little effect after the acquisition of their specific exemptions from the pope. How Abbess Reimerswaal might have fared with a determined Nicholas von Cusa in residence as bishop of her diocese, one cannot say. But Rijnsburg's more pro-active tactic of paying for the best professional legal services and the sisters' cultivation of influential protectors worked more effectively than Abbess Verena von Stuben's stalling and negotiating over details, procedure, and jurisdiction.

Überwasser

Like Sonnenburg and Rijnsburg, Überwasser was a noble house in which the abbess held the status of a minor territorial ruler and was also attended by a retinue of court officials such as chamberlain and cupbearer.[37] Converting this kind of establishment to a reformed Benedictine convent, one without private property and with enclosure, was a wrenching experience. The cloister chronicle and account book, written by at least two hands— the earlier of which opposed the Observance—includes accounts of two reforms of the cloister by Observants in 1460 and 1483. The later hand is probably that of reform Abbess Sophia Dobbers (1483–1509) herself.[38] The writer opposing the Observance attributes the bishop's action of imposing a reform prioress to a political intrigue. This writer tells how, when the old abbess died in 1460, the sisters elected a certain Countess von Werth to succeed her. But the newly appointed bishop of Münster, Johann von Baiern, in an act of "political revenge," refused to confirm her and, instead, brought in Richmodis von der Horst from the Observant cloister of the Machabäer (Maccabees) in Cologne. The chronicler asserts that Countess von Werth was denied the appointment because her influential friends in the Cologne cathedral chapter had prevented Johann from becoming bishop of Cologne. The writer goes on to relate rather bitterly how Richmodis was brought in instead at great cost to the convent.

> The bishop wanted to reform this cloister; and thus did not confirm the above mentioned lady. He fetched a lady out of the clois-

ter in Cologne called the Maccabees; this was [Richmodis] von der Horst. The bishop brought the lady here in great state at the cloister's expense. When she was installed, the two days [of ceremonies] cost more than 150 gulden. The lady and those who came with her were here for a year and three months.[39]

Although Schulze concludes that Abbess Richmodis left because the hostility of the Überwasser sisters drove her away, Linneborn suggests that she may have felt that the reform was well enough established.[40] Abbess Richmodis's successor, chosen from within the cloister, remained in office for twenty years, but either a rigorous reform was not carried out or laxity crept back in. New provisions issued at her death specified, for instance, that during a transition period the sisters could keep their servants and did not have to sing the choral hours.[41]

In 1483 a concerted effort was made finally to convert the Überwasser cloister from a house of secular canonesses to a reformed Benedictine one. This time the bishop enlisted the support of the city council, the nobles, the cathedral chapter, the emperor, and the pope.[42] Against such a powerful, united front the women could do little to resist and were given one year to decide if they wished to remain in the cloister or transfer to another. Over the heads of the sisters and contrary to their choice, the cathedral chapter appointed Hilburgis von Norrendyn as abbess, who came with three reforming sisters from the Benedictine convent of St. Aegidius. From February to the following June, the inhabitants of the cloister lived as two opposing camps. The chronicler recounts the tense situation and its outcome: "The sisters who were supposed to reform here ate in the abbey [and] the others in St. Ludger's chapel, from the feast of St. Agatha [February 5th] until St. Boniface day [June 5th]. Then [a week later] the old sisters departed and left the cloister to them."[43] What precipitated this crisis was the death of the reform abbess from St. Aegidius. The old sisters had quickly elected a new abbess, one opposed to reform, and had installed her in the abbess's apartments. At the same time, however, the three Observant sisters elected Sister Sophia Dobbers at St. Aegidius. The bishop's commissioners hastily confirmed Sophia, brought her to the convent, and installed her on Sunday. Now another hand, friendly to the reform, writes,

Then on Monday and Tuesday the commissioners and the mayor came and requested the sisters to leave. This was on Thursday

[June 12th]. So on that day they left. . . . Item: sixteen sisters departed of their own will on that day and were each given ten gulden. [Later they would receive a pension of twenty gulden annually as payment for the dowries they had brought to the convent.][44]

A few of the old sisters later returned. The chronicle goes on to recount with evident satisfaction how Abbess Sophia built a new refectory, a dormitory, and a cloister wall, remaining abbess of Überwasser until her death in 1509.

The most significant differences between the successful conversion of Überwasser to an Observant house—albeit after repeated attempts—and the less effective efforts at Sonnenberg and Rijnsberg were the imposition of an Observant abbess and the combined authority represented by the city council, the local nobility, and the cathedral chapter under the leadership of a forceful reforming bishop. Against such odds women who were unwilling to live under the Observance had no choice but to move to another cloister. The choice of transfer with a pension was, however, open to them.

Freiburg

Johannes Meyer describes how at Freiburg, where three cloisters were reformed in 1465, the sisters' resistance was worn down by talking at them. In his *Book of the Reform of the Dominican Order* Meyer relates how—one after another—first he, then a local nobleman, then three city officials talked to the women for days on end "until the sisters began to make progress." Referring to himself in the third person, Meyer writes that he (the reformer)

> told the sisters what God gave him to say, imploring them and exhorting them as much as he could. And, after he had said all he could on behalf of God and the order, the wise Lord Thüring von Hallweil, Landvogt [the duke's governor] and marshal, spoke most reasonably in the name of his most gracious Lord, Duke Sigismund of Austria. After that the city of Freiburg spoke through three eloquent intelligent men. And although the sisters at first were all unwilling and in no way wanted to be enclosed and reformed nor

to accept any sisters from cloisters of the Observance, the good father persevered with the help of God and exhorted the gentlemen also to persevere whenever he saw any wavering. Thus from day to day the sisters began to relent and to submit themselves to the spiritual life.[45]

Meyer's method of exhortation and persuasion was not altogether successful, since only five of the ten sisters at the Magdalen cloister accepted the reform; the other five "ran away secretly at night by means of the stream that flowed through the cloister." Meyer calls them "foolish, ignorant" women.[46] But at the other two Freiburg cloisters, Adelhausen and St. Agnes, the women opted to try the Observance. The transition was not without problems, however, for three years after the reform of Adelhausen, Meyer writes of only mixed success so far. He still had hopes for a good outcome.

> But note, the sisters were given a year to try it. And those who did not wish to remain could transfer to another cloister. But the prioress died before the year was up and a sister from Unterlinden was made prioress and many sisters left for other cloisters that are not reformed. And so a different sister, from [the cloister of] St. Katharina at Colmar, was made prioress, and thus the beginning was more gradual. But it is to be hoped that Adelhausen will bear great fruit.[47]

Johannes Busch, in contrast, used more of a carrot-and-stick method to effect reform. He typically assembled all the sisters in the refectory, read out Cusa's reform decree, and promised the Jubilee indulgence for compliance but excommunication for disobedience. This procedure was the same for both men's and women's houses.[48] Brigitte Degler-Spengler reports that during the "reform years" there was a great deal of shifting between cloisters "and not only to cloisters of the same order."[49] Often most or all of the old sisters departed, leaving only the reform sisters in charge. At Villingen, for example, before the arrival of Ursula Haider's party of reform sisters, the Bicken cloister had just six nuns. Of these, the chronicle says, five left and only one elected to stay.[50]

In some cases those who left later decided to return. At Gertrudenberg in 1475, two young sisters eagerly welcomed the reformers, though five departed. The five, however, found life outside the cloister no longer to their liking and elected to return.[51] Similarly, at Kirchheim four sisters elected to leave, with three of them returning. This was, however, not a happy situation because Magdalena Kremer's chronicle reports that they continued to resist the reform. Unwilling to accept the rules on enclosure, one sister simply climbed over the wall, complaining that she "had to take care of her business and could no longer send messages outside."[52] In the most drastic cases of resistance, such as at Derneburg in 1442, the nuns who refused the reform were packed onto wagons and transported to other cloisters against their will.[53]

At Söflingen, the sisters who refused to accept the Observance were forcibly removed from the cloister by the city of Ulm's troops and given two weeks to think the matter over. Eight of thirty-six women, including five novices, elected to return. No sister was prevented from returning and those who did were allowed to live there under the reform with special dispensations, such as the right to receive visits from friends.[54] The others, however, remained outside the cloister where they carried on a three-year legal battle for reinstatement, seeking help from the pope, the emperor, secular princes, and the cities. In lawsuits heard in Strasbourg and Rome, a monetary settlement at last was reached in 1486, amounting to a hefty sum of 5,300 gulden. Although the women did not regain control of their cloister, those sisters who elected to transfer to other houses were granted the right to take their dowries and personal property with them.[55]

Wienhausen

At Wienhausen, "recalcitrant" sisters were also transported to other houses. Here again we have two differing accounts of the circumstances surrounding the forced expulsions: one by reformer Johannes Busch and another by a sister at Wienhausen who was critical of the proceedings. Busch relates how in 1469 he went with three prelates and Duke Otto of Lüneburg and Braunschweig to institute the reform of Wienhausen. Duke Otto summarily gathered Abbess Katharina von Hoya and all the sisters in the refectory and announced to them, "The Lord [bishop] of Hildesheim and I desire that you should accept the reform; this shall be carried out. Those of you who wish to be reformed, go to the right side of the refectory, and those who do not wish it to the left." Busch indicates that the sisters defied the order and, he reports, "immediately all the nuns went to the left."[56]

The Wienhausen chronicle gives a more nuanced version.[57] Rather than the women's disobedience, which Busch stresses, the writer emphasizes their loyalty to the abbess. She states that it was not out of rebellion that the nuns stood with her but out of solidarity. Thus the chronicler relates,

> So that one could see which [sisters] wished to comply and which would show themselves to be disobedient, they ordered that these should stand on one side and those on the other side in two groups. Then they saw that all went to stand by the abbess, not out of rebellion, as one might think, but to show their obedience to their abbess from whom they did not want to be parted living or dead, except for one who went to the other side. But, as soon as she saw that her sisters had joined the abbess, she went over to that side.

The chronicler goes on to recount in disparaging language how the duke "slyly" separated the abbess from the sisters, "locked up" those who were officers in a separate house, and interrogated the abbess again by herself, "angrily" taking away her keys and deposing her from office. Then he put her and the cellaress in a wagon and sent them away without the sisters' knowledge to Derneburg. Finally, he "lured" the officers out and sent them off to different cloisters.[58]

One wonders what the duke feared from these women. But it should be remembered that Duke Wilhelm had gotten into a melee with the nuns at Mariensee. There Busch relates a comical but violent scene in which the duke and several women fell in a pile on the ground and the duke had to fight his way out of the tangle. Busch tells how the duke first seized an obstinate nun and tried to draw her to the carriage:

> [But] she fell back flat on the ground, the duke on the top of her, and the other nuns on the top of the duke, each pushing the other onto him, so that the duke could not raise himself from off her, especially as his arms were crushed beneath her scapular. . . . At length he got one arm away from her, and with it pushed off the nuns who were lying upon him, hitting them and drawing blood from their arms.

In this rather unseemly encounter, the impetuous duke seems to have come out better than the women. Indeed, Busch remarks, "he was a man and the nuns were like children, without strength."[59] Against such choleric secular rulers, women had little recourse, unless they could call upon more powerful family allies.

After Abbess von Hoya was transported to another cloister and a new reform abbess and officers from Derneburg were brought in, the reform met with little further resistance. The chronicler recounts bitterly how the sisters had to turn in their cash, tableware, cooking utensils, and other valuables, which the reform abbess from Derneburg sold off "in a thievish manner" and "to the great detriment of the cloister." The women had to bring out their "golden chain, set with jewels and pearls from which hung pictures of several saints." The Bursfeld reformers had objected to excess splendor and possession of private devotional art that should have been held in common. The Wienhausen chronicler rejects this, lamenting that "the paintings of the saints and their decorations were looked down on and many good practices and traditions were abolished and declared to be foolery, with the result that many a previously peaceful soul was cast into sadness and anxiety."[60]

Busch, on the other hand, complains that the women at Wienhausen had misunderstood the meaning of the common life. They thought that they were observing the rule of poverty because they kept their purses with their private money in a common chest to which one sister had the key. When one wanted to buy something, "she went to the keeper of the key and asked her to open the chest. And she always agreed, permitting her to take as much as she wanted of her money, for it was her property." Although they ate in a common refectory, Busch objects, they provided their own food: "One had much and lived well and another sitting beside her had less and was poor."[61] This was not the common life as Busch understood it. The Wienhausen chronicle sees the situation from a different perspective, however, saying that "before the reform each one provided her own [food] herself, whatever she was entitled to for her needs, so that the cloister's assets might be preserved in a good state and might multiply."[62]

The chronicler is highly critical of Duke Otto and the reformers, particularly the abbess of Derneburg, who was placed in charge of the cloister. But the chronicler has nothing but praise for Susanna Potstock, the commoner who was brought in with the Observant party to take over as reform prioress at Wienhausen. The writer calls her a "person of humility and many virtues," and concedes in a fair-minded way that "this Susanna carried out her office faithfully, industriously, and fairly, dealing with her nuns like a mother with her daughters [and] helping them in spiritual and material matters."[63] Later chosen as abbess, Susanna remained for thirty-two years and died in 1501 while engaged in introducing the reform at the cloister of Medingen.

St. Katharina, Nuremberg

Another cloister from which there are two differing accounts, one by a male reformer and another by one of the sisters, is the Dominican cloister of St. Katharina in Nuremberg. This convent was discussed briefly in Chapter 3. In the annals of the Dominican reform, the men's convent at Nuremberg was the second in the German provinces to become Observant after Conrad of Prussia had established his first house at Colmar in 1389. An attempt was made at this very early stage to reform the women's house as well. But this was before Conrad had founded the first Observant women's convent at Schönensteinbach. Moreover, it was undertaken by men alone, without Observant women to institute it and was a dismal failure.

Johannes Meyer recounts the women's resistance and the violent scene in his *Book of the Reform*. Conrad had obtained a mandate from the pope for the reform and enclosure of the women's cloister. In Meyer's account, it is the women who do the shoving when the prior and city councilmen tell them what the pope has ordered.

> The prior charged the sisters, earnestly and with virtuous humility, to obey and admonished them to be enclosed. When the sisters heard this, they resisted and, with very offensive behavior and unladylike manners and gestures rebelled against submission to the pope and godly obedience. Then the prior ordered that they should restrain such openly disobedient sisters and hobble their feet; and he ordered one brother to lift up the foot of one sister. Then she said, "I will not be bound by anyone but this citizen, my cousin." So the burgher went and started to do as she had said and knelt at her feet. And she gave him a wicked shove with her foot,

hitting the worthy man so furiously that he fell over backwards on to the ground. And the storm of anger was so great that the prior, with his brothers and the city councilmen, had to leave, for his admonition was making no headway.[64]

Meanwhile, the sisters took council with "wise seculars and learned priests" who advised them that they should not allow the papal bull to be read to them. For if they did not hear it, they could not be held to it or placed under the ban. The sisters therefore refused to admit the reformers again. Nevertheless, the Observants managed to sneak into the cloister while workmen were leaving it. The sisters tried to drive them out by swinging a large crucifix and screaming so loudly that they could not hear the bull being read out. The brothers responded by drawing forth sacks of flour which they threw in the women's faces so that they could not see. As a result of the melee, Master General Raymond of Capua decided only to enclose the house but not to force the women to adopt a stricter way of life against their will.[65]

Thirty-two years later, in 1428, a second attempt was undertaken, this time with the aid of ten women Observants from Schönensteinbach and with a different outcome. The second effort was initiated when the movement had been well established and after Schönensteinbach had begun to achieve its famous reputation. Though still in the early days of the Dominican Observance, four women's houses had already been reformed and the Observance at the Nuremberg men's house was now over thirty years old. Thus, the women at St. Katharina knew the Dominican men and also that support for the Observants within the city was growing.

Prior of the Dominican nun's house, Johannes Nider sent a letter to the prioress at Schönensteinbach, requesting a party of Observant sisters. The group that arrived in Nuremberg included the indomitable Katharina von Mühlheim, whose letter home (as well as Nider's to the sisters at Schönensteinbach) has been discussed in Chapter 3. Nider himself later included an account of the reform in book III, chapter 3 of his *Formicarius* (Ant Hill), composed in 1437. In addition to Nider's text, there are Johannes Meyer's version and another account written by one of the women—probably an Observant. Nider depicts the events as an example of the power of prayer to overcome both the women's resistance and that of their influential allies in the city council. Because the council had agreed to carry out the reform only if the women accepted it willingly, much depended on winning the consent of the sisters.[66] Nider asserts that the reform party from Schönen-steinbach was "openly" brought into the cloister. This is contradicted by Johannes Meyer's account that they entered secretly at night, indeed even before the divided city council had finished debating the issue.[67] Yet Nider maintains that council members in the opposition were present and that their purpose was to hear the views of the Nuremberg sisters. Nider was extremely anxious and had asked in his sermon on that day for prayers for an outcome that would be pleasing to God.[68] To everyone's amazement, including Nider's, the women agreed.

The other account, written soon after the reform by one of the sisters, mentions nothing about disagreement—internal or external. It is, however, more accurate about the chronology of events, giving exact dates of the one-week delay, during which the reform party was not permitted to enter the cloister. In the woman's account, the focus is strongly on the legality of the Observant take-over: the sisters' vote, the transfer of their possessions to the common chest, and the disposition of their funds. As the writer indicates, not all the sisters agreed to this: "Here one will find written how the Observance was begun and how many of the sisters from before the Observance remained in the cloister, how many of them left, what [posses-sions] they turned over, what of their property was sold and for what amount, and how the money was invested again." The author records that thirty-five sisters resided at St. Katharina before the arrival of the ten reformers. She also recounts, "[T]he sisters agreed to the holy Observance except for eight sisters who said that it would be too difficult for them." Five sisters transferred to Engelthal and three to Frauenaurach. Yet, as men-tioned above, this writer stated that "all the sisters of this convent were present and they all gave their votes to the above named Johannes Nider to choose a prioress."[69]

We are not privy to the discussion that preceded the sisters agreeing to the reform, since all of the accounts were written by Observants and none reported the details of the exchange. Nider's narrative stresses the power of prayer and Meyer's the persuasiveness of Nider and Master General Texer-ius. The sister's report, on the other hand, focuses on the procedural pro-priety of the take-over by constructing a record of the actions taken and accounting for the funds collected. What is tantalizingly missing from all the accounts is a description of the interactions between the reformers from

Schönensteinbach and the sisters who remained or transferred. Letters do survive, however, written later by reform prioress at Nuremberg, Kunigunda Haller (1468–97). This correspondence, in which Haller advises the sisters at St. Gall, as was seen in Chapter 3, gives an impression of effective leadership and of a woman as committed to Observant ideals as the male reformers. Still, without the city council's request, the widow Schreiber's intention to take her fortune to Alsace, and Nider's intercession (including his eight-point letter soliciting a reform party), the Schönensteinbach sisters would not have taken over at St. Katharina. But they did so, whether reluctantly or not, in a cooperative effort with male activists.

Klingental

A final example of women's successful resistance to the reform—in fact, the most notorious and large-scale failure of the Observants—was at Klingental, Basel's most elite and wealthiest cloister. The struggle has been admirably described by Renée Weis-Müller in her insightful study of the case. Already in 1423, when the women's cloister of St. Maria Magdalena an den Steinen in Basel had been reformed, the sisters at Klingental took evasive action to prevent the Observance from being carried to them. Claiming that poor oversight by the Dominicans had damaged their cloister spiritually and materially, they were able to disengage from their superiors and to place themselves under the jurisdiction of the bishop of Constance.[70] In spite of this, the Dominicans undertook to reform them in 1480, with the aim of regaining control of the wealthy cloister. Even if the campaign may have begun ideologically, Rudolf Wackernagel suggests that any higher aims were soon replaced by those of "pure power and dominance."[71]

Lined up on opposing sides and with convent women at the center of the conflict was an array of constituencies, including two of the wealthiest and most prominent rival clans in Basel. On the one side, opposing the reform, was the family of former Prioress Clara zu Rhein, which included some of the cloister's leading benefactors. On the other side were the von Eptingens, who had donated more than 8,000 gulden to the cloister. Supporters of the reform, besides the Dominicans and Carthusians, included the town council and the city confederacies of Bern, Obwalden, and Nidwalden. Arrayed against it were the secular clergy; the bishop of Basel, the Augustinians; the confederacies of Zürich, Lucern, and Schwyz; the rural aristocracy; and, eventually, Archduke Sigismund of Austria.[72] The city council itself, although in favor of the Observants, was subdivided into factions that wanted only moderate reform and those that opposed any compromises.

Into this tinderbox were sent thirteen Observant sisters from Engelport in Guebwiller. When the Dominican officials read out the reform bull, the unwilling sisters drowned them out with shouting and threatened the reformers. The city bailifs then responded by locking the recalcitrant women into their cells. Subsequently, thirty-nine of the forty-one Klingental sisters left the cloister rather than be reformed. Under threat of excommunication (for leaving without permission), nine of them eventually returned.[73] Now on the outside, the evicted Klingental women waged intensive financial warfare against the reform party. Having taken one of the convent's seals with them (besides their personal fortunes), the old Klingental sisters proceeded to collect the cloister's rents and draw out its funds. When the reformers were required to pay pensions and settlements to those who had left, there was no money and the reformers were forced to mortgage the cloister's assets at a fraction of their value to raise the cash. Soon tenants began to refuse to pay rents to either group until the conflict was resolved.[74] Besides cashiering the cloister's assets, the evicted sisters effectively mustered the support of powerful aristocratic friends, who blockaded the roads to Basel. Count Oswald von Thierstein, Archduke Sigismund's regional administrator, imposed an embargo on Basel's grain trade and confiscated rents and produce from lands in Alsace owned by Basel citizens.[75] After two years, the cloister stood on the edge of total financial ruin. Fearing the impact on the city of such an enormous fiscal collapse and the effects of the grain embargo, the mayor and town council changed allegiance and abandoned support for the reform party.

Although the financial debacle had brought the Observant reformers to their knees, the death blow was dealt by a bizarre chain of events in which the visiting archbishop of Granea, Andrea Zamometić, during his stay in Basel issued a call for a general church council directed against Pope Sixtus IV. Because Zamometić happened to have a distant connection to Stephan Irmi, the prior of the Basel male Dominican convent, who had spearheaded the reform effort, Pope Sixtus IV reversed his support for the reform of

Klingental and ruled in favor of the evicted sisters. He ordered the party of Observants to return home to Engelport and gave the cloister back to the old Klingental sisters with all their rights and possessions. Stephan Irmi was removed as prior and the Dominican men's house forced to pay enormous damages of 11,000 gulden.[76]

Now thoroughly disgusted, both groups of women subsequently dissociated themselves from the Dominicans. The old Klingental sisters changed their order and habit, officially joining the Augustinians. The reforming sisters, embittered over what they considered a betrayal by their Dominican overseers, wandered from cloister to cloister for years before finding a home at an Observant house of the Augustinian order.[77] The prioress of their original home convent of Engelport, Elsbeth Dürner, was also deposed. In August of 1482 she wrote angrily to a friend, "[H]ow the convent and I have been disloyally slandered with lies and interfered with in respect to the prelates of the holy church and the master of our order, by which means they try to make inroads and violently exercise their dominance over us. In such a manner are we treated by the men at Basel."[78]

The original sisters at Klingental who had successfully opposed the Observant movement felt that their form of piety was in no way inferior. Indeed, until the reform sisters arrived, new members of their community had always adopted the traditional practices. To them, the thirteen reformers from Alsace were upstart intruders who had no right to change the established ways. To the women of the reform, on the other hand, Observantism constituted a purer piety.

The victory here for the opponents of the Observance illustrates the importance of financial considerations as a factor in the reform of women's cloisters. The impact of the threatened financial collapse of Klingental on the city of Basel underscores the significant role women's houses played in the economic life of cities. Likewise, the convent sisters' networks of allies and the pressure they could bring to bear make clear the women's political influence even from inside the cloister walls. The complex interaction of economic, political, and religious forces involved in reform efforts meant that the outcome often depended on which group—the Observants or their opponents—could mobilize the more powerful secular and clerical forces. Where women resorted to delaying tactics, law suits, political influence, or economic pressure to slow the process or make it costly to secular constituencies, they were able to avert reform or retain some of their assets.

Resistance to Reform in Men's Convents

Lest it appear that men did not oppose the reform as violently or more successfully than women, a brief look at the case of the men's Dominican house in Basel is useful. This reform in 1429 was possibly the most contentious and hard-fought effort of all and probably the reason Klingental had undertaken to separate from the order. Johannes Meyer, himself later a resident of this house, gives a partisan account in chapters 23 and 24 of his *Book of the Reform of the Dominican Order*.[79] Meyer was one of the most committed hard-liners among the early Observants, especially on the issue of poverty. As he tells it, there were many citizens of Basel who urged the reform of the men's house after the women's cloister of St. Maria Magdalena an den Steinen had become Observant in 1423, but there were also many citizens against it. Few of the convent's inhabitants themselves were willing. Therefore the Basel city council wrote to Master General of the order, Bartholomeus Texerius, requesting him to use his authority to institute the reform. When Texerius, along with the German provincial and the city council, tried to introduce the reform by bringing in four brothers from the Observant house in Nuremberg, the resident friars fought against them with "devilish violence and hellish power." Meyer relates bitterly how discord "in the entire city" forced the Obervants to withdraw.

> [A]lso the sisters of the cloister of Klingental and their lay friends, the powerful and the common, were so at odds and hateful that great divisiveness and discord affected the entire city of Basel, such that the master of the order [Texerius] had to leave and the city council withdrew its support. The brothers who had been sent from Nuremberg had to withdraw. And the nastiness and disobedience of the brothers and sisters was so great that several books could be written about it.

Texerius was driven out of the city by an armed force of noblemen and commoners and forced to take refuge in Bern. After excommunicating the rebels, Texerius is reputed by Meyer to have declared, "I will have a convent that keeps the rule of the order in a spiritual way, or die!"[80]

Concerned to see the ban lifted, Basel citizens sent a number of conciliatory messages. Finally, a delegation of citizens along with the four brothers who had led the fight against the reform traveled to Bern to beg forgiveness and the removal of the ban. Describing the reconciliation, Meyer writes: "When the four brothers lay prostrate before the master [Texerius] and he, intending to absolve them from the ban, had started to speak the words of absolution, he began to recall what he had suffered in this matter and his heart was so moved that he proceeded to weep so profusely that he was unable to speak and another father had to absolve the brothers in his place."[81] Yet not all went smoothly thereafter when the exiled reformers from Nuremberg returned to institute the Observance. Even though the rebels were encouraged to stay and were given special privileges allowing them to eat meat, to sleep on regular bedding, and the like, nearly all of them left, one after the other, for unreformed houses. The convent, nevertheless, recovered and Basel went on to become a leading center of the Observance, although it did not succeed in reforming Klingental despite three attempts.

Perhaps the Klingental women were more effective in averting reform because the wealth and status of their house far exceeded that of any other cloister in the city. The approaching financial collapse of such a major institution was a matter grave enough to outweigh the desire for religious change and would have averted the reform even without the clerical intrigues and internal reverses that undermined the position of the Observants. Above all, these violent controversies reveal the strong public engagement in issues involving its convents and the active participation of the citizenry at Basel in matters of reform even before the more radical Reformation of the sixteenth century.

Excursus: The Problematic Issue of Enclosure

Besides economic factors, the most contested element in the Observants' program was clearly the question of enclosure. For reasons both religious and non-religious, women resented and resisted this infringement of their freedom. At the sister-house in Emmerich, for example, Sister Nese in gheen Nijelant outspokenly opposed it on religious grounds because, as the sister-book narrator attests, "it seemed to her that there was more humility and holiness in a life of simple poverty than if one had every need satisfied and lived under the coersion of the rule."[82] At the cloister of Herzebrock, Observant writer Anna Roede tells in her chronicle of Sister Alheit Vollen-spit's anxiety over the idea of being enclosed.

> At first this same sister Alheit could not well accept that she should be enclosed. At last she was won over by good exhortations. So she desired from the prior at Osterberg that he and the convent would give [us] the painting of "Our Lady of Suffering" that we now have in our choir—for it belonged to him. And she wanted to have it here and to go before it daily and lament her sufferings. In this manner she agreed to be enclosed. So [the picture] was given.[83]

In other cases, however, opposition was less amenable to persuasion. At the Clarissan cloister of Brixen, Maria von Wolkenstein wrote to her brother Leo: "My dearest, faithful Brother, we are letting you know that we do not want to stay in this cloister with all the bad things happening. Therefore, I call on you as a true brother to help me transfer to another cloister. And God knows that we want to keep the rule. But the additions and so many amendments are more than the entire rule." In another letter Maria complains that she can no longer have visitors or send notes in and out easily: "They have closed up all the holes that Ulrich used."[84] After the Dominican convent of St. Agnes in Strasbourg was enclosed, notes were passed in and out through "secret underground openings." Some of the sisters sneaked outside and, together with their friends and supporters, tried to frighten the enclosed Observant sisters by placing bundles of wood and kindling under the dormitory.[85]

Despite reformist propaganda, enclosure was in most cases not an older practice that was being reinstated but a new one. Although claustration had been mandated in the rule for nuns *(Regula ad moniales)* composed by Caesarius of Arles (501–573), it was not part of either the Benedictine or the Augustinian rule.[86] Except for a few orders, such as the Cistercians and the Poor Clares, enclosure was not widely practiced before 1298 when Pope Boniface VIII (1294–1303) decreed in the bull *Periculoso* that all nuns who had taken solemn vows and were living under an accepted rule were to be perpetually cloistered. Even after *Periculoso,* most nuns remained unenclosed, opting to wait and see if the decrees would be reversed or actually enforced.[87]

Perhaps stronger than the church's pressure on women was that of the secular population over social problems arising from open cloisters. In Basel so many complaints were heard about nuns being on the streets at night that city bailiffs were finally ordered to arrest them.[88] It was, thus, not the church hierarchy alone but in many cases public demand and political pressure that progressively mandated enclosure as necessary to a "safe and honorable" alternative to marriage. Here the interests of the patrician classes were most involved. In Venice, where preachers in the early sixteenth century repeatedly compared convents to public brothels, clausura laws were finally introduced, transforming cloisters into what Jutta Sperling provocatively has called "safe-deposits of patrician blood and bodies that the state depended upon for the reproduction of its aristocracy."[89] Yet beyond the social imperative of protecting the purity and moral reputation of the wealthy classes, a fiscal problem was created when women in religious establishments did not take solemn vows and could leave their communities at any time to make claims on family inheritances.[90] Accordingly, for the affluent lay public, enclosure was often an economic issue as well as a moral and social one.

From a religious point of view, however, the idea of withdrawal from the world and of living in seclusion had roots that went back to the earliest monastic communities and the desert hermits. Accordingly, the first women's convents were founded away from towns where living removed from the world was practiced as part of the nun's vocation.[91] Schönensteinbach itself was established in an abandoned convent in a forest. Yet, as Thomas Lentes explains, in referring to the enclosure ceremony at its founding: the primary aim was not really outward but inward enclosure, the creation of an inner space for meditation:

> The establishing of enclosure, the separation from the world, is not understood—in the way that is often asserted—as a prison for regimented women, but as the creation of a visual inner space for meditation on the passion ['memoria passionis']. . . . Ultimately, the aim is not the outward but the inward enclosure of the nuns

. . . the turning of the eyes away from the world and fixing the gaze on the crucified one as an essential step in the reform of the inner person.[92]

Withdrawal from the world did not apply only to women but was proposed as an ideal for Observant men as well. Accordingly, Dominican Master General Raymond of Capua's directives stress the primacy of solitude and meditation.[93] After the men's convent at Basel was reformed, for example, a wall was erected and the Observant brothers were permitted to leave their house no more than once a week. Instead of traveling about, they were expected to devote themselves to prayer, study, and meditation.[94] This constituted a significant departure from the Dominican order's traditional emphasis on preaching and a shift of focus toward a form of interiorized piety like that practiced by the New Devout who themselves discouraged public preaching and the "vanity" it encouraged.[95] Similarly, the reform statutes for Observant Franciscans of Saxony, issued in 1467, permitted the brothers to preach, but they were admonished to return to the cloister immediately afterward.[96] Worrying that pastoral care would interfere with meditation and devotions, Nicholas von Cusa advocated that it should be delegated to the parish priests.[97] The degree of sentiment on this issue as a reform measure is registered in the anonymous tract *Reformatio Sigismundi,* which circulated at the Council of Basel and aggressively demanded that strict enclosure be instituted for men and "no monk should be seen on the streets at all."[98]

But what did claustration mean for women and how was it practiced? Like other measures, there were degrees of enclosure. Nicholas von Cusa's reform statutes for Rijnsburg state, for example, that sisters might leave the cloister with the vicar of Utrecht's permission.[99] On a day-to-day basis, however, nuns only had contact with outsiders through the "speaking window," the "rotating window" (through which things were passed in and out), and the "confession window." The only persons allowed to enter Observant cloisters were the confessor and the provost. The confessor lived in a house of his own outside the cloistered area but heard confessions and administered communion through a window between the nuns' choir and the outer church—sometimes called the "little Jesus window."[100] In reformed convents, a separate altar was often built for the nuns in their own choir where they sang the monastic hours by themselves, as the Wienhausen chronicle records.[101] Hamburger quotes Anna von Buchwald at Preetz, explaining how she made a private choir for the sisters because the clerics and the laity were "in the way" during communion.

> All our predecessors took communion at the high altar, on account of which we were often obstructed by clerics and the laity, who were always standing about there. Because of this I had one altar enclosed in our choir . . . there we henceforth undertook to take communion, and I had the doors to the choir closed. . . . I had the ironwork between the choir and the sanctuary made.[102]

Likewise a sister at Ebstorf writes (c. 1490), "In the third year of the reform, the altar in the choir was taken down and a small chapel was built with a communion window. Before this they [the sisters] had gone to the altar."[103]

Perhaps it is not surprising that Observant women wrote a good deal about enclosure. Magdalena Kremer indicates, for example, that claustration was often difficult and required fortitude. In her chronicle of the reform of Kirchheim (c. 1490), she writes a short, sermon-like commentary on the subject:

> [W]e read that Josephus wrote of St. Mary Magdalene that from the day that she was converted, she never looked at any man again. And that is to be believed, because she left the world completely and fled from all men into the wilderness. . . . After she suffered temptation and affliction she was driven by the spirit of God into the inner desert where God fed her by his angels for more than thirty years. And I have written this as an illustration that we should not become complacent, but be alert and always cautious and stout hearted with great fortitude, not only each one for herself, but also each to the other.[104]

Other accounts from sixteenth-century Observant women, long accustomed to living enclosed and ideologically opposed to the Lutherans who tried to open their cloisters, describe how they resisted the attempts. Sister Eva Neyler's (d. 1575) first-person narrative recounting efforts to convert the Dominican sisters of Pforzheim to the new faith reports with alarm how the divider between the outer church and the nuns' choir was torn out "so that you could see all the way to the dormitory." Without the grille to shield them from view, Sister Eva reports, the women responded by slinking down as far as possible in their seats during religious services so that "no one could see us, except when we came in and went out, and [we] pulled our veils so low that they could see neither nose nor mouth. Thus the people crowded around that they might view us and practically stood on each other's heads." Adding to this circus atmosphere, the locks were taken off of their doors, the sisters were plagued by men entering the cloister unannounced and especially by the provost coming into their cells, offering to get them a husband, and kissing them. Sister Eva exclaims indignantly, "We would scarcely have been sure of our honor if we had not protected each other." She relates the women's collective strategy for heading off the provost, how they clustered around whenever he spoke to any sister alone. Confused, the provost complained that he "could not speak a word to any of them without two or three others showing up. So we said it was our custom."[105] After the twenty-three choir nuns were finally permitted to leave Pforzheim in 1564 and moved to the unreformed cloister of Kirchberg in Württemberg, they reinstated enclosure, even though Kirchberg was an open convent. In her account of their reform of Kirchheim, Sister Eva reports matter-of-factly how the old residents all left their house rather than be enclosed:

> [T]he cloister was daily overrun with secular people, which was very difficult for us and we did not want to suffer it for the long term, for it was because of this that we had left Pforzheim, that we might again keep the Observance as we are committed to. But the [seven] Kirchberg women did not want to accept it, did not want to be enclosed, nor to lose their friends and serving maids or to take on our Observance which was intolerable to them. We would have liked to keep them, but they did not want to stay and went out to their friends in the world.[106]

Similarly, Abbess Caritas Pirckheimer (d. 1532) and the Poor Clares of Nuremberg fought every attempt of the city council to open their cloister, even the uncovering of a window that would allow visitors to see the sisters when they conversed.[107] These women, ideologically committed to seclusion and used to the autonomy they enjoyed within it, felt safe within their cloister but anxious about contact with the outside world. Indeed, in some narratives by Observant women in the fifteenth century, claustration is employed as a means of freeing themselves from outside interference and control. Some used it, as did Prioress Barbara Bernheimer at Kirchheim, to fend off the machinations of an intrusive overlord; they refused the tyrannical duke or his representatives into the cloister to negotiate with them by saying it was against the sisters' regulations.[108]

The most unusual instance, however, is the case of women self-imposing enclosure at the cloister of St. Katharina at St. Gall. Here, as previously noted, a small group of sisters in the house, had adopted the common life under the influence of the religiously charismatic Angela Varnbühler. Later, when Angela was elected prioress, she began a correspondence, asking for advice on how to institute the Observance with Kunigunda Haller, prioress at Nuremberg, whose letters were copied into the sister-book. After several years under their own self-fashioned form of the Observance, the sisters decided to enclose themselves, as Prioress Varnbühler asserts in the convent chronicle, "We enclosed our cloister with the unanimous will of the sisters' council (Ratschwestern) and of the entire convent." Later the women also decided to cover the "speaking window." This Prioress Varnbühler explains, saying, "not being seen is not part of the rule of the Order, but it is a heavenly grace":

> We covered our conversation window with [perforated] tin by unanimous decision of the senior sisters and of the whole convent on the Saturday before the feast day of St. Thomas Aquinas, to the praise of Almighty God. And separated ourselves from the view of our friends out of love for our heavenly bridegroom, that we might become more focused on the holy, worthy sacraments and might better keep the three essential vows, which we are pledged to observe. May God in heaven strengthen us in His praise and increase His grace and reward with good—as He Himself is good—all those who helped and advised us. Oh, inwardness, what a help thou art to spirituality.[109]

The measure was hotly disputed by the nuns' families and by the citizens of St. Gall, who did not take kindly to being shut out by the sisters. But the nuns held to their decision. When Prioress Kunigunda Haller received word of it, she wrote from Nuremberg:

> I learned of the closing and covering of your window. Oh, how it lifted my heart and I rejoiced in the immeasurable goodness of God, who in such a fatherly way is helping you to overcome. From day to day you will experience the great grace and succor of God that will come to you because of this. From what manifold false images, sins and temptations you will be preserved. This you will experience often with God's help. It is scarcely possible that a spiritual person may escape untroubled from looking at the world. A well-guarded eye makes a spirit turned inward.[110]

The convent of St. Katharina possessed six German copies of Thomas à Kempis's *Imitation of Christ,* one of which had been given to them by Kunigunda Haller.[111] Whether or not Haller's advice had anything to do with Kempis's book cannot be determined, but its first chapter, "On the Imitation of Christ and Contempt for all the World's Vanites," ends with a similar admonition: "Think often of that wise word: 'The eye is not satisfied with seeing nor the ear filled with hearing.' Be zealous therefore to separate your heart from the love of things which are seen, and to turn it to the things which are not seen."[112] In this unusual instance, enclosure has changed its orientation. Rather than being shut in, the women at St. Gall voted to shut the world out, much to the consternation of the town. The reversal—self-enclosure—might be explained, beyond its religiously ascetic significance, as a kind of taking control and limiting influence from the outside.

Caroline Bynum has stated that if we are to know "which aspects of reality [medieval people] were rejecting and which they were affirming when they 'renounced the world,' where they felt themselves able to make choices, and what they felt to be the important differences in the roles open to them or imposed upon them, we must find ways of answering these questions from the works they actually wrote."[113] Perhaps a look here at another text by an Observant woman will help to explain what was being rejected and affirmed in renouncing the world. At least one effect of enclosure was the development of a rich life of the imagination which generated literary works undertaking imaginary pilgrimages and journeys "into the interior"of the individual. One such work is an exercise composed by Margareta Ursula von Masmünster (d. 1447/48), prioress at the Penitents' cloister St. Maria Magdalena an den Steinen in Basel and one of the reformers who came there from Unterlinden. In a work called "The Spiritual Sea Voyage," she invites the sisters to go with her on an imaginary voyage that will take nine weeks and end at Easter. This spiritual journey is designed to free the participants from "the raging sea of old bad habits" and disorderly life.[114] The text states that after vespers on Septuagesima Sunday the group of those who want to make the trip will set out together. But before they "leave," the sisters are instructed to "say farewell to their friends." During the "holy time" they are not to go to the visiting window.[115] And prior to undertaking the inward pilgrmage, the participants must make an accounting, both outwardly and inwardly, by making their confession and receiving communion before the group is to "depart."

Each week of the voyage the travelers will focus on a particular aspect of Christ's passion, observing complete silence until Easter Wednesday. As long as they are on the trip, they must practice humility, patience, love, and obedience among one another. They are to continue to carry out their offices with exceptional integrity and be punctual in all things. With special prayers and flagellations (five blows), they are to immerse themselves in the sufferings of Christ during the Passion. On the ship they will take with them the angels, patriarchs, prophets, and "David to play the harp."[116] The work describes the symbolism of the parts of the ship (which represents the soul) and the pilgrim's equipment. Visiting imaginary churches and staying at imaginary inns, the travelers at last arrive at "the holy grave." It is an exercise reminiscent of Ursula Haider's theatrical pilgrimages to the seven churches of Rome and the Holy Land, as well as of Felix Fabri's work for women, the "Sionpilgerin" (Zion Pilgrim, 1492), which it predates. In a similarly imaginative way, the chronicle of the Bicken cloister relates several of Ursula Haider's (d. 1498) dramatic ceremonies and candelight processions that she enacted with the Poor Clares at Villingen.

Another theatrical exercise in the same manuscript, and possibly also by Margareta Ursula von Masmünster, is called "Going with Jesus into the Desert." This imaginary pilgrimage takes the participants on a visit to the desert fathers, spending a day with each hermit. Here again the participants leave the world, and live in the "wilderness" where they "flee all creatures and observe silence."[117] In a series of departures, the sisters practice virtues, resist the evil spirit, break the will, and detach themselves from worldly inclinations. By renouncing the world, they are imitating the desert hermits, purifying themselves and undertaking a journey into the interior of the soul.

The renunciation of the world in order to undertake an interior pilgrimage is a fundamentally different concept from that of enclosure to protect the chastity of the nun; yet the concepts are linked. In the iconography of the Observance, which borrows from Marian iconography, enclosure is most often depicted by the image of the enclosed garden (*hortus conclusus*) of the Old Testament Song of Songs (4.12), the Marian symbol of chastity. At the same time, however, it represents a spiritual love garden in which the dialogue between the soul and its divine spouse takes place. This scene of interior, spiritual communion is depicted in numerous devotional texts like the *Garden of Devotion,* Antwerp, 1487 (Fig. 4). It is in this garden of the soul that the believer cultivates spiritual virtues, which are symbolized as trees and plants in works such as *The King's Summa* (*Somme le Roi,* thirteenth century). Thus, a fifteenth- century illustration shows women watering trees of virtue under Christ's supervision as head gardener (Fig. 5).[118]

On another level, Observant imagery links the enclosed garden with the popular symbol of the garden of heavenly paradise, that ultimate goal toward which all humankind is striving. In medieval devotional illustrations this heavenly realm is frequently conflated with the garden of the Incarnation in images that show the Madonna and child seated within a walled enclosure—usually in company with several saints. A manuscript illustration of this type from the Dominican convent of Heilig Kreuz in Regensburg depicts the four reform sisters who came from Nuremberg to introduce the Observance (c. 1490). Here, each of the women (and the niece of the donor, a novice in a white veil) is shown kneeling in front of an enclosed garden containing the Virgin and child with Saints Catherine, Margaret, Ursula, and Apollonia (Fig. 6).[119] Here, as in other texts and illustrations of reform literature, the cloister is idealized as the earthly precursor to the garden of heavenly paradise. Thus Barbara von Benfelden writes (c. 1468/ 77) of the reform of St. Agnes's in Strasbourg, referring to the cloister as "a special herb garden" and asserting that, after it was reformed, "this convent sent out green shoots, grew, and increased in virtue and spirituality."[120]

This symbolism of interority and enclosure, representing the cloistered life, the soul, the conscience, or the chaste heart as a garden in which

Fig. 4   (above and opposite) Hoofkijn van devotien (Garden of Devotion), Antwerp, Gerhard Leeu, 1487.

Fig. 5   *Somme le Roi*. Bodleian Library, Oxford, MS 283, fol. 99v. Fifteenth century.

Fig. 6 Illustration (c. 1490) from a choir book of Cloister Heilig Kreuz, Regensburg, showing beside the donor and her niece (novice in white veil) four reforming sisters from St. Katharina, Nuremberg.

virtues and spirituality are nurtured, was taken up and cultivated by Observants on a large scale in numerous devotional allegories that reached a high point of production in the fifteenth and sixteenth centuries. Dietrich Schmidtke's definitive study of late-medieval garden allegories identifies over fifty works of this genre produced in German- and Netherlandish-speaking areas that still survive in hundreds of copies.[121] As a symbol with imagery that both appealed to women and powerfully represented the Observant ideals of interiority and withdrawal from the world, it is not surprising that some ninety percent of these manuscripts stem from the libraries and scriptoria of convents of Observant women. They are texts that incorporate the intimate phraseology of the Song of Songs, that most popular of all late-medieval books on love. Typically, they begin with quotations from the canticle, such as, "I have come to my garden" (5.1) or "A garden enclosed is my sister, my spouse" (4.12), expressions that romanticize and spiritualize withdrawal from the world. In the discourse of Observant spirituality, seen, for example, in Kunigunda Haller's letters and Angela Varnbühler's chronicle, withdrawal from the world is represented as a gift of love to the heavenly bridegroom.[122] In this unusual case, women can be seen discussing and fashioning their own form of observance.

It was, thus, under the leadership of the fervently religious Angela Varnbühler that enclosure was appropriated, self-imposed and transformed into a kind of heroic asceticism akin to the radical piety of the female spiritual athletes in the Dominican sister-books of the fourteenth century. That the St. Gall sisters knew and read these earlier women's works is indicated by the copies they possessed in their cloister library. Indeed, the Observants were not slow to see the utility of appropriating such works to the reform or to copy and circulate them. The correspondence between Prioress Varnbühler and Prioress Haller, the use of the fourteenth-century women's texts, and the creation of new ones demonstrate some of the ways in which Observants defined the discourse. After assuming power, they exercised it through text production and dissemination, even influencing what works from earlier periods would be handed down. It was, accordingly, with the authorization and encouragement to write, engendered by the momentum of the reform, that women in Observant houses produced their own histories. And it was through these networks that advice was shared and texts distributed. Thus the documents that survive are largely those generated by and constitutive of the reforms.

As in the case of the reform at St. Katharina, in Nuremberg virtually all the surviving accounts are by Observants. But while the women, who took part with men in the reform effort, use the discourse generated by the Observance, their writings often have different agendas. Meyer, a fundamentalist convinced of the rightness of the Observant cause, was chiefly interested in chronicling the progress of the reform at large. Nider, although he had written the letter asking for ten reform sisters from Schönensteinbach in order that the Nuremberg brothers should not be made "a laughingstock," stressed in his report the workings of the Holy Spirit and the miraculous conversion of the Nuremberg women rather than the contribution of the sisters from Schönensteinbach. The observant sister, on the other hand, names in her account not only the reformers but all of the rank and file sisters affected by the reform, including those who left the cloister. Compiling a narrative for the legal record of procedures and the disposition of funds, she shows a mindfulness of the implications for the cloister's privileges and monetary assets. Thus, while working in alliance with men in the reform effort, women constructing their own history often emphasized different concerns.

After becoming an enclosed house, literally a community turned inward, the St. Gall sisters began industriously reading, exchanging, and copying devotional literature and dramatically expanded their library. Not only at St. Gall and Nuremberg but also at many reformed houses, women living enclosed took advantage of the authorization to participate through their networks in the religious conversation going on not only among Observant cloisters but in the larger population as well. The result was an unparalleled burst of scribal activity in the scriptoria of women's houses of the Observance, as will be seen in the chapter to follow.

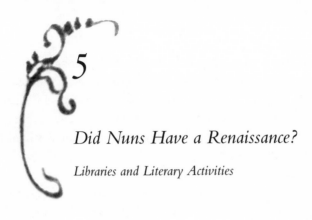

5

Did Nuns Have a Renaissance?

Libraries and Literary Activities

So let us then in the prime of our lives not be indolent or slothful, but with all vigor apply ourselves to the study of grammar until we have arrived at the knowledge of rightly reading, understanding and composing prose or verse. And let us now plant and seed the garden of our intelligence, so that we may eat the sweet fruit all the days of our lives.

—A sister at Ebstorf, c. 1490

Joan Kelly-Gadol, David Herlihy, and others have debated the provocatively phrased question: "Did women have a Renaissance?"[1] In this chapter I shall argue that in at least some Observant cloisters they did. It was not the same "rebirth" that men in the secular and religious worlds were experiencing at this time, but a contemporaneous, alternative, intense flowering of scribal, literary, and religious activity focused on the production of texts in Latin and especially the vernacular.

About the education of women in Observant cloisters a considerable amount is known, particularly at Ebstorf whose library contains a history of the house, an account of its reform,[2] as well as some essays written by female students in the fifteenth century. Earlier chapters in this study have discussed the teaching of Latin as part of the reform initiative. The Ebstorf reform account, composed in Latin c. 1490 by one of the sisters, eulogizes education and exhorts the sisters not to falter in their efforts to acquire it.

Therefore we ought to work hard for a good foundation and apply ourselves with all vigor to our lessons, so that the golden jewel of education—however modest—should not be lost in this revered place by our negligence and idleness. Rather let us make every effort that it shall increase from day to day. For if we were to lose gold or silver, the loss might be recouped, but if the foundation of learning were to be lost, it would do irreparable damage to the religious life. For whenever in cloisters the acquisition of learning goes into decline, the result most assuredly is the destruction of the religious life as well.[3]

In the first years after the Observance was instituted at Ebstorf (1464/70) under the direction of Prioress Metta von Niendorf (d. 1495), the women devoted themselves to copying new liturgical books as fast as they could. One sister recounts:

In three years the prioress arranged for the production of six large books which she also had decorated artistically, page by page, with gold letters and illuminations. For there were artists among the sisters who understood this craft. In the first year of her priorate she had three sisters—for the sake of speed—copy a lectionary. Another part, the winter section, was copied by one sister alone. Likewise, Sister N [Elisabeth von Nigendorp] transcribed two great antiphonals and also a hymnal for the prioress, also two processionals, one for the provost and the other for the prioress, all decorated with illuminations and gold.[4]

The account goes on to relate how the women labored mightily to produce for themselves two more antiphonals, two hymnals (not yet completed), two great psalters, a collectar, an evangeliar, and two lectionaries. A cloister chronicle, composed by the same sister in 1487, lists twenty-seven massive manuscripts that the women copied (breviaries, collectars, graduals, gospelbooks, psalters, antiphonals, lectionaries, hymnals) and proudly names the six sisters who accomplished this monumental work. Ending her account, the sister exclaims enthusiastically, "All of these books are as dear to us as precious pearls because of the sweet and delightful writings that they contain."[5]

What remains of the library at Ebstorf, which had its greatest growth during this period, are 51 volumes, most of them in Latin.[6] As with other libraries assembled in women's cloisters at the end of the Middle Ages, the greater part has not survived. Most were destroyed by fire (as was the great library at Adelhausen, where 300 volumes burnt up in 1410), decimated by military conflicts, or dispersed during the Protestant Reformation. Andreas Rüther and Hans-Jochen Schiewer list nearly all of the South-German Dominican women's cloister libraries as lost.[7]

Still, a handful of collections have survived, at least in part. Prominent among these is the collection that once existed at St. Nicolaus in undis (Strasbourg) which was partially rescued when author Daniel Sudermann (1550–c. 1631) purchased some of its manuscripts as the library was being broken up in 1592 after Strasbourg had become Protestant.[8] At St. Katharina (St. Gall) the late-medieval library once contained some 500 volumes, of which 105 are still extant.[9] Larger still was the collection at St. Katharina in Nuremberg which, by the end of the fifteenth century, had accumulated between 500 and 600 volumes. Almost all of its manuscripts were acquired after the cloister was reformed in 1428 and almost half of these volumes were copied by the sisters themselves.[10] Examining the records of the library's holdings before 1500, Werner Williams-Krapp found that during its first 133 years the convent of St. Katharina had acquired only 36 books. By the end of the fifteenth century, however, the sisters copied and acquired so many vernacular works that they possessed, according to Karin Schneider, "the largest collection of German language manuscripts known in the Late Middle Ages."[11]

This was not the only cloister to experience a "literature explosion" in this century. It is estimated that more than eighty percent of the manuscripts that made up the libraries of Observant cloisters were produced or acquired in the period after the reform.[12] Although only ten percent of men's and women's religious houses belonged to the Observance, nearly ninety percent of German manuscripts owned by convents come from this very small number of reformed women's houses.[13] It is clear from several accounts that one of the things reform sisters usually brought with them was books for copying. At Medingen, for example, four Observant sisters arrived in 1467 from Pforzheim, carrying with them ten manuscripts and specific instructions that the German non-liturgical books were to be returned to Pforzheim upon the death of the reformers.[14] To exchange works for copying, Observant women's cloisters organized an extensive interlibrary loan system and began industriously expanding their collections in order to satisfy an increasing demand for devotional literature in the vernacular. The circulation of these texts suggests that Observant convents were often in closer contact with Observant houses of other orders than they were with non-reformed convents of their own order.[15]

Reading, both communal and individual, was an important part of the daily regimen of Observant cloisters. The chronicle of cloister Medingen related that during meals one of the youngest nuns read aloud from the rule, from the lives of the saints, or other text.[16] According to the reform statutes for St. Katharina in Nuremberg, reading was done in the work room as well as at evening meals and included some Latin texts.[17] A list of what the women heard still survives in a catalogue containing an impressive 370 table readings made by a sister at St. Katharina between 1455 and 1499.[18]

In his "Book of Offices" for Dominican sisters, Johannes Meyer provides a plan for the education of novices.[19] Here Meyer recommends that each prioress should assign "pious, God-fearing sisters educated in the liberal arts" to instruct the young sisters in "the art of 'grammatticka'." Besides the study of Latin, so that they can understand the liturgy, Meyer urges that the novices devote themselves to texts that will teach them what he calls "the Godly art," that is, piety. Meyer goes so far as to recommend a list of eleven works, which include: "Hugo's book of proper training" (Hugh of St. Victor's "Rule for Novices"), the *Cloister of the Soul*, "The Meditations of St. Bernard," the "Meditations and Prayers of St. Anselm," *The Lives of the Saints*, Heinrich Seuse's *Little Book of Eternal Wisdom*, the *Goad of Love*, Thomas à Kempis's *Imitation of Christ*, Thomas Peuntner's *Little Book of Loving God*, Rudolf von Ems's *Barlaam and Josaphat*, the "Book of the Virtues and Vices," and "other similar books."[20] These, he recommends, should be read not all at once but a little bit at a time, a program that would have lent itself well to readings at table. Meyer's instructions also included a system for cataloguing a library.[21]

The list of table readings at St. Katharina (Nuremberg) includes a description of the contents of each volume, annotations that reveal the cataloguer's considerable familiarity with the texts. Besides saints' lives and many mystical and moral works like those Meyer recommended, the list contains readings dealing with practical, applied spirituality. For example, the entry for volume N 14 identifies the manuscript as

[a] little book containing, first, a good lesson entitled: "Whoever wishes to better his life completely." After that comes the question,

"Whether one can acquire one virtue without acquiring the others," "How one may have all of them," and "What it means to humble oneself under God's mighty hand," and many good teachings about why people are more inclined toward evil than toward good, and what the conscience is and what true piety is and about the three powers of the soul and four praiseworthy virtues, and about the holy sacrament and a good prayer to Our Lord, and the rule of the Dominican order, and three sermons that [Johannes] Tauler preached, and about the mass and the rule of divine love. This little book was copied by the sisters.

Another entry, O 18, states: "A little book, containing a very good prayer and an exhortation on the saints and on the holy sacrament and the Last Supper and about the sufferings of Christ and the Imitation of Christ. This book was copied by Sister Clara Paumgartner and is located in the choir."[22] A thorough cataloguer, the cloister librarian includes the names of copyists, donors, and information on volumes received as gifts from other cloisters, such as in N 28, "the life of Saint Margaret was sent to us from Tulln," or E 62, "a book of the lives of St. Peter and St. Paul, a gift sent to Prioress Haller from Colmar." The cataloguer also records the sisters' donation of many books to other cloisters, explaining, "[T]here were so many surplus books and often three and four copies of the same work, which were too many, and the sisters at Regensburg, Gotteszell, and elsewhere had such a deficiency."[23] Here one glimpses the active interchange going on in women's Observant networks, both within and across orders, in their efforts to help build up their libraries.

In 1469 Meyer dedicated two books to the prioress of St. Nicolaus in undis in Strasbourg. His dedication asks that she distribute his text among all cloisters of the Dominican order that understood German.[24] Accordingly, copies were sent to the sisters at St. Gall and distributed even among Observant houses outside the order, as is seen in the copy made at St. Gall and sent as a gift to the Augustinian sisters of Inzigkofen. Its affectionate dedication reflects the close relations between Observants of different orders: "And this book we wish to be a sign of our eternal friendship and love for you, and yours for us, in constant faithfulness to God until the time that we will be written into the book of life where we will assuredly be united eternally before God's face . . . an affectionate jewel from us to you."[25] Evidence of a similar cordial exchange of books between the Dominican sisters at St. Gall and the Poor Clares at the reformed cloister in Villingen is found in a manuscript, sent to St. Gall by the Clarissan sisters, that contains a collection of poems on birds and fish composed by Prioress Ursula Haider (d. 1498). A notation in the manuscript states, "The esteemed, devout women of the Villingen Poor Clares gave us these little birds and minnows. May God bless them eternally! God be praised!"[26] Another manuscript formerly in the library of cloister Inzigkofen contains texts copied by eleven different hands at four cloisters, including St. Katharina in St. Gall, Schönensteinbach, the Augustinian cloister in Pillenreuth, and possibly St. Katharina in Nuremberg.[27]

At St. Katharina in St. Gall the sisters were permitted to copy books in their free time, as long as they did not neglect their other duties. A writer in the St. Katharina sister-book expresses enormous satisfaction and delight with the fine quality of books copied and illuminated in the women's scriptorium, exclaiming that these are "such beautiful books; anyone who sees them will not believe that a woman could do such good work." The cloister chronicle proudly names the scribes and the sister-book asserts, "[I]t is not improper for a sister to write her name into a book that she has copied, as long as it is not out of vanity. It is often remembered for more than one hundred years and benefits a sister's soul."[28] Fine copying and library building thus became a way of adding to the prestige of the house as well as meeting a need for group and individual reading material.[29]

This is not to say that there was no women's copying of books before the fifteenth century. Indeed, a manuscript illumination c. 1310 shows a Cistercian sister with pen and scraper (for erasures), copying a text.[30] The Oetenbach sister-book (c. 1340) records that when the widow and mystic, Ita von Hohenfels, came to Oetenbach, "there came with her three women. One could write and illuminate, the other could paint, and the third embroider. . . . Thus they and other sisters copied books, so that each year the scriptorium earned ten marks by illuminating and copying" (an amount equivalent to the annual upkeep of three sisters).[31] But in the fifteenth century the volume of books copied increased exponentially. At St. Katharina in Nuremberg the sisters produced in their scriptorium between 250 and 300 manuscripts.[32] Other libraries, such as that at St. Katharina (St. Gall), contain manuscripts from the fifteenth century almost exclusively.

Having about 250 books before the reform, the library doubled in size between 1484 and 1507.[33]

Not all growth in libraries can be attributed to the Observance. Some scholars argue that the trend may have been part of a larger cultural phenomenon in fifteenth-century society at large.[34] And this point is well taken. Many of the books in cloister libraries were donated by secular friends and relatives of the sisters. Karin Schneider has shown that many works considered primarily to be "nuns' literature" actually were brought to the cloister by sisters or were gifts from laypersons.[35] Yet it remains to be explained why the same extraordinary growth did not occur in the libraries of houses that were not reformed. For example, in the east-middle German territories, which remained largely unaffected by the Observance, there was little increase in copying and transmission of vernacular literature. The convent libraries of the province of Saxony contain only a few manuscripts relative to the large numbers in the province of Teutonia.[36] Comparing libraries of two Dominican convents, St. Katharina at Nuremberg and the unreformed Dominican convent of Engelthal (near Nuremberg), Williams-Krapp found that Engelthal had a larger library in the fourteenth century but still possessed only fifty-four German books in 1444, while the collection at St. Katharina had grown exponentially.[37] If such growth were a general cultural phenomenon, it would be expected to have affected libraries at all cloisters. The particular impetus for this activity at reformed women's houses was, as has been noted, the desire of Observants to provide vernacular table readings and suitable materials with which to educate newly reformed women in the spirituality of the Observance. Even the vernacular Bible, which in the thirteenth and fourteenth centuries had been considered dangerous in the hands of beguines and nuns, now became part of the library collections of Dominican women.[38] At the reformed Cistercian abbey of Lichtenthal (Baden-Baden), the list of table readings made by cloister librarian, Sister Regula, provides for the entire Bible to be read completely through every year.[39]

Women Become Translators

Since part of the reform program was to promote private as well as communal reading, the Observants also encouraged the translation of devotional works. A few of the women identified as translators of works from Latin include Claranna von Hochenburg (d. 1423) at Schönensteinbach, Elizabeth Kempf (d. 1485) and Dorothea von Kippenheim (d. 1425 or fl.c. 1508/1516) at Unterlinden, Anna Ebin (d. 1485) at Pillenreuth, Aleydis Ruyskop (d. 1507) at Rolandswerth, and Sister Regula (d. 1478) at Lichtenthal.[40]

The librarian responsible for providing the texts to be read at table, Sister Regula, explains in her introduction to *Das Leben Jesu* her method and reason for making the translation.

> This book is called "The Life of Jesus" and is translated from the Latin of the Holy Gospel into German in the briefest form, out of affection and love for those who are not educated to understand Latin and therefore sometimes are frustrated when they have much to read. For them this book is fashioned so that they themselves will inwardly awaken in sympathetic contemplation.[41]

Regula hastens to assure the reader that her translation has been approved by the authorities, saying, "Our Lord of Mulbrunn (Maulbronn) and Master Berthold have pronounced this book good and proper" and suitable to be read at table.[42]

But that Regula sometimes chafed under the censorship of the authorities and contested their decision can be seen in her "Book of the Holy Maidens and Women" (Fig. 7). In the manuscript to this collection of women saints' lives that Regula compiled, she states at one point, "Here I wanted to write a vision of St. Catherine's birth, but it was not allowed. So be it." But Regula left a blank space for it in the manuscript anyway. The "vision" or insight about St. Catherine's birth was apparently a revelation of Regula's own, one she says "God gave [her] to understand."[43] Such revelations were being increasingly censured. At the Council of Constance (1414–17), for example, Jean Gerson cautioned confessors not to accept as true any revelations from women without subjecting them to minute scrutiny.[44]

Nevertheless, at least ten manuscripts survive in which Sister Regula commented on and edited texts according to her own lights.[45] In her collection of saints' lives, drawn from sixteen different sources, Regula leaves out some of the most violent scenes, replacing them with the disapproving

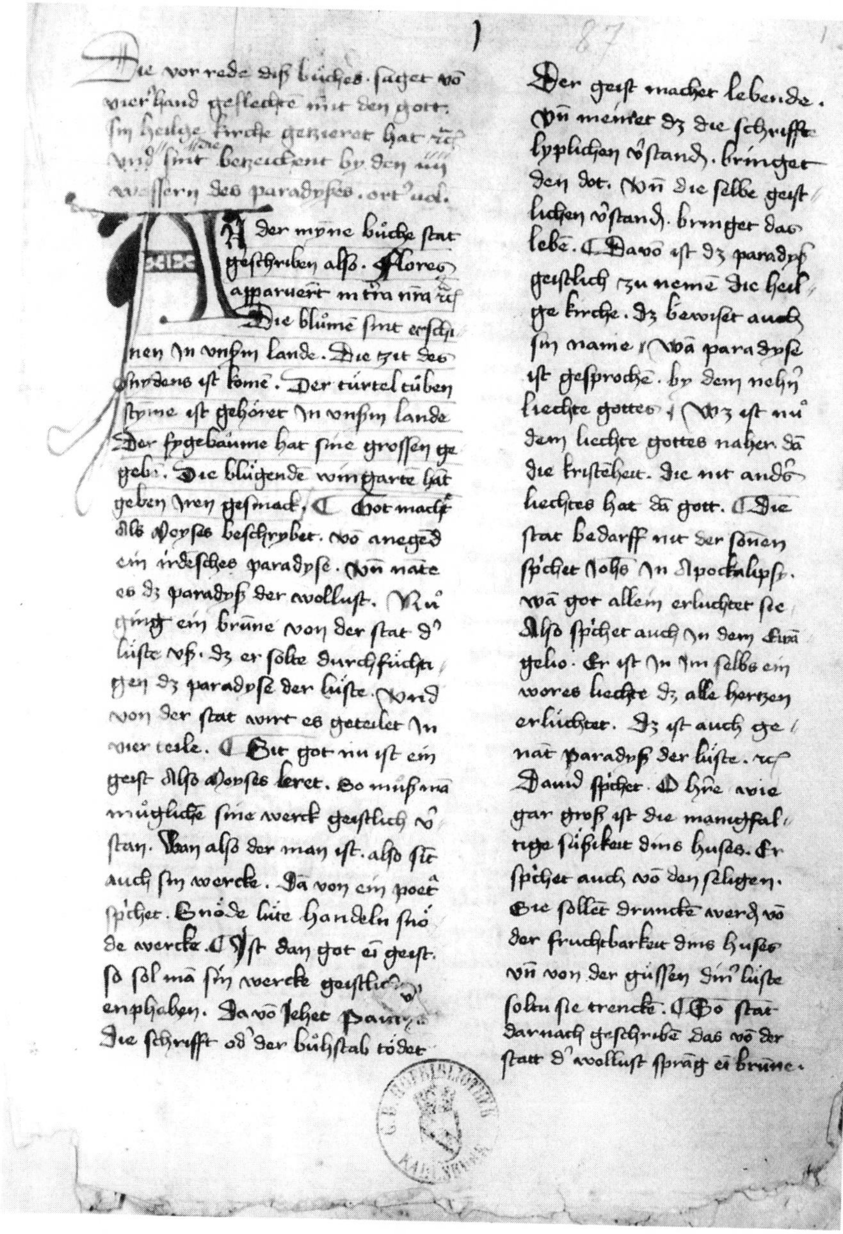

Die vor rede diß buches saget vo
vier hand geslechte mit den gott
sin heilige kirche gezierет hat etc.
Und sint bezeichent by den iiij
wassern des paradyses. ort uel.
Als der myne buche stat
geschriben alsô. Flores
apparuerunt in terra nostra etc.
Die blume sint erschi
nen In unsrm lande. Die zit des
snydens ist kome. Der turtel tuben
styme ist gehoret In unsrm lande
Der fygebaume hat sine grossen ge
geben. Die bluyende wingarte hat
geben iren gesmack. Got macht
als Moyses beschrybet. vo anegend
ein irdesches paradyse. Un nante
es dz paradyß der wollust. Nu
gieng ein brune von der stat d'
luste uß. dz er solte durchfuchti
gen dz paradyse der luste. Und
von der stat wirt es geteilet In
vier teile. Bit got nu ist ein
geist also Moyses leret. So muß ma
mugliche sine werck geistlich v'
stan. Wan also der man ist. also sie
auch sin wercke. da von ein poet
spricht. Snode lute handeln sno
de wercke. Ist dan got ei geist.
so sol ma sin wercke geistlich
enphahen. Da vo sehet Paulus
die schrifft od' der buchstab todet

Der geist machet lebende.
Un meinet dz die schrifft
lyplichen v'standen bringet
den dot. Un die selbe geist
lichen v'standen bringet das
lebe. Davo ist dz paradys
geistlich zu neme die heili
ge kirche. Dz bewiset auch
sin name. Wa paradyse
ist gesprochen. by dem nehsten
liechte gottes. Wz ist nu
dem liechte gottes naher da
die kristeheit. die nit ande
liechtes hat da gott. Die
stat bedarff nit der sunen
spricht Johannes In Apocalipsi.
wa got allem erluchtet sie
Also spricht auch In dem Ewa
gelio. Er ist In im selbs ein
wores liecht dz alle hertzen
erluchtet. Dz ist auch ge
nant paradyß der luste. etc.
David spricht. O herre wie
gar groß ist die manigfal
tige süßikeit dins huses. Er
spricht auch vo den seligen.
Sie sollent drunken werden vo
der fruchtbarkeit dins huses
un von der gussen din' luste
soltu sie trencke. So stat
darnach geschribe das vo der
statt d' wollust sprang ei brune.

Fig. 7. The handwriting of Sister Regula, "Buch von den heiligen Mägden und Frauen" (Book of Holy Maidens and Women, c. 1460), MS L69, fol. 1r (Kloster Lichtenthal) Badische Landesbibliothek Karlsruhe.

words, "and other even more devilish tortures, which are not useful to write or hear." At other times she excises miracles and expresses her own opinion on the works: "They are not needed for a godly life. . . . [T]he clear mirror of [St. Francis's] virtuous life is sufficient for us to follow."[45] In including her own comments, adding to and cutting out portions of the works she copied or translated, Sister Regula demonstrates her own engagement with the texts and confidence in her evaluations of them. Although she does not write the vision of St. Catherine's birth, she resists the censors ideologically by leaving space for it, perhaps hoping for a change of opinion.

Women's Works

At Nuremberg, Katharina Tucher (d. 1448), a widow and an avid reader who entered the cloister of St. Katharina as a lay sister sometime around 1433, did record visions and brought them with her to the convent along with twenty-four books, which she had copied herself. These included numerous mystical texts, devotional works and sections of the Bible, in addition to her own revelations.[47] The *Revelations,* written down between 1418 and 1421, take the form of dreams and dialogues between herself and Jesus, Mary, her confessor, or other figures. Yet their format is ambiguous, so that these conversations might be construed as religious insights or reported dreams rather than supernatural phenomena or visions that were subject to censorship. In one dream sequence Katharina speaks in the voice of a soul accompanying her divine Lord on a hunt, then as a lamb. In another she is a dove flying abroad with her mate. These dialogues and dream-visions serve mainly to illustrate edifying points or to bring Katharina to repentance and into a closer relationship with her spiritual spouse.

At the Bicken cloister in Villingen, another sister, most likely the indefatigable Ursula Haider, left behind an account of her own visions and revelations. Later compiler of the cloister history, Sister Juliana Ernst, reports that they were found in 1638 among the "old books in the infirmary." Sister Juliana copied excerpts from these visions verbatim ("von wort zue wort") into the chronicle.[48] The visions include conversations with Mary Magdalene and "a Dominican," either Heinrich Seuse or Johannes Tauler.

They contain echos of Seuse's *Little Book of Eternal Wisdom,* to which Sister Ursula was particularly devoted but also passages lifted from Tauler's sermons. Juliana says that some of Ursula's mystical chapters "were too lofty for [her] childish understanding" and therefore she left them out.[49] These visions superficially resemble those of earlier works. But they seem to have more the character of insights that occurred to Prioress Ursula while contemplating a particular question arising from her reading of certain mystical texts. She wishes, for example, to know how Mary Magdalene felt when she saw her beloved Lord departing for the last time at his ascension. Standing before her reliquary, she prays: "Oh, chosen creature of God, mirror of penitence, Holy Mary Magdalene, I recall to you all the love that you felt in the presence of your beloved and ask that you give me to understand the great lamentation that you felt for your most beloved master when he ascended into heaven before your eyes."[50] Ursula then goes on to expand on this question for sixteen lines before a voice, which seems to come from the reliquary, answers her. The vision has more the character of a didactic homily or devotional meditation than a revelation like those of the mystical writers of the fourteenth century.[51]

Ursula was a composer of verse as well. Either alone or together with some of the other Bicken cloister Clares, she composed a collection of some seventy emblematic poems entitled "Our Lady's Little Fish and Birds," a copy of which they sent as a gift to the Dominican sisters of St. Katharina at St. Gall. Only the gift copy at St. Gall survives and is designated with the notation that it was sent by the Poor Clares at Villingen. Each poem in the collection names one kind of bird or fish and pairs it with a virtue and the name of a particular sister.[52] All the names are those of actual residents of the Bicken cloister, for example, "The Green Finch (Cecilia Bayer)" and "The Hawk (Anna Bruhi)." Each poem carries a didactic message: "I am called the Green Finch / and am well known to [God's] spiritual children. / My song exhorts you / to advance daily in discipline and virtue. / Then, with your sisters you will put out green shoots / in lovely May, like a flower in bloom." Or, "Hawk is my name. Solitude is my song. / Jesus, the Lord, embraced me in love / when He hung alone and comfortless upon the cross. / At all times keep your spirit turned inward and in harmony. / For then you will arrive at the highest good / and enter eternally into God's secret hiding place."[53] While the poems (reproduced here without rhyme or meter) may be artistically naive, they testify to the creative atmosphere at Villingen under Prioress Ursula Haider and to the nature of other literary activities going on in the cloister.

The Bicken cloister chronicle also contains two of Ursula Haider's New Year's addresses from 1495 and 1496, which were copied word-for-word into Juliana's account. The four-page New Year's address from 1495, former Prioress Haider's "spiritual gift" to the sisters, was delivered from her bed in the infirmary and opens with an apparent reference to the plaques representing locations in the Holy Land that she had placed throughout the cloister: "Dearest spiritual children, for your sakes I have spent a long time walking about and have traversed the whole of blessed Jerusalem and all the holy places and stations to see if I might perhaps buy or turn up something that I could bring to Villingen to my sickbed and there distribute to my own dearest spiritual children for New Year's." Prioress Ursula tells how on the way she met a noble merchant from whom she bought "a beautiful temple" at a bargain price and in spite of her poverty, saying, "I returned with my purchased treasure to the Black Forest to my dark little sickroom."[54] She goes on to describe the fantastic temple, reminiscent of that in Parzival's castle of the Grail. But the temple, as her audience realized from the outset, is a spiritual one that symbolizes the martyred body of Christ. This New Year's address constitutes a kind of homily preached by their former prioress, probably continuing a New Year's tradition that began when Ursula was still in office and addressed the community regularly as was permitted on certain occasions.

At Freiburg Sister Magdalena Beutler (1407–1458) of the house of Poor Clares composed another kind of work, a long meditation on the Our Father ("Erklärung des Vater Unsers" or "Paternoster-Gebetsbuch"). She assembled texts from many sources to form a series of seventy-seven prayers, all of them beginning with the phrase, "Our Father who art in heaven."[55] Sister Veronika Ainkürn, at the reformed Cistercian cloister of Kirchheim am Ries, composed a set of prayers titled, "Sequence or Interpretation of the Psalter" (c. 1520/30). When Sister Agnes Bühler (d. 1562) made a copy of it, she noted, "This little book belonged to the devout and spiritual sister Veronika Ainkürn. She composed and wrote it herself by the grace of the Holy Spirit." The work of 125 pages, now at the convent of Neresheim, survives in only this one copy, but Arnold Schromm cites it as evidence of other original works that are no longer extant.[56] Similarly, in

Alsace at the Clarissan cloister of Alspach, a Sister Margetha von Kent-zingen (fl. 1459) is said to have composed a work on the Passion of Christ. A cloister necrology dating from the eighteenth century states that Marga-retha "led a very holy and austere life. It seems Christ revealed to her many secrets of his holy suffering. The book in which she wrote her visions with words and colored illustrations is still in our hands."[57] If this illustrated work has survived, its present location is unknown.

Women also composed works in Latin. For example, Aleydis Ruyskop (d. 1507), a distinguished scholar at cloister Rolandswerth (Nonnenwerth), composed seven Latin homilies on St. Paul and is praised for her learning by the humanist writer Johannes Butzbach (1478–1526). In 1509 Butzbach dedicated to Ruyskop his "On Distinguished Learned Women." In his "Little Book about Famous Painters" (1505), he names Gertrud von Bü-chel, an accomplished painter also at the convent of Rolandswerth.[58] At Unterlinden a Latin vita of Prioress Elisabeth Kempf (d. 1485) was com-posed, probably by her successor Agatha Gossembrot. Prioress Kempf her-self translated numerous works into German, including the Unterlinden sister-book, to which she also made additions.[59]

Only recently have women writers who resided in religious houses founded by the Common Life movement in the Low Countries and upper Rhine region begun to receive attention. In his study of Windesheim can-onesses, Wybren Scheepsma lists twelve works, including a two-volume autobiography, composed by Alijt Bake, a sister at the Galilea cloister in Ghent, where she became prioress in 1445.[60] Inspired by the example of Colette of Corbie, Alijt attempted a reform of her cloister only to run afoul of the male leadership of the Windesheim Congregation, which took exception to her mystical and religious writings. When Alijt did not accept their admonitions, they removed her as prioress and exiled her to a convent in Antwerp, probably Facons. That same year (1455) the leaders of the chapter issued a prohibition against women writing revelations or concern-ing themselves with theological matters.[61]

At Facons, Sister Jacomijne Costers was stricken with plague in 1489 but miraculously recovered. Afterward she wrote "Vision and Example," a description of how, during her illness, she was taken on a journey through purgatory and hell, where she witnessed the fate that befalls the unrepen-tant. She received from Christ a program of reform that she was to insti-tute.[62] Among Jacomijne's friends and supporters at Facons was Sister

Mechthild van Rieviren (d. 1497), who wrote her own "biography" of spiritual experiences and revelations.[63]

In Utrecht, Bertha Jacobs (Suster Bertken, 1427–1514) was a canoness at the Jerusalem convent and later an anchoress at the Buurkerck (Maria de Mindere), where she lived enclosed for fifty-seven years. Two books of her work, *On the Passion of Our Dear Lord Jesus Christ* (1515/16) and a collection of tracts, prayers, and poems (1518) were published after her death.[64] Maria van Hout (Maria van Oisterwijk, c. 1499–1547), was educated in the beguine house, Bethlehem, in Oisterwijk. In 1545 she moved with two other sisters to Cologne and there took up residence at the Carthusian house of St. Barbara. Maria penned five religious tracts and fourteen letters of spiritual guidance (Sendbriefe), which were published by Melchior von Neusz in Cologne (1531).[65] Another anonymous woman writer in Oisterwijk (1463–1540), whose familiarity with cloister life indicates she may have spent her later years in a religious house, composed the mystical *Pearl* (published 1535) and the *On the Temple of Our Soul* (1543).[66]

In addition to devotional works, prayers, and exercises—such as Margareta Ursula von Masmünster's (d. 1447/48) spiritual "Sea Voyage," discussed above—women in the Common Life and Observant movements also composed texts describing their way of life. Two such works include that of Salome Sticken, prioress of Diepenveen, "Rule of Life" (1435/39), composed for a convent in Westphalia, and a handbook on ceremonies by Katharina von Mühlheim.[67] In this manual Katharina describes all the feast days and ceremonies, explaining how they are to be prepared for and celebrated. Handbooks such as Anna von Buchwald's "Book in the Choir" for the sisters at Preetz are, besides chronicles, among the most typical kinds of writing of fifteenth-century prioresses.

Private Prayer-books and Devotional Anthologies

Much larger in number than the original works written by convent women are religious anthologies and private prayer-books of all kinds compiled by sisters in the Common Life movement as well as in convents of the regular orders. Gerhard Achten points to a veritable "explosion" of private prayer-books created in the second half of the fifteenth century, most of them as yet unexamined by scholars.[68] Of the fifty-one surviving volumes of the library at Ebstorf, nearly one-third are personal prayer-book anthologies—ten in Latin and six in Low German. Surveying them, Helmar Härtel remarks that although all originated at Ebstorf, they are various in their contents.

> One clearly orders the prayers according to the church year, another according to the Lenten period, another relates almost all the prayers to the eucharist. None of them is a liturgical prayer-book; [and] only in one case are prayers from the mass present in significant numbers. [Rather] each book represents an individual collection of religious texts, usually without attribution as to author, and no prayer-book is a copy of any other. Central themes are the devout visualization of the sufferings of Christ, the veneration of the Savior's Mother and, in the Low German books, particularly the communion.[69]

Sisters of the Common Life also occupied themselves with compiling personal collections of texts and notes for private meditation in their own cells.[70] The Emmerich book of sisters mentions, for example, Sister Mechtelt van Kalker's habit of writing "devout things" in a book. Anne Bollmann suggests that Sister Mechthelt would have been copying prayers, writing personal resolutions or quotations from her spiritual reading.[71] Studying a rediscovered woman's prayer-book (dated 1497), from the Weissfrauen cloister in Erfurt, Adolar Zumkeller asserts that the compiler's selections show "the influence of the *devotio moderna* with its simple, affective immersion in the life of the historical Jesus and its piety focused on the practice of the spiritual life." Yet in his analysis of the owner's spirituality, Zumkeller does not give credit to the sisters for their part in these developments through selecting the excerpts collected in their personal devotional anthologies. Rather, he observes, "the reform efforts of a Nicholas of Cusa and later cloister visitors were not without fruit."[72] Clearly, there is much more to be learned about women's religious belief and practice from examining what the sisters chose for their individually compiled prayer-books and personal anthologies. What topics and images did they leave out? Through which networks did they acquire the texts? And, above all, how did their collective preferences affect the spiritual discourse connecting not only cloisters but also relatives among the laity with whom they exchanged information and books.

Along with making anthologies of prose texts, women in the fifteenth century collected songs and made them into books. The libraries of Ebstorf, Marienberg, Medingen, Pfullingen, and Wienhausen all contained song-books compiled in the fifteenth and early sixteenth centuries. The Wien-hausen book, for example, includes fifteen melodies with thirty-six Low German, seventeen Latin, and six mixed-language songs. Except for a few secular ones and religious contractures of folk songs, the texts are religious.[73] Echoing Zumkeller's assessment of the Erfurt prayer-book anthology, Ida Riggert-Mindermann describes these collections of verses as characteristic of "the mysticism associated with the Devotio Moderna."[74] Here, again, the networks through which women received and shared these songs and verses need to be studied.

In addition to copying large numbers of books for their libraries, fifteenth-century women also illustrated them.[75] The St. Katharina cloister in Nuremberg, which accumulated the largest library of vernacular works of its day, also developed its own style of book illustration. Among the artists who can be identified is Barbara Gwichtmacher (d. 1491), who at Nuremberg illuminated a breviary and a two-volume missal (1452). Margarete Karteuser copied and, together with four other sisters, illuminated an eight-volume antiphonal (1458–1470). Other sisters at Nuremberg, whose names are not known, illustrated the "Legend of St. Vincent" (c. 1452) and the sister-book, *Lives of the Sisters of Töss* (Fig. 8).[76] At Freiburg, miniaturist Sibilla von Bondorf, a sister at the Clarissan house (c. 1478–83) and later in Strasbourg (1483–1524) illustrated numerous works, including a life of St. Clara in thirty-three full-page images and a life of St. Elisabeth (Figs. 9 and 10).[77] Surveying manuscript illumination in women's cloisters of the upper Rhine region, art historian Christian von Heusinger identifies centers in Strasbourg, Colmar, Basel, and Freiburg, commenting that virtually all of the works originated at reformed houses.[78] While, in many cases, new liturgical books were mandated by the reforms, the decoration of saints' lives (including those of Clare and Elisabeth) and of the sister-book of Cloister Töss indicate an interest in female role models and literature about women as well as their history. Like women's reading preferences, their choices to illustrate particular works and their selection of scenes and images are ripe for further investigation. This is true as well for most of the works produced

Fig. 8. Illustration of Elsbeth Stagel (d. c. 1360), composing the *Lives of the Sisters of Töss.* Manuscript copied c. 1454 in the scriptorium of St. Katharina (Nuremberg) Stadtbibliothek Nürnberg, MS Cent. V 10a, fol. 3r.

Fig. 9. Clare of Assisi with Pope Gregory IX. One of 33 illustrations by Sibilla von Bondorf for a Life of St. Clare (c. 1490). Badische Landesbibliothek Karlsruhe, MS Thennenbach 4, fol. 138r.

Fig. 10.   Illustration by Sibilla von Bondorf of Clare of Assisi writing with pen and scraper.
Badische Landesbibliothek Karlsruhe, ms Thennenbach 4, fol. 157r.

by women which have only been mentioned here, but which will, it is hoped, be the subject of other studies.

Transcribing and Reconstructing Sermons

Another area of intense activity, besides copying, illustrating, translating, or composing devotional texts, tracts, handbooks and chronicles, was the collecting and trading of sermons among women in Observant convents. Although it is clear that sermons had been an important part of library collections in earlier centuries, in the fifteenth century they multiplied dramatically as nuns compiled anthologies of contemporary sermons—both those by visitors and their own "house preachers." In the library of the Nazareth sisterhouse at Geldern, sermons constituted fully one-third of the collection, while in the eighty-six surviving manuscripts from the library of St. Nicolaus in undis (Strasbourg) alone there are 850.[79] As communal reading material, they constituted an important part of the daily literary fare of the refectory. At St. Katharina in Nuremberg, for example, the catalogue of table readings shows that some of the most frequently used works were sermons of local pastor Albrecht Fleischmann, whose texts the sisters had transcribed and kept for devotional reading.[80] The sisters' collection contains, as well, many others that were preached at their cloister.

These sermons, as they were heard and later reread and studied, constituted a significant part of the women's education and continuing spiritual instruction. At Nuremberg it was a good education, for there many of the speakers were men with formidable academic qualifications, such as the distinguished visiting scholar Johannes Streler, dean of the theological faculty in Vienna, and the most frequent guest, Gerhard Comitis, lector at the Dominican men's convent.[81] The female audience for these sermons at St. Katharina was literate and thoroughly grounded in a knowledge of the scriptures and religious-devotional and sermon literature. At Basel, the women of the Penitents' cloister St. Maria Magdalena an den Steinen were favored with guest sermons by participants attending the great church council held there from 1431 to 1449. An array of eminent speakers, including Johannes of Brandenturn (later cardinal), Heidelberg professor Nikolaus of Jauer, illustrious Vienna University scholar Johannes Coeli, and others spoke in the convent church.[82] Accordingly, the attitudes of the sisters reflect those of the preachers of the day.[83]

As the female branch of the Order of Preachers, Dominican nuns saw it as part of their mission to transcribe, collect, and share sermons with other cloisters. Parties of reforming sisters often brought with them or sent collections from their home cloister. It was, for example, the sisters from St. Maria Magdalena an den Steinen, coming to reform the Strasbourg cloister of St. Nicolaus in undis, who most likely brought with them the sermons preached at their house by the delegates at the Council of Basel.[84] Because of this, often the only copies that exist of the vernacular sermons of many preachers are those preserved by nuns at cloisters where they were delivered. For instance, twenty-eight sermons given in the years 1493 and 1494 by Johannes Pauli, otherwise known as the author of the satirical moral tales, *Schimpf and Ernst* (1522), were transcribed and kept by a nun at the Bicken cloister in Villingen.[85] Thirty-nine sermons delivered by preachers at Nuremberg survive only in one manuscript containing summaries made by the sisters at St. Katharina.[86] Similarly, in Strasbourg sisters at St. Nicolaus in undis and those at the convent of the Penitents of St. Maria Magdalene made many of the only copies of sermons in the vernacular by the most popular preacher of the day, Johannes Geiler von Kaysersberg. They even saw some of them into print. The series published in 1510 as *The Souls' Paradise* was taken down by Susanna Hörwart and Ursel Stingel at the cloister of the Penitents and corrected for publication by Geiler himself.[87]

Evidence of the women's careful reading and use of these sermons as materials for study is shown by the "Ebstorf Collection of Homilies," delivered by house preachers and transcribed by a nun during the years 1497–1516. In the margins of the manuscript are notes by a later nun's hand from around 1515/1520.[88] Similarly, Adolar Zumkeller, in his study of the personal prayer-book of a sister at the Weissfrauen cloister, cites several entries referring to points made by the convent's confessor with the notation, "These words were preached by Father Confessor, Georg."[89] Besides efforts to internalize the pastor's words, a practice common to both sister-houses of the Windesheim Congregation and cloisters of the Observance, the making of anthologies of house sermons preached by the convent's own lectors served as a way of honoring one's confessor and enhancing the reputation of the cloister.[90]

While Dietrich Schmidtke identifies the individual practice of recording the sermons one has heard as particularly characteristic of the fifteenth-century reform movement, sermons were transcribed, read, and studied earlier, but before the thirteenth century primarily in Latin rather than the vernacular.[91] A fourteenth-century manuscript of sermons from a women's house in Cologne contains, for example, the notation, "We are writing down some of his [Bishop Ailbret's] words . . . so that they will remain in our memory. For blessed are those that hear the word and keep it, as Our Lord says."[92] Wolfgang Stammler found notes on a sermon by Johannes Tauler in a manuscript from Klingental along with the nun's comment, "This is the part of the sermon that I liked best."[93] In the fifteenth century, however, vernacular transcriptions increased exponentially. There are personal collections of sermons, sermon notes, and synopses made by women like Sister Agnes Sachs at St. Nicolaus in undis in Strasbourg (1434–37), and Katherina Gurdelers at the St. Agnes cloister in Trier (c. 1500). A manuscript copy of Agnes Sachs's collection confirms: "These sermons were heard by Agnes, daughter of Stefan Sachs. And she kept them in her heart and wrote them down and wrote them again from her transcript."[94]

The Art of Transcribing

The questions of how and when women transcribed sermons have created controversy. In 1957 Wolfgang Stammler asserted that most of the German sermons from the Middle Ages that have come down to us were reconstructed after the service from memory, mostly in women's convents.[95] This assertion has been challenged by Paul-Gerhard Völker who argued that a transcript made from memory would unavoidably have gaps in the development of the theme due to the impossibility of noting down the exact words of the speaker at a time when no system of German shorthand yet existed.[96] Thus a partial transcription should differ stylistically from an original work. Comparing texts, however, Völker finds that there is no identifiable difference between transcriptions and "authentic" texts. Moreover, written copies of sermons show no more gaps or inconsistencies in content and form than other types of literature. He therefore concludes that in most cases the preacher himself must have written or read and corrected the transcripts.[97] Indeed, many were never delivered at all but sermons composed to be read. The most prominent examples are those by St.

Bernard of Clairvaux, which Jean Leclercq asserted were never preached in the form that we have them.[98]

Puzzling, however, are the many manuscripts that contain prefaces in which the scribes make no mention that their texts have been corrected. Instead, they take full responsibility for the errors in their versions. For example, a series of twenty-four sermons on the Passion of Christ, preached to the sisters at St. Nicolaus in undis by Peter of Breslau in 1445, begins with the caveat:

> No one should think that they [the sermons] are word-for-word, for that was beyond my capabilities. I confess my understanding [to be] too weak and my mind too foolish. Rather, many words have been left out that embellished the sermons, [those] that make ardent, devout hearts eager to listen and which show masterful artistry and cleverness, that paltry understanding and imprecise hearing could not retain. For, if I were to write the sermons in perfection of word and precept, I would need the intellect and the grace of the preacher.[99]

More than a modesty topos, this introduction seems to refer to the actual difficulties and shortcomings of transcription. Similarly, the nun who compiled the twenty-eight sermons delivered at the Bicken cloister in Villingen by Johannes Pauli (1493–94) writes, "Let it be known that, if in these transcribed sermons not all points have been so delightfully presented, masterfully rehearsed, and precisely drawn, it is not the fault of the lector but of the poor scribe. She earnestly desires that you will forgive her and pray for her."[100] No mention is made here of the text being corrected or even approved by Pauli himself. This transcription differs, for example, from the "Basel sermons," which are accompanied by the notation that they have been "checked and corrected by two eminent masters who were also participants in this same council."[101]

Völker asserts that he knows of only two cases of actual simultaneous transcription. One is that of Caritas Pirckheimer (1467–1532), prioress of the Clarissan cloister in Nuremberg, who wrote down the sermons of Stephan Fridolin (c. 1430–1498), as the manuscript says, "from this worthy father's mouth word for word." The second case is that of a male scribe who copied the sermons of an Augustinian lector (unidentified) "while he spoke."[102] There are, however, other accounts of apparently simultaneous note-taking, such as that reported in the Diepenveen book of sisters, which says of Sister Liesbeth van Delft (d. 1423): "And when our Father [Johannes Brinckerinck] gave a collation, she sat and wrote it down from his mouth on her tablet.[103] As early as 1523, followers of Martin Luther had begun taking down Luther's German sermons using a shorthand system invented by Georg Rörer. Rörer, along with Kaspar Cruciger and Stephan Roth, friends from student days and all efficient Latin note-takers, combined Latin shorthand with Rörer's 800 special abbreviations to record Luther's words, translating them simultaneously into Latin and afterward converting them back into German again.[104]

Although no formal shorthand for German existed in the medieval period, ancient Roman systems were used earlier in the dictation of patristic works and for taking notes at lectures.[105] A pupil of Hugh of St. Victor (d. 1141) is known to have transcribed lectures by writing notes on wax tablets and then taken them to the master to be corrected. The famous sermons of Bernard of Clairvaux, some assert, may have been simultaneously transcribed by listeners, and later edited by him.[106]

How well nuns would have been able to do this is a question raised by Kurt Ruh, who provides as an example two versions of a sermon by Heinrich Riss, O.P. (d. 1494). One version, dated 1486, is found in a manuscript from St. Katharina in Nuremberg and the other in a Zürich manuscript of unknown provenance dating from c. 1480–90. The Zürich text is a carefully worked out, scholarly "literary" sermon, while the copy from St. Katharina has gaps and lacks all of the rhetorical elements, careful formulations, and erudite wording of the other version. Ruh concludes his comparison with the remark, "This is how a transcript by the much admired nuns equipped with amazing memory looks!"[107] If nothing else, Ruh's example should convince anyone, who has lingering doubts about whether women actually wrote down sermons, that they did. What Ruh aims to demonstrate here is the difficulty of reproducing a text adequately from memory.

Yet perhaps the "nun with the good memory" should not be dismissed so quickly, or at least not left in this state of literary limbo. It may be that the nun's text was not a literary effort at all. Ruh lists four categories of written sermons:

1. Texts written by the preacher himself.
2. Texts transcribed by someone else but checked by the preacher.
3. Texts reconstructed from memory by auditors.
4. Translations from Latin.[108]

Yet, as Gerrit Zieleman has suggested, a different perspective may come from an additional category, "reworked sermons" *(reportationes),* which includes "notes and partial transcriptions."[109] While these sets of notes were often revised, they were not recomposed as either sermons for reading or literary productions. Rather, they were used as devotional aids of the type common in houses of the Sisters of the Common Life to enable the auditor to retain and internalize the important points presented in the sermon. Women in sister-houses took notes on the "collations," those nonliturgical, moral addresses delivered to the sisters usually on Sunday or feastday afternoons. For women, particularly, the collation was a spiritual high point of the week; they had fewer other resources than the Brothers. In order to meditate on the lessons, the women often made notes on the talks and copied them into personal devotional books as a way of keeping these spiritual "points" in memory and to study them again later.[110]

It is clear that making summaries or notes on sermons in order to assimilate and reflect on them was also practiced in Observant houses outside the *devotio moderna.* At Inzigkofen, a later chronicle reports an entry from the old cloister chronicle, "anno 1520 and a few years thereafter," about an occasion in which a sermon of Martin Luther's was read at table and the women made notes from it, at least until the confessor found out.

> At this time it happened that a sermon was lent to our convent that the above-mentioned doctor [Luther] had made about the Lord's Prayer. This was read at table and pleased all so much that some copied down some points from it. But immediately afterward our father confessor Phillip gave an exortation ordering that those who had copied down something of Luther's teaching, be it little or much, should turn it in or do without communion.[111]

The chronicle of the Bicken cloister reports that Ursula Haider required her novices to write sermon summaries as an exercise: "She wanted the novices, when they listened to the sermons, to write them down word for word, as much as each one according to her ability was able to grasp. And when they had summarized them, she had them brought to her, read them over thoroughly, and corrected what was missing or omitted."[112] Writing out notes is also mentioned in the Diepenveen book of sisters, which describes Sister Alijt Bruuns, saying, "She was very desirous of hearing the word of God in the collation and wrote the most memorable points on her tablet in order to retain them and afterward to write them on paper."[113] These references indicate that some women were well practiced in both taking notes and writing summaries that recorded the main points of sermons.

Besides making personal synopses, women reconstructed sermons to share and honor, as well as preserve, the words of their house preacher. One such collection was made by Maria van Pee (Pede), prioress (1465–1480/82) at the cloister of Jericho in Brussels. In her anthology of the sermons of Jan Storm, Maria modestly states in the prologue:

> I have compiled this book from many collations that were preached in our convent over five years by a worthy priest who was our confessor. . . . I lament from the bottom of my heart that I am so inept in my understanding that I could not remember in order to write word for word all the beautiful quotations and authorities of the saints that he gathered in his sermons, [and] the way he interpreted them so beautifully. But I have only been able to retain the simple meaning contained in them, as closely as I could.[114]

To differentiate texts that were merely copied from those that were reconstructed from notes, fifteenth-century scribes sometimes indicated in their manuscripts that texts were copied from "authentic" documents and had been checked or corrected. In these cases, the scribe usually explained that she did not take them down herself but had copied them from other manuscripts. Thus, Zieleman posits, sermons that lack such a statement of source authenticity are often reconstructed texts.[115]

Hans-Jochen Schiewer offers another explanation for the differences in style and quality of sermon reproductions. He argues that the polished pieces must have been made by nuns who had requested copies of the sermons they heard from their confessors or guest preachers and who then copied these into their collections. Citing complaints from preachers about nuns asking them for copies of their sermons, Schiewer concludes that actual transcriptions by women are likely the exception rather than the rule.[116] Yet even if such exceptions constitute only a small percentage of extant sermons, they represent a substantial number, given the thousands of German and Dutch sermons that have survived, most of them still unstudied and many even uncatalogued.[117]

Were Convent Women Writers of Sermons?

Although women lacked the formal education accorded to men, it seems clear from their accounts that notetaking and recomposing collations were skills that many practiced and became adept at. Thomas Mertens argues that women reconstructed and wrote out finished sermons in a manner that tried to assimilate and imitate the style and authority of their confessor.[118] Sometimes this involved writing out the text from an outline borrowed from the preacher, as Sister Janne Colijns most likely did. In recomposing their confessors' texts, women assumed male roles, effectively becoming co-authors or "ghost writers" as Mertens concludes:

> In copying out the sermons of their father confessor, the sisters took over his role completely. This is the most striking aspect of their work. They wrote complete, well-structured texts in which an authoritative "I" speaks to the beloved sisters. They took up their role as genuine ghost writers, and precisely because they played it so convincingly, modern researchers have disbelieved the claims made in the prologues that a sister wrote the sermons.[119]

Certainly no one would expect women, without a comparable education, to write in as polished a manner as university-educated men. That some had greater natural gifts, more education to begin with, and were more adept than others in reproducing a text from notes is probable. Many, as has been shown, simply never regarded their writings as "literary" efforts but only as devotional aids. Yet even these non-literary texts and "reportationes" are valuable in their own right as records of what women listeners thought was interesting, relevant, and worth recording. In this regard, accuracy of transcription is less important than the fact that nuns wrote these texts at all. At a minimum, such notes, summaries, and transcriptions testify to the intense engagement of fifteenth-century women as participants in the religious conversation.

From the point of view of "New Philology," of course, the accuracy issue is irrelevant, since each text has validity in its own right. Editors seeking to reconstruct "authentic" texts may have a vested interest in establishing original authorship, but as examples of the discourse of the time, all texts are part of the conversation. What is clear is that the primary collectors, consumers, and users of vernacular sermons were women. From reconstructing the texts of others it is not a great leap to constructing one's own; and on specific occasions prioresses were themselves required to formally address their communities, no doubt sometimes incorporating parts of sermons they had read. The New Year's addresses "preached" by Prioress Ursula Haider to the sisters at Villingen, discussed above, were not an unusual occurrence. Instructions for prioresses in the ceremonial and in the "Sister-Book" of St Katharina St. Gall state that at Christmas and on the Feast of the Annunciation, "the prioress shall deliver a brief spiritual exhortation to the sisters of such material as will ignite their hearts in godly love, renew and increase their good desires to serve God with ardent love until death. She should also exhort them, through true repentance and penance and confession, to extirpate all the sins of their past life by the power of the birth of our Savior Jesus Christ."[120] Likewise, Magdalena Kremer includes edifying exhortations of her own for readers of her chronicle of the reform of Kirchheim that are very much in the style of a sermon. She writes, for example,

> The honor of God and the welfare of souls, the devotion and love of the people for this cloister, the godly service in the cloister and the good, harmonious life of the sisters, all this and other good things the enemy of mankind cannot tolerate. He caused this cloister so much suffering that it cannot all be written. The benevolent almighty God imposed this [on us] in fatherly good faith, who only imposes or allows things to happen for a good purpose. For, the teachers tell us, the evil spirit tempts men in order to deceive them. One person tempts another in order to know him. [But] God

tempts an individual in order to test him. God especially wants to prove the good people through the evil ones, for otherwise they would not be distinguishable from one another. God also says in the Gospel, it is necessary that vexation should come upon us. But woe to him from whom the vexation comes; it would be better for him that a millstone were hung about his neck and [he] were sunk in the depths of the sea. Thus a famous, well-educated and pious master and priest in the cathedral chapter at Strasbourg once preached that the devil's messsengers were more evil than the devil himself.[121]

Magdalena's many references in her chronicle to the Gospels, church fathers, sermons, and the words of the cloister's confessor represent material she assimilated or appropriated for her text in the same way that preachers freely borrowed from other sources in preparing their sermons. In many passages, she quotes in Latin and demonstrates her familiarity with the Old and New Testaments. Here Magdalena uses sermons she has heard or read, pieces that spoke particularly to her in some way, as support for arguments she makes in a text of her own. This kind of layered composition with references and quotations from other sources may be typical of the sermon form, but is clearly something new in women's writing.

Writing Chronicles and Histories of Reform

Finally, as is evident from the primary sources on the reform used in this study, women in Observant convents were encouraged to write their own histories. These fifteenth-century chronicles, housebooks, and historical accounts differ from the earlier foundation legends and the sister-books composed in the fourteenth century. Containing few vitae of the traditional sort, they focus instead on tracing the history and growth of the community continuously from its inception up to the present day. Rather than following any established form, these tend to be hybrid works that combine together diverse mixtures of records and narrative. Within the amalgam there are often examples of women's assimilation of the art of preaching, such as Elisabeth Muntprat's (d. 1531) introduction to the sister-book of St. Katharina, St. Gall.

For the opening, Elisabeth adopts a ceremonious tone, using long peri-odic phrasing, expressive of the solemnity she deems appropriate to begin-ning such a book. Her account is intended to document the legitimacy and worthiness of the community's past and to inspire present and future generations of readers to carry on the tradition and to fulfill the vision of the founders. Beginning with a kind of short sermon, Elsbeth writes,

> Jesus Christ, our own heavenly spouse, we desire to place here as a solid foundation stone and underpinning on which all heavenly edifices, not made by hands but by the grace of the Holy Spirit, are built. In the words of St Paul, He is a right-angled corner-stone—for He rules all things with His power ordering them har-moniously and strongly—and a keystone, which holds together in the bond of love all those who give themselves to his honor. The same, who through His mercy in this place has begun to work His grace and planted our worthy convent, we ask that He will water it with His sweet, loving spirit . . . so that those who come after us may know and understand how our worthy convent was estab-lished and has grown . . . that what our predecessors built up with such great effort shall not fall into decline, but rather the earnest-ness and love of spirituality, which our predecessors possessed shall with God's help grow in us and in those who follow after us to the increase of the Holy Observance.[122]

Magdalena Kremer adopts a similar tone when she compares the sisters of her convent to the children of Israel and the women's hardships to those of Old and New Testament saints, saying, "God always imposes great worry and suffering on his dear friends."[123] In her first *Chronicle of Herzebrock* (c. 1538), Anna Roede also sermonizes on the evils of the day. Citing Matthew 11:12, she exhorts her sisters to examine their consciences: "Oh, what an ardent flame [of devotion] there once was in holy Christiandom and what is there now?!"[124] These kinds of miniature sermons and exhortations by women are often found embedded within the most diverse historical narra-tives. They are frequently interspersed among inventories of holdings, fi-nancial records, letters, copies of documents, necrologies, vitae, accounts of miracles, information on the running of the cloister and the performance of the liturgy. Perhaps the most eclectic is Anna von Buchwald's "Book in the Choir," which has been described as "a chronicle, diary, account book, Rule and liturgical handbook, all combined into one."[125] Similarly, the cloister annals of Heiningen are "a colorful mixture of chronicle, inventory of properties, account book, necrology, and written contracts."[126] What these chronicles, housebooks, and annals all express, however, is the desire to leave an accurate record.

Since all chronicles covering more than one generation are based on earlier written and oral accounts, the earliest history of the convent is necessarily drawn from whatever older documents may have survived. The new histories written in the fifteenth century and thereafter take pains to state their sources and often lament the inadequacies in the older records. Thomas Head points to women's taking over "primary custodianship" of the traditions of their own communities as a development that arises for the first time in the early modern period.[127] It is a development that received strong impetus in the fifteenth century from Observant reformers, especially Benedictines and Dominicans, who issued mandates that each convent should write its own history.[128] Thus chroniclers often write with a "before" and "after" perspective on the Observance. The scrupulous sister compiling the chronicle of Pfullingen (c. 1525) writes, for example,

> Exactly how many sisters have died since the founding of the cloister to the introduction of the Observance we are not sure. We find no more than 214. But we have heard of some in particular, whose names we do not find recorded. Therefore we do not know the correct total. . . . And that is the reason that we do not know the number of the first [founding] sisters. The book in which they were listed was written in the year 1400 [i.e., over a century earlier].[129]

The necrology of the Poor Clares of Alspach, written in the eighteenth century, gives an insight into the reasons for the loss of the cloister's older documents.

> From the first one hundred years after the establishment of our order, little or nothing is to be found, doubtless because of the deterioration and loss of our old writings, chronicles, and annals which have become partly unreadable due to being buried in the

ground during times of war. Partly also because the Conventual fathers confiscated many of them when we in 1442 withdrew from their jurisdiction and joined the Observants.[130]

This concern with accuracy is especially present in those works that combine an inventory of properties with the historical narrative, such as the *Hausbuch* of Cloister Maihingen (begun c. 1522). Here, the chronicle states, shall be recorded "each abbess's term in office, what events took place during that time, also most of the donors and benefactors, and all the anniversary services that have been endowed up until now and many other things that are necessary and useful to know."[131] At the death or resignation of each abbess, the account accordingly gives the exact value of the assets and debts passed on to her successor. Of Abbess Barbara Goldschelk (1481–1500) the book relates, for example, "The old Mother Superior, Barbara, called the new [abbess] to her and handed over to her in the presence of the eldest sisters and the two treasurers eleven hundred gulden. And all the debts of the convent were paid so that we did not owe a heller."[132] Later, in recounting a conflict between the cloister and Count Ludwig XIII of Öttingen over taxes, the chronicler warns future abbesses to guard their privileges and not give in to pressure, "because once one agrees to a tax or other infringement of the cloister's immunity, it will always remain thus."[133] Such strict accounting was important at Maihingen because the convent was in financial difficulties at the time the housebook was compiled. One of its purposes was to record and analyze precisely the causes of the cloister's economic decline so as to bring about a recovery and keep future abbesses from making the same mistakes.[134]

Combining old written documents with eyewitness accounts by the oldest living members of the community, the new chronicles attempt to lend authority to their narratives by specifically citing and often naming their first-hand sources. Anna Roede writes, for example in her *Later Chronicle of Herzebrock* (c. 1553), "What is written hereafter I gathered together out of rent contracts, deeds, letters of immunity, and the old writings that the abbesses in these years left behind." As her witness, she writes, "All this . . . I heard from the blessed Sophia Mysener and a few other old sisters."[135] Likewise, in Anna's earlier *Chronicle of Herzebrock* (1538), she writes, "This I heard from the old sisters who were here before the reform and who had heard of it also from other old sisters."[136] Part of the increased sensitivity to accuracy and the identification of sources grew out of the interest of the Observance in record keeping. Thus the chronicler at Pfullingen at first laments her inadequate information about the earliest sisters, but later writes with satisfaction, "But from the time of the Observance onward, 1461, ninety-five sisters died, whose names and dates of death have been written down diligently."[137]

Examining thirty-five Observant convent histories, all of them from men's houses, Constance Proksch's study of reform and history writing in the late Middle Ages (1994) posits the "reform chronicle" as a distinct historiographic type, characterized by a particular structure and point of view. Proksch defines it as essentially "antithetical" in form, since the accounts typically describe a period of decline prior to the reform. They then contrast this phase with a flowering of cloister life after the successful introduction of the Observance, which is depicted as a critical turning point in the history of the cloister.[138] Like previous monastery chronicles, the reform chronicle is not written for outside consumption or even primarily for future generations, but for the current residents of the house with the purpose of connecting them to their past and making them aware of their traditions and responsibilities. Indeed, most reform chronicles were composed in a late or declining phase of the Observance. Thus their aim is to inspire the current generation to persevere in or renew the reform.[139] Like the account at Ebstorf, these works tend to idealize the reform. Anna Roede looking back on the days of the beginning of the Observance, writes in her *Later Chronicle of Herzebrock* (c. 1553) of reform Abbess Sophie von Münster (1463–1500): "In this abbess' time the reform flourished with all spirituality and love and peace and harmony. The divine office was strictly observed day and night. . . . Oh, if only things were still as at that time!"[140] Even chronicles written at a later period, such as that of St. Gertrude in Cologne (1670), number the prioresses from this starting point, designating them as the first, second, third, etc. "after the reform." Prioresses before the Observance are not numbered.[141] At Wienhausen, the old account c. 1470, from which the Chronicle of 1692 was compiled, similarly shifts from very brief résumés of each prioress before the Observance to longer and much more detailed narratives and inventories after 1469.

Observant cloisters of the regular orders were not alone in encouraging the writing of chronicles and other kinds of texts. Wybren Scheepsma identifies in women's houses of the Common Life movement at least "fifteen different historiographical or biographical texts."[142] Like the chronicles in convents of the Observance, these texts are often of a hybrid nature. Anne Bollman describes the Emmerich book of sisters as a combination of "hagiography, spiritual exercise, memorial, and cloister history."[143] Containing little in the way of mystical visions, revelations, or the radical asceticism of the spiritual athletes in the fourteenth-century sister-books, the vitae in the later books of the Sisters of the Common Life offer an ideal that is attainable by ordinary people.[144] As the prologue added to the Diepenveen book of sisters in 1524 (probably by Sister Griet Essink), explains, "because it would be impossible for me to describe all the virtues, I have undertaken here to gather only a few, so that we may imitate their virtues and example." Concluding, she writes, "But let us consider these few as an example to live by and recognize that to imitate them will, in our own weakness, be challenge enough."[145] Similarly, the author of the book of sisters of the Master Geert House, Deventer, states: "Let us listen with fervent desire to the way these women, our fellow sisters, devoted themselves to Christ, lest we should think it impossible to imitate what they accomplished, who were here before us in this place and almost at the same time."[146] Bollmann explains that reading the lives of the "charismatic founders" and of successive generations was seen as a powerful means of teaching and "socializing" novices to keep alive the devout piety of the founders. Like the reform chronicles of the Observance, these works convey a view of decline and renewal. They provide a sense of endangered spirituality and of threats to the survival of the community. Pointing to the recurrent threat to the community of plague, Bollmann emphasizes that the collections of vitae serve in a way as "ars moriendi," that is, texts that teach how to live by teaching how to die well.[147] Besides the Emmerich book of sisters, those of Diepenveen and the Master Geert House of Deventer have been edited, but other versions and fragments of texts from other houses are still being recovered and have yet to be edited.[148]

Although R. R. Post laid to rest any assertions that adherents of the *devotio moderna* could be viewed as Renaissance humanists, Thomas Mertens has demonstrated how the movement, nevertheless, revived several early Christian literary genres by composing new works based on these older models. In addition to "collation books," influenced by the *Collationes patrum* of John Cassian (d. 435), the New Devout composed "Lives of the Sisters" and "Lives of the Brothers" based on the older "Lives of the

Fathers" *(Vitae patrum).* These incorporated the Early Christian practice of "farewell discourses," carefully recording any "edifying 'point' made by a sister on her deathbed."[149] Composing new vernacular works on these early Christian models was not a practice limited only to men's houses of the Brethren of the Common Life.

Scheepsma has characterized women's important role in the Common Life movement—a contribution largely ignored until recently—as a "second religious women's movement."[150] Like the thirteenth-century "women's religious movement" posited by Grundmann which spawned the large number of beguine foundations, this new wave of women's communities, spread in the last decades of the fourteenth and in the fifteenth centuries across the northwest of Europe and Germany, far outnumbering new foundations for men. Grundmann theorized that the extraordinary flowering of women's writing that coincided with the founding of beguine houses in the thirteenth century arose from the reciprocal influences of beguine spirituality and mendicant preaching. In a similar way, the fifteenth century saw a new productive pairing of religious enthusiasm and involvement with preaching in the sister-houses and convents of the Common Life as well as in the convents of the Observance. In this later period, however, women focused on collecting, reconstructing, and exchanging sermons. In some cases, as the next chapter will show, they also edited and revised them for distribution to the laity.

Women's avid engagement with sermons in the fifteenth century was but part of a larger engagement with vernacular texts of many kinds. Indeed, it was the shift to their own language, along with the authorization to write in it, that brought many more women into the conversation. Beyond that, use of the vernacular affected the nature of the discussion by creating a different relationship to the text and the Word, overall a different religious sensibility. Women's transcription and dissemination of vernacular sermons were encouraged by preachers such as Johannes Geiler von Kaysersberg because, among other things, they were useful in furthering the aims of the reform. What was probably not so clear was that women, in reconstructing sermon texts from notes, became co-authors of the sermons and assumed male roles.

The increasing shift to the language of the laity in the production and exchange of devotional literature by monastic women was a fundamental structural change that empowered them to participate in a broader range of literary activities than ever before. Use of the vernacular also furthered the exchange of books between female monastic networks and the laity. Observant women's copying and dissemination of manuscripts preserved not only their own works but played an important part in determining which others would receive wider circulation. Their scribal activities disseminated works such as the devotional garden allegories, of which some hundreds of copies survive from this period, and affected which works from earlier periods would be passed on. As previously mentioned, it was the Observants' copying and circulating of the fourteenth-century sisterbooks as reading material for newly reformed women's cloisters that rescued these texts from oblivion. Only one manuscript of the sister-books survives from the fourteenth century as compared with twenty from the fifteenth century. Of these, almost all are from the scriptoria of Observant convents, most of them women's houses.[151] Along with these visionary vitae, the women copied works of earlier mystical writers, including Heinrich Seuse (d. 1366) and the sermons of Meister Eckhart (d. 1327/28) and Johannes Tauler (d. 1361). Four-fifths of their extant texts are found in manuscripts from the fifteenth century.[152] It was, however ironically, the copies made by Observants that contributed to the repopularizing of these mystical writers. Here, again, women's collective reading preferences must be taken into account as a significant factor in textual transmission. Moreover, even sister-books from an earlier century must be read in the context of the reform to which they owe their survival.

In the creation of a literary culture for women, both the reform effort and the shift to the vernacular played a part. They were factors that produced a new form of agency by enabling participation in literate discourse on a larger scale and in wider networks than previously. Present-day researchers seeking to construct a literary chronology for women thus find that a traditional secular periodization is often a poor fit. For convent women in particular, scribal and literary production are more closely linked to reform movements and religious currents. In the case of fifteenth-century Observant sisters, the reform-related compilation of sermon anthologies, cloister histories, books of sisters, manuals, and devotional works, in addition to translating and copying of texts constitute a renaissance—if not in the conventional sense then at least as an intense flowering of literary engagement on the part of monastic women.

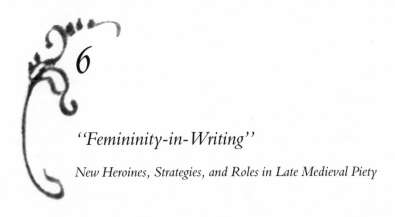

6

"Femininity-in-Writing"

New Heroines, Strategies, and Roles in Late Medieval Piety

This book was finished, to the honor of God and Mary his dear Mother, on epiphany of the year 1503. . . . I knew that I was not qualified, but when I saw that it
would not be done by anyone else, I undertook this task out of love for God and
my fellow sisters. I hope I have written nothing except what is true before God
and would be affirmed by truthful and credible sisters. Although I confess the work
to have been often irksome and I often unwillling, the inner compulsion that I felt
and the sweet fragrance that I as well as others perceived at times when I was very
immersed in it strengthened me in this good work. May it be to the praise and
glory of God and all of those who are written about in this book. May we follow
their example, encourage one another, renew ourselves, and after our labors in this
short life join in their company.

—Book of Sisters, St. Agnes, Emmerich (1503)

Here I begin a little book of the origins of the cloister of Engelthal and the magni-
tude of grace which God brought forth in these women at the beginning and
thereafter. . . . [God] is powerful in benevolence to his friends, for He alone rules
all things, blessing some and not others.

—Christine Ebner, Little Book of the Overwhelming Burden of Grace (c. 1340)

The question has often been raised why medieval women chose to employ
certain literary forms and whether these forms and poses represent something characteristically feminine. Complicating the issue has been the
problem of recovering texts that were not mediated by male redactors.
Indeed, before the fourteenth century only very few texts can be ascribed
to women that were not transmitted by male scribes and mentors. Beginning about 1320, however, works began to appear in which confessors are
conspicuously absent as authors and collaborators. These "nuns' books," as
they were often labeled, were long regarded by literary historians as particularly characteristic of women's writing and frequently cited as clear
examples of a unique *Frauenmystik*. Early commentators thought they knew

what this was and, throughout the nineteenth century and even up to middle of the twentieth, characterized them as examples of "feminine" hysteria, poor imitations of men's mystical writing and works of "misguided aspirations," "inferior talent," and "bad taste."[1] As late as 1964, literary historian Josef Quint described sister-books as "sick," pseudo-mystical works that "exhaust themselves in strange visions."[2] These and other such women's writings were explained as hallucinations of the overheated brain that resulted from a misunderstanding of theology and the faith itself. At worst they were regarded as symptoms of a cultural decline, not only decadent but pathological and downright dangerous.[3]

Such judgments, proceeding as they did from established views of doctrinal and psychological correctness, continued to be promulgated until mid-century. By this time, however, scholars had begun to reexamine and rehabilitate nuns' books. Arguing that these works should be removed from the category of mystical writings altogether, medievalists assigned them, instead, to the genre of hagiographic texts. Looked at in this way, as examples of saints' lives, fourteenth-century nuns' vitae do not seem sick or theologically misguided at all. In structure and literary conventions these works fit well within a long and respected tradition accepted for men's vitae. As has been shown, Anna von Munzingen's Adelhausen sister-book was probably modeled on Gérard de Frachet's *Vitae fratrum,* an account of the lives of the early Dominican brothers.[4] Moreover, the practices of self-mortification the sister-books depict belong to a long tradition of voluntary suffering exercised in order to atone for evil and to show devotion to Christ. It is a tradition that dates back through monasticism and to the desert fathers of the third and fourth century.[5] The fasting, self-flagellation, and other asceticisms practiced in men's convents were frequently recommended to women by their male spiritual mentors. In one often-cited example, Venturino da Bergamo (1304–1346) sent Katharina von Gueberschwihr, prioress at Unterlinden, a gift of several scourges along with instructions that she and the sisters should discipline themselves nightly in the church, giving their bared shoulders seven lashes for each verse of a *Miserere.*[6]

To understand the meaning of these ostensibly female and hysterical, radically ascetic practices—particularly the trances and visions that are recounted in the sister-books—one needs to look at their function within the larger system of cultural beliefs and consider their role as strategies and instruments operating within a particular social order. In hagiographic writings, the genre to which such works have now been tentatively reassigned, ascetic practices, miracles and paramystical phenomena are everywhere present and constitute what Peter Dinzelbacher identifies as essential "evidence of holiness." Indeed, Dinzelbacher states that there is scarcely any thirteenth-century saint's legend without dreams, visions, and supernatural appearances.[7] In the sister-books they serve as proof of a sister's holy life. Indeed, to have spiritual trances and visions was considered the particular mark of the elect, the outward sign of those chosen by God to receive His special grace and recognition. As Christine Ebner's (d. 1356) *Little Book of the Overwhelming Burden of Grace* reports, women at the cloister of Engelthal received so much "grace" that there was only one sister who did not experience trances, and she appears suspect.[8] Not only sisters but entire cloisters competed with one another in the effort to show themselves preferred by God. To the degree that these literary idealizations of spiritual grace represent actual practices—itself a debatable assertion—the arduous fasting and night vigils they portray could well have been conducive to the fainting spells or hallucinations that conferred this important special status. Lest one think that the cultural reward structure that made this extreme behavior worthwhile is unique to the Middle Ages, Siegfried Ringler suggests a tour of the training facilities of modern-day olympic athletes, which to the physically unfit look much like torture chambers.[9]

Examining the literary form of sister-books, Ringler argues that the female authors wrote the way they did "not because they did not know any better," as earlier critics had assumed, "but because they chose to." That is, these texts were consciously crafted examples of a specific literary genre designed to make a particular kind of statement.[10] By depicting the spiritual blessings bestowed on the community through its most exceptional members, its spiritual giants of the past, fourteenth-century sister-books served as advertisements of God's favor and the spiritual power and importance of a cloister. As a political strategy illustrating the virtue of the women's lives, these works served to protect and enhance the prestige of a religious house.[11] If women more than men were drawn to trances, visions, and radical asceticism—or, at least, to depicting them in their writing—it may have been because these phenomena opened avenues of influence that were not otherwise available to them. Indeed, visionary phenomena and radical asceticism could elevate female mystics even above priests by placing them in direct relationship with God.[12] This intimate relationship—expressed in fainting and trances—was understood by men such as Jacques de Vitry to be a kind of conjugal intimacy, "the King lying with his bride."[13] It awed and fascinated Vitry, for such intimacy was inaccessible to him as a man.

For visionary women, to be one of God's chosen intimates was to be privy to divine knowledge and even to speak on behalf of God with an authoritative voice in a climate in which women were otherwise strictly prohibited from publicly expressing theological views. Empowered by their mystical aura, a few women acquired considerable influence.[14] The celebrated mystic at Engelthal, Christine Ebner, author of the Engelthal sister-book as well as her own revelations, became so renowned that in 1350 she was visited by King Charles (later Emperor Charles IV) accompanied by a retinue of dukes and counts, all of whom knelt before her and asked for her blessing.[15] In addition to the authority conferred by the role of spokesperson for God, extreme asceticism, weeping, praying, and fasting were means to acquire power to blunt the wrath of God. By becoming conduits—agents and brokers—of divine mercy, these women also gained the authority to mitigate the sufferings of souls in purgatory.[16] Their charismatic suffering and self-abnegation were thus not, as many scholars have asserted, an internalization of male misogyny but, as Bynum asserts, a kind of rebellion. They functioned as an effective strategy countering the church's exclusion of women from preaching and speaking out on religious subjects.[17] As noted in Chapter 1, this kind of asceticism also served an important altruistic purpose: it provided noble women living in voluntary poverty with a vast source of spiritual wealth that could be freely dispensed as charity.[18] Thus, Bynum continues, substituting one's own suffering through illness and austere practices for the guilt of others is not a "symptom"—it is "theology."[19]

Earlier, Herbert Grundmann had suggested that women's mystical turn—"the route to the inside"—was a path taken because women's religious needs were not being met.[20] Yet it might also be understood as a road taken because women had previously been so effectively silenced: a route to speech. Generally, the social groups affected by a loss of status tend to be the most conscious of alternative modes of expression, linguistic registers, and the power of language.[21] Certainly the mystic, Mechthild of Magdeburg [c. 1208–c. 1282/94]—a patrician beguine living in an ever more marginal, endangered position and one of the first women ever to write in German—used her native vernacular in a totally unprecedented way. In portraying mystical encounters of the soul with the divine, Mechthild created abstract nouns, invented compound verbs, and fashioned new meanings. Juxtaposing verse and prose narratives, dialogues, prayers, and visions, she depicted ecstatic states in ways never before imagined. Mechthild's astonishing work *The Flowing Light of the Godhead* (c. 1250/82) broke not only the bounds of the old Low German language and its usage, but it shattered women's long observed, near total silence in their own tongue.[22] Authorized, indeed, commanded to write by the divine greeting she received in her visions, Mechthild gained an audience and a following for her literary self-expression and achieved notoriety even during her own lifetime.

While Mechthild was encouraged and her work translated by male redactors, in the fifteenth century women's visionary writings had become objects of suspicion as concern grew within the church over the influence wielded by female mystics. Officials were increasingly uneasy over the activism and the mass followings stirred up by holy women like Birgitta of Sweden (c. 1303–1373). Women's revelatory writings were considered particularly subversive because the direct line to God that they established created an alternative hierarchy that bypassed the authorities. The church responded with censorship, the issuance of guidelines on how to distinguish authentic from false visions, and a strategy of containment to restore the balance of power.[23] Soon the relationship between clerics and visionary women changed from encouragement to caution. Men who, like Jacques de Vitry (c. 1160–1240), Thomas de Cantimpré (c. 1200–c. 1272) and others had been fascinated by female mystics and collaborated with them in the recording of their visions, now warned against the dangers of false visions and excess.[24]

With the censoring of visionary writings, mysticism as a secure and effective route to influence for women was all but closed off. Thus it is not surprising that in the fifteenth century one should find them writing in a different voice and in other genres not thought of as female. The very idea that women wrote in a mystical-visionary mode because that was their nature appears absurd when they were forced to seek another outlet and, accordingly, used other literary modes. Bynum asks the telling question: if women became mystics "because they are intrinsically more emotional, imaginative, religious, or hysterical than men, why did it take centuries for this to emerge?"[25]

New Literary Strategies, New Heroines

Women had, of course, always been able to write in other modes. And when a different strategy was called for in the fifteenth century, they produced other kinds of texts: reform chronicles and accounts, handbooks, devout biographies, as well as religious tracts and devotional texts. Growing out of the religious movements of the fifteenth century, these writings are characterized by a very different voice. Like their antecedents, the earlier sister-books, these new chronicles and vitae portray the exceptional piety and religious devotion of past members of the community. Unlike the earlier sister-books, however, they are largely devoid of the "feminine" trances and spiritual ecstasies that nineteenth-century commentators had come to expect. Instead, they relate the religious and political struggles of the community and the introduction of the reform. Rather than celebrating the convent's visionary or radically ascetic spiritual giants, these texts commemorate the leadership of capable abbesses and their accomplishments for the community, especially those who reinvigorated its spiritual life. In writing their own history, fifteenth-century Observant women present a view of themselves that is based less on extreme asceticism than on character and competence.

Although these annals and reform chronicles were composed at Observant houses, male supervisors did not figure substantially in their composition beyond encouraging women to keep records and write their own cloister histories. This is true both for accounts in the reform of the regular orders and for collections of biographies composed by sisters at convents of the New Devout, where, despite strong ties, the sisters and brothers kept at a strictly discrete distance from each other.[26] Similarly, chronicles of Observant houses manifest less contact with male mentors than earlier works, principally because under the Observance only the confessor and provost had even limited access to the cloister. Like the earlier sister-books, fifteenth-century chronicles also have political and propagandistic aims, presenting a kind of collective portrait of the convent that depicts idealized figures of the past in order to demonstrate the convent's spiritual power and to inspire the present generation.[27] Most were written or supervised by abbesses, prioresses, or their assistants, who largely determined their content. For example, the author of the *Hausbuch* of cloister Maihingen explains who is to have charge of the chronicle and what it is to contain.

> Now, since an abbess has much to do and is burdened with temporal as well as spiritual things, this book should always be entrusted to a prioress and placed in her hands to be in charge of it so that what is written is entered by her or by others with the advice of the abbess and approved by both, whatsoever is useful and necessary and what will serve for the betterment or as a warning, and also what happens during the term of each abbess.[28]

As artifacts of the Observance, these works portray the reform abbess as a new kind of heroine. She is depicted as a spiritually vibrant woman and a dynamic leader, strong not only in character but, above all, in business sense. In many cases, she is represented as the real moving force behind the reform. Anna Roede's second chronicle of Herzebrock tells how abbess Sophia von Stromberg herself initiated the Observance by soliciting the bishop for help in finding monks experienced in reform, who would assist her to institute enclosure. She relates, "[Abbess Sophia] managed to acquire, with the help of good people [and] by making many humble requests, two good men from the convent [of Osterberg], two old pious men." Anna specifies that this was "three years before the reform."[29] In 1463, Abbess Stromberg died and was succeeded by the even more effective Sophia von Münster who pursued the reform with "great labor and industry." Under Sophia's leadership the formerly impoverished cloister began to flourish both spiritually and fiscally after Sophia, an effective and assertive manager, lobbied for an inheritance for one of the sisters and secured donations to the cloister. In addition to Herzebrock, the energetic Abbess Sophia oversaw the reform of three other cloisters: Malgarten, St. Gertrudenberg, and Gerden.[30]

Even more active and imposing was Ebstorf's prioress, Mechthild von Niendorf (d. 1495), who is described as the reformer of six cloisters. In elegiac terms, the author of the convent chronicle compares Prioress Mechthild to an eagle and the sisters under her guidance to eaglets.

[S]he is the firm lover of the monastic life, the actual foundress of the reform, first in our cloister [and then in others.] Like an eagle that holds its young up to the sun to test their fitness in its blaze and leaves the remains of its food for the other birds to enjoy, so this inordinately beloved mother shared the grace she had received from God with other cloisters. Four lay near to our area and the fifth in the diocese from which she stemmed, namely, Meyburg. To these regions she led her daughters, those of whom she knew that they could bravely endure the brilliance of the sun, under the regimen of the new monastic life, . . . setting an example by her own life.[31]

This eulogy, based on Latin models, differs in style from most women's chronicles and shows the strong emphasis at Ebstorf of training novices in Latin grammar and composition. The portrait, thus, resembles those of earlier heroic abbesses in the works of Hrosvit and Bertha.

Expressive of the Observants' program opposing elitism in cloisters, the new reform abbess is often portrayed as indifferent to social rank. Herzebrock chronicler, Anna Roede, a goldsmith's daughter who was very sensitive to class differences, repeatedly asserts in her account that nobility of character is superior to nobility of rank. She praises Abbess Sophia, under whom she served as cloister secretary, for not being swayed by such distinctions, asserting: "[D]uring the term of this abbess, the reform blossomed in all spirituality, in love and peace, in unity. . . . She was no respecter of persons and did not consider whether one was of the nobility or not, as St. Benedict says in the rule. And because humility flowered in her, so she brought forth much fruit in those under her."[32]

At Wienhausen, where the chronicle reports resistance to the reform, the writer portrays the loyalty of the sisters to their old noble abbess, Katharina von Hoya. At the same time, however, the account emphasizes the humility and virtue of Susanna Potstock, the young commoner who was brought in by the abbess of Derneburg to institute the Observance and replace the high ranking aristocrat, Katharina von Hoya. Susanna proves her own nobility of character by quietly joining the deposed Abbess von Hoya in the wagon that was to take her away. Only after expressing empathy and demonstrating her humility by leaving the cloister together with the old abbess does Susanna return to accept the office of prioress. Having proved herself to be a leader of outstanding character, she eventually gains the support of the sisters. The chronicle states that the new abbess served for thirty-two years "with the greatest care and industry."[33]

Although not at all uniform or conforming to a standard monastic chronicle format, women's hybrid texts serve some of the same political functions as earlier sister-books.[34] For the abbesses who supervised the writing of these chronicles a chief aim, as examples have shown, was the protection of their houses. The narratives are not constructed only with contemporary audiences in mind, but often as political instruments to aid and advise future prioresses. Besides advice, they incorporate and often copy into the text fiscal and legal documents for the safeguarding of the house and the sisters who will come after them. Because nunneries were always more vulnerable than men's convents to fiscal encroachment and interference from outside, a major theme in women's chronicles is the struggle to maintain their immunity from secular jurisdiction. Unlike the earlier sister-books, which defended and legitimated the women's community through a strategy of demonstrating its spiritual power and influence, fifteenth-century women's chronicles attempt to establish a documentary paper trail of legality. Thus their narratives name names and recount "for the record" and for future generations how secular rulers tried, sometimes successfully, to exact duties and assert control over them in violation of the convent's official guarantees of exemption from secular authority. In these anecdotes, prioresses are shown networking effectively and helping each other. In one example, a warning and object lesson for future prioresses, the *Hausbuch* of cloister Maihingen relates how Count Ludwig XIII of Oettingen (d. 1486) demanded payment of a tax, which Abbess Barbara Goldschelck (1481–1500) refused to remit. To collect the tax, the count confiscated one of the convent's horses. Consulting her old steward, the abbess discovers that the steward has been paying this tax secretly himself in order to avoid difficulties with the count. Alarmed at the setting of a precedent that will infringe on the cloister's sovereignty, Abbess Barbara writes to her colleague, Magdalena von Oettingen, who was abbess of Kirchheim am Ries (1446–1496) and also the count's cousin. This tactic was effective, for the account relates that Abbess Magdalena

> wrote a strongly worded letter to her cousin, Count Ludwig, reprimanding him that he should wish to persecute the poor cloister

in such an unjust manner, saying in the letter that the holy mother, St. Birgitta, would punish him and that he would fall from his horse and break a foot, as later happened. But he scorned the warning. A few days afterward, when the count rode to Landshut to see the duke, he fell on entering the palace and broke his leg. Then he remembered what the abbess of Kirchheim had written and called on God and St. Birgitta to help him. And he ordered that the [sisters] at Maihingen be given back their horse. And he was laid up for a considerable time and afterward never again taxed the cloister. Later he came here on crutches and was a good friend to us.

To prove the veracity of the story, the Maihingen chronicler interjects a personal remark (a typical strategy in women's texts), asserting, "Lest anyone should think this is made up, our old sister Veronica herself saw him standing on crutches in front of the speaking window and was there when the settlement was agreed on."[35]

Other women's chronicles transcribe into their narrative papal letters of exemptions, deeds establishing property rights, records of donations, accounts of the acquisition of relics, histories and genealogies of famous founders that connect their houses to influential protectors—anything that will establish and defend their claims of independence.[36] Speaking directly and personally into the record, Anna Roede, for example, documents the donation of a farm, saying, "This I found written in the old missal and the actual deed must have burnt up."[37] To establish the legitimacy of other bequests received, Anna provides the names of the donors and the story behind each gift. Likewise, the *Hausbuch* of Maihingen lists for the benefit of future abbesses the names of bishops who exempted the cloister from taxes and details the papal gift of the cloister's relics.

Chronicles also function to exonerate the women via the official record of possible blame for damage to the cloister's economic base. Anna Roede tells the women's side of the story, documenting how the damage was not incurred by the sisters themselves but was caused by feuds, poor stewards, and corrupt suppliers. Anna specifically identifies the people at fault. When she does not directly name them, she warns ominously, "God knows their names!"[38] As mentioned earlier, the women at Kirchheim unter Teck resisted Count Eberhard's attempts to reverse the reform and to starve them

out. To gain public support, they composed and circulated a flier that detailed their grievances against him. As a strategem, the sisters named names,
listing all the persons who had helped them. This flier Magdalena Kremer
copied verbatim into her account. At another point, she portrays the sisters'
spirited resolve to hold out and describes their defiance during the seige:

> It should also be known for the betterment of all those who shall
> come after us that in all our affliction, grief, and privation our
> singing and reading never diminished, rather we sang even more,
> . . [and] the soldiers surrounding the convent said to each other,
> "Oh, dear God, how can the women sing so joyfully in such suf-
> fering?" And they told us afterward that they had benefitted greatly
> from it. And all who were in the town were also amazed and
> improved by the unceasing religious services.[39]

The most important political purpose of the chronicles is, of course, to
protect and to perpetuate the reform. Resistance to the forces that would
weaken the cloister's spirituality is thus one of the most prominent themes
of these texts. But threats to the Observance are not always external. At
Ebstorf, for example, the chronicler admonishes her sisters to resist the
danger posed by laziness and slothfulness, and not to take for granted what
others have accomplished by hard work. As she reminds her readers, the
present generation has been privileged "to grow up in the reform from
childhood, as in a rose garden."[40] The writers typically look back on the
early days of the reform as a kind of golden age. Thus Anna Roede writes
of the earlier flowering of the reform when Sophia von Münster was abbess
(1463–1500) and exclaims, "But a real reform lasts generally not above one
hundred years. In the first fifty years it blooms and in the second fifty years
it wanes, just as do the days, unfortunately, before our eyes. May God make
us better."[41]

As texts whose aim is to protect, perpetuate, and shape the Observance,
reform chronicles create a different image of women from the portraits
they drew of themselves in the mystical sister-books of the fourteenth-
century. These fifteenth- and early sixteenth-century narratives portraying
reform sisters defying the secular authorities for the sake of the Observance
or abbesses colluding to protect the interests of their communities depict
women who are more *in* the world than out of it. Instead of the ecstatic

faints, trances, and visions foregrounded in the sister-books, the authors emphasize fortitude, assertiveness, and industry. In the light of these depictions and of Hrosvit's and Bertha's portraits of heroic abbesses from a much earlier period, the idea that what is unique about women's writing is something female, in the sense of mystical, must be reexamined. To be sure, visions and radical asceticism could still function as effective routes to power despite increased censorship, as will be seen in the case of Magdalena Beutler, but the route was perilous and had to be embarked on differently.

Femininity-in-Writing?

While working on his study *Women Writers of the Middle Ages* (1984), Peter Dronke related that a number of friends and colleagues asked him, "Do you think there is something about these women writers that distinguishes their work from that of men?" Dronke always replied that he "was not searching for a Platonic Form, Femininity-in-writing, which would manifest itself similarly in every female text." Nevertheless, he did identify a common denominator in the women's texts he studied. This was a certain "immediacy," their authors' way of looking at themselves "more concretely and more searchingly" than many of their male contemporaries.[42] Beyond this, what other qualities have been proposed to characterize women's writing?

Early feminist critics, approaching the question from a literary theoretical point of view, compared men's rational, logical, hierarchical, and linear language to women's a-rational, contra-logical, circular, or non-hierarchical self-expression. They also identified in some women's works a unique focus on bodily sensations and images—a way of writing the body.[43] Historians, on the other hand, use terms like emotional, intuitive, subjective, sentimental, narcissistic, spontaneous, or "focused on the inner life" to describe the way women write.[44] Caroline Walker Bynum employed the term feminine (even when referring to writers like Heinrich Seuse) to mean "affective, exuberant, lyrical, and filled with images."[45] In his survey of women's convents in Basel, Rudolf Wackernagel identified as characteristic of late-medieval women's chronicles what he described as a "tone of sweetness" or "winsomeness."[46] Other literary historians, however, have noted only women's "clumsy syntax," "poor word choice," "labored rhymes," "simple rhyme schemes," or the "need for training."[47]

In the chronicles surveyed in the present study, a kind of "immediacy" related to the quality Dronke identifies can be seen in their personal tone. The female chroniclers often include themselves in their texts or interrupt the third-person narrative with first-person comments. Thus the Pfullingen chronicler states, "As I write this, I have great hopes" that the Lord will not abandon the community. The writers address the reader directly, using the familiar ("du") form and terms of endearment such as "dearest beloved." Near the end of her account, the Pfullingen chronicler says, "Pray to God for the writer. She composed this for you out of love."[48] Angela Varnbühler, the prioress at St. Gall, begins the chronicle of the convent of St. Katharina with herself and her entrance into the cloister, then shifts to "we," saying, "In the year 1441, I, Engel Varnbühler, was born on Pentecost Wednesday, entered the cloister in 1453 on the day after Corpus Christi, and took orders on the Feast of St. Margaret. . . . In 1459 we began the common life."[49] Similarly, Abbess Sophia Dobbers begins her entries on the reform of Überwasser with the words, "In 1483, I arrived."[50] Other female chroniclers interject frequent personal comments. Anna Roede poignantly relates, "[Abbess Sophia von Münster] died in my arms." Speaking of hard times at the hands of the Lutherans, she exclaims, "Oh what sad children we were then" and "Oh God, what wonders we lived through in our time and what is still to come before the Judgment Day!"[51] The women's sense of sisterhood is expressed in frequent references to their community as "we" and to their house as "our" cloister.[52] More often than men's chronicles, women's cloister histories include and name individual members of the rank and file.

Similar to chronicles, the personal tone of books of sisters composed at convents and sister-houses of the New Devout also tends to be inclusive and collective. Anne Bollmann notes that the Emmerich collection of biographies treats lay sisters in the same way as choir sisters, regardless of rank. Bollmann speaks of a "we-author" and describes the writing process in these works as "interactive," a conglomerate of collective memories of sisters that were generated by oral interviews and discussions about the deceased. The author acts as "the pen" of her community, recording the flow of the collective memory.[53]

Besides their vividness of affect and more intimate tone, women's chronicles differ formally from those of men. Although the women authors are aware that they are writing for posterity, they are largely unfamiliar with the standard forms of the chronicle and tend to invent their own idiosyncratic formats, often interspersing their accounts within other documents.[54] Stylistically, they demonstrate a much wider variation of training—often a lack of training—in grammar and rhetoric. The ability to read is clearly not the same skill as the ability to write, and thus many women's chronicles are filled with elliptical expressions, partially articulated ideas, repetitions, non-chronological sequences, incomplete and run-on sentences. Frequently agitated or polemical, these accounts bear all the marks of orality, resembling spoken conversations or dictated texts more than deliberately crafted literary compositions. Because they are written in regional dialects, the vocabulary tends to be that of the idiomatic spoken language of the particular locality and is less homogeneous than the German written by male monastics who traveled about. In short, women's language is generally not school language. The brothers, who have gone through a long process of education, think and express themselves differently even in the vernacular from female chroniclers who, despite their familiarity with the sermon form and its conventions, have little experience with the practice and style of history writing. The non-standard form, content, and manner of expression of these convent chronicles illustrate well just how much training influences what and how people write.

Skeptical of the possibility of discerning a feminine voice at all in medieval women's mystical works, Ursula Peters argued that literary historians cannot distinguish "a specifically female level of expression" but only the "ideological production of programmatic preconceptions about women."[55] The dilemma here, as described by Hamburger, is the effort by feminist critics to recover female voices from the past, while at the same time arguing that the female author is only a medium for the voice of male supervisors who "mouth the dominant discourse." But while Hamburger admits the significant influence on women of male spiritual advisors, he is not willing to grant them the status of "ventriloquists."[56] With fifteenth- and early sixteenth-century texts the problem of mediation can be approached differently because the number and variety of works composed by women is substantial enough to allow comparison of parallel works composed by men and women. One can, for example, contrast cloister annals by women at women's houses with those composed by male chroniclers at men's houses or by male chroniclers at women's houses. My focus here will be on works in the vernacular, the language that women considered their own, but which was used by male authors when writing for women or for the less well-educated laity, particularly the nobility. How do these male-authored vernacular texts resemble their feminine counterparts?

Not surprisingly, men's chronicles, even those written in the vernacular, tend to be consciously constructed as literary works observing literary conventions. Gallus Öhem's German *Chronicle of the Monastery of Reichenau* [c. 1505/8], for example, begins with a dedication and prologue.[57] The dedication is to the current abbot and contains an elaborate modesty topos deprecating Öhem's own "artistry" and "wisdom," despite the fact that he had studied at two universities. The concept of artistry in writing as expressed here is a very different approach and tone from that encountered in most female-authored chronicles. Öhem goes on to explain that he has organized his work in three parts: founders, abbots, and the privileges and services of princes and nobility. Addressing his work "to the Swabian nobility," he also includes the coats of arms of members of the convent and donors.

Histories written by women, in contrast, tend to be smaller in scale and particular in focus.[58] They concentrate more on internal events and on the spirituality of the members than do similar chronicles by their male compatriots. When external conflicts are narrated they most often deal with the women's struggles to resist secular control. The men's reform chronicles, on the other hand, deal more with power conflicts that affect the standing of the cloister in the world. They rarely touch on the day-to-day religious life within the house or that of the individual members of the community. The German *Chronicle of the Monastery of St. Gall* (c. 1490), for example, centers on the history of the ongoing warfare between the abbey and the town, over which the abbey tried to assert its jurisdiction. The abbey's chronicler insists on calling St. Gall a "monastery city" even though the town had declared itself a "free imperial city."[59] Much of his account is an inventory of the property destroyed in this conflict and plans for a new monastery to be built elsewhere, which is described in extremely detailed legal language. Reference to the spiritual or inner life of the members of the community is minimal here as well. Likewise, Raphael Hanisch's vernacular account (1510/20) of the conflict between rival houses of Conventual and Observant Franciscans in Breslau (Wroclaw) makes no mention of the religious differences between the two groups.[60] Rather, Hanisch details the politics and tactics of a struggle in which the Observants lose and with-draw from Breslau. Generally, the men's accounts lack the inward focus and more intimate tone of the "we" and the "our" that is found in the women's narratives. By these criteria, anyone reading two anonymous accounts could, most likely, identify which one was written by a male and which by a female chronicler.

But what about a male chronicler writing about a women's house? An example of this kind of vernacular text can be found in Lambert Slaggert's German *Chronicle of Cloister Ribnitz,* a history of a house of Poor Clares composed by its confessor, 1523–32. Slaggert opens first with a history of the Franciscan order, then of the Poor Clares and a geneology of the princes of Mecklenburg, before he begins the story of Ribnitz.[61] Although Slaggert recounts the events in the administration of each abbess in turn, his history records many political events and conflicts external to this cloister. Clearly written with the ruling family in mind, whose history Slaggert narrates, the work does not highlight the outstanding abbesses, but treats each one in turn in a more or less formulaic way. Often cryptically concealing more than it reveals, Slaggert's work is the more remarkable for what it does not say about the women. Of Elisabeth of Mecklenburg, the cloister's seventh abbess, who was forced to resign during the reform of 1493, Slaggert only comments, "For many reasons which are better kept silent than written about, she lost the support of the sisters who refused to recognize her as abbess any longer or be under obedience to her." Whether this was because she supported or opposed the reform is not made clear, although Slaggert intimates that the change was imposed from outside and instituted with great difficulty. A second reform requiring the sisters to give up their private property was carried out in 1509. Here the first to comply was Elisabeth's successor, Abbess Dorothea von Mecklenburg. Slaggert reports laconically that her action was imitated by the others, but "with great unwillingness" and with "no real love for it."[62] More details about the women's role and reaction to the reform are not forthcoming. Indeed, except for the names of those in the ducal family who were inhabitants of the cloister, little is said about the lives or deeds of any sisters other than the abbesses, who are portrayed as unexceptional, routinely going through the motions of being abbess.

In contrast to Slaggert's chronicle of Ribnitz, the histories composed by women, as already noted, typically celebrate the community's outstanding leaders and portray them as exceptional for their virtue, spirituality, or leadership and administrative abilities. Yet, at the same time, the works tend to be more inclusive of sisters other than abbesses and prioresses. While the women are in the foreground of these stories, men are often included in the role of helpers. Tore Nyberg observes that men in the chronicles of Maihingen and Altomünster fall into two categories: they are either helpers or "threats [usually secular men] to the integrity of the cloister or to monastic life as an expression of feminine distinction."[63] In most of the women's accounts surveyed in this study the sisters portray themselves as the initiators or co-initiators of the of the activities within the cloister and the men as working with them in a common endeavor. Recalling the early days of the Observance at Herzebrock under Abbess Sophia von Münster, Anna Roede portrays the men as helpers, recounting how there were not enough sisters to sing the hours antiphonally as the sisters wished, so the provost and confessor made up one choir and the sisters the other. She reports how the two men copied new choir books "and helped us day and night, so that the divine service would be primary."[64]

Despite the typical use of "we" and "our" in their cloister histories and a few accounts of women in opposition to men, as in Magdalena Kremer's narrative about women's march on Rome to secure readmittance to the order, the texts contain few direct remarks on gender. Those that do comment tend to describe instances in which women succeeded where men did not. The Ebstorf chronicle tells how the convent had first been occupied by a group of male canons who received a vision that the altar would be served by nuns. Sometime later one of the canons, while searching for a golden ring that he had lost, knocked over a candlestick, starting a fire that burned the house to the ground. The canons then abandoned the site. Wishing to refound a religious community in that place, a local count asked his sister, who was a Benedictine nun, to send women of her order who "would gladly embrace poverty out of love for God." In this way, the ring that the men had lost passed to the women. The Ebstorf chronicler goes on to explain that the ring that each sister receives on entering the order symbolizes her betrothal to the divine bridegroom and is a consecration "so sublime and great" that it is "second only to that of the priest."[65] Even more than in men's works, women depict themselves as distinguished by their religious calling.

Another narrative about a woman succeeding where men failed describes the founding of the Bridgettine community at Maihingen. It tells how the men who first started what was to be a Bridgettine double convent were unable to get a contingent of women to come to Maihingen from the older community already established at Gnadenberg. The *Hausbuch* of Maihingen relates the story of an enterprising widow, Anna Kerg, who would later become a lay sister in the house. Anna was frustrated by the men's inability to get results and so took up the cause herself. Soliciting letters of invitation from the local count and from the Abbess of Kirchheim am Ries, the energetic Anna took them herself to Gnadenberg. Here the *Hausbuch* comments, "So the dear Sister Anna went there with the two letters and accomplished more than the brothers had in ten years."[66]

Karen Glente argues that male authors see women as essentially passive while female writers depict them as active. Comparing works about visionary women, Glente examined Thomas de Cantimpré's vita of Margaret of Ypres (d. 1237) and Jacques de Vitry's biography of Marie of Oignies (d. 1213) with Katharina von Gueberschwihr's vitae of the charismatic women at Unterlinden (c. 1320). While the accounts are not contemporary, Glente justifies her selection by citing the extreme paucity of any unmediated texts at all by women. She argues that male authors, Vitry and Cantimpré, depict women primarily in terms of gender. Katharina of Gueberschwihr, on the other hand, portrays them as "people (Menschen) who happen to be women."[67] While the men consider visionary women to be highly exceptional and other, Katharina distinguishes degrees of piety in her models and encourages the sisters in her cloister to imitate the spirituality of these women as an incrementally achievable goal. Both Thomas de Cantimpré and Jacques de Vitry depict God as the initiator and the women as merely acquiescing in being chosen by him. In contrast, Katharina von Gueberschwihr focuses on the women's active role in initiating the mystical contact. She describes the women who levitate as seeking to raise themselves toward heaven. Here there is a reciprocal complementarity, a working together of the women's piety and God's grace.[68] This difference of perspective on agency is, likewise, an important aspect of women's self-representation in fifteenth-century reform chronicles.

An examination of fifteenth- and early-sixteenth-century collections of vitae of religious women in Observant convents and sister-houses of the New Devout offers a perspective on how the conventions of composing nuns' vitae had changed. Unlike their predecessors in the fourteenth century, fifteenth- and sixteenth-century collections of vitae depict the sisters as examples of virtue in practical day-to-day activities rather than as exceptional spiritual athletes interceding for souls in manly fashion. Theirs is a world of very hard work in which heroism is embodied through examples such as the handicapped sister in the Emmerich book of sisters (c. 1503) who spun cloth year after year with bleeding fingers because of a severe burn she had suffered earlier.[69] These women display ardent spirituality, humility, selflessness, and practical virtues rather than visions and feats of asceticism that were frowned upon by the censors.

The Case of Magdalena Beutler

That visionary works continued to be composed by women despite censorship of them should not surprise. What does perhaps surprise, however, is the way they were reinvented to pass muster in the language and service of reform. Mystical texts or revelations were written, for example, by Alijt Bake, Jacomijne Costers, and Magdalena Beutler, all of whom also single-handedly undertook reforms of their convents. Here Magdalena Beutler (1407–1458), known as Magdalena of Freiburg and a sister at the house of Poor Clares in that city, will serve as a case in point.[70] By casting herself as a visionary in the cause of the Observance, Sister Magdalena gained control not only over her own convent but became one of the best known, albeit most controversial, women of her time. Her original vita, compiled either by her confessor or by Sister Elisabeth Vögtin, Madgalena's contemporary in the cloister, has been lost. But two different versions in texts composed before Magdalena's death (1458) survive in manuscript copies from 1491 and 1656/57.[71] What is remarkable is how well Sister Magdalena seems to have grasped what only a few women before her understood, namely, the power of visionary and para-mystical episodes to gain influence over others both within and outside the cloister. Magdalena was clearly aware of this, but consistently claimed reform as her aim and justification.

The "Magdalenen-Buch" (1491) tells how in 1429 on the eve of the Feast of the 11,000 Virgins, Magdalena, then twenty-two, miraculously vanished for three days. All the sisters, their confessor, and their steward searched the cloister for her without finding a trace. On the second night, as the downcast sisters were assembled in the choir to perform their office, two knocks were heard and a letter fluttered down into their midst. The note turned out to be a message from the missing Magdalena, written in her own blood. It exhorted the sisters not to grieve or to search further, for she was "a prisoner of God" and in a place where the Lord wanted her to be. Urging the sisters to adopt voluntary poverty, Magdalena admonished them portentously, "God help you in the future, when I a miserable child and prisoner of God shall preach poverty to you."[72]

On the third day, when the women came into the choir for matins, they discovered Magdalena lying before the altar "as though dead." The sisters tried to revive her, but she did not respond until three hours later, when the vita reports:

> [S]he gave a great sigh and began to move. The sisters went to her, raised her up, and began to speak with her, but she remained silent, spoke not a word to anyone, but embraced each of the sisters in turn and then went and laid herself before the altar. After a while she took pen and paper and wrote to the women of the cloister that they should earnestly and diligently turn to God, for the Lord had revealed to her the great and unutterable pain that their deceased sisters suffered . . . who had been so devoted to material possessions and did not want to hold all goods in common.

Magdalena's disappearance, her letter from "the other world," and her dramatic return had a profound effect on the convent. The "Magdalenen-Buch" reports that, as a result, the sisters "abandoned themselves and completely dedicated themselves to voluntary poverty and to other austerities which they earlier had resolutely resisted."[73] This amateur theatrical staged by Magdalena in order bring her sisters to the point of accepting reform had worked brilliantly. Always a somewhat controversial member of the community, Magdalena afterward came to be regarded as a visionary and was able through further disappearances and visions to keep religious fervor in her cloister at a high pitch.

The daughter of an equally flamboyant mother, Magdalena was perhaps predestined for this role. Johannes Meyer describes how her mother, the wealthy widow Margareta von Kenzingen, had placed the five-year-old Magdalena in the cloister of the Poor Clares and then abandoned her own large fortune in order to take up a life of poverty and ministry to the sick in the city of Marburg where she lived unrecognized. Some time later, her vita relates, she was wrongfully accused of theft and sentenced to death by drowning. Only when Margareta was brought forward to be executed did a priest from Freiburg recognize her and testify that she was an honorable person, and moreover, of a very prominent family. Margareta was released and afterward entered the newly reformed Dominican cloister of Unterlinden in Colmar. From Unterlinden she later went with a group of Observants to undertake the reform of the St. Maria Magdalena an den Steinen cloister in Basel where she remained until her death, revered there as one of the cloister's most illustrious mystics.[74]

About four years before her death, Margareta had become concerned about the unreformed house of Poor Clares in Freiburg where her daughter (now age seventeen) was living. Believing that the cloister was not spiritual enough, she tried to have Magdalena moved to an Observant house. The daughter, however, refused to leave the Clares, won her case in a hearing before the city council, and—it seems—decided instead to imitate her illustrious mother by reforming the Clarissan cloister herself. In this she succeeded and went on to achieve even greater notoriety than her well-known mother.

Magdalena's awareness of the power of visionary experiences and the supernatural to gain influence and the right to speak with authority is matched by her reformist zeal and her conviction that the end justifies the means. Scrupulously wording her statements so that they contained no untruths if taken literally, Magdalena had perpetrated her first small deception, her disappearance, for what, she believed, was a good cause. Seeing its remarkable result, Magdalena became convinced that she wanted to become a martyr for reform. Perhaps she realized that she could have an even more powerful effect by orchestrating her own canonization. Accordingly, a year later Magdalena prophesied that in thirty-four days she would die. This she announced along with the news that she had requested God to grant an indulgence to all who would "honor His name" or "perform a good work during her life or after her death."[75] Moreover, she petitioned God to guarantee that all would be saved who were present at her death. At this point her plan seems to have gotten out of control, for the news spread quickly beyond the cloister. On the appointed day, Epiphany of the year 1431, hordes of lay people and prominent church officials streamed into Freiburg on foot, on horseback, and in every kind of wagon, jamming the city to witness the death of the now famous prophet.

Despite Magdalena's best efforts, she failed to die on that day. Tearfully, she was forced to announce that God had miraculously spared her, much to the consternation of most onlookers and particularly Observant reformer, Johannes Nider, who pronounced it a self-deception.[76] Indeed, Magdalena's scheme had backfired and she was discredited. But not entirely, for although Magdalena had lost credibility in the eyes of the public and most churchmen, her Clarissan sisters remained loyal to her and esteemed her to the end of her life as a true visionary. Even before her death at age fifty-one in 1458, the sisters began collecting her revelations, compiling her vita, and afterward referred to her as "our good, blessed Magdalena."[77] Even outside her cloister the failed effort at martyrdom had contributed to her notoriety. Beyond the two fifteenth-century versions of her vita containing her revelations (each set filling some 200 to 300 manuscript pages), three fragmentary vitae survive that include letters and accounts about her.[78] Karen Greenspan points out that, besides the revelations, at least two devotional works sometimes attributed to a Sister Magdalena exist in over forty manuscripts and eleven printed copies.[79] Although Schleussner maintained that the two longer vitae were both probably written by male Franciscans, it is also possible that the author of the earlier manuscript, the "Magdalenen-Buch" (1491), was sister Elisabeth Vögtin. The cloister's "Gedenkbuch" states that Vögtin wrote about Magdalena's "blessed life and virtues" to which she had been an eyewitness.[80] While not deciding the issue, it may at least be possible here to shed some light on the question by applying some of the criteria this study has identified as characteristic of women's writings in this period.

Like many women's texts, the 1491 "Magdalenen-Buch" follows no conventional format. It is a hodgepodge of letters, songs, prayers, exercises, visions, and biography in no chronological sequence, while the other version (composed from some of the same sources) is organized chronologically. The 1491 text has many more first-person interjections, references to "us" and to "our mother" [superior] and, above all, a warmer, more intimate tone than that of the later version. It speaks, for example, of touching, grasping, holding, and hugging the visionary Magdalena, as the sisters tried to revive her. In contrast, the other version recounts rather matter-of-factly,

"They found her lying right before the altar in front of the Holy Sacrament, appearing as though dead. Then they read matins with great fear and trembling."[81] Unlike this more impersonal version, the 1491 text depicts a later intimate scene of the sisters sitting together in a circle around Magdalena as she speaks of her supernatural experience until late into the night: "The sisters were full of joy and all went to her and sat in a circle around her and listened to her words and talked with her until midnight when the bell struck twelve."[82] The prayers and revelations, either dictated or written by Magdalena herself, that form the largest portion of the two works seem stylistically unimproved. The prayers constitute a kind of stream-of-consciousness devotional monologue, a sort of religious rap, which has not fared well with critics. The revelations are difficult to read because of their lack of punctuation and run-on sentences. Often didactic in nature, they comprise admonitions and lessons in which Magdalena preaches to her sisters a spiritual way of life. Many of the visions are introduced with rubrics such as, "Here She Teaches the Sisters How They Should Pray Devoutly" or "How the Holy Body of Our Lord Pays for All Our Sins." Others relate visual and auditory revelations, but are prudently recounted as perceived "not in God's actual words, but heard as though in a dream" or "in a heavenly, light sleep."[83]

The interesting question that arises here is whether Magdalena, in her bid to acquire influence and to use it in the cause of the reform, consciously styled herself after earlier famous visionary women, most notably Hildegard of Bingen and Mechthild of Hackeborn (or Mechthild of Magdeburg). This question arises because in one of her dream-visions of the realm of the blessed, she reports seeing two figures whom she identifies as Hildegard and Mechthild. She addresses them and Mechthild answers, "I am God's servant Mechthildis . . . and with me is the blessed Hildegard [Hilgartdis]. . . . God revealed to us much that we had to make known to the world so that men should profess that they were created for nothing other than to praise and serve the eternal God."[84] The reference here could be to Mechthild of Magdeburg, whose controversial writings had been translated from the original Middle Low into Middle High German about 1350. Although Mechthild was thought to have been largely forgotten by the fifteenth century, Sara Poor has traced the reception of Mechthild's *Flowing Light of the Godhead* both as a complete text and as excerpts in anthologies that circulated in fifteenth-century women's convents.[85] The other possibility is that

Magdalena was referring to another Helfta mystic, Mechthild of Hackeborn (1241–1298), whose Latin *Book of Special Grace* was also excerpted for collections.[86] Similarly, Hildegard of Bingen's visionary works were believed to have been forgotten, yet a look at the library catalogue from the years 1455–1499 at St. Katharina in Nuremberg lists a work called "The Prophecies of Saint Hildegard."[87] Gertrud Lewis points out that Hildegard was listed in the official index of saints and revered as such in fifteenth-century Germany.[88]

Clearly, Magdalena was not alone among fifteenth-century women writers in citing other female mystics. Not only have scholars underestimated how much contact women's convents had with each other, but also how much women knew about other mystics. Anne Bollmann points to Alijt Bake, visionary author, reformer, and prioress of the Galilea cloister in Ghent, who cites the writings of Catherine of Siena (1347–1380), Mechthild of Magdeburg, and Mechthild of Hackeborn. Not only does it appear that Magdalena Beutler patterned herself on Hildegard and Mechthild, but Alijt Bake states in her autobiography that she is "walking the path" of Colette of Corbie, saying, "For just as Sister Colette was a mother of our order in the reformation of the holy religion, I should also be a mother of our order in the reformation of the inner life."[89]

Both Magdalena and Alijt were likely also affected by the model of reform activism represented by Catherine of Siena whose biography was well known among convent women from the many copies given by families to their daughters on entering a cloister. Both the St. Gall and Nuremberg St. Katharina libraries contain several copies of it.[90] It is also clear that the mystical model was still a very powerful one. Probably because of her visions, Alijt was chosen prioress of the Galilea Cloister in Ghent even though she was only thirty and had made her profession only five years before.[91] Yet the price was high. Alijt Bake was censured and exiled by the Windesheim authorities (and died a year later) while Magdalena Beutler was publicly discredited. Even the latest edition of the *Verfasserlexikon* refers to her as an "hysteric."[92] In contrast, Catherine of Siena, who paid the price for her extreme asceticism by an early death at age thirty-three, enjoyed the protection of Dominican Master General Raymond of Capua, who composed her vita himself. Among other things, he saw its importance for promoting the Dominican reform. Yet even Catherine was forced to defend herself against suspicions about the authenticity of her visions.[93]

Like Magalena Beutler's revelations, the mystical writings of Alijt Bake do not fit into standard categories. They are, like many women's writings, a loosely organized, hybrid mix of genres: visionary revelations, spiritual lessons, and every-day experiences in a sort of diary format, a mix that Bollmann identifies as "rapiarium" (anthology of extracts) structure.[94] These kinds of books, compiled by Devout Sisters for personal study and contemplation, contained short anecdotes, aphorisms, extracts, and meditations designed to foster spiritual growth. Like the anthologies, Alijt's writings are intended for "convent-internal" or personal use. A characteristic that Natalie Davis identified as typical of women's histories also applies here. Like those Davis surveyed, these works are particular in focus, designed for a specific community, an intimate, convent-internal setting and in-house consumption.[95] Although Prioress Bake was well read in classical, patristic texts, and the mystical literature of her time (she refers to sermons by Johannes Tauler and to works by Rulman Merswin and Jordanus von Quedlinburg), she chose to compose edifying religious manuals for the sisters.[96] Books of advice, such as Anna von Buchwald's "Book in the Choir," Elsbeth Muntprat's sister-book at St. Gall, and Katharina von Mühlheim's handbook of instructions for ceremonies seem to be a form particularly favored by female writers. Like Alijt's books for edification and instruction, these works take cognizance of the literary requirements and the circumstances of life in a community of sisters. Women's needs for different kinds of books can be illustrated by the vita of Andries Yserens in the book of sisters of the Lamme-van-Dieze House in Deventer. Sister Andries spent twenty years in the kitchen, serving in the office of kitchen mistress, before being chosen to head her community. Finding it more difficult to concentrate on spiritual exercises while preparing food than while doing other work such as spinning, Sister Andries used cherry pits to keep her place in her devotions.[97] The ideology of the Modern Devotion and the living situation in sister-houses required a different way of reading, one that favored texts written in small, discrete units as points to ponder while working. Because women lacked the years of education and structured time needed to study or write works requiring sustained concentration, accommodations made to their circumstances influenced the forms of literature they produced.

Like Magdalena Beutler, who was influenced by the writing of earlier female mystics and composed revelations of her own, adapting them to the religious issues and movements of her day, Alijt Bake was a reader and user of texts. Even though her writings remained largely unknown, Bollmann shows that they were, nevertheless, copied and transmitted anonymously under new titles and in adaptations.[98] Indeed, by compiling religious anthologies, women created new texts of their own. Choosing works that appealed to their interests and excerpting their meaningful points, they passed on these preferences in written form.[99] Likewise, by taking notes and writing up summaries of sermon highlights that they wished to retain, women were participating in shaping the religious discourse of the day by formulating it in their own words. Alijt Bake, for example, adapted and reflected on sermons by Johannes Tauler and others in writings of her own.[100] In this way, many women in fifteenth-century religious houses became not only consumers but producers of religious literature.

Women as Consumers, Contributors, and Disseminators of the Literature of Piety

In the transcribing and sharing of collections of their own house sermons, women took part in an absorbing activity that involved them in a conversation not only within networks of Observant houses but with the laity as well. Moreover, both house-sermon transcriptions and many of the vernacular devotional works that the sisters copied and exchanged for their own use also were circulated to devout friends and family members outside the cloister. Because little in the way of theology and devotional literature had been written specifically for a lay reading public in the vernacular, interest was high and women's convent libraries became an important source for the religious texts that circulated, were copied, and eventually printed for the laity. These texts, written for a monastic readership, were borrowed mainly from women's convent libraries which, unlike those at men's houses, consisted primarily of works in German.[101] As illustrated by these kinds of exchanges, it was the alliance of reform and lay piety—not just one or the other—that brought vernacular religious literature to its greatest distribution.[102] That this was not an insignificant development can be demonstrated by the number of late medieval devotional books, saints' lives, religious songs, and tracts that were published in editions far larger than any that secular fictional writing ever achieved. Together they constitute some seventy to eighty percent of the total production of works in the late Middle Ages.[103] Their significance for at least one female reader is candidly expressed in the Emmerich book of sisters which describes Sister Lijsbet Kaels's love of books, saying she "had a large number of devotional books and she used to call them her 'bellows.' For, she said, 'with these I blow upon my heart and ignite the flame so that it glows with love for my God.' "[104]

That women were, indeed, a large part of the audience for German devotional texts, read aloud or privately, and for vernacular preaching in the fifteenth and early sixteenth centuries is illustrated by attendance at sermons. Larissa Taylor points out that women in the audience outnumbered men four to one.[105] Of the vernacular sermons that have come down to us, virtually all were copied in the women's religious houses where they were preached and were transcribed for individual study. Accordingly, researching German-language sermons for the fifteenth century literally means reading literature that was meant primarily for religious women.[106] Besides transcribing sermons, women also edited them for a lay readership. Susanna Hörwart and Ursula Stingel at the Magdalen cloister in Strasbourg not only transcribed for publication many of the sermons of Strasbourg preacher Johannes Geiler von Kaysersberg, but a letter from Geiler (dated 1499) explains that Prioress Hörwart edited his enclosed sermon to make it appropriate for lay readers. Geiler's letter addressed to the sisters at the Freiburg house of the Penitants of St. Maria Magdalena states:

> Know that our mother prioress at Strasbourg [Susanna Hörwart] did not want to make the sermon available to the laity [as it was preached to the sisters] but selected from it what she considered appropriate for lay persons, adding to and subtracting from it as she saw fit. I am sending it to you enclosed. You may distribute it to whomever you wish so that God will be glorified by all of us, both religious and lay people, now and forever. Amen.[107]

Elsewhere, Geiler refers to the same Prioress Susanna as "a lover of God and of her neighbor, a builder and upholder of the reform and of the spiritual life."[108]

It is clear here that these women's engagement in reformed spirituality had more than merely an internal focus. It is of a piece with the greater rank-and-file engagement in religious issues and especially reformed preaching in the two decades preceding the Reformation. As collectors, choosers, transmitters, and consumers of religious literature, convent women must be taken into account as participants in the late-medieval conversation on spirituality. Their involvement—itself a kind of empowerment—was an outgrowth of the Observant movement.

Observant Women and the Reformation

In the battle for church renewal it is perhaps ironic that the Observant reformers should have been the staunchest opponents of the Lutheran and Zwinglian reforms. And female Observants were the most resistant of all.[109] Women in non-observant cloisters such as Töss and Oetenbach in Zürich had a less strict form of enclosure and were, thus, more open to the new teachings. At Oetenbach, Lutheran relatives of cloistered nuns made concerted efforts to bring these women into contact with the preachers of the new faith and so "to curb the influence of the Dominicans." In 1522 the Zürich city council arranged for Huldrych Zwingli (1484–1531) to preach at the convent of Oetenbach. Speaking in the cloister church, Zwingli declared monasticism to be "hypocrisy." Accounts report that after Zwingli's sermons "several women declared themselves to be enthusiastic followers of the reformer." Soon the convent split into two parties: a majority group which held fast to the old faith and a minority one which followed Zwingli and was dubbed "the Lutherans." By 1525, when most of the Zürich citizenry had adopted the Zwinglian persuasion, the city council took over Oetenbach and its property. The cloister was opened and the women who remained were required to engage in useful work for the benefit of the poor and to wear ordinary women's clothing.[110]

Reports of the nearby Conventual cloister of Töss record that it too split into opposing factions. At first the faction supporting the new faith applied to the Zürich authorities to exempt them from singing the office at matins. They asked to read it instead, "due to the extreme cold" which made for "poor singing." Later they petitioned to end it altogether. Still not wishing to leave the convent, however, they proposed to spend their time there "more profitably," to increase their allowances, to wear ordinary clothing, and to end claustration. Finally, in 1525 the majority petitioned for dissolution of the cloister. Although most of the women left the house, a few continued to live there on fixed allowances.[111] Halter comments that in general the Conventual women's convents presented less opposition to the new faith than the Observant houses, citing particularly the Inselkloster in Bern and St. Katharina in St. Gall, both of which resisted tenaciously to the last.[112]

At St. Gall, cathedral organist Fridolin Sicher touchingly describes the nuns' sad procession to the church when the town council required the sisters of St. Katharina to attend sermons on the new faith there.

> Then the women went forth shamefacedly two by two with the youngest in front according to age. But they showed little joy or eagerness: old, sick, limping women with great swollen eyes, for clearly they had found this going out a great hardship. It appears that those who were there would have preferred to stay separated from the world in their cloister until death. Otherwise they would have left [the house] before this, considering the quantity of scorn and denigration of their order that had been preached to them [and] they would gladly have gone into the world, had they wished it and [would have] been treated mildly enough by the people, but none of them wanted to come out.[113]

Of the fifty-one inhabitants of the cloister, three eventually renounced their vows. Two of the three married, but one soon left her husband and entered another cloister at Kreuzlingen. Vogler points out that St. Katharina was "a thorn in the flesh" to St. Gall, since it lay inside the city walls even though its extensive properties completely encircled the city. After the city had joined the Zwinglian camp, marauding parties of townsfolk began periodically vandalizing the cloister and its properties. To save the books and other precious items, Sister Regula Keller tried to smuggle them out to other convents. Eventually, however, the city council took over St. Katharina, effectively ending all semblance of monastic life there. Not one to give up, Regula Keller remained near by, living with a small community of women. Despite repeated arrests, she waged a continuous forty-year legal battle for reinstatement of the convent.[114]

In their chronicles there are many first-hand accounts from the women themselves about the conflicts with the Lutheran new sect. Eva Madgalena

Neyler's (d. 1575) chronicle of the Dominican house in Pforzheim, which had been reformed in 1443 by sisters from St. Katharina in Nuremberg, tells how the thirty-nine sisters solemnly resisted for eight years. Neyler asserts with satisfaction that "by God's grace [they] wore out eighteen preachers."[115] At last the nuns received permission to move as a group out of the territory of the Margrave of Baden to a dilapidated cloister (Kirchberg) near Sulz on the Neckar that was inhabited by seven non-observant nuns. Here they instituted a reform according to the Observance, which, as recounted above, drove away the house's seven original inhabitants.[116]

At the Dominican cloister of Steinheim, near Marbach, which had been reformed by sisters from Unterlinden in 1478, an anonyomus nun kept a diary from 1553 to 1566. In it she kept a record for posterity of the sisters' struggle against Duke Ulrich of Württemberg and his efforts to convert the women to Protestantism and gain control of their cloister. The diary's editor, Konrad Rothenhäusler, comments that as late as 1570 Protestant church officials in Württemberg reported how little headway the Reformation had made in women's cloisters, even though all of the men's houses had long been reformed.[117] After fifty soldiers had been quartered in their cloister, the diary relates, intimidation and threats forced the women to accept the duke as their "protector" and hand over their letters of exemption from secular jurisdiction. Mass and the singing of the Office were forbidden, yet the sisters secretly continued to "read the Hours at midnight two by two in the refectory," refusing to accept the new faith, the author insists, "not out of defiance" but because they could not act "against their consciences." The anonymous sister's account breaks off with the women's fate still uncertain. Rothenhäusler reports that the sisters remained in their cloister, continuing to perform the office in secret, until the last one died sometime around 1580. Its author explains, the diary was written as a "protest to God and the world" to document how the sisters unjustly were forced by threats of violence to give up their privileges and yet remained true to the old faith.[118] At Herzebrock, Anna Roede's second chronicle gives an Observant women's perspective on Lutheran assertions that the Word of God was not reaching the cloisters. Anna writes indignantly that the sisters were each "as well trained as that [Lutheran] priest, for they all understood well what they sang and read, [both] the Old Testament and the New."[119]

Although the overwhelming majority of Observant women's houses rejected the new sects, not all of them did. At Münster, for example, the sisters at Überwasser, which had been reformed in 1483, joined the Anabaptists early on. Their chronicle tells how the majority of the sisters, including the chronicler herself, Elisabeth Fridaghes, was won over by the new teachings. Shortly after reporting favorably on Bernard Rothmann's Palm Sunday sermon in 1533, the chronicle breaks off, after its author and most of the sisters joined Rothmann's sect. From other accounts it is known that only the prioress and two sisters held to the old beliefs. Yet, although the Anabaptist sisters abandoned the rule, they continued to live for a time in the convent, circulating in town as agitators for Rothmann's party.[120] In contrast, the sisters at Marienthal (Niesing), another Münster house of Augustinian nuns, first founded as a house of Sisters of the Common Life, rejected the Lutheran teachings. Their chronicle relates how the Anabaptist mobs drove them out of their cloister. Among the crowd were sisters from Überwasser, who urged the Marienthal women to have themselves baptized.[121]

According to Jonathan Grieser, these two reformed convents, Überwasser, an old aristocratic Benedictine house of former canonesses, and Marienthal, a former sister-house, established only in the fifteenth century and then becoming an enclosed Augustinian cloister, belie the conventional wisdom about the relationship between religious houses and social class. For in this case it was Marienthal, the house of less prestigious burgher daughters—the sisters, aunts and offspring of city council members—who opposed the Anabaptist movement, taking sides against the town council during its struggle against the prince-bishop. Meanwhile, the aristocratic nuns of cloister Überwasser joined the Anabaptist council members. Accordingly, Grieser cautions against "identifying convents too closely with particular social classes or groups." Citing the activities of the Überwasser sisters in agitating for the Anabaptist cause, Grieser asserts, "we must begin to view women as participants as well as victims."[122] The issue here is not a simple one, for the aristocratic house had clearly had conflicts with prince-bishops in the past. During the reform by Observants in 1483, which was supported by the bishop and the town council together, all the old sisters had left. Who replaced them and what the social composition of the house was by 1533 needs further study.[123]

Sigrid Schmitt has demonstrated that in Strasbourg the social make up of women's religious houses often changed dramatically in the wake of the reforms. Her study illustrates how class struggles within the city council over the social ambitions of the rising urban patriciate played a decisive role in the reform of women's convents by Observants in the fifteenth century and by Protestants in the sixteenth. Support for the Observants was related to the desire for broader access to cloisters by the daughters of the wealthy and powerful municipal magistrate class.[124] Jutta Sperling's study of convents in the city of Venice similarly concludes that enclosure was linked to social status and constituted less an attempt to subjugate women than a way to preserve the purity, exclusivity, and isolation of the aristocratic caste. While the open communities of religious tertiaries were available to women of the less elite classes, the enclosure of nuns symbolized the inaccessibility of these houses to all but the very few of the highest ranks of society. It constituted part of a larger cultural system of transactions that affected whole families and their social rank.[125]

Conclusion

It is clear that the Observant reforms of the fifteenth century cannot be viewed—as they so often have been—simply as efforts by men to subordinate women or of the church hierarchy to enforce *Periculoso* (the papal decree of enclosure). Nor can the Observant movement be seen as just a repetition of many waves of reform that preceded it. Rather, the fifteenth-century movement was bound up with a larger shift that connected the nuns and the populace as a whole and was disruptive of old power structures. Indeed, one of the most striking things about the introduction of the Observance at men's as well as women's houses was the impassioned and sometimes even violent involvement of the city populace. A very powerful force that resonated with the interests of the laity, reform discourse merged on the one hand with the struggle of the increasingly powerful urban magistrate class for greater access and control of religious institutions and, on the other, with the maneuvers of territorial rulers to consolidate their power at the expense of the lesser aristocracy. The fact that the Observance was imposed even in cloisters where all of the aristocratic inhabitants opposed it is symptomatic of the waning power of the women's noble families, as Schmitt shows. The acceptance of larger numbers of daughters of the burgher class after the reform in Strasbourg bears witness to the pressure being exerted from below to open cloisters to a wider spectrum of society.[126] To this end, reform was a powerful tool in the hands of religious activists of the burgher class like Johannes Nider, Johannes Busch, and Johannes Meyer. Whether they intended it or not, the Observance was effective in dislodging the nobility, both female and male, from long entrenched positions of authority and exclusivity within the religious orders and in opening them up to a new influx of devout religious.

These changes were rarely achieved without bringing in a new prioress and reform sisters to take over the principal offices and institute the Observance. For these women, participation in the reform effort provided not only an avenue of religious engagement but, for non-noble reform prioresses such as Susanna Potstock, a career advancement. In cases where women acted independently, as did Magdalena Beutler, reform was an opportunity to employ the old, still viable (though dangerous) visionary model for acquiring influence. For other women, however, Observant activism and literary exchange constituted a new way to have a voice in the larger conversation on spirituality, a way that did not depend on the mysticism or asceticism that had in earlier centuries been the only routes to religious influence for women.

In 1524, a prologue and epilogue were added (probably by Sister Griet Essink) to the book of sisters at the Diepenveen convent of St. Mary and St. Agnes, a work that also contains a long account of the reform of Hilwartshausen (on the Weser) by three of the Diepenveen sisters. In the prologue, Sister Griet refers to her convent with traditional imagery, calling it "an orchard" (bomgoert) and referring to the virtues of the women as "devout plants" that blossomed there. Concluding, she remarks, "nobody should think that there are not more sisters whose lives we ought to describe. [For] many devout sisters have died in this place and amongst them there were many whose virtues would definitely be worth recording."[127] This comment could apply equally well to the attempt of the present study to survey women writers in the fifteenth and early sixteenth centuries using the literary portraits made by women in the Observant movement. It has not been possible here to treat sufficiently all of the writers and works that are "worth recording," but only to outline a field that is still virtually untouched.

Women's literary historians have, for example, often raised the question why female contemporaries of Christine de Pizan did not write their own "cities of ladies." As it turns out, and this study has tried to show, they did. Contemporaries in actual communities of ladies composed sister-books and convent chronicles that celebrate, not the mythological figures of Pizan's virtual city, but women much closer at hand: former inhabitants of these communities. These works commemorate in a similar way female moral virtue, spiritual achievements, and the deeds of heroic prioresses and ordinary sisters. Yet, as this example also shows, the potential benefits of cross-fertilization in the study of women writers in the Anglo-French and German-Dutch worlds of the Middle Ages have long gone unrecognized, as researchers construct histories of women independently on both sides of a linguistic and cultural divide. Clearly, the pool of works by medieval women authors needs to be enlarged across national and linguistic borders. More inclusive interdisciplinary studies need to be undertaken that will encompass new geographical and linguistic categories such as those suggested by Jacqueline Wogan-Brown.[128]

The chronicles produced in real cities of ladies by female writers of the fifteenth century Observant movement constitute complex collective strategies, works that were not only generated by the reform but, at the same time, sought to shape, validate, and perpetuate it. Differing in form, style, and content from the master narrative, women's accounts portray female reformers as leaders and initiators in their own right. Seen from women's perspective, the reform efforts appear more broadly based, multi-faceted, and involved with social change. As more of their texts come to light, what remains is to study them individually and to establish their place in literary-historical studies. As these new voices from the eve of the Reformation demonstrate, the past changes: it looks different with women sharing center stage.

NOTES

Introduction

1. Unless otherwise indicated, all translations are mine. The author of the book does not give her name, but Anne Bollmann and Nikolaus Staubach suggest that it was most probably Mechtelt Smeeds. See *Schwesternbuch und Statuten des St. Agnes–Konvents in Emmerich,* ed. with introduction by Anne Bollmann and Nikolaus Staubach, Emmericher Forschungen 17 (Emmerich: Emmericher Geschichtsverein, 1998), 15–17, 38. For the English title, I have used the term "book of sisters" to distinguish the works written in the fifteenth and sixteenth centuries at sisterhouses of the Common Life or New Devout from the fourteenth-century Dominican "sister-books." See Wybren Scheepsma, " 'For hereby I hope to rouse some to piety' ": Books of Sisters from Convents and Sister-Houses Associated with the 'Devotio moderna' in the Low Countries," in *Women, the Book, and the Godly,* 2 vols., ed. Lesley Smith and Jane Taylor (Cambridge: Brewer, 1995), 28.

2. Since this project was begun more than six years ago, a large number of studies are in progress and a list-serve, "Mittelalterliche Frauenklöster," organized by Katrinette Bodarwé for exchange of information on medieval women's communities has been established. See www.frauenkloester.de.

Three fifteenth-century chronicles that I have not been able to include are Sophie von Stolberg's chronicle of Helfta and the chronicles of Lüne and Heligkreuz (Braunschweig). Nor was the original of Anna von Buchwald's "Buch im Chor" accessible, because it was being restored. See Jo Ann McNamara, *Sisters in Arms: Catholic Nuns through Two Millennia* (Cambridge, Mass.: Harvard University Press, 1996), 302; Hans Patze, "Klostergründung und Klosterchronik," in *Blätter für deutsche Landeskunde* 113 (1977): 115–16; and Heike Uffmann, " 'Wie in einem Rosengarten . . . .' Die Ebstorfer Klosterreform im Spiegel von Chronistik und Tischlesung," in *"In Treue und Hingabe": 800 Jahre Kloster Ebstorf,* ed. Marianne Elster and Horst Hoffmann (Uelzen: Becker, 1997), 215. The chronicle of the Clarissan cloister in Nuremberg was not included because it is not clear whether it was composed by the sisters or by lay chronicler Nikolaus Glasberger. See Lotte Kurras and Franz Machilek, eds., *Caritas Pirckheimer, 1467–1532,* Ausstellung der Katholischen Stadtkirche Nürnberg, June 26–August 8, 1982 (Munich: Prestel, 1982), 98.

3. Scheepsma, " 'For hereby I hope to rouse some to piety,' " 1:30. For more on the *devotio moderna* movement, see Chapter 2.

4. John Van Engen, "The Virtues, the Brothers, and the Schools," *Revue Bénédictine* 98 (1988): 178.

5. Gerhard Rehm, *Die Schwestern vom gemeinsamen Leben im nordwestlichen Deutschland. Untersuchungen der Devotio moderna und des weiblichen Religiösentums,* Berliner Historische Studien 11, Ordensstudien 5 (Berlin: Dunker and Humblot, 1985), 16.

6. Wybren Scheepsma, *Deemoed en devotie: De koorvrouwen van Windesheim en hun geschriften* (Amsterdam: Prometheus, 1997), forthcoming in English translation, *The Canonesses of Windesheim and their Writings* (Woodbridge, Suffolk: Boydell and Brewer). More recently, six of the Sisters of the Common Life have been included in Kurt Ruh's history of mystical writers in the West, *Geschichte der abendländischen Mystik,* vol. 4 (Munich: Beck, 1999). In addition, Anne Bollmann is currently at work on a study of the books of sisters produced in women's communities of the Modern Devout.

7. Matthäus Bernards, *Speculum Virginum: Geistigkeit und Seelenleben der Frau im Hochmittelalter* (Cologne: Böhlau, 1955), 1.

8. Marie-Luise Ehrenschwendtner, "'Puella litteratae': The Use of the Vernacular in the Dominican Convents of Southern Germany," in *Medieval Women in their Communities,* ed. Diane Watt (Toronto: University of Toronto Press, 1997), 50.

9. Francis Rapp, "Zur Spiritualität in elsässischen Frauenklöstern am Ende des Mittelalters," in *Frauenmystik im Mittelalter,* ed. Peter Dinzelbacher and Dieter R. Bauer (Ostfildern: Schwaben Verlag, 1985), 347; and Andreas Rüther and Hans-Jochen Schiewer, "Die Predigthandschriften des Straßburger Dominikanerinnenklosters St. Nikolaus in Undis," in *Die deutsche Predigt im Mittelalter,* ed. Volker Mertens and Hans-Jochen Schiewer (Niemeyer: Tübingen, 1992): 177.

10. Elke Dißelbeck-Tewes, *Frauen in der Kirche. Das Leben der Frauen in den mittelalterlichen Zisterzienserklöstern Fürstenberg, Graefental und Scheldenhorst* (Cologne: Böhlau, 1989), 93.

11. Caroline Walker Bynum, *Holy Feast and Holy Fast: The Religious Significance of Food to Medieval Women* (Berkeley and Los Angeles: University of California Press, 1987), 16; and Daniel Bornstein, "Women and Religion in Late Medieval Italy: History and Historiography," in *Women and Religion in Medieval and Renaissance Italy,* ed. Daniel Bornstein (Chicago: Chicago University Press, 1996), 10.

12. Jeffrey Hamburger, *The Visual and the Visionary: Art and Female Spirituality in Late Medieval Germany* (New York: Zone Books, 1998), 14. See also idem, *Nuns as Artists: The Visual Culture of a Medieval Convent* (Berkeley and Los Angeles: University of California Press, 1977).

13. Bonnie Anderson and Judith Zinsser, *A History of their Own: Women in Europe from Prehistory to the Present* (New York: Harper and Row, 1988–89), 1:xiii.

14. Gabrielle Spiegel, *The Past as Text: The Theory and Practice of Medieval Historiography* (Baltimore: Johns Hopkins University Press, 1997), 74.

15. Joan Ferrante, *To the Glory of Her Sex: Women's Roles in the Composition of Medieval Texts* (Bloomington: Indiana University Press, 1997), 3.

16. Aside from Hrosvit, Bertha of Vilich, and the Helfta mystics, most texts by women before the fourteenth century were dictated to male confessors, scribes, or collaborators. For a list of medieval women writers, see Barbara Newman, *From Virile Woman to Woman Christ* (Philadelphia: University of Pennsylvania Press, 1995), 317–20. On the difficulty of distinguishing female voices, see Catherine M. Mooney, *Gendered Voices: Medieval Saints and Their Interpreters* (Philadelphia: University of Pennsylvania Press, 1999).

17. All of these are now being resourcefully reexamined by scholars such as Marilyn Oliva in *The Convent and Community in Late Medieval England: Female Monasteries in the Diocese of Norwich, 1350–1540* (Woodbridge, Suffolk: Boydell, 1998), 6–7, 61, 78–79, 215–16.

18. Sully Roecken and Carolina Brauckmann, *Margaretha Jedefrau* (Freiburg: Kore, 1989), 1:16.

19. Eileen Power, *Medieval English Nunneries, c. 1275 to 1535* (Cambridge: Cambridge University Press, 1922). Lina Eckenstein, in her path-breaking work *Women under Monasticism* (1896; repr. New York: Russel and Russel, 1963), deplores the frequent medieval depictions of the nun as "a slothful and hysterical," if not a "dissolute" character, viii.

20. Shulamith Shahar, *The Fourth Estate: A History of Women in the Middle Ages,* trans. Chaya Galai (London: Methuen, 1983), 48.

21. Caroline Walker Bynum, "Religious Women in the Later Middle Ages," in *Christian Spirituality. High Middle Ages and Reformation,* ed. Jill Raitt, Bernard McGinn, and John Meyendorff (New York: Crossroad, 1987), 136.

22. Hamburger, *The Visual,* 15–16; Ursula Peters, "Frauenliteratur im Mittelalter? Überlegungen zur Trobiaritzpoesie, zur Frauenmystik und zur feministischen Literaturbetrachtung," *Germanisch-Romanische Monatsschrift,* n.F. 38 (1988), 50.

23. Albrecht Classen, "New Voices in the History of German Women's Literature from the Middle Ages to 1600: Problems and New Approaches," *German Studies Review* 23 (2000): 13, 18.

24. [Bartolomea Ricciboni] *Life and Death in a Venetian Convent: The Chronicle and Necrology of Corpus Domini, 1395–1436,* ed. and trans. Daniel Bornstein (Chicago: Chicago University Press, 2000),

22. See also other titles in the Chicago series, The Other Voice in Early Modern Europe, edited by Margaret L. King and Albert Rabil Jr.

25. [Bartolomea Riccoboni] *Life and Death in a Venetian Convent*, 3.

26. Johannes Helmrath, *Das Basler Konzil 1431–1449: Forschungsstand und Probleme* (Cologne: Böhlau, 1987), 348.

27. Kaspar Elm, ed., *Reformbemühungen und Observanzbestrebungen im spätmittelalterlichen Ordenswesen*, Berliner Historische Studien 14, Ordensstudien 6 (Berlin: Dunker und Humblot, 1989), 16–17. Thoma Vogler's inventory of the library of the Observant Dominican sisters at St. Katharina in St. Gall in the fifteenth century contains, for example, six German copies of Thomas à Kempis's *Imitation of Christ*. See *Geschichte des Dominikanerinnen-Klosters St. Katharina in St Gallen 1228–1607* (Fribourg, Switzerland: Paulus, 1938), 247, 267.

28. Walter Ziegler, "Reformation and Klosterauflösung. Ein ordensgeschichtlicher Vergleich," in *Reformbemühungen und Observanzbestrebungen im spätmittelalterlichen Ordenswesen*, ed. Kaspar Elm, Berliner Historische Studien 14, Ordensstudien 6 (Berlin: Dunker und Humblot, 1989), 591; Euan Cameron, *The European Reformation* (Oxford: Clarendon, 1991), 42.

29. Constance Proksch, *Klosterreform und Geschichtsschreibung im Spätmittelalter* (Cologne: Böhlau, 1994).

30. Gerda Lerner, *The Creation of Feminist Consciousness* (New York: Oxford University Press, 1993), vii–viii.

31. Jo Ann Kay McNamara, *Sisters in Arms: Catholic Nuns through Two Millennia* (Cambridge, Mass.: Harvard University Press, 1993), 417.

32. Johannes Meyer, *Das Buch der Reformacio Predigerordens*, ed. Benedictus Maria Reichert, Quellen und Forschungen zur Geschichte des Dominikanerordens in Deutschland 3 (Leipzig: Harrassowitz, 1909), 14.

33. McNamara, *Sisters,* 417.

34. Joan Ferrante, *To the Glory of Her Sex: Women's Roles in the Composition of Medieval Texts* (Bloomington: Indiana University Press, 1997), 5–6.

35. Friedrich Techen, ed. *Die Chroniken des Klosters Ribnitz* (Meklenburgische Geschichtsquellen 1 (Schwerin: Bärensprungsche Hofdruckerei, 1909), 10.

36. Herman Hallauer, "Nikolaus von Kues und das Brixener Klarissenkloster," *Mitteilungen und Forschungsbeiträge der Cusanus-Gesellschaft* 6 (1967): 76.

37. Werner Williams-Krapp, "Observanzbewegung, monastische Spiritualität und geistliche Literatur im 15. Jahrhundert," *Internationales Archiv für Sozialgeschichte der deutschen Literatur* 20 (1995): 3.

38. Williams-Krapp, "Observanzbewegung, monastische Spiritualität," 3; Karin Schneider, "Die Bibliothek des Katharinenklosters in Nürnberg und die städtische Gesellschaft," in *Studien zum städtischen Bildungswesen des späten Mittelalters und der frühen Neuzeit,* ed. Bernd Moeller et. al (Göttingen: Vandenhoeck and Ruprecht, 1983), 70–71; Eugen Hillenbrand, "Die Observantenbewegung in der deutschen Ordensprovinz der Dominikaner," in *Reformbemühungen und Observanzbestrebungen im spätmittelalterlichen Ordenswesen,* ed. Kaspar Elm, Berliner Historische Studien 14, Ordensstudien 6 (Berlin: Dunker and Humblot, 1989), 269; Regina D. Schiewer, "Sermons for Nuns of the Dominican Observance Movement," in *Medieval Monastic Preaching,* ed. Carolyn Muessig (Leiden: Brill, 1998), 78.

39. Juliana Ernst (1588–1641), editor of the Chronicle of the Bicken Cloister in Villingen, states that she found two New Year's addresses from 1495 and 1496 given by former prioress Ursula Haider (d. 1498), saying, "I will cite them here word for word as they came from her mouth." See [Juliana Ernst,] *Die Chronik des Bickenklosters zu Villingen,* ed. Karl Jordan Glatz, Bibliothek des Litterarischen Vereins in Stuttgart 151 (Tübingen: Fues, 1881), 43. The editor of the Chronicle of Inzigkofen says, "Here I cite from the old house chronicler: 'In the year 1520 . . .';" see "Die Geissenhof'sche Chronik des Klosters Inzigkofen," ed. Theodor Dreher, *Freiburger Katholisches Kirchenblatt* 38 (1894): col. 476. This old chronicle was begun in 1525 by Apollonia Besserer (1492–1538) and Elisabeth Muntprat (d. 1555). See Werner Fechter, *Deutsche Handschriften des 15. und 16. Jahrhunderts aus der Bibliothek des ehemaligen Augustinerchorfrauenstifts Inzigkofen* (Sigmaringen: Thorbecke, 1997), 1, 28, 34. Johannes Meyer's editing of three sister-books is discussed below and in Chapter 2.

40. See the introduction by editor Horst Appuhn to the *Chronik und Totenbuch des Klosters Wienhausen* (Wienhausen: Kloster Wienhausen, 1986), v–viii.

41. [Anna von Munzingen,] "Dis sint die gnade, die vnser Herre hett getan semlichen swestern in disem closter ze Adelnhusen," in "Die Chronik der Anna von Munzingen. Nach der ältesten Abschrift mit Einleitung und Beilagen," ed. J. König, *Freiburger Diozesan Archiv* 13 (1880): 192.

42. Preetz, Archiv, Klosterpreetz, MS 1, fol. 142v. Translation cited from Jeffrey Hamburger, *The Visual and the Visionary: Art and Female Spirituality in Late Medieval Germany* (New York: Zone, 1998), 5.

43. Augsburg, Staatsarchiv MS Kloster Maria Maihingen MüB 1, fol. 77v. See also Alfred Schröder, "Das Hausbuch des Klosters Maihingen. Quellenkritische Untersuchungen," *Archiv für die Geschichte des Hochstifts Augsburg* 6 (1929): 769–74.

44. Johannes Gatz, "Pfullingen," *Alemania Franciscana Antiqua* 17 (1972): 191. The original manuscript of this chronicle is now lost, but a transcription was published in 1913. This transcription reads: "For as long as I have been in [the cloister] I am very hopeful that the Lord will not abandon us." See "Anno dni MCCL an Sant Martins tag da ist dis Closter Pfullingen an gefangen worden," in "Duae Relationes circa Monasterium Brixinense O. Clar.," ed. Maximilianus Straganz, *Archivum Franciscanum Historicum* 6 (1913): 538–44, at 544.

45. "Innumerabiles grates . . ." [Chronicle of Ebstorf, 1487], in "Litterarisches und geistiges Leben in Kloster Ebstorf am Ausgange des Mittelalters," ed. Conrad Borchling, *Zeitschrift des historischen Vereins für Niedersachsen* 4 (1905): 406.

46. Klaus Grubmüller's analysis of the layering in the Töss sister-book identifies six stages in the work's construction. A prologue and a vita of Elisabeth Bechlin were added, for example, by another sister—possibly from material by Elsbeth Stagel—before other accretions and, as a final stage, Johannes Meyer's abridgements and his additions of an epilogue and an aditional prologue in the fifteenth century. See Klaus Grubmüller, "Die Viten der Schwestern von Töss und Elsbeth Stagel: Überlieferung und literarische Einheit," *Zeitschrift für deutsche Philologie* 98 (1969): 171–204; Alois Haas, "Elsbeth Stagel," in *Die deutsche Literatur des Mittelalters: Verfasserlexikon*, ed. Wolfgang Stammler and Karl Langosch (Berlin: de Gruyter, 1995), 9: col. 224; and Werner Fechter "Johannes Meyer OP," in *Die deutsche Literatur des Mittelalters: Verfasserlexikon*, 6 (1987), col. 483.

47. *Das St. Katharinentaler Schwesternbuch. Untersuchung, Edition, Kommentar*, ed. Ruth Meyer, Münchener Texte und Untersuchungen 104 (Tübingen: Niemeyer, 1995), 66–72. Meyer also made an abridged, alphabetical version of the Adelhausen sister-book, a register of the convents' inhabitants, but the original work by Anna von Munzingen survives. See. J. König, "Die Chronik der Anna von Munzingen. Nach der ältesten Abschrift mit Einleitung und Beilagen," *Freiburger Diözesan-Archiv* 13 (1880): 130–225.

48. Ursula Peters, *Religiöse Erfahrung als literarisches Faktum: Zur Vorgeschichte und Genese frauenmystischer Texte des 13. und 14. Jahrhunderts* (Tübingen: Niemeyer, 1988), 133, 182.

49. "Chronik des Schwesternhauses Marienthal, genannt Niesinck in Münster," in *Berichte der Augenzeugen über das Münstersche Wiedertäuferreich*, ed. Carl Cornelius, 419–41, Geschichtsquellen des Bisthums Münster 2 (1853; repr. Münster: Aschendorff, 1965); and "Klosterchronik Überwasser während der Wirren 1531–33," ed. Rudolf Schulze, in *Quellen und Forschungen zur Geschichte der Stadt Münster*, vol. 2, ed. Eduard Schulte, 149–66 (Münster: Aschendorff, 1926). Similarly, the only published excerpts from the journals of Prioresses of Frauen-Chiemsee, Magdalena Auer (d. 1494) and Ursula Pfaffinger (d. 1528) are those for the years 1503–4, recounting the war of succession between the Palatinate and Bavaria; however, these may have been written by a scribe. See Ernst Geiß, ed., "Relation der Aebtissin Ursula der Pfäffingerin von Frauen-Chiemsee über den pfälzisch-bayerischen Erbfolge-Krieg," *Oberbayerisches Archiv für vaterländische Geschichte* 8 (1847): 224–36; Rudolf Rainer, "Magdalena Auer," in *Die deutsche Literature des Mittelalters: Verfasserlexikon*, ed. Kurt Ruh et al., 1: col. 516 (Berlin: de Gruyter, 1978); Helgard Ulmschneider, "Ursula Pfäffinger," *Verfasserlexikon*, 7:cols. 551–52 (1987); and Charlotte Woodford, *Nuns as Historians in Early Modern Germany* (Oxford: Clarendon, 2002), 68–70.

50. See Gabrielle Spiegel, "History, Historicism, and the Social Logic of the Text in the Middle Ages," *Speculum* 65 (1990): 64; idem, "Theory into Practice: Reading Medieval Chronicles," in *The Medieval Chronicle: Proceedings of the 1st International Conference on the Medieval Chronicle, Driebergen/Utrecht, July 13–16, 1996*, ed. Erik Kooper, 1–12 (Amsterdam and Atlanta: Rodopi, 1999); Lynn Hunt, ed., *The New Cultural History* (Berkeley and Los Angeles: University of California Press, 1989); and Anton Kaes, "New Historicism and the Study of German Literature," *The German Quarterly* 62 (1989): 210–19.

51. Rolf Sprandel, "Frauengeschichten in der Geschichtsschreibung des spätmittelalterlichen Deutschland," in *Aufgaben, Rollen und Räume von Frau und Mann*, ed. Jochen Martin and Renate Zoepffel (Munich: Alber, 1989), 2:737.

Chapter 1

1. "Chronik des Schwesternhauses Marienthal, genannt Niesinck in Münster," in *Berichte der Augenzeugen über das Münstersche Wiedertäuferreich*, ed. Carl Cornelius, Geschichtsquellen des Bisthums Münster 2 (1853; repr. Münster: Aschendorff, 1965), lxxxiii.

2. See Mary C. Erler and Maryanne Kowaleski, "Introduction: A New Economy of Power Relations: Female Agency in the Middle Ages," in *Gendering the Master Narrative: Women and Power in the Middle Ages*, ed. Erler and Kowaleski (Ithaca: Cornell University Press, 2003), 1–16.

3. Erler and Kowaleski, "Introduction"; and Susan Frye and Karen Robertson, eds., *Maids and Mistresses, Cousins and Queens: Women's Alliances in Early Modern England* (Oxford: Oxford University Press, 1999).

4. Sully Roecken and Carolina Brauckmann, *Margaretha Jedefrau*, vol. 1 (Freiburg: Kore, 1989), 41.

5. Petra Rohde, "Die Freiburger Klöster zwischen Reformation und Auflösung," in *Geschichte der Stadt Freiburg im Breisgau*, ed. Heiko Haumann and Hans Schadek, vol. 2 (Stuttgart: Theiss, 1994), 421.

6. Marilyn Oliva, *The Convent and Community in Late Medieval England: Female Monasteries in the Diocese of Norwich, 1350–1540* (Woodbridge, Suffolk: Boydell, 1998), 148.

7. Ibid., 149, 157; Joan Ferrante, *To the Glory of Her Sex: Women's Roles in the Composition of Medieval Texts* (Bloomington: Indiana University Press, 1997), 68; Penelope D. Johnson, *Equal in Monastic Profession: Religious Women in Medieval France* (Chicago: University of Chicago Press, 1991), 56.

8. Roberta Gilchrist comments on the "stereotyping"of women's religious houses as "poor, scandalous, passive institutions." Even recent reassessments of the historical evidence for nunneries, she asserts, "devalue female religious experience." See *Gender and Material Culture: The Archeology of Religious Women* (London: Routledge, 1993), 1, 23. Marilyn Oliva has noted that histories of monasticism, such as the first volume of David Knowles's standard work "omitted any mention of nuns," saying that "evidence for female monasteries was 'non-existent'." In fact, Oliva argues, a great deal of evidence exists about female houses "in the very same documents" that Knowles and others used to study male monasteries while they were dismissing women's convents as "unimportant." The problem, she argues, has been relying too heavily on anecdotal evidence left by men which has resulted in a negative picture of nuns that "trivializes their functions and diminished their significance." See Oliva, *Community*, 2–4, 7.

9. "Vahe ich an etwaz zu schreyben von den heiligen swestern, dy gewesen seyn zu Weyler," in "Mystisches Leben in dem Dominikanerinnenkloster Weiler bei Esslingen im 13. und 14. Jahrhundert," ed. Karl Bihlmeyer, *Würtembergische Vierteljahrshefte für Landesgeschichte*, n.F. 25 (1916): 68.

10. Jutta Giesela Sperling, *Convents and the Body Politic in Late Renaissance Venice* (Chicago: University of Chicago Press, 1999), 39.

11. Shulamith Shahar, *The Fourth Estate: A History of Women in the Middle Ages*, trans. Chaya Galai (London: Methuen, 1983), 42.

12. [Magdalena Kremer,] "Wie diß loblich closter zu Sant Johannes Baptisten zu Kirchen under

deck prediger-ordens reformiert ist worden und durch woelich personen," in *Geschichte des Herzogtums Wuerttemberg unter der Regierung der Graven,* ed. Christian Friedrich Sattler, 2d ed. (Tübingen: Reiss, 1773–77), 4:157.

13. "Das Schwesternbuch von Sankt Agnes," in *Schwesternbuch und Statuten des St. Agnes–Konvents in Emmerich,* ed. with introduction by Anne Bollmann and Nikolaus Staubach, Emmericher Forschungen 17 (Emmerich: Emmericher Geschichtsverein, 1998), 240–42.

14. In discussing the origins of earlier beguine communities, historians have stressed as a contributing factor many women's rejection of marriage. This view is expressed by Daniela Müller, Claudia Opitz, Peter Dinzelbacher, and Ute Weinmann. Their positions are summarized in Martina Spies, *Beginengemeinschaften in Frankfurt am Main: Zur Frage der genossenschaftlichen Selbstorganisation von Frauen im Mittelalter* (Dortmund: Ebersbach, 1998), 25–28. On beguines' rejection of marriage, see also Walter Simons, *Cities of Ladies: Beguine Communities of the Medieval Low Countries 1200–1565* (Philadelphia: University of Pennsylvania Press, 2001), 68–76. Feminist Rebekka Habermas sees the development of beguine houses as a kind of emancipatory revolt against the limited roles assigned to women in medieval society, the formation of a "feminine alternative culture." See "Die Beginen—eine 'andere' Konzeption von Weiblichkeit?" in *Die ungeschriebene Geschichte. Historische Frauenforschung, Dokumentation 5. Historikerinnentreffen April 1984,* ed. Wiener Historikerinnen (Vienna: Wiener Frauenverlag, 1984), 200.

15. "Schwesternbuch von Sankt Agnes," ed. Bollmann and Staubach, 71. The book of sisters of the Master Geert House in Deventer relates a similar account of Sister Gese Broeckelants, who likewise, entered the women's community when her parents promised her in marriage. "When this good sister was still living with her parents and was not yet very old, she was promised in marriage to a man. When she heard that, she was extremely depressed and wept a great deal. And since she knew of no help from anyone, she turned to our dear Lord. And went therefore to the church, prostrated herself before the holy sacrament, and asked our Lord to free her of this burden [and] she would serve Him eternally. And as she lay there and offered herself to our dear Lord, she thought the words came to her, she should go to Deventer and ask for a place in Master Geert's House. And before she rose from the spot where she had been praying, she promised God her chastity;" *Hier beginnen sommige stichtige punten van onsen oelden zusteren (naar het te Arnhem berustende Handschrift Uitgegeven,* ed. Dirk de Man (The Hague: Nijhoff, 1919), 9–10, fols. 1v–2r.

16. [Katharina von Gueberschwihr,] "Les 'Vitae sororum d'Unterlinden,' Edition critique du manuscrit 508 de la Bibliothèque de Colmar," ed. Jeanne Ancelet-Hustache, *Archives d'histoire doctrinale et littéraire du moyen age* 5 (1930): 374–76.

17. See, for example [Bartolomea Riccoboni,] *Life and Death in a Venetian Convent: The Chronicle and Necrology of Corpus Domini, 1395–1436,* ed. and trans. Daniel Bornstein (Chicago: Chicago University Press, 2000), 91.

18. Caroline Walker Bynum, *Holy Feast and Holy Fast: The Religious Significance of Food to Medieval Women* (Berkeley and Los Angeles: University of California Press, 1987), 226.

19. Shahar, *Fourth Estate,* 8–9.

20. Sperling, *Convents,* 25; Elke Disselbeck-Tewes, *Frauen in der Kirche. Das Leben der Frauen in den mittelalterlichen Zisterzienserklöstern Fürstenberg, Graefental and Scheldenhorst,* Dissertationen zur mittelalterlichen Geschichte 8 (Cologne: Böhlau, 1989), 61, 63.

21. [Elsbeth Stagel?] *Das Leben der Schwestern zu Töß, beschrieben von Elsbet Stagel samt der Vorrede von Johannes Meier und dem Leben der Prinzessin Elisabet von Ungarn,* ed. Ferdinand Vetter, Deutsche Texte des Mittelalters 6 (Berlin: Weidmann, 1906), 85, 94.

22. [Anna von Munzingen,] "Dis sint die gnade, die vnser Herre hett getan semlichen swestern in disem closter ze Adelnhusen," in "Die Chronik der Anna von Munzingen. Nach der ältesten Abschrift mit Einleitung und Beilagen," ed. J. König, *Freiburger Diözesan-Archiv* 13 (1880): 176.

23. Renée Weis-Müller, *Die Reform des Klosters Klingental und ihr Personenkreis,* Baseler Beiträge zur Geschichtswissenschaft 59 (Basel and Stuttgart: Helbing and Lichtenhahn, 1956), 38.

24. Shahar, *Fourth Estate,* 8.

25. Lina Eckenstein, *Women under Monasticism* (1896; repr. New York: Russel and Russel, 1963), 149.

26. Bruce Venarde, *Women's Monasticism and Medieval Society: Nunneries in France and England, 890–1215* (Ithaca: Cornell University Press, 1997), 101.

27. [Anna Roede,] "Anna Roedes spätere Chronik von Herzebrock," ed. Franz Flaskamp, *Jahrbuch der Gesellschaft für Niedersächsische Kirchengeschichte* 68 (1970), 122–23.

28. "Die Stiftung des Klosters Oetenbach und das Leben der seligen Schwestern daselbst, aus der Nürnberger Handschrift," ed. H. Zeller-Werdmüller and Jakob Bächthold, *Zürcher Taschenbuch* 12 (1889), 230. These humorous anecdotes, so different in style from Johannes Meyer's didactic ones, differentiate the earlier text material from later additions.

29. St. Gall, Stiftsbibliothek, MS St. Katharina, Wil, "Klosterchronik," Nr. 87, fol. 95r; and Thoma Vogler, *Geschichte des Dominikanerinnen–Klosters St. Katharina in St. Gallen 1228–1607* (Fribourg, Switzerland: Paulus, 1938), 29.

30. Karl Grube, *Johannes Busch Augustinerpropst zu Hildesheim: Ein katholischer Reformator des 15. Jahrhunderts* (Freiburg: Herder, 1881), 184, 280 n. 38.

31. Arcangela's views on enforcement of the decrees of the Council of Trent appeared in her *La semplicità ingannata*, published posthumously in 1654. See Sperling, *Convents*, 31, 35.

32. Eileen Power, *Medieval English Nunneries, c. 1275–1535* (Cambridge: Cambridge University Press, 1922), 4, 5.

33. Cited in Joanne Baker, "Female Monasticism and Family Strategy: The Guises and Saint Pierre de Reims," *Sixteenth Century Journal* 28 (1975): 1092–93.

34. Sperling, *Convents*, 69, xiv.

35. Ibid., 61, 63, 71.

36. St. Gall, Stiftsbibliothek, MS St. Katharina, Wil, "Klosterchronik," Nr. 87, fol. 17v; Vogler, *St. Katharina*, 53.

37. Maria Hüffer, *Die Reformen der Abtei Rijnsburg im 15. Jahrhundert* (Münster: Aschendorff, 1937), 131.

38. Hüffer, *Die Reformen*, 73.

39. Rudolf Schulze, *Das adelige Frauen- (Kanonissen-) Stift der Hl. Maria (1040–1773) und die Pfarre Liebfrauen-Überwasser zu Münster Westfalen* (Münster: Aschendorff, 1952), 33.

40. Eckenstein, *Monasticism*, 152; Baker, "Family," 1100.

41. Jo Ann Kay McNamara, *Sisters in Arms: Catholic Nuns through Two Millennia* (Cambridge, Mass.: Harvard University Press, 1996), 179, 191; Merry Wiesner-Hanks, ed. *Convents Confront the Reformation: Catholic and Protestant Nuns in Germany*, trans. Joan Skocir and Merry Wiesner-Hanks (Milwaukee: Marquette University Press, 1996), 14.

42. Schulze, *Kanonissen*, 31.

43. Ulrich Faust, ed., *Die Frauenklöster in Niedersachsen, Schleswig-Holstein und Bremen*, Germania Benedictina 11: Norddeutschland (St. Ottilien: EOS-Verlag, 1984), 25.

44. McNamara, *Arms*, 185.

45. Hrosvitha of Gandersheim, *Hrosvithae Opera*, ed. Helene Homeyer (Paderborn: Schöningh, 1970), 465.

46. Schulze, *Kanonissen*, 29.

47. McNamara, *Arms*, 223.

48. Schulze, *Kanonissen*, 30–31.

49. McNamara, *Arms*, 224.

50. Katherine Gill, "'Scandala': Controversies Concerning Clausura and Women's Religious Communities in Late Medieval Italy," in *Christendom and its Discontents*, ed. Scott Waugh and Peter Diehl (Cambridge: Cambridge University Press, 1996), 183.

51. Oliva, *Convent*, 26.

52. Faust, *Frauenklöster*, 27.

53. [Bertha of Vilich,] *Mater spiritualis: The Life of Adelheid of Vilich*, trans. Madelyn Dick (Toronto: Peregrina, 1994), 24–25.

54. [Bertha of Vilich,] *Mater spiritualis*, 31–32.

55. John B. Freed, "Urban Development and the 'Cura Monialium' in Thirteenth-Century Germany," *Viator* 3 (1972): 319.

56. *Chronik und Totenbuch des Klosters Wienhausen,* ed. Horst Appuhn (Wienhausen: Kloster Wienhausen, 1986), fols. 30–31. Regarding the date and historical layering of this chronicle, see Chapter 4, note 57.

57. R. Krauß, "Geschichte des Dominikaner-Frauenklosters Kirchberg," *Württembergische Vierteljahreshefte* n.f. 3 (1894): 297. Marilyn Oliva has established that for English cloisters in the diocese of Norwich between 1350 and 1540 "the vast majority of nuns came not from the aristocracy, but rather from medieval society's middling social ranks. See Oliva, *Convent,* 7.

58. Hermann Tüchle, "Süddeutsche Klöster vor 500 Jahren, ihre Stellung in Reich und Gesellschaft," *Blätter für deutsche Landesgeschichte* 109 (1973): 120.

59. Emil Erdin, *Das Kloster der Reuerinnen Sancta Maria Magdalena an den Steinen zu Basel von den Anfängen bis zur Reformation (etwa 1230–1529)* (Fribourg: Paulus, 1956), 46.

60. Vogler, *St. Katharina,* 53; *Das St. Katharinentaler Schwesternbuch. Untersuchung, Edition, Kommentar,* ed. Ruth Meyer, Münchener Texte und Untersuchungen 104 (Tübingen: Niemeyer, 1995), 202; [Bartolomea Riccoboni,] *Life and Death in a Venetian Convent: The Chronicle and Necrology of Corpus Domini, 1395–1436,* ed. and trans. Daniel Bornstein (Chicago: Chicago University Press, 2000), 17.

61. Johannes Meyer, *Ämterbuch,* ed. Sarah DeMaris, Monumenta ordinis fratrum praedicatorum historica (Rome: Institutum Historicum Fratrum Praedicatorum, in press.) I am grateful to Sarah DeMaris for providing me an advance copy of her manuscript.

62. Johannes Kist, *Das Klarissenkloster in Nürnberg bis zum Beginn des 16. Jahrhunderts* (Nuremberg: Sebaldus, 1929), 105.

63. "Anno dni MCCL an Sant Martins tag da ist dis Closter Pfullingen an gefangen worden," in "Duae Relationes circa Monasterium Brixinense O. Clar.," ed. Maximilianus Straganz, *Archivum Franciscanum Historicum* 6 (1913): 542; see also Johannes Gatz, "Pfullingen," *Alemania Franciscana Antiqua* 17 (1972): 188.

64. Disselbeck-Tewes, *Zisterzienserklöstern,* 183–84.

65. Ibid., 146, 183–84, 309; Lydal Roper, *The Holy Household: Women and Morals in Reformation Augsburg* (Oxford: Clarendon, 1989), 42.

66. Disselbeck-Tewes, *Zisterzienerklöstern,* 184.

67. Brigitte Degler-Spengler, *Das Klarissenkloster Gnadental in Basel 1289–1529,* Quellen und Forschungen zur Basler Geschichte 3 (Basel: Reinhardt, 1969), 33–34.

68. Cited in Ulrich P. Ecker, "Die Geschichte des Klosters S. Johannes-Baptista der Dominikanerinnen zu Kirchheim unter Teck," (Ph.D. diss., University of Freiburg, 1985), 30; Marie-Claire Däniker-Gysin, *Geschichte des Dominikanerinnenklosters Töß 1233–1525,* Neujahrsblatt der Stadtbibliothek Winterthur 289 (Winterthur: Ziegler, 1957), 46–47.

69. Vogler, *St. Katharina,* 32–33. In 1474 Elisabeth Muntprat brought with her to the cloister interest on a deposit of 230 gulden held by the city of Überlingen. Her Father gave an additional 200 gulden to endow anniversary prayers for his soul. Later Elisabeth also received an annuity of five gulden from an uncle. Ibid., 31.

70. Karl Suso Frank, *Das Klarissenkloster Söflingen: Ein Beitrag zur franziskanischen Ordensgeschichte Süddeutschlands und zur Ulmer Kirchengeschichte* (Stuttgart: Kohlhammer, 1980), 76; Weis-Müller, *Klingental,* 44.

71. Däniker-Gysin, *Töß,* 47.

72. Johnson, *Monastic,* 173, 219.

73. Oliva, *Convent,* 21.

74. Gustav Voit, *Engelthal—Geschichte eines Dominikanerinnenklosters,* vol. 1, Schriftenreihe der Altnürnberger Landschaft 26 (Nuremberg: Koru and Berg, 1977), 77; Ecker, *Kirchheim,* 24–27; Kist, *Klarissenkloster,* 17–18.

75. Kist, *Klarissenkloster,* 81.

76. Ibid., 78–79.

77. Rudolf Wackernagel, *Geschichte der Stadt Basel*, vol. 2 (Basel: Helbing and Lichtenhahn, 1916), 692–93.

78. Erdin, *Reuerinnen*, 41, 81.

79. Annette Barthelmé, *La Réforme dominicaine au XVe siècle en Alsace et dans l'ensemble de la province de Teutonie*, Collection d'études sur l'histoire du droit et des institutions de l'Alsace 7 (Strasbourg: Heitz, 1931), 138–39.

80. Brigitte Hilberling, *700 Jahre Kloster Zoffingen, 1257–1957* (Constance: Merk, 1957), 48; Däniker-Gysin, *Töß*, 48; Voit, *Engelthal*, 1:62.

81. Johannes Meyer, *Das Buch der Reformacio Predigerordens*, vol. 2, ed. Benedictus Maria Reichert, Quellen und Forschungen zur Geschichte des Dominikanerordens in Deutschland 3 (Leipzig: Harrassowitz, 1909), 85.

82. Canisia Jedelhauser, *Geschichte des Klosters und der Hofmark Maria-Medingen von den Anfängen im 13. Jahrhundert bis 1606*, Quellen und Forschungen zur Geschichte des Dominikanerordens in Deutschland 34 (Leipzig: Harrassowitz, 1936), 91; Lotte Kurras, "Ein Bildzeugnis der Reformtätigkeit des Nürnberger Katharinenklosters für Regensburg," *Mitteilungen des historischen Vereins für die Geschichte der Stadt Nürnberg* 68 (1981), 294.

83. Jedelhauser, *Maria-Medingen*, 91.

84. Johannes Linneborn, "Die Reformation der westfälischen Benediktiner-Klöster im 15. Jahrhundert durch die Bursfelder Congregation," *Studien und Mitteilungen zur Geschichte des Benedictinerordens* 21 (1900): 319–22; Schulze, *Stift*, 147.

85. Münster, Nordrhein-Westfälisches Staatsarchiv Münsterscher Studienfonds, Stift Überwasser, Akten Nr. 799, fol. 86v; and Schulze, *Stift*, 147–48, 376.

86. Hilberling, *Zoffingen*, 29.

87. Andreas Rüther, *Bettelorden in Stadt und Land. Die Straßburger Mendikantenkonvente und das Elsaß im Spätmittelalter*, Berliner Historische Studien 26, Ordenstudien 11 (Berlin: Dunker and Humblot, 1997), 285. Disselbeck-Tewes sets the value of twenty-four schillings at one gulden in 1457. See *Zisterzienserklöstern*, 309. Roper cites the annual income of a stonemason at about twenty-one gulden in 1475. See Roper, *Household*, 42.

88. St. Gall, Stiftsbibliothek, MS St. Katharina, Wil, "Klosterchronik," Nr. 87, fols. 8v, 42r. See also Vogler, *St. Katharina*, 49.

89. "Sorores karissime . . ." [Ebstorf reform account, c. 1490,] in "Litterarisches und geistiges Leben in Kloster Ebstorf am Ausgange des Mittelalters," ed. Conrad Borchling, *Zeitschrift des historischen Vereins für Niedersachsen* 4 (1905): 393.

90. Ida-Christine Riggert, *Die Lüneburger Frauenklöster*, Quellen und Untersuchungen zur Geschichte Niedersachsens im Mittelalter 19 (Hanover: Hahn, 1996), 107, 110, 140.

91. Dieter Brosius, "Die Lüneburger Klöster und ihr Verhältnis zum Landesherrn," in *Das Benediktinerinnenkloster Ebstorf im Mittelalter: Vorträge einer Tagung im Kloster Ebstorf vom 22. bis 24. Mai 1987*, ed. Klaus Jaitner and Ingo Schwag (Hildesheim: LAX, 1988), 143–44; Riggert, *Lüneburger*, 97.

92. Voit, *Engelthal*, 1:28.

93. Anne Roede, *Spätere Chronik*, 96–97.

94. Since the manuscript was unavailable due to its restoration and digitalization for on-line accessibility, references are to Gustav von Buchwald, "Anne von Buchwald, Priorin des Klosters Preetz 1494–1508," *Zeitschrift der Gesellschaft für Schleswig-Holsteinische Geschichte* 9 (1897): 14–15.

95. von Buchwald, "Anne von Buchwald," 40.

96. Helmar Härtl, "Die Bibliothek des Klosters Ebstorf am Ausgang des Mittelalters," in *'In Treue und Hingabe': 800 Jahre Kloster Ebstorf*, ed Marianne Elster and Horst Hoffmann, Schriften zur Uelzener Heimatkunde 13 (Uelzen: Becker, 1997), 111.

97. Buchwald, "Preetz," 37–38.

98. Weis-Müller, *Klingental*, 33.

99. Buchwald, "Preetz," 41.

100. Faust, *Frauenklöster*, 30.

101. Erdin, *Reuerinnen*, 91.

102. Weis-Müller, *Klingental*, 31–32.

103. Linneborn, "Bursfelder," 21 (1900): 62. Johannes Meyer's "Ämterbuch" includes a list of plants recommended for the cloister garden. See J. König, "Die Chronik der Anna von Munzingen. Nach der ältesten Abschrift mit Einleitung und Beilagen," *Freiburger Diözesan-Archiv* 13 (1880): 206, Beilage 1 (appendix 1).

104. "Innumerabiles grates . . ." [Chronicle of Ebstorf, 1487], in "Litterarisches und geistiges Leben in Kloster Ebstorf am Ausgange des Mittelalters," ed. Conrad Borchling, *Zeitschrift des historischen Vereins für Niedersachsen* 4 (1905): 405.

105. Elfriede Kelm, "Das Buch im Chore der Preetzer Klosterkirche. Nach dem Original dargestellt," *Schriften des Vereins für Schleswig-Holsteinische Kirchengeschichte*, 30/31 (1974/75): 18.

106. Kelm, "Das Buch im Chore," 19; Buchwald, "Preetz," 22.

107. Kist, *Klarissenkloster*, 27. The reform regulations governing the Clarissen sisters at Pfullingen state that letters sent outside the cloister were to be read by the prioriess, Gatz, "Pfullingen," 202.

108. Letter from maria von Wolkenstein to Leo von Wolkenstein, December 1455, in Appendix to Hermann Hallauer, "Nikolaus von Kues und das Brixener Klarissenkloster," *Mitteilungen und Forschungsbeiträge der Cusanus-Gesellschaft* 6 (1967): 117.

109. Max Miller, *Die Söflinger Briefe und das Klarissenkloster Söflingen bei Ulm im Spätmittelalter* (Würzburg: Triltsch, 1940), 80, 89; Frank, *Söflingen*, 100.

110. Letter from Genovera Vetter to Johannes Spieß, August 1482, in Appendix to Miller, *Briefe*, 194.

111. Frank, *Söflingen*, 100.

112. Miller, *Briefe*, 164.

113. Frank, *Söflingen*, 100–101.

114. Ursula Peters, *Religiöse Erfahrung als literarisches Faktum: Zur Vorgeschichte und Genese frauenmystischer Texte des 13. und 14. Jahrhuderts* (Tübingen: Niemeyer, 1988), 193.

115. [Elsbeth Stagel?] *Töß*, ed. Vetter, 27.

116. "Sorores karissime . . . ," ed. Borchling, 395.

117. *Schwesternbuch von Sankt Agnes*, ed. Bollmann and Staubach, 255.

118. Vogler, *St. Katharina*, 62. Volger's reference to folio 43r of the St. Gall, Stiftsbibliothek, MS St. Katharina, Wil, "Schwesternbuch," Nr. 89, is incorrect. I have been unable to locate the correct folio.

119. Härtel, "Ebstorf," 111–12.

120. Disselbeck-Tewes, *Frauen*, 206.

121. Riggert, *Lüneburger*, 299, 325.

122. Voit, *Engelthal*, 1:55.

123. St. Gall, Stiftsbibliothek, MS St. Katharina, Wil, "Schwesternbuch," Nr. 89, fol. 180; Vogler, *St. Katharnia*, 75.

124. Weis-Müller, *Klingental*, 26.

125. Erdin, *Reuerinnen*, 105–7.

126. "Die Stiftung des Klosters Oetenbach," ed. Zeller-Werdmüller and Bächthold, 227–28. The Oetenbach sister-book is one of the three that Johannes Meyer edited. For a summary of his cuts and additions, see *Das St. Katharinentaler Schwesternbuch. Untersuchung, Edition, Kommentar*, ed. Ruth Meyer, Münchener Texte und Untersuchungen zur deutschen Literatur des Mittelalters 104 (Tübingen: Niemeyer, 1995), 66–72.

127. [Anna von Munzingen,] "Dis sint die gnade . . . , ed. König, 163.

128. Buchwald, "Preetz," 36. Reporting on one of her frequent trips to Lübeck to purchase stores, Anna writes in 1496, "[When] I was in Lübeck, I bought 100 pounds of almonds at 2.5 schillings a pound totaling 12.5 marks, which I got for you again from the previous year because almonds were so expensive; idem. 36.

129. Kelm, "Buch," 15.

130. Buchwald, "Preetz," 36.

131. St. Gall, Stiftsbibliothek, MS St. Katharina, Wil, "Klosterchronik," Nr. 87, fol. 40r. I have not been able to find the letter from Haller that Volger cites. See Vogler, *St. Katharina,* 65, 66, note 1. Gudrun Gleba reports organs being repaired or purchased new at Herzebrock, Gertrudenberg, St. Ägidien, and Malgarten. See *Reformpraxis und materielle Kultur: Westfälische Frauenklöster im Mittelalter* (Husum: Matthiesen, 2000), 167.

132. Roede, *Spätere Chronik,* 130.

133. Edeltraud Klueting, *Das Bistum Osnabrück 1: Das Kanonissenstift und Benediktinerinnenkloster Herzebrock,* Germania Sacra n.F. 21 (Berlin: de Gruyter, 1986), 220; Roede, "Spätere Chronik," 129.

134. Friedrich Techen, ed., *Die Chroniken des Klosters Ribnitz,* Mecklenburgische Geschichtsquellen 1 (Schwerin: Bärensprungsche Hofdruckerei, 1909), 10.

135. Eckenstein, *Monasticism,* 223. Many of these artistic activities have been brought to light recently in Jeffrey Hamburger's seminal studies, *Nuns as Artists* and *The Visual and the Visionary.*

136. Jeffrey Hamburger, *Nuns as Artists: The Visual Culture of a Medieval Convent,* California Studies in the History of Art 37 (Berkeley and Los Angeles: University of California Press, 1997), 37–51; Victoria Joan Moessner, "The Medieval Embroideries of Convent Wienhausen," in *Studies in Cistercian Art and Architecture,* ed. Meredith Lillich (Kalamazoo, Mich.: Cistercian Publications, 1987), 3:170; Marie Schuette, *Deutsche Wandteppiche* (Leipzig: Bibliographisches Institut, 1938), 45–46. A tapestry from the last quarter of the fifteenth century showing two Dominican nuns weaving a tapestry is reproduced in Winfried Wilhelmy, *Drache, Greif und Liebesleut': Mainzer Bildteppiche aus spätgotischer Zeit. Ausstellungskatalog,* Schriften des Bischöflichen Dom- und Diözesanmuseums Mainz (Mainz: Philipp von Zabern, 2000), 18.

137. "Sorores karissime . . . ," ed. Borchling, 392.

138. Buchwald, "Preetz," 47; Jeffrey Hamburger, *The Visual and the Visionary: Art and Female Spirituality in Late Medieval Germany* (New York: Zone Books, 1998), 98–99.

139. [Juliana Ernst,] *Die Chronik des Bickenklosters zu Villingen,* ed. Karl Jordan Glatz, Bibliothek des Litterarischen Vereins in Stuttgart 151 (Tübingen: Fues, 1881), 42. Juliana cites from an old manuscript found in the infirmary, which she identifies as written by former prioress Haider.

140. [Juliana Ernst,] *Die Chronik,* 65.

141. "Sorores karissime . . . ," ed. Borchling, 394–95.

142. Weis-Müller, *Klingental,* 21–22.

143. Frank, *Söflingen,* 106.

144. Grube, *Busch,* 142.

145. Jutta Prieur, *Das Kölner Dominikanerinnenkloster St. Gertrud am Neumarkt,* Kölner Schriften zu Geschichte und Kultur (Cologne: dme-Verlag, 1983), 467; Erdin, *Reuerinnen,* 119; Linneborn, "Bursfelder," 565.

146. *Schwesternbuch von Sankt Agnes,* ed. Bollmann and Staubach, 116, 208 n. 12, 252 n. 2.

147. Ibid., 246.

148. "Chronik des Schwesternhauses," ed. Cornelius, 427.

149. Degler-Spengler, *Gnadental,* 54.

150. Huffer, *Rijnsburg,* 128.

151. Jo Ann McNamara, "The Need to Give: Suffering and Female Sanctity in the Middle Ages," in *Images of Sainthood in Medieval Europe,* ed. Timea Szell (Ithaca: Cornell University Press, 1991), 203.

152. [Bertha of Vilich,] *Adelheid,* trans. Madelyn Dick, 28–29.

153. McNamara, "Suffering," 213.

154. Hieronymus Wilms, *Das Beten der Mystikerinnen dargestellt nach den Chroniken der Dominikanerinnenklöster zu Adelhausen, Dießenhofen, Engeltal, Kirchberg, Oetenbach, Töß und Unterlinden,* Quellen und Forschungen zur Geschichte des Dominikanerordens in Deutschland 11 (Leipzig: Harrassowitz, 1918), 50.

155. Marie-Luise Ehrenschwendtner, "'Puellae litteratae': The Use of the Vernacular in the Dominican Convents of Southern Germany," in *Medieval Women in their Communities,* ed. Diane Watt (Toronto: University of Toronto Press, 1997), 59.

156. A nineteenth-century abridged edition and continuation by Georg Geissenhof of the old chronicle begun by Elisabeth Mundprat and Apollonia Besserer was published by Theodor Dreher. See "Die Geissenhof'sche Chronik des Klosters Inzigkofen," ed. Theodor Dreher, *Freiburger Katholisches Kirchenblatt* 38 (1894): col. 423. See also Werner Fechter, *Deutsche Handschriften des 15. und 16. Jahrhunderts aus der Bibliothek des ehemaligen Augustinerchorfrauenstifts Inzigkofen* (Sigmaringen: Thorbecke, 1997), 1.

157. Augsburg, Staatsarchiv, MS Kloster Maria Maihingen MüB 1, fol. 14r. See also Nyberg, Tore, *Dokumente und Untersuchungen zur inneren Geschichte der drei Brigittenklöster Bayerns 1420–1570*, Quellen und Erörterungen zur bayerischen Geschichte, n.F. 26, vol. 2 (Munich: Beck, 1974), 163. Although the scribe has not been identified, materials for the *Housebook* were assembled by Prioress Walburga Scheffler and a successor who identifies herself only as "Prioress Anna."

158. Buchwald, "Preetz," 17, 20–21.

159. [Katharina von Gueberschwihr,] "Vita," 338.

160. Hamburger, *Artists*, 88–90; Francis Rapp, "Zur Spiritualität in elsässischen Frauenklöstern am Ende des Mittelalters," in *Frauemystik im Mittelalter*, ed. Peter Dinzelbacher and Dieter R. Bauer (Ostfildern: Schwabenverlag, 1985), 354–55; Gertrud Jaron Lewis, *By Women, for Women, about Women: The Sister-Books of Fourteenth-Century Germany* (Toronto: Pontifical Institute of Medieval Studies, 1996), 146–47; [Elsbeth Stagel?] *Töß*, 84; Thomas Lentes, "Die Gewänder der Heiligen. Ein Diskussionsbeitrag zum Verhältnis von Gebet, Bild und Imagination," in *Hagiographie und Kunst der Heiligenkult in Schrift, Bild und Architektur*, ed. G. Kerscher (Berlin: D. Reimer, 1993), 140; Engène Honeé, "Image and Imagination in the Medieval Culture of Prayer: A Historical Perspective," in *The Art of Devotion in the Late Middle Ages in Europe, 1300–1500*, ed. Henk van Os (Princeton: Princeton Unversity Press, 1994), 171.

161. Ellen Ross, *The Grief of God: Images of the Suffering Jesus in Medieval England* (Oxford: Oxford University Press, 1997), 125.

162. [Elsbeth Stagel?] *Töß*, 31.

163. Bynum, *Feast*, 401 n. 81; idem, *Jesus as Mother: Studies in the Spirituality of the High Middle Ages* (Berkeley and Los Angeles: University of California Press, 1982), 194. The "Tagebuch der Angela von Holfels," diary of Sister Angela Holfels (1465–1539) at the Augustinian convent of St. Agnes in Trier contains a sort of personal account book of prayers said; Hamburg, Staats- und Universitätsbibliothek MS Theol. 8 2064.

164. Ross, *Grief*, 126, McNamara, "Suffering," 216, idem, *Arms*, 376. For women like Clare of Assisi who were "not intended" to preach, Degler-Spengler asserts, St. Francis had prescribed a mission of prayer and strict fasting. See *Gnadental*, 12. Similarly, Patricia Ranft asserts, St. Dominic established a contemplative base at Prouille for women to be "partners in the apostolate" by supporting the work of the order through prayer," *Women and the Religious Life in Premodern Europe* (New York: St. Martin's Press, 1996), 70–71.

165. Bynum, *Feast*, 120, 129.

166. Barbara Newman, *From Virile Woman to Woman Christ: Studies in Medieval Religion and Literature* (Philadelphia: University of Pennsylvania Press, 1995), 122.

167. [Katharina von Gueberschwihr,] "Vita," 345.

168. Michael Goodich, "The Contours of Female Piety in Later Medieval Hagiography," *Church History* 50 (1981): 28–29.

169. Ross, *Grief*, 126.

170. *Hier beginnen sommige stichtigë punten van onsen oelden zusteren*, ed. Dirk de Man (The Hague: M. Nijhoff, 1919), 245–46. See also John Van Engen, *Devotio Moderna: Basic Writings* (New York: Mahwah: Paulist Press, 1988), 131.

171. Hiltrud Gnüg and Renate Möhrmann, eds. *Frauen Literatur Geschichte: Schreibende Frauen vom Mittelalter bis zur Gegenwart* (Stuttgart: Metzler, 1999), xi. See also Margaret Bäurle and Luzia Braun, "Klöster und Höfe—Räume literarischer Selbstentfaltung," in idem, 2.

Chapter 2

1. Herbert Grundmann, *Religious Movements in the Middle Ages: The Historical Links between Heresy, the Mendicant Orders, and the Women's Religious Movement in the Twelfth and Thirteenth Century, with the Historical Foundations of German Mysticism*, ed. and trans. Stephen Rowen (Notre Dame: University of Notre Dame Press, 1995).

2. Even the question how to translate the term "religiöse Frauenbewegung" is controversial: should it be "religious women's movement" or "women's religious movement?" The latter is how Rowen's recent translation renders it most of the time. Questioning whether such a movement may not actually have existed much earlier in the Middle Ages, Jo Ann McNamara argues that women's religious communities have always tended to be invisible to the historical record, at least "until a male preacher, cleric or monastic community adopted them into the world of account-books and charters," *Sisters in Arms: Catholic Nuns through Two Millennia* (Cambridge, Mass.: Harvard University Press, 1996), 236, 239. Brigitte Degler-Spengler, on the other hand, objects to Grundmann's terminology. She doubts that one should speak of a "religious women's movement" at all. Instead, she suggests the terms "religious lay persons' movement," "feminine religious movement," or, less simply, "religious movement among women." See "Die religiöse Frauenbewegung des Mittelalters: Conversen-Non-nen-Beginen," *Rottenburger Jahrbuch für Kirchengeschichte* 3 (1984), 86. Ute Weinmann has proposed the designation "social-religious movement," a label Ulrike Denne identifies as preferred by medievalists in the former East Germany. Cited in Ulrike Denne *Die Frauenklöster im spätmittelalterlichen Freiburg im Breisgau* (Freiburg: Alber, 1997), 10. Peter Dinzelbacher rejects Grundmann's term on the grounds that it does not correspond to any "medieval expression." See his "Rollenverweigerung, religiöser Auf-bruch und mystisches Erleben mittelalterlicher Frauen," in *Mittelalterliche Frauenmystik*, ed. Peter Din-zelbacher (Paderborn: Schöningh, 1993), 59. The most systematic objections, however, have been lodged by Martina Wehrli-Johns, who challenges Grundmann's view of the importance of the apostolic poverty movement. She argues that his excessive fascination with the concept of voluntary poverty caused him to overlook the more important development of the twelfth-century "penitential move-ment." See Martina Wehrli-Johns, "Voraussetzungen und Perspektiven mittelalterlicher Laienfrömmig-keit seit Innozenz III. Eine Auseinandersetzung mit Herbert Grundmanns 'Religiösen Bewegungen,'" *Mitteilungen des Instituts für österreichische Geschichtsforschung* 104 (1996): 291–94, 301, 305.

3. Grundmann, *Religious Movements*, 234.

4. Ibid., 7–9, 19–21; Brigitte Degler-Spengler, "'Zahlreich wie die Sterne des Himmels': Zister-zienser, Dominikaner und Franziskaner vor dem Problem der Inkorporation von Frauenklöstern," *Rottenburger Jahrbuch für Kirchengeschichte* 4 (1985): 37; Penelope D. Johnson, *Equal in Monastic Profession: Religious Women in Medieval France* (Chicago: University of Chicago Press, 1991), 4. Even earlier than Robert and Norbert, who received official permission to preach in 1096 and 1118, Bruce Venarde points to wandering preachers already afoot at mid-century. See *Women's Monasticism and Medieval Society: Nunneries in France and England, 890–1215* (Ithaca: Cornell University Press, 1997), 57.

5. Brigitte Degler-Spengler, "Die religiöse Frauenbewegung des Mittelalters: Conversen-Non-nen-Beginen," *Rottenburger Jahrbuch för Kirchengeschichte* 3 (1984): 79, 76. The Order of Canons Regular of Prémontré was founded by Norbert of Xanten in 1120. It constituted a middle step between the contemplative life of the earlier orders and the active life of the friars of the thirteenth century.

6. Venarde, *Nunneries*, xii, 87, 92, 126–28. On the "Frauenfrage," see also Walter Simons, *Cities of Ladies: Beguine Communities of the Medieval Low Countries 1200–1565* (Philadelphia: University of Pennsylvania Press, 2001), x–xi, 111; Ernest McDonnell, *The Beguines and Beghards in Medieval Culture with Special Emphasis on the Belgian Scene* (1954; repr. New York: Octagon, 1969), 83–85; Karl Bücher *Die Frauenfrage im Mittelalter*, 2d ed. (Tübingen: Laupp, 1910).

7. Degler-Spengler, "zahlreich," 41.

8. Ibid., 43; Annemarie Halter, *Geschichte des Dominikanerinnen-Klosters Oetenbach in Zürich 1234–1525* (Winterthur: Keller, 1956), 17, Grundmann, *Movements*, 91.

9. Grundmann, *Movements*, 75.

10. Amalie Fößel and Anette Hettinger, *Klosterfrauen, Beginen, Ketzerinnen. Religiöse Lebensformen von Frauen im Mittelalter* (Idstein: Schulz-Kirchner, 2000), 47. According to McDonnell, neither Cologne nor Strasbourg ever possessed more than two men's beghard houses, *Beguines and Beghards,* 253.

11. Despite the Cistercians' moratorium, women's houses had increased from 15 to 220 between 1150 and 1250. Degler-Spengler, "zahlreich," 44–45; Gustav Voit, *Engelthal—Geschichte eines Dominikanerinnenklosters,* 2. vols., Schriftenreihe der Altnürnberger Landschaft 26 (Nuremberg: Koru and Berg, 1977): 1:40.

12. The Dominicans, the Franciscans, as well as the Cistercians attempted to stem the flow by requiring that nuns be strictly cloistered and stipulating that only houses having endowments sufficient to make them completely self-supporting would be accepted. Degler-Spengler, "zahlreich," 43, 48; Voit, *Engelthal,* 1:40; Grundmann, *Movements,* 91; Halter, *Oetenbach,* 17.

13. Besides acquiescing to special requests by influential friends and relations among the higher nobility, the popes themselves wanted to regulate unincorporated and unstructured women's communities to guard against uncontrolled diversity and keep women from falling into heresy. Degler-Spengler, "zahlreich," 40, 46, 48.

14. Grundmann, *Movements,* 81. Hadewijch's dates have been contested, see Wybren Scheepsma, "Hadewijch und die 'Limburgse Sermoenen'. Überlegungen zu Datierung, Identität und Autentizität," in *Deutsche Mystik im abendländischen Zusammenhang: Neuerschlossene Texte, neue methodische Ansätze, neue theoretische Konzepte,* ed. Walter Haug and Wolfram Schneider-Lastin, 653–82 (Tübingen: Niemeyer, 2000).

15. [Magdalena Kremer] "Wie diß loblich closter zu Sant Johannes baptisten zu kirchen under deck prediger-ordens reformiert ist worden und durch woelich personen," in *Geschichte des Herzogtums Wuerttemberg unter der Regierung der Graven,* 2d ed., ed. Christian Friedrich Sattler (Tübingen: Reiss, 1773–77), 4:218.

16. Dinzelbacher, "Rollenverweigerung," 59–60.

17. The sister-books of Töss, Katharinental, Adelhausen, Engelthal, and probably Oetenbach contain foundation histories that were incorporated into these works in the fourteenth century. To the Töss sister-book, a prologue that had existed separately as a latin text, "De monasterio sororum in Thosse" was translated and added in the fourteenth century, as was that attached to the vitae in the Katharinental sister-book. Engelthal contains an account of the cloister's founding that was part of the work's original conception. Here Christina Ebner seems to have combined historical information from the cloister's book of properties and rents (1312) with a legendary tale about a harpist who left the retinue of Elisabeth of Hungary to take up a religious life. In this work the foundation story forms part of the first vita. A foundation narrative was added to the Unterlinden sister-book by Prioress Elisabeth Kempf in the fifteenth century, and one to the Kirchberg book in 1691, probably by the Dominican Pius Kessler. The Weiler and Gotteszell works do not contain foundation accounts. See. Susanne Bürkle, *Literatur im Kloster: Historische Funktion und rhetorische Legitimation frauenmystischer Texte des 14. Jahrhunderts* (Tübingen and Basel: Francke, 1999), 179–92, esp. 180–82; *Das St. Katharinentaler Schwesternbuch. Untersuchung, Edition, Kommentar,* ed. Ruth Meyer, Münchner Texte und Untersuchungen 104 (Tübingen: Niemeyer, 1995), 76–79, 141; and the entries in Kurt Ruh et al., *Die deutsche Literatur des Mittelalters: Verfasserlexikon,* 11 vols. (Berlin: de Gruyter, 1978–); Voit, *Engelthal,* 1:20–21. For a listing and a comprehensive overview, see Gertrud Jaron Lewis, *By Women, for Women, about Women: The Sister-Books of Fourteenth-Century Germany* (Toronto: Pontifical Institute of Medieval Studies, 1996).

18. "Die Stiftung des Klosters Oetenbach und das Leben der seligen Schwestern daselbst, aus der Nürnberger Handschrift," ed. H. Zeller-Werdmüller and Jakob Bächthold, *Zürcher Taschenbuch* 12 (1889): 223–24.

19. Ibid., 226–27.

20. "Stiftung," ed. Zeller-Werdmüller and Bächthold, 218–20.

21. On the dating of this foundation account to the fourteenth century see Bürkle, *Literatur im Kloster,* 181 note 66, and *Das St. Katharinentaler,* ed. Meyer, 76–79.

22. *St. Katharinentaler*, ed. Meyer, 142–43.

23. Ulrich Ecker points out that a major donor was later often designated as a "founder," and earned the title retroactively by the gift of goods and privileges, regardless of when the endowment was actually made. See Ulrich P. Ecker, "Die Geschichte des Klosters S. Johannes-Baptista der Dominikanerinnen zu Kirchheim unter Teck" (Ph.D. diss., University of Freiburg, 1985), 18, note 1.

24. Voit, *Engelthal*, 1:23. An even older German cloister chronicle and account book, composed by Engelthal prioress Elsbet Schenkin von Klingenburg, dates from 1312. See Suzanne Bürkle, *Literature*, 186.

25. [Christine Ebner,] *Der Nonne von Engelthal: Büchlein von der Gnaden Überlast*, Karl Schröder, ed., Bibliothek des Litterarischen Vereins in Stuttgart 108 (Tübingen: Litterarischer Verein, 1871), 2–3. Christine includes a moving account of the beguines' charismatic spirituality as they are learning to sing the Hours before their induction as Dominicans. She relates:

In the first Advent when they sang the Hours, their first singing mistress was named Hailrat. She was wondrously beautiful and sang exceptionally well and learned quickly and was very devoted to Our Lord. This showed in her life and in all her works. Now, when they came to the fourth Sunday in Advent, they were singing matins, and when they came to the fifth response "Virgo Israel," and the verse, "In caritate perpetua," she sang in German and sang so incredibly beautifully that one would have thought it was the voice of an angel. The verse reads in German: "I have loved you with an eternal love and have drawn you to me in my mercy." This verse our Lord spoke as a prophecy to the human race. The convent was so filled with devotion that they all fell to the floor in a swoon and lay there until they came back to themselves. Then they sang matins to the end with even greater devotion (6–7).

26. [Katharina von Gueberschwihr,] "Les 'Vitae sororum d'Unterlinden.' Edition critique du manuscrit 508 de la Bibliothèque de Colmar," ed. Jeanne Ancelet-Hustache, *Archives d'histoire doctrinale et littéraire du moyen age* 5 (1930): 317–517; idem, *Lebensbeschreibung der ersten Schwestern des Klosters der Dominikanerinnen zu Unterlinden von deren Priorin Catharina von Gebsweiler*, trans. Elisabeth Kempf, [1415–1485], ed. Ludwig Clarus (Regensburg: Mainz, 1863); and Karl-Ernst Greith, "Elisabeth Kempfs Übersetzung und Fortsetzung der 'Vitae sororum' der Katharina von Gueberschwihr," *Annuaire de la Société d'Histoire et d'Archéologie de Colmar* 32 (1984): 28–29.

27. [Katharina von Gueberschwihr,] *Lebensbeschreibung*, trans. Kempf, ed. Clarus, 31–33.

28. Simons, *Cities*, 108, 143. Similarly, Fößel and Hettinger, comment on the phenomenon of women helping beguine women, *Klosterfrauen*, 51.

29. *St. Katharinental*, ed. Meyer, 144.

30. "Anno dni MCCL an Sant Martins tag da ist dis Closter Pfullingen an gefangen worden," in "Duae Relationes circa Monasterium Brixinense O. Clar.," ed. Maximilianus Straganz, *Archivum Franciscanum Historicum* 6 (1913): 538; and Johannes Gatz, "Pfullingen," *Alemania Franciscana Antiqua* 17 (1972): 170.

31. "Anno dni MCCL . . . ," ed. Straganz, 538.

32. Müller, "Frauenklöster," 14; Gerhard Rehm, *Die Schwestern vom gemeinsamen Leben im nordwestlichen Deutschland. Untersuchungen zum Devotio moderna und des weiblichen Religiösentums*, Berliner Historische Studien 11, Ordensstudien 5 (Berlin: Dunker und Humblot, 1985), 30. Franz Felten points out that the distinction between canonesses and nuns is easier to make in theory than in practice where one encounters numerous transitional forms. See "Frauenklöster und -stifte im Rheinland im 12. Jahrhundert. Ein Beitrag zur Geschichte der Frauen in der religiösen Bewegung des hohen Mittelalters," in *Reformidee und Reformpolitik im spätsalisch-frühstaufischen Reich*, ed. Stefan Weinfurter, Quellen und Abhandlungen zur Mittelrheinischen Kirchengeschichte 68 (Mainz: Seibert, 1992), 193.

33. [Hrosvit of Gandersheim,] "Primordia coenobii Gandeshemensis," in *Hrosvithae Opera*, ed. Helene Homeyer (Paderborn: Schöningh, 1970), 450–72; and [Bertha of Vilich,] "Vita Adelheidis

Abbatissae Vilicensis," ed. Oswald Holger-Egger, in *Monumenta Germaniae Historica: Scriptorum*, ed. Pertz, Holger-Egger et al., vol. 15, part 2, pp. 754–63.

34. Cited from [Bertha of Vilich,] *Mater spiritualis: The Life of Adelheid of Vilich*, trans. Madelyn Bergen (Toronto: Peregrina Press, 1994), 22–23.

35. Gertrud Jaron Lewis, *By Women, for Women, about Women: The Sister-Books of Fourteenth-Century Germany* (Toronto: Pontifical Institute of Medieval Studies, 1996), 53–54; J. König, ed., "Die Chronik der Anna von Munzingen. Nach der ältesten Abschrift mit Einleitung und Beilagen," *Freiburger Diözesan-Archiv* 13 (1880): 150–51. This is disputed, however, by Bürkle, *Kloster*, 162–79. See also Gérard de Frachet, *Lives of the Brethren of the Order of Preachers 1206–1259*, trans. Placid Conway (London: Burns, Oates, and Washbourne, 1924), v.

36. Lewis, *Sister-Books*, 54–56.

37. Cited in ibid., 52.

38. Walter Blank, "Die Nonnenviten des 14. Jahrhunderts. Eine Studie zur hagiographischen Literatur des Mittelalters unter besonderer Berücksichtigung der Visionen und ihrer Lichtphänomene" (Ph.D. diss., University of Freiburg, 1962), 92; and Otto Langer, *Mystische Erfahrung und spirituelle Theologie. Zu Meister Eckharts Untersuchungen mit der Frauenfrömmigkeit seiner Zeit*, Münchener Texte und Untersuchungen zur deutschen Literatur des Mittelalters 91 (Munich and Zürich: Artemis, 1987), 60.

39. [Stagel?,] *Töß*, ed. Vetter, 87. Klaus Grubmüller's analysis of the layering in the construction of the Töss sister-book places the vita of Elisabeth Bechlin at the third (of six) stages in the development of the text. This vita and a prologue were added by another sister, possibly from material by Elsbeth Stagel, before later accretions and Johannes Meyer's editing. See Klaus Grübmuller, "Die Viten der Schwestern von Töss und Elsbeth Stagel: Überlieferung und literarische Einheit," *Zeitschrift für deutsche Philologie* 98 (1969): 171–204.

40. Veronika Gerz-von Büren, *Geschichte des Clarissenklosters St. Clara in Kleinbasel 1266–1529*, Quellen und Forschungen zur Basler Geschichte 2 (Basel: Reinhardt, 1969), 96. Benedictine cloisters housed on the average only five, ten, or at most twenty monks. Perhaps the saddest example was the once great abbey of St. Gall, which in 1411 had only two conventuals left: One had elected the other abbot and the second held all the remaining cloister offices and their incomes. As the "abbot" was neither educated nor a priest, the monastic offices had to be performed by Benedictines from other cloisters, or by mendicants, or sometimes even by pensioners who were clothed in monk's habits.

See also Gerhard Spahr, "Die Reform im Kloster St. Gallen 1417–1441." *Schriften des Vereins für Geschichte des Bodensees und seiner Umgebung* 75 (1957): 20–25, 35. Spahr asserts that St. Gall's revenues, which in 1275 had amounted to 1043 marks silver, had shrunk to only 371 marks in 1354. Monasteries like St. Gall, which accepted only nobles, could not attract sufficient numbers. Many members lived separately in their own houses or castles, spent their time hunting or fighting, were illiterate, and brought their "Hausfrauen" with them to church.

41. Franz Haffner, *Die kirchlichen Reformbemühungen des Speyrer Bischofs Matthias von Rammung in vortridentinischer Zeit (1464–1478)* (Speyer: Pilger, 1961), 71–72. Johannes Helmrath points out that in the diocese of Geneva in the fifteenth century, twenty-nine percent of the priests had concubines, see "Reform als Thema der Konzilien des Spätmittelalters," in *Christian Unity: The Council of Ferrara-Florenz 1438/39–1449*, ed. Giuseppe Alberigo (Louvain: Louvain University Press, 1991), 88. Adalbert Mischlewski comments that in Memmingen the general preceptor of the order of St. Anthony, Peter Mitte de Caprariis, paid 380 gulden for his daughter's wedding in 1461 out of funds belonging to the monastery; see "Spätmittelalterliche Reformbemühungen im Antoniterorden," in *Reformbemühungen und Observanzbestrebungen im spätmittelalterlichen Ordenswesen*, ed. Kaspar Elm, Berliner Historische Studien 14, Ordensstudien 6 (Berlin: Dunker and Humblot, 1989), 167.

42. Jutta Prieur, *Das Kölner Dominikanerinnenkloster St. Gertrud am Neumarkt*, Kölner Schriften zu Geschichte und Kultur (Cologne: dme-Verlag, 1983). 93.

43. Letter from the Clarissan sisters to the Nuremberg city council [c. 1410], in appendix to Johannes Kist, ed., *Das Klarissenkloster in Nürnberg bis zum Beginn des 16. Jahrhunderts* (Nuremberg: Sebaldus, 1929), 154–62, at 156.

44. Francis Rapp, "Zur Spiritualität in elsässischen Frauenklöstern am Ende des Mittelalters," in *Frauenmystik im Mittelalter,* ed. Peter Dinzelbacher and Dieter R. Bauer (Ostfildern: Schwaben Verlag, 1985), 349.

45. Annemarie Halter, *Geschichte des Dominikanerinnen-Klosters Oetenbach in Zürich 1234–1525* (Winterthur: Keller, 1956), 121–22.

46. Karl Suso Frank, *Das Klarissenkloster Söflingen: Ein Beitrag zur franziskanischen Ordensgeschichte Süddeutschlands und zur Ulmer Kirchengeschichte* (Ulm: Stuttgart: Kohlhammer, 1980), 96–97.

47. Ulrich Ecker, "Die Geschichte des Klosters S. Johannes-Baptista der Dominikanerinnen zu Kirchheim unter Teck" (Ph.D. diss., University of Freiburg, 1985), 158. Yet noble visitors, especially a cloister's patrons, are frequently mentioned being entertained at women's convents including Adelhausen in Freiburg and Klingental in Basel. Not only patrons but also family members dined with the sisters in a large external refectory at Klingental during parish fairs. At the Dominican house of Töss women left the cloister to take the waters at a spa; records in Bern from 1439 report nuns traveling about the city at night. See Sully Roecken and Carolina Brauckmann, *Margareta Jedefrau,* vol. 1 (Freiburg: Kore, 1989), 87; Renée Weis-Müller, *Die Reform des Klosters Klingental und ihr Personenkreis,* Baseler Beiträge zur Geschichtswissenschaft 59 (Basel and Stuttgart: Helbing and Lichtenhahn, 1956), 32; Marie-Claire Däniker-Gysin, *Geschichte des Dominikanerinnenklosters Töß 1233–1525,* Neujahrsblatt der Statbibliothek Winterthur 289 (Winterthur: Ziegler, 1957), 54.

48. Weis-Müller, *Klingental,* 46–47.

49. Arnold Schromm, *Die Bibliothek des ehemaligen Zisterzienserinnenklosters Kirchheim am Ries: Buchpflege und geistiges Leben in einem Frauenstift,* Studia Augustana 9 (Tübingen: Niemeyer, 1998), 91.

50. Barbara Frank, *Das Erfurter Peterskloster im 15. Jahrhundert. Studien zur Geschichte der Klosterreform und der Bursfelder Union,* Veröffentlichungen des Max-Planck-Instituts für Geschichte 34, Studien zur Germania Sacra 2 (Göttingen: Vandenhoeck and Ruprecht, 1973), 85.

51. Halter, *Oetenbach,* 106.

52. Hermann Tüchle, "Süddeutsche Klöster vor 500 Jahren, ihre Stellung in Reich und Gesellschaft," *Blätter für deutsche Landesgeschichte* 109 (1973): 112.

53. Gerhard Taddey, *Das Kloster Heiningen von der Gründung bis zur Aufhebung,* Veröffentlichungen des Max-Planck-Instituts für Geschichte 14 (Göttingen: Vandenhoeck and Ruprecht, 1966), 96.

54. Brigitte Hilberling, *700 Jahre Kloster Zoffingen, 1257–1957* (Constance: Merk, 1957), 28–29, 34.

55. [Anna Roede,] "Anna Roedes spätere Chronik von Herzebrock," ed. Franz Flaskamp, *Jahrbuch der Gesellschaft für Niedersächsische Kirchengeschichte* 68 (1970): 92–93.

56. Letter from the Clarissan sisters to the Nuremberg city council [c. 1410], in Kist, ed., *Klarissenkloster,* 159; Georg Pickel, "Geschichte des Klaraklosters in Nürnberg," *Beiträge zur bayerischen Kirchengeschichte* 19 (1913): 158–59. A similar rivalry was reported at Katharinental in Johannes Meyer's *Buch der Reformacio Predigerordens,* ed. Benedictus Maria Reichert, Quellen und Forschungen zur Geschichte des Dominikanerordens in Deutschland 2 (Leipzig: Harrassowitz, 1908), 62. On the two Saint Johns, see Hans-Jochen Schiewer, "Die beiden Sankt Johannsen, ein dominikanischer Johannes-Libellus und das literarische Leben im Bodenseeraum um 1300," *Oxford German Studies* 22 (1993): 21–54; and Jeffrey Hamburger, *St. John die Divine: The Deified Evangelist in Medieval Art and Theology* (Berkeley and Los Angeles: University of California Press, 2002), 65–82.

57. Emil Erdin, *Das Kloster der Reuerinnen Sancta Maria Magdalena an den Steinen zu Basel von den Anfängen bis zur Reformation (etwa 1230–1529)* (Fribourg: Paulus, 1956), 49.

58. Medard Barth, "Dr. Johannes Kreutzer (gest. 1468) und die Wiederaufrichtung des Dominikanerinnenklosters Engelporten in Gebweiler. Kritisch und geschichtlich behandelt," *Archiv für elsässische Kirchengeschichte* 8 (1933): 193–94.

59. Ida-Christine Riggert, *Die Lüneburger Frauenklöster,* Quellen und Untersuchungen zur Geschichte Niedersachsens im Mittelalter 19 (Hanover: Hahn, 1996), 316–17.

60. Max Miller, *Die Söflinger Briefe und das Klarissenkloster Söflingen bei Ulm im Spätmittelalter* (Würzburg: Triltsch, 1940), 40–41; Frank, *Söflingen,* 101–2.

61. Riggert, *Lüneburger,* 277. For an earlier period, much has been written about whether the

famous house of Gandersheim should be designated as a Benedictine convent or a "Stift" (a canoness house). For a summary, see Bert Nagel, *Hrosvit von Gandersheim* (Stuttgart: Metzler, 1965), 47–48.

62. The cloister of Klingental, for example, called itself "Dominican" up until 1429 when it tried to disconnect from the order and place itself instead under the jurisdiction of the bishop of Constance as an Augustinian house of choir nuns. In 1480 the Dominicans tried to win it back by attempting a reform. Weis-Müller states, "In form, Klingental was definitely a cloister, but its character was something like that of a 'Stift' (a canoness house), not one with a strict way of life based on the Aachen statutes [which prescribed a common life], but one like many other houses"; *Klingental*, 16, 39. To complicate matters further, there were also regular canonesses (canonici regulares) who took vows, lived a common life without private property, wore a habit, lived enclosed and were more like regular nuns than like secular canonesses (canonici saeculares). See Ulrich Faust, ed., *Die Frauenklöster in Niedersachsen, Schleswig-Holstein und Bremen*, Germania Benedictina 11 (St. Ottilien: EOS-Verlag, 1984), 27.

63. Dietrich Schmidtke, *Studien zur dingallegorischen Erbauungsliteratur des Mittelalters. Am Beispiel der Gartenallegorie*, Hermea, Germanistische Forschungen n.F. 43 (Tübingen: Niemeyer, 1982), 264.

64. Joseph Lortz, *The Reformation in Germany*, 2 vols., trans. Ronald Walls (New York: Herder, 1968), 1:110; Bernd Moeller, "Piety in Germany around 1500," in *The Reformation in Medieval Perspective* (Chicago: Quadrangle, 1971), 51, 53, 60.

65. John Van Engen, "The Virtues, the Brothers, and the Schools," *Revue Bénédictne* 98 (1988): 178; Van Engen, ed. and trans., *Devotio Moderna: Basic Writings* (Mahwah, N.Y.: Paulist Press, 1988), 14; Kaspar Elm, "Die Brüderschaft vom gemeinsamen Leben. Eine geistliche Lebensform zwischen Kloster und Welt, Mittelalter und Neuzeit," in *Ons geestelijk erf* 59 (1985): 470–96. For summaries of the aims and practices of the Brothers and Sisters of the Common Life, see Albert Hyma, *The Christian Renaissance: A History of the "Devotio Moderna,"* 2d ed. (Hamden, Conn.: Archon, 1965); Regnerus Richardus Post, *The Modern Devotion: Confrontation with Reformation and Humanism*, Studies in Medieval and Reformation Thought 3 (Leiden: Brill, 1968); Francis Oakley, *The Western Church in the Later Middle Ages* (Ithaca: Cornell University Press, 1979), 100–113; Kaspar Elm, " 'Vita regularis sine regula': Bedeutung, Rechtsstellung und Selbstverständnis des mittelalterlichen und frühneuzeitlichen Semireligiosentums," in *Häresie und vorzeitige Reformation im Spätmittelalter*, ed. Frantsiek Smahel and Elisabeth Müller-Lückner, 239–73 (Munich: Oldenburg, 1998); and Otto Gründler, "Devotio Moderna," in *Christian Spirituality: High Middle Ages and Reformation*, ed. Jill Raitt, 176–93 (New York: Crossroad, 1989).

66. Van Engen, *Devotio*, 12, 19, 30; Heiko Oberman, "Preface," in *Devotio Moderna: Basic Writings*, ed. John Van Engen (Mahwah, N.Y.: Paulist Press, 1988), 2; Gerhard Rehm, *Die Schwestern vom gemeinsamen Leben im nordwestlichen Deutschland. Untersuchungen der Devotio moderna und des weiblichen Religiösentums*, Berliner Historische Studien 11, Ordensstudien 5 (Berlin: Dunker and Humblot, 1985), 61.

67. Rehm, *Schwestern*, 98–101.

68. Ibid., 108–9.

69. *Van den doechden der vuriger ende stichtiger susteren van Diepen veen (Handschrift D)*, ed. D. A. Brinkerink (Leiden: Sijthoff's, 1904). The book of sisters of Diepenveen relates the reform of cloister Hilwartshausen on pages 341–68.

70. *Van den doechden*, ed. Brinkerink, 22.

71. Elm, "Verfall," 233–34. Particularly, the Benedictine reformers were influenced by the ideas of the *Devotio moderna*. Uwe Neddermeyer shows, for example, that 130 of the total 800 copies of a Kempis's *Imitatio Christi* were made by Observant Benedictines; see " 'Radix Studii et Speculum Vitae' Verbreitung und Rezeption der 'Imitatio Christi' in Handschriften und Drucken bis zur Reformation," in *Studien zum 15. Jahrhundert: Festschrift für Erich Meuthen*, vol. 1, ed. Johannes Helmrath et al., 465, 475.

72. Bernhard Neidiger, "Erzbischöfe, Landesherren und Reformkongregationen. Initiatoren und treibende Kräfte der Klosterreformen des 15. Jahrhunderts im Gebiet der Diözese Köln," *Rheinische Vierteljahrsblätter* 54 (1990): 76; Katherine Walsch, "The Observance: Sources for a History of the Observant Reform Movement in the Order of Augustinian Friars in the Fourteenth and Fifteenth Centuries," *Rivista di Storia della Chiesa in Italia* 31 (1977): 40–41; and Elm, "Verfall," 189.

73. Berndt Hamm, "Von der spätmittelalterlichen Reformatio zur Reformation: Der Prozeß normativer Zentrierung von Religion und Gesellschaft in Deutschland," *Archiv für Reformationsgeschichte* 84 (1993): 12.

74. The earliest successes were, in fact, not due to the central authorities. According to Walsh, they occurred "as spontaneous independent initiatives, sometimes with secular encouragement, in several different regions by individuals associated with a particular convent, locality, or spiritual tradtion"; Walsh, "Observance," 41, Helmrath, "Basler Konzil," 349.

75. David Burr, *The Spiritual Franciscans: From Protest to Persecution in the Century after Saint Francis* (University Park: Pennsylvania State University Press, 2001), 303–4.

76. Joan Marie Richards, *Franciscan Women: The Colettine Reform of the Order of Saint Clare in the Fifteenth Century* (Ph.D. diss., University of California, Berkeley, 1989).

77. Duncan Nimmo, "The Franciscan Regular Observance: The Culmination of Medieval Franciscan Reform," in *Reformbemühungen und Observanzbestrebungen im spätmittelalterlichen Ordenswesen*, ed. Kaspar Elm, Berliner Historische Studien 14, Ordensstudien 6 (Berlin: Dunker und Humblot, 1989), 195, 202; Duncan Nimmo, "Reform at the Council of Constance: The Franciscan Case," in *Renaissance and Renewal in Church History*, ed. Derek Baker, Studies in Church History 14 (Oxford: Blackwell, 1977), 161; Paul Nyhus,"The Franciscan Observant Reform in Germany," in *Reformbemühungen und Observanzbestrebungen im spätmittelalterlichen Ordenswesen*, ed. Kaspar Elm, Berliner Historische Studien 14, Ordensstudien 6 (Berlin: Dunker und Humblot, 1989), 215; Brigitte Degler-Spengler, *Das Klarissenkloster Gnadental in Basel 1289–1529*, Quellen und Forschungen zur Basler Geschichte 3 (Basel: Reinhardt, 1969), 72; Kurt Ruh, *Geschichte der abendländischen Mystik*, vol. 4 (Munich: Beck, 1999), 209–10.

78. Francis Xavier Martin, "The Augustinian Observant Movement," in *Reformbemühungen und Observanzbestrebungen im spätmittelalterlichen Ordenswesen*, ed. Kaspar Elm, Berliner Historische Studien 14, Ordensstudien 6 (Berlin: Dunker and Humblot, 1989), 333–36.

79. Werner Williams-Krapp, "Frauenmystik und Ordensreform," in *Literarische Interessenbildung im Mittelalter*, ed. Joachim Heinzle (Stuttgart: Metzler, 1993), 305. Sabine von Heusinger suggests, however, that Catherine's Dominican biographers fashioned her as the standardbearer for the Observant reform. See "Catherine of Siena and the Dominican Order," in *Siena e il suo territorio nel Rinascimento: Renaissance Siena and its Territory*, ed. Mario Ascheri (Siena: Leccio, 2000), 45–50.

80. Meyer, *Reformacio*, 3:198; Bernhard Neidiger, "Selbstverständnis und Erfolgschancen der Dominikanerobservanten: Beobachtungen zur Entwicklung in der Provinz Teutonia und im Basler Konvent (1388–1510)," *Rottenburger Jahrbuch für Kirchengeschichte* 17 (1998): 68; Eugen Hillenbrand, "Die Observantenbewegung in der deutschen Ordensprovinz der Dominikaner," in *Reformbemühungen im spätmittelalterlichen Ordenswesen*, ed. Kaspar Elm, Berliner Historische Studien 14, Ordensstudien 6 (Berlin: Dunker und Humblot, 1989), 221.

81. Neidiger, "Selbstverständnis," 81, 83; [Bartolomea Riccoboni,] *Convent*, 5.

82. Petrus Becker, "Erstrebte und erreichte Ziele benediktinischer Reformen im Spätmittelalter," in *Reformbemühungen und Ordensbestrebungen im spätmittelalterlichen Ordenswesen*, ed. Kaspar Elm, Berliner Historische Studien 14, Ordensstudien 6 (Berlin: Dunker and Humblot, 1989), 24.

83. Proksch, *Klosterreform*, 243; Gebhard Spahr, "St. Gallen," 69; Helmrath, *Konzil*, 143.

84. Karl Grube, *Johannes Busch Augustinerpropst zu Hildesheim: Ein katholischer Reformator des 15. Jahrhunderts* (Freiburg: Herder, 1881), 52; Barbara Frank, *Peterskloster*, 51; Becker, "Ziele," 27.

85. Gerhard Müller, "Reform und Reformation. Zur Geschichte von spätmittelalterlicher und früher Neuzeit," *Jahrbuch der Gesellschaft für niedersächsische Kirchengeschichte* 83 (1985): 21.

86. "Sorores karissime . . . ," in "Litterarisches und geistiges Leben im Kloster Ebstorf am Ausgange des Mittelalters," ed. Conrad Borchling, *Zeitschrift des historischen Vereins für Niedersachsen* 4 (1905), 389.

87. Hillenbrand, "Observantenbewegung," 235.

88. Neidiger, "Selbstverständnis," 68, 90; Nyhus, "Franciscan," 210; Hillenbrand, "Observantenbewegung," 246.

89. [Johannes Busch,] *Des Augustinerpropstes Iohannes Busch Chronicon Windeshemense und Liber de*

reformatione monasteriorum, ed. Karl Grube, Geschichtsquellen der Provinz Sachsen und angrenzender Gebiete 19 (Halle: Hendel, 1886), 610–11; Jeffrey Hamburger, *The Visual and the Visionary. Art and Female Sanctity in Late Medieval Germany* (New York: Zone, 1998), 88.

90. Cited from Hamburger, *The Visual and the Visionary*, 88. As a sign of their commitment to poverty, Thomas of Prussia, the brother of Conrad, even supervised the tearing down of one of the two towers at the women's cloister of Schönensteinbach because it was "too splendid and inconsistent with the poverty of Christ." See Seraphin Dietler, *Chronik des Klosters Schönensteinbach*, ed. Johann von Schlumberger (Guebwiller: Boltz, 1897), 314. It was only after these initial strictures were loosened that the Dominican reform gathered momentum, even though poverty remained an issue that would continue to divide Franciscan Observants.

91. Proksch, *Klosterreform*, 209; Barbara Frank, *Peterskloster*, 51.

92. Rudolf Schulze, *Das adelige Frauen- (Kanonissen-) Stift der Hl. Maria (1040–1773) und die Pfarre Liebfrauen-Überwasser zu Münster Westfalen (gegründet 1040): Ihre Verhältnisse und Schicksale* (Münster: Aschendorff, 1952), 145, 375 n. 10.

93. Gabriel Löhr, *Die Teutonia im 15. Jahrhundert: Studien und Texte vornehmlich zur Geschichte ihrer Reform*, Quellen und Forschungen zur Geschichte des Dominikanerordens in Deutschland 19 (Leipzig: Harrassowitz, 1924), 3; Franz Egger, *Beiträge zur Geschichte des Predigerordens. Die Reform des Baseler Konvents 1429 und die Stellung des Ordens am Baseler Konzil 1431–1448* (Bern: Lang, 1991), 89–90.

94. Egger, *Baseler*, 90; Martin, "Augustinian," 338. Dominican Observants founded numerous lay confraternities to promote religious devotion among lay men and women, the largest one being the enormously popular rosary brotherhood established in 1475. See Anne Winston-Allen, *Stories of the Rose: The Making of the Rosary in the Middle Ages* (University Park: Penn State Press, 1997), 78–79, and Winston-Allen, "Tracing the Origins of the Rosary: German Vernacular Texts," *Speculum* 68 (1993): 629–36.

95. Barbara Frank, *Peterskloster*, 53; Proksch, *Klosterreform*, 7; Kaspar Elm, "Die Franziskanerobservanz als Bildungsreform," in *Lebenslehren und Weltentwürfe in Übergang vom Mittelalter zur Neuzeit: Politik-Bildung-Naturkunde-Theologie. Bericht über Kolloquien der Kommission zur Erforschung der Kultur des Spätmittelalters*, ed. Hartmut Boockmann, Bernt Moeller and Karl Stackmann, Abhandlungen der Akademie der Wissenschaften in Göttingen, Phil.-hist. Klasse, F. 3, no. 179 (Göttingen: Vandenhoeck, 1989), 202; Franz Machilek, "Der Klosterhumanismus in Nürnberg um 1500," *Mitteilungen des Vereins für Geschichte der Stadt Nürnberg* 64 (1977): 10–45.

96. Proksch, *Klosterreform*, 215.

97. Schulze, *Überwasser*, 148–49.

98. At Chemnitz, the citizenry in 1485 built a monastery for the Observants, dedicated by the donor families with "affection for the Observants who, through their exemplary life, their devout celebration of the holy sacraments, and their assiduous hearing of confessions worked tirelessly for the kingdom of God"; Lucius Teichmann, "Die franziskanische Observanzbewegung in Ost-Mitteleuropa und ihre politisch-nationale Komponente im böhmisch-schlesischen Raum," *Archiv für schlesische Kirchengeschichte* 49 (1991): 209.

99. Johannes Kist, "Klosterreform im spätmittelalterlichen Nürnberg," *Zeitschrift für bayerische Kirchengeschichte* 32 (1963): 32.

100. Hillenbrand, "Observantenbewegung," 268.

101. Karin Schneider, "Die Bibliothek des Katharinenklosters in Nürnberg und die städtische Gesellschaft," in *Studien zum städtischen Bildungswesen des späten Mittelalters und der frühen Neuzeit*, ed. Bernd Moeller et al. (Göttingen: Vandenhoeck und Ruprecht, 1983), 75; Meyer, *Reformacio*, 3:66–67. At Soest, the town council called for reform, citing the need for "religious services to be increased" and prayers said "with regularity." See Theodor Rensing, "Die Reformbewegung in den westfälischen Dominikanerklöstern," *Westfalen* 17 (1932): 96. Johannes Nider's account of this reform can be found book III, chapter 3 of his *Formicarius* (1437), published in a facsimile edition by Hans Biedermann, ed., [Johannes Nyder] *Formicarius* (Graz: Akademischer Druck- und Verlagsanstalt, 1971), and in Meyer's *Reformacio*, 3:60–69.

102. Letter from Prioress Adelheid von Aue to Johannes Meyer (1464), in Dietler, *Chronik,* ed. Schlumberger, 466.

103. Bernd Moeller, "Religious Life in Germany on the Eve of the Reformation," in *Pre-Reformation Germany,* ed. Gerald Strauß (New York: Harper and Row, 1972), 25.

104. Nyhus, "Franciscan," 217. Euan Cameron asserts that laymen felt more and more that the church was their church and they wished to control its personnel and behavior, in *The European Reformation* (Oxford: Clarendon, 1991), 60.

105. Dietler, *Chronik,* ed. Schlumberger, 340.

106. Letter from Maria von Wolkenstein and convent sisters at Brixen to Maria's brothers, Oswald, Leo, and Friedrich von Wolkenstein (August 1455) in appendix to Hermann Hallauer, "Nikolaus von Kues und das Brixener Klarissenkloster," *Mitteilungen und Forschungsbeiträge der Cusanus-Gesellschaft* 6 (1967): 111.

107. Nyhus, "Franciscan," 212–13.

108. Meyer, *Reformacio,* 3:131.

109. Maria Huffer, *Die Reformen in der Abtei Rijnsburg im 15. Jahrhundert* (Münster: Aschendorff, 1937), 91.

110. Weis-Müller, *Klingental,* 173.

111. Voit, *Engelthal,* 1:58.

112. [Juliana Ernst,] *Die Chronik des Bickenklosters zu Villingen,* ed. Karl Jordan Glatz, Bibliothek des Litterarischen Vereins in Stuttgart 151 (Tübingen: Fues, 1881), 30.

113. Erdin, *Reuerinnen,* 51.

114. Halter, *Oetenbach,* 84–85; Hillenbrand, "Observantenbewegung," 244.

115. "Chronik des Schwesternhouses Marienthal, genannt Niesinck in Münster," in *Berichte der Augenzeugen über das Münstersche Wiedertäuferreich,* ed. Carl Cornelius, Geschichtsquellen des Bisthums Münster 2 (1853; repr. Münster: Aschendorff, 1965), 421.

116. Wilhelm Eberhard Schwarz, "Studien zur Geschichte des Klosters der Augustinerinnen Mariental, genannt Niesing zu Münster," *Zeitschrift für vaterländische Geschichte und Altertumskunde* 72 (1914): 56.

117. Pickel, *Klarakloster,* 197. Similarly, the city of Gmünd reserved to itself jurisdiction not only over admission of novices, but replacement of servants, and cloister finances, Gerhard Metzger, "Der Dominikanerorden in Württemberg am Ausgang des Mittelalters," *Blätter für württembergische Kirchengeschichte,* n.F. 46 (1942): 40.

118. Manfred Schulze, *Fürsten und Reformation. Geistliche Reformpolitik weltlicher Fürsten vor der Reformation,* Spätmittelalter und Reformation, neue Reihe 2 (Tübingen: Mohr, 1991), 9; Dieter Mertens, "Monastische Reformbewegungen des 15. Jahrhunderts: Ideen-Ziele-Resultate," in *Reform von Kirche und Reich zur Zeit der Konzilien von Konstanz (1414–1418) und Basel (1431–1449),* ed. Ivan Hlavácek and Alexander Patschovsky (Constance: Universitätsverlag Konstanz, 1996), 163.

119. Schulze, *Fürsten,* 130; Cameron, *Reformation,* 60.

120. At the Reformreichstag of 1495, Emperor Maximilian voiced his concern that God's wrath was already being felt in "severe pestilences and the human plagues called the evil 'pox' to a degree not seen in human memory." Maximilian charged the princes in attendance with seeing that God's commandments and those of the church were being heeded. They must themselves avoid sin "more than they had in the past" and do good works. Schulze, *Fürsten,* 115, 117, 130. Concerned, many enlisted in the Observant cause and undertook the reform of convents in their territories.

121. Servatius Wolfs, "Dominikanische Observanzbestrebungen: Die Congregatio Hollandiae (1464–1517)," in *Reformbemühungen und Observanzbestrebungen im spätmittelalterlichen Ordenswesen,* ed. Kaspar Elm, Berliner Historische Studien 14, Ordensstudien 6 (Berlin: Dunker and Humblot, 1989), 283.

122. Pickel, *Klarakloster,* 193.

123. Schulze, *Fürsten,* 26; Ecker, "Kirchheim," 156–57, 166–67, 336.

124. Letter of Count Ulrich of Württemberg to the women's convent of Sylo in Sélestat (April

1478) in appendix to *Geschichte des Herzogtums Wuerttemberg unter der Regierung der Graven,* ed. Christian Friedrich Sattler (Tübingen: Reiss, 1773–77), 3:98.

125. [Magdalena Kremer,] "Wie diß loblich kloster zu Sant Johannes Baptisten zu Kirchen under deck prediger-ordens reformiert ist worden und durch woelich personen," in *Geschichte des Herzogtums Wuerttemberg unter der Regierung der Graven,* ed. Christian Friedrich Sattler, 2d. ed. (Tübingen: Reiss, 1773–77), 4:156.

126. Teichmann, "Observanzbewegung," 209.

127. Hillenbrand, "Observantenbewegung," 246.

128. Elm, "Verfall," 227; Wolfs, "Congregatio," 279. Elector Ludwig von der Pfalz (d. 1436), influenced by his wife, Princess Mechthild of Savoy (1390–1438), who as a girl had been schooled by Observants and whose two sisters had entered the reformed cloister of St. Colett, called in French friars from Touraine in 1426 to reform the Franciscan cloister of Heidelberg. See Frank, *Söflingen,* 81–82. Piety was clearly not the only reason for founding a monastery. Elector Frederick I von der Pfalz (d. 1476) founded a Dominican monastery at Heidelberg to promote learning, especially the study of the arts and theology. Likewise, Count Ulrich of Württemberg constructed a new cloister in Stuttgart which he turned over to Observant Dominicans, recruited from the university city of Nuremberg, who brought with them a large number of books and provided the Duke with a prestigious community of scholars for his court seat. See Hillenbrand, "Observantenbewegung," 253–54.

129. "Schwesternbuch von Sankt Agnes," ed. Bollmann and Staubach, 10–11, 74.

130. See, for example, the account of Jde Ruijtkens, ibid., 205.

131. Cited from Eileen Power, *Medieval English Nunneries, c. 1275 to 1535* (Cambridge: Cambridge University Press, 1922), 679.

132. Ulrich Ecker, "Die Reform der Freiburger Dominikanerinnenklöster Adelhausen, St. Agnes und St. Maria Magdalena, 1465," Zulassungsarbeit zur wissenschaftlichen Prüfung für das Lehramt an Gymnasien, Freiburg i. Br., 1976, 31–32.

133. Weis-Müller, *Klingental,* 161, 165.

134. Meyer, *Reformacio,* 3:135–45.

135. Däniker-Gysin, *Töß,* 24–25.

136. Duncan Nimmo suggests that the council embodied "the highest aspirations" but failed in the task it had set itself; "Constance," 159. Others argue that the council failed because it focused its energies on resolving the schism and settling conflicting economic interests. Nevertheless, Stump cites "the solemn, public example" which it set and "the expectation of renewal which this produced" as encouraging the self-reform of those present. For a summary of other views, see Phillip Stump, *The Reforms of the Council of Constance,* Studies in the History of Christian Thought 53 (Leiden: Brill, 1994), 17, 138, 156; Helmrath, "Reform," 107.

137. Joachim Homeyer, *500 Jahre Äbtissinnen in Medingen* (Uelzen: Becker, 1994), 34; Franz Schrader, *Die ehemalige Zistersienserinnenabtei Marienstuhl vor Egeln. Ein Beitrag zur Geschichte der Zistersienserinnen und der nach-reformatorischen Restbestände des Katholizismus im ehemaligen Herzogtum Magdeburg,* Erfurter Theologische Studien 16 (Leipzig: St. Benno–Verlag, 1965), 40; Helmrath "Reform," 143.

138. Neidiger, "Selbstverständnis," 73; Helmrath, *Basler Konzil,* 350; Dieter Stievermann, "Die württembergischen Klosterreformen des 15. Jahrhunderts: Ein bedeutendes landeskirchliches Strukturelement des Spätmittelalters und ein Kontinuitätsstrang zum ausgebildeten Landeskirchentum der Frühneuzeit," *Zeitschrift für Württembergische Landesgeschichte* 44 (1985): 99.

139. Constance Proksch, *Klosterreform und Geschichtsschreibung im Spätmittelalter* (Cologne: Böhlau, 1994), 1; Philip Soergel, *Wondrous in His Saints: Counter-Reformation Propaganda in Bavaria* (Berkeley and Los Angeles: University of California Press, 1993), 18; Kaspar Elm, "Reform- und Observanzbestrebungen im spätmittelalterlichen Ordenswesen. Ein Überblick," in *Reformbemühungen und Observanzbestrebungen im spätmittelalterlichen Ordenswesen,* ed. Kaspar Elm, Berliner Historische Studien 14, Ordenstudien 6 (Berlin: Dunker und Humblot, 1989), 3–4; Elm, "Verfall und Erneuerung des Ordenswesens im Spätmittelalter: Forschungen und Forschungsaufgaben" in *Untersuchungen zu Kloster und Stift,* Veröffentlichungen des Max-Planck-Instituts für Geschichte 68, Studien zur Germania Sacra 14

(Göttingen: Vandenhoeck and Ruprecht, 1980), 237; Erich Methuen, *Das 15. Jahrhundert*, 2d. ed., Oldenbourg Grundriß der Geschichte 9 (Munich: Oldenbourg, 1984), 3.

140. See, particularly, Rolf Kießling, *Bürgerliche Gesellschaft und Kirche in Augsburg im Spätmittelalter: Ein Beitrag zur Strukturanalyse der oberdeutschen Reichsstadt,* Abhandlungen zur Geschichte der Stadt Augsburg 19 (Augsburg: Mühlberger, 1971), 354–59.

Chapter 3

1. [Magdalena Kremer,] "Wie diß loblich closter zu Sant Johannes baptisten zu kirchen under deck prediger-ordens reformiert ist worden und durch woelich personen," in *Geschichte des Herzogtums Wuerttemberg under der Regierung der Graven,* ed. Christian Friedrich Sattler, 2d. ed. (Tübingen: Reiss, 1773–77), 4:218–19.

2. Ulrich Ecker, "Die Geschichte des Klosters S. Johannes-Baptista der Dominikanerinnen zu Kirchheim unter Teck" (Ph.D. diss., University of Freiburg, 1985), 104, 165–72, 181–86.

3. [Magdalena Kremer,] "Wie diß loblich closter," 223.

4. Seraphin Dietler, *Chronik des Klosters Schönensteinbach,* ed. Johann von Schlumberger (Guebwiller: Boltz, 1897), 222. Conrad of Prussia's rules, "Ordinationen für reformierte Dominikanerinnen" (1397), are contained in Basel, Universitätsbibliothek, MS E III 13, fols. 29v–31v.

5. Johannes Meyer, *Buch der Reformacio Predigerordens,* ed., Benedictus Maria Reichert, Quellen und Forschungen zur Geschichte des Dominikanerordens in Deutschland 3 (Leipzig: Harrassowitz, 1909), 32–33.

6. Dietler, *Chronik,* ed. Schlumberger, 422; Thomas Lentes, "Bild, Reform, und Cura Monialium: Bilderverständnis und Bildergebrauch im 'Buch der Reformacio Predigerordens' des Johannes Meyer (1485)," in *Dominicains et Dominicaines en Alsace (XIIIe–XXe Siècle): Acts du Colloque de Guebwiller, 8–9 avril 1994,* ed. Jean-Luc Eichenlaub (Colmar: Editions d'Alsace, 1996), 183. Paul Stinzi, on the other hand, lists Elisabeth as the third prioress. See "Schönensteinbach," *Annuaire de la Société d'Histoire Sundgauvienne* (1964): 73.

7. Jean-Charles Winnlen, *Schönensteinbach: Une Communauté religieuse féminine 1138–1792* (Altkirch: Société d'histoire Sundgauvienne, 1993), 41; Meyer, *Reformacio,* 3:37–38, 3:21, 47.

8. Bernhard Thorr, "Die Dominikanerinnen von Schönensteinbach," *Annuaire de la Société d'Histoire Sundgauvienne* (1975): 47.

9. From the cloisters they reformed, Schönensteinbach women went on with other groups to St Maria Magdalena an den Steinen (Basel, 1423), Himmelskron (Worms, 1429), and Dominican houses at Tulln (in Austria, 1436), Pforzheim (1442), as well as Brünn (1466). See Meyer, *Reformacio,* 3:iv–v; Winnlen, *Schönensteinbach,* 64; Ferdinand Seibt, ed., *Bohemia Sacra: Das Christentum in Böhmen 973–1973* (Düsseldorf: Schwann, 1974), 77; Vladimír Koudelka, "Zur Geschichte der böhmischen Dominikanerprovinz im Mittelalter," *Archivum fratrum Praedicatorum* 26 (1956): 155. Hieronymus Wilms lists also St. Marien at Medingen (1468) and Katharinental (1482). See *Das älteste Verzeichnis der deutschen Dominikanerinnenklöster,* Quellen und Forschungen zur Geschichte des Dominikanerordens 24 (Leipzig: Harrassowitz, 1928), 33, 36.

10. St. Maria Magdalena an den Steinen (Basel, 1423), Himmelskron (Worms, 1429), and Dominican houses at Tulln (in Austria, 1436), Pforzheim (1441), as well as Brünn. See Meyer, *Reformacio,* 3: iv–v, 3:79, 103.

11. St. Maria Magdalena an den Steinen had twelve sisters when it was reformed by women from Unterlinden in 1423 and increased to forty by 1446, even though it had sent groups to reform Himmelskron (with help from Schönensteinbach, 1429), St. Nicolaus in undis (1431), St. Michael's Insel at Bern (1439), and afterward Hasenpfuhl (c. 1463), and St. Agnes, Freiburg (1465). Dietler, *Chronik,* ed. Schlumberger, 371; Emil Erdin, *Das Kloster der Reuerinnen Sancta Maria Magdalena an den Steinen zu Basel von den Anfängen bis zur Reformation (etwa 1230–1529)* (Fribourg: Paulus, 1956), 65–70, 94.

12. [Barbara von Benfelden,] "Von zunemunge der geistlicheit und uff gang der tugenden der swestern dis conventes des klosters sancte Agnesen," in appendix to Annette Barthelmé, ed., *La Réforme*

dominicaine au Xve siècle en Alsace et dans l'ensenble de la province de Teutonie, Collection d'études sur l'histoire du droit et des institutions de l'Alsace 7 (Strasbourg: Heitz, 1931), 189.

13. Gnadental, the Clarissan house at Basel, was reformed by women from Alspach (Alsace), the first Observant house of Poor Clares. Brigitte Degler-Spengler, *Das Klarissenkloster Gnadental in Basel 1289–1529,* Quellen und Forschungen zur Basler Geschichte 3 (Basel: Reinhardt, 1969), 35; Andreas Rüther, *Bettelorden in Stadt und Land. Die Straßburger Mendikantenkonvente und das Elsaß im Spätmittelalter,* Berliner Historische Studien 26, Ordensstudien 11 (Berlin: Dunker and Humblot, 1997), 315. For more on the Nuremberg Clarissans, see Johannes Kist, "Klosterreform im spätmittelalterlichen Nüremberg," *Zeitschrift für bayerische Kirchengeschichte* 32 (1963): 44.

14. Virgil Redlich, *Johann Rode von St. Matthias bei Trier* (Münster: Aschendorff, 1923), 87–90.

15. Sister Johanna, a Poor Clare, had already left Gnadental before it was reformed, for the Observant Dominican house of St. Maria Magdalena an den Steinen—both of them in Basel; Degler-Spengler, *Gnadental,* 77.

16. Studying cloisters in Freiburg, Ulrich Ecker found that unreformed houses declined between 1454 and 1490 in gifts and professions, while Observant convents tended to attract more of both. Ecker contrasted Adelhausen (reformed in 1465) with St. Katharina of the same city (which was not reformed). Comparing city property owned by the two cloisters, Ecker found that at mid-century both cloisters' holdings were approximately the same (St. Katharina owning 874 sq. meters and Adelhausen 975); by 1500, however, the unreformed cloister's holdings had shrunk to 189 sq. meters and Adelhausen's had grown to 2,982. See Ulrich Ecker, "Die Reform der Freiburger Dominikanerinnenklöster Adelhausen, St. Agnes und St. Maria Magdalena, 1465," Zulassungsarbeit zur wissenschaftlichen Prüfung für das Lehramt an Gymnasien, Freiburg i. Br., 1976, 45. Gudrun Gleba cites similar increases in donations to cloisters after a reform. See *Reformpraxis und materielle Kultur: Westfälische Frauenklöster im späten Mittelalter,* Historische Studien 462 (Husum: Matthiesen, 2000), 176–77.

17. Ecker, "Kirchheim," 180–81.

18. [Magdalena Kremer,] "Wie diß loblich closter," ed. Sattler, 159; Ecker, "Kirchheim," 80.

19. Gerhard Metzger, "Der Dominikanerorden in Württemberg am Ausgang des Mittelalters," *Blätter für württembergische Kirchengeschichte,* n.F. 46 (1942): 16.

20. Jutta Gisela Sperling, *Convents and the Body Politic in Late Renaissance Venice* (Chicago: University of Chicago Press, 1999), 116.

21. See Karen Greenspan, "Erklärung des Vaterunsers: A Critical Edition of a 15th-Century Mystical Treatise by Magdalena Beutler of Freiburg" (Ph.D. diss., University of Massachusetts, 1984), 6, 52–53; Wilhelm Oehl, *Deutsche Mystikerbriefe des Mittelalters, 1100–1550* (Munich: Georg Müller, 1931), 520; Wilhelm Schleussner, "Magdalena von Freiburg. Eine pseudomystische Erscheinung des späteren Mittelalters, 1407–1458," *Der Katholik* 87 (1907): 207–16.

22. Caroline Walker Bynum, "Religious Women in the Later Middle Ages," in *Christian Spirituality: High Middle Ages and Reformation,* ed. Jill Raitt, Gernard McGinn, John Meyendorff (New York: Crossroad, 1987), 122.

23. Similarly, Othlon, a monk of St. Emmeram in Regensburg, wrote in the eleventh century of Chunihilt, Berthgit, Chunitrud, Tecla, Lioba, and Waltpurgis, pious women who had come from England. See Lina Eckenstein, *Women under Monasticism* (1896; repr. New York: Russel and Russel, 1963), 135, 138–39.

24. St. Dominic dispatched a group from his first foundation at Prouille to teach the women of San Sisto the Dominican way of life. Heribert Christian Scheeben, "Die Anfänge des zweiten Ordens," *Archivum fratrum Praedicatorum* 2 (1932): 284–315.

25. "Die Stiftung des Klosters Oetenbach und das Leben der seligen Schwestern daselbst, aus der Nürnberger Handschrift," ed. H. Zeller-Werdmüller and Jakob Bächthold, *Zürcher Taschenbuch* 12 (1889), 236. Besides Abbess Adelheid's reform of Vilich and of St. Maria of Cologne, McNamara cites Himiltrude and Hauwide, abbesses, who in the eleventh century reformed the convents of St. Glodesind and St. Peter in Metz. In the early twelfth century Abbess Rissende of Faremoutiers asked for help from the abbesses of Chelles and Joarre, "who had successfully reformed their own houses;" McNamara, *Sisters,* 227.

26. Renée Weis-Müller, *Die Reform des Klosters Klingental and ihr Personenkreis,* Baseler Beiträge zur Geschichtswissenschaft 59 (Basel: Helbing and Lichtenhahn, 1956), 112–13; and Annette Barthelmé, ed., *La Réforme dominicaine au XVe siècle en Alsace et dans l'ensemble de la province de Teutonie,* Collection d'études sur l'histoire du droit et des institutions de l'Alsace 7 (Strasbourg: Heitz, 1931), 59–60.

27. The remnant community subsequently grew to fifty; Dietler, *Chronik,* ed. Schlumberger, 409–16.

28. Metzger, "Dominikanerorden," 46 (1942): 53–54; Martin Crusius, *Schwäbische Chronik,* 2 vols., trans. Johann Jakob Moser (Frankfurt: Metzler and Erhard, 1733), 2:109.

29. Weis-Müller, *Klingental,* 49–50.

30. Johannes Busch reports that when Prior Bernhard at Hamersleben requested reformers to send to Stendal, he asked Prioress Helena at Marienberg for women who were "well informed, zealous for the reform and could be models for others in their manner of living and discipline in cloister life." Karl Grube, *Johannes Busch Augustinerpropst zu Hildesheim: Ein katholischer Reformator des 15. Jahrhunderts* (Freiburg: Herder, 1881), 217.

31. St. Gall, Stiftsbibliothek, MS St. Katharina, Wil, "Schwesternbuch," Nr. 89, fol. 20r. Prioress Haller also remonstrates, "[I]n thirteen years, I have sent eighteen sisters to [reform] other cloisters" (fol. 20r).

32. Dietler, *Chronik,* ed. Schlumberger, 326–27.

33. Brigitte Hilberling, *700 Jahre Kloster Zoffingen, 1257–1957* (Constance: Merk, 1957), 27.

34. Grube, *Busch,* 210.

35. Johannes Linneborn, "Die Reformation der westfälischen Benedictiner-Klöster im 15. Jahrhundert durch die Bursfelder Congregation," *Studien und Mitteilungen zur Geschichte des Benedictinerordens* 21 (1900): 56.

36. [Juliana Ernst,] *Die Chronik des Bickenklosters zu Villingen,* ed. Karl J. Glatz, Bibliothek des Litterarischen Vereins in Stuttgart 151 (Tübingen: Fues, 1881), 25.

37. [Magdalena Kremer,] "Wie diß loblich closter," ed. Sattler, 154–55. The eighth sister was Barbara Bernheim who was chosen to head the group.

38. Letter from Katharina von Mühlheim to the prioress and sisters at Schönensteinbach (11 April 1436), in Dietler, *Chronik,* ed. Schlumberger, 406.

39. Seibt, *Bohemia Sacra,* 77.

40. Letter from Katharina von Mühlheim, in Dietler, *Chronik,* ed. Schlumberger, 406.

41. Letter from Johannes Nider to the prioress and sisters at Schönensteinbach (25 October 1428) in Dietler, *Chronik,* ed. Schlumberger, 363–66. Twenty-seven years later Nicholas of Cusa used a much more subtle and complementary approach when he wrote to the Observant cloister of Poor Clares at Nuremberg to request reforming sisters for Brixen saying:

> [W]e have heard repeatedly, how many brothers and sisters of the Observance have been sent out from several of your reformed cloisters in Nuremberg to many cloisters in other places and have seeded the Observance where it has sprung up and through whom such an honorable and upright Observance has been planted and has taken root . . . , [and] has elevated your order, the city of Nuremberg, and the praise of yourselves and your cloister. Because of this we beg earnestly that you will want—for God's increase and that of your order, for the observance of your rule, and also for our sakes—to send three or four sisters from your cloister.

Letter from Nicholas of Cusa to the abbess and Clarissan sisters at Nuremberg (12 August 1455), in appendix to Hermann Hallauer, ed. "Nikolaus von Kues und das Brixener Klarissenkloster," *Mitteilungen und Forschungsbeiträge der Cusanus-Gesellschaft* 6 (1967): 113.

42. Letter from Sister Tecla to her pupils at marienberg, cited by Busch in [Johannes Busch,] *Des Augustinerpropstes Iohannes Busch Chronicon Windeshemense und Liber de reformatione monasteriorum,* ed. Karl Grube, Gesichtsquellen der Provinz Sachsen und angrenzender Gebiete 19 (Halle: Hendel, 1886), 627; Grube, *Busch,* 201–7. Often the women they taught were eager to learn. When three Observant

sisters arrived at Fischbeck (on the Weser) from the Magdalen cloister at Hildesheim, Abbess Armgard von Rheden, who had little formal education, attended all the Latin and other classes. Busch claims that, under Abbess Armgard, Fischbeck became a sort of training center, taking in sisters from other houses to be instructed and sending them back with Observants from Fischbeck to teach at their own cloisters. Grube, *Busch*, 161, 234.

43. Grube, *Busch*, 205–7, [Busch,] *Liber de reformatione*, 624–26.

44. [Magdalena Kremer,] "Wie diß loblich closter," ed. Sattler, 157.

45. Magdalena Kremer herself was made sacristan, scriptrix, mistress of novices, and head singer. Christina von Rheinau, "a very earnest and devout sister," was named assistant bursar and door-keeper. Katharina Meyger was to make rounds, and Laysister Fida (Fidela) took over as mistress of the kitchen. [Magdalena Kremer,] "Wie diß loblich closter," ed. Sattler, 157; Ecker, "Kirchheim," 101, 104–5, 169–70.

46. Katharina entered Schönensteinbach in 1418. If she had been fourteen, the minimum age of admittance for Observants, she could not have been any younger than sixty-two when she undertook the reform of Brünn in 1466 as leader of the women's party. Seibt, *Bohemia sacra*, 77; Meyer, *Reformacio*, 2:66; Dietler, *Chronik*, ed. Schlumberger, 306, 371, 408; and Vladimír Koudelka, "Zur Geschichte der böhmischen Dominikanerprovinz im Mittelalter. II. Die Männer und Frauenklöster," *Archivum Fratrum Praedicatorum* 26 (1956): 156.

47. Heike Uffmann, "'. . . wie in einem Rosengarten . . . .' Die Ebstorfer Klosterreform im Spiegel von Chronistik und Tischlesung," in *"In Treue und Hingabe": 800 Jahre Kloster Ebstorf*, ed. Marianne Elster and Horst Hoffmann (Uelzen: Becker, 1997), 219–220. For more on Mechthild, see Chapter 6.

48. Dietler, *Chronik*, ed. Schlumberger, 463, 486; Weis-Müller, *Klingental*, 126. Other veterans include Edelin von Aue, for twenty-four years prioress of St. Katharina (Colmar) before reforming Adelhausen in Freiburg; and Barbara Krebs, twenty-six years subprioress at St.Katharina (Colmar) before reforming Sylo (Sélestat) and later St. Gertrude (Cologne). See Meyer, *Reformacio*, 2:113, 118, 146; Dietler, *Chronik*, ed. Schlumberger, 475, 487; Jutta Prieur, *Das Kölner Dominikanerinnenkloster St. Gertrud am Neumarkt*, Kölner Schriften zu Geschichte und Kultur (Cologne: dme-Verlag, 1983), 110.

49. Dietler, *Chronik*, ed. Schlumberger, 274, 327, 343.

50. Ibid., 349; Erdin, *Reuerinnen*, 66.

51. Margareta Regenstein went to St. Maria Magdalena an den Steinen (Basel), Himmelskron (Hochheim), and finally Hasenpfuhl (Speyer), where she became prioress after the second attempt there succeeded in 1463. See Dietler, *Chronik*, ed. Schlumberger, 461–62; Meyer, *Reformacio*, 2:111–12. Margareta Zorn took part in successful reforms at Unterlinden, St. Maria Magdalena an den Steinen, Himmelskron, and a failed effort to reform the Penitants of St. Maria Magdalena in Strasbourg in 1436. See Dietler, *Chronik*, ed. Schlumberger, 319, 388. No more accurate than the assertion that Observants were naive and inexperienced women is the claim that they were simple girls from non-affluent backgrounds. While it is true that the Benedictine reform made a concerted effort to eliminate class privileges and that the trend throughout all orders was toward more open admissions policies, examination of the background of a sample group of Dominican Observants sent from Unterlinden to St. Maria Magdalena an den Steinen (Basel)—untypical, perhaps, only in its early date, 1423—reveals that more than half of the thirteen reforming sisters were members of the nobility. See Erdin, *Reuerinnen*, 46.

52. [Magdalena Kremer,] "Wie diß loblich closter," ed. Sattler, 200.

53. Ecker, "Kirchheim," 188–92.

54. Ibid., 165, 177.

55. Meyer, *Reformacio*, 3:118; [Juliana Ernst,] *Chronik*, ed. Glatz, 34; Gustav Voit, *Engelthal— Geschichte eines Dominikanerinnenklosters*, 2 vols., Schriftenreihe der Altnürnberger Landschaft 26 (Nuremberg: Koru and Berg, 1977), 1:61.

56. Meyer, *Reformacio*, 3:67–68.

57. Ibid., 3:65.

58. "Also vindt man hie geschriben wie die obseruantz angefangen ist worden," in "Die Refor-

mation des Katharinenklosters zu Nürnberg im Jahr 1428," ed. Theodor von Kern, *Jahresbericht des historischen Vereins für Mittelfranken* 31 (1863): 9–10, 11–12.

59. Linneborn, *Bursfelder*, 21 (1900): 319–20. Similarly, in the transition period at St. Agnes in Strasbourg, sisters were not required to fast, abstain from meat, or get up to sing the Hours at matins. And they retained a window where they could visit with their families. McNamara, *Sisters*, 411.

60. Ecker, "Kirchheim," 182. Similarly, reformers at Engelthal asserted that no one should be "forced to an extremity," but rather all must love and serve God "with a fervent heart." Voit, *Engethal*, 1:62.

61. Max Miller, *Die Söflinger Briefe und das Klarissenkloster Söflingen bei Ulm im Spätmittelalter* (Würzburg: Triltsch, 1940), 57. An unconventional method of winning over resisters is recounted, however, in the Diepenveen book of sisters (after 1478) which describes the reform of the Augustinian house of Hilwartshausen (on the Weser). When three reformers from Diepenveen arrived, the Hilwartshausen sisters were violently agitated and ran about the cloister, calling them "devils." The narrator relates how the Mother Superior, giving a tour of her convent to head reformer Stine Groten, came upon an angry resident who had thrown herself on the ground in a fit. Sister Stine, thinking her to be ill, said, "Dear Mother, let her be given some wine to drink and she will be better." The effect was instantaneous: the account relates that, "when the sister heard that [Stine Groten] was so kind, her hostility vanished. She changed completely and thereafter regarded her with affection." The account goes on to give an idealized picture of Sister Stine's winning personality and manner of earning affection by her good example; *Van den doechden der vuriger ende stichtiger sustern van Diepen veen, Handschrift D*, ed. D. A. Brinkerink (Leiden: Sijthoff, 1904), 354.

62. "Das Schwesternbuch von Sankt Agnes," in *Schwesternbuch und Statuten des St. Agnes–Konvents in Emmerich*, ed. Anne Bollmann and Nikolaus Staubach, Emmericher Forschungen 17 (Emmerich: Emmericher Geschichtsverein, 1998), 10 n. 30, 73–74.

63. Ibid., 205.

64. Augsburg, Staatsarchiv, MS Kloster Maria Maihingen MüB 1, fol. 6r. See also Arnold Schromm, *Die Bibliothek des ehemaligen Zisterzienserinnenklosters Kirchheim am Ries: Buchpflege und geistiges Leben in einem Frauenstift*, Studia Augustana 9 (Tübingen: Niemeyer, 1998), 86; Tore Nyberg, *Dokumente und Untersuchungen zur inneren Geschichte der drei Brigittenklöster Bayerns 1420–1570*, 2 vols., Quellen und Erörterungen zur bayerischen Geschichte, n.F. 26 (Munich: Beck, 1972–74), 2:154.

65. Augsburg, Staatsarchiv, MS Kloster Maria Maihingen MüB 1, fol. 6r–6v; Nyberg, *Dokumente*, 2:154.

66. The women stated that they urgently wished to take part in the jubilee indulgence and the "holy reform which was being preached throughout Saxony." See Gerhard Taddey, *Das Kloster Heiningen von der Gründung bis zur Aufhebung*, Veröffentlichungen des Max-Planck-Instituts für Geschichte 14 (Göttingen: Vandenhoeck and Ruprecht, 1966), 95–96. See also Grube, *Busch*, 180.

67. Kurt Ruh, *Geschichte der abendländischen Mystik*, 4 vols. (Munich: Beck, 1990–1999), 4:252–54; Wybren Scheepsma, *Deemoed en devotie: De koorvrouwen van Windesheim en hun geschriften* (Amsterdam: Prometheus, 1997), 175–79.

68. Degler-Spenger, *Gnadental*, 75. Likewise, in 1497 seven Dominican sisters at Cronschwitz in Saxony asked for assistance from the Elector in instituting a reform, against the wishes of the other sisters in their house and their provincial. The women stated that they wanted to be reformed so as "not to end their days in such a miserable state." See Helmut Thurm, *Das Dominikaner-Nonnenkloster Cronschwitz bei Weida* (Jena: Fischer, 1942), 83; Manfred Schulze, *Fürsten und Reformation. Geistliche Reformpolitik weltlicher Fürsten vor der Reformation*, Spätmittelalter und Reformation, n.F. 2 (Tübingen: Mohr, 1991), 144.

69. Lina Eckenstein praises her as "a woman of great intelligence and strong character." See Eckenstein, *Monasticism*, 421; also J. A. Giesel, "Eine Heggbacher Chronik," *Württembergische Vierteljahreshefte* 2 (1879): 221. Instituting her reforms gradually and on her own responsibility, Eckenstein asserts, Elisabeth began with the younger sisters, allowing the elder nuns to keep to their old ways at first, bringing them incrementally to an Observant interpretation of the rule. Among the women

mentioned by Johannes Busch is the elderly Abbess von Möllenbeck at Fischbeck (on the Weser), who was moved by the spirit of reform but herself too old to effect it and thus requested help from the Observant house of Wülfinghausen. This she received in the form of Sister Armengard von Rheden, whom we have already met. Armengard not only instituted Observant practices at Fischbeck but oversaw the reform of three neighboring cloisters: Wenningsen, Marienwerder, and Barsinghausen. See Grube, *Busch*, 161, 234.

70. "Inzigkofen Ursprung," ed. Johannes Pflummern, in "A.B.C., Zur Geschichte des Nonnenklosters Inzigkofen," ed. Georg Ludwig Stecher, *Diözesanarchiv von Schwaben* 21 (1903): 68; "Die Geissenhof'sche Chronik des Klosters Inzigkofen," ed. Theodor Dreher, *Freiburger Katholisches Kirchenblatt* 38 (1894): col. 441; Werner Fechter, *Deutsche Handschriften des 15. und 16. Jahrhunderts aus der Bibliothek des ehemaligen Augustinerchorfrauenstifts Inzigkofen* (Sigmaringen: Thorbecke, 1997), 5, 8.

71. The questions are preserved in the chronicle at Sigmaringen, Fürstlich Hohenzollernsche Hofbibliothek, MS 68, vol. 1, fols. 30r–43v; "Inzigkofen Ursprung," ed. Pflummern, 68; Fechter, *Deutsche Handschriften*, 8–9. The rules were those drawn up by Cardinal Branda de Castiglione, "reformer" for the German lands after the Council of Constance.

72. Meyer, *Reformacio*, 3:80–91; Dietler, *Chronik*, ed. Schlumberger, 388–400.

73. Meyer, *Reformacio*, 3:122–45.

74. Sigrid Schmitt, *Geistliche Frauen und städtische Welt. Stiftsdamen-Klosterfrauen-Beginen und ihre Umwelt am Beispiel der Stadt Straßburg im Spätmittelalter (1250–1530)*, forthcoming.

75. Barthelmé, *La Réforme*, 188. Barthelmé includes in her appendix a transcription of the rest of the narrative about St. Agnes, 188–92.

76. Heribert Christian Scheeben, ed. "Handschriften I," *Archiv der deutschen Dominikaner* 1 (1937): 188.

77. Strasbourg, Bibliothèque Nationale et Universitaire de Strasbourg, MS 2934, fols. 243v–248v; Barthelmé, *La Réforme*, 179, 188–92. Sigrid Schmitt deals extensively with the reform of St. Margaret's in her forthcoming "Geistliche Frauen und städtische Welt. Stiftsdamen-Klosterfrauen-Beginen und ihre Umwelt am Beispiel der Stadt Straßburg im Spätmittelalter (1250–1530)," Habilitationsschrift, University of Mainz, 2000. I am grateful to Dr. Schmitt for allowing me to read chapters from her book manuscript.

78. Letter from Prioress Adelheid von Aue to Johannes Meyer (1464) in Dietler, *Chronik*, ed. Schlumberger, 463. Meyer also compiled a history of the Inselkloster in Bern, as Meyer himself states, "with the industry and help of sister Anna von Sissach." See Claudia Engler," Anna von Sissach," *Die deutsche Literatur des Mittelalters: Verfasserlexikon*, ed. Kurt Ruh et al. (Berlin: de Gruyter, 1978–), 11: cols. 107–8; Wolfram Schneider-Lastin, "Die Fortsetzung des Ötenbacher Schwesternbuchs und andere vermißte Texte in Breslau," *Zeitschrift für deutsches Altertum* 124 (1995): 203–4; The lost work of Elisabeth Meringer and the just recently rediscovered Inselkloster Chronicle illustrate the fate of many such works belonging to women's cloisters, including, for example, the original chronicle and texts of Ursula Haider at the Bickenkloster, Villingen. An eighteenth-century account reports that, during an inventory of property at Villingen by Imperial Commissioner von Gleichenstein in 1782, there were found "some antiquated chests and cabinets full of old books and writings. From these only the largest or those with the best bindings were selected and the rest thrown into the oven" to keep the nuns from retrieving them. See Karl J. Glatz, "Auszüge aus den Urkunden des Bickenklosters in Villingen," *Zeitschrift für die Geschichte des Oberrheins* 32 (1880): 308.

79. Letter from Prioress Adelheid von Aue to Johannes Meyer (1464) in Dietler, *Chronik*, ed. Schlumberger, 464–65.

80. Meyer, *Reformacio*, 3:113–14. They were to take over the offices of prioress and subprioress at Sylo. Two other sisters, Elisabeth Ringler and Margaret Meyer were selected to serve as sacristan/head singer and as assistant bursar. A fifth, Elsbeth von Rathsamhausen, had only recently made her profession.

81. Dietler, *Chronik*, ed. Schlumberger, 463, 486–87; Prieur, *St. Gertrud*, 110–111; Weis-Müller, *Klingental*, 126.

82. Letter from Prioress Adelheid von Aue to Johannes Meyer (1464) in Dietler, *Chronik*, ed. Schlumberger, 466–67.

83. Meyer, *Reformacio*, 3:112–13.

84. Vogler, *St. Katharina*, 25.

85. St. Gall, Stiftsbibliothek, MS St. Katharina, Wil, "Schwesternbuch," Nr. 89, fols. 5v–6r. A similar account is found in Angela Varnbühler's "Chronicle," cited by Vogler, *St. Katharina*, 27.

86. St. Gall, Stiftsbibliothek, MS St. Katharina, Wil, "Chronik," Nr. 87, fol. 5v; Vogler, *St. Katharina*, 40.

87. St. Gall, Stiftsbibliothek, MS St. Katharina, Wil, "Schwesternbuch," Nr. 89, fol. 32r; Vogler, *St. Katharina*, 56–57.

88. St. Gall, Stiftsbibliothek, MS St. Katharina, Wil, "Schwesternbuch," Nr. 89, fol. 29r.

89. Ibid., fols. 26r–26v.

90. Ibid., fol. 139r.

91. Vogler, *St. Katharina*, 59.

92. Elfriede Kelm, "Das Buch im Chore der Preetzer Klosterkirche. Nach dem Original dargestellt," *Schriften des Vereins für Schleswig-Holsteinische Kirchengeschichte*, 30/31 (1974/75): 29.

93. Gustav von Buchwald, "Anna von Buchwald, Priorin des Klosters Preetz 1494–1508," *Zeitschrift der Gesellschaft für Schleswig-Holsteinische Geschichte* 9 (1879): 19.

94. Buchwald, "Preetz," 20–21.

95. Ibid., 40–41.

96. Ibid., 57–58.

97. Ibid., 56.

98. Ibid., 62.

99. Wolfgang Müller, "Die Villinger Frauenklöster des Mittelalters und der Neuzeit," in *200 Jahre Kloster St. Ursula, Villingen*, ed. Helmut Heinrich and Gisela Sattler (Villingen: Kloster St. Ursula, n.d.), 22–23; [Juliana Ernst,] *Chronik*, ed. Glatz, 66–68.

100. [Juliana Ernst,] *Chronik*, ed. Glatz, 66–85.

101. Ibid., 121–22.

102. Max Straganz, "Die ältesten Statuten des Klarissenklosters zu Brixen (Tirol)," *Franziskanische Studien* 6 (1919): 148.

103. "Anno dni MCCL an Sant Martins tag da ist dis Closter Pfullingen an gefangen worden," in "Duae Relationes circa Monasterium Brixinense O. Clar.," ed. Maximilianus Straganz, *Archivum Franciscanum Historicum* 6 (1913): 535, 539–40; Hallauer, "Klarissencloster," 95; and Wilhelm Baum, *Nikolaus Cusanus in Tirol. Das Wirken des Philosophen und Reformators als Fürstbischof von Brixen* (Bozen: Athesia, 1983), 125.

104. "Chronik des Schwesternhauses Marienthal, genannt Niesinck in Münster," in *Berichte der Augenzeugen über das Münstersche Wiedertäuferreich*, ed. Carl Cornelius, Geschichtsquellen des Bisthums Münster 2 (1853; repr. Münster: Aschendorff, 1965), 434–35.

105. [Magdalena Kremer,] "Wie diß loblich closter," ed. Sattler, 241–43.

106. "Anno dni MCCL," ed. Straganz, 542–43; Johannes Gatz, "Pfullingen," *Alemania Franciscana Antiqua* 17 (1972): 188.

107. "Anno dni MCCL," ed. Straganz, 542.

108. Paul Stinzi, "Schönensteinbach," *Annuaire de la Société d'Histoire Sundgauvienne* (1964): 59–60, 63–65.

109. See, for example, Magdalena Kremer's account of Ursula Surgend at St. Katharina in Colmar and her part in the reform mission to Sylo in Sélestat: [Kremer,] *Kirchheim*, 224–25.

110. For the confrontation between the Brigittine cloister of Maihingen and Count Ludwig XIII of Oettingen, see Chapter 6.

Chapter 4

1. Katharina von Hoya, quoted in [Johannes Busch,] *Des Augustinerpropstes Iohannes Busch Chronicon Windeshemense und Liber de reformatione monasteriorum*, ed. Karl Grube, Geschichtsquellen der Provinz Sachsen und angrenzender Gebiete 19 (Halle: Hendel, 1886), 630.

2. Katharina von Hoya, *Des Augustinerpropstes Iohannes Busch*, 592–93, cited from Eileen Power's translation, *Medieval English Nunneries, c. 1275–1535* (Cambridge University Press, 1922), 680.

3. Rolf Kiessling, *Bürgerliche Gesellschaft und Kirche in Augsburg im Spätmittelalter. Ein Beitrag zur Strukturanalyse der oberdeutschen Reichsstadt*, Abhandlungen zur Geschichte der Stadt Augsburg 19 (Augsburg: Mühlberger, 1971), 298.

4. Johannes Meyer, *Das Buch der Reformacio Predigerordens*, ed. Benedictus Maria Reichert, Quellen und Forschungen zur Geschichte des Dominikanerordens in Deutschland 3 (Leipzig: Harrassowitz, 1909), 3:14.

5. Karl Grube, *Johannes Busch Augustinerpropst zu Hildesheim: Ein katholischer Reformator des 15. Jahrhunderts* (Freiburg: Herder, 1881), 122–23.

6. Grube, *Johannes Busch*, 88; Gustav Voit, *Engelthal—Geschichte eines Dominikanerinnenklosters*, 2 vols., Schriftenreihe der Altnürnberger Landschaft 26 (Nuremberg: Koru and Berg, 1977), 1:58.

7. Dieter Stievermann, "Gründung, Reform und Reformation des Frauenklosters zu Offenhausen," *Zeitschrift für württembergische Landesgeschichte* 47 (1988): 172; Merry E. Wiesner, "Ideology Meets the Empire: Reformed Convents and the Reformation," in *Germania Illustrata: Essays Presented to Gerald Strauss*, ed. Susan Karant-Nunn and Andrew Fix (Kirksville, Mo.: Sixteenth-Century Essays and Studies, 1991), 184.

8. Meyer, *Reformacio*, 3:102.

9. Gebhard Spahr, "Die reform im Kloster St. Gallen 1417–1441," *Schriften des Vereins für Geschichte des Bodensees und seiner Umgebung* 75 (1957): 62.

10. *Chronik und Totenbuch des Klosters Wienhausen*, ed. Horst Apphuhn (Wienhausen: Kloster Wienhausen, 1986), 26.

11. Paul Nyhus, "The Franciscan Observant Reform in Germany," in *Reformbemühungen und Observanzbestrebungen im spätmittelalterlichen Ordenswesen*, ed. Kaspar Elm, Berliner Historische Studien 14, Ordensstudien 6 (Berlin: Dunker and Humblot, 1989), 216; Lucius Teichmann, "Die franziskanische Observanzbewegung in Ost-Mitteleuropa und ihre politisch-nationale Komponente im böhmisch-schlesischen Raum," *Archiv für schlesische Kirchengeschichte* 49 (1991): 208, 210.

12. Annemarie Halter, *Geschichte des Dominikanerinnen-Klosters Oetenbach in Zürich 1234–1525* (Winterthur: Keller, 1956), 118.

13. Marie-Claire Däniker-Gysin, *Geschichte des Dominikanerinnenklosters Töß 1233–1525*, Neujahrsblatt der Stadtbibliothek Winterthur 289 (Winterthur: Ziegler, 1957), 24, 28; Dietrich Schmidtke, *Studien zur dingallegorischen Erbauungsliteratur des Mittelalters. Am Beispiel der Gartenallegorie*, Hermaea, Germanistische Forschungen, n.F. 43 (Tübingen: Niemeyer, 1982), 260.

14. [Busch,] *Liber de reformatione*, 630.

15. Renée Weis-Müller, *Die Reform des Klosters Klingental und ihr Personenkreis*, Baseler Beiträge zur Geschichtswissenschaft 59 (Basel: Helbing and Lichtenhahn, 1956), 196; Thoma Vogler, *Geschichte des Dominikanerinnen-Klosters St. Katharina in St. Gallen 1228–1607* (Fribourg, Switzerland: Paulus, 1938), 22; Spahr, "St. Gallen,"62.

16. See Sigrid Schmitt, "Geistliche Frauen und städtische Welt. Stiftsdamen-Klosterfrauen-Beginen und ihre Umwelt am Beispiel der Stadt Straßburg im Spätmittelalter (1250–1530)," Habilitationsschrift, University of Mainz, 2002.

17. Bruno Griesser, "Die Reform des Klosters Rechentshofen in der alten Speyrer Diözese durch Abt Johann von Maulbronn 1431–1433," *Archiv für mittelrheinische Kirchengeschichte* 8 (1956): 276–77.

18. Rudolf Schulze, *Das adelige Frauen- (Kanonissen-) Stift der Hl. Maria (1040–1773) und die Pfarre Liebfrauen-Überwasser zu Münster, Westfalen* (Münster: Aschendorff, 1952), 150; Ulrich Faust, ed., *Germania Benedictina 11: Norddeutschland* (St. Ottilien: EOS-Verlag, 1984), 26–27.

19. Griesser, "Rechentshofen," 273, 277. Similarly relatives of the nuns at St. Walburg, in Eich-

stätt, opposed reform on the grounds that their daughters were of the nobility and too delicate to bear the rigors of a strictly observant life, Jakob Marx, *Geschichte des Erzstifts Trier, das ist der Stadt Trier und des Landes, als Churfürstenthum und als Erzdiöcese, von den ältesten Zeiten bis zum Jahre 1816*, 3 vols., (1856–64; repr. Aalen: Scientia, 1969), 3:500.

20. Staatsarchiv Nürnberg, Rep. 12 a, n. 3, fol. 5; Voit, *Engelthal*, 1:54.

21. Barbara Frank, *Das Erfurter Peterskloster im 15. Jahrhundert. Studien zur Geschichte der Klosterreform und der Bursfelder Union*, Veröffentlichungen des Max-Planck-Instituts für Geschichte 34, Studien zur Germania sacra 2 (Göttingen: Vandenhoeck and Ruprecht, 1973), 57.

22. Stievermann, "Offenhausen," 171.

23. For a list of literary works, see Karl Knötig, *Die Sonnenburg im Pustertal* (Bozen: Athensia, 1985), 40.

24. Morimichi Watanabe, "Nicholas of Cusa and the Tyrolese Monasteries: Reform and Resistance," *History of Political Thought* 7 (1986): 61.

25. Wilhelm Baum, *Nikolaus Cusanus in Tirol. Das Wirken des Philosophen und Reformators als Fürstbischof von Brixen* (Bozen: Athesia, 1983), 126.

26. Rudolf Humberdrotz, *Die Chronik des Klosters Sonnenburg (Pustertal)*, 2 vols., Schlern-Schriften 226 (Innsbruck: Wagner, 1963), 33.

27. Reform statutes for Sonnenburg drawn up by Nicholas of Cusa after a visit to the cloister on November 29, 1453; in Appendix to Hermann Hallauer, "Eine Visitation des Nikolaus von Kues im Benediktinerinnenkloster Sonnenburg," *Mitteilungen und Forschungsbeiträge der Cusanus-Gesellschaft* 6 (1967): 120–21.

28. Chief among the sticking points was the simultaneous battle between Cusa and the convent over legal claims to three villages, especially grazing rights around the village of Enneberg. Verena, who always suspected Cusa of greed for power and materialistic motives, insisted that this matter had to be settled before the reform could be discussed. Cusa naively insisted that they were in no way connected. Accordingly, the fight over Enneberg continued to escalate in tandem with the hardening of lines over the reform. For more on the conflict over Enneberg, see Baum, *Cusanus*, 189–99, and Albert Jäger, *Der Streit des Cardinals Nicolaus von Cusa mit dem Herzoge Sigmund von Österreich als Grafen von Tirol*, 2 vols. (Innsbruck: Wagner, 1861), 1:41–58.

29. Cusa's conditions called for Verena to "come to the great church at Bruneck when many people would be there. Then she should throw herself on the ground before the altar while the priests prayed the seven penitential psalms and sprinkled her with holy water. After which she might rise and swear on a crucifix to be obedient to the church in the future. Then she should be struck on the shoulders with a staff and required to keep the censures." Verena was also required to pray for the souls of those who had fallen in the battle at Enneberg for which she was held entirely guilty. Knötig, *Sonnenburg*, 39–40.

30. Memorandum by Abbess Verena von Stuben, March 1454, in Appendix to Hallauer, "Sonnenburg," 125. Verena kept a detailed record of the preceedings with the Cardinal, including copies of the letters that passed between them with explanatory notes. This record is found in Innsbrück, Tiroler Landesarchiv, MS 2336, "Missiv-Buch des Klosters Sonnenburg: Was sich mit dem Cardinal Nicolai Cusan und der Abtissin Verena von Stuben zugetragen," at 150. Verena's memorandum continues:

> Second: that I and the convent should be locked in so that his Grace has control over the key, [and] he will lock and unlock it as he wills and for his business. Third: that a common bailiff should be placed in charge of the convent's property and shall manage it and the convent. Fourth: The same bailiff shall be responsible to supply the subprioress with food, clothing, and all that she requires for the women, and I, as abbess, shall not contradict.

31. Baum, *Cusanus*, 179.

32. Maria Hüffer, *Die Reformen in der Abtei Rijnsburg im 15. Jahrhundert* (Münster: Aschendorff, 1937), 103.

33. Ibid., 8–9, 75–78.

34. Ibid., 83, 90–91, 95, 103–4, 109–10.

35. Ibid., 114–21, 125–26.

36. For one bull alone the women owed seventy-four gold ducats, plus one hundred paid to a cardinal, twelve to two lawyers, thirty to a private solicitor, eight to the chamberlain for arranging the audience, fifty to two signatories, three hundred in travel expenses, and more. Ibid., 134–35.

37. Schulze, *Liebfrauen-Überwasser*, 33.

38. "Klosterchronik Überwasser während der Wirren 1531–33," in *Quellen und Forschungen zur Geschichte der Stadt Münster*, ed. Eduard Schulte (Münster: Aschendorff, 1926), 2:151.

39. Münster, Nordrhein-Westfälisches Staatsarchiv, Münsterscher Studienfonds, Stift Überwasser, Akten Nr. 799 (Cloister Annals), fol. 85r; see also Schulze, *Liebfrauen-Überwasser*, 144.

40. Schulze, *Liebfrauen-Überwasser*, 144; Johannes Linneborn, "Die Reformation der westfälischen Benedictiner-Klöster im 15. Jahrhundert durch die Bursfelder Congregation," *Studien und Mitteilungen zur Geschichte des Benedictinerordens* 21 (1900): 317 n. 2. Perhaps Linneborn meant on the model of Engelthal where specific sisters were named as assistants and successors to take over the offices when the reform sisters would return to Nuremberg. See Voit, *Engelthal*, 1:61.

41. Linneborn, "Bursfelder," 319; Schulze, *Liebfrauen-Überwasser*, 144–46.

42. Linneborn, "Bursfelder," 318.

43. Schulze, *Liebfrauen-Überwasser*, 375.

44. Münster, Nordrhein-Westfälisches Staatsarchiv, Münsterscher Studienfonds, Stift Überwasser, Akten Nr. 799, fol. 86v; see also Schulze, *Liebfrauen-Überwasser*, 149, 375–76.

45. Meyer, *Reformacio*, 3:121; Seraphin Dietler, *Chronik des Klosters Schönensteinbach*, ed. Johann von Schlumberger (Guebwiller: Boltz, 1897), 481.

46. Meyer, *Reformacio*, 3:120.

47. Ibid., 1:118; Gustav Voit reports that at Engelthal the sisters who elected to leave took their pensions with them, *Engelthal*, 1:60.

48. Busch made a list of all the convent's inhabitants and interviewed each one individually. See Grube, *Busch*, 142.

49. Degler-Spengler, Brigitte, *Das Klarissenkloster Gnadental in Basel 1289–1529*, Quellen und Forschungen zur Baseler Geschichte 3 (Basel: Reinhardt, 1969), 77; Isenard Frank, "Der Anschluß des Salzburger Dominikanerklosters Freisach an die österreichischen Observanten, 1502–1503," *Archivum Fratrum Praedicatorum* 52 (1982): 222 n. 11.

50. [Juliana Ernst,] *Die Chronik des Bickenklosters zu Villingen*, ed. Karl Jordan Glatz, Bibliothek des Litterarischen Vereins in Stuttgart 151 (Tübingen: Fues, 1881), 34–35.

51. Roswitha Poppe, "Gertrudenberg," in *Die Frauenklöster in Niedersachsen, Schleswig-Holstein und Bremen*, ed. Ulrich Faust, Germania Benedictina 11: Norddeutschland (St. Ottilien: EOS-Verlag, 1984), 478.

52. [Magdalena Kremer,] "Wie diß loblich kloster zu Sant Johannes Baptisten zu Kirchen under deck prediger-ordens reformiert ist worden und durch wolich personen," in *Geschichte des Herzogtums Wuerttemberg unter der Regierung der Graven*, ed. Christian Friedrich Sattler (Tübingen: Reiss, 1777), 4:164, 221–22.

53. Grube, *Busch*, 88.

54. Max Miller, *Die Söflinger Briefe und das Klarissenkloster Söflingen bei Ulm im Spätmittelalter* (Wurzburg: Triltsch, 1940), 38, 54, 56–57.

55. Ibid., 38; Karl Suso Frank, *Das Klarissenkloster Söflingen: Ein Beitrag zur franziskanischen Ordensgeschichte Süddeutschlands und zur Ulmer Kirchengeschichte* (Stuttgart: Kohlhammer, 1980), 95.

56. [Busch,] *Liber de reformatione*, 630.

57. Although the manuscript of the chronicle is dated 1692, editor Horst Appuhn states that the text must have been copied from an older Low German one, probably from around 1470, the time of the reform, as can be seen by the names incorrectly rendered from the Low German, as well as from errors in dates, and names of provosts left out of the record before 1470. After 1470 the dates are correct and the record is complete. Appuhn comments that "in the High German version one can still perceive

the powerful Low German style in which the accounts from the time of abbesses Katharina von Hoya and Susanna Potstock are recorded." *Chronik Wienhausen,* ed. Appuhn, v–vi, viii.

58. Ibid., 19, 20–21.

59. [Busch,] *Liber de reformatione,* here quoted in Power, *Nunneries,* 679.

60. *Chronik Wienhausen,* ed. Appuhn, 22–23.

61. [Busch,] *Liber de reformatione,* 633–34.

62. *Chronik Wienhausen,* ed. Appuhn, 25.

63. Ibid., 24–25.

64. Meyer, *Reformacio,* 3:13.

65. Johannes Kist, "Klosterreform im spätmittelalterlichen Nürnberg," *Zeitschrift für bayerische Kirchengeschichte* 32 (1963): 34.

66. Theodor von Kern, "Die Reformation des Katharinenklosters zu Nürnberg im Jahr 1428," *Jahresbericht des historischen Vereins für Mittelfranken* 31 (1863), 3.

67. Meyer, *Reformacio,* 3:65.

68. Kern, *Katharinenkloster,* 3.

69. The account, "Also vindt man hie geschriben wie die obseruantz angefangen ist worden . . . ," is transcribed in its entireity in Kern, *Katharinenkloster,* 7–12, here 7, 8–10.

70. Weis-Müller, *Klingental,* 41, 65.

71. Ibid., 16, 65–66; Wackernagel, *Basel,* 2:837.

72. Weis-Müller, *Klingental,* 58–59, 118.

73. Ibid., 128, 132; Wackernagel, *Basel,* 2:835. Weis-Müller speculates that some were children whose care their guardians did not want to take on, *Klingental,* 134.

74. Weis-Müller, *Klingental,* 114, 116–17, 243.

75. Ibid., 172.

76. Ibid., 54, 56, 181, 188–89.

77. Annette Barthelmé, *La Réforme dominicaine au XVe siècle en Alsace et dans l'ensemble de la province de Teutonie,* Collection d'études sur l'histoire du droit et des institutions de l'Alsace 7 (Strasbourg: Heitz, 1931), 115; Weis-Müller, *Klingental,* 17, 111, 125–26.

78. Elsbeth Dürner to Wilhelm von Rappoltstein, 9 August 1482, in *Rappoltsteinisches Urkundenbuch 759–1500,* ed. Karl Albrecht, 5 vols. (Colmar: Waldmeyer, 1891–1898), 5:304.

79. Meyer, *Reformacio,* 3:72–75.

80. Ibid., 3:70, 74.

81. Ibid., 3:74.

82. *Schwesternbuch und Statuten des St. Agnes–Konvents in Emmerich,* ed. Anne Bollman and Nikolaus Staubach, Emmericher Forschungen 17 (Emmerich: Emmericher Geschichtsverein, 1998), 214.

83. Anna Roede, "Anna Roedes spätere Chronik von Herzebrock," ed. Franz Flaskamp, *Jahrbuch der Gesellschaft für Niedersächsische Kirchengeschichte* 68 (1970): 115. For more on enclosure and particularly the art within cloisters, see Jeffrey Hamburger's chapter, "Art, Enclosure, and The Pastoral Care of Nuns," in idem, *The Visual and The Visionary: Art and Female Spirituality in Late Medieval Germany,* 35–109 (New York: Zone Books, 1998).

84. Maria von Wolkenstein to Leo von Wolkenstein, October/November 1455, in appendix to Hallauer, *Kues,* 116; and Maria to Leo, December 1455, idem, 117.

85. Meyer, *Reformacio,* 3:136–37.

86. Marilyn Oliva, *The Convent and Community in Late Medieval England: Female Monasteries in the Diocese of Norwich, 1350–1540* (Woodbridge, Suffolk: Boydell, 1998), 34; Elizabeth Makowski, *Canon Law and Cloistered Women: "Periculoso" and Its Commentators, 1298–1545* (Washington, D.C.: Catholic University of America Press, 1997), 28–29.

87. Makowski, *Canon Law,* 1, 10–11, 31, 74–75, 110; Brigitte Degler-Spengler, " 'Zahlreich wie die Sterne des Himmels': Zistersienser, Dominikaner und Franziskaner vor dem Problem der Inkorporation von Frauenklöstern," *Rottenburger Jahrbuch für Kirchengeschichte* 4 (1985): 40–41; Patricia Ranft, *Women and the Religious Life in Premodern Europe* (New York: St. Martin's Press, 1996), 69.

88. Weis-Müller, *Klingental*, 32. Power, *Nunneries*, describes attempts to impose claustration as "dictated by a real social necessity," 661.

89. Jutta Gisela Sperling, *Convents and the Body Politic in Late Renaissance Venice* (Chicago: University of Chicago Press, 1999), 13, 120.

90. Merry Wiesner-Hanks, ed., *Convents Confront the Reformation: Catholic and Protestant Nuns in Germany*, trans. Joan Skocir and Merry Wiesner-Hanks (Milwaukee: Marquette University Press, 1996), 21. See also Ranft, *Religious*, 96–97.

91. Oliva, *Convent*, 22, 24.

92. Thomas Lentes, "Bild, Reform und Cura Monialium; Bildverständnis und Bildergebrauch im 'Buch der Reformacio Predigerordens' des Johannes Meyer (d. 1485)," in *Dominicains et Dominicaines en Alsace (XIIIe–XXe Siècle): Actes du colloque de Guebwiller, 8–9 avril 1994*, ed. Jean-Luc Eichenlaub (Colmar: Editions d'Alsace), 180. Justifying enclosure for women, Ranft argues that in founding the order Saint Dominic "saw two types of life as necessary and complementary to achieve the over-all goal of the Order of Preachers, the active life of Martha and the contemplative life of Mary." Dominic and his group were involved in an active apostolate, but, as a first step, he established a contemplative base at Prouille for women who were to be, Ranft asserts, "partners in the apostolate" and "the lifeblood" of the order. Of the two types, the contemplative life was intended to be superior. Ranft maintains that women were given the superior role in the eyes of the Dominicans, a fact which, she attests "has been little noted." See Ranft, *Women*, 70–71.

93. McNamara, *Sisters*, 402. In other orders, the Observance did not begin in cities like Rome, Milan or Bologna, but in hermitages and cloisters in isolated locations. In its early stages, the movement emphasized the "Vita eremitica" as the norm for monastics. See Kaspar Elm, "Die Fransiskanerobservanz als Bildungsreform," in *Leben und Weltentwürfe im Übergang vom Mittelalter zur Neuzeit. Politik-Bildung-Naturkunde-Theologie. Bericht über Kolloquien der Kommission zur Erforschung der Kultur des Spätmittelalters*, ed. Hartmut Bookmann, Bernt Moeller, and Karl Stackmann, 204. Thus reform statutes for Colmar and other Dominican men's houses substitute life in a closed community for daily ministering in the world. See Gerhard Metzger, "Der Dominikanerorden in Württemberg am Ausgang des Mittelalters," *Blätter für württembergische Kirchengeschichte*, n.F. 46 (1942): 19–20.

94. Franz Egger, *Beiträge zur Geschichte des Predigerordens. Die Reform des Baseler Konvents 1429 und die Stellung des Ordens am Baseler Konzil 1431–1448* (Bern: Lang, 1991), 77, 89–90; Gabriel Löhr, *Die Teutonia im 15. Jahrhundert: Studien und Texte vornehmlich zur Geschichte ihrer Reform*, Quellen und Forschungen zur Geschichte des Dominikanerordens in Deutschland 19 (Leipzig: Harrassowitz, 1924), 3.

95. Egger, *Beiträge*, 90; Grube, *Busch*, 22–23. For the Observant Dominicans of the Congregation of Holland, Johannes Uytenhove's regulations *(De Reformatione*, 1471) require enclosure as a aid to keeping the rule. See Servatius Wolfs, "Dominikanische Observanzbestrebungen: Die Congregatio Hollandiae (1464–1517)," in *Reformbemühungen und Observanzbestrebungen im spätmittelalterlichen Ordenswesen*, ed. Kaspar Elm, Berliner Historische Studien 14, Ordenssudien 6 (Berlin: Dunker and Humblot, 1989), 282.

96. Manfred Schulze, *Fürsten und Reformation. Geistliche Reformpolitik weltlicher Fürsten vor der Reformation*, Spätmittelalter und Reformation, n.F. 2 (Tübingen: Mohr, 1991), 102. Moreover, the Bursfeld Congregation forbade free traffic in and out of men's cloisters and also mandated enclosure; Grube, *Busch*, 224, 238; and Spahr, "St. Gallen," 35.

97. Johannes Linneborn, "Die Bursfelder Kongregation während der ersten hundert Jahre ihres Bestandes," *Deutsche Geschichtsblätter* 14 (1912/13): 28.

98. Tore Nyberg, "Der Brigittenorden im Zeitalter der Ordensreformen," in *Reformbemühungen und Observanzbestrebungen im spätmittelalterlichen Ordenswesen*, ed. Kaspar Elm, Berliner Historische Studien 14, Ordensstudien 6 (Berlin: Dunker and Humbolt, 1989), 391.

99. Hüffer, *Rijnsburg*, 90.

100. St. Gall, Stiftsbibliothek, MS St. Katharina, Wil, Vogler 87, fol. 24r; see also Volger, St. Katharina, 50; Barthelmé, *La Réform*, 186; Ida-Christina Riggert, *Die Lüneburger Frauenklöster*, Quellen und Untersuchungen zur Geschichte Niedersachsens im Mittelalter 19 (Hanover: Hahn, 1996), 239, 279–80.

101. *Chronik Wienhausen*, ed. Appuhn, 26.

102. Preetz, Archiv, Klosterpreetz, "Buch im Chor," fol. 154r, translation cited from Jeffrey Hamburger, *The Visual and the Visionary: Art and Female Spirituality in Late Medieval Germany* (New York: Zone Books, 1998), 69, 488 n. 158.

103. "Sorores karissime . . ." [Ebstorf reform account, c. 1490], in the appendix to "Litterarisches und geistiges Leben in Kloster Ebstorf am Ausgange des Mittelalters," ed. Conrad Borchling, *Zeitschrift des historischen Vereins für Niedersachsen* 4 (1905): 388–96, here 392.

104. [Kremer,] "Wie diß loblich closter," 220–21.

105. [Eva Magdalena Neyler,] "Item diß nachgeschriben geschicht und gewalt des vyntz von Gott," in "Die Vertreibung der Klosterfrauen aus Pforzheim," ed. Dr. Holzwarth, *Katholische Trösteinsamkeit* 12 (1858): 205–54, here 235–36, 247–48. Another version of Eva Neyler's account, from an eighteenth-century copy, was edited by Karl Rieder in "Zur Reformationsgeschichte des Dominikanerinnenklosters zu Pforzheim," *Freiburger Diözesan-Archiv* n.F. 18 (1917): 321–60.

106. Eva Neyler's account of the arrival at Kirchberg is transcribed from Stuttgart, Landesbibliothek, Cod. hist. 4 330, fol. 221r–224v, in R. Krauß, "Geschichte des Dominikaner-Frauenklosters Kirchberg," *Württembergische Vierteljahreshefte*, n.F. (1894): 318–19. A transcription from an eighteenth-century manuscript is found in Rieder, "Reformationsgeschichte," 360–66, here 361.

107. Katharina M. Wilson, ed., *Women Writers of the Renaissance and Reformation* (Athens: University of Georgia Press, 1987), 290–91.

108. [Kremer,] "Wie diß loblich closter," 160. An example of a radically committed Observant, Sister Bartolomea Riccoboni writes of the enclosure of the Dominican house of Corpus Domini at Venice in 1394, saying, "Just imagine what joy lingered in those minds that had for so long yearned to be enclosed for love of the Lord Jesus Christ!" Later she says that the women's fervor reached such a point that "going to the windows bothered them terribly," [Bartolomea Riccoboni,] *Life and Death in a Venetian Convent: The Chronicle and Necrology of Corpus Domini, 1395–1436*, ed. and trans. Daniel Bornstein (Chicago: University of Chicago Press, 2000), 33, 35.

109. St. Gall, Stiftsbibliothek, MS St. Katharina, Wil, "Klosterchronik," Nr. 87, fol. 22r and fol. 45r. See also Vogler, *St. Katharina*, 46, 50–51.

110. St. Gall, Stiftsbibliothek, MS St. Katharina, Wil, "Schwesternbuch," Nr. 89, fol. 31r. See also Vogler, *St. Katharina*, 51 n. 3. "Gesicht" has the meaning of both countenance and sight.

111. Vogler, *St. Katharina*, 247, 267.

112. Thomas à Kempis, *The Imitation of Christ*, trans. E. M. Blaiklock (Nashville: Thomas Nelson, 1979), 24.

113. Caroline Walker Bynum, *Jesus as Mother: Studies in the Spirituality of the High Middle Ages* (Berkeley and Los Angeles: University of California Press, 1982), 6.

114. Strasbourg, Bibliothèque Municipale, MS 563, fol. 22r. That the work must have circulated widely in a much abridged version is indicated by the copy in the Freiburg Universitätsbibliothek, MS 202, fols. 189v–191v, which, unlike the Strasbourg manuscript, does not mention Margareta von Masmünster's name. Excerpts from the work can be found in Florenz Landmann, "Zwei Andachtsübungen von Straßburger Klosterfrauen am Ende des Mittelalters," *Archiv für Elsässische Kirchengeschichte* 6 (1931): 222–28. Dietrich Schmidtke cites ten manuscript copies, "Margaret Ursula von Masmünster," in *Die deutsche Literatur des Mittelalters: Verfasserlexikon*, ed. Kurt Ruh et al. (Berlin: de Gruyter, 1985), 5: cols. 1250–51.

115. Strasbourg, Bibliothèque Municipale, MS 563, fol. 23r.

116. Freiburg, Universitätsbibliothek, MS 202, fol. 191r.

117. Strasbourg, Bibliothèque Municipale, MS 563, fol. 16r. See also Landmann, "Andachtsübungen," 220.

118. See Derek Pearsall and Elizabeth Salter, *Landscapes and Seasons of the Medieval World* (Toronto: University of Toronto Press, 1973), 71 and plate 25b. Imagery of the devout soul in the garden also recalls Jesus' appearance to Mary Magdalene when she mistook him for the gardener.

119. Lotte Kurras, "Ein Bildzeugnis der Reformtätigkeit des Nürnberger Katharinenklosters für

Regensburg," *Mitteilungen des historischen Vereins für die Geschichte der Stadt Nürnberg* 68 (1981): 295. See also Anne Winston-Allen, *Stories of the Rose: The Making of the Rosary in the Middle Ages* (University Park: Pennsylvania State University Press, 1997), 89–98.

120. [Barbara von Benfelden.] "Von zunemunge der geistlicheit und uff gang der tugenden der swestern," transcribed in appendix to Annette Barthelmé, *La Réforme dominicaine au Xve siècle en Alsace et dans l'ensemble de la province de Teutonie,* Collection d'études sur l'histoire du droit et des institutions de l'Alsace 7 (Strasbourg: Heitz, 1931), 189–92, here 189. This account is only found in Strasbourg, Bibliothèque Nationale et Universitaire de Strasbourg, MS 2934, fols. 243v–248r, here 244r.

121. Schmidtke, *Erbauungsliteratur,* 474, 493, 506, 509, 529. See also Anne Winston-Allen, "'Minne' in Spiritual Gardens of the Fifteenth Century," in *Canon and Canon Transgression in Medieval German Literature,* ed. Albrecht Classen (Göppingen: Kümmerle, 1993), 153–62.

122. St. Gall, Stiftsbibliothek, MS St. Katharina, Wil, "Schwesternbuch," Nr. 89, fols. 31r–31v; St. Gall, Stiftsbibliothek, MS St. Katharina, Wil, "Klosterchronik," Nr. 87, fols. 22r, 45r. See also Volger, *St. Katharina,* 46, 50–51.

Chapter 5

1. Joan Kelly-Gadol, "Did Women Have a Renaissance?" in *Becoming Visible: Women in European History,* ed. Renate Bridenthal and Claudia Koonz, 137–64 (Boston: Houghton Mifflin, 1977); David Herlihy, "Did Women have a Renaissance?: A Reconsideration," *Medievalia et Humanistica,* n.s. 13 (1985): 1–22.

2. "Sorores karissime . . . ," ed. Conrad Borchling, in "Litterarisches und geistiges Leben im Kloster Ebstorf am Ausgange des Mittelalters," *Zeitschrift des historischen Vereins für Niedersachsen* 4 (1905): 395. See also Wilhelm Spangenberg, Sophia Wichelmann, and Hans E. Seidat, *Ebstorf aus der Chronik* (Uelzen: Becker, 1982), 100, and Heike Uffmann, "'. . . wie in einem Rosengarten . . .' Die Ebstorfer Klosterreform im Spiegel von Chronistik und Tischlesung," in *'In Treue und Hingabe': 800 Jahre Kloster Ebstorf,* ed. Marianne Elster and Horst Hoffmann (Uelzen: Becker, 1997), 215–16.

3. "Sorores karissime . . . ," ed. Borchling, in "Kloster Ebstorf," 395.

4. Ibid., 391–92.

5. From the Ebstorf Chronicle, "Innumerabiles grates . . . ," ed. Borchling, in "Kloster Ebstorf," 407.

6. Helmar Härtel, "Die Bibliothek des Klosters Ebstorf am Ausgang des Mittelalters," in *'In Treue und Hingabe:' 800 Jahre Kloster Ebstorf,* ed. Elster and Hoffmann, 109–21; idem, "Die Klosterbibliothek Ebstorf. Reform und Schulwirklichkeit am Ausgang des Mittelalters," in *Schule und Schüler im Mittelalter,* ed. Martin Kintzinger, 245–58 (Cologne: Böhlau, 1996).

7. Only remnants remain of the libraries at Schönensteinbach, St Maria Magdalena an den Steinen (Basel), Liebenau (near Friedrichshafen), Himmelskron (Hochheim), St. Katharina (Colmar), the "Insel" cloister in Bern, St. Agnes in Strasbourg, Engelport (Guebwiller), Sylo (Sélestat), and the Dominican women's convents at Pforzheim, Hasenpfuhl, Altenhohenau, Medingen, Medlingen, and Tulln. See Andreas Rüther and Hans-Jochen Schiewer, "Die Predigthandschriften des Straßburger Dominikanerinnenklosters St. Nikolaus in undis," in *Die deutsche Predigt im Mitttelalter,* ed. Volker Mertens and Hans-Jochen Schiewer (Niemeyer: Tübingen, 1992), 172–73; Heiko Haumann and Hans Schadek, eds., *Geschichte der Stadt Freiburg im Breisgau,* 2 vols. (Stuttgart: Theiss, 1994), 1:439.

8. Rüther and Schiewer, "Predigthandschriften," 169; Hans Hornung, "Der Handschriftensammler D. Sudermann und die Bibliothek des Straßburger Klosters St. Nikolaus in Undis," *Zeitschrift für Geschichte des Oberrheins* 107 (1959): 338–99; idem, "Daniel Sudermann als Handschriftensammler: Ein Beitrag zur Straßburger Bibliotheksgeschichte" (Ph.D. diss., University of Tübingen, 1956).

9. Thoma Vogler, *Geschichte des Dominikanerinnen-Klosters St. Katharina in St. Gallen 1228–1607* (Fribourg, Switzerland: Paulus, 1938), 151, 233–70.

10. Karin Schneider, "Die Bibliothek des Katharinenklosters in Nürnberg und die Städtische Gesellschaft," in *Studien zum Städtischen Bildungswesen des späten Mittelalters und der frühen Neuzeit,* ed.

Bernd Moeller et al. (Göttingen: Vandenhoeck and Ruprecht, 1983), 71; and Eugen Hillenbrand, "Die Observantenbewegungen der deutschen Ordensprovinz der Dominikaner," in *Reformbemühungen und Observanzbestrebungen im spätmittelalterlichen Ordenswesen*, ed. Kaspar Elm, Berliner Historische Studien 14, Ordensstudien 6 (Berlin: Dunker und Humblot, 1989), 269.

11. Werner Williams-Krapp, "Observanzbewegung, monastische Spiritualität und geistliche Literatur im 15. Jahrhundert," *Internationales Archiv für Sozialgeschichte der deutschen Literatur* 20 (1995), 3; Schneider, "Bibliothek," 70.

12. Williams-Krapp, "Observanzbewegung," 3.

13. Regina Schiewer, "Sermons for Nuns of the Dominican Observance Movement," in *Medieval Monastic Preaching*, ed. Carolyn Muessig (Leiden: Brill, 1998), 78.

14. Canisia Jedelhauser, *Geschichte des Klosters und der Hofmark Maria-Medingen von den Anfängen im 13. Jahrhundert bis 1606*, Quellen und Forschungen zur Geschichte des Dominikanerordens in Deutschland 34 (Leipzig: Harrassowitz, 1936), 91. Similarly, a letter from reform prioress Anna Sneberger at St. Agnes in Freiburg lists the books she and three reforming sisters brought from Basel. [Sneberger, Anna.] Letter to the sisters at St. Maria Magdelena an den Steinen, Basel, 15 July 1465. In "Frauengeschichte/ Geschlechtergeschichte/Sozialgeschichte. Forschungsfelder-Forschungslücken: eine bibliographische Annäherung an das späte Mittelalter," ed. Gabriela Signori. In *Lustgarten und Dämonenpein: konzept von Weiblichkeit im Mittelalter und Früher Neuzeit*, ed. Annette Kuhn and Bea Lundt, 29–53 (Dortmund: Ebersbach, 1997), at 34–35.

15. Werner Williams-Krapp, "German and Dutch Legendaries of the Middle Ages: A Survey," in *Hagiography and Medieval Literature: A Symposium*, ed. Hans Bekker-Nielsen (Odense: Odense University Press, 1981), 70.

16. Ida-Christine Riggert, *Die Lüneburger Frauenklöster*, Quellen und Untersuchungen zur Geschichte Niedersachsens im Mittelalter 19 (Hanover: Hahn, 1996), 276.

17. Burkhard Hasebrink, "Tischlesung und Bildungskultur im Nürnberger Katharinenkloster. Ein Beitrag zu ihrer Rekonstruktion," in *Schule und Schüler im Mittelalter. Beiträge zur europäischen Bildungsgeschichte des 9. bis 15. Jahrhunderts*, ed. Martin Kintzinger, Sönke Lorenz, and Michael Walter, Beihefte zum Archiv für Kulturgeschichte 42 (Cologne: Böhlau, 1996), 204.

18. A. Hauber, "Deutsche Handschriften in Frauenklöstern des späteren Mittelalters," *Zentralblatt für Bibliothekswesen* 31 (1914): 349; Hasebrink, "Tischlesung," 202.

19. Meyer's work, a translation and adaptation for women of Humbert of Romans's (1194–1277) *Liber de instructione officialium ordinis praedicatorum*, is currently being edited by Sarah DeMaris for the series Monumenta ordinis fratrum praedicatorum historica.

20. Meyer's list of titles reads:

daz buch hugonis von der zücht [De institutione novitiorum] Daz buch von dem closter der sel [Claustrum animae] Die betrachtung sancti bernhardi, Die betrachtung vnd gepet Anshelmi Collationes patrum daz ist die red der altveter vnd der altveter leben daz leben vnd die marter der heiligen [Der Heiligen Leben] Daz buchlin der wisheit daz do heist horologium eterne sapientie vnd daz büchlin daz da heist Stimulus amoris vnd das büchlin daz do heist von dem nach volgen christi [Imitatio Christi] daz buch von der mynn gotz [Büchlein von der Liebhabung Gottes] daz buch Baarlaam daz buch von den tugenden vnd vntugenden vnd ander des gelich der bücher.

Hasebrink, "Tischlesung," 195–96.

21. J. König, "Die Chronik der Anna von Munzingen. Nach der ältesten Abschrift mit Einleitung und Beilagen," *Freiburger Diözesan-Archiv* 13 (1880): 202–4.

22. This catalogue of manuscripts, "Jtem die her nach geschriben pücher hat der convent hie zu sant Kathereyn . . . ," compiled 1455–99 by one of the sisters, is edited by Franz Jostes in appendix II to *Meister Eckhart und seine Jünger. Ungedruckte Texte zur Geschichte der deutschen Mystik*, Collectanea Friburgensis 4 (Fribourg, Switzerland: Kommissionsverlag der Universitätsbuchhandlung, 1894), 115–59, here 153, 157.

23. Ibid., 129, 155, 160. The convent of St. Katharina had sent a reform party to Tulln in 1436.
24. Hornung, "Daniel," 1:110a.
25. Cited in Hauber, "Handschriften," 356.
26. St. Gall, Stiftsbibliothek, Cod. 1919, fols. 315v–316r; Vogler, *St. Katharina*, 82.
27. Freiburg, Universitätsbibliothek, MS 490. See also Werner Fechter, *Deutsche Handschriften des 15. und 16. Jahrhunderts aus der Bibliothek des ehemaligen Augustinerchorfrauenstifts Inzigkofen* (Sigmaringen: Thorbecke, 1997), 120–26.
28. St. Gall, Stiftsbibliothek, MS St. Katherina, Wil, "Schwesternbuch," Nr. 89, fol. 177r.
29. At Überwasser, the account books of reform prioress Sophia Dobbers record sums paid in the year 1496—thirteen years after the reform—to purchase, commission, bind or illuminate at least eighteen books, that included, besides the usual liturgical ones, a *Vitae patrum*, the *Sermones Bernhardi*, a printed "school book," and printed psalters. See Rudolf Schulze, *Das adelige Frauen- (Kanonissen-) Stift der Hl. Maria (1040–1773) und die Pfarre Liebfrauen-Überwasser zu Münster, Westfalen* (Münster: Aschendorff, 1952), 378 n. 21.
30. Reproduced in Katrin Graf, *Bildnisse schreibender Frauen im Mittelalter 9. bis Anfang 13. Jahrhundert* (Basel: Schwabe, 2002), plate 2.
31. "Die Stiftung des Klosters Oetenbach und das Leben der seligen Schwestern daselbst, aus der Nürnberger Handschrift," ed. H. Zeller-Werdmüller and Jakob Bächthold, *Zürcher Taschenbuch* 12 (1889): 231, Gertrud Jaron Lewis, *By Women, for Women, about Women: The Sister-Books of Fourteenth-Century Germany* (Toronto: Pontifical Institute of Medieval Studies, 1996), 273 n. 19. Alison Beach has illustrated in detail the scribal activities of nuns in the twelfth century. See "The Female Scribes of Twelfth-Century Bavaria" (Ph.D. diss., Columbia University, 1996) and idem *Women as Scribes: Book Production and Monastic Reform in Twelfth-Century Bavaria* (Cambridge: Cambridge University Press, 2004).
32. Hillenbrand, "Observantenbewegung," 269; Schneider, "Bibliothek," 71.
33. Vogler, *St. Katharina*, 151.
34. Klaus Graf, "Ordensreform und Literatur in Augsburg während des 15. Jahrhunderts," in *Literarisches Leben in Augsburg während des 15. Jahrhunderts*, ed. Johannes Janota and Werner Williams-Krapp (Tübingen: Niemeyer, 1995), 100, 112, 115, 137; Christoph Roth, *Literatur und Klosterreform: Die Bibliothek der Benediktiner von St. Mang zu Füssen im 15. Jahrhundert*, Studia Augustana 10 (Tübingen: Niemeyer, 1998), 10–11.
35. Cited in Elisabeth Schraut, "Kunst im Frauenkloster: Überlegungen zu den Möglichkeiten der Frauen im mittelalterlichen Kunstbetrieb am Beispiel Nürnberg," in *Auf der Suche nach der Frau im Mittelalter*, ed. Bea Lundt (Munich: Fink, 1991), 112. See Karin Schneider, "Die Bibliothek des Katharinenklosters in Nürnberg und die städtische Gesellschaft," in *Studien zum städtischen Bildungswesen des späten Mittelalters und der frühen Neuzeit*, ed. Bernd Moeller et al., 70–82 (Göttingen: Vandenhoeck and Ruprecht, 1983).
36. Williams-Krapp, "Observanzbewegung," 2.
37. Werner Williams-Krapp, "Die Bedeutung der reformierten Klöster des Predigerordens für das literarische Leben in Nürnberg im 15. Jahrhundert," paper presented at the conference on "Die literarische und materielle Kultur der Frauenklöster im späten Mittelalter und in der frühen Neuzeit (ca. 1350–1550), February 24–26, 1999, Herzog August Bibliothek Wolfenbüttel, p. 8. I am grateful to Prof. Williams-Krapp for sending me a copy of his paper.
38. Marie-Luise Ehrenschwendtner, " 'Puellae litteratae': The Use of the Vernacular in the Dominican Convents of Southern Germany," in *Medieval Women in their Communities*, ed. Diane Watt (Toronto: University of Toronto Press, 1997), 52–53; Williams-Krapp, "Observanzbewegung," 4.
39. Gerhard Stamm, "Klosterreform und Buchproduktion: Das Werk der Schreib- und Lesemeisterin Regula," in *750 Jahre Zisterzienserinnen-Abtei Lichtenthal: Faszination eines Klosters* (Sigmaringen: Thorbecke, 1995), 63–64.
40. Johannes Meyer, *Das Buch der Reformacio Predigerordens*, 2 vols., ed. Benedictus Maria Reichert, Quellen und Forschungen zur Geschichte des Dominikanerordens in Deutschland 2 (Leipzig: Harras-

sowitz, 1908–09), 63. At the end of a collection of sermons at Unterlinden (Colmar, Bibliothèque de la Ville de Colmar, MS 717II, fol. 324v) stands the colophon, "I sister Dorothea von Kippenheim, a convent sister . . . translated this book from Latin into German for the praise of God," Christian von Heusinger, "Studien zur oberrheinischen Buchmalerei und Graphik im Spätmittelalter" (Ph.D diss., University of Freiburg, 1953), 139. See also Hans Rupprich, *Die deutsche Literatur vom späten Mittelalter bis zum Barock. I. Das ausgehende Mittelalter, Humanismus und Renaissance 1370–1520*, Geschichte der deutschen Literatur von den Anfängen bis zur Gegenwart 4.1 (Munich: Beck, 1970), 323, 330; Werner Williams-Krapp, "Dorothea von Kippenheim," in *Die deutsche Literatur des Mittelalters: Verfasserlexikon*, ed. Wolfgang Stammler, Karl Langosch, and Kurt Ruh (Berlin: de Gruyter, 1980), 2: 217–18. Another Dorothea von Kippenheim at Unterlinden translated works around 1508/16 and may have been confused with the earlier Dorothea (d. 1425). See Karl-Ernst Greith, "Ulrich von Augsburg," in *Verfasserlexikon*, 9:1244; idem, "Eine deutsche Übersetzung der 'Vita Sancti Udalrici' des Bern von Reichenau aus Unterlinden in Colmar," in *Durch abenteuer muess man wagen vil: Festschrift für Anton Schwob zum 60. Geburtstag*, ed. Wernfried Hofmeister and Bernd Steinbauer (Innsbruck: Institut für Germanistik, 1997), 111; idem, "Elisabeth Kempf (1415–1485). Priorin und Übersetzerin in Unterlinden zu Colmar," *Annuaire de la Société et d'Archéologie de Colmar* 29 (1980/81): 47–73; Siegfried Ringler, "Anna Ebin," in *Die deutsche Literatur des Mittelalters: Verfasserlexikon*, ed. Kurt Ruh et al. (Berlin: de Gruyter, 1980), 2:cols. 295–97; Gertrud Jaron Lewis, *Bibliographie zur deutschen Frauenmystik des Mittelalters*, Bibliographien zur deutschen Literatur des Mittelalters 10 (Berlin: Schmidt, 1989), 419; Lina Eckenstein, *Women under Monasticism* (1896; repr. New York: Russel and Russel, 1963), 428; Stamm, "Lichtenthal," 65; idem, "Regula, Lichtenthaler Schreibmeisterin," *Die deutsche Literatur des Mittelalters: Verfasserlexikon*, ed. Kurt Ruh et al. (Berlin: de Gruyter, 1989), 7: col. 1131–34; Karl-Ernst Greith, "Die Leben-Jesu-Übersetzung der Schwester Regula aus Lichtenthal," *Zeitschrift für deutsches Altertum und deutsche Literatur* 119 (1990); 22–37; idem, "Heiligenverehrung und Hagiographie im Kloster Unterlinden zu Colmar," in *Dominicans et Dominicaines en Alsace, XIII–XXe Siècle*, ed. Jean-Luc Eichenlaub (Colmar: Archives Départementales du Haut-Rhin, 1996), 171; Felix Heinzer and Gerhard Stamm, *Die Handschriften der Badischen Landesbibliothek in Karlsruhe. XI. Die Handschriften von Lichtenthal* (Wiesbaden: Harrassowitz, 1987), 173.

41. Karlsruhe, Badische Landesbibliothek, MS Lichtental 70, fol. 187r; Greith, "Schwester Regula," 33.

42. Karlsruhe, Badische Landesbibliothek, MS Lichtental 70, frontis leaf; Stamm, "Kloster-reform," 64.

43. Karlsruhe, Badische Landesbibliothek, MS Lichtental 69, fol. 46r; Stamm, "Klosterreform," 65.

44. Ute Stargardt, "Male Clerical Authority in the Spiritual (Auto)biographies of Medieval Holy Women," in *Women as Protagonists and Poets in the German Middle Ages: An Anthology of Feminist Approaches to Middle High German Literature*, ed. Albrecht Classen (Göppingen: Kümmerle, 1991), 210.

45. Greith, "Schwester Regula," 32.

46. Karlsruhe, Badische Landesbibliothek, MS L 69, fol. 206v; Stamm, "Klosterreform," 66.

47. [Katharina Tucher,] *Die 'Offenbarungen' der Katharina Tucher*, ed. Ulla Williams and Werner Williams-Krapp, Untersuchungen zur deutschen Literaturgeschichte 98 (Tübingen: Niemeyer, 1998), 1–23; Karin Schneider, "Katharina Tucher," in *Die deutsche Literatur des Mittelalters: Verfasserlexikon*, ed. Kurt Ruh et al. (Berlin: de Gruyter, 1992), cols. 1132–34.

48. [Juliana Ernst,] *Die Chronik des Bickenklosters zu Villingen*, ed. Karl Jordan Glatz, Bibliothek des Litterarischen Vereins in Stuttgart 151 (Tübingen: Fues, 1881), 96–97.

49. Ernst, *Chronik*, 139.

50. Ibid., 108.

51. Ringler attributes to Haider a more "objective understanding" of the nature of divine revelation, saying that it can also include the answer to a specific question "found in certain (mystical) texts." Thus she freely incorporates the writings of Johannes Tauler as part of her own "revelations." See Siegfried Ringler, "Ursula Haider," in *Die deutsche Literatur des Mittelalters: Verfasserlexikon*, ed. Wolfgang Stammler and Karl Langosch, (Berlin: de Gruyter, 1981), 3: cols. 402–3.

52. St. Gall, Stiftsbibliothek, Cod. 1919, fols. 304v–316r; Carl Greith, *Die deutsche Mystik im Prediger-Orden (von 1250–1530) nach ihren Grundlehren, Liedern und Lebensbildern* (1861; repr. Amsterdam: Rodopi, 1965), 277–88; Vogler, *St. Katharina*, 82, 250.

53. St. Gall, Stiftsbibliothek, Cod. 1919, fol. 305r–305v.

54. [Ernst,] *Chronik*, 43, 44.

55. Karen Greenspan, "Erklärung des Vaterunsers: A Critical Edition of a 15th-Century Mystical Treatise by Magdalena Beutler of Freiburg (Ph.D. diss., University of Massachusetts, 1984), 105–298; Peter Dinzelbacher, "Magdalena von Freiburg," in *Die deutsche Literatur des Mittelalters: Verfasserlexikon,* ed. Wolfgang Stammler and Karl Langosch (Berlin: de Gruyter, 1985), 5: col. 1120.

56. Kloster Neresheim, MS Ne 8, frontice leaf; Arnold Schromm, *Die Bibliothek des ehemaligen Zisterzienserinnenklosters Kirchheim am Ries: Buchpflege und geistiges Leben in einem Frauenstift,* Studia Augustana 9 (Tübingen: Niemeyer, 1998), 130, 155.

57. Ernst Herrgott, "Necrologium von Alspach," *Alemania Franciscana Antiqua* 13 (1969): 62. This Margartha von Kentzingen is apparently not the same person as Margareta von Kenzingen, the mother of Magdalena Beutler, who died in 1428. I thank Martina Backes for bringing this work to my attention.

58. Eckenstein, *Monasticism,* 428; Rupprich, *Mittelalter,* 675; Edith Ennen, *Frauen im Mittelalter* (Munich: Beck, 1984), 142. At this writing I have not been able to access the principal source on Aleydis Raiscop which is K. Kossert, *Aleydis Raiscop: Die Humanistin von Nonnenwerth,* Gocher Schriften 6 (Goch: H. Werner, 1985).

59. Colmar, Bibliothèque de la Ville, MS 508, fols. 137r–141v, vita of Elisabeth Kempf by Agatha Gosembrot; Herzog-August-Bibliothek, Wolfenbüttel, MS Extravagantes 164, 1, fols. 2r–151r, Elisabeth Kempf's translation of the "Vitae Sororum" of Unterlinden with additions. See also Karl-Ernst Greith, "L'activité littéraire des dominicaines d'Unterlinden aux XIVe et XVe siècles," in *Les Dominicaines d'Unterlinden, ed.* Madeleine Blondel and Jeffrey Hamburger (Paris: Somogy, 2000), 1:166; idem, "Elisabeth Kempf," 47–73; Claudia Bartholemy; "Élisabeth Kempf, prieure à Unterlinden: une vie entre traduction et tradition," in *Les Dominicaines d'Unterlinden,* ed. Madeleine Blondel and Jeffrey Hamburger (Paris: Somogy, 2000), 1:167–70.

60. The largest part of Alijt Bake's works are contained in Brussels, Koninklijke Bibliotheek, MS 643–644 and Universiteitsbibliotheek, Ghent, MS 3854. For other manuscripts of her works see Wybren Scheepsma, *Deemoed en devotie: De koorvrouwen van Windesheim en hun geschriften* (Amsterdam: Prometheus, 1997), 175–202; 253–59, 355–56. Most have been edited by Bernhard Spaapen in the series "Middeleeuwse Passienmystiek," II–V in *Ons geestelijk erf* 40–43 (1966–69). See also Kurt Ruh, *Geschichte der abendländischen Mystik* (Munich: Beck, 1999), 4:252–67.

61. Scheepsma, *Deemoed,* 385; Ruh, *Mystik,* 254.

62. Vienna, Österreichische Nationalbibliothek, MS s.n. 12.827, fols. 1r–28r; ed. Scheepsma, "De helletocht van Jacomijne Costers (d. 1503)," *Ons geestelijk erf* 70 (1996): 157–85. For information on other works by her, see Scheepsma, *Deemoed,* 154–68, 248–50, 384.

63. Vienna, Österreichische Nationalbibliothek, MS s.n. 12.827, fols. 45v–57r. See Scheepsma, *Deemoed,* 167–74, 250–51, 384.

64. *Van dye passie ons liefsherren ihū christi* (Leiden: Seuersz, 1515/16). For a facsimile edition of both books, see A. M. J. van Buuren, ed., *Suster Bertken. Twee bij Jan Seversz in Leiden verschenen boekjes ('s-Gravenhage, Koninklijke Bibliotheek, 227 G 46) in facsimile uitgegeven* (Utrecht: Uti, 1989); Ruh, *Mystik,* 268–76.

65. *Der rechte wech zo der Euangelischer volkomenheit* (Cologne: Neusz, 1531); Ruh, *Mystik,* 277–89.

66. *Margarita Euangelica. Een devote boecxken geheeten Die Evangelische Peerle* (Utrecht: Berntsen, 1535), *[Van] den Tempel onser sielen* (facsimile edition), ed. Albert Ampe (Antwerp: Russbroecgenootschap, 1968); Ruh, *Mystik,* 290–312.

67. English translation: John Van Engen, *Devotio Moderna* (Mahwah, N.Y.: Paulist Press, 1988), 176–86. Stadtbibliothek, Nuremberg, MS Cent VII 16, fols. 8v–260r, Katharina von Mühlheim, "Handbook for the Sacristan;" Walter Fries, "Kirche und Kloster zu St. Katharina in Nürnberg," *Mitteilungen des Vereins für Geschichte der Stadt Nürnberg* 25 (1924): 46.

68. Gerard Achten, *Das christliche Gebetbuch im Mittelalter: Andachts- und Stundenbücher in Handschrift und Frühdruck*, Staatsbibilothek Preussischer Kulturbesitz, exhibition catalogue 13 (Wiesbaden: Reichert, 1980), 44.

69. Härtel, "Bibliothek," 113–14.

70. Thomas Mertens, "Collatio und Codex im Bereich der Devotio Moderna," in *Der Codex im Gebrauch*, ed. Christel Meier, Dagmar Hüpper, and Hagen Keller, Münstersche Mittelalter-Schriften 70 (Munich: Fink, 1996), 177.

71. *Schwesternbuch und Statuten des St. Agnes–Konvents in Emmerich*, ed. Anne Bollmann and Niko- laus Staubach, Emmericher Forschungen 17 (Emmerich: Emmericher Geschichtsverein, 1998), 253, 253 n. 8.

72. Münnerstadt (Bad Kissingen), Augustinerklosterbibliothek, MS 406, fols. 1–8, 181–310; Adolar Zumkeller, "Vom geistlichen Leben im Erfurter Weissfrauenkloster am Vorabend der Reformation. Nach einer neu aufgefundenen handschriftlichen Quelle," in *Reformatio ecclesiae: Beiträge zu kirchlichen Reformbemühungen von der Alten Kirche bis zur Neuzeit. Festgabe für Erwin Iserloh*, ed. Remigius Bäumer (Paderborn: Schöningh, 1980), 257–58. An example of a personal anthology is Badische Landesbiblio- thek, Karlsruhe, Cod. Schwarzach 19, fols. 1r–265v (1480) compiled, and some texts possibly com- posed, by Anna Schott at the cloister of St. Agnes and St. Margaret, Strasbourg.

73. Kloster Wienhausen, MS 9, fols. 1–39; Paul Alpers, ed., "Das Wienhausener Liederbuch," *Niederdeutsches Jahrbuch* 38 (1943–47): 1–41; Victoria Joan Moessner, "The Medieval Embroideries of Convent Wienhausen," in *Studies in Cistercian Art and Architecture 3*, ed. Meredith Lillich (Kalamazoo, Mich.: Cistercian Publications, 1987), 163; Klosterbibliothek Ebstorf, MS VI 17, fols. 1–62; Eduard Schröder, ed., "Die Ebstorfer Liederhandschrift," *Jahrbuch des Vereins für Niederdeutsche Sprachforschung* 15 (1889): 1–32; Johannes Gatz, "Pfullingen," *Alemania Franciscana Antiqua* 17 (1972): 213–15; Franz Jostes, ed., "Eine Werdener Liederhandschrift aus der Zeit um 1500," *Jahrbuch des Vereins für Niederdeut- sche Sprachforschung* 14 (1888): 60–89; Johannes Janota, "Werdener Liederbuch" in *Die deutsche Literatur des Mittelalters: Verfasserlexikon*, ed. Kurt Ruh et al. (Berlin: de Gruyter, 1999), 10: cols. 883–86; Walther Lipphardt, "Niederdeutsche Reimgedichte und Lieder des 14. Jahrhunderts in den mittelalterlichen Orationalien der Zisterzienserinnen von Medingen und Wienhausen," *Niederdeutsches Jahrbuch* 95 (1972): 66–131. Although Lipphardt reproduces only songs from the fourteenth century, he lists the provenance of twelve Medingen manuscripts from the fifteenth and early sixteenth centuries containing songs.

74. Ida-Christine Riggert-Mindermann, "Monastisches Leben im Kloster Ebstorf und den ande- ren Heideklöstern während des Spätmittelalters," in *'In Treue und Hingabe': 800 Jahre Kloster Ebstorf*, ed. Marianne Elster and Horst Hoffmann (Uelzen: Becker, 1997), 198; Jeffrey Hamburger, *Nuns as Artists. The Visual Culture of a Medieval Convent*, California Studies in the History of Art 37 (Berkeley and Los Angeles: University of California Press, 1997), 120. Walther Lipphardt, "Die liturgische Funktion deutscher Kirchenlieder in den Klöstern niedersächsischer Zisterzienserinnen des Mittelalters," *Zeit- schrift für Katholische Theologie* 94 (1972): 158–98; Preussische Staatsbibliothek, Berlin, MS germ. octav. 185, fols. 1–322 (Deventersche Liederhandschrift.)

75. In addition to literary production, there is some evidence of an increase in artistic activity in weaving, painting, and commissioning of works for the building projects undertaken in reformed cloisters. At Preetz, Anna von Buchwald commissioned a statue of the Virgin for the new altar and more than twenty-eight paintings for the renovated cloister. The Wienhausen chronicle records that in 1488 three sisters restored the paintings in their choir. See Jeffrey Hamburger, *The Visual and the Visionary. Art and Female Spirituality in Late Medieval Germany* (New York: Zone Books, 1998), 73; and *Chronik und Totenbuch des Klosters Wienhausen*, ed. Horst Appuhn (Wienhausen: Kloster Wienhausen, 1986), 28. See also Hamburger's insightful treatment of the series of drawings made by sisters at the Observant convent of St. Walburga in Eichstätt around 1500, *Nuns as Artists: The Visual Culture of a Medieval Convent*, California Studies in the History of Art 37 (Berkeley and Los Angeles: University of California Press, 1997). Tapestry making was, as Hamburger points out, difficult, costly, and less com- mon than is supposed; Hamburger, *Nuns*, 37. Nevertheless, in 1500 the nuns at Lüne began producing

them. See Riggert-Mindermann, "Ebstorf," 204. Other centers from which a substantial number of fifteenth-century weavings and tapestries survive are Wienhausen (even earlier famed for its weaving), Isenhagen, Ebstorf, and St. Katharina in Nuremberg, which had the largest and most famous manufacture of the period. At Fischbeck an historical tapestry was made to preserve the cloister's own foundation history in picture form. See Erich Kittel, *Kloster and Stift St. Marien in Lemgo, 1265–1965. Festschrift anlässlich des 700-jährigen Bestehens* (Detmold: Naturwissenschaftlicher und historischer Verein für das Land Lippe, 1965), 22–23.

76. Leipzig, Deutsches Buch-und Schriftmuseum, Kl. I 42; Nuremberg, Stadtbibliothek, MS Cent V, 10a, fol. 3r; MS Cent V, App. 34, p–w; MS Cent III, 86; and MS Cent VI, 43g. See Karl Fischer, "Die Buchmalerei in den beiden Dominikanerklöstern Nürnbergs" (Ph.D. diss., University of Erlangen, 1928), 69–80.

77. Karlsruhe, Badische Landesbibliothek, MS Thennenbach 4; Deutsches Buch- und Schriftmuseum, Leipzig, Klemm Collection MS I, 104. Max Miller asserts that she did not go to Strasburg. See Max Miller, *Die Söflinger Briefe und das Klarissenkloster Söflingen bei Ulm im Spätmittelalter* (Würzburg: Triltsch, 1940), 206 n. 24; David Brett-Evans, "Sibilla von Bondorf—Ein Nachtrag," *Zeitschrift für deutsche Philologie* 86 (1967), Sonderheft: 91–98; Detlef Zinke and Angela Karasch, *Verborgene Pracht: Mittelalterliche Buchkunst aus acht Jahrhunderten in Freiburger Sammlungen* (Lindenberg: Fink, 2002), 116–19; *Clara und Franciscus von Assisi: Eine Spätmittelalterliche alemannische Legende der Magdalena Steimerin, mit 8 Miniaturen aus der Pergamenthandschrift der Badischen Landesbibliothek Karlsruhe*, afterward Christian von Heusinger (Constance: Simon and Koch, 1959); Clara Bruins, *Chiara d'Assisi come 'altera Maria': Le miniature della vita di Santa Chiara nel manoscritto Tennenbach-4 di Karlsruhe*, Iconographia Franciscana 12 (Rome: Instituto storico dei Cappuccini, 1999); and Rainer Kößling, ed., *Leben und Legende der heiligen Elisabeth. Nach Dietrich von Apolda. Mit 14 Miniaturen der Handschrift von 1481* (Leipzig: Insel, 1999).

78. Christian von Heusinger, "Studien zur oberrheinischen Buchmalerei und Graphik im Spätmittelalter" (Ph.D. diss., University of Freiburg, 1953), 70–110; idem, "Spätmittelalterliche Buchmalerei in oberrheinischen Frauenklöstern," *Zeitschrift für die Geschichte des Oberrheins* 107 (1959): 160.

79. Monika Costard, "Predigthandschriften der Schwestern vom gemeinsamen Leben. Spätmittelalterliche Predigtüberlieferung in der Bibliothek des Klosters Nazareth in Geldern," in *Die deutsche Predigt im Mittelalter*, ed. Volker Mertens and Hans-Jochen Schiewer (Tübingen: Niemeyer, 1993), 211; Hans-Jochen Schiewer and Volker Mertens, *Repertorium der ungedruckten deutschsprachigen Predigten des Mittelalters. Der Berliner Bestand. Vol. I: Die Handschriften aus dem Straßburger Dominikanerinnenkloster St. Nikolaus in undis und benachbarte Provenienzen* (Tübingen: Niemeyer, in press).

80. Hasebrink, "Tischlesung," 205.

81. Ibid., 209. For a sample list of guest preachers at St. Katharina see Peter Renner, "Spätmittelalterliche Klosterpredigten aus Nürnberg," *Archiv für Kulturgeschichte* 41 (1959): 209–17.

82. Hans-Jochen Schiewer, "Universities and Vernacular Preaching. The Case of Vienna, Heidelberg, and Basle," in *Medieval Sermons and Society: Cloister, City, University: Proceedings of International Symposia at Kalamazoo and New York*, ed. Jacqueline Hamesse (Louvain-la-Neuve: Fédération Internationale des Instituts d'études médiévales, 1998), 393. These sermons are contained in MSS Staatsbibliothek, Berlin, germ. quart. 206; MS germ. quart. 166 (both from St. Nicolaus in undis, Strasbourg), and MS germ. fol. 741 (from cloister Medlingen, reformed by sisters from Schönensteinbach.)

83. Costard, for example, characterizes sermons intended for an educated convent audience as focused on spritual themes rather than on miracles and saints' legends that were more prominent in parish sermons. See Monika Costard, "Zwischen Mystik und Moraldidaxe. Deutsche Predigten des Fraterherren Johannes Veghe und des Dominikaners Konrad Schlatter in Frauenklöstern des 15. Jahrhunderts," *Ons geestelijk erf* 69 (1995): 247.

84. Rüther and Schiewer, "Predigthandschriften," 179.

85. Berlin, Staatsbibliothek, MS germ. quart. 1069, fols. 1–240; Wolfgang Müller, "Die Villinger Frauenklöster des Mittelalters und der Neuzeit," in *200 Jahre Kloster St. Ursula, Villingen*, ed. Helmut Heinrich and Gisela Sattler (Villingen: Kloster St. Ursula, n.d.), 23.

86. Schriesheim (Heidelberg), Sammlung Eis, Cod. 114, fols. 39r–253v; Renner, "Klosterpredigten," 203.

87. Inserted at the end of the second main point of chapter 33 is the comment "up to this point the sermons were written down from Dr. Kaysersberg's mouth by Sister Susanna Hörwart of Augsburg, prioress of the Penitants [of St. Mary Magdalene] here in Strasbourg, . . . Thereafter, they were diligently continued to the end by Sister Ursel Stingel." Johannes Geiler von Kaysersberg, *Sämtliche Werke,* ed. Gerhard Bauer (Berlin: de Gruyter, 1995), 3:680.

88. Ebstorf Klosterbibliothek, Cod. VI 5, fols. 1–347; Cod. VI g, fols. 1–206; Borchling, "Ebstorf," 383.

89. Zumkeller, "Weissfrauenkloster," 253; see note 72 above.

90. Costard, "Mystik," 238, 241, 243; Paul-Gerhard Völker, "Die Überlieferungsformen mittelalterlicher deutscher Predigten," *Zeitschrift für deutsches Altertum und deutsche Literatur* 92 (1963): 219.

91. Dietrich Schmidtke, "Zur Geschichte der Kölner Predigt im Spätmittelalter: Einige neue Predigernamen," in *Festschrift für Ingeborg Schröber zum 65. Geburtstag,* ed. Dietrich Schmidtke and Helga Schüppert, Beiträge zur Geschichte der deutschen Sprache und Literatur 95 (Tübingen: Niemeyer, 1973, 340; and Alison I. Beach, "Female Scribes of Twelfth-Century Bavaria" (Ph.D. diss., Columbia, 1996).

92. Hamburg, Universitätsbibliothek, Cod. theol. 12°2205 (excerpts of sermons of Johannes Tauler preached at St. Gertrud, Cologne, fourteenth-century manuscript); Jutta Prieur, *Das Kölner Dominikanerinnenkloster St. Gertrud am Neumarkt,* Kölner Schriften zu Geschichte und Kultur (Cologne: dme-Verlag, 1983), 405. See also Philipp Strauch, "Kölner Klosterpredigten des 13. Jahrhunderts," *Jahrbuch des Vereins für Niederdeutsche Sprachforschung* 37 (1911): 21–48.

93. Einsiedeln, Stiftsbibliothek, MS 277, fol. 221r–221v; Wolfgang Stammler, "Tauler in Basel," in *Johannes Tauler: Ein deutscher Mystiker. Gedenkschrift zum 600. Todestag,* ed. Ephrem Filthaut (Essen: Driewer, 1961), 75.

94. Berlin, Staatsbibliothek, MS germ. quart. 206, fols. 37v–314v; Hornung, "Sudermann," 2:25–27. Since Agnes heard these preachers in different churches of Strasbourg, she must either have recorded them before she entered the cloister or perhaps entered as a lay sister since they were allowed to go in and out. Katherina Gurdelers's collection of 74 sermons and sermon summaries is found in Universitätsbibliothek, Hamburg, Cod. theol. 2065. See also Werner Wegstein, "Katherina Gurdelers," in *Die deutsche Literatur des Mittelalters: Verfasserlexikon,* ed. Kurt Ruh et al. (Berlin: de Gruyter, 1981), 3: cols. 326–37.

95. Wolfgang Stammler, "Predigt," in *Deutsche Philologie im Aufriß,* 3 vols., 2d rev., ed. Wolfgang Stammler (Berlin: Schmidt, 1952–1957), 2:982–83.

96. Völker, "Überlieferungsformen," 215–16.

97. Ibid., 215, 223. See also Hans-Jochen Schiewer, "Spuren von Mündlichkeit in der mittelalterlichen Predigtüberlieferung. Ein Plädoyer für exemplarisches und beschreibend-interpretierendes Edieren," *Editio* 6 (1992): 65–66, 68.

98. Völker, "Überlieferungsformen," 224–25; Jean Leclercq, *Recueil d'Etudes sur Saint Bernard et ses écrits,* vol. 1 (Rome: Edizioni di storia e letteratura, 1962), 193–212. But see Christopher Holdsworth, "Were the Sermons of St. Bernard on the Song of Songs ever Preached?" in *Medieval Monastic Preaching,* ed. Carolyn Muessig (Leiden: Brill, 1998), 295–318.

99. Berlin, Staatsbibliothek, MS germ. quart. 22; Völker, Überlieferungsformen," 217. See also the transcriber's comment in Staatsbibliothek Berlin, MS germ. oct. 63, fol. 48r–48v. In introducing her rewritten transcript of a sermon by Geiler von Kaysersberg (c. 1500), this sister at St. Nicolaus in undis, Strasbourg, wrote earnestly, "But as different from each other as a painted person is from a living one, just as different is the sound of inanimate writing compared to the living words that he spoke. For the grace and fire of the Holy Spirit that accompanied the living words cannot be expressed in writing. Nevertheless, at the request of devout hearts, this lesson has been written down as well as possible by this frail and simple person just as she heard it from his mouth."

100. Robert G. Warnock, ed., *Die Predigten Johannes Paulis,* Münchener Texte und Untersuchungen zur Literatur des deutschen Mittelalters 26 (Munich: Beck, 1970), 3. See above note 85.

101. Schiewer, "Mündlichkeit," 66–67.

102. Munich, Bayerisches Nationalmuseum, MS 3801; Universitätsbibliothek Augsburg (Fürstliche Öttingen-Wallersteinsche Sammlung) MS III.1 qu.41. See Völker, "Überlieferungsformen," 218.

103. "[S]oe sat sij ende schrief hem dat uutten monde in hoer tafel," Thomas Mertens, "Postum Auteurschap de Collaties van Johannes Brinckerinck," in *600 Jahr Kapittel van Windesheim*, ed. A. J. Hendrikman et al., Middeleeuwse Studies 12 (Nijmegen: Centrum voor Middeleeuwse Studies, Katholieke Universiteit Nijmegen, 1996), 87; *Van den doechden der vuriger ende stichtiger sustern van Diepenveen, Handschrift D*, ed. D. A. Brinkerink (Leiden: Sijthoff, 1904), 253–54.

104. Curt Dewischeit, *Georg Rörer, ein Geschwindschreiber Luthers* (Berlin: Schrey, 1899), 1–11; Laurenz Schneider and G. Blauert, *Geschichte der deutschen Kurzschrift* (Wolfenbüttel: Heckner, 1936), 43–46.

105. Gerrit Cornelius Zieleman, "Das Studium der deutschen und niederländischen Predigten des Mittelalters," in *Sô predigent etelîche: Beiträge zur deutschen und niederländischen Predigt im Mittelalter*, ed. Kurt Otto Seidel, Göppinger Arbeiten zur Germanistik 378 (Göppingen: Kümmerle, 1982), 19.

106. Holdsworth, "St. Bernard," 313–16.

107. Nuremberg, Stadtbibliothek Cod. cent. VII, 13, fols. 71r–74r; Zentralbibliothek Zürich, Cod. D 231 (638), fols. 163r–194r; Kurt Ruh, "Heinrich Riß," in *Die deutsche Literatur des Mittelalters: Verfasserlexikon*, ed. Kurt Ruh et al. (Berlin: de Gruyter, 1992), 8: cols. 83–86.

108. Kurt Ruh, "Deutsche Predigtbücher des Mittelalters," *Vestigia bibliae* 3 (1981): 12–13.

109. Zieleman, "Predigten," 19, 21.

110. Mertens, "Collatio," 177–79; John Van Engen, "The Virtues, the Brothers, and the Schools," *Revue Bénédictine* 98 (1988): 189.

111. "Die Giessenhof'sche Chronik des Klosters Inzigkofen," ed. Theodor Dreher, *Freiburger Katholisches Kirchenblatt* 38 (1894): cols. 476–77.

112. [Ernst,] *Chronik*, 40.

113. Deventer, Stads-en Athenaeumbibliotheek, MS Suppl. 198 (101 E 26), fol. 81v; Mertens, "Collatio," 177 n. 82, 179.

114. Brussels, Koninklijke Bibliotheek, MS 4367–4368, fol. 3r–3v; Zieleman, "Studium," 17, 20, 38–39. See also Mertens, "Ghostwriting," in press.

115. Zieleman, "Studium," 17.

116. Schiewer, "Mündlichkeit, 66–67; Berlin, Staatsbibliothek, MS germ. quart. 206, fol. 103r; printed in Volker Mertens and Hans-Jochen Schiewer, "Erschließung einer Gattung: Edition, Katalogisieriug und Abbildung der deutschsprachigen Predigt des Mittelalters," *Editio* 4 (1990): 93–111; at 107–11.

117. The inventory of German sermons in the Staatsbibliothek Preußischer Kulturbesitz, Berlin, alone consists of some 3,000, of which approximately 2,100 are unpublished. See Hans-Jochen Schiewer, "German Sermons in the Middle Ages," in *The Sermon*, ed. Beverly Kienzle, trans Debra Stoudt. Typologie des sources du moyen âge occidental 81–83 (Turnhout, Belgium: Brepols, 2000), 886. Currently the DFG-Forschungsprojekt "Repertorium der ungedruckten deutschsprachigen Predigten des Mittelalters," under the direction of Professors Volker Mertens (Freie Universität Berlin) and Hans-Jochen Schiewer (Universität Freiburg), is cataloging them and has completed volume I: *Die Handschriften aus dem Straßburger Dominikanerinnenkloster St. Nikolaus in undis und benachbarte Provenienzen* (Tübingen: Niemeyer, in press). See also Volker Mertens and Hans-Jochen Schiewer, "Erschliessung einer Gattung: Edition, Katalogisierung und Abbildung der deutschsprachigen Predigt des Mittelalters," *Editio* 4 (1990): 93–111.

Moreover, comments such as those prefacing a sermon preached by Geiler von Kaysersberg at the cloister of St. Nicolaus in undis seems unequivocal. Here, a sister writes," The grace and fire of the Holy Spirit that accompanied the living words cannot be expressed in writing. Nevertheless, at the request of devout hearts, this lesson has been written down as well as possible by this frail and simple person, just as she heard it from his mouth." Berlin, Staatsbibliothek, MS germ. oct. 63, fol. 48v.

118. Thomas Mertens, "Ghostwriting Sisters: The Preservation of Dutch Sermons of Father Con-

fessors in the Fifteenth and Early Sixteenth Century," in *Seeing and Knowing: Women and learning in medieval Europe 1200–1600* , ed. Anneke Mulder-Bakker (Turnhout: Brepols, in press). I am grateful to Professor Mertens for sending me advance copy from his forthcoming article.

119. Mertens, "Ghostwriting," in press; Koninklijke Bibliotheek, Brussels, MS II 298 (cat. 1997), sermons of Jan Storm reconstructed by Janne Colijns.

120. Vogler, *St. Katharina*, 76.

121. [Magdalena Kremer,] "Wie diß loblich Kloster zu Sant Johannes Baptisten zu Kirchen under deck prediger-ordens reformiert ist worden und durch woelich personen," in *Geschichte des Herzogtums Wuerttemberg unter der Regierung der Graven,* ed. Christian Friedrich Sattler, 2d ed. (Tübingen: Reiss, 1773–77), 4:159.

122. St. Gall, Stiftsbibliothek, MS St. Katharina, Wil, "Schwesternbuch," fol. 1r.

123. [Kremer,] "Wie diß loblich Kloster," 205.

124. [Anne Roede,] "Chronik des Klosters Herzebrock," ed. Franz Flaskamp, *Osnabrücker Mitteilungen* 74 (1967): 55.

125. Hamburger, *Visual,* 67.

126. Gerhard Taddey, *Das Kloster Heiningen von der Gründung bis zur Aufhebung,* Veröffentlichungen des Max-Planck-Instituts für Geschichte 14 (Göttingen: Vandenhoeck and Ruprecht, 1966), 11.

127. Thomas Head, "Hrosvith's 'Primordia' and the Historical Tradition of Monastic Communities," in *Hrosvit of Gandersheim: "Rara avis in Saxonia?"* ed. Katharina M. Wilson, Medieval and Renaissance Monograph Series 7 (Ann Arbor, Mich.: Medieval and Renaissance Collegium, 1987), 144. Head cites Natalie Davis, "Gender and Genre: Women as Historical Writers (1400–1820)," in *Beyond their Sex. Learned Women of the European Past,* ed. Patricia Labalme (New York: New York University Press, 1980), 153–82.

128. Edeltraud Klueting, *Das Bistum Osnabrück 1: Das Kanonissenstift und Benediktinerinnenkloster Herzebrock,* Germania Sacra n.F. 21 (Berlin: de Gruyter, 1986), 255; Uffmann, "Rosengarten," 215.

129. "Anno dni MCCL an Sant Martins tag da ist dis Closter Pfullingen an gefangen worden," ed. Max Straganz, in "Duae relationes circa Monasterium Brixinense O. Clar.," *Archivum Franciscanum Historicum* 6 (1913): 543.

130. Herrgott, "Necrologium," 62.

131. Augsburg, Staatsarchiv, MS Kloster Maria Maihingen MüB 1, fol. 2r; Tore Nyberg, *Dokumente und Untersuchungen zur inneren Geschichte der drei Brigittenklöster Bayerns 1420–1570,* 2 vols., Quellen und Erörterungen zur bayerischen Geschichte, n.F. 26 (Munich: Beck, 1972–74), 2:147; idem, "Das Hausbuch des Klosters Maihingen," *Jahrbuch des Vereins für Augsburger Bistumsgeschichte* (1971): 142.

132. Augsburg, Staatsarchiv, MS Kloster Maria Maihingen MüB 1, fol. 53v; Nyberg, "Hausbuch," 161.

133. Augsburg, MS Kloster Maihingen MüB 1, fol. 138r.

134. Nyberg, "Hausbuch," 162–63.

135. [Anna Roede,] "Anna Roede's spätere Chronik von Herzebrock," ed. Franz Flaskamp, *Jahrbuch der Gesellschaft für Niedersächsische Kirchengeschichte* 68 (1970): 88, 94–95, 123.

136. [Roede,] "Chronik," 55. With a similar concern for authenticity, the chronicler at Maihingen asserts, "this book is compiled from many written texts and from pious, truthful old sisters . . . also from the witness of the old first sisters of our [Bridgettine] convent [founded 1481] who were themselves present and heard and saw many things," MS Kloster Maihingen MüB 1, fol. 2r.

137. "Anno dni MCCL an Sant Martins tag da ist dis Closter Pfullingen an gefangen worden," ed. Straganz, in "Duae relationes," 543.

138. Constance Proksch, *Klosterreform und Geschichtsschreibung im Spätmittelalter* (Cologne: Böhlau, 1994), 11, 206; Uffmann, "Rosengarten," 215.

139. Hans-Werner Goetz, "Zum Geschichtsbewußtsein in der alemannisch-schweizerischen Klosterchronik des hohen Mittelalters (11.–13. Jh.)," *Deutsches Archiv für Erforschung des Mittelalters* 44 (1988): 462, 478–79, 485–86; Proksch, *Klosterreform,* 207, 280–81.

140. [Roede,] "Spätere Chronik," 124; Borchling, "Litterarisches," 369.

141. Prieur, *St. Gertrud,* 113.

142. Wybren Scheepsma, "'For hereby I hope to rouse some to piety': Books of Sisters from Convents and Sister-Houses Associated with the 'Devotio moderna' in the Low Countries," in *Women, the Book, and the Godly,* 2 vols., ed. Lesley Smith and Jane Taylor (Cambridge: Brewer, 1995), 1:31.

143. *Schwesternbuch,* ed. Bollman and Staubach, 17.

144. Scheepsma, "Books of Sisters," 28, 34–35, 39.

145. Deventer, Stads- of Athenaeumbibliotheek, MS Suppl. 198 [101 E 26], fols. 1r, 388r. (This is not the 1534 text edited by D. A. Brinkerink, but an unedited 1524 version with additions probably by Sister Griet Essink.); Scheepsma, "Books of Sisters," 37.

146. *Hier beginnen sommige stichtige punten van onsen oelden zusteren,* ed. Dirk de Man (The Hague: Nijhoff, 1919), 7; Scheepsma, "Books of Sisters," 35. See also John van Engen, *Devotio Moderna: Basic Writings* (Mahwah, N.Y.: Paulist Press, 1988), 122.

147. *Schwesternbuch,* ed. Bollman and Staubach, 18, 22.

148. See Bollmann, "Weibliche Diskurse: Die Schwesternbücher der *devotio moderna* zwischen Biographie und geistlicher Konversation," in *Kultur, Geschlecht, Körper,* ed. Genus–Münsteraner Arbeitskreis für Gender Studies, 241–84 (Münster: Agenda, 1999), and idem forthcoming dissertation, University of Groningen.

149. Thomas Mertens, "The Modern Devotion and Innovation in Middle Dutch Literature," in *Medieval Dutch Literature in its European Context,* ed. Erik Kooper, Cambridge Studies in Medieval Literature (New York: Cambridge University Press, 1995), 232–36.

150. Scheepsma, *Deemoed,* 381.

151. Gertrud Jaron Lewis, *By Women, for Women, about Women: The Sister-Books of Fourteenth-Century Germany* (Toronto: Pontifical Institute of Medieval Studies, 1996), 286–89.

152. Werner Williams-Krapp, "Dise ding sind dennoch nit ware zeichen der heiligkeit.' Zur Bewertung mystischer Erfahrung im 15. Jahrhundert," *Zeitschrift für Literaturwissenschaft und Linguistik* 20 (1990): 61–62.

Chapter 6

1. H. Pyritz, *Die Minneburg, nach der Heidelberger Pergamenthandschrift (CPG 455),* Deutsche Texte des Mittelalters 43 (Berlin: Akademie, 1950), lxxii. Cited in Otto Langer, *Mystische Erfahrung und spirituelle Theologie. Zu Meister Eckharts Auseinandersetzung mit der Frauenfrömmigkeit seiner Zeit,* Münchener Texte und Untersuchungen zur deutschen Literatur des Mittelalters 91 (Munich: Artemis, 1987), 13, 48; and Josef Quint, "Mystik," in *Reallexikon der deutschen Literaturgeschichte,* ed. Paul Merker, Wolfgang Stammler et al., 2d ed. (Berlin: de Gruyter, 1965), 2:550.

2. Quint, "Mystik," 2:550.

3. Langer, *Mystische Erfahrung,* 10, 12, 16; Caroline Walker Bynum, *Holy Feast and Holy Fast* (Berkeley and Los Angeles: University of California Press, 1987), 209; Georg Kunze, "Studien zu den Nonnenviten des deutschen Mittelalters" (Ph.D. diss., University of Hamburg, 1952), 54; and Walter Blank, "Die Nonnenviten des 14. Jahrhunderts. Eine Studie zur hagiographischen Literatur des Mittelalters unter besonderer Berücksichtigung der Visionen und ihrer Lichtphänomene" (Ph.D. diss, University of Freiburg, 1962), 115. See also Gabriele L. Strauch, "Mechthild von Magdeburg and the Category 'Frauenmystik'," in *Women as Protagonists and Poets in the German Middle Ages,* ed. Albrecht Classen, Göppinger Arbeiten zur Germanistik 528 (Göppingen: Kümmerle, 1991), 171–86.

4. [Anna von Munzingen,] "Die Chronik der Anna von Munzingen. Nach der ältesten Abschrift mit Einleitung und Beilagen," ed. J. König, *Freiburger Diözesan-Archiv* 13 (1880): 150–51.

5. Giles Constable, *Attitudes Toward Self-Inflicted Suffering in the Middle Ages* (Brookline, Mass: Hellenic College Press, 1982), 9, 14. Georg Kunze and Engelbert Krebs point to male vitae containing self abnegations such as pouring cold water on food in order to diminish the enjoyment of it and phenomena like levitation. See Kunze, "Nonnenviten," 163; and Engelbert Krebs, "Die Mystik in Adelhausen. Eine vergleichende Studie über die 'Chronik' der Anna von Munzingen und die thauma-

tographishe Literatur des 13. und 14. Jahrhunderts als Beitrag zur Mystik im Predigerorden," in *Festgabe, Heinrich Finke*, ed. Gottfried Buschbell (Münster: Aschendorff, 1904), 98, 99.

6. Wilhelm Oehl, *Deutsche Mystikerbriefe des Mittelalters, 1100–1550* (Munich: Georg Müller, 1931), 287–88; and Jeffrey Hamburger, *The Visual and the Visionary. Art and Female Spirituality in Late Medieval Germany* (New York: Zone Books, 1998), 303.

7. Peter Dinzelbacher, "Die 'Vita et Revelationes' der Wiener Begine Agnes Blannbekin (d. 1315) im Rahmen der Viten- und Offenbarungsliteratur ihrer Zeit," in *Frauenmystik im Mittelalter*, ed. Peter Dinzelbacher and Dieter R. Bauer (Ostfildern: Schwabenverlag, 1985), 165.

8. Hieronymus Wilms, *Das Beten der Mystikerinnen, dargestellt nach den Chroniken der Dominikaner-innenklöster zu Adelhausen, Dießenhofen, Engeltal, Kirchberg, Oetenbach, Töß und Unterlinden*, Quellen und Forschungen zur Geschichte des Dominikanerordens in Deutschland 11 (Leipzig: Harrassowitz, 1918), 6.

9. Siegfried Ringler, "Die Rezeption mittelalterlicher Frauenmystik als wissenschaftliches Problem dargestellt am Werk der Christine Ebner," in *Frauenmystik im Mittelalter*, ed. Peter Dinzelbacher and Dieter R. Bauer (Ostfildern: Schwabenverlag, 1990), 197.

10. Siegfried Ringler, *Viten- und Offenbarungsliteratur in Frauenklöstern des Mittelalters. Quellen und Studien*, Münchener Texte und Untersuchungen zur deutschen Literatur des Mittelalters 72 (Munich: Artemis, 1980), 9, 11.

11. Blank, "Nonnenviten," 87; Ringler, "Rezeption," 191; Kunze, "Studien," 104.

12. Joan Ferrante, *To the Glory of Her Sex: Women's Roles in the Composition of Medieval Texts* (Bloomington: Indiana University Press, 1997), 140.

13. Glente, "Mystikerinnen," 252. See also Oehl, *Mystikerbriefe*, 195.

14. Marilyn Oliva, *The Convent and Community in Late Medieval England: Female Monasteries in the Diocese of Norwich, 1350–1540* (Woodbridge, Suffolk: Boydell, 1998), 213; and Claire Sahlin, "The Prophetess as Preacher: Birgitte of Sweden and the Voice of Prophecy," *Medieval Sermon Studies* 40 (1997), 29.

15. Anna Groh Seeholtz, *Friends of God: Practical Mystics of the Fourteenth Century* (1934; repr. New York: AMS Press, 1970), 132; and Leonard P. Hindsley, *The Mystics of Engelthal: Writings from a Medieval Monastery* (New York: St. Martin's Press, 1998), 71.

16. Ellen Ross, *The Grief of God: Images of the Suffering Jesus in Medieval England* (Oxford: Oxford University Press, 1997), 13, 126, 128, 138.

17. Bynum, *Feast*, 200, 208–9, 218.

18. Ibid, *Feast*, 208; Ross, *Grief*, 138; and Jo Ann Kay McNamara, "The Need to Give: Suffering and Female Sanctity in the Middle Ages," in *Images of Sainthood in Medieval Europe*, ed. Timea Szell (Ithaca: Cornell University Press, 1991), 199–221.

19. Bynum, *Feast*, 206.

20. Herbert Grundmann, *Religious Movements in the Middle Ages: The Historical Links between Heresy, the Mendicant Orders, and the Women's Religious Movement in the Twelfth and Thirteenth Century, with the Historical Foundations of German Mysticism*, trans. Stephen Rowen (Notre Dame: Notre Dame University Press, 1995), 134.

21. Gabrielle Spiegel, "Theory into Practice: Reading Medieval Chronicles," in *The Medieval Chronicle: Proceedings of the 1st International Conference on the Medieval Chronicle*, Driebergen/Utrecht, 13–16 July 1996, ed. Erik Kooper (Amsterdam: Rodopi, 1999), 5.

22. Mechthild of Magdeburg, *The Flowing Light of the Godhead*, trans. Frank Tobin (New York: Paulist Press, 1998). See also Sara S. Poor, "Mechthild von Magdeburg, Gender and the 'Unlearned Tongue,'" *Journal of Medieval and Early Modern Studies* 31 (2001): 213–50.

23. Werner Williams-Krapp, " 'Dise ding sind dennoch nit ware zeichen der heiligkeit.' Zur Bewertung mystischer Erfahrung im 15. Jahrhundert," *Zeitschrift für Literaturwissenschaft und Linguistik* 20 (1990): 63–69. For Johannes Meyer's seven criteria for distinguishing true from false visions, see *Das Buch der Reformacio Predigerordens*, ed. Benedictus M. Reichert, Quellen und Forschungen zur Geschichte des Dominikanerordens in Deutschland 2 and 3 (Leipzig: Harrassowitz, 1908–09), 2:57–61. In

his forward to the St. Katharinental Sisterbook, Meyer concludes with the words, "But my dear Sisters, I have confidence in you, that you can harvest the flowers from the grass and like the bee extract the nourishment from the flower." *Das Katharinentaler Schwesternbuch. Untersuchung, Edition, Kommentar,* ed. Ruth Meyer, Münchener Texte und Untersuchungen 104 (Tübingen: Niemeyer, 1995), 141.

24. Johannes Tauler, for example, had corresponded with and visited Margareta Ebner at Medingen. See Manfred Weitlauff, "Margareta Ebner," in *Die deutsche Literatur des Mittelalters: Verfasserlexikon,* ed. Kurt Ruh et al. (Berlin: de Gruyter, 1980), 2:304; and Oehl, *Mystikerbriefe,* 349. John Coakley, "Friars as Confidants of Holy Women in Medieval Dominican Hagiography," in *Images of Sainthood in Medieval Europe,* ed. Renate Blumenfeld-Kosinski and Timea Szell (Ithaca: Cornell University Press, 1991), 222–46; and idem, "Gender and the Authority of the Friars. The Significance of Holy Women for Thirteenth-Century Franciscans and Dominicans," *Church History* 60 (1991): 460.

25. Caroline Walker Bynum, *Jesus as Mother: Studies in the Spirituality of the High Middle Ages* (Berkeley and Los Angeles: University of California Press, 1982), 172–73.

26. Wybren Scheepsma, *Deemoed en devotie: De koorvrouwen van Windesheim en hun geschriften* (Amsterdam: Prometheus, 1997), 385.

27. Spiegel, "Theory," 2, 9.

28. Augsburg, Staatsarchiv, MS Kloster Maria Maihingen MüB 1, fol. 2r; Tore Nyberg, *Dokumente und Untersuchungen zur inneren Geschichte der drei Brigittenklöster Bayerns 1420–1570,* 2 vols., Quellen und Erörterungen zur bayerischen Geschichte, n.F. 26 (Munich: Beck, 1972–74), 2:147.

29. [Anna Roede,] "Anna Roedes spätere Chronik von Herzebrock," ed. Franz Flaskamp, *Jahrbuch der Gesellschaft für Niedersächsische Kirchengeschichte* 68 (1970): 114; and Gudrun Gleba, *Reformpraxis und materielle Kultur: Westfälische Frauenklöster in Mittelalter* (Husum: Matthiesen, 2000), 68.

30. [Roede,] "Spätere Chronik," ed. Flaskamp, 119–20, 121–23.

31. "Innumerabiles grates . . ." [Chronicle of Ebstorf, 1487], ed. Conrad Borchling, in appendix to "Litterarisches und geistiges Leben in Kloster Ebstorf am Ausgange des Mittelalters," *Zeitschrift des historischen Vereins für Niedersachsen* 4 (1905): 396–407, here 401–2.

32. [Roede,] "Spätere Chronik," ed. Flaskamp, 124. Other qualities of an ideal reform abbess are portrayed in the description of Jutteldis von Bevern who headed the group of sisters sent from Herzebrock with a mandate to reform Gertrudenberg in 1475. Parts of a lost chronicle, written in the early sixteenth century by a contemporary of Jutteldis, are preserved by citations in Johann Itel Sandhoff's chronicle of Gertrudenberg from 1759. Sandhoff asserts that he is citing "word for word" a text written by "a pious sister who lived at the time of [Abbess] Jutteldis," Gleba, *Reformpraxis,* 69, 121; Hans-Hermann Breuer, ed. *Die Gertrudenberger Chronik des Johann Itel Sandhoff vom Jahre 1759* (Osnabrück: Schöningh, 1939), 2. The chronicle narrates how Jutteldis and her party, together with the three sisters who remained at the start of the reform, energetically undertook the revitalization of the cloister. Jutteldis is praised as a beautiful and highly intelligent noblewoman who "conversed in a gracious manner with persons of both high and low rank." She is described as strict but motherly, diplomatic, and not affected or misled in her decision making by "envious persons or prattlers;" Gleba, *Reformpraxis,* 124–25; Breuer, *Gertrudenberger,* 47. The laudatory account goes on to relate a miracle of multiplication of grain and bread for the poor. Jutteldis, also capable in business matters, likewise multiplied the cloister's monetary holdings through wise land purchases and her own inheritance. Portrayed as an exemplary manager, she is credited with making improvements to the cloister's buildings without placing the house in debt "as before the reform."

33. *Chronik und Totenbuch des Klosters Wienhausen,* ed. Horst Appuhn (Wienhausen: Kloster Wienhausen, 1986), 19–29. On the date and transmission of this chronicle, see Chapter 4 of this study, note 57.

34. On the monastic chronicle as a literary form see Hans Patze, "Klostergründung und Klosterchronik," *Blätter für deutsche Landesgeschichte* 113 (1977): 89–121; Volker Honemann, "Klostergründungsgeschichten," in *Deutsche Literatur des Mittelalters: Verfasserlexikon,* ed. Kurt Ruh et al. (Berlin: de Gruyter, 1983), 4: cols. 1239–1247; Hans-Werner Goetz, "Zum Geschichtsbewußtsein in der alemannisch-schweizerischen Klosterchronik des hohen Mittelalters (11.–13. Jh)," *Deutsches Archiv für Erfor-*

schung des Mittelalters 44 (1988): 455–88; Klaus Schreiner, "Verschriftlichung als Faktor monastischer Reform. Funktionen von Schriftlichkeit im Ordenswesen des hohen und späten Mittelalters," in *Pragmatische Schriftlichkeit im Mittelalter,* ed. Hagen Keller, 37–75, Münstersche Mittelalter-Schriften 65 (Munich: Fink, 1992); Constance Proksch, *Klosterreform und Geschichtsschreibung im Spätmittelalter* (Cologne: Böhlau, 1994); Rolf Sprandel, *Chronisten als Zeitzeugen. Forschungen zur spätmittelalterlichen Geschichtsschreibung in Deutschland* (Vienna: Böhlau, 1994); See also Natalie Z. Davis, "Gender and Genre: Women as Historical Writers (1400–1820)," in *Beyond Their Sex: Learned Women of the European Past,* ed. Patricia Labalme, 153–82 (New York: New York University Press, 1980); Gabrielle Spiegel, *The Past as Text: The Theory and Practice of Medieval Historiography* (Baltimore, Md.: Johns Hopkins Uinversity Press, 1997); idem, "Theory into Practice: Reading Medieval Chronicles," in *The Medieval Chronicle: Proceedings of the 1st International Conference on the Medieval Chronicle,* Driebergen/Utrecht 13–16 July, 1996, ed. Erik Kooper, 1–12 (Amsterdam: Rodopi, 1999); Charlotte Woodford, *Nuns as Historians in Early Modern Germany* (Oxford: Clarendon Press, 2002).

35. Augsburg, Staatsarchiv, MS Kloster Maria Maihingen MüB 1, fols. 138v–139r. See also Nyberg, *Brigittenklöster,* 2:252–54.

36. Sophia von Stolberg's chronicle of Neu-Helfta lists the family and names of the founding donors, so that the sisters will know them. See Hans Patze, "Klostergründung und Klosterchronik," *Blätter für Landesgeschichte* 113 (1977): 115. Similarly, Anna Roede begins her first chronicle of Herzebrock with Charlemagne and the bishops of Osnabrück, on the model of Erwin Ertman's *Osnabrücker Bischofschronik,* perhaps in order to connect the cloister with illustrious figures of the past. See [Anna Roede,] "Chronik des Klosters Herzebrock," ed. Franz Flaskamp, *Osnabrücker Mitteilungen* 74 (1967): 38–39.

37. [Anna Roede,] "Spätere Chronik,"ed. Flaskamp, 109.

38. Ibid., 97.

39. [Magdalena Kremer,] "Wie diß loblich closter zu Sant Johannes Baptisten zu Kirchen under deck prediger-ordens reformiert ist worden und durch woelich personen," ed. Christian Friedrich Sattler, in *Geschichte des Herzogtums Wuerttemberg unter der Regierung der Graven,* 2d ed. (Tübingen: Reiss, 1773–77), 4:180–81.

40. "Sorores karissime . . ." [Ebstorf reform account, c. 1490], ed. Conrad Borchling, in appendix to "Litterarisches und geististiges Leben in Kloster Ebstorf am Ausgange des Mittelalters," *Zeitschrift des historischen Vereins für Niedersachsen* 4 (1905): 388–96, here 390, 395.

41. [Anna Roede,] "Spätere Chronik," ed. Flaskamp, 124.

42. Peter Dronke, *Women Writers of the Middle Ages: A Critical Study of Texts from Perpetua (d. 203) to Marguerite Porette (d. 1310)* (Cambridge: Cambridge University Press, 1984), x.

43. Robyn Warhol and Diane Price Herndl, eds., *Feminisms: An Anthology of Literary Theory and Criticism* (New Brunswick, N.J.: Rutgers University Press, 1991), 331.

44. Albrecht Classen, "The Implications of Feminist Theory on the Study of Medieval German Literature. Also an Introduction," in *Women as Protagonists and Poets in the German Middle Ages: An Anthology of Feminist Approaches to Middle High German Literature,* ed. Albrecht Classen, Göppinger Arbeiten zur Germanistik 528 (Göppingen: Kümmerle, 1991), ix; Laurie Finke, *Feminist Theory, Women's Writing* (Ithaca: Cornell University Press, 1992), 32; Shulamith Shahar, *The Fourth Estate: A History of Women in the Middle Ages,* trans. Chaya Galai (London: Methuen, 1983), 60; and Danielle Regnier-Bohler, "Literary and Mystical Voices," in *A History of Women in the West II. Silences of the Middle Ages,* ed. Christiane Klapisch-Zuber (Cambridge, Mass.: Harvard University Press, 1992), 444.

45. Bynum, *Feast,* 105.

46. Rudolf Wackernagel, *Geschichte der Stadt Basel,* 3 vols. (Basel: Helbling und Lichtenhahn, 1907–1924), 2:689.

47. Anne Holtorf, "Ebstorfer Liederbuch," in *Die deutsche Literatur des Mittelalters: Verfasserlexikon,* ed. Kurt Ruh et al. (Berlin: de Gruyter, 1980): 2: col. 313; and Helga Schüppert, "Söflinger Briefe," in *Verfasserlexikon* 9: col. 15.

48. Johannes Gatz, "Pfullingen," *Alemania Franciscana Antiqua* 17 (1972): 191. But see the tran-

scription, "Anno dni MCCL an Sant Martins tag da ist dis Closter Pfullingen an gefangen worden," ed. Maximilianus Straganz, in "Duae Relationes circa Monasterium Brixinense O. Clar.," *Archivum Franciscanum Historicum* 6 (1913): 538–44, at 544. Straganz's transcription reads, "For as long as I have been in [the cloister], I am hopeful that the Lord will not abandon us in the future."

49. St. Gall, Stiftsbibliothek, MS St. Katharina, Wil, "Klosterchronik," Nr. 87, fol. 5v; and Thoma Vogler, *Geschichte des Dominikanerinnen-Klosters St. Katharina in St. Gallen 1228–1607* (Fribourg, Switzerland: Paulus, 1938), 27, 46.

50. Rudolf Schulze, *Das adelige Frauen- (Kanonissen-) Stift der Hl. Maria (1040–1771) und die Pfarre Liebfrauen-Überwasser zu Münster, Westfalen* (Münster: Aschendorff, 1952), 375.

51. [Anna Roede,] "Spätere Chronik," ed. Flaskamp, 135, 137, 142.

52. Münster, Nordrhein-Westfälisches Staatsarchiv Münsterscher Studienfonds, Stift Überwasser, Akten Nr. 799 (cloister annals), fol. 86v; see also Schulze, *Überwasser*, 148. A German account in the chronicle of cloister Heiningen begins, "Our cloister Heiningen was founded . . . ," Hildesheim, Dombibliothek, Cod. Bev. 546b, fol. 7v. Magdalena Kremer narrates the reformers' activities in the first person, saying, "When we arrived at Kirchheim . . . ," "Wie diß loblich closter," 156.

53. Anne Bollmann, "Weibliche Diskurse: Die Schwesternbücher der *devotio moderna* zwischen Biographie und geistlicher Konversation," in *Kultur, Geschlecht, Körper*, ed. Genus–Münsteraner Arbeitskreis für Gender Studies (Münster: Agenda, 1999), 259, 247, 249, 250. After the house had accepted a rule and was enclosed, it attracted women from a higher social stratum than that of the older sisters.

54. Only Anna Roede in her first chronicle models the first part on Ertwin Ertman's chronicle of the bishops of Osnabrück. See Franz Flaskamp, "Chronik des Klosters Herzebrock," *Osnabrücker Mitteilungen* 74 (1976): 38, 46–53.

55. Ursula Peters, "Frauenliteratur im Mittelalter? Überlegungen zur Trobairitzpoesie, zur Frauenmystik und zur feministischen Literaturbetrachtung," *Germanisch-Romanische Monatsschrift*, n.F. 38 (1988): 49, quoted in Hamburger, *Visual*, 16.

56. Hamburger, *Visual*, 15, 29.

57. [Gallus Öhem,] *Die Chronik des Gallus Öhem*, ed. Karl Brandi, Quellen und Forschungen zur Geschichte der Abtei Reichenau 2 (Heidelberg: Winter, 1893).

58. Natalie Davis, "Gender and Genre: Women as Historical Writers (1400–1820)," in *Beyond their Sex. Learned Women of the European Past,* ed. Patricia Labalme (New York: New York University Press, 1980), 156, 160, 174.

59. "Kurze Chronik des Gotzhuses St. Gallen (1360–1490)," ed. J. Hardegger, *Mitteilungen zur vaterländischen Geschichte* 2 (1863): 1, 8.

60. [Raphael Hanisch,] "Chronik der böhmischen Observantenprovinz (c. 1510/20)," ed. Nikolaus Pol, *Jahrbücher der Stadt Breslau*, ed. Johann Gustav Büsching (Breslau: Friedrich Korn, 1819), 3:15–25. See also Lucius Teichmann, "Die franziskanische Observanzbewegung in Ost-Mitteleuropa und ihre politisch-nationale Komponente im böhmisch-schlesischen Raum," *Archiv für schlesische Kirchengeschichte* 49 (1991): 205–18.

61. Fredrich Techen, ed., *Die Chroniken des Klosters Ribnitz*, Mecklenburgische Geschichtsquellen 1 (Schwerin: Bärensprungsche Hofdruckerei, 1909), 12, 66–70, 71–74.

62. Ibid., 121–22, 125.

63. Tore Nyberg, "Das Hausbuch des Klosters Maihingen," *Jahrbuch des Vereins für Augsburger Bistumsgeschichte* 5 (1971): 156.

64. [Anna Roede,] "Spätere Chronik," ed. Flaskamp, 117.

65. "Innumerabiles grates . . ." [Chronicle of Ebstorf, 1487], ed. Conrad Borchling, in appendix to "Litterarisches und geistiges Leben in Kloster Ebstorf am Ausgange des Mittelalters," *Zeitschrift des historischen Vereins für Niedersachsen* 4 (1905): 396–407, here 401–2, here 398, 399.

66. Augsburg, Staatsarchiv, MS Kloster Maria Maihingen MüB 1, fol. 8r; see also Nyberg, *Brigittenklöster,* 156–57.

67. Karen Glente, "Mystikerinnen aus männlicher und weiblicher Sicht: Ein Vergleich zwischen

Thomas von Cantimpré und Katharina von Unterlinden," in *Religiöse Frauenbewegungen und mystische Frömmigkeit im Mittelalter,* ed. Peter Dinzelbacher and Dieter R. Bauer (Cologne: Böhlau, 1988), 259, 263.

68. Ibid., 259, 261–62.

69. Rolf Limbeck, *Der St. Agneskonvent zu Emmerich,* Emmericher Forschungen 16 (Emmerich: Emmericher Geschichtsverein, 1998), 191.

70. See Wybren Scheepsma, *Deemoed en devotie: De koorvrouwen van Windesheim en hun geschriften* (Amsterdam: Prometheus, 1997), 384–85; and Kurt Ruh, *Geschichte der abendländischen Mystik. Vol. 4: Die niederländische Mystik des 14. bis 16. Jahrhunderts* (Munich: Beck, 1999), 253–54.

71. Wilhelm Schleussner, "Magdalena von Freiburg. Eine pseudomystische Erscheinung des späteren Mittelalters, 1407–1458," *Der Katholik* 87 (1907): 15–18, 201; and Peter Dinzelbacher and Kurt Ruh, "Magdalena von Freiburg," in *Die deutsche Literatur des Mittelalters: Verfasserlexikon,* Kurt Ruh et al. (Berlin: de Gruyter, 1985), 5: cols. 1118–19; and Karen Greenspan, "Erklärung des Vaterunsers: A Critical Edition of a 15th-Century Mystical Treatise by Magdalena Beutler of Freiburg" (Ph.D. diss., University of Massachusetts, 1984), 12–20. The "Magdalenen-Buch," Mainz Stadtbibliothek, Cod. II 16, copied in 1491 by sister Margarethe Alden at the Cistercian convent of St. Agnes in Mainz, is unedited. The other version of Magdalena's vita is found in a copy c. 1656/57 held by the Freiburg, Universitätsbibliothek MS 185.

72. Magdalena's letter, excerpted in (M) Mainz, Stadtbibliothek, Cod. II 16, fols. 17v–18r, is recorded in (F) Freiburg, Universitätsbibilothek MS 185, pp. 39–40. See Schleussner, "Magdalena," 31. It is also printed in Oehl, "Mystikerbriefe," 252.

73. Mainz, Stadtbibliothek, Cod. II 16, fols. 18r, 19v; and Schleussner, "Magdalena," 110, 112.

74. Heinrich Denifle, "Das Leben der Margareta von Kenzingen," *Zeitschrift für deutsches Altertum* 19 (1876): 478–91.

75. Freiburg, Universitätsbibilothek MS 185, p. 106; and Schleussner, "Magdalena," 118.

76. Schleussner, "Magdalena," 120–21; and Kaspar Schieler, *Magister Johannes Nider aus dem Orden Prediger-Brüder: Ein Beitrag zur Kirchengeschichte des 15. Jahrhunderts* (Mainz: Kirchheim, 1885), 119–20.

77. Schleussner, "Magdalena," 18.

78. Ibid., 16–18, 199–201; and Dinzelbacher and Ruh, "Magdalena," 5: cols. 1118–19.

79. Greenspan, "Erklärung," 2, note 3. In other manuscripts the works are anonymously transmitted. Dinzelbacher, on the other hand, does not attribute to her "Die goldene Litanei." See Dinzelbacher and Ruh, "Magdalena," 5: cols. 1118–21.

80. Schleussner, "Magdalena," 202; and Martina Backes, "Zur literarischen Genese frauenmystischer Viten und Visionstexte am Beispiel des Freiburger 'Magdalenenbuches'," in *Literarische Kommunikation und soziale Interaktion: Studien zur Institutionalität mittelalterlicher Literatur,* ed. Beate Keller et al., 251–60 (Bern: Lang, 2001).

81. Freiburg, Universitätsbibilothek MS 185, p. 41; and Schleussner, "Magdalena," 110.

82. Mainz, Stadtbibliothek Cod. II 16, fols. 19r–19v; and Schleussner, "Magdalena," 112.

84. Mainz, Stadtbibliothek, Cod. II 16, fols. 149r, 151v, 141v, 194r.

84. Ibid., fol. 152v.

85. Sara S. Poor, "Mechthild von Magdeburg, Agency, and the Problem of Female Authorship," (work in progress.) I thank her for allowing me to read an advance copy of this chapter of her manuscript.

86. Even a cursory look turns up parts of the text in women's libraries at Unterlinden, Inzigkofen, and Kirchheim am Ries. See Karl-Ernst Greith, "L'activité littéraire des dominicaines d'Unterlinden aux XIVe et XVe siècles," in *Les Dominicaines d'Unterlinden,* ed. Madeleine Blondel and Jeffrey Hamburger (Paris: Somogy, 2000), 1:165; Werner Fechter, *Deutsche Handschriften des 15. und 16. Jahrhunderts aus der Bibliothek des ehemaligen Augustinerchorfrauenstifts Inzigkofen* (Sigmaringen: Thorbecke, 1997), 143; and Arnold Schromm, *Die Bibliothek des ehemaligen Zisterzienserinnenklosters Kirchheim am Ries: Buchpflege und geistiges Leben in einem Frauenstift,* Studia Augustana 9 (Tübingen: Niemeyer, 1998), 220, 232–33. Margot Schmidt finds eight complete texts and seventy-nine manuscripts with excerpts and fragments

of Mechthild's *Liber specialis gratiae*, "Mechthild von Hackeborn," in *Die deutsche Literatur des Mittelalters: Verfasserlexikon,* ed. Wolfgang Stammler, Karl Langosch, and Kurt Ruh (Berlin: de Gruyter, 1987), 6: col. 253.

87. "Sant Hilgarten weiszagung." See Franz Jostes, ed., *Meister Eckhart und seine Jünger. Ungedruckte Texte zur Geschichte der deutschen Mystik,* Collectanea Friburgensis 4 (Fribourg, Switzerland: Kommissionsverlag der Universitätsbuchhandlung, 1894), 135. This is most likely a copy of Johannes Tortsch's *Bürde der Welt,* composed in German around 1424/33, which contains prophecies attributed to Hildegard of Bingen. See *Diss biechlin saygt an die wayssagung vo[n] zükunfftiger betrübtnusz. Wölliche grausmen betrübtnusz vns klärlichen aussprechen ist. Sannt Birgitta. Sannt. Sybilla. Sant Gregorius. Sant Hilgart. Sant Joachim. Vnd wirt genant die Bürde der welt,* Augsburg: Hans Schönsperger, 1522. The work (GW 4401) was first published in 1482.

88. Gertrud Jaron Lewis points out that Hildegard was listed in the *Martyrologium romanorum.* See "Hildegard von Bingen (1098–1179)," in *Medieval Germany: An Encyclopedia,* ed. John Jeep (New York: Garland, 2001), 358.

89. Anne Bollmann, "Being a Women on My Own": Alijt Bake (1415–1455) as Reformer of the Inner Self," in *Seeing and Knowing: Women and Learning in Medieval Europe 1200–1600,* ed. Anneke Mulder-Bakker (Turnhout: Brepols, in press). I am grateful to Anne Bollman for allowing me to read her forthcoming article. See also Ruh, *Mystik,* 4:264–65.

90. See Vogler, *St.Katharina,* 266, 269. Raymond of Capua's biography of Catherine is also titled "Der Rosengarten." Jostes, *Texte,* 134–35.

91. Ruh, *Mystik,* 4:253–54.

92. Dinzelbacher and Ruh, "Magdalena," in *Die deutsche Literatur des Mittelalters: Verfasserlexikon,* ed. Kurt Ruh et al. (Berlin: de Gruyter, 1985), 5: col. 1120.

93. Peter Dinzelbacher, ed., *Mittelalterliche Visionsliteratur: Eine Anthologie* (Darmstadt: Wissenschaftliche Buchgesellschaft, 1989), 197–201.

94. Bollmann, "Being," forthcoming.

95. See above note 58. Anne Bollmann, "Weibliche Diskurse. Die Schwesternbücher der *Devotio moderna* zwischen Biographie und geistlicher Konversation," in *Kultur, Geschlecht, Körper,* ed. Genus–Münsteraner Arbeitskreis für gender studies (Münster: Agenda, 1999), 241, 248, 258.

96. Bollmann, "Being," forthcoming.

97. Bollmann, "Diskurse," 251–52.

98. Bollmann, "Being," forthcoming.

99. Thomas Mertens, "The Modern Devotion and Innovation in Middle Dutch Literature, in *Medieval Dutch Literature in its European Context,* ed. Erik Kooper, Cambridge Studies in Medieval Literature (New York: Cambridge University Press, 1995), 229; and idem, "Rapiarium," in *Dictionnaire de spiritualité,* ed. Joseph de Guibert, Marcel Viller, and Ferdinand Cavallera (Paris: Beauchesne, 1988), 13: cols. 114–19.

100. Anne Bollmann, "A Woman Mystic at the Dawn of the Modern Era: Alijt Bake (1415–c. 1455) as a 'Reformer of the Inner Life'" (paper delivered at the 37th International Congress of Medieval Studies, Kalamazoo, Mich., May 4, 2002); and idem, "Being," forthcoming. Women's networks and the libraries they helped to build brought women into contact with a larger range of texts than has been recognized. As indicated earlier in connection with Magdalena Beutler's reading, manuscripts such as those from the early sixteenth century at the Cologne Observant houses of St. Cecilia and St. Maria Magdalena contain, as just one example, parts of works by Mechthild of Hackeborn and Gertrude the Great of Helfta excerpted in German translation. These manuscript anthologies of passages from these and other authors were compiled mostly by men for women as private devotional and table readings for the spiritual year. See Dietrich Schmidtke, *Studien zur dingallegorischen Erbauungsliteratur des Mittelalters. Am Beispiel der Gartenallegorie,* Hermaea, Germanistische Forschungen, n.F. 43 (Tübingen: Niemeyer, 1982), 45–46, 97–99.

101. Schmidtke, *Studien,* 265; and Werner Williams-Krapp, "Ordensreform und Literatur im 15. Jahrhundert," *Jahrbuch der Oswald von Wolkenstein Gesellschaft* 4 (1986): 42.

102. Klaus Graf, "Ordensreform und Literatur in Augsburg während des 15. Jahrhunderts," in *Literarisches Leben in Augsburg während des 15. Jahrhunderts*, ed. Johannes Janota and Werner Williams-Krapp (Tübingen: Niemeyer, 1995), 137.

103. Thomas Cramer, *Geschichte der deutschen Literatur im späten Mittelalter* (Munich: DTV, 1990), 168.

104. *Schwesternbuch und Statuten des St. Agnes–Konvents in Emmerich*, ed. Anne Bollmann and Niko-laus Staubach, Emmericher Forschungen 17 (Emmerich: Emmericher Geschichtsverein, 1998), 228–29.

105. Larissa Tayor, *Soldiers of Christ: Preaching in Late Medieval and Reformation France* (Oxford: Oxford University Press, 1992), 172.

106. Regina Schiewer, "Sermons for Nuns of the Dominican Observance Movement," in *Medieval Monastic Preaching*, ed. Carolyn Muessig (Leyden: Brill, 1998), 75.

107. L. Dacheux, *Die ältesten Schriften Geilers von Kaysersberg* (1882; repr. Amsterdam: Rodopi, 1965), 223–24. The sermon that Susanna Hörwart edited is that delivered at the Strasbourg cloister of the Penitants on December 27, 1498. See *Johannes Geiler von Kaysersberg. Sämtliche Werke*, 3 vols., ed. Gerhard Bauer (Berlin: de Gruyter, 1989–95), 3: viii–ix.

108. Geiler von Kaysersberg, *Werke*, 3:viii.

109. Merry Wiesner-Hanks, ed. *Convents Confront the Reformation: Catholic and Protestant Nuns in Germany*, trans. Joan Skocir and Merry Wiesner-Hanks (Milwaukee: Marquette University Press, 1996), 16; and Annette Barthelmé, *La Réforme dominicaine au Xve Siècle en Alsace et dans l'ensemble de la province de Teutonie*, Collection d'études sur l'histoire du droit et des institutions de l'Alsace 7 (Strasbourg: Heitz, 1931), 151.

110. Annemarie Halter, *Geschichte des Dominikanerinnenklosters Oetenbach in Zürich 1234–1525* (Winterthur: Keller, 1956), 145, 146, 162–63.

111. Marie-Claire Däniker-Gysin, *Geschichte des Dominikanerinnenklosters Töß 1233–1525*, Neujahrs-blatt der Stadtbibliothek Winterthur 289 (Winterthur: Ziegler, 1957), 67–69.

112. Halter, *Oetenbach*, 144 n. 8.

113. Vogler, *St. Katharina*, 178–79.

114. Ibid., 183, 186–87, 167, 188–217.

115. R. Krauß, "Geschichte des Dominikaner-Frauenklosters Kirchberg," *Württembergische Viertel-jahreshefte*, n.F. 3 (1894): 292.

116. See above Chapter 4, note 106.

117. Konrad Rothenhäusler, *Standhaftigkeit der altwürttembergischen Klosterfrauen im Reformations-Zeit-alter* (Stuttgart: Verlag der Aktien-Gesellschaft "Deutsches Volksblatt," 1884), 15.

118. Ibid., 180–81, 188, 193, 16, 187.

119. [Anna Roede,] "Spätere Chronik," ed. Flaskamp, 138.

120. [Elisabeth Fridaghes], "Klosterchronik Überwasser während der Wirren 1531–33," ed. Rudolf Schulze, in *Quellen und Forschungen zur Geschichte der Stadt Münster i. W*, ed. Eduard Schulte (Münster: Aschendodrff, 1924–26), 2:159.

121. "Chronik des Schwesternhouses Marienthal, genannt Niesinck in Münster," ed. Carl Adolf Cornelius, in *Berichte der Augenzeugen über das Münstersche Wiedertäuferreich*, Gesichtsquellen des Bis-thums Münster 2 (1853; repr. Münster: Aschendorff, 1965), 433–34.

122. Johathan D. Grieser, "A Tale of Two Convents: Nuns and Anabaptists in Münster, 1533–1535," *Sixteenth Century Journal* 26 (1995): 46.

123. On conflicts between the convent and the prince-bishops who were sometimes allied with the city council on the issue of reform and sometimes at odds with it, see Gleba, *Reformpraxis*, 71.

124. Sigrid Schmitt, "Geistliche Frauen und städtische Welt. Stiftsdamen–Klosterfrauen–Beginen und ihre Umwelt am Beispiel der Stadt Straßburg im Spätmittelalter (1250–1530)" (Habilitationsschrift, University of Mainz, 2002). I am grateful to Sigrid Schmitt for allowing me to read chapters of her soon-to-be-published Habilitationsschrift.

125. See Chapter 1 above, and Jutta Gisela Sperling, *Convents and the Body Politic in Late Renaissance Venice* (Chicago: University of Chicago Press, 1999), 61, 63–64, 68.

126. Schmitt, "Geistliche Frauen." See also above, note 124.

127. Deventer, Stads- of Athenaeumbibliotheek, MS Supp-l. 198 [101 E 26], fols. 1r and 387v; cited here from Wybren Scheepsma's translation in " 'For hereby I hope to rouse some to piety': Books of Sisters from convents and Sister-Houses Associated with the 'Devotio moderna' in the Low Countries," in *Women, the Book, and the Godly*, 2 vols., ed. Lesley Smith and Jane Taylor, 1:27–40 (Cambridge: Brewer, 1995), 37.

128. Jacqueline Wogan-Browne, "Powers of Record, Powers of Example: Hagiography and Women's History," in *Gendering the Master Narrative: Women and Power in the Middle Ages,* ed. Mary C. Erler and Maryanne Kowaleski (Ithaca: Cornell University Press, 2003), 91–93.

SELECTED BIBLIOGRAPHY

PRIMARY SOURCES

Manuscripts that have been transcribed, whether critically edited or not, are located with the printed works rather than the manuscript sources. All texts by women are listed under the name of the author rather than the editor; anonymous works under the title or incipit.

Manuscripts

Augsburg, Staatsarchiv
MS Kloster Maria Maihingen MüB 1 (Chronicle of Maihingen, compiled by Prioress Walburga Scheffler and "Prioress Anna," 1522–25, extracts published in Nyberg, *Dokumente*, 146–272)

Basel, Universitätsbibliothek
E III 13 (Konrad von Preussen, "Ordinacionen für reformierte Dominikanerinnen," 1397, fols. 29v–31v)

Berlin, Staatsbibliothek
MS germ qu. 22 (24 sermons of Peter of Breslau transcribed at St. Nicolaus in undis, 1445)
MS germ. qu. 166 (Basel reform sermons, 1434, fols. 256r–354r)
MS germ. qu. 206 (Agnes Sachs's sermon collection, 1434–37, fols. 37v–314v)
MS germ. oct. 63 (Simultaneous transcription of a sermon by Johannes Geiler von Kaysersberg, preached in 1489 at St Nicolaus in undis, fols. 48r–68r)

Bloomington, Lilly Library, University of Indiana
MS Ricketts 198: Johannes Meyer, "Ämterbuch" and "Buch der Ersetzung," illuminated by a pupil of Barbara Gwichtmacher at St. Katharina, Nuremberg, c. 1460

Brussels, Koninklijke Bibliotheek
MS II 298 [cat. 1997] (43 Sermons of Jan Storm, some transcribed by Janne Colijns, 1507)
MS 643–44 (Texts by Alijt Bake, most edited by Scheepsma or Spaapen)
MS 4367–68 (78 sermons of Jan Storm transcribed by Maria van Pee, 1466/67)

Colmar, Bibliothèque de la Ville de Colmar
MS 508 (Vita of Elisabeth Kempf by Agatha Gossembrot, 15th century, fols. 137r–141v)
MS 717 II (Anthology of sermons, meditations, and hagiographic texts translated by Dorothea von Kippenheim, after 1516)

Constance, Kloster Zoffingen, Archiv
MS Rechnungs- und Chronikbuch

Deventer, Stads- of Athenaeumbibilotheek
MS Suppl. 198 [101 E 26] (Diepenveen Book of Sisters, 1524, with additions probably by Sister Griet Essink; a different version from the 1534 text edited by Brinkerink)

Ebstorf, Evangelischer Damenstiftsbibliothek
MS V 3 (Song book, 15th century)
MS VI 5 and MS VI 6 (Sermon collection with marginal notes, 1497/1515)
MS VI 17 (Ebstorf Liederhandschrift, 16th century)

Einsiedeln, Stiftsbibliothek
MS 277 (Notes from a sermon of Johannes Tauler preached at Klingental, 14th century, fol. 221r–221v)

Freiburg, Augustinermuseum
MS 11731 (Antiphonal with illuminations, several by Sibilla von Bondorf, c. 1476)

Freiburg, Erzbischöfliches Archiv
MS Ha 534 (Abridged version [compiled 1854] of the old Chronicle of Inzigkofen, published in shortened form by Dreher)

Freiburg, Stadtarchiv
MS 108 (Johannes Meyer, "Ämterbuch" and "Buch der Ersetzung," c. 1482–84)

Freiburg, Universitätsbibilothek
MS 185 (Vita of Magdalena Beutler, copied 1656/57)
MS 202 ("Die geistliche Meerfahrt," abridged version, fols. 189v–191v)
MS 490 (Anthology compiled by sisters at 4 cloisters: St. Katharina, St. Gall; Schönensteinbach; Pillenreuth; and St. Katharina, Nuremberg (?), 1461, 1465, 1473, 1492)
MS 1131 (Sequentiary, some illuminations by Sibilla von Bondorf, c. 1476)

Ghent, Universiteitsbibliotheek
MS 3854 (Texts by Alijit Bake, most edited by Scheepsma or Spaapen)

Hamburg, Staats- und Universitätsbibliothek
MS Theol. 8° 2064 (Tagebuch der Angela von Holfels, 1507–39)
MS Theol. 2065 (Katherina Gurdeler's summaries of sermons and collations of Jakob van Burigh, c. 1500)
MS Theol. 12° 2205 (Summaries of sermons preached by Johannes Tauler at St. Gertrud, Cologne, 14th century)

Hildesheim, Dombibliothek
Cod. Bev. 546b (Chronik des Klosters Heiningen)

Innsbrück, Tiroler Landesregierungsarchiv
MS 2336 (Missiv-Buch des Klosters Sonnenburg, "Was sich mit dem Cardinal Nicolai Cusan und der Äbtissin Verena von Stuben zugetragen," c. 1460)

Karlsruhe, Badische Landesbibliothek
MS Lichtental 69 ("Buch von den heiligen Mägden und Frauen," compiled and translated by Sister Regula, c. 1460)
MS Lichtental 70 ("Leben Jesu" and "Elsässische Legenda aurea," translated by Sister Regula, c. 1450, fols. 1r–187v,332r–391v)
MS Lichtental 82 ("Legende von den 10 000 Märtyrern," probably translated by Sister Regula, 1445–50, fols. 142r–157r)
MS Schwarzach 19 (Anthology of devotional texts compiled and some perhaps written by Anna Schott, c. 1480)
MS Thennenbach 4 (Life of St. Clare with 33 illustrations by Sibilla von Bondorf, c. 1490)

Leipzig, Deutsches Buch- und Schriftmuseum, Deutsche Bücherei
MS Klemm Collection I, 104 (Vita of Elisabeth of Hungary, illuminated by Sibilla von Bondorf, 1481)
MS Kl. I 42 (Breviary, illuminated by Barbara Gwichtmacher, c. 1452/57)

London, British Museum
MS Add. 15686 (Clarissan rule with 8 illustrations by Sibilla von Bondorf, 15th century)
MS Add. 15710 (Life of St. Francis with 70 illustrations by Sibilla von Bondorf, 15th century)

Mainz, Stadtbibliothek
Cod. II 16 (Das Magdalenen-Buch, 1491)

Munich, Bayerisches Hauptstaatsarchiv
Cod. Kloster Altomünster Literale 29 (Chronicle of Altomünster, completed 1538, extracts published in Nyberg, *Dokumente*, 273–95)
Cod. Kloster Frauenchiemsee Literale 88 (historical, legal, and economic accounts of Abbesses Magdalena Auer, 1467–94, and Ursula Pfaffinger, 1494–1528)

Munich, Bayerisches Nationalmuseum
MS 3801 (Sermons of Stephan Fridolin [d. 1498] simultaneously transcribed by Caritas Pirckheimer)

Munich, Staatliche Graphische Sammlung
Inv. Nr. 39 837–39 845 (Life of St. Francis, 9 illustrations by Sibilla von Bondorf, 15th century)

Münnerstadt (Bad Kissingen), Augustinerklosterbibliothek
MS 406 (Anthology of prayers and meditations from the Erfurt, Weissfrauenklosterbibliothek, 1497)

Münster, Nordrhein-Westfälisches Staatsarchiv
Münsterscher Studienfonds, Stift Überwasser, Akten Nr. 799 (Cloister Annals, Überwasser, 1460–90)

Neresheim, Klosterbibliothek Neresheim
MS Ne 8 ("Diß ist ain ordnung oder auß tailung des psalters Beatus vir," composed by Veronika Ainkürn, d. 1546, fols. 1–125)

Selected Bibliography

Nuremberg, Germanisches Nationalmuseum
MS 2261 ("Schwester Katrei," tract translated by Anna Eyb [Ebin], c. 1465–82, fols. 70r–115v)

Nuremberg, Stadtbibliothek
MS Cent III, 86 and 87 (2 vols., missal copied by sisters at St. Katharina, Nuremberg, and illuminated by Barbara Gwichtmacher, c. 1452/63)
MS Cent V, 10a (Sister-book of Cloister Töß, illuminated by a pupil of Barbara Gwichtmacher, c. 1454, fols. 1r–84v; also contains sister-books of St. Katharinental and Oetenbach, edited by Johannes Meyer)
MS Cent V, App. 34 p–w (8 vols., Antiphonal copied by Margarete Kartheuser and illuminated by 5 hands, 1458–70)
MS Cent VI, 43g (Vita of St. Vincent, illuminated by pupils of Barbara Gwichtmacher, c. 1462)
MS Cent VII, 13 (Notes on a sermon by Heinrich Riß preached at St. Katharina, c. 1486, fols. 71r–74r)
MS Cent VII, 16 (Handbook for the sacristan composed by Katharina von Mühlheim, c. 1428/36, fols. 8v–260r)

Preetz, Archiv, Klosterpreetz
MS 1 (Anna von Buchwald, "Buch im Chor," 1471–87, and other writings)

Schriesheim (Heidelberg), Sammlung Eis
Cod. 114 (39 sermon summaries by sisters at St. Katharina, Nuremberg, 15th century)

Sigmaringen, Fürstlich Hohenzollernsche Hofbibliothek
MS 68 (4 vols., Chronicle of Inzigkofen, begun 1525 by Elisabeth Muntprat and Apollonia Besserer, recopied before 1760 with letters and documents added and modernized spelling)

St. Gall, Stiftsbibliothek
MS St. Katharina, Wil, "Klosterchronik," Nr. 87 (Chronicle of St. Katharina, St. Gall, 1450–1528, begun by Angela Varnbühler)
MS St. Katharina, Wil, "Schwesternbuch," Nr. 89 (Sister-book of St. Katharina, St. Gall, the majority written 1483–86 by Elisabeth Muntprat)

Strasbourg, Bibliothèque Nationale et Universitaire de Strasbourg
MS 2934 ("Buch der Reformacio Predigerordens" with additions by Barbara von Benfelden)

Strasbourg, Bibliothèque Municipale
MS 563 ("Die geistliche Meerfahrt," by Margareta Ursula von Masmünster, late 15th century, fols. 19r–36r; excerpts in Landmann, "Andachtsübungen")

Wolfenbüttel, Herzog-August-Bibliothek
MS Extravagantes 164, 1 (Eilsabeth Kempf's translation and continuation of the "Vitae Sororum" of Unterlinden and her abridged adaptation of the "Liber miraculorum," before 1485)
MS 1159 Novi. (Chronicle and memorabilia, Cloister Heilig Kreuz, Braunschweig, 1485/1506)

Printed Works

Sister-books, Chronicles, and Other Works by Women, Named and Unnamed

Anonymous. *Margarita Euangelica. Een devote boecxken geheeten Die Evangelische Perle.* Utrecht: Berntsen, 1535.

Anonymous. *[Van] den Tempel onser sielen.* Facsimile edition. Edited by Albert Ampe. Antwerp: Russbroecgenootschap, 1968.

Adelheid von Aue. Letter, 21 November 1464. In *Seraphin Dietler's Chronik des Klosters Schönensteinbach,* ed. Johannes von Schlumberger, 464–67. See Dietler, *Chronik.*

"Also vindt man hie geschriben wie die obseruantz angefangen ist worden. . . ." In "Die Reformation des Katharinenklosters zu Nürnberg im Jahre 1428," ed. Theodor von Kern, 7–12. See Kern, "Katharinenkloster."

[Anna von Munzingen.] "Dis sint die gnade, die vnser Herre hett getan semlichen swestern in disem closter ze Adelnhusen." In "Die Chronik der Anna von Munzingen. Nach der ältesten Abschrift mit Einleitung und Beilagen," ed. J. König, 153–92. See J. König, "Die Chronik."

"Anno dni MCCL an Sant Martins tag da ist dis Closter Pfullingen an gefangen worden." In "Duae Relationes circa Monasterium Brixinense O. Clar.," ed. Maximilianus Straganz, 538–44. See Straganz, "Monasterium Brixinense."

Bake, Alijt. "De autobiografie van Alijt Bake." In "Middeleeuwse Passienmystiek III," ed. with introduction by Bernhard Spaapen. *Ons geestelijk erf* 41 (1967): 209–301, 321–50.

———. "De brief uit de ballingschap." In "Middeleeuwse Passienmystiek IV," ed. with introduction by Bernhard Spaapen. *Ons geestelijk erf* 41 (1967): 351–67.

———. "De lessen van Palmzondag." In "Middeleeuwse Passienmystiek V. De kloosteronderrichtingen van Alijt Bake, 2," ed. with introdiction by Bernhard Spaapen. *Ons geestelijk erf* 42 (1968): 225–61.

———. "De louteringsnacht van de actie." In "Middeleeuwse Passienmystiek V. De kloosteronderrichtingen van Alijt Bake, 3," ed. with introduction by Bernhard Spaapen. *Ons geestelijk erf* 42 (1968): 374–421.

———. "De trechter en de spin." In "Metaforen voor mystiek leiderschap van Alijt Bake," ed. with introduction by Wybren Scheepsma. *Ons geestelijk erf* 69 (1995): 222–34.

———. "'Van die memorie der passien ons heren' van Alijt Bake," ed. with introduction by Wybren Scheepsma. *Ons geestelijk erf* 68 (1994): 106–28.

———. "De vier Kruiswegen." In "Middeleeuwse Passienmystiek II," ed. with introduction Bernhard Spaapen. *Ons geestelijk erf* 40 (1966): 5–64.

———. "De weg der victorie." In "Middeleeuwse Passienmystiek V. De kloosteronderrichtingen van Alijt Bake, 4," ed. with introduction by Bernhard Spaapen. *Ons geestelijk erf* 43 (1969): 270–304.

———. "De weg van de ezel." In "Middeleeuwse Passienmystiek V. De kloosteronderrichtingen van Alijt Bake, 1," ed. with introduction by Bernhard Spaapen. *Ons geestelijk erf* 42 (1966): 5–32.

[Barbara von Benfelden.] "Von zunemunge der geistlicheit und uff gang der tugenden der swestern dis conventes des klosters sancte Agnesen." In *La Réforme dominicaine au XVe siècle en Alsace et dans l'ensenble de la province de Teutonie,* ed. Annette Barthelmé, 189–92. See Barthelmé, *Réforme.*

[Bertha of Vilich.] *Mater Spiritualis: The Life of Adelheid of Vilich.* Translated by Madelyn Bergen Dick. Toronto: Peregrina, 1994.

———. "Vita Adelheidis Abbatissae Vilicensis." In *Monumenta Germaniae,* ed. Oswald Holger-Egger, vol. 15, part 2: 754–63. See G. H. Pertz, Oswald Holger-Egger et al., *Monumenta Germaniae.*

Beutler, Magdalena. "Erklärung des Vaterunsers." In "'Erklärung des Vaterunsers.' A Critical Edition of a Fifteenth-Century Mystical Treatise by Magdalena Beutler of Freiburg," ed. Karen Greenspan, 105–298. See Greenspan, "Erklärung."

Christine de Pizan. *The Book of the City of Ladies.* Translation and introduction by Rosalind Brown-Grant. London: Penguin, 1999.

———. "Le Livre du dit de Poissy." In *Oeuvres poétiques de Christine de Pisan,* ed. Maurice Roy, 2:159–222. 1886; reprint, New York: Johnson, 1965.

"Chronik des Schwesternhauses Marienthal, genannt Niesinck in Münster." In *Berichte der Augenzeugen über das Münstersche Wiedertäuferreich,* ed. Carl Cornelius, 419–41. Geschichtsquellen des Bisthums Münster 2. 1853; reprint, Münster: Aschendorff, 1965.

Chronik und Totenbuch des Klosters Wienhausen. Edited by Horst Appuhn. Wienhausen: Kloster Wienhausen, 1986.

Costers, Jacomijne. "Visioen en exempel." In "De helletocht van Jacomijne Costers (d. 1503)," ed. with introduction by Wybren Scheepsma. *Ons geestelijk erf* 70 (1996): 157–85.

[Dürner, Elsbeth.] Letter, 9 August 1482. In *Rappoltsteinisches Urkundenbuch 759–1500.* 5 vols., ed. Karl Albrecht, 5:304. See Albrecht *Urkundenbuch.*

[Ebner, Christine.] *Der Nonne von Engelthal: Büchlein von der Gnaden Überlast.* Edited by Karl Schröder. Bibliothek des Litterarischen Vereins in Stuttgart 108. Tübingen: Litterarischer Verein, 1871.

[Elisabeth von Kirchberg.] "Leben heiliger alemannischer Frauen des Mittelalters IV. Die Nonnen von Kirchberg bei Haigerloch." Edited by Anton Birlinger. *Alemannia* 11 (1883): 1–20.

———. "Unserm herren Jhesu Christo zu ewigem lob. . . ." In "Aufzeichnungen über das Mystische Leben der Nonnen von Kirchberg bei Sulz Predigerordens während des XIV. und XV. Jahrnunderts," ed. F. W. E. Roth, 103–21. See Roth, "Aufzeichnungen."

[Ernst, Juliana.] *Die Chronik des Bickenklosters zu Villingen.* Edited by Karl Jordan Glatz. Bibliothek des Litterarischen Vereins in Stuttgart 151. Tübingen: Fues, 1881.

"Es was ain seilgú schwester, dú hiess . . ." [Katharinental Sister-Book]. In "Leben heiliger alemannischer Frauen des Mittelalters V. Die Nonnen von St. Katharinental bei Dieszenhofen," ed. Anton Birlinger. *Alemannia* 15 (1887): 150–83.

[Fridaghes, Elisabeth.] "Klosterchronik Überwasser während der Wirren 1531–33." Edited by Rudolf Schulze. In *Quellen und Forschungen zur Geschichte der Stadt Münster,* ed. Edward Schulte, 2:149–66. Münster: Aschendorff, 1926.

[Haider, Ursula.] "Die Sinngedichte der Schwestern von St. Katharina in St. Gallen und in Villingen." In *Die deutsche Mystik im Prediger-Orden (von 1250–1530) nach ihren Grundlehren, Liedern und Lebensbildern,* ed. Carl Greith, 277–88. See Carl Greith, *Mystik.*

Hier beginnen sommige stichtige punten van onsen oelden zusteren (naar het te Arnhem berustende Handschrift uitgegeven). Edited by Dirk de Man. The Hague: M. Nijhoff, 1919.

Hrosvit of Gandersheim. *Hroswitha von Gandersheim, Werke in deutscher Übertragung. Mit einem Beitrag zur frühmittelhochdeutschen Dichtung.* Edited and translated by Helene Homeyer. Munich, Paderborn, Vienna: Schöningh, 1973.

————. *Hrosvithae Opera.* Edited by Helene Homeyer. Paderborn: Schöningh, 1970.

"Innumerabiles grates . . ." [Chronicle of Ebstorf, 1487.] In "Litterarisches und geistiges Leben in Kloster Ebstorf am Ausgange des Mittelalters," ed. Conrad Borchling, appendix, 396–407. See Borchling, "Kloster Ebstorf."

"Inzigkofen Ursprung." Edited by Johannes Pflummern. In "A.B.C., Zur Geschichte des Nonnenklosters Inzigkofen," ed. Georg Ludwig Stecher. *Diözesanarchiv von Schwaben* 21 (1903): 65–72.

[Jacobs, Bertha.] *Suster Bertken. Twee bij Jan Seversz in Leiden verscheuen boekjes ('s-Gravenhage. Koninklijke Bibliotheek, 227 G 46) in facsimile uitgegeven.* Utrecht: Uti, 1989.

————. *Van dye passie ons liefsherren ihū christi.* Leiden: Seversz, 1515/16.

"Jtem die her nach geschriben pŭcher hat der convent hie zu sant Kathereyn. . . ." In *Meister Eckhart und seine Jünger. Ungedruckte Texte zur Geschichte der deutschen Mystik,* ed. Franz Jostes, 114–60. See Jostes, *Eckhart.*

[Katharina von Gueberschwihr.] *Lebensbeschreibungen der ersten Schwestern des Klosters der Dominikanerinnen zu Unterlinden von deren Priorin Catharina von Gebsweiler.* Edited by Ludwig Clarus. Regensburg: Manz, 1863.

————. "Vitae sororum." In "Les 'vitae sororum d'Unterlinden.' Edition critique du manuscrit 508 de la Bibliothèque de Colmar," ed. Jeanne Ancelet-Hustache. *Archives d'histoire doctrinale et littéraire du moyen age* 5 (1930): 317–517.

Katharina von Mühlheim. Letter, 11 April 1436. In *Seraphin Dietler's Chronik des Klosters Schönensteinbach,* ed. Johannes von Schlumberger, 405–6. See Dietler, *Chronik.*

[Kremer, Magdalena.] "Wie diß loblich closter zu Sant Johannes baptisten zu kirchen under deck prediger-ordens reformiert ist worden und durch woelich personen." In *Geschichte des Herzogtums Wuerttemberg unter der Regierung der Graven,* ed. Christian Friedrich Sattler, 4:152–247. See Sattler, *Wuerttemberg.*

Letter of the Clarissan Sisters to the Nuremberg City Council (c. 1410). In *Das Klarissenkloster in Nürnberg bis zum Beginn des 16. Jahrhunderts,* ed. Johannes Kist, appendix, 154–62. See Kist, *Klarissenkloster.*

"Levensbeschrijvingen van devote zusters te Deventer." Edited with introduction by Wilhelmus Johannes Kühler. *Archief voor de geschiedenis van het aartsbisdom Utrecht* 36 (1910): 9–68 (introduction, 1–8).

Maria von Hout (van Oisterwijk). *Der rechte wech zo der evangelischer volkomenheit.* Cologne: Neusz, 1531.

Maria von Wolkenstein. Letters (1455). In "Nikolaus von Kues und das Brixener Klarissenkloster," ed. Hermann Hallauer, appendix, 111–12, 116–18. See Hallauer, "Brixener Klarissenkloster."

Mechthild of Magdeburg. *The Flowing Light of the Godhead.* Translated by Frank Tobin. New York: Paulist Press, 1998.

[Neyler, Eva Magdalena.] "Item diß nachgeschriben geschicht und gewalt des vyntz von Gott über unß und unßer gotzhuß hat sich also erhept." Edited by Dr. Holzwarth, *Katholische Trösteinsamkeit* 12 (1858): 203–54.

————. "Item diß nachgeschriben geschieht und gewalt des vyntz von Got über unß und unßer gotzhuß hat sich also erhept." In "Zur Reformationsgeschichte des Dominikanerinnenklosters zu Pforzheim," ed. Karl Rieder, 321–60. See Rieder, "Pforzheim," in *Freiburger Diözesan-Archiv* n.F. 18 (1917): 311–66.

"Nonnenbriefe aus dem Kloster Ebstorf." In *Ebstorf aus der Chronik,* ed. Wilhelm Spangenberg and Sophia Wichelmann, 91–101. See Spangenberg, *Ebstorf.*

[Riccoboni, Bartolomea.] *Life and Death in a Venetian Convent: The Chronicle and Necrology of Corpus Domini, 1395–1436.* Edited and translated by Daniel Bornstein. Chicago: Chicago University Press, 2000.

[Roede, Anna.] "Chronik des Klosters Herzebrock." Edited with introduction by Franz Flaskamp. *Osnabrücker Mitteilungen* 74 (1967): 37–79.

———. "Anna Roedes spätere Chronik von Herzebrock." Edited with introduction by Franz Flaskamp. *Jahrbuch der Gesellschaft für Niedersächsische Kirchengeschichte* 68 (1970): 75–146.

Das St. Katharinentaler Schwesternbuch. Untersuchung, Edition, Kommentar. Edited by Ruth Meyer. Münchener Texte und Untersuchungen zur deutschen Literatur des Mittelalters 104. Tübingen: Niemeyer, 1995.

"Das Schwesternbuch von Sankt Agnes." In *Schwesternbuch und Statuten des St. Agnes–Konvents in Emmerich,* ed. Anne Bollmann and Nikolaus Staubach, 31–307. Emmericher Forschungen 17. Emmerich: Emmericher Geschichtsverein, 1998.

[Sneberger, Anna.] Letter to the sisters at St. maria Magdelena an den Steinen, Basel, 15 July 1465. In "Frauengeschichte/Geschlechtergeschichte/Sozialgeschichte. Forschungs-felder-Forschungslücken: eine bibliographische Annäherung an das späte Mittelalter," ed. Gabriela Signori, 34–35. In *Lustgarten und Dämonenpein: Konzepte von Weiblichkeit im Mittelalter und Früher Neuzeit,* ed. Annette Kuhn and Bea Lundt, 29–53. Dortmund: Ebersbach, 1997.

"Sorores karissime . . ." [Ebstorf reform account, c 1490.] In "Litterarisches und geististiges Leben in Kloster Ebstorf am Ausgange des Mittelalters," ed. Conrad Borchling, appendix, 388–96. See Borchling, "Kloster Ebstorf."

[Stagel, Elsbeth?] *Das Leben der Schwestern zu Töß, beschrieben von Elsbet Stagel samt der Vorrede von Johannes Meier und dem Leben der Prinzessin Elisabet von Ungarn.* Edited by Ferdinand Vetter. Deutsche Texte des Mittelalters 6. Berlin: Weidmann, 1906.

[Sticken, Salome.] "A Way of Life for sisters." [Vivendi formula.] In *Devotio Moderna: Basic Readings,* ed. and trans. John Van Engen, 176–86. Mahwah, N.Y.: Paulist Press, 1988.

"Die Stiftung des Klosters Oetenbach und das Leben der seligen Schwestern daselbst, aus der Nürnberger Handschrift." Edited by H. Zeller-Werdmüller and Jakob Bächthold. *Zürcher Taschenbuch* 12 (1889): 213–76.

"Tagebuch der Dominikanerin von Steinheim." In *Standhaftigkeit der altwürttembergischen Klosterfrauen im Reformations-Zeitalter,* ed. Konrad Rothenhäusler, 179–93. See Rothenhäusler, *Klosterfrauen.*

Tucher, Katharina. *Die 'Offenbarungen' der Katharina Tucher.* Edited by Ulla Williams and Werner Williams-Krapp. Untersuchungen zur deutschen Literaturgeschichte 98. Tübingen: Niemeyer, 1998.

"Vahe ich an etwaz zu schreyben von den heiligen swestern, dy gewesen seyn zu Weyler" [Weiler Sister-Book.] In "Mystisches Leben in dem Dominikanerinnenkloster Weiler bei Esslingen im 13. und 14. Jahrhundert," ed. Karl Bihlmeyer, 68–85. See Bihlmeyer, "Mystisches Leben."

Van den doechden der vuriger ende stichtiger sustern von Diepen veen, Handschrift D. Edited by D. A. Brinkerink. Leiden: Sijthoff, 1904.

[Verena von Stuben.] Memorandum (March 1454). In "Eine Visitation des Nikloaus von Kues im Benediktinerinnenkloster Sonnenburg," ed. Hermann Hallauer, 123–25. See Hallauer, "Sonnenburg."

Vetter, Genoveva. Letters. In *Die Söflinger Briefe und das Klarissenkloster Söflingen bei Ulm im Spätmittelalter*, ed. Max Miller, 193–97. See Miller, *Söflinger Briefe*.

"Wer got lob und danck wil sagen umb die uberflüssigen genad, . . ." [Gotteszell Sister-Book.] In "Aufzeichnungen über das Mystische Leben der Nonnen." ed. F. W. E. Roth. *Alemania* 21 (1893): 123–48.

Other Printed Primary Sources

Albrecht, Karl, ed. *Rappoltsteinisches Urkundenbuch 759–1500.* 5 vols. Colmar: Waldmeyer, 1891–98.

Alpers, Paul, ed. "Das Wienhausener Liederbuch." *Niederdeutsches Jahrbuch* 38 (1943–47): 1–41.

[Busch, Johannes.] *Des Augustinerpropstes Iohannes Busch Chronicon Windeshemense und Liber de reformatione monasteriorum.* Edited by Karl Grube. Geschichtsquellen der Provinz Sachsen und angrenzender Gebiete 19. Halle: Hendel, 1886.

Clara und Franciscus von Assisi: Eine spätmittelalterliche alemannische Legende der Magdalena Steinerin, mit 8 Miniaturen aus der Pergamenthandschrift der Badischen Landesbibiliothek Karlsruhe, afterward by Christian von Heusinger. Constance: Simon and Koch, 1959.

Crusius, Martin. *Schwäbische Chronik.* 2 vols. Translated by Johann Jakob Moser. Frankfurt: Metzler and Erhard, 1733.

[Cusa, Nicholas of.] Draft of reform statutes for Sonnenburg Abbey (1453). In "Eine Visitation des Nikolaus von Kues im Benediktinerinnenkloster Sonnenburg," ed. Hermann Hallauer, appendix, 120–23. See Hallauer, "Sonnenburg."

Dacheux, L., ed. *Die ältesten Schriften Geilers von Kaysersberg.* 1882; reprint, Amsterdam: Rodopi, 1965.

Denifle, Heinrich, ed. "Das Leben der Margareta von Kenzingen." *Zeitschrift für deutsches Altertum* 19 (1876): 478–91.

Dietler, Seraphin. *Seraphin Dietler's Chronik des Klosters Schönensteinbach.* Edited by Johann von Schlumberger. Guebwiller: Boltz, 1897.

Frachet, Gérard de. *The Lives of the Brethren of the Order of Preachers 1206–1259.* Translated by Placid Conway. London: Burns, Oates, and Washbourne, 1924.

Geiler von Kaysersberg, Johannes. *Das Evangeli buch. das buoch der Evangelien durch das gantz jar. Mitt Predig vnd vßlesungen durch den wirdigen hochgelerten Doctor Johannes Geiler von Keisersperg . . . vnd dz vß seinem mund von wort zu wort geschrieben.* Straßburg: Johannes Grieninger, 1515.

———. *Johannes Geiler von Kaysersberg. Sämtliche Werke.* 3 vols. Edited by Gerhard Bauer. Berlin: de Gruyter, 1989–95.

Geiß, Ernst, ed. "Relation der Aebtissin Ursula der Pfäffingerin von Frauen-Chiemsee über den pfälzisch-bayerischen Erbfolge-Krieg." *Oberbayerisches Archiv für vaterländische Geschichte* 8 (1847): 224–36.

"Die Geissenhof'sche Chronik des Klosters Inzigkofen." Edited by Theodor Dreher. *Freiburger Katholisches Kirchenblatt* 38 (1894): cols. 405, 421–24, 441–44, 460–63, 475–79, 489–93, 505–9, 521–24, 537–42, 555–60, 570–76, 589–92, 604–6, 638–40, 650–52, 666–69, 684–87, 697–99, 713–16, 732–34, 766–68, 794–97, 813–16, 826–28.

Greith, Carl, ed. *Die deutsche Mystik im Predigerorden (von 1250–1530) nach ihren Grundlehren, Liedern und Lebensbildern.* 1861; reprint, Amsterdam: Rodopi, 1965.

[Hanisch, Raphael.] "Chronik der böhmischen Observantenprovinz (c. 1510/20)." Edited by Nikolaus Pol. In *Jahrbücher der Stadt Breslau,* ed. Johann Gustav Büsching, 3:15–25. Breslau: Friedrich Korn, 1819.

Jostes, Franz, ed. "Eine Werdener Liederhandschrift aus der Zeit um 1500," *Jahrbuch des Vereins für niederdeutsche Sprachforschung* 14 (1888): 60–89.

Kempis, Thomas à. *The Imitation of Christ.* Translated by E. M. Blaiklock. Nashville, Tenn.: Thomas Nelson, 1979.

König, J. "Die Chronik der Anna von Munzingen. Nach der ältesten Abschrift mit Einleitung und Beilagen." *Freiburger Diözesan-Archiv* 13 (1880): 129–236.

Kößling, Rainer, ed. *Leben und Legende der heiligen Elisabeth. Nach Dietrich von Apolda. Mit 14 Miniaturen der Handschrift von 1481.* Leipzig: Insel, 1999.

"Kurze Chronik des Gotzhuses St. Gallen (1360–1490)." Edited by J. Hardegger. *Mitteilungen zur vaterländischen Geschichte* 2 (1863): 1–109.

Lipphardt, Walther, ed. "Niederdeutsche Reimgedichte und Lieder des 14. Jahrhunderts in den mittelalterlichen Orationalien der Zisterzienserinnen von Medingen und Wienhausen." *Niederdeutsches Jahrbuch* 95 (1972): 66–131.

Meyer, Johannes. *Ämterbuch.* Edited by Sarah DeMaris. Monumenta Ordinis fratrum praedicatorum historica. Rome: Insititutum Historicum Fratrum Praedicatorum, forthcoming.

———. *Das Buch der Reformacio Predigerordens.* 2 vols. Edited by Benedictus Maria Reichert. Quellen und Forschungen zur Geschichte des Dominikanerordens in Deutschland 2 and 3. Leipzig: Harrassowitz, 1908–9.

———. "Epistel brief zu den swestren predigerordens, 1470." Edited by Heribert Christian Scheeben. *Archiv der deutschen Dominikaner* 1 (1937): 186–89.

[Nider, Johannes.] *Formicarius.* Edited by Hans Biedermann. Graz: Akademischer Druck- und Verlagsanstalt, 1971.

———. Letter, 25 October 1428. In *Seraphin Dietler's Chronik des Klosters Schönensteinbach,* ed. Johannes von Schlumberger, 362–66. See Dietler, *Chronik.*

Nyberg, Tore, ed. *Dokumente und Untersuchungen zur inneren Geschichte der drei Brigittenklöster Bayerns 1420–1570.* Quellen und Erörterungen zur bayerischen Geschichte n.F. 26. 2 vols. Munich: Beck, 1972–74.

Pertz, G. H., Oswald Holger-Egger, et al., *Monumenta Germaniae historica inde ab anno Christi quingentesimo usqve ad Annum millesimum et quingentesimum. Scriptorum.* 33 vols. Hannover: Hahn, 1888; reprint, Stuttgart: Hiersemann, 1991.

Öhem, Gallus. *Die Chronik des Gallus Öhem.* Edited by Karl Brandi. Quellen und Forschungen zur Geschichte der Abtei Reichenau 2. Heidelberg: Winter, 1893.

Roth, R. W. E, ed. "Aufzeichnungen über das Mystische Leben der Nonnen von Kirchberg bei Sulz Predigerordens während des XIV. und XV. Jahrnunderts." *Alemania* 21 (1893): 103–48.

Sandhoff, Johann Itel. *Die Gertrudenberger Chronik des Johann Itel Sandhoff vom Jahre 1759.* Edited by Hans-Hermann Breuer. Osnabrück: Schöningh, 1939.

Scheepsma, Wybren, ed. "Twee onuitgegeven traktaatjes van Alijt Bake." *Ons geestelijk erf* 66 (1992): 145–67.

Schröder, Eduard, ed. "Die Ebstorfer Liederhandschrift," *Jahrbuch des Vereins für niederdeutsche Sprachforschung* 15 (1889): 1–32.

Slaggert, Lambert. "Lambert Slaggerts Chronik." In *Die Chroniken des Klosters Ribnitz,* ed. Friedrich Techen, 63–171. See Techen, *Ribnitz.*

Sattler, Christian Friedrich, *Geschichte des Herzogtums Wuerttemberg unter der Regierung der Graven.* 4 vols. 2d ed. Tübingen: Reiss, 1773–77.

Straganz, Maximilianus, ed. "Duae relationes circa Monasterium Brixinense O. Clar." *Archivum Franciscanum Historicum* 6 (1913): 531–45.

Techen, Friedrich, ed. *Die Chroniken des Klosters Ribnitz.* Mecklenburgische Geschichtsquellen I. Schwerin: Bärensprungsche Hofdruckerei, 1909.

[Tortsch, Johannes.] *Diss biechlin saygt an die wayssagung von[n] zükunfftiger betrübnusz. Wölliche grausmen betrübtnusz vns klärlichen aussprechen ist. Sannt Birgitta. Sannt Sybilla. Sant Gregorius. Sant Hilgart. Sant Joachim. Vnd wirt genant die Bürde der welt.* Augsburg: Hans Schönsperger, 1522.

Ulrich V von Würtemberg, Count. Letter, 8 April 1478. In *Geschichte des Herzogtums Wuertemberg unter der Regierung der Graven.* 4 vols. 2d ed. Edited by Christian Friedrich Sattler, 3:98–99. Tübingen: Reiss, 1773–77.

[Uytenhove, Johannes.] "Tractatus 'Pro Reformatione.'" Edited by Raymond Martin. *Analecta sacri Ordinis fratrum praedicatorum* 16 (1923–24): 46–48, 279–303.

Warnock, Robert G., ed. *Die Predigten Johannes Paulis.* Münchener Texte und Untersuchungen zur Literatur des deutschen Mittelalters 26. Munich: Beck 1970.

SECONDARY SOURCES

Achten, Gerard. *Das Christliche Gebetbuch im Mittelalter: Andachts- und Stundenbücher in Handschrift und Frühdruck.* Staatsbibliothek Preussischer Kulturbesitz, exh. cat. 13. Wiesbaden: Reichert, 1980.

Ahlgren, Gillian T. W. *Teresa of Avila and the Politics of Sanctity.* Ithaca: Cornell University Press, 1996.

Albert, Peter. "Johannes Meyer, ein oberdeutscher Chronist des fünfzehnten Jahrhunderts." *Zeitschrift für die Geschichte des Oberrheins* 52, n.F. 13 (1998): 255–63.

———. "Zur Lebensgeschichte des Dominikanerchronisten Johannes Meyer." *Zeitschrift für die Geschichte des Oberrheins* 60, n.F. 21 (1906): 504–10.

Ammann, Alfred. "Die Klosterfrauen in St. Katharinental und die Reformation." *Katholische Schweizerblätter,* n.F. 9 (1893): 240–50.

Andermann, Ulrich. "Zur Erforschung mitelalterlicher Kanonissenstifte: Aspekte zum Problem der weiblichen 'vita canonica.'" In *Geistliches Leben und standesgemässes Auskommen: Adelige Damenstifte in Vergangenheit und Gegenwart,* ed. Kurt Andermann, 11–42. Tübingen: Bibliotheca Academica, 1998.

Anderson, Bonnie S., and Judith P. Zinsser. *A History of Their Own: Women in Europe from Prehistory to the Present.* 2 vols. New York: Harper and Row, 1988–89.

Appuhn, Horst. *Kloster Medingen.* Munich: Deutscher Kunstverlag, 1974.

Armgart, Martin. "Ein fehlgeschlagener Reformversuch des Speyrer Dominikanerinnenklosters im Jahr 1442." In *Palatia Historica. Festschrift für Ludwig A. Doll,* ed. Pirmin Spieß, 247–77. Mainz: Gesellschaft für mittelrheinische Kirchengeschichte, 1994.

Backes, Martina. "Literarische Interessenbildung im mittelalterlichen Südwesten am Beispiel der Stadt Freiburg/Br." In *"Ze hove und an der strázen." Die deutsche Literatur des Mittelalters und ihr "Sitz im Leben." Festschrift für Volker Schupp,* ed. Anna Keck and Theodor Nolte, 1–11. Stuttgart and Leipzig: S. Hirzel, 1999.

———. "Zur literarischen Genese frauenmystischer Viten und Visionstexte am Beispiel des Freiburger 'Magdalenenbuches.'" In *Literarische Kommunikation und soziale Interaktion:*

Studien zur Institutionalität mittelalterlicher Literatur, ed. Beate Keller et al., 251–60. Bern: Lang, 2001.

Bailey, Michael D. *Battling Demons: Witchcraft, Heresy, and Reform in the Late Middle Ages.* University Park, Pa.: Penn State Press, 2003.

Baker, Joanne. "Female Monasticism and Family Strategy: The Guises and Saint Pierre de Reims." *Sixteenth Century Journal* 28 (1975): 1091–1108.

Baltrusch-Schneider, Dagmar. "Klosterleben als alternative Lebensgestaltung im Fränkischen Reich." In *Weibliche Lebensgestaltung im frühen Mittelalter,* ed. Hans-Werner Goetz, 45–64. Cologne: Böhlau, 1991.

Barker, Paula S. Datsko. "Caritas Pirckheimer: A Female Humanist Confronts the Reformation." *Sixteenth Century Journal* 26 (1995): 259–72.

Barth, Medard. "Dr. Johannes Kreutzer (gest. 1468) und die Wiederaufrichtung des Dominikanerinnenklosters Engelporten in Gebweiler. Kritisch und geschichtlich behandelt." *Archiv für elsässische Kirchengeschichte* 8 (1933): 181–208.

———. "Die Haltung beim Gebet in elsässischen Dominikanerinnenklöstern des 15. und 16. Jahrnunderts." *Archiv für elsässische Kirchengeschichte* 13 (1938): 141–48.

Barthelmé, Annette. *La Réforme dominicaine au XVe siècle en Alsace et dans l'ensemble de la province de Teutonie.* Collection d'études sur l'histoire du droit et des institutions de l'Alsace 7. Strasbourg: Heitz, 1931.

Bartholemy, Claudia. "Élisabeth Kempf, prieure à Unterlinden: une vie entre traduction et tradition." In *Les Dominicaines d'Unterlinden,* 2 vols., ed. Madeleine Blondel and Jeffrey Hamburger, 1:167–70. Paris: Somogy, 2000.

Bartlett, Anne Clark. *Male Authors, Female Readers.* Ithaca: Cornell University Press, 1995.

Bauer, Gerhard. "Johannes Geiler von Kaysersberg: Ein Problemfall für Drucker, Herausgeber, Verleger, Wissenschaft und Wissenschaftsförderung." *Daphnis* 5 (1994): 559–89.

Bauerreiss, Romuald. *Kirchengeschichte Bayerns.* 7 vols. St. Ottilien: EOS, 1949–75.

Baum, Wilhelm. *Nikolaus Cusanus in Tirol. Das Wirken des Philosophen und Reformators als Fürstbischof von Brixen.* Bozen: Athesia, 1983.

Bäurle, Margaret and Luzia Braun. "Klöster und Höfe—Räume literarischer Selbstentfaltung." In *Frauen Literatur Geschichte" Schreibende Frauen vom Mittelalter bis zur Gegenwart,* ed. Hiltrud Gnüg and Renate Möhrmann, 1–15. Stuttgart: Metzler, 1985.

Beach, Alison I. "The Female Scribes of Twelfth-Century Bavaria." Ph.D. diss., Columbia University, 1996.

———. "Voices from a Distant Land: Fragments of a Twelfth-Century Nuns' Letter Collection." *Speculum* 77 (2002): 34–54.

———. *Women as Scribes: Book Production and Monastic Reform in Twelfth-Century Bavaria.* Cambridge: Cambridge University Press, 2004.

Becker, Petrus. "Benediktinische Reformbewegungen im Spätmittelalter. Ansätze, Entwicklungen, Auswirkungen." In *Untersuchungen zu Kloster und Stift,* 167–87. Veröffentlichungen des Max-Planck-Instituts für Geschichte 68, Studien zur Germania Sacra 14. Göttingen: Vandenhoeck und Ruprecht, 1980.

———. "Erstrebte und erreichte Ziele benediktinischer Reformen im Spätmittelalter." In *Reformbemühungen und Ordensbestrebungen im spätmittelalterlichen Ordenswesen,* ed. Kaspar Elm, 23–34. Berliner Historische Studien 14, Ordensstudien 6. Berlin: Dunker and Humblot, 1989.

Bell, David. *What Nuns Read: Books and Libraries in Medieval English Nunneries.* Cistercian Studies 158. Kalamazoo, Mich.: Cistercian Publications, 1995.

Bernards, Matthäus. *Speculum Virginum: Geistigkeit und Seelenleben der Frau im Hochmittelalter.* Cologne: Böhlau, 1955.

———. "Zur Seelensorge in den Frauenklöstern des Hochmittelalters." *Revue Bénédictine* 66 (1956): 256–68.

Bihlmeyer, Karl. "Mystisches Leben in dem Dominikanerinnenkloster Weiler bei Esslingen im 13. und 14. Jahrhundert." *Württembergische Vierteljahrshefte für Landesgeschichte.* n.F. 25 (1916): 61–93.

———. "Die schwäbische Mystikerin Elsbeth Achler von Reute (gest. 1420) und die Überlieferung ihrer Vita." In *Festgabe Philipp Strauch zum 80. Geburtstag,* ed. Georg Baesecke and Ferdinand Joseph Schneider, 88–109. Halle: Niemeyer, 1932.

Billinkoff, Jodi. *The Avila of Saint Teresa: Religious Reform in a Sixteenth-Century City.* Ithaca: Cornell University Press, 1989.

Birlinger, Anton. "Amores Soeflingensis." *Alemannia* 3 (1875): 86–88, 140–48.

Blank, Walter. "Die Nonnenviten des 14. Jahrhunderts. Eine Studie zur hagiographischen Literatur des Mittelalters unter besonderer Berücksightigung der Visionen und ihrer Lichtphänomene." Ph.D. diss., University of Freiburg, 1962.

Boffey, Julia. "Women Authors and Women's Literacy in Fourteenth- and Fifteenth-Century England." In *Women and Literature in Britain, 1150–1500,* ed. Carol Meale, 159–82. Cambridge: Cambridge University Press, 1993.

Bollmann, Anne. " 'Being a Woman on My Own': Alijt Bake (1415–1455) as Reformer of the Inner Self." In *Seeing and Knowing: Women and Learning in Medieval Europe 1200–1600,* ed. Anneke Mulder-Bakker. Tournhout, Belgium: Brepols, in press.

———. "Weibliche Diskurse: Die Schwesternbücher der *devotio moderna* zwischen Biographie und geistlicher Konversation." In *Kultur, Geschlecht, Körper,* ed. Genus— Münsteraner Arbeitskreis für Gender Studies, 241–84. Münster: Agenda, 1999.

Bookmann, Hartmut. "Über den Zusammenhang von Reichsreform und Kirchenreform." In *Reform von Kirche und Reich: Zur Zeit der Konzilien von Konstanz (1414–1418) und Basel (1431–1449),* ed. Ivan Hlavácek and Alexander Patschovsky, 203–14. Konstanz: Universitätsverlag Konstanz, 1996.

Borchling, Conrad, ed. "Litterarisches und geistiges Leben in Kloster Ebstorf am Ausgange des Mittelalters." *Zeitschrift des historischen Vereins für Niedersachsen* 4 (1905): 361–420.

Bornstein, Daniel. "Women and Religion in Late Medieval Italy: History and Historiography." In *Women and Religion in Medieval and Renaissance Italy,* ed. Daniel Bornstein, 1–27. Chicago: University of Chicago Press, 1996.

Böse, Kristin. "Der Magdalenenteppich des Erfurter Weißfrauenklosters im Spiegel des spätmittelalterlichen Reformgedankens. Bildinhalt und Herstellungsprozeß." In *Lesen, Schreiben, Sticken und Erinnern,* ed. Gabriela Signori, 53–89. Bielefeld: Verlag für Regionalgeschichte, 2000.

Borst, Arno. *Mönche am Bodensee (610–1525).* Sigmaringen: Thorbecke, 1978.

Bossert, Gustav. "Die Quellen zur Reformationsgeschichte des Dominikanerinnenklosters in Pforzheim." *Zeitschrift für Geschichte des Oberrheins,* n.F. 34 (1919): 465–85.

Brandmüller, Walter. "Causa reformationis. Ergebnisse und Probleme der Reformen des Konstanzer Konzils." *Annuarium Historiae Conciliorum* 13 (1981): 49–66.

Brett-Evans, David. "Sibilla von Bondorf—Ein Nachtrag." *Zeitschrift für deutsche Philologie* 86 (1967), Sonderheft: 91–98.

Bridenthal, Renate, Claudia Koonz, and Susan Stuard, eds. *Becoming Visible: Women in European History.* 2d ed. Boston: Houghton Mifflin, 1987.

Brosius, Dieter. "Die Lüneburger Klöster und ihr Verhältnis zum Landesherrn." In *Das Benediktinerinnenkloster Ebstorf im Mittelalter: Vorträge einer Tagung im Kloster Ebstorf vom 22. bis 24. Mai 1987,* ed. Klaus Jaitner and Ingo Schwab, 135–56. Hildesheim: Lax, 1988.

Bruckner, Albert. "Zum Problem der Frauenhandschrift im Mittelalter." In *Aus Mittelalter und Neuzeit. Gerhard Kallen zum 70. Geburtstag,* ed. Josef Engel, 171–83. Bonn: Hanstein, 1957.

Bruins, Clara. *Chiara d'Assisi come 'altera Maria': Le miniature della vita di Santa Chiara nel manoscritto Tennenach-4 di Karlsruhe.* Iconographia Franciscana 12. Rome: Instituto storico dei Cappucini, 1999.

Bryant, Gwendolyn. "Caritas Pirckheimer: The Nuremberg Abbess." In *Women Writers of the Renaissance and Reformation,* ed. Katharina M. Wilson, 287–303. Athens: University of Georgia Press, 1987.

Bücher, Carl. *Die Frauenfrage im Mittelalter.* Tübingen: Laupsch, 1882.

Buchwald, Gustav von. "Anna von Buchwald, Priorin des Klosters Preetz 1494–1508." *Zeitschrift der Gesellschaft für Schleswig-Holsteinische Geschichte* 9 (1897): 3–98.

Bürkle, Susanne. *Literatur im Kloster: Historische Funktion und rhetorische Legitimation frauenmystischer Texte des 14. Jahrhunderts.* Tübingen and Basel: Francke, 1999.

———. "Weibliche Spiritualität und imaginierte Weiblichkeit." *Zeitschrift für deutsche Philologie* 113 (1994): 116–43.

Burr, David. *The Spiritual Franciscans: From Protest to Persecution in the Century after Saint Francis.* University Park: Pennsylvania State University Press, 2001.

Bynum, Caroline Walker. *Holy Feast and Holy Fast: The Religious Significance of Food to Medieval Women.* Berkeley and Los Angeles: University of California Press, 1987.

———. *Jesus as Mother: Studies in the Spirituality of the High Middle Ages.* Berkeley and Los Angeles: University of California Press, 1982.

———. "Religious Women in the Later Middle Ages." In *Christian Spirituality. High Middle Ages and Reformation,* ed. Jill Raitt, Bernard McGinn, and John Meyendorff, 121–39. New York: Crossroad, 1987.

Cameron, Euan. *The European Reformation.* Oxford: Clarendon, 1991.

Classen, Albrecht. "Footnotes to the German Canon: Maria von Wolkenstein and Argula von Grumbach." In *The Politics of Gender in Early Modern Europe,* ed. Jean R. Brink et al., 131–48. Sixteenth Century Essays and Studies 12. Kirksville, Mo.: Sixteenth Century Studies Journal Publishers, 1989.

———. "The Implications of Feminist Theory on the Study of Medieval German Literature. Also an Introduction." In *Women as Protagonists and Poets in the German Middle Ages: An Anthology of Feminist Approaches to Middle High German Literature,* ed. Albrecht Classen, i–xxi. Göppinger Arbeiten zur Germanistik 528. Göppingen: Kümmerle, 1991.

———. "New Voices in the History of German Women's Literature from the Middle Ages to 1600: Problems and New Approaches." *German Studies Review* 23 (2000): 13–31.

Coakley, John. "Friars as Confidants of Holy Women in Medieval Dominican Hagiography." In *Images of Sainthood in Medieval Europe,* ed. Renate Blumenfeld-Kosinski and Timea Szell, 222–46. Ithaca: Cornell University Press, 1991.

———. "Gender and the Authority of the Friars. The Significance of Holy Women for Thirteenth-Century Franciscans and Dominicans." *Church History* 60 (1991): 445–60.

Constable, Giles. *Attitudes Toward Self-Inflicted Suffering in the Middle Ages.* Brookline, Mass: Hellenic College Press, 1982.

———. *The Reformation of the Twelfth Century*. Cambridge: Cambridge University Press, 1996.

———. "Renewal and Reform in Religious Life: Concepts and Realities." In *Renaissance and Renewal in the Twelfth Century*, ed. Robert L. Benson and Giles Constable, 37–67. Cambridge: Harvard University Press, 1982.

Costard, Monika. "Predigthandschriften der Schwestern vom gemeinsamen Leben: Spätmittelalterliche Predigtüberlieferung in der Bibliothek des Klosters Nazareth in Geldern." In *Die deutsche Predigt im Mittelalter*, Internationales Symposium am Fachbereich Germanistik der Freien-Universität Berlin vom 3–6 Oktober 1989, ed. Volker Mertens and Hans-Jochen Schiewer, 194–222. Tübingen: Niemeyer, 1993.

———. "Zwischen Mystik und Moraldidaxe. Deutsche Predigten des Fraterherren Johannes Veghe und des Dominikaners Konrad Schlatter in Frauenklöstern des 15. Jahrhunderts." *Ons geestelijk erf* 69 (1995): 235–59.

Cramer, Thomas. *Geschichte der deutschen Literatur im späten Mittelalter*. Munich: DTV, 1990.

Cross, Claire. " 'Great Reasoners in Scripture': the Activities of Women Lollards." In *Medieval Women*, ed. Derek Baker, 359–80. Oxford: Blackwell, 1978.

Dacheux, L. *Die ältesten Schriften Geilers von Kaysersberg*. 1882; reprint, Amsterdam: Rodopi, 1965.

———. *Johannes Geiler von Kaisersberg. Ein katholischer Reformator am Ende des 15. Jahrhunderts*. Freiburg: Herder, 1877.

Däniker-Gysin, Marie-Claire. *Geschichte des Dominikanerinnenklosters Töß 1233–1525*. Neujahrsblatt der Stadtbibliothek Winterthur 289. Winterthur: Ziegler, 1957.

Davis, Natalie Z. "Gender and Genre: Women as Historical Writers (1400–1820)." In *Beyond their Sex. Learned Women of the European Past*, ed. Patricia Labalme, 153–82. New York: New York University Press, 1980.

———. " 'Women's History' in Transition: The European Case." *Feminist Studies* 1 (1976): 83–103.

Degler-Spengler, Brigitte. *Das Klarissenkloster Gnadental in Basel 1289–1529*. Quellen und Forschungen zur Basler Geschichte 3. Basel: Reinhardt, 1969.

———. "Observanten außerhalb der Observanz. Die franziskanischen Reformen "sub ministris." *Zeitschrift für Kirchengeschichte* 89 (1978): 354–71.

———. "Die religiöse Frauenbewegung des Mittelalters: Conversen-Nonnen-Beginen." *Rottenburger Jahrbuch für Kirchengeschichte* 3 (1984): 75–88.

———. " 'Zahlreich wie die Sterne des Himmels': Zisterzienser, Dominikaner und Franziskaner vor dem Problem der Inkorporation von Frauenklöstern." *Rottenburger Jahrbuch für Kirchengeschichte* 4 (1985): 37–50.

———. "Zisterzienserorden und Frauenklöster. Anmerkungen zur Forschungsproblematik." In *Die Zisterzienser. Ordensleben zwischen Ideal und Wirklichkeit*, ed. Kaspar Elm, 213–220. Ergänzungsband, Schriften des rheinischen Museumsamtes 18. Cologne: Rheinland-Verlag, 1982.

DeMeyer, Albert. *La Congrégation de Hollande ou la réforme dominicaine en territoire bourguignon (1465–1515)*. Liège: Soledi, 1946.

Denne, Ulrike. *Die Frauenklöster im spätmittelalterlichen Freiburg im Breisgau*. Freiburg: Alber, 1997.

Dersch, Wilhelm. *Hessisches Klosterbuch: Quellenkunde zur Geschichte der im Regierungsbezirk Kassel, der Provinz Oberhessen und dem Fürstentum Waldeck gegründeten Stifter, Klöster und*

Niederlassungen von geistilchen Genossenschaften. Veröffentlichungen der Historischen Kommission für Hessen und Waldeck 12. Marburg: Elwert, 1915.

Dewischeit, Curt. *Georg Rörer, ein Geschwindschreiber Luthers.* Berlin: Schrey, 1899.

Dinzelbacher, Peter. *Mittelalterliche Visionsliteratur: Eine Anthologie.* Darmstadt: Wissenschaftliche Buchgesellschaft, 1989.

———. *Religiöse Frauenbewegung und mystische Frömmigkeit im Mittelalter.* Köln: Böhlau, 1988.

———. "Rollenverweigerung, religiöser Aufbruch und mystisches Erleben mittelalterlicher Frauen." In *Mittelalterliche Frauenmystik,* ed. Peter Dinzelbacher, 27–76. Paderborn: Schöningh, 1993.

———. "Die 'Vita et Revelationes' der Wiener Begine Agnes Blannbekin (1315) im Rahmen der Viten- und Offenbarungsliteratur ihrer Zeit." In *Frauenmystik im Mittelalter,* ed. Peter Dinzelbacher and Dieter R. Bauer, 152–77. Ostfildern: Schwabenverlag, 1985.

Dinzelbacher, Peter, and Dieter Bauer, eds. *Frauenmystik im Mittelalter.* Ostfildern: Schwabenverlag, 1985.

Dinzelbacher, Peter, and Kurt Ruh. "Magdalena von Freiburg." In *Die deutsche Literatur des Mittelalters: Verfasserlexikon,* ed. Kurt Ruh et al., 5: cols. 1117–21. Berlin: de Gruyter, 1985.

Dißelbeck-Tewes, Elke. *Frauen in der Kirche. Das Leben der Frauen in den mittelalterlichen Zisterzienserklöstern Fürstenberg, Graefental und Scheldenhorst.* Dissertationen zur mittelalterlichen Geschichte 8 (Cologne: Böhlau, 1989).

Doelle, Ferdinand. *Die Observanzbewegung in der sächsischen Franziskanerprovinz (Mittel- und Ostdeutschland) bis zum Generalkapitel von Parma 1529.* Reformationsgeschichtliche Studien und Texte, 30 and 31. Münster: Aschendorff, 1918.

Driscoll, Michael S. "Penance in Transition: Popular Piety and Practice." In *Medieval Liturgy: A Book of Essays,* ed. Lizette Larson-Miller, 121–63. New York: Garland, 1997.

Dronke, Peter. *Women Writers of the Middle Ages: A Critical Study of Texts from Perpetua (d. 203) to Marguerite Porete (d. 1310).* Cambridge: Cambridge University Press, 1984.

Duffy, Eamon. *The Stripping of the Altars: Traditional Religion in England, c. 1400–1580.* New Haven: Yale University Press, 1992.

Eckenstein, Lina. *Women under Monasticism.* 1896; reprint, New York: Russel and Russel, 1963.

Ecker, Ulrich. P. "Die Geschichte des Klosters S. Johannes-Baptista der Dominikanerinnen zu Kirchheim unter Teck." Ph.D. diss., University of Freiburg, 1985.

———. "Die Reform der Freiburger Dominikanerinenklöster Adelhausen, St. Agnes und St. Maria Magdalena, 1465." Zulassungsarbeit zur wissenschaftlichen Prüfung für das Lehramt an Gymnasien, Freiburg i. Br., 1976.

Eckhard, Michael. "Bildstickereien aus Kloster Lüne als Ausdruck der Reformation des 15. Jahrhunderts." *Die Diözese Hildesheim in Vergangenheit und Gegenwart* 53 (1985): 63–78.

Egger, Franz. *Beiträge zur Geschichte des Predigerordens. Die Reform des Baseler Konvents 1429 und die Stellung des Ordens am Baseler Konzil 1431–1448.* Bern: Lang, 1991.

Ehrenschwendtner, Marie-Luise. "'Puellae litteratae': The Use of the Vernacular in the Dominican Convents of Southern Germany." In *Medieval Women in their Communities,* ed. Diane Watt, 49–71. Toronto: Univeristy of Toronto Press, 1997.

Eisele, Friedrich. "Das Klosterleben der regulierten Augustiner-Chorfrauen von Inzigkofen." *Freiburger Diözesan Archiv* 65 (1937): 125–55.

Selected Bibliography

Elm, Kaspar. "Die Brüderschaft vom gemeinsamen Leben. Eine geistliche Lebensform zwischen Kloster und Welt, Mittelalter und Neuzeit." *Ons geestelijk erf* 59 (1985): 470–96.

———. "Die Franziskanerobservanz als Bildungsreform." In *Lebenslehren und Weltentwürfe im Übergang vom Mittelalter zur Neuzeit. Politik-Bildung-Naturkunde-Theologie. Bericht über Kolloquien der Kommission zur Erforschung der Kultur des Spätmittelalters*, ed. Hartmut Boockmann, Bernt Moeller, and Karl Stackmann, 201–13. Abhandlungen der Akademie der Wissenschaften in Göttingen, Phil-hist. Klasse, Folge 3, No. 179. Göttingen: Vandenhoeck, 1989.

———. *Literarische Formen des Mittelalters: Florilegien, Kompilationen, Kollektionen*. Wolfenbüttler Mittelalter-Studien 15. Wiesbaden: Harrassowitz, 2000.

———, ed. *Reformbemühungen und Observanzbestrebungen im spätmittelalterlichen Ordenswesen*. Berliner Historische Studien 14, Ordensstudien 6. Berlin: Duncker and Humblot, 1989.

———. "Reformen und Kongregationsbildungen der Zisterzienser in Spätmittelalterlicher und früher Neuzeit." *Die Zisterzienser. Ordensleben zwischen Ideal und Wirklichkeit. Eine Ausstellung des Landschaftsverbandes Rheinland. Aachen 3 July–28 September, 1980*, ed. Kaspar Elm and Peter Joerissen, 243–54. Schriften des Rheinischen Museumamtes 10. Cologne: Rheinlandverlag, 1980.

———. "Verfall und Erneuerung des Ordenswesens im Spätmittelalter: Forschungen und Forschungsaufgaben." In *Untersuchungen zu Kloster und Stift*, 188–238. Veröffentlichungen des Max-Planck-Instituts für Geschichte 68, Studien zur Germania Sacra 14. Göttingen: Vandenhoeck und Ruprecht, 1980.

———. "'Vita regularis sine regula': Bedeutung, Rechtsstellung und Selbstverständnis des mittelalterlichen und frühneuzeitlichen Semireligiosentums." In *Häresie und vorzeitige Reformation im Spätmittelalter*, ed. Frantisek Smahel and Elisabeth Müller-Lückner, 239–73. Munich: Oldenburg, 1998.

———. "Westfälisches Zisterziensertum und die spätmittelalterliche Reformbewegung." *Westfälische Zeitschrift* 128 (1978): 9–32.

Elm, Kaspar, and Peter Joerissen, eds. *Die Zisterzienser. Ordensleben zwischen Ideal und Wirklichkeit*. Schriften des Rheinischen Museumsamtes 10. Cologne: Rheinland Verlag, 1981.

Engelbert, Pius. "Die Bursfelder Benediktinerkongregation und die spätmittelalterlichen Reformbewegungen." *Historisches Jahrbuch* 103 (1983): 35–55.

Ennen, Edith. *Frauen im Mittelalter*. Munich: Beck, 1984.

Erdin, Emil. *Das Kloster der Reuerinnen Sancta Maria Magdalena an den Steinen zu Basel von den Anfängen bis zur Reformation (etwa 1230–1529)*. Fribourg: Paulus, 1956.

Erler, Mary C. *Women, Reading, and Piety in Late Medieval England*. Cambridge: Cambridge University Press, 2002.

Erler, Mary C., and Maryanne Kowaleski, eds. "Introduction: A New Economy of Power Relations: Female Agency in the Middle Ages," in *Gendering the Master Narrative*, ed. Erler and Kowaleski, 1–16. (Ithaca: Cornell University Press, 2003).

———. *Women and Power in the Middle Ages*. Athens: University of Georgia Press, 1988.

Faust, Ulrich, ed. *Die Frauenklöster in Niedersachsen, Schleswig-Holstein und Bremen*. Germania Benedictina 11: Norddeutschland. St. Ottilien: EOS-Verlag, 1984.

———. "Monastisches Leben in den Lüneburger Klöstern." In *Das Benediktinerinnenkloster Ebstorf im Mittelalter. Vorträge einer Tagung im Kloster Ebstorf vom 22. bis 24. März 1987*, ed. Klaus Jaitner and Ingo Schwab, 27–40. Hildesheim: Lax, 1988.

Fechter, Werner. *Deutsche Handschriften des 15. und 16. Jahrhunderts aus der Bibliothek des ehemaligen Augustinerchorfrauenstifts Inzigkofen.* Sigmaringen: Thorbecke, 1997.

———. "Johannes Meyer, O.P." In *Die deutsche Literatur des Mittelalters: Verfasserlexikon,* ed. Kurt Ruh et al., 6:cols. 474–89. Berlin: de Gruyter, 1983.

Felten, Franz J. "Frauenklöster und -stifte im Rheinland im 12. Jahrhundert. Ein Beitrag zur Geschichte der Frauen in der religiösen Bewegung des hohen Mittelalters." In *Reformidee und Reformpolitik im spätsalisch-frühstaufischen Reich,* ed. Stefan Weinfurter, 189–200. Quellen und Abhandlungen zur Mittelrheinischen Kirchengeschichte 68. Mainz: Seibert, 1992.

Ferrante, Joan. *To the Glory of Her Sex: Women's Roles in the Composition of Medieval Texts.* Bloomington: Indiana University Press, 1997.

Finke, Laurie. *Feminist Theory, Women's Writing.* Ithaca: Cornell University Press, 1992.

Fischer, Karl. "Die Buchmalerei in den beiden Dominikanerklöstern Nürnbergs." Ph.D. diss., University of Erlangen, 1928.

Flaskamp, Franz. "Die Chroniken des Klosters Herzebrock." *Osnabrücker Mitteilungen* 73 (1966): 38–54.

———. "Sophie von Münster Äbtissin zu Herzebrock." *Jahrbuch des Vereins für westfälische Kirchengeschichte* 63 (1970): 7–11.

Fößel, Amalie, and Anette Hettinger. *Klosterfrauen, Beginen, Ketzerinnen. Religiöse Lebensformen von Frauen im Mittelalter.* Idstein: Schulz-Kirchner, 2000.

Frank, Barbara. *Das Erfurter Peterskloster im 15. Jahrhundert. Studien zur Geschichte der Klosterreform und der Bursfelder Union.* Veröffentlichungen des Max-Planck-Instituts für Geschichte 34, Studien zur Germania sacra 2. Göttingen: Vandenhoeck and Ruprecht, 1973.

———. "Subiaco, ein Reformkonvent des späten Mittelalters." *Quellen und Forschungen aus italienischen Archiven und Bibliotheken* 15 (1972): 526–656.

Frank, Isenard W. "Der Anschluß des Salzburger Dominikanerklosters Friesach an die österreichischen Observanten, 1502–1503." *Archivum Fratrum Praedicatorum* 52 (1982): 219–266.

Frank, Karl Suso. *Das Klarissenkloster Söflingen: Ein Beitrag zur franziskanischen Ordensgeschichte Süddeutschlands und zur Ulmer Kirchengeschichte.* Ulm, Stuttgart: Kohlhammer, 1980.

Freed, John B. "Urban Development and the 'Cura Monialium' in Thirteenth-Century Germany." *Viator* 3 (1972): 311–27.

Fries, Walter. "Kirche und Kloster zu St. Katharina in Nürnberg." *Mitteilungen des Vereins für Geschichte der Stadt Nürnberg* 25 (1924): 1–143.

Frye, Susan, and Karen Robertson, eds. *Maids and Mistresses, Cousins and Queens: Women's Alliances in Early Modern England.* Oxford: Oxford University Press, 1999.

Gand, Friedrich. *Maria-Reuthin. Dominikanerinnenkloster und Hohenberger Grablege.* Göppingen: Kümmerle, 1973.

Garber, Rebecca. *Feminine Figurae: Representations of Gender in Religious Texts by Medieval Women Writers, 1100–1375.* New York and London: Routledge, 2003.

Gasser, Vincenz. "Das Benediktinerinnenstift Sonnenburg im Pustertal." *Studien und Mitteilungen aus dem Benediktiner- und Zisterzienserorden* 9 (1888): 39–57, 251–58.

Gatz, Johannes. "Pfullingen." *Alemania Franciscana Antiqua* 17 (1972): 169–216.

Gehring, Hester McNeal Reed. "The Language of Mysticism in South German Dominican Convent Chronicles of the XIVth Century." Ph.D. diss, University of Michigan, 1957.

Gerz-von Büren, Veronika. *Geschichte des Clarissenklosters St. Clara in Kleinbasel 1266–1529.* Quellen und Forschungen zur Basler Geschichte 2. Basel: Reinhardt, 1969.

Giesel, J. A. "Eine Heggbacher Chronik." *Württembergische Vierteljahrshefte* 2 (1879): 220–23, 259–65.

Gilchrist, Roberta. *Gender and Material Culture: The Archaeology of Religious Women*. London: Routledge, 1993.

Gill, Katherine. "Open Monasteries for Women in Late Medieval and Early Modern Italy: Two Roman Examples." In *The Crannied Wall: Women, Religion, and the Arts in Early Modern Europe*, ed. Craig Monson, 15–47. Ann Arbor: University of Michigan Press, 1992.

———. "'Scandala': Controversies Concerning Clausura and Women's Religious Communities in Late Medieval Italy." In *Christendom and its Discontents*, ed. Scott Waugh and Peter Diehl, 177–203. Cambridge: Cambridge University Press, 1996.

———. "Women and the Production of Religious Literature in the Vernacular, 1300–1500." In *Creative Women in Medieval and Early Modern Italy*, ed. E. Ann Matter and John Coakley, 64–104. Philadelphia: University of Pennsylvania Press, 1994.

Glatz, Karl J. "Auszüge aus den Urkunden des Bickenklosters in Villingen." *Zeitschrift für die Geschichte des Oberrheins* 32 (1880): 274–308.

Gleba, Gudrun. *Reformpraxis und materielle Kultur: Westfälische Frauenklöster im Mittelalter*. Husum: Matthiesen, 2000.

Glente, Karen. "Mystikerinnen aus männlicher und weiblicher Sicht: Ein Vergleich zwischen Thomas von Cantimpré und Katherina von Unterlinden." In *Religiöse Frauenbewegungen und Mystische Frömmigkeit im Mittelalter*, ed. Peter Dinzelbacher and Dieter R.Bauer, 251–64. Cologne: Böhlau, 1988.

Goetz, Hans-Werner. "Zum Geschichtsbewußtsein in der alemannisch-schweizerischen Klosterchronik des hohen Mittelalters (11.–13. Jh.)" *Deutsches Archiv für Erforschung des Mittelalters* 44 (1988): 455–88.

Goodich, Michael. "The Contours of Female Piety in Later Medieval Hagiography." *Church History* 50 (1981): 20–32.

Gnüg, Hiltrud and Renate Möhrmann. *Frauen Literatur Geschichte: Schreibende Frauen vom Mittelalter bis zur Gegenwart*. Stuttgart: Metzler, 1999.

Graf, Klaus. "Ordensreform und Literatur in Augsburg während des 15. Jahrhunderts." In *Literarisches Leben in Augsburg während des 15. Jahrhunderts*, ed. Johannes Janota and Werner Williams-Krapp, 100–159. Tübingen: Niemeyer, 1995.

Greenspan, Karen. "Erklärung des Vaterunsers: A Critical Edition of a 15th-Century Mystical Treatise by Magdalena Beutler of Freiburg." Ph.D. diss, University of Massachusetts, 1984.

Greith, Karl-Ernst. "L'activité littéraire des dominicaines d'Unterlinden aux XIVe et XVe siècles." In *Les Dominicaines d'Unterlinden*, 2 vols., ed. Madeleine Blondel and Jeffrey Hamburger, 1:160–66. Paris: Somogy, 2000.

———. "Eine deutsche Übersetzung der 'Vita Sancti Udalrici' des Bern von Reichenau aus Unterlinden in Colmar." In *Durch abenteuer muess man wagen vil: Festschrift für Anton Schwob zum 60. Geburtstag*, ed. Wernfried Hofmeister and Bernd Steinbauer, 109–18. Innsbruck: Institut für Germanistik, 1997.

———. "Elisabeth Kempf (1415–1485). Priorin und Übersetzerin in Unterlinden zu Colmar." *Annuarie de la Société d'Histoire et d'Archéologie de Colmar* 29 (1980/81): 47–73.

———. "Elisabeth Kempfs Überstetzung und Fortsetzung der 'Vitae sororum' der Katharina von Gueberschwihr." *Annuaire de la Société d'Histoire et d'Archéologie de Colmar* 32 (1984): 27–42.

————. "Heiligenverehrung und Hagiographie im Kloster Unterlinden zu Colmar." In *Dominicans et Dominicaines en Alsace, XIII –XXe siècle. actes du colloque de Guebwiller 8–9 Avril 1994,* ed. Jean-Luc Eichenlaub, 167–72. Colmar: Archives Départementales du Haut-Rhin, 1996.

————. "Die Leben-Jesu-Übersetzung der Schwester Regula aus Lichtenthal." *Zeitschrift für deutsches Altertum und deutsche Literatur* 119 (1990): 22–37.

————. "Ulrich von Augsburg." In *Die deutsche Literatur des Mittelalters: Verfasserlexikon,* ed. Kurt Ruh et al., 9:cols. 1240–45. Berlin: de Gruyter, 1995.

Greven, Joseph. *Die Anfänge der Beginen. Ein Beitrag zur Geschichte der Volksfrömmigkeit und des Ordenswesens im Hochmittelalter.* Vorreformationsgeschichtliche Forschungen 8. Münster: Aschendorff, 1912.

Grieser, D. Jonathan. "A Tale of Two Convents: Nuns and Anabaptists in Münster, 1533–1535." *Sixteenth Century Journal* 26 (1995): 31–48.

Griesser, Bruno. "Die Reform des Klosters Rechentshofen in der alten Speyerer Diözese durch Abt Johann von Maulbronn 1431–33." *Archiv für Mittelrheinische Kirchengeschichte* 8 (1956): 270–84.

Grube, Karl. *Johannes Busch Augustinerpropst zu Hildesheim: Ein katholischer Reformator des 15. Jahrhunderts.* Freiburg: Herder, 1881.

Grubmüller, Klaus. "Die Viten der Schwestern von Töss und Elsbeth Stagel." *Zeitschrift für deutsches Altertum* 98 (1969): 171–204.

Grundmann, Herbert. "Die Frauen und die Literatur im Mittelalter. Ein Beitrag zur Frage nach der Entstehung des Schrifttums in der Volkssprache." *Archiv für Kulturgeschichte* 26 (1936): 129–61.

————. *Religious Movements in the Middle Ages: The Historical Links between Heresy, the Mendicant Orders, and the Women's Religious Movement in the Twelfth and Thirteenth Century, with the Historical Foundations of German Mysticism.* Translated by Stephen Rowen. Notre Dame: University of Notre Dame Press, 1995.

Haas, Alois. "Elsbeth Stagel." In *Die deutsche Literatur des Mittelalters: Verfasserlexikon,* ed. Kurt Ruh et al., 9: cols 219–25. Berlin: de Gruyter, 1995.

Habermas, Rebekka. "Die Beginen—eine 'andere' Konzeption von Weiblichkeit?" In *Die ungeschriebene Geschichte. Historische Frauenforschung, Dokumentation 5. Historikerinnentreffen April 1984,* ed. Wiener Historikerinnen, 199–207. Vienna: Wiener Frauenverlag, 1984.

Haffner, Franz. *Die kirchlichen Reformbemühungen des Speyrer Bischofs Matthias von Rammung in vortridentinischer Zeit (1464–1478).* Speyer: Pilger, 1961.

Hallauer, Hermann. "Eine Visitation des Nikolaus von Kues im Benediktinerinnenkloster Sonnenburg." *Mitteilungen und Forschungsbeiträge der Cusanus-Gesellschaft* 4 (1964): 104–25.

————. "Nikolaus von Kues und das Brixener Klarissenkloster." *Mitteilungen und Forschungsbeiträge der Cusanus-Gesellschaft* 6 (1967): 75–123.

Halter, Annemarie. *Geschichte des Dominikanerinnenklosters Oetenbach in Zürich 1234–1525.* Winterthur: Keller, 1956.

Hamburger, Jeffrey F. "La bibliothèque d'Unterlinden et l'art de la formation spirituelle." In *Les Dominicaines d'Unterlinden,* ed. Madeleine Blondel and Jeffrey Hamburger, 2 vols., 1:110–59. Paris: Somogy, 2000.

————. *Nuns as Artists. The Visual Culture of a Medieval Convent.* California Studies in the History of Art 37. Berkeley and Los Angeles: University of California Press, 1997.

————. *The Visual and the Visionary. Art and Female Spirituality in Late Medieval Germany.* New York: Zone Books, 1998.

Hamm, Berndt. "Von der spätmittelalterlichen reformatio zur Reformation: Der Prozeß normativer Zentrierung von Religion und Gesellschaft in Deutschland." *Archiv für Reformationsgeschichte* 84 (1993): 7–81.

Härtel, Helmar. "Die Bibliothek des Klosters Ebstorf am Ausgang des Mittelalters." In *'In Treue und Hingabe:' 800 Jahre Kloster Ebstorf,* ed. Marianne Elster and Horst Hoffmann, 109–21. Schriften zur Uelzener Heimatkunde 13. Uelzen: Becker, 1997.

————. "Klosterbibliotheken zwischen Reform und Reformation. Studien zur niedersächsischen Bibliotheksgeschichte im ausgehenden 15. und beginnenden 16. Jahrhundert." In *Probleme der Bearbeitung mittelalterlicher Handschriften,* ed. Helmar Härtel et al., 121–31. Wolfenbütteler Forschungen 30. Wiesbaden: Harrassowitz, 1986.

————. "Die Klosterbibliothek Ebstorf. Reform und Schulwirklichkeit am Ausgang des Mittelalters." In *Schule und Schüler im Mittelalter,* ed. Martin Kintzinger, 245–58. Cologne: Böhlau, 1996.

Hasebrink, Burkhard. "Tischlesung und Bildungskultur im Nürnberger Katharinenkloster. Ein Beitrag zu ihrer Rekonstruktion." In *Schule und Schüler im Mittelalter. Beiträge zur europäischen Bildungsgeschichte des 9. bis 15. Jahuhunderts,* ed. Martin Kintzinger, Sönke Lorenz, and Michael Walter, 187–216. Beihefte zum Archiv für Kulturgeschichte 42. Cologne: Böhlau, 1996.

Hauber, A. "Deutsche Handschriften in Frauenklöstern des späteren Mittelalters." *Zentralblatt für Bibliothekswesen* 31 (1914): 341–73.

Haug, Franz, and Johann Adam Kraus. "Urkunden des Dominikanerinnenklosters Stetten in Gnadental bei Hechingen 1261–1802." *Hohenzollerische Jahreshefte* 17 (1957): 321–444.

Haumann, Heiko, and Hans Schadek, eds. *Geschichte der Stadt Freiburg im Breisgau.* 3 vols. Stuttgart: Theiss, 1992–96.

Häussler, Max. *Felix Fabri aus Ulm und seine Stellung zum geistigen Leben seiner Zeit.* Beiträge zur Kulturgeschichte des Mittelalters und der Renaissance 15. Berlin, Leipzig: Teubner, 1914.

Haverkamp, Alfred. "Leben in Gemeinschaften: Alte und neue Formen im 12. Jahrhundert." In *Aufbruch—Wandel–Erneuerung: Beiträge zur 'Renaissance' des 12. Jahrhunderts,* ed. Georg Wieland, 11–44. Stuttgart: Frommann-holzboog, 1995.

Head, Thomas. "Hrosvith's 'Primordia' and the Historical Tradition of Monastic Communities." In *Hrosvit of Gandersheim: Rara avis in Saxonia?* ed. Katharina M. Wilson, 143–64. Medieval and Renaissance Monograph Series 7. Ann Arbor, Mich.: Medieval and Renaissance Collegium, 1987.

Heimpel, Hermann. "Das deutsche 15. Jahrhundert. In Krise und Beharrung." In *Die Welt zur Zeit des Konstanzer Konzils.* Reichenauvorträge im Herbst 1964, ed. Theodor Mayer, 9–29. Vorträge und Forschungen 9. Stuttgart Thorbecke, 1965.

Heinen, Hadamut. "Beiträge zur Geschichte des Klosters Rolandswerth (Nonnenwerth)." *Annalen des historischen Vereins für den Niederrhein* 128 (1936): 1–41.

Heinrich, Helmut, and Gisela Sattler, eds. *200 Jahre Kloster St. Ursula Villingen.* Villingen: Kloster St. Ursula, n.d.

Heinzer, Felix. "Handschriften und Drucke des 15. und 16. Jahrhunderts aus der Benediktinerinnenabtei Frauenalb. Eine bibliotheksgeschichtliche Skizze." *Bibliothek und Wissenschaft* 20 (1986): 93–124.

————. "Lichtenthaler Bibliotheksgeschichte als Spiegel der Klostergeschichte." *Zeitschrift für Geschichte des Oberrheins* 136 (1988): 35–62.

Heinzer, Felix, and Gerhard Stamm. *Die Handschriften der Badischen Landesbibliothek in Karlsruhe: XI. Die Handschriften von Lichtenthal.* Wiesbaden: Harrassowitz, 1987.

Helmbold, Marie Luise. *Geschichte des Stiftes Fischbeck bei der Weser.* Göttingen: Edition Studentica, 1982.

Helmrath, Johannes. *Das Basler Konzil 1431–1449: Forschungsstand und Probleme.* Cologne: Böhlau, 1987.

————. "Reform als Thema der Konzilien des Spätmittelalters." In *Christian Unity. The Council of Ferrara-Florenz 1438/39–1449,* ed. Giuseppe Alberigo, 75–152. Louvain: Louvain University Press, 1991.

————."Theorie und Praxis der Kirchenreform." *Rottenburger Jahrbuch für Kirchengeschichte* 11 (1992): 41–70.

Herlihy, David. "Did Women have a Renaissance?: A Reconsideration." *Medievalia et Humanistica* n.s. 13 (1985): 1–22.

Hengst, Karl, ed. *Westfälisches Klosterbuch: Lexikon der vor 1815 errichteten Stifte und Klöster von ihrer Gründung bis zur Aufhebung.* 2 vols. Veröffentlichungen der Historischen Kommission für Westfalen 44. Münster: Aschendorff, 1992–94.

Herrgott, Ernst. "Necrologium von Alspach." *Alemania Franciscana Antiqua* 13 (1969): 59–83.

Heusinger, Christian von. "Spätmittelalterliche Buchmalerei in oberrheinischen Frauenklöstern." *Zeitschrift für die Geschichte des Oberrheins* 107 (1959): 136–60.

————. "Studien zur oberrheinischen Buchmalerei und Graphik im Spätmittelalter." Ph.D. diss., University of Freiburg, 1953.

Heusinger, Sabine von. "Catherine of Siena and the Dominican Order." In *Siena e il suo territorio nel Rinascimento,* ed. Mario Ascheri, 43–51. Siena: Leccio, 2000.

————. *Johannes Mulberg, O.P. (d. 1414): Ein Leben im Spannungsfeld von Dominikanerobservanz und Beginenstreit.* Quellen und Forschungen zur Geschichte des Dominikanerordens, n.F. 9. Berlin: Akademie, 2000.

Hilberling, Brigitte. *700 Jahre Kloster Zoffingen, 1257–1957.* Constance: Merk, 1957.

Hillenbrand, Eugen. "Die Observantenbewegung in der deutschen Ordensprovinz der Dominikaner." In *Reformbemühungen und Observanzbestrebungen im spätmittelalterlichen Ordenswesen,* ed. Kaspar Elm, 219–71. Berliner Historische Studien 14, Ordensstudien 6. Berlin: Dunker and Humblot, 1989.

Hindsley, Leonard P. *The Mystics of Engelthal: Writings from a Medieval Monastery.* New York: St. Martin's Press, 1998.

Hinnebusch, William A. *The History of the Dominican Order.* 2 vols. New York: Alba House, 1966–73.

Hlaváček, Ivan, and Alexander Patschovsky, eds. *Reform von Kirche und Reich zur Zeit der Konzilien von Konstanz (1414–1418) und Basel (1431–1449).* Konstanz: Universitätsverlag Konstanz, 1996.

Hoffmann, Horst, and Marianne Elster. *In Treue und Hingabe": 800 Jahre Kloster Ebstorf.* Ebstorf: Cloister Ebstorf, 1997.

Hofmeister, Philipp. "Liste der Nonnenklöster der Bursfelder Kongregation." *Studien und Mitteilungen zur Geschichte des Benediktinerordens* 53 (1935): 77–102.

Holdsworth, Christopher. "Were the Sermons of St. Bernard on the Song of Songs ever

Preached?" In *Medieval Monastic Preaching*, ed. Carolyn Muessig, 295–318. Leiden: Brill, 1998.

Hollywood, Amy. *The Soul as Virgin Wife: Mechthild of Magdeburg, Marguerite Porete, and Meister Eckhart.* Notre Dame, Ind.: University of Notre Dame Press, 1995.

Holtorf, Anne. "Ebstorfer Liederbuch." In *Die deutsche Literatur des Mittelalters: Verfasserlexikon*, ed. Kurt Ruh et. al., 2: cols. 312–14. Berlin: de Gruyter, 1980.

Homeyer, Joachim. *500 Jahre Äbtissinnen in Medingen.* Uelzen: Becker, 1994.

Honemann, Volker. "Klostergründungsgeschichten." In *Die deutsche Literatur des Mittelalters: Verfasserlexikon*, ed. Kurt Ruh et. al., 4: cols. 1239–1247. Berlin: de Gruyter, 1983.

Honée, Eugène. "Image and Imagination in the Medieval Culture of Prayer: A Historical Perspective." In *The Art of Devotion in the Late Middle Ages in Europe, 1300–1500*, ed. Henk van Os, 157–74. Princeton: Princeton University Press, 1994.

Hopfenzitz, Josef. "Das Brigittenkloster Maihingen (1437–1607)." *Jahrbuch des Vereins für Augsburger Bistumsgeschichte* 3 (1969): 27–85.

Hornung, Hans. "Daniel Sudermann als Handschriftensammler: Ein Beitrag zur Straßburger Bibliotheksgeschichte." Ph.D. diss., University of Tübingen, 1956.

———. "Der Handschriftensammler D. Sudermann und die Bibliothek des Straßburger Klosters St. Nikolaus in Undis." *Zeitschrift für Geschichte des Oberrheins* 107 (1959): 338–99.

Hotchin, Julie. "Enclosure and Containment: Jutta and Hildegard at the Abbey of St. Disibod." *Magistra* 2 (1996): 103–23.

———. "Female Religious Life and the 'Cura monialium' in Hirsau Monasticism, 1080 to 1150." In *Listen Daughter: The 'Speculum virginum' and the Formation of Religious Women in the Middle Ages*, ed. Constant Mews, 59–83. New York: Palgrave, 2001.

Howell, Martha, Suzanne Wemple, and Denise Kaiser. "A Documented Presence: Medieval Women in Germanic Historiography." In *Women in Medieval History and Historiography*, ed. Susan Mosher Stuard, 101–31. Philadelphia: University of Pennsylvania Press, 1987.

Hubrath, Margarete. "Monastische Memoria als Denkform in der Viten- und Offenbarungsliteratur aus süddeutschen Frauenklöstern des Spätmittelalters." *Zeitschrift für Literaturwissenschaft und Linguistik* 27 (1997): 22–38.

Huemer, Blasius. "Verzeichnis der deutschen Zisterzienserinnenklöster." *Studien und Mitteilungen zur Geschichte des Benediktinerordens* n.F. 6 (1916): 1–47.

Hüffer, Maria. *Die Reformen in der Abtei Rijnsburg im 15. Jahrhundert.* Münster: Aschendorff, 1937.

Humberdrotz, Rudolf, ed. *Die Chronik des Klosters Sonnenburg (Pustertal). Eingeleitet und aus der Originalhandschrift ediert von Rudolf Humberdrotz*, 2 vols. Vol. 1: *1597–1766*. Schlern-Schriften 226. Innsbruck: Wagner, 1963.

Hunt, Lynn, ed. *The New Cultural History.* Berkeley and Los Angeles: University of California Press, 1989.

Hyma, Albert. *The Christian Renaissance: A History of the "Devotio Moderna."* 2d ed. Hamden, Conn.: Archen, 1965.

Jäger, Albert. *Der Streit des Cardinals Nicolaus von Cusa mit dem Herzoge Sigmund von Österreich als Grafen von Tirol.* 2 vols. Innsbruck: Wagner, 1861.

Jaitner, Klaus. "Das Benediktinerinnenkloster Ebstorf im Mittelalter (ca. 1165–1550)." In *Das Benediktinerinnenkloster Ebstorf im Mittelalter. Vorträge einer Tagung im Kloster Ebstorf vom 22. Bis 24. Mai 1987*, ed. Klaus Jaitner and Ingo Schwab, 1–25. Veröffentlichungen der Historischen Kommission für Niedersachsen und Bremen 37. Hildesheim: Lax, 1988.

———. "Kloster Ebstorf." In *Die Frauenklöster in Niedersachsen, Schleswig-Holstein und Bremen,* ed. Ulrich Faust, 165–92. Germania Benedictina 11. St. Ottilien: EOS, 1984.

Janota, Johannes. "Werdener Liederbuch." In *Die deutsche Literatur des Mittelalters: Verfasserlexikon,* ed. Kurt Ruh et. al., 10: cols. 883–86. Berlin: de Gruyter, 1999.

Janota, Johannes, and Werner Williams-Krapp, eds. *Literarisches Leben in Augsburg während des 15. Jahrhunderts.* Tübingen: Niemeyer, 1995.

Jászai, Géza, ed. *Monastisches Westfalen: Kloster und Stifte 800–1800.* Münster: Westfälisches Landesmuseum für Kunst und Kulturgeschichte, 1982.

Jedelhauser, Canisia. *Geschichte des Klosters und der Hofmark Maria-Medingen von den Anfängen im 13. Jahrhundert bis 1606.* Quellen und Forschungen zur Geschichte des Dominikanerordens in Deutschland 34. Leipzig: Harrassowitz, 1936.

Johnson, Penelope D. *Equal in Monastic Profession: Religious Women in Medieval France.* Chicago: University of Chicago Press, 1991.

———. "'Mulier et Monialis': The Medieval Nun's Self-Image." *Thought* 64 (1989): 242–53.

Jones, Rufus Matthew. *The Flowering of Mysticism. The Friends of God in the Fourteenth Century.* 1939; reprint, New York: Hafner, 1971.

Jostes, Franz, ed. *Meister Eckhart und seine Jünger. Ungedruckte Texte zur Geschichte der deutschen Mystik.* Collectanea Friburgensis 4. Fribourg, Switzerland: Kommissionsverlag der Universitätsbuchhandlung, 1894.

Kaes, Anton. "New Historicism and the Study of German Literature." *The German Quarterly* 62 (1989): 210–19.

Kells, Kathleen. E. "Christine Pisan's 'le Dit de Poissy': An Exploration of an Alternative Lifestyle for Aristocratic Women in Fifteenth-Century France." In *New Images of Medieval Women" Essays Toward a Cultural Anthropology,* ed. Edelgard DuBruck, 103–18. Medieval Studies 1. Lewiston, N.Y.: Mellen, 1989.

Kelly-Gadol, Joan. "Did Women Have a Renaissance?" In *Becoming Visible: Women in European History,* ed. Renate Bridenthal and Claudia Koonz, 137–64. Boston: Houghton Mifflin, 1977.

Kelm, Elfriede. "Das Buch im Chore der Preetzer Klosterkirche. Nach dem Original dargestellt." *Schriften des Vereins für Schleswig-Holsteinische Kirchengeschichte* 30/31 (1974/75): 7–35.

Kern, Theodor von. "Die Reformation des Katharinenklosters zu Nürnberg im Jahr 1428." *Jahresbericht des historischen Vereins für Mittelfranken* 31 (1863): 1–20.

Ketsch, Peter. *Frauen im Mittelalter.* 2 vols. Studien Materialien 19. Düsseldorf: Schwann, 1984.

Kieckhefer, Richard. "A Church Reformed though Not Deformed?" *Journal of Religion* 74 (1994): 240–49.

Kienzle, Beverly. *The Sermon.* Typologie des Sources du Moyen Age Occidental 81–83. Turnhout: Brepols, 2000.

Kienzle, Beverly Mayne, and Pamela J. Walker, eds. *Women as Preachers and Prophets through Two Millennia of Christianity.* Berkeley and Los Angeles: University of California Press, 1998.

Kiessling, Rolf. *Bürgerliche Gesellschaft und Kirche in Augsburg im Spätmittelalter. Ein Beitrag zur Strukturanalyse der oberdeutschen Reichsstadt.* Abhandlungen zur Geschichte der Stadt Augsburg 19. Augsburg: Mühlberger, 1971.

Kist, Johannes. *Das Klarissenkloster in Nürnberg bis zum Beginn des 16. Jahrhunderts.* Nuremberg: Sebaldus, 1929.

———. "Klosterreform im spätmittelalterlichen Nürnberg." *Zeitschrift für bayerische Kirchengeschichte* 32 (1963): 31–45.

Kittel, Erich. *Kloster und Stift St. Marien in Lemgo, 1265–1965. Festschrift anlässlich des 700jährigen Bestehens.* Detmold: Naturwissenschaftlicher und historischer Verein für das Land Lippe, 1965.

Klapisch-Zuber, Christiane, "The Medievalist: Women and the Serial Approach." In *Writing Women's History*, ed. Michelle Perrot, trans. Felicia Pheasant, 25–33. Oxford: Blackwell, 1992.

———, ed. *Silences of the Middle Ages.* Vol. 2 of *A History of Women in the West.* Cambridge, Mass.: Harvard University Press, 1992.

Klueting, Edeltraud. *Das Bistum Osnabrück 1: Das Kanonissenstift und Benediktinerinnenkloster Herzebrock.* Germania Sacra n.F.21. Berlin: de Gruyter, 1986.

Knetsch, Peter. *Frauen im Mittelalter.* 2 vols. Düsseldorf: Schwann, 1983–84.

Knötig, Karl. *Die Sonnenburg im Pustertal.* Bozen: Athensia, 1985.

Koch, M. Aquinata. *Geschichte des Klosters St. Katharina in Wil.* Wil: n.p., 1928.

König, J. "Zur Geschichte der Freiburger Klöster." *Freiburger Diözesan-Archiv* 12 (1878): 291–303.

Kooper, Erik, ed. *The Medieval Chronicle: Proceedings of the 1st International Conference on the Medieval Chronicle.* Driebergen/Utrecht 13–16 July 1996. Amsterdam: Rodopi, 1999.

Koudelka, Vladimír. "Zur Geschichte der böhmischen Dominikanerprovinz im Mittelalter." *Archivum fratrum Praedicatorum* 26 (1956): 127–60.

Kramer, Dewey Weiss. " 'Arise and Give the Convent Bread': Christine Ebner, the Convent Chronicle of Engelthal, and the Call to Ministry among Fourteenth-Century Religious Women." In *Women as Protagonists and Poets in the German Middle Ages: An Anthology of Feminist Approaches to Middle High German Literature*, ed. Albrecht Classen, 187–206. Göppingen: Kümmerle, 1991.

Krämer, Sigrid. *Handschriftenerbe des deutschen Mittelalters.* Mittelalterliche Bibliothekskataloge Deutschlands und der Schweiz, Supplements 1–3. Munich: Beck, 1989–90.

Krauß, R. "Geschichte des Dominikaner-Frauenklosters Kirchberg." *Württembergische Vierteljahreshefte* 3 (1894): 291–332.

Krebs, Engelbert. "Die Mystik in Adelhausen. Eine vergleichende Studie über die 'Chronik' der Anna von Munzingen und die thaumatographische Literatur des 13. und 14. Jahrhunderts als Beitrag zur Mystik im Predigerorden." In *Festgabe, Heinrich Finke*, ed. Gottfried Buschbell, 41–105. Münster: Aschendorff., 1904.

Kristeller, Paul Oskar. "The Contribution of Religious Orders to Renaissance Thought and Learning." *The American Benedictine Review* 21 (1970): 1–55.

Kristeller, Paul Oskar, and Edward P. Mahoney, eds. *Medieval Aspects of Renaissance Learning. Three Essays by P. O. Kristeller.* Duke Monographs in Medieval and Renaissance Studies, 1. Durham, N.C.: Duke University Press, 1974.

Krug, Rebecca. *Reading Families: Women's Literate Practice in Late Medieval England.* Ithaca: Cornell University Press, 2002.

Kühler, Wilhelmus Johannes. *Johannes Brinckerinck en zijn klooster te Diepenveen.* 2d ed. Leiden: van Leewen, 1914.

Kuhn-Rufus, Maren. "Frauenzisterze, Landesherrschaft und Reichsfreiheit. Kloster Wald, die Grafschaft Sigmaringen in Vorderösterreich." *Zeitschrift für württembergische Landesgeschichte* 46 (1987): 11–85.

———. "Frauenzisterze und Vogtei. Kloster Wald und die Grafschaft Sigmaringen." *Zeitschrift für württembergische Landesgeschichte* 45 (1986): 25–101.

———. "Zisterzienserinnen in Deutschland." In *Die Zisterzienser, Ordensleben zwischen Ideal und Wirklichkeit*, ed. Kaspar Elm and Peter Joerissen, 125–47. Schriften des rheinischen Museumsamtes 10. Cologne: Rheinland Verlag, 1981.

Kurras, Lotte. "Ein Bildzeugnis der Reformtätigkeit des Nürnberger Katharinenklosters für Regensburg." *Mitteilungen des historischen Vereins für die Geschichte der Stadt Nürnberg* 68 (1981): 293–96.

Kurras, Lotte, and Franz Machilek, eds. *Caritas Pirckheimer, 1467–1532*. Ausstellung der Katholischen Stadtkirche Nürnberg, June 26–August 8, 1982. Munich: Prestel, 1982.

Kunze, Georg. "Studien zu den Nonnenviten des deutschen Mittelalters." Ph.D. diss, University of Hamburg, 1952.

Ladner, Gerhart. B. *The Idea of Reform: Its Impact on Christian Thought and Action in the Age of the Fathers.* Cambridge Mass: Harvard University Press, 1959.

Landmann, Florenz, ed. "Johannes Kreutzer aus Gebweiler (gest. 1468) als Mystiker und Dichter Geistlicher Lieder: Die Unterweisung an eine Klosterfrau und zwei Sammelwerke: Ein Geistlicher Mai und eine geistliche Ernte." *Archives de l'église d'Alsace* 8 (1957): 21–62.

———. "Zwei Andachtsübungen von Straßburger Klosterfrauen am Ende des Mittelalters." *Archiv für Elsässische Kirchengeschichte* 6 (1931): 217–28.

Langen, Elvira. "Eine neue Quelle für die Kenntnis des mystischen Lebens in Kloster Pillenreuth. Ph. D. diss., University of Heidelberg, 1961.

Langer, Otto. *Mystische Erfahrung und spirituelle Theologie. Zu Meister Eckharts Auseinandersetzung mit der Frauenfrömmigkeit seiner Zeit.* Münchener Texte und Untersuchungen zur deutschen Literatur des Mittelalters 91. Munich and Zurich: Artemis, 1987.

Larrier, René. *Francophone Women Writers of Africa and the Caribbean.* Gainesville, Fla.: University of Florida Press, 2000.

Laufner, Richard. "Die Bibliothek von St. Agneten und der Weberbach in Trier im 15. und 16. Jahrhundert." *Kurtrierisches Jahrbuch* 9 (1969): 121–28.

———. "St. Agneten an der Weberbach. Ein Beitrag zur Trierer Kirchen- und Kulturgeschichte." *Kurtrierisches Jahrbuch* 8 (1968): 112–28.

Lauterbach, Klaus H. *Geschichtsverständnis, Zeitdidaxe und Reformgedanke an der Wende zum 16. Jahrhungert: Das oberrheinische 'Buchli der hundert capiteln' im Kontext des spätmittelalterlichen Reformbiblizismus.* Forschungen zur oberrheinischen Landesgeschichte 33. Freiburg: K. Alber, 1985.

Lawler, Jennifer. *Encyclopedia of Women in the Middle Ages.* London: McFarland, 2001.

Leclercq, Jean. "Monastic and Scholastic Theology in the Reformers of the Fourteenth to Sixteenth Century." In *From Cloister to Classroom: Monastic and Scholastic Approaches to Truth*, ed. Rozanne Elder, 178–201. Kalamazoo, Mich.: Cistercian Publications, 1986.

———. *Recueil d'Etudes sur Saint bernard et ses écrits.* Vol. 1. Rome: Edizioni di storia e letteratura, 1962.

Lee, Andrew. "Materialien zum geistigen Leben des späten fünfzehnten Jahrhunderts im Sankt Katharinenkloster zu Nürnberg." Ph.D. diss, University of Heidelberg, 1969.

Selected Bibliography

Lee, Paul. *Nunneries, Learning and Spirituality in Late Medieval English Society: The Dominican Priory of Dartford*. Rochester, N.Y.: York Medieval Press, 2001.

Leinweber, Josef. "Provinzialsynode und Kirchenreform im Spätmittelalter." In *Reformatio ecclesiae: Beiträge zu kirchlichen Reformbemühungen von der Alten Kriche bis zur Neuzeit. Festgabe für Erwin Iserloh*. ed. Remigius Bäumer, 113–28. Paderborn: Schöningh, 1980.

Lentes, Thomas. "Bild, Reform und Cura Monialium: Bildverständnis und Bildergebrauch im 'Buch der Reformacio Predigerordens' des Johannes Meyer (d. 1485)." In *Dominicains et Dominicaines en Alsace (XIIIe–XXe Siècle): Actes du colloque de Guebwiller, 8–9 avril 1994*, ed. Jean-Luc Eichenlaub, 177–95. Colmar: Editions d'Alsace, 1996.

———. "Die Gewänder der Heiligen. Ein Diskussionsbeitrag zum Verhältnis von Gebet, Bild und Imagination." In *Hagiographie und Kunst der Heiligenkult in Schrift, Bild und Architektur*, ed. G. Kerscher, 120–51. Berlin: D. Reimer, 1993.

———. "'Tauler im Fegefeuer' oder der Mystiker als Exempel. Formen der Mystik-Rezeption im 15. Jahrhundert. Mit einem Anhang zum Sterbeort Taulers und Textabdruck." In *Contemplata aliis tradere. Studien zum Verhältnis von Literatur und Spiritualität*, ed. Claudia Brinker et al., 111–56. Bern: Lang, 1995.

Lerner, Gerda. *The Creation of Feminist Consciousness*. 2 vols. New York: Oxford University Press, 1993.

Lewis, Gertrud Jaron. *Bibliographie zur deutschen Frauenmystik des Mittelalters*. Bibliographien zur deutschen Literatur des Mittelalters 10. Berlin: Schmidt, 1989.

———. *By Women, for Women, about Women: The Sister-Books of Fourteenth-Century Germany*. Toronto: Pontifical Institute of Medieval Studies, 1996.

———. "Hildegard von Bingen (1098–1179)." In *Medieval Germany: An Encyclopedia*, ed. John Jeep, 358–59. New York: Garland, 2001.

Limbeck, Rolf. *Der St. Agneskonvent zu Emmerich*. Emmericher Forschungen 16. Emmerich: Emmericher Geschichtsverein, 1998.

Linneborn, Johannes. "Die Bursfelder Kongregation während der ersten hundert Jahre ihres Bestandes." *Deutsche Geschichtsblätter* 14 (1912/13): 3–30, 33–58.

———. "Die Reformation der westfälischen Benedictiner-Klöster im 15. Jahrhundert durch die Bursfelder Congregation." *Studien und Mitteilungen zur Geschichte des Benedictinerordens* 20 (1899): 266–314, 531–70; 21 (1900): 53–68, 315–32, 554–78; 22 (1901): 48–71, 396–418.

Lipphardt, Walther. "Die liturgische Funktion deutscher Kirchenlieder in den Klöstern Niedersächsischer Zisterzienserinnen des Mittelalters." *Zeitschrift für Katholische Theologie* 94 (1972): 158–98.

Loes, Gabriel. M. "Villingen: Klarissen." *Alemania Franciscana Antiqua* 3 (1957): 45–76.

Löhr, Gabriel Maria. *Die Teutonia im 15. Jahrhundert: Studies und Texte vornehmlich zur Geschichte ihrer Reform*. Quellen und Forschungen zur Geschichte des Dominikanerordens in Deutschland 19. Leipzig: Harrassowitz, 1924.

———. "Die zweite Blütezeit des Kölner Dominikanerklosters (1464–1525)." *Archivum Fratrum Praedicatorum* 19 (1949): 208–54.

Lortz, Joseph. *The Reformation in Germany*. 2 vols. Translated by Ronald Walls. New York: Herder, 1968.

———. "Zur Problematik der kirchlichen Misstände im Spätmittelalter." *Trierer theologische Zeitschrift* 58 (1949): 1–26, 212–27, 257–79, 347–57.

Lossen, Richard. "Der pfälzische Staat und die Klöster im Ausgang des Mittelalters." Ph.D. diss., University of Freiburg, 1907.

Lynch, Joseph. *The Medieval Church: A Brief History.* London: Longmann, 1992.

Machilek, Franz. "Die Frömmigkeit und die Krise des 14. und 15. Jahrhunderts." *Mediaevalia Bohemica* 4 (1971): 209–27.

———. "Der Klosterhumanismus in Nürnberg um 1500." *Mitteilungen des Vereins für Geschichte der Stadt Nürnberg* 64 (1977): 10–45.

———. "Reformorden und Ordensreformen in den böhmischen Ländern vom 10. bis 18. Jahrhundert." In *Bohemia sacra: Das Christentum in Böhmen 973–1973,* ed. Fredinand Seibt, 63–80. Düsseldorf: Schwann, 1974.

Makowski, Elizabeth. *Canon Law and Cloistered Women: "Periculoso" and Its Commentators, 1298–1545.* Washington, D.C.: Catholic University of America Press, 1997.

Martin, Francis Xavier. "The Augustinian Observant Movement." In *Reformbemühungen und Observanzbestrebungen im spätmittelalterlichen Ordenswesen,* ed. Kaspar Elm, 325–45. Berliner Historische Studien 14, Ordensstudien 6. Berlin: Dunker and Humblot, 1989.

Märtl, Claudia. "'pos verstockt weyber'?: Der Streit um die Lebensform der Regensburger Damenstifte im ausgehenden 15. Jahrhundert." In *Regensburg, Bayern und Europa. Festschrift für Kurt Reindel zum 70. Geburtstag,* ed. Lothar Kolmer and Peter Segl, 365–87. Regensburg: Universitätsverlag, 1995.

———. "Der Reformgedanke in den Reformschriften des 15. Jahrhunderts." In *Reform von Kirche und Reich zur Zeit der Konzilien von Konstanz (1414–1418) und Basel (1431–1449),* ed. Ivan Hlavácek and Alexander Patschovsky, 91–108. Konstanz: Universitätsverlag, 1996.

Marx, Jakob. *Geschichte des Erzstifts Trier, das ist der Stadt Trier und des Landes, als Churfürstenthum und als Erzdiöcese, von den ältesten Zeiten bis zum Jahre 1816,* 3 vols. in 5 parts. 1856–64; reprint, Aalen: Scientia, 1969.

Matheis-Rebaud, Christel. "'Die Predigt mit dem Gebet für die sieben Tage der Woche' von Johann Geiler von Kaysersberg (1445–1510): Ein Beispiel für die religiöse und spirituelle Unterweisung von Klosterfrauen am Ende des Mittelalters; Erstmalig veröffentlicht mit Übersetzung ins Französische." *Revue Mabillon* n.F. 63 (1991): 207–39.

Matter, E. Ann, and John Coakley, eds. *Creative Women in Medieval and Early Modern Italy: A Religious and Artistic Renaissance.* Philadelphia: University of Pennsylvania Press, 1994.

McDonnell, Ernest. *The Beguines and Beghards in Medieval Culture with Special Emphasis on the Belgian Scene.* 1954; reprint, New York: Octagon, 1969.

McLeod, Enid. *The Order of the Rose. The Life and Ideas of Christine de Pizan.* Totowa, N.J.: Rowan and Littlefield, 1976.

McNamara, Jo Ann Kay. "The Need to Give: Suffering and Female Sanctity in the Middle Ages." In *Images of Sainthood in Medieval Europe,* ed. Timea Szell, 199–221. Ithaca: Cornell University Press, 1991.

———. *Sisters in Arms: Catholic Nuns through Two Millennia.* Cambridge, Mass.: Harvard University Press, 1996.

Meale, Carol. *Women and Literature in Britain 1150–1500.* Cambridge: Cambridge University Press, 1993.

Meier, Ludwig. "Zur Geschichte des Berner Dominikanerinnenklosters im 15. Jahrhundert." *Archivum Fratrum Praedicatorum* 45 (1975): 201–11.

Mertens, Dieter. "Der Humanismus und die Reform des Weltklerus im deutschen Südwesten." *Rottenburger Jahrbuch für Kirchengeschichte* 11 (1992): 11–28.

———. "Klosterreform als Kommunikationsereignis." In *Formen und Funktionen öffentlicher*

Kommunikation im Mittelalter, ed. Gerd Althoff, 397–420. Vorträge und Forschungen 51. Stuttgart: Thorbecke, 2001.

———. "Monastische Reformbewegungen des 15. Jahrhunderts: Ideen-Ziele-Resultate." In *Reform von Kirche und Reich zur Zeit der Konzilien von Konstanz (1414–1418) und Basel (1431–1449)*, ed. Ivan Hlaváček and Alexander Patschovsky, 157–81. Constance: Universitätsverlag Konstanz, 1996.

Mertens, Thomas. "Collatio and Codex im Bereich der Devotio Moderna." In *Der Codex im Gebrauch*, ed. Christel Meier, Dagmar Hüpper, and Hagen Keller, 163–82. Münstersche Mittelalter-Schriften 70. Munich: Fink, 1996.

———. "Ghostwriting Sisters: The Preservation of Dutch Sermons of Father Confessors in the Fifteenth and Early Sixteenth Ceutury." In *Seeing and Knowing: Women and Learning in Medieval Europe 1200–1600*, ed. Anneke Mulder-Bakker. Turnhout, Belgium: Brepols, in press.

———. "Middle Dutch Sermons: Manuscript Tradition and Research Situation." *Medieval Sermon Studies* 40 (1997): 46–50.

———. "The Modern Devotion and Innovation in Middle Dutch Literature." In *Medieval Dutch Literature in its European Context*, ed. Erik Kooper, 226–41. Cambridge Studies in Medieval Literature. New York: Cambridge University Press, 1995.

———. "Postum Auteurschap de Collaties van Johannes Brinckerinck." In *600 Jaar Kapittel van Windesheim*, ed. A. J. Hendrikman et al., 85–97. Middeleeuwse Studies, 12. Nijmegen: Centrum voor Middeleeuwse Studies, Katholieke Universiteit Nijmegen, 1996.

———. "Rapiarium." in *Dictionnaire de spiritualité*, ed. Joseph de Guibert, Marcel Viller, and Ferdinand Cavallera, 13: cols. 114–19. Paris: Beauchesne, 1988.

———. "Texte der modernen Devotion als Mittler zwischen kirchlicher und persönlicher Reform." *Niederdeutsches Wort* 34 (1994): 63–74.

Mertens, Volker. "Theologie der Mönche—Frömmigkeit der Laien? Beobachtungen zur Textgeschichte von Predigten des Hartwig von Erfurt." In *Literatur und Laienbildung im Spätmittelalter und in der Reformationszeit. Symposium Wolfenbüttel 1981*. Germanische Symposien Berichtsbände 5. Stuttgart: Metzler, 1984.

Mertens, Volker, and Hans-Jochen Schiewer, eds. *Die deutsche Predigt im Mittelalter.* Tübingen: Niemeyer, 1989.

———. "Erschliessung einer Gattung: Editon, Katalogisierung und Abbildung der deutschsprachigen Predigt des Mittelalters." *Editio* 4 (1990): 93–111.

Metzger, Gerhard. "Der Dominikanerorden in Württemberg am Ausgang des Mittelalters." *Blätter für württembergische Kirchengeschichte*, n. s. 46 (1942): 4–60; 47 (1943): 1–20.

Meuthen, Erich. *Das 15. Jahrhundert.* 2d. ed. Munich: Oldenbourg, 1984.

Meyer, Johannes. "Johannes Busch und die Klosterreform des fünfzehnten Jahrhunderts." *Jahrbuch der Gesellschaft für niederländische Kirchengeschichte* 47 (1949): 43–53.

———. "Zur Reformationsgeschichte des Klosters Lüne." *Zeitschrift der Gesellschaft für niedersächsische Kirchengeschichte* 14 (1909): 161–222.

Miethke, Jürgen. "Kirchenreform auf den Konzilien des 15. Jahrhunderts. Motive-Methoden-Wirkungen. In *Studien zum 15. Jahrhundert. Festschrift für Erich Meuthen*, 2 vols., ed. Johannes Helmrath, Heribert Müller, and Helmut Wolff, 1:13–42. Munich: Oldenbourg, 1994.

Miller, Max. *Die Söflinger Briefe und das Klarissenkloster Söflingen bei Ulm im Spätmittelalter.* Würzburg: Triltsch, 1940.

———. "Der Streit um die Reform des Barfüßerklosters in Ulm und des Klarissenklosters in Söflingen und seine Beilegung, 1484–1487." In *Aus Archiv und Bibliothek. Studien aus Ulm und Oberschwaben*, ed. Alice Rössler, 175–93. Weißenborn: Konrad, 1969.

Mischlewski, Adalbert. "Monastisches Ideal und Bürgerinteressen: Das Problem der Klausur bei den Memminger Augustinerinnen." *Analecta Augustiniana* 53 (1990): 455–66.

———. "Spätmittelalterliche Reformbemühungen im Antoniterorden." In *Reformbemühungen und Observanzbestrebungen im spätmittelalterlichen Ordenswesen*, ed. Kaspar Elm, 153–69. Berliner Historische Studien 14, Ordensstudien 6. Berlin: Dunker and Humblot, 1989.

Moeller, Bernd. "Die frühe Reformation in Deutschland als Umbruch." In *Wissenschaftliches Symposion des Vereins für Reformationsgeschichte 1996*, ed. Bernd Moeller and Stephen E. Buckwalter, 76–91. Schriften des Vereins für Reformationsgeschichte, 199. Gütersloh: Gütersloh Verlagshaus, 1998.

———. "Piety in Germany around 1500." In *The Reformation in Medieval Perspective*, ed. Steven Ozment, 50–75. Chicago: Quadrangle, 1971.

———. "Religious Life in Germany on the Eve of the Reformation." In *Pre-Reformation Germany*, ed. Gerald Strauß, 13–35. New York: Harper and Row, 1972.

Moessner, Victoria Joan. "The Medieval Embroideries of Convent Wienhausen." In *Studies in Cistercian Art and Architecture 3*, ed. Meredith Lillich, 161–77. Kalamazoo, Mich.: Cistercian Publications, 1987.

Monson, Craig. "Introduction." In *The Crannied Wall: Women, Religion, and the Arts in Early Modern Europe*, 1–14. Ann Arbor: University of Michigan Press, 1992.

Mooney, Catherine M. *Gendered Voices: Medieval Saints and Their Interpreters*. Philadelphia: University of Pennsylvania Press, 1999.

Mortier, Daniel Antonin. *Histoire des maitres généraux de l'Ordre des Frères Prêcheurs*. 7 vols. Paris: Picard, 1903–14.

Mulder-Bakker, Anneke, ed. *Seeing and Knowing: Women and Learning in Medieval Europe 1200–1600*. Turnhout, Belgium: Brepols, in press.

Müller, Anneliese. "Studien zur Besitz- und Sozialgeschichte des Dominikanerinnenklosters St. Katharinental bei Dießenhofen." Ph.D. diss., University of Tübingen, 1971.

Müller, Gerhard. "Nachricht von der Reformation im Kloster Lüne, so von einer papistischen Jungfrau ehemals aufgesetzt." *Annalen der Braunschweig-Lüneburgischen Churlande* 7 (1793): 378–93.

———. "Reform und Reformation. Zur Geschichte von spätmittelalter und früher Neuzeit." *Jahrbuch der Gesellschaft für niedersächsische Kirchengeschichte* 83 (1985): 9–29.

———. "Reformation und Visitation sächsischer Klöster gegen Ende des 15. Jahrhunderts." *Neues Archiv für sächsische Geschichte und Altertumskunde* 38 (1917): 46–74.

Müller, Wolfgang. "Die Villinger Frauenklöster des Mittelalters und der Neuzeit." In *200 Jahre Kloster St. Ursula Villingen*, ed. Helmut Heinrich and Gisela Sattler, 14–31. Villingen: Kloster St. Ursula, n.d.

Müntz, Marc. "Freundschaften und Feindschaften in einem spätmittelalterlichen Frauenkloster. Die sogenannten Söflinger Briefe." In *"Meine in Gott geliebte Freundin." Freundschaftsdokumente aus klösterlichen und humanistischen Schreibstuben*, ed. Gabriela Signori, 107–16. Religion in der Geschichte. Kirche, Kultur und Gesellschaft 4. Bielefeld: Verlag für Regionalgeschichte, 1998.

Muschg, Walter. *Die Mystik in der Schweiz 1200–1500*. Frauenfeld und Leipzig: Huber, 1935.

Nagel, Bert. *Hrosvit von Gandersheim*. Stuttgart: Metzler, 1965.

Neddermeyer, Uwe. " 'Radix Studii et Speculum Vitae' Verbreitung und Rezeption der

'Imitatio Christi' in Handschriften und Drucken bis zur Reformation." In *Studien zum 15. Jahrhundert: Festschrift für Erich Meuthen*, 2 vols., ed. Johannes Helmrath et al., 1:457–81. Munich: Oldenbourg, 1994

Neidiger, Bernhard. "Der Armutsbegriff der Dominikanerobservanten: Zur Diskussion in den Konventen der Provinz Teutonia (1389–1513)." *Zeitschrift für die Geschichte des Oberrheins* 145 (1997): 117–58.

———. "Erzbischöfe, Landesherren und Reformkongregationen. Initiatoren und treibende Kräfte der Klosterreformen des 15. Jahrhunderts im Gebiet der Diözese Köln." *Rheinische Vierteljahrsblätter* 54 (1990): 19–77.

———. *Mendikanten zwischen Ordensideal und städtischer Realität*. Berliner Historische Studien 5. Berlin: Duncker und Humblot, 1981.

———. "Die Observanzbewegungen der Bettelorden in Südwestdeutschland." *Rottenburger Jahrbuch für Kirchengeschichte* 11 (1992): 175–96.

———. Selbstverständnis und Erfolgschancen der Dominikanerobservanten: Beobachtungen zur Entwicklung in der Provinz Teutonia und im Basler Konvent (1388–1510)." *Rottenburger Jahrbuch für Kirchengeschichte* 17 (1998): 67–122.

———. "Stadtregiment und Klosterreform in Basel." In *Reformbemühungen und Observanzbestrebungen im spätmittelalterlichen Ordenswesen*, ed. Kaspar Elm, 539–67. Berliner Historische Studien 14, Ordensstudien 6. Berlin: Dunker and Humblot, 1989.

Newman, Barbara. *From Virile Woman to Woman Christ: Studies in Medieval Religion and Literature*. Philadelphia: University of Pennsylvania Press, 1995.

Nimmo, Duncan. "The Franciscan Regular Observance. The Culmination of Medieval Franciscan Reform." In *Reformbemühungen und Observanzbestrebungen im spätmittelalterlichen Ordenswesen*, ed. Kaspar Elm, 189–205. Berliner Historische Studien 14, Ordensstudien 6. Berlin: Dunker and Humblot, 1989.

———. "Reform at the Council of Constance: The Franciscan Case." In *Renaissance and Renewal in Church History*, ed. Derek Baker, 159–74. Studies in Church History 14. Oxford: Blackwell, 1977.

———. *Reform and Division in the Medieval Franciscan Order, from Saint Francis to the Foundation of the Capuchins*. Rome: Capuchin Historical Institute, 1987.

Nolte, Ernst. *Quellen und Studien zur Geschichte des Nonnenklosters Lüne bei Lüneburg. I. Teil: Die Quellen. Die Geschichte Lünes von den Anfängen bis zur Klostererneuerung 1481*. Studien zur Kirchengeschichte Niedersachsens 6. Göttingen: Vandenhoeck, 1932.

Nothegger, Florentin. "Brixen/Südtirol." *Alemania Franciscana Antiqua* 17 (1972): 243–54.

Nowicki-Pastuschka, Angelika. *Frauen in der Reformation: Untersuchung zum Verhalten von Frauen in den Reichsstädten Augsburg und Nürnberg zur reformatorischen Bewegung zwischen 1517 und 1537*. Pfaffenweiler: Centaurus, 1990.

Nyberg, Tore. "Der Brigittenorden im Zeitalter der Ordensreformen." In *Reformbemühungen und Observanzbestrebungen im spätmittelalterlichen Ordenswesen*, ed. Kaspar Elm, 373–96. Berliner Historische Studien 14, Ordensstudien 6. Berlin: Dunker and Humblot, 1989.

———. "Das Hausbuch des Klosters Maihingen." *Jahrbuch des Vereins für Augsburger Bistumsgeschichte* 5 (1971): 143–68.

Nyhus, Paul L. "The Franciscan Observant Reform in Germany." In *Reformbemühungen und Observanzbestrebungen im spätmittelalterlichen Ordenswesen*, ed. Kaspar Elm, 207–17. Berliner Historische Studien 14, Ordensstudien 6. Berlin: Dunker and Humblot, 1989.

———. "The Observant Reform Movement in Southern Germany." *Franciscan Studies* 32 (1972): 154–67.

Oakley, Francis. *The Western Church in the Later Middle Ages*. Ithaca: Cornell University Press, 1979.

Obermann, Heiko. "Preface." In *Devotio Moderna: Basic Writings*, ed. John van Engen, 1–3. Mahwah, N.Y.: Paulist Press, 1988.

Ochsenbein, Peter. "Latein und Deutsch im Alltag oberrheinischer Dominikanerinnenklöster des Spätmittelalters." In *Latein und Volkssprache im deutschen Mittelalter 1100–1500*, ed. Nikolaus Henkel and Nigel Palmer, 42–51. Tübingen: Niemeyer, 1992.

———. "Spuren der Devotio moderna im spätmittelalterlichen Kloster St. Gallen." *Studien und Mitteilungen zur Geschichte des Benediktinerordens* 101 (1990): 475–96.

Oehl, Wilhelm. *Deutsche Mystikerbriefe des Mittelalters, 1100–1550*. Munich: Georg Müller, 1931.

Oliva, Marilyn. *The Convent and Community in Late Medieval England: Female Monasteries in the Diocese of Norwich, 1350–1540*. Woodbridge, Suffolk: Boydell, 1998.

O'Mara, V. M. "Preaching to Nuns in Late Medieval England." In *Medieval Monastic Preaching*, ed. Carolyn Muessig, 93–119. Leiden: Brill, 1998.

Opitz, Claudia. *Evatöchter und Bräute Christi: Weiblicher Lebenszusammenhang und Frauenkultur im Mittelalter*. Weinheim: Deutscher Studien Verlag, 1990.

Parisse, Michel. "Die Frauenstifte und Frauenklöster in Sachsen vom 10. bis zur Mitte des 12. Jahrhunderts." In *Salier und das Reich*, 2 vols., ed. Stefan Weinfurter, 2:465–501. Sigmaringen: Thorbecke, 1991.

Patschovsky, Alexander. "Der Reformbegriff zur Zeit der Konzilien von Konstanz und Basel." In *Reform von Kirche und Reich*, ed. Ivan Hlavácek and Alexander Patschovsky, 7–28. Konstanz: Universitätsverlag Konstanz, 1996.

Patze, Hans. "Klostergründung und Klosterchronik." *Blätter für deutsche Landesgeschichte* 113 (1977): 89–121.

Pearsall, Derek, and Elizabeth Salter. *Landscapes and Seasons of the Medieval World*. Toronto: University of Toronto Press, 1973.

Peters, Ursula. "Das 'Leben' der Christine Ebner: Textanalyse und kulturhistorischer Kommentar." In *Abendländische Mystik im Mittelalter. Symposion Kloster Engelberg 1984*, ed. Kurt Ruh, 402–22. Stuttgart: Metzler, 1986.

———. "Frauenliteratur im Mittelalter? Überlegungen zur Trobiaritzpoesie, zur Frauenmystik und zur feministischen Literaturbetrachtung." *Germanisch-Romanische Monatsschrift* n.F. 38 (1988): 35–56.

———. "Frauenmystik im 14. Jahrhundert; Die 'Offenbarungen' der Christine Ebner." In *Weiblichkeit oder Feminismus? Beiträge zur interdisziplinären Frauentagung, Konstanz 1983*, ed. Claudia Opitz, 213–27. Weingarten: Drumlin, 1984.

———. *Religiöse Erfahrung als literarisches Faktum: Zur Vorgeschichte und Genese frauenmystischer Texte des 13. und 14. Jahrhunderts*. Tübingen: Niemeyer, 1988.

———. "Vita religiosa und spirituelles Erleben: Frauenmystik und frauenmystische Literatur im 13. und 14. Jahrhundert." In *Deutsche Literatur von Frauen*, 2 vols., ed. Gisela Brinker-Gabler, 1:88–109. Munich: Beck, 1988.

Petroff, Elizabeth Alvilda. "Male Confessors and Female Penitants": Possibilities for Dialogue." In *Body and Soul: Essays on Medieval Woman and Mysticism*, ed. Elizabeth A. Petroff, 139–60. New York and Oxford: Oxford University Press, 1994.

———. *Medieval Women's Visionary Literature*. Oxford: Oxford University Press, 1986.

Pfanner, Josef. *Briefe von, an und über Caritas Pirckheimer aus den Jahren 1498–1530.* Landshut: Solanus, 1966.

———. *Das Gebetbuch der Caritas Pirckheimer.* Landshut: Solanus, 1961.

———. *Medieval Women's Visionary Literature.* Oxford: Oxford University Press, 1986.

Pfleger, Luzian. "Geiler von Kaysersberg und das Magdalenenkloster zu Straßburg." *Strassburger Diözesanblatt* 37 (1918): 24–31, 56–63.

———. *Kirchengeschichte der Stadt Strassburg im Mittelalter.* Colmar: Alsatia, 1941.

———. *Zur Geschichte des Predigtwesens in Straßburg vor Geiler von Kaysersberg.* Straßburg: Herder, 1907.

———. "Der Personalbestand der Straßburger Klöster in Jahre 1442." *Archiv für Elsässische Kirchengeschichte* 12 (1937): 72.

Pickel Georg. "Geschichte des Klaraklosters in Nürnberg." *Beiträge zur bayerischen Kirchengeschichte* 19 (1913): 145–72, 193–211, 241–59.

Poor, Sara S. *Mechthild von Magdeburg and her Book: Gender and the Making of Textual Authority.* Philadelphia: University of Pennsylvania Press, 2004.

Popp, Marianne. "Die Dominikanerinnen im Bistum Regensburg." *Beiträge zur Geschichte des Bistums Regensburg* 12 (1978): 259–308.

Poppe, Roswitha. "Gertrudenberg." In *Die Frauenklöster in Niedersachsen, Schleswig-Holstein und Bremen,* ed. Ulrich Faust, 475–86. Germania Benedictina 11: Norddeutschland. St. Ottilien: EOS-Verlag, 1984.

Post, Regnerus Richardus. *The Modern Devotion: Confrontation with Reformation and Humanism.* Studies in Medieval and Reformation Thought 3. Leiden: Brill, 1968.

Power, Eileen. *Medieval English Nunneries, c. 1275 to 1535.* Cambridge: Cambridge University Press, 1922.

Prieur, Jutta. *Das Kölner Dominikanerinnenkloster St. Gertrud am Neumarkt.* Kölner Schriften zu Geschichte und Kultur. Cologne: dme-Verlag, 1983.

Proksch, Constance. *Klosterreform und Geschichtsschreibung im Spätmittelalter.* Cologne: Böhlau, 1994.

Quint, Josef. "Mystik." In *Reallexikon der deutschen Literaturgeschichte,* 4 vols., 2d. ed., ed. Paul Merker, Wolfgang Stammler et al., 2:544–68. Berlin: de Gruyter, 1965.

Raitt, Jill, ed. *Christian Spirituality: High Middle Ages and Reformation.* New York: Crossroad, 1989.

Ranft, Patricia. *Women and the Religious Life in Premodern Europe.* New York: St. Martin's Press, 1996.

———. *Women and Spiritual Equality in Christian Tradition.* Basingstoke: Macmillan, 1998.

Rankl, Helmut. *Das Vorreformatorische landesherrliche Kirchenregiment in Bayern (1378–1526).* Miscellanea Bavarica Monacensia 34. Munich: Kommissionsbuchhandlung Wölfle, 1971

Rapp, Francis. "L'Observance et la Réformation en Alsace (1522–1560)." *Revue d'histoire de l'Église de France* 174 (1979): 41–54.

———. *Réformes et réformation à Strasbourg. Église et société dans le diocèse de Strasbourg (1450–1525).* Association des publications près les universités de Strasbourg. Collection de l'Instutut des Hautes Études Alsaciennes 23. Paris: Ophrys, 1974.

———. "Zur Spiritualität in elsässischen Frauenklöstern am Ende des Mittelalters." In *Frauenmystik im Mittelalter,* ed. Peter Dinzelbacher and Dieter R. Bauer, 347–65. Ostfildern: Schwaben Verlag, 1985.

Redlich, Virgil. *Johann Rode von St. Matthias bei Trier.* Münster: Aschendorff, 1923.

———. *Tegernsee und die deutsche Geistesgeschichte im 15. Jahrhundert.* Schriften zur bayerischen Landesgeschichte 9. 1931; reprint, Aalen: Scientia, 1974.

Régnier-Bohler, Danielle. "Literary and Mystical Voices." In *A History of Women in the West II. Silences of the Middle Ages,* ed. Christiane Klapisch-Zuber, 427–82. Cambridge, Mass.: Harvard University Press, 1992.

Rehm, Gerhard. *Die Schwestern vom gemeinsamen Leben im nordwestlichen Deutschland. Untersuchungen der Devotio moderna und des weiblichen Religiösentums.* Berliner Historische Studien 11, Ordensstudien 5. Berlin: Dunker and Humblot, 1985.

Reichert, Benedictus M. "Zur Geschichte der deutschen Dominikaner und ihrer Reform." *Römische Quartalschrift für Altertumskunde und für Kirchengeschichte* 10 (1896): 299–311.

Remling, Franz Xavier *Urkundliche Geschichte der Abteien und Klöster in Rheinbayern.* 2 vols. in 1. 1836; reprint, Primasens: Johann Richter, 1973.

Renevy, Denis, and Christiania Whitehead, eds. *Writing Religious Women: Female Spiritual and Textual Practices in Late Medieval England.* Toronto: University of Toronto Press, 2000.

Renner, Peter, ed. *Die Denkwürdigkeiten der Äbtissin Caritas Pirckheimer.* St. Ottilien: EOS, 1982.

———. "Spätmittelalterliche Klosterpredigten aus Nürnberg." *Archiv für Kulturgeschichte* 41 (1959): 201–17.

Rensing, Theodor. "Die Reformbewegung in den westfälischen Dominikanerklöstern." *Westfalen* 17 (1932): 91–97.

Riddy, Felicity. " 'Women talking about the things of God': A Late Medieval Sub-Culture." In *Women and Literature in Britain, 1150–1500,* ed. Carol Meale, 104–27. Cambridge: Cambridge Universtiy Press, 1993.

Riechert, Ursula. *Oberschwäbische Reichsklöster im Beziehungsgeflecht mit Königtum, Adel und Städten.* Europäische Hochschulschriften III/301. Frankfurt: Lang, 1986.

Rieder, Karl. "Zur Reformationsgeschichte des Dominikanerinnenklosters zu Pforzheim." *Freiburger Diözesan-Archiv* n.F. 18 (1917): 311–66.

Riggert, Ida-Christine. *Die Lüneburger Frauenklöster.* Quellen und Untersuchungen zur Geschichte Niedersachsens im Mittelalter 19. Hanover: Hahn, 1996.

Riggert-Mindermann, Ida-Christine. "Monastisches Leben im Kloster Ebstorf und den anderen Heideklöstern während des Spätmittelalters." In *'In Treue und Hingabe': 800 Jahre Kloster Ebstorf,* ed. Marianne Elster and Horst Hoffmann, 197–211. Uelzen: Becker, 1997.

Ringler, Siegfried. "Anna Ebin." In *Die deutsche Literatur des Mittelalters: Verfasserlexikon,* ed. Kurt Ruh et al., 2: cols. 295–97. Berlin: de Gruyter, 1980.

———. "Die Rezeption mittelalterlicher Frauenmystik als wissenschaftliches Problem dargestellt am Werk der Christine Ebner." In *Frauenmystik im Mittelalter,* ed. Peter Dinzelbacher and Dieter Bauer, 178–200. Ostfildern: Schwabenverlag, 1990.

———. "Ursula Haider." In *Die deutsche Literatur des Mittelalters: Verfasserlexikon,* ed. Kurt Ruh et al., 3: cols. 399–403. Berlin: de Gruyter, 1981.

———. Viten- und Offenbarungsliteratur in Frauenklöstern des Mittelalters. Quellen und Studien. Münchener Texte und Untersuchungen zur deutschen Literatur des Mittelalters 72. Munich: Artemis, 1980.

Roecken, Sully, and Carolina Brauckmann. *Margaretha Jedefrau.* 2 vols. Freiburg: Kore, 1989, 1995.

Rohde, Petra. "Die Freiburger Klöster zwischen Reformation und Auflösung." In *Geschichte der Stadt Freiburg,* ed. Heiko Haumann and Hans Schadek, 2:418–45. Stuttgart: Theiss, 1994.

Roper, Lyndal. *The Holy Household: Women and Morals in Reformation Augsburg.* Oxford: Clarendon, 1989.

Ross, Ellen. *The Grief of God: Images of the Suffering Jesus in Medieval England.* Oxford: Oxford University Press, 1997.

Roth, Christoph. *Literatur und Klosterreform: Die Bibliothek der Benediktiner von St. Mang zu Füssen im 15. Jahrhundert.* Studia Augustana 10. Tübingen: Niemeyer, 1998.

Roth, F. W. E. "Zur Geschichte der Mystik im Kloster St. Thomas an der Kyll." *Studien und Mitteilungen zur Geschichte des Benediktinerordens und seiner Zweige* 37 (1916): 182–86.

Rothenhäusler, Konrad. *Die Abteien und Stifte des Herzogthums Württemberg im Zeitalter der Reformation.* Stuttgart: Verlag "Deutsches Volksblatt," 1884.

———. *Standhaftigkeit der altwürttembergischen Klosterfrauen im Reformations-Zeitalter.* Stuttgart: Verlag der Aktien-Gesellschaft "Deutsches Volksblatt," 1884.

Rublack, Ulinka. "Female Spirituality and the Infant Jesus in Late Medieval Dominican Convents." *Gender and History* 6 (1995): 37–57.

Rudolf, Rainer. "Magdalena Auer." In *Die deutsche Literatur des Mittelalters: Verfasserlexikon,* ed. Kurt Ruh et al., 1: col. 516. Berlin: de Gruyter, 1978.

Ruh, Kurt, ed. *Altdeutsche und altniederländische Mystik.* Darmstadt: Wissenschaftliche Buchgesellschaft, 1964.

———. "Deutsche Predigtbücher des Mittelalters." *Vestigia bibliae* 3 (1981): 11–30.

———. *Geschichte der abendländischen Mystik.* 4 vols. Munich: Beck, 1990–1999.

———. "Heinrich Riß." In *Die deutsche Literatur des Mittelalters: Verfasserlexikon,* ed. Kurt Ruh et al., 8: cols. 83–86. Berlin: de Gruyter, 1992.

———. "Die Schwesternbücher der Niederlande." *Zeitschrift für deutsches Altertum und deutsche Literatur* 126 (1997): 167–73.

Rupprich, Hans. *Die deutsche Literatur vom späten Mittelalter bis zum Barock. I. Das ausgehende Mittelalter, Humanismus und Renaissance 1370–1520.* Geschichte der deutschen Literatur von den Anfängen bis zur Gegenwart 4.1. Beck: Munich, 1970.

Rüther, Andreas. *Bettelorden in Stadt und Land. Die Straßburger Mendikantenkonvente und das Elsaß im Spätmittelalter.* Berliner Historische Studien 26, Ordenstudien 11. Berlin: Dunker and Humblot, 1997.

———. "Bischof, Bürger, Bettelbrüder. Straßburgs Mendikanten zwischen bischöflicher Herrschaft und städtischer Landnahme." In *Könige, Landesherren und Bettelorden in West- und Mitteleuropa bis zur frühen Neuzeit,* ed. Dieter Berg, 61–82. Saxonia Franciscana. Beiträge zur Geschichte der sächsischen Franziskanerprovinz 10. Werl: Dietrich-Coelde, 1998.

———. "Geistliche Prosa aus Frauenklöstern in Schlesischen Bibliotheken." In *La vie quotidienne des moines et chanoines réguliers au Moyen Age et Temps Modernes,* 2 vols., ed. Marek Derwich, 2:499–502. Wroclaw: Institut d'Historie de l'Université de Wroclaw, 1995.

———. "Schreibbetrieb, Bücheraustausch und Briefwechsel: Der Konvent St. Katharina in St. Gallen während der Reform." In *Vita Religiosa im Mittelalter. Festschrift für Kaspar Elm zum 70. Geburtstag,* ed. Franz Felten and Nikolas Jaspert, 653–77. Berlin: Duncker and Humblot, 1999.

Rüther, Andreas, and Hans-Jochen Schiewer. "Die Predigthandschriften des Straßburger Dominikanerinnenklosters St. Nikolaus in Undis." In *Die deutsche Predigt im Mittelalter,* ed. Volker Mertens and Hans-Jochen Schiewer, 169–93. Niemeyer: Tübingen, 1992.

Rüttgart, Antje. "Die Diskussion um das Klosterleben von Frauen in Flugschriften der frühen Reformationszeit." In *"In Christo ist weder man noch weyb": Frauen in der Zeit der*

Reformation und der katholischen Reform, ed. Anne Conrad and Caroline Gritschke, 69–94. Münster: Aschendorff, 1999.

Sahlin, Claire. "The Prophetess as Preacher: Birgitta of Sweden and the Voice of Prophecy." *Medieval Sermon Studies* 40 (1997): 29–44.

Schadek, Hans, and Jürgen Treffeisen. "Klöster im spätmittelalterlichen Freiburg, Frühgeschichte, Sozialstruktur, Bürgerpflichten." In *Geschichte der Stadt Freiburg im Breisgau,* 2 vols. *Vol I: Von den Anfängen bis zum 'Neuen Stadtrecht' von 1520*, ed. Heiko Haumann and Hans Schadek, 1:421–67. Stuttgart: Theiss, 1994.

Schäfer, Karl Heinrich. *Die Kanonissenstifter im deutschen Mittelalter. Ihre Entwicklung und innere Einrichtung im Zusammenhang mit dem altchristlichen Sanctimonialentum.* Stuttgart: Enke, 1907.

Scheepsma, Wybren. *Deemoed en devotie: De koorvrouwen van Windesheim en hun geschriften.* Amsterdam: Prometheus, 1997.

———. "'For hereby I hope to rouse some to piety': Books of Sisters from Convents and Sister-Houses Associated with the 'Devotio moderna' in the Low Countries." In *Women, the Book, and the Godly*, 2 vols. ed. Lesley Smith and Jane Taylor, 1:27–40. Cambridge: Brewer, 1995.

———. "Hadewijch und die 'Limburgse Sermoenen.' Überlegungen zu Datierung, Identität und Autentizität." In *Deutsche Mystik im abendländischen Zusammenhang: Neuerschlossene Texte, neue methodische Ansätze, neue theoretische Konzepte*, Kolloquium Kloster Fischingen 1998, ed. Walter Haug and Wolfram Schneider-Lastin, 653–82. Tübingen: Niemeyer, 2000.

———. "Twee onuitgegeven traktaatjes van Alijt Bake." *Ons Geestelijk erf* 66 (1992): 145–67.

Schieler, Kaspar. *Magister Johannes Nider aus dem Orden Prediger-Brüder: Ein Beitrag zur Kirchengeschichte des 15. Jahrhunderts.* Mainz: Kirchheim, 1885.

Schiewer, Hans-Jochen. "Auditionen und Vision einer Begine. Die 'Selige Schererin', Johannes Mulberg und der Basler Beginenstreit. Mit einem Textabdruck." In *Die Vermittlung geistlicher Inhalte im deutschen Mittelalter*, ed. Timothy R. Jackson, Nigel Palmer, and Almut Suerbaum, 289–317. Tübingen: Niemeyer, 1996.

———. "Die beiden Sankt Johannsen, ein dominikanischer Johannes-Libellus und das literarische Leben im Bodenseeraum um 1300." *Oxford German Studies* 22 (1993): 21–54.

———. "German Sermons in the Middle Ages." In *The Sermon*, ed. Beverly Kienzle, trans. Debra Stoudt, 861–961. Typologie des Sources du moyen âge occidental 81–83. Turnhout, Belgium: Brepols, 2000.

———. "Spuren von Mündlichkeit in der mittelalterlichen Predigtüberlieferung. Ein Plädoyer für exemplarisches und beschreibend-interpretierendes Edieren." *Editio* 6 (1992): 64–79.

———. "Typ und Polyfunktionalität." *Jahrbuch für Internationale Germanistik* 24 (1992): 44–47.

———. "Universities and Vernacular Preaching. The Case of Vienna, Heidelberg, and Basle." In *Medieval Sermons and Society: Cloister, City, University: Proceedings of International Symposia at Kalamazoo and New York*, ed. Jacqueline Hamesse, 387–96. Louvain-la-Neuve: Fédération Internationale des Instituts d'études médiévales, 1998.

———. "'Uslesen': Das Weiterwirken mystischen Gedankenguts im Kontext dominikanischer Frauengemeinschaften." In *Deutsche Mystik im abenländischen Zusammenhang: Neuerschlossene Texte, neue methodische Ansätze, neue theoretische Konzepte. Kolloquium Klo-*

ster Fischingen 1998, ed. Walter Haug and Wolfram Schneider-Lastin, 581–601. Tübingen: Niemeyer, 2000.

Schiewer, Hans-Jochen, Volker Mertens et al., eds. *Repertorium der ungedruckten deutschsprachigen Predigten des Mittelalters. Der Berliner Bestand.* Vol. 1: *Die Handschriften aus dem Straßburger Dominikanerinnenkloster St. Nikolaus in undis und benachbarte Provenienzen.* Tübingen: Niemeyer, in press.

Schiewer, Regina D. "Die Entdeckung der mittelniederdeutschen Predigt: Überlieferung, Form, Inhalte." *Oxford German Studies* 26 (1997): 24–72.

———. "Sermons for Nuns of the Dominican Observance Movement." In *Medieval Monastic Preaching,* ed. Carolyn Muessig, 75–92. Leiden: Brill, 1998.

Schlechter, Armin. "Eine deutsche mystische Handschrift der Straßburger Dominikanerin Anna Schott aus der Bibliothek von Johann Nikolaus Weislinger." *Zeitschrift für Geschichte des Oberrheins* 145 (1997): 462–73.

Schleussner, Wilhelm. "Magdalena von Freiburg. Eine pseudomystische Erscheinung des späteren Mittelalters, 1407–1458." *Der Katholik* 87 (1907): 15–32, 109–27, 199–216.

Schmid, Karl. "Adel und Reform in Schwaben." In *Gebetsgedenken und adliges Selbstverständnis im Mittelalter,* ed. Karl Schmid, 359–76. Sigmaringen: Thorbecke, 1983.

Schmidt, Margot. "Mechthild von Hackeborn." In *Die deutsche Literatur des Mittelalters: Verfasserlexikon,* ed. Kurt Ruh et al., 6: col. 251–60. Berlin: de Gruyter, 1987.

Schmidt, Paul Gerhard. "'Amor transformat amantem in amatum': Bernhard von Waging an Nicolaus Cusanus über die Vision einer Reformunwilligen Nonne." In *Poetry and Philosophy in the Middle Ages. Festschrift for Peter Dronke,* ed. John Marenbon. Leiden: Brill, 2001.

Schmidt, Wieland. "Johannes Kreutzer, ein elsässischer Prediger des 15. Jahrhunderts." In *W. Schmidt. Kleine Schriften. Festgabe der Universitätsbibliothek der Freien Universität Berlin für Wieland Schmidt zum 65. Geburtstag,* 227–59. Wiesbaden: Harrassowitz, 1969.

Schmidtke, Dietrich. "Geistliche Schiffahrt. Zum Thema des Schiffes der Buße im Spätmittelalter." *Beiträge zur Geschichte der deutschen Sprache und Literatur* 91 (1969): 357–85; 92 (1970): 115–77.

———. *Studien zur dingallegorischen Erbauungsliteratur des Mittelalters. Am Beispiel der Gartenallegorie.* Hermaea. Germanistische Forschungen n.F. 43. Tübingen: Niemeyer, 1982.

———. "Zur Geschichte der Kölner Predigt im Spätmittelalter: Einige neue Predigernamen." In *Festschrift für Ingeborg Schröber zum 65. Geburtstag,* ed. Dietrich Schmidtke and Helga Schüppert, 328–61. Beiträge zur Geschichte der deutschen Sprache und Literatur 95. Tübingen: Niemeyer, 1973.

Schmitt, Sigrid. "Geistliche Frauen und städtische Welt. Stiftsdamen—Klosterfrauen—Beginen und ihre Umwelt am Beispiel der Stadt Straßburg im Spätmittelalter (1250–1530)." Habilitationsschrift, University of Mainz, 2002.

Schmitz-Kallenberg, Ludwig. *Monasticon Westfaliae.* Münster: Universitäts-Buchhandlung, 1909.

Schneider, Karin. "Beziehungen zwischen den Dominikanerinnenklöstern Nürnberg und Altenhohenau im ausgehenden Mittelalter. Neue Handschriftenfunde." In *Würzburger Prosastudien II: Untersuchungen zur Literatur und Sprache des Mittelalters,* ed. Peter Kesting, 211–18. Medium Aevum 31. Munich: Fink, 1975.

———. "Die Bibliothek des Katharinenklosters in Nürnberg und die städtische Gesellschaft." In *Studien zum städtischen Bildungswesen des späten Mittelalters und der frühen Neuzeit,* ed. Bernd Moeller et. al., 70–82. Göttingen: Vandenhoeck and Ruprecht, 1983.

————. "Katharina Tucher." In *Die deutsche Literatur des Mittelalters: Verfasserlexikon*, ed. Kurt Ruh et al., 8: cols. 1132–34. Berlin: de Gruyter, 1992

Schneider, Laurenz and G. Blauert. *Geschichte der deutschen Kurzschrift*. Wolfenbüttel: Heckner, 1936.

Schneider-Lastin, Wolfram. "Die Fortsetzung des Ötenbacher Schwesternbuchs und andere vermißte Texte in Breslau." *Zeitschrift für deutsches Altertum* 124 (1995): 201–10.

Schrader, Franz. *Die ehemalige Zisterzienserinnenabtei Marienstuhl von Egeln. Ein Beitrag zur Geschichte der Zisterzienserinnen und der nachreformatorischen Restbestände des Katholizismus im ehemaligen Herzogtum Magdeburg*. Erfurter Theologische Studien 16. Leipzig: St. Benno–Verlag, 1965.

————. *Ringen, Untergang und Überleben der katholischen Klöster in den Hochstiften Magdeburg und Halberstadt von der Reformation bis zum Westfälischen Frieden*. Katholisches Leben und Kirchenreform im Zeitalter der Glaubensspaltung, 37. Münster: Aschendorff, 1977.

Schraut, Elisabeth. "Kunst im Frauenkloster: Überlegungen zu den Möglichkeiten der Frauen im mittelalterlichen Kunstbetrieb am Beispiel Nürnberg." In *Auf der Suche nach der Frau im Mittelalter*, ed. Bea Lundt, 81–114. Munich: Fink, 1991.

Schreiner, Klaus. "Benediktinische Klosterreform als zeitgebundene Auslegung der Regel." In *Blätter für württembergische Kirchengeschichte* 86 (1986): 105–95.

————. "Dauer, Niedergang, und Erneuerung klösterlicher Observanz im hoch- und spätmittelalterlichen Mönchtum. Krisen, Reform- und Institutionalisierungsprobleme in der Sicht und Deutung betroffener Zeitgenossen." In *Institutionen und Geschichte*, ed. Gert Melville, 295–342. Cologne: Böhlau, 1992.

————. "Mönchtum im Geist der Benediktinerregel. Erneuerungswille und Reformstreben im Kloster Blaubeuren während des hohen und späten Mittelalters." In *Blaubeuren*, ed. Hansmartin Decker-Hauff and Immo Eberl, 93–176. Sigmaringen: Thorbecke, 1986.

————. "Verschriftlichung als Faktor monastischer Reform. Funktionen von Schriftlichkeit im Ordenswesen des hohen und späten Mittelalters." In *Pragmatische Schriftlichkeit im Mittelalter*, ed. Hagen Keller, 37–75. Münstersche Mittelalter-Schriften 65. Munich: Fink, 1992.

Scribner, Robert W. "Elements of Popular Belief." In *Handbook of European History 1400–1600: Late Middle Ages, Renaissance, and Reformation*, 2 vols., ed. Thomas A Brady Jr. et al., 1:231–262. Leiden: Brill, 1994.

Schröder, Alfred. "Das Hausbuch des Klosters Maihingen. Quellenkritische Untersuchung." *Archiv für die Geschichte des Hochstifts Augsburg* 6 (1929): 765–76.

Schromm, Arnold. *Die Bibliothek des ehemaligen Zisterzienserinnenklosters Kirchheim am Ries: Buchpflege und geistiges Leben in einem Frauenstift*. Studia Augustana 9. Tübingen: Niemeyer, 1998.

Schrörer, Alois. "Der Anteil der Frau an der Reformation in Westfalen." In *Reformatio ecclesiae. Beiträge zur kirchlichen Reformbemühungen von der Alten Kirche bis zur Neuzeit. Festgabe für Erwin Iserloh*, ed. Remigius Bäumer, 641–60. Paderborn: Schöningh, 1980.

Schuette, Marie. *Deutsche Wandteppiche*. Leipzig: Bibliographisches Institut, 1938.

Schulenburg, Jane Tibbets. *Forgetful of Their Sex: Sanctity and Society, ca. 500–1100*. Chicago: University of Chicago Press, 1998.

————. "Women's Monastic Communities, 500–1100: Patterns of Expansion and Decline." *Signs: Journal of Women in Culture and Society* 14 (1989): 162–92.

Schulze, Manfred. *Fürsten und Reformation. Geistliche Reformpolitik weltlicher Fürsten vor der Reformation. Spätmittelalter und Reformation,* n.R. 2. Tübingen: Mohr, 1991.

Schulze, Rudolf. *Das adelige Frauen- (Kanonissen-) Stift der Hl. Maria (1040–1773) und die Pfarre Liebfrauen-Überwasser zu Münster Westfalen.* Münster: Aschendorff, 1952.

———. "Bilder aus der Geschichte des Klosters Überwasser." *Westfälischer Merkur* (1920) Nr. 435, 586, (1921) Nr. 47, 75, 110, 411, 436, 599.

Schüppert, Helga. "Söflinger Briefe." In *Deutsche Literatur des Mittelalters: Verfasserlexikon,* ed. Kurt Ruh et. al., 9: cols. 12–16. Berlin: de Gruyter, 1995.

Schwarz, Wilhelm Eberhard. "Studien zur Geschichte des Klosters der Augustinerinnen Marienthal, genannt Niesing zu Münster." *Zeitschrift für vaterländische Geschichte und Altertumskunde* 72 (1914): 47–151.

Schwitalla, Johannes. "Frauen als Autorinnen in der reformatorischen Öffentlichkeit. Der Streit um das Recht des öffentlichen Wortes." In *Geschlechterkonstruktionen in Sprache, Literatur und Gesellschaft: Gedenkschrift für Gisela Schoenthal,* ed. Elisabeth Cheauré, 281–304. Freiburg i. Br.: Rombach, 2002.

Seeholtz, Anna Groh. *Friends of God: Practical Mystics of the Fourteenth Century.* 1934; reprint, New York: AMS Press, 1970.

Seibt, Ferdinand, ed. *Bohemia sacra: Das Christentum in Böhmen 973–1973.* Düsseldorf: Schwann, 1974.

———. "Geistige Reformbewegungen zur Zeit des Konstanzer Konzils." In *Das Konstanzer Konzil,* ed. Remigius Bäumer, 323–44. Wege der Forschung 15. Darmstadt: Wissenschaftliche Buchgesellschaft, 1977.

Seidel, Kurt. O., ed. *Sô predigent etelîche. Beiträge zur deutschen und niederländischen Predigt im Mittelalter.* Göppingen: Kümmerle, 1982.

750 Jahre Dominikanerinnenkloster Adelhausen Freiburg im Breisgau. Edited by Adelhausenstiftung Freiburg zu Breisgau. Freiburg: Adelhausenstiftung, 1985.

Shahar, Shulamith. *The Fourth Estate: A History of Women in the Middle Ages.* Translated by Chaya Galai. London: Methuen, 1983.

Signori, Gabriela, ed. *Lesen, Schreiben, Sticken und Erinnern: Beiträge zur Kultur- und Sozialgeschichte mittelalterlicher Frauenklöster.* Bielefeld: Verlag für Regionalgeschichte, 2000.

———. "Die Söflinger Liebesbriefe oder die vergessene Geschichte von Nonnen, die von Liebe träumen." *Metis* 4 (1995): 14–23.

Simons, Walter. *Cities of Ladies: Beguine Communities of the Medieval Low Countries 1200–1565.* Philadelphia: University of Pennsylvania Press, 2001.

Smalley, Beryl. *The Study of the Bible in the Middle Ages.* Oxford: Blackwell, 1952.

Smith, Susan L. *Power of Women: A Topos in Medieval Art and Literature.* Philadelphia: University of Pennsylvania Press, 1995.

Soergel, Philip M. *Wondrous in His Saints: Counter-Reformation Propaganda in Bavaria.* Berkeley and Los Angeles: University of California Press, 1993.

Spahr, Gebhard. "Die Reform im Kloster St. Gallen 1417–1441." *Schriften des Vereins für Geschichte des Bodensees und seiner Umgebung* 75 (1957): 13–80.

Spahr, Kolumban. "Nikolaus von Cues, das adelige Frauenstift Sonnenburg OSB und die mittelalterliche Nonnenklausur." *Cusanus Gedächtnisschrift,* ed. Nikolaus Grass, 307–26. Innsbruck: Wagner, 1970.

Spangenberg, Wilhelm, Sophia Wichelmann, and Hans E. Seidat, eds. *Ebstorf aus der Chronik.* Uelzen: Becker, 1982.

Spätling, Luchesius. "Das Klarissenkloster in Brixen." *Franziskanische Studien* 37 (1955): 365–88.

Sperling, Jutta Gisela. *Convents and the Body Politic in Late Renaissance Venice.* Chicago: University of Chicago Press, 1999.

Spiegel, Gabrielle. "History, Historicism, and the Social Logic of the Text in the Middle Ages." *Speculum* 65 (1990): 59–86.

———. *The Past as Text: The Theory and Practice of Medieval Historiography.* Baltimore, Md.: Johns Hopkins University Press, 1997.

———. "Theory into Practice: Reading Medieval Chronicles." In *The Medieval Chronicle: Proceedings of the 1st International Conference on the Medieval Chronicle,* Driebergen/Utrecht, 13–16 July, 1996, ed. Erik Kooper, 1–12. Amsterdam and Atlanta: Rodopi, 1999.

Spies, Martina. *Beginengemeinschaften in Frankfurt am Main. Zur Frage der genossenschaftlichen Selbstorganisation von Frauen im Mittelalter.* Dortmund: Ebersbach, 1998.

Sprandel, Rolf. *Chronisten als Zeitzeugen. Forschungen zur spätmittelalterlichen Geschichtsschreibung in Deutschland.* Vienna: Böhlau, 1994.

———. "Frauengeschichten in der Geschichtsschreibung des spätmittelalterlichen Deutschland." In *Aufgaben, Rollen und Räume von Frau und Mann,* 2 vols., ed. Jochen Martin and Renate Zoepffel, 2:731–49. Munich: Alber, 1989.

Stamm, Gerhard. "Klosterreform und Buchproduktion: Das Werk der Schreib- und Lesemeisterin Regula." In *750 Jahre Zisterzienserinnen-Abtei Lichtenthal: Faszination eines Klosters,* ed. Harald Siebenmorgen et al., 63–70. Sigmaringen: Thorbecke, 1995.

———. "Regula, Lichtenthaler Schreibmeisterin." In *Die deutsche Literatur des Mittelalters: Verfasserlexikon,* ed. Kurt Ruh et al., 7: cols. 1131–34. Berlin: de Gruyter, 1989.

Stammler, Wolfgang. *Gottsuchende Seelen.* Germanistische Bücherei 1. Munich: Hueber, 1948.

———. "Predigt." In *Deutsche Philologie im Aufriß,* 3 vols, 2d rev. ed., ed. Wolfgang Stammler, 2: cols. 980–1004. Berlin: Schmidt, 1952–57.

———. "Tauler in Basel." In *Johananes Tauler: Ein deutscher Mystiker. Gedenkschrift zum 600. Todestag,* ed. Ephrem Filthaut, 75–76. Essen: Driewer, 1961.

Stargardt, Ute. "Male Clerical Authority in the Spiritual (Auto)biographies of Medieval Holy Women." In *Women as Protagonists and Poets in the German Middle Ages: An Anthology of Feminist Approaches to Middle High German Literature,* ed. Albrecht Classen, 209–38. Göppingen: Kümmerle, 1991.

Staubach, Nikolaus. "Pragmatische Schriflichkeit im Bereich der Devotio Moderna." In *Frühmittelalterliche Studien* 25 (1991): 418–61.

———. "Von der persönlichen Erfahrung zur Gemeinschaftsliteratur. Entstehungs und Rezeptionsbedingungen geistlicher Reformtexte im Spätmittelalter." In *Ons geestelijk erf* 68 (1994): 200–228.

Stegmaier-Breinlinger, Renate. " 'Die hailigen Stett Rom und Jerusalem': Reste einer Ablaßsammlung im Bickenkloster in Villingen." *Freiburger Diözesan-Archiv* 91 (1971): 176–201.

Stein, Frederick Marc. "The Religious Women of Cologne 1120–1320." Ph.D. diss. Yale University, 1977.

Stievermann, Dieter. "Gründung, Reform und Reformation des Frauenklosters zu Offenhausen." *Zeitschrift für württembergische Landesgeschichte* 47 (1988): 149–202.

———. *Landesherrschaft und Klosterwesen im spätmittelalterlichen Württemberg.* Sigmaringen: Thorbecke, 1989.

————. "Die württembergischen Klosterreformen des 15. Jahrhunderts: Ein bedeutendes landeskirchliches Strukturelement des Spätmittelalters und ein Kontinuitätsstrang zum ausgebildeten Landeskirchentum der Frühneuzeit." *Zeitschrift für Württembergische Landesgeschichte* 44 (1985): 65–103.

Stinzi, Paul. "Schönensteinbach." *Annuaire de la Société d'Histoire Sundgauvienne* (1964): 49–74.

Stoudt, Debra. "The Influence of Preaching on Dominican Women in Fourteenth-Century Teutonia." *Medieval Sermon Studies* 44 (2000): 53–67.

Straganz, Maximilianus, ed. "Die ältesten Statuten des Klarissenklosters in Brixen (Tirol). *Franziskanische Studien* 6 (1919): 143–70.

Strauch, Gabriele. "Mechthild von Magdeburg and the Category of 'Frauenmystik.'" In *Women as Protagonists and Poets in the German Middle Ages: An Anthology of Feminist Approaches to Middle High German Literature*, ed. Albrecht Classen, 171–86. Göppingen: Kümmerle, 1991.

Strauch, Philipp, ed. "Kölner Klosterpredigten des 13. Jahrhunderts." *Jahrbuch des Vereins für niederdeutsche Sprachforschung* 37 (1911): 21–48.

————. *Margaretha Ebner und Heinrich von Nördlinngen. Ein Beitrag zur Geschichte der deutschen Mystik.* 1882; reprint, Amsterdam: P. Schippers, 1966.

Stuard, Susan Mosher, ed. *Women in Medieval History and Historiography.* Philadelphia: University of Pennsylvania Press, 1987.

Stump, Phillip. *The Reforms of the Council of Constance.* Studies in the History of Christian Thought 53. Leiden: Brill, 1994.

Sullivan, Donald. "Nicholas of Cusa as Reformer: The Papal Legation to the Germanies, 1451–52." *Medieval Studies* 36 (1974): 382–428.

Summit, Jennifer. *Lost Property: The Woman Writer and English Literary History, 1380–1589.* Chicago: University of Chicago Press, 2000.

Sydow, Jürgen. "Sichtbare Auswirkungen der Klosterreform des 15. Jahrhunderts." *Rottenburger Jahrbuch für Kirchengeschichte* 11 (1992): 209–21.

Taddey, Gerhard. *Das Kloster Heiningen von der Gründung bis zur Aufhebung.* Veröffentlichungen des Mas-Planck Instituts für Geschichte 14. Göttingen: Vandenhoeck and Ruprecht, 1966.

Taylor, Jane, and Lesley Smith. *Women, the Book, and the Godly. Selected Proceedings of the St. Hilda's Conference.* 2 vols. Rochester, N.Y.: Brewer, 1993.

Taylor, Larissa. *Soldiers of Christ: Preaching in Late Medieval and Reformation France.* Oxford: Oxford University Press, 1992.

Teichmann, Lucius. "Die franziskanische Observanzbewegung in Ost-Mitteleuropa und ihre politisch-nationale Komponente im böhmisch-schlesischen Raum." *Archiv für schlesische Kirchengeschichte* 49 (1991): 205–18.

Theil, Bernhard. "Die Reform des Klosters Gotteszell im 15. Jahrhundert." *Gmünder Studien* 1 (1976): 9–34.

Tinsley, David. "Medieval German Studies as a Paradigm for Gender Studies." In *Medieval German Voices in the 21st Century: The Paradigmatic Function of Medieval German Studies for German Studies*, ed. Albrecht Classen, 123–44. Amsterdam and Atlanta: Rodopi, 2000.

Thompson, Sally. "Why English Nunneries Had No History: A Study of English Nunneries Founded after the Conquest." In *Medieval Religious Women I: Distant Echoes*, ed. John A. Nichols and Lillian T. Shank, 131–49. Kalamazoo, Mich.: Cistercian Publications, 1984.

———. *Women Religious: The Founding of English Nunneries after the Conquest.* Oxford: Clarendon, 1991.

Thorr, P. Bernhard. "Die Dominikanerinnen von Schönensteinbach." *Annuaire de la Société d'Histoire Sundgauvienne* (1975): 47–56.

Thurm, Helmut. *Das Dominikaner-Nonnenkloster Cronschwitz bei Weida.* Jena: Fischer, 1942.

Totah, Mary David. "Undivided Heart: Another Look at Enclosure." *Cistercian Studies Quarterly* 33.3 (1998): 345–68.

Tüchle, Hermann. *Kirchengeschichte Schwabens.* Vol. 2. Stuttgart: Schwabenverlag, 1954.

———. "Süddeutsche Klöster vor 500 Jahren, ihre Stellung in Reich und Gesellschaft. *Blätter für deutsche Landesgeschichte* 109 (1973): 102–23.

Uffmann, Heike. "Innen und außen: Raum und Klausur in reformierten Nonnenklöstern des späten Mittelalters." In *Lesen, Schreiben, Sticken und Erinnern: Beiträge zur Kultur- und Sozialgeschichte mittelalterlicher Frauenklöster,* 185–212. Bielefeld: Verlag für Regionalgeschichte, 2000.

———. " '. . . wie in einem Rosengarten . . .' Die Ebstorfer Klosterreform im Spiegel von Chronistik und Tischlesung." In *'In Treue und Hingabe': 800 Jahre Kloster Ebstorf,* ed. Marianne Elster and Horst Hoffmann, 213–24. Uelzen: Becker, 1997.

Uhrle, Susanne. *Das Dominikanerinnenkloster Weiler bei Eßlingen 1230–1571/92.* Veröffentlichungen der Kommission für geschichtliche Landeskunde in Baden-Württemberg, Series B, 49. Stuttgart: Kohlhammer, 1968.

Ulmschneider, Helgard. "Ursula Pfäffinger." In *Die deutsche Literatur des Mittelalters: Verfasserlexikon,* ed. Kurt Ruh et al., 7: cols. 551–52. Berlin: de Gruyter, 1987.

Urbanski, Silke. " 'Der Begevenen Kinder Frunde.' Soziale und politische Gründe für das Scheitern eines Reformversuchs am Kloster Havestehude 1482." In *Recht und Alltag im Hanseraum. Gerhard Theuerkauf zum 60. Geburtstag,* ed. Silke Urbanski, Christian Lamschus, and Jürgen Ellermeyer, 411–28. Lüneburg: Deutsches Salzmuseum, 1993.

Van Engen, John. "The Church in the Fifteenth Century." In *Handbook of European History, 1400–1600: Late Middle Ages, Renaissance, and Reformation,* vol. 1, ed. Thomas Brady et al. Grand Rapids, Mich.: Eerdmans, 1995.

———. *Devotio Moderna: Basic Writings.* Translated by John Van Engen. Mahwah, N.Y.: Paulist Press, 1988.

———. "The Virtues, the Brothers, and the Schools." *Revue Bénédictine* 98 (1988): 178–217.

van Houts, Elisabeth. "Women and the Writing of History in the Early Middle Ages." *Early Medieval Europe* 1 (1992): 53–68.

Venarde, Bruce L. *Women's Monasticism and Medieval Society: Nunneries in France and England, 890–1215.* Ithaca: Cornell University Press, 1997.

Vierling, Josef, Fridolin. *Das Ringen um die Letzten dem Katholizismus treuen Klöster Straßburgs zur Zeit der Reformation und Gegenreformation.* Straßburger Beiträge zur neueren Geschichte 8. Straßburg: Herder, 1913.

Vogler, M. Thoma (Katharina). *Geschichte des Dominikanerinnen-Klosters St. Katharina in St. Gallen 1228–1607.* Fribourg, Switzerland: Paulus, 1938.

Voit, Gustav. *Engelthal—Geschichte eines Dominikanerinnenklosters.* 2 vols. Schriftenreihe der Altnürnberger Landschaft 26. Nuremberg: Koru and Berg, 1977.

Völker, Paul-Gerhard. "Die Überlieferungsformen mittelalterlicher deutscher Predigten." *Zeitschrift für deutsches Altertum und deutsche Literatur* 92 (1963): 212–27.

Wackernagel, Rudolf. *Geschichte der Stadt Basel.* 3 vols. Basel: Helbing and Lichtenhahn, 1907–24.

Walsh, Katherine. "The Observance: Sources for a History of the Observant Reform Movement in the Order of Augustinian Friars in the Fourteenth- and Fifteenth Centuries." *Rivista di Storia della Chiesa in Italia* 31 (1977): 40–67.

———. "Papstum und Ordensreform in Spätmittelalter und Renaissance: Zur Wechselwirkung von Zentralgewalt und lokaler Initiative." In *Reformbemühungen und Observanzbestrebungen im spätmittelalterlichen Ordenswesen,* ed. Kaspar Elm, 411–30. Berliner Historische Studien 16, Ordensstudien 6. Berlin: Dunker and Humblot, 1989.

Walter, Robert. "Beatus Rhenanus et Sebastian Brant. L'Affaire des Pénitents de Sainte Marie-Madelaine." *Revue d'Alsace* 107 (1981): 61–70.

Walz, Angelus. *Dominikaner und Dominikanerinnen in Süddeutschland 1225–1966.* Freising: Kyrios, 1967.

Warhol, Robyn, and Diane Price Herndl, eds. *Feminisms: An Anthology of Literary Theory and Criticism.* New Brunswick, N.J.: Rutgers University Press, 1991.

Warren, Nancy. *Spiritual Economies: Female Monasticism in Later Medieval England.* Philadelphia: University of Pennsylvania Press, 2001.

Watanabe, Morimichi. "Nicholas of Cusa and the Reform of the Roman Curia." In *Humanity and Divinity in Renaissance and Reformation: Essays in Honor of Charles Trinkaus,* ed. John W. O'Malley et al., 185–203. Studies in the History of Christian Thought 51. Leyden: Brill, 1993.

———. "Nicholas of Cusa and the Tyrolese Monasteries: Reform and Resistance." *History of Political Thought* 7 (1986): 53–72.

Watt, Diane, ed. *Medieval Women and their Communities.* Toronto: University of Toronto Press, 1997.

Wegstein, Werner. "Katharina Gurdelers." In *Die deutsche Literatur des Mittelalters: Verfasserlexikon,* ed. Kurt Ruh, et al., 3: cols. 326–27. Berlin: de Gruyter, 1981.

Wehrli-Johns, Martina. *Geschichte des Zürcher Predigerkonvents (1230–1524).* Mendikanten zwischen Kirche, Adel und Stadt. Zürich: Rohr, 1980.

———. "Das mittelalterliche Beginentum—Religiöse Frauenbewegung oder Sozialidee der Scholastik?" In *Fromme Frauen oder Ketzerinnen?: Leben und Verfolgung der Beginen im Mittelalter,* ed. Martina Wehrli-Johns and Claudia Opitz, 25–51. Basel: Herder, 1998.

———. "Voraussetzungen und Perspektiven mittelalterlicher Laienfömmigkeit seit Innozenz III. Eine Auseinandersetzung mit Herbert Grundmanns 'Religiösen Bewegungen.'" *Mitteilungen des Instituts für österreichische Geschichtsforschung* 104 (1996), 216–309.

Weinbrenner, Ralph. *Klosterreform im 15. Jahrhundert zwischen Ideal und Praxis: Der Augustiner-Eremit Andres Proles (1429–1503) und die privilierte Observanz.* Spätmittelalter und Reformation, n.R. 7. Tübingen: Mohr, 1996.

Weinmann, Ute. *Mittelalterliche Frauenbewegungen: Ihre Beziehungen zur Orthodoxie und Häresie.* Pfaffenweiler: Centaurus, 1990.

Weis-Müller, Renée. *Die Reform des Klosters Klingental und ihr Personenkreis.* Baseler Beiträge zur Geschichtswissenschaft 59. Basle and Stuttgart: Helbing and Lichtenhahn, 1956.

Weitlauff, Manfred. "Margareta Ebner." In *Die deutsche Literatur des Mittelalters: Verfasserlexikon,* ed. Kurt Ruh, et al., 2: cols. 303–6. Berlin: de Gruyter, 1980.

Wemple, Suzanne Fonay. "Monastic Life of Women from the Merovingians to the Ottonians." In *Hrosvit of Gandersheim: Rara avis in Saxonia?,* ed. Katharina M. Wilson, 35–54.

Medieval and Renaissance Monograph Series 7. Ann Arbor, Mich.: Medieval and Renaissance Collegium, 1987.

Wicher, P. J. "Das ehemalige Nonnenkloster O.S.B. zu Admont." *Studien und Mitteilungen des Benediktinerordens* 2 (1881): 75–84, 288–319.

Wichner, Jacob. *Kloster Admont in der Steiermark und seine Beziehungen zur Kunst.* Vienna: Brzezowsky, 1888.

Wiesner, Merry E. "Ideology Meets the Empire: Reformed Convents and the Reformation." In *Germania Illustrata: Essays Presented to Gerald Strauss*, ed. Susan Karant-Nunn and Andrew Fix, 181–96. Kirksville, Mo.: Sixteenth Century Essays and Studies, 1991.

Wiesner-Hanks, Merry. *Convents Confront the Reformation: Catholic and Protestant Nuns in Germany.* Translated by Joan Skocir and Merry Wiesner-Hanks. Millwaukee, Wis.: Marquette University Press, 1996.

———. "Women's Response to the Reformation." In *The German People and the Reformation*, ed. R. Po-Chia Hsia, 148–71. Ithaca: Cornell University Press, 1988.

Wilhelmy, Winfried. *Drache, Greif und Liebesleut': Mainzer Bildteppiche aus spätgotischer Zeit.* Mainz: Philipp von Zabern, 2000.

Williams, Ulla, and Werner Williams-Krapp, eds. *Die "Offenbarungen" der Katharina Tucher.* Tübingen: Niemeyer, 1998.

Williams-Krapp, Werner. "Die Bedeutung der reformierten Klöster des Predigerordens für das literarische Leben in Nürnberg im 15. Jahrhundert." Paper delivered at the Conference on "Die Literatur und materielle Kultur der Frauenklöster im späten Mittelalter und in der frühen Neuzeit (ca. 1350–1550), February 24–26, 1999, Herzog Albrecht Bibliothek, Wolfenbüttel.

———. "'Dise ding sind dennoch nit ware zeichen der heiligkeit.' Zur Bewertung mystischer Erfahrung im 15. Jahrhundert." *Zeitschrift für Literaturwissenschaft und Linguistik* 20 (1990): 61–71.

———. "Dorothea von Kippenheim." In *Die deutsche Literatur des Mittelalters: Verfasserlexikon*, ed. Kurt Ruh, et al., 2: col. 217–18. Berlin: de Gruyter, 1980.

———. "Frauenmystik und Ordensreform." In *Literarische Interessenbildung im Mittelalter*, ed. Joachim Heinzle, 301–13. Stuttgart and Weimar: Metzler, 1993.

———. "German and Dutch Legendaries of the Middle Ages: A Survey." In *Hagiography and Medieval Literature: A Symposium*, ed. Hans Bekker-Nielsen, 66–75. Odense: Odense University Press, 1981.

———. "Mittelalterliche deutsche Heiligenpredigtsammlungen und ihr Verhältnis zur homiletischen Praxis." In *Die deutsche Predigt im Mittelalter*, ed. Volker Mertens and Hans-Jochen Schiewer, 352–60. Tübingen: Niemeyer, 1993.

———. "Observanzbewegung, monastische Spiritualität und geistliche Literatur im 15. Jahrhundert. *Internationales Archiv für Sozialgeschichte der deutschen Literatur* 20 (1995): 1–15.

———. "Ordensreform und Literatur im 15. Jahrhundert." *Jahrbuch der Oswald von Wolkenstein Gesellschaft* 4 (1986): 41–51.

Wilms, Hieronymus. *Das älteste Verzeichnis der deutschen Dominikanerinnenklöster.* Quellen und Forschungen zur Geschichte des Dominikanerordens 24. Leipzig: Harrassowitz, 1928.

———. *Das Beten der Mystikerinnen dargestellt nach den Chroniken der Dominikanerinnenklöster zu Adelhausen, Dießenhofen, Engeltal, Kirchberg, Oetenbach, Töß und Unterlinden.* Quellen und Forschungen zur Geschichte des Dominikanerordens in Deutschland 11. Leipzig: Harrassowitz, 1918.

————. *Geschichte der deutschen Dominikanerinnen 1206–1916*. Dülmen i. W.: Laumann, 1920.

Wilson, Katharina M., ed. *Women Writers of the Renaissance and Reformation*. Athens: University of Georgia Press, 1987.

Wilts, Andreas. *Beginen im Bodenseeraum*. Sigmaringen: Thorbecke, 1994.

Winnlen, Jean Charles. *Schönensteinbach: Une Communauté religieuse féminine 1138–1792*. Altkirch: Société d'histoire Sundgauvienne, 1993.

Winston, Anne. "Tracing the Origins of the Rosary: German Vernacular Texts." *Speculum* 68 (1993): 619–36.

Winston-Allen, Anne. "Gardens of Heavenly and Earthly Delight: Medieval Gardens of the Imagination." *Neuphilologische Mitteilungen* 99(1998): 83–92.

————. "'Minne' in Spiritual Gardens of the Fifteenth Century." In *Canon and Canon Transgression in Medieval German Literature*, ed. Albrecht Classen, 153–62. Göppingen: Kümmerle, 1993.

————. "Rewriting Women's History: Medieval Nuns' Vitae by Johannes Meyer." In *Medieval German Voices in the 21st Century: The Paradigmatic Function of Medieval German Studies for German Studies*, ed. Albrecht Classen, 145–54. Atlanta and Amsterdam: Rodopi, 1999.

————. *Stories of the Rose: The Making of the Rosary in the Middle Ages*. University Park, Pa.: Pennsylvania State University Press, 1997.

Wittmer, Karl. "Reformversuche im Dominikanerinnen-Kloster St. Katharina zu Straßburg, 1492–1493." *Archiv für elsässische Kirchengeschichte* 16 (1943): 419–25.

Wogan-Browne, Jocelyn and Marie-Elisabeth Henneau. "Introduction: Liege, the Medieval 'Woman Question,' and the Question of Medieval Women." In *New Trends in Feminine Spirituality: The Holy Women of Liege and their Impact*, ed. Juliette Dor, Lesley Johnson, and Jocelyn Wogan-Browne, 1–32. Medieval Women: Texts and Contexts 2. Turnhout, Belgium: Brepols, 1999.

Wolfs, Servatius, Petrus. "Congregatio Hollandica: Reformkongregation im Predigerorden." *Ons geestellijk erf* 22 (1948): 165–83.

————. "Dominikanische Observanzbestrebungen: Die Congregatio Hollandiae (1464–1517)." In *Reformbemühungen und Observanzbestrebungen im spätmittelalterlichen Ordenswesen*, ed. Kaspar Elm, 273–92. Berlin: Dunker and Humblot, 1989.

————. "Reformversuche und Reformen in der Ordensprovinz Saxonia, 1456–1468." *Archivum Fratrum Praedicatorum* 52 (1982): 145–54.

Woodford, Charlotte. *Nuns as Historians in Early Modern Germany*. Oxford: Clarendon, 2002.

Wrede, Adolf. *Die Einführung der Reformation im Lüneburgischen durch Herzog Ernst den Bekenner*. Göttingen: Dietrich, 1887.

Zarri, Gabriella. "Gender, Religious Institutions, and Social Discipline: The Reform of the Regulars." In *Gender and Society in Renaissance Italy*, ed. Judith C. Brown and Robert C. Davis, 193–212. London: Addison Wesley, Longman, 1998.

Zigeler, Walter. "Reformation und Klosterauflösung. Ein ordensgeschichtlicher Vergleich." In *Reformbemühungen und Observanzbestrebungen im spätmittelalterlichen Ordenswesen*, ed. Kaspar Elm, 585–614. Berliner Historische Studien 14, Ordensstudien 6. Berlin: Dunker und Humblot, 1989.

Zieleman, Gerrit Cornelius. "Overleveringsvormen van middeleeuwse preken in de landstaal." *Nederlands archief voor kerkgeschiedenis* 59 (1978–79): 11–20.

————. "Das Studium der deutschen und niederländischen Predigten des Mittelalters." In

Selected Bibliography

Sô predigent etelîche: Beiträge zur deutschen und niederländischen Predigt im Mittelalter, ed. Kurt Otto Seidel, 5–48. Göppinger Arbeiten zur Germanistik 378. Göppingen: Kümmerle, 1982.

Zinke, Detlef, and Angela Karasch. Verborgene Pracht: Mittelalterliche Buchkunst aus acht Jahrhunderten in Freiburger Sammlungen. Lindenberg: Fink, 2002.

Zschoch, Hellmut. Klosterreform und monastische Spiritualität im 15. Jahrhundert. Conrad von Zenn OESA und sein "Liber de vita monastica." Beiträge zur historischen Theologie 75. Tübingen: Mohr, 1988.

Zumkeller, Adolar. "Johannes von Staupitz und die klösterliche Reformbewegung." Analecta Augustiniana 52 (1989): 29–49.

———. "Martin Luther und sein Orden." Analecta Augustiniana 25 (1962): 254–90.

———. "Vom geistlichen Leben im Erfurter Weissfrauenkloster am Vorabend der Reformation. Nach einer neu aufgefundenen handschriftlichen Quelle." In Reformatio ecclesiae: Beiträge zu kirchlichen Reformbemühungen von der Alten Kirche bis zur Neuzeit. Festgabe für Erwin Iserloh, ed. Remigius Bäumer, 231–258. Paderborn: Schöningh, 1980.

INDEX

References in parenthesis refer to the religious order with which a community was affiliated or associated.

Index

sermons (*continued*)
female audiences and, 11, 16, 188–89, 231
note-taking and summaries as devotional aids, 192–94
table readings, 188
transcribing and reconstructing, 188–97, 203, 231
Sigismund of Austria, Archduke, 93–94, 124–25, 135, 149
sister-books, 68, 75, 205–7
aims, 70, 75 207, 210–11, 213
foundation narratives, 12, 68–76, 252 n. 17
genre, 206–7
use by Observants, 166, 204
versus books of sisters, 239 n. 1
Slaggert, Lambert, 220
Söflingen, near Ulm (Clariss.), xviii, 46–47, 77, 79, 112, 142
Sonnenburg, near Brunico (Bened.), xviii, 133. *See also* Verena von Stuben
sources, xviii, 4–5, 12–14
Sperling, Jutta, 23, 31, 236
Stagel, Elsbeth, 13–14, 242 n. 46
St. Agnes, Emmerich (sister-house/August.), xviii
book of sisters: accounts of sisters, 1, 24–25, 55–57, 183, 205, 223, 231; rule and enclosure, 25, 93, 112, 152–53
St. Agnes, Mainz (Cist.), xviii, 289 n. 71
St. Agnes, Strasbourg (Dom.), 88, 94, 115–16, 153. *See also* Barbara von Benfelden
St. Agnes, Trier (August.), xviii, 190, 250 n. 163
Steinheim an der Murr (Dom.), xviii
journal, 234
Sticken, Salome, 182
St. Katharina, Colmar (Dom.), xviii, 102, 117. *See also* Adelheid von Aue
St. Katharina, Nuremberg (Dom.), xviii, 86–87, 99, 100, 145–48. *See also* Haller, Kunigunda
early reform effort, 130, 146
library of, 11, 171, 172–73, 184
reform account, 111, 147, 167
second reform effort, 110–11, 146–47
St. Katharina, St. Gall or Sankt Gallen (Dom.), xviii, 38, 41, 48, 103, 158–59, 233
chronicle. *See* Varnbühler, Angela
library of, 171, 173–74
sister-book. *See* Muntprat, Elisabeth

St. Katharinental, Diessenhofen (Dom.), xviiii
sister-book, 14, 69–70, 73
St. Klara, Freiburg (Clariss.), xviii, 101, 184.
See also Beutler, Magdalena
St. Klara, Nuremberg (Clariss.), xviii, 39, 77, 79, 91, 100, 157, 329 n. 2
chronicle, 329 n. 2
St. Maria Magdalena. *See* Penitents of St. Maria Magdalena
St. Nicolaus in undis, Strasbourg (Dom.), xi, xviii, 40, 77, 114–15, 171, 173, 188
sermon collection, 188, 190, 191, 281 n. 99
Summit, Jennifer, xiv
Sylo, Sélestat (Dom.), 23–24, 92, 103, 104. *See also* Adelheid von Aue

Teutonia, Dominican province of, 94
Texerius, Bartholomeus, 110–11, 151–52
Thomas de Cantimpré, 209, 222
Töss, Winterthur (Dom.), xviii, 38, 131, 232–33
sister-book, 28, 47, 60, 76. *See also* Stagel, Elsbeth
Tucher, Katharina, 178

Überwasser, Münster (Canoness./Bened.), xviii, 32, 40, 85, 86, 111–12, 138, 235.
See also Fridaghes, Elisabeth
cloister annals, 40–41, 138–40, 235
Ulrich of Württemberg, count, 77, 91
Unterlinden, Colmar (Dom.), xviii, 99
foundation account. *See* Kempf, Elisabeth
sister-book. *See* Katharina von Gueberschwihr

Varnbühler, Angela, 47, 118, 217
chronicle, 118, 158, 166
Verena von Stuben, 133–37, 269 n. 29, n. 30
vernacular language, shift to, 203–4, 230–31
Vigin, Agnes, 40, 114–15
Vilich, near Bonn (canoness./Bened.). *See* Bertha of Vilich
Vogler, Thoma, 118
voice, "female," 4, 16, 21, 218

Weiler, near Esslingen (Dom.)
sister-book, 23, 252 n. 17
Weissfrauen, Erfurt (Penit.), xviii, 183, 189